To Tom

Dad & Ch...

THE RUNNING BACKS

By the same author THE PRO QUARTERBACK

THE RUNNING BACKS

by Murray Olderman

Drawings and Diagrams by Murray Olderman

Prentice-Hall, Inc., Englewood Cliffs, New Jersey

Printed in the United States of America · T

Prentice-Hall International, Inc., London
Prentice-Hall of Australia, Pty. Ltd., Sydney
Prentice-Hall of Canada, Ltd., Toronto
Prentice-Hall of India Private Ltd., New Delhi
Prentice-Hall of Japan, Inc., Tokyo

Front End Paper and Back End Paper: Vernon J. Biever Photos

Acknowledgments

The man with the football, the running back, exposes the calculated violence and the compelling suspense of the game that's a microcosm of our times. The pro quarterback, detailed in a previous book, is the man who sets these forces in action and has been appropriately glamorized. The running back is the man who produces the action, the centrifugal force in the patterned swirl of moving bodies.

He has the ability to dominate by his physical presence, and this makes him the natural focal point in watching football. The reference frame is in that most basic tactic, advancing on the ground behind a friendly escort against a hostile opponent. Involved are all the elements which epitomize the appeal of football—strength, speed, intrigue, finesse and motivated spirit.

"Keep 'em honest" is the prevailing philosophy of offense, and you keep 'em honest by making the defense respect the running threat. Without the type of back to enforce that threat, the offense generally falters. So the running back has been historically vital to success.

This book traces his beginnings, his development, his growing importance and the recognition of his worth. Jim Thorpe, the pioneer of professional football, was a running back. So was Red Grange, the game's first status symbol. Jim Brown was the ultimate prototype and the highest paid performer of his time. The rewards, financial and esthetic, accrue to such moderns as Donny Anderson and O. J. Simpson.

What follows is an attempt at strategic analysis of his role and a study of personal histories and character to reveal and humanize the traits that go into the making of a running back—and provide conjunctively a picture of professional football as it evolved and is played today.

—MURRAY OLDERMAN

v

Contents

To Nancy, Lorraine, Marcia, Mark
. . . and necessarily in that order

Introduction

To catalog and detail the exploits of some 75 professional football running backs from Jim Thorpe to O. J. Simpson obviously requires research. By definition, research is investigation directed to the discovery of some fact by careful study of a subject. In the pursuit of these studies, I was aided by the unstinting cooperation of the official family of professional football—to be specific, Don Weiss of the Commissioner's office, Harold Rosenthal of the American Football League, Jim Heffernan and Joe Browne of the National Football League, and Seymour Siwoff of the Elias Sports Bureau.

For technical assistance, I am indebted to such fine tacticians as Coach Paul Brown of Cincinnati, Coach Allie Sherman of the New York Giants, Coach Weeb Ewbank of the New York Jets, Coach Vince Lombardi of the Washington Redskins, and Dick Gallagher, director of Pro Football's Hall of Fame.

I am also grateful for the cooperation extended to me by the stars of this book— the running backs themselves. And finally I appreciate the many gentlemen of the press who have written about these men, past and present, to provide a forum of background knowledge.

Thank you, all.

—Murray Olderman

PART I

1. Running: A Force of Football

Willie Heston, one of the legendary early All-Americans, was also one of the first highly paid running backs in the embryo days of pro football with the Canton Bulldogs.

"Football is, and always will be, a running game first," said Vince Lombardi. And men like Jimmy Taylor (31), in dark uniform, carried out that philosophy. He's plunging for a score against Kansas City in the first Super Bowl game.

Rod Hanna Topeka *Capital-Journal*

The name of Thomas "Swede" Hanson won't create a great flutter among football historians. It shows up minutely in the records of the Philadelphia Eagles as the leading ground gainer of the 1934 season, when he rushed for 805 yards. Swede was a locally produced hero and a single-minded man. He went to Temple University and majored in football. After a hard day's practice on the field, Swede re-charged his batteries in the classroom by dozing through a lecture in a course called Sports Theories.

The instructor, a self-professed football expert, interrupted his rest abruptly during an oral quiz when he snapped, "Mr. Hanson! It's the fourth quarter, score tied, your team's ball on your own 45, fourth down and two to go. What would you do?"

Swede yawned placidly. "I'd tell the quarterback," he said, "to give me the ball."

Swede radiated confidence in the most elemental method of advancing a football, and a generation later nothing has changed. A man with a ball crooked in the elbow of his arm, advancing against the opposition, is still the primary force in the sophisticated sport they call professional football. It's basic. "I see a flash of color," says Tommy Mason, the running back of the Los Angeles Rams, "and I go the other direction."

"Personally," says Vince Lombardi, the tactician of the Washington Redskins, "I like running. To me, that's football. Football is, and always will be, a running game first."

On a late afternoon in 1823, the autumnal sky yellowing to dusk over the famed Rugby School in England, a slender young student named William Webb Ellis caught an oval ball kicked in a game called "football." The game was in an exasperating scoreless tie as Master Ellis cradled the ball. Under the rules extant he was obliged to kick the ball. He knew he was too far away to achieve a successful boot for a score; curfew was already knelling on the belltower, so he did the only sensible thing under the circumstances. He put the ball under his arm and ran. His startled opponents, never having encountered such a tactic, failed to react and William Webb Ellis ran the length of the field for a touchdown.

"Unbecoming a gentleman," muttered the opposition. "Bloody foul."

But appreciation of Ellis' ingenious act soon followed and imbedded in a musty wall at Rugby there is a tablet which reads, in part:

"This stone commemorates the exploit of William Webb Ellis who with a fine disregard of the rules of football, as played in his time, first took the ball in his arms and ran with it. . . ."

It was the first recorded run and laid the foundation of the game which has become known as American football, officially inaugurated by Princeton and Rutgers in 1869. In the century of football action which has elapsed, it was inevitable that as skills increased, men would start laying wagers on the respective abilities of the players, and the next thing you know they'd be playing for money. In eastern Ohio, the enthusiastic citizenry of small industrial cities like Canton and Massillon induced famous college athletes to join their teams on weekends for professional jousts.

The runner as the ultimate force in football was epitomized by the great Jimmy Brown of Cleveland.

In 1905, the great Willie Heston of Michigan's famous "point-a-minute" teams signed with the Canton Bulldogs for $600 a game, a scandalous sum for that period, more than one would have to pay for the Model T motor car which was already on Henry Ford's drawing board. Willie, a 190-pound running terror, was considered a big man at the turn of the century and was in demand because the football practiced was highly physical, two tightly massed teams practicing the old cliché of the irresistible force and the immovable object. The forward pass, which later obviated a lot of the head-to-head combat, was still illegal and unused.

But there were wily methods to counter the force of someone like Heston. Away from the Spartan living of the Michigan training table, he had put on 50 pounds, which didn't help his mobility. The field on which the Canton Bulldogs played the Massillon Tigers was frozen. On Canton's first play, Willie received the ball from the center and swept gingerly around his right end. As he got past the line of tugging bodies, his feet skidded on a patch of hidden ice, which the Massillon backers had thoughtfully covered with straw. Willie's feet went higher than a can-can dancer's, and his body hit the ice with a thud, whereupon all the Massillon men fell on fat Willie like he was a cushion and in the crush knocked him out. After Willie was dragged to the sidelines, Massillon went on to win the game.

Eventually, there were refinements introduced to the pro game and to the running aspects of it, as the teams organized into leagues and the National Football League was born in 1920. One of the teams was the Brooklyn Dodgers, coached by an erudite gentleman named Col. John McEwan. He doubled as a teacher of English at West Point. John "Stumpy" Thomason, a product of Georgia Tech, was a running back for the Dodgers who also called the signals. One day in practice, Stumpy asked the Colonel, "How do I run this play?"

"Young man," replied the professor, "dispatch yourself with the utmost precision and proceed as far as your individual excellency will permit."

This dependence on "individual excellency" has made running an exciting art in professional football because all the lavish preparations, all the intricate designs of the play patterns are subordinate to the talent of the great ones—Jimmy Brown, who brought running to its most exquisite level as a fullback at Cleveland, didn't always need a carefully charted path to blast his way through teams.

When the circles and X's were transferred to the field of action, the human element became a paramount factor in the success of a play. In the January 1959 Pro Bowl game, Coach Jim Lee Howell of the New York Giants, handling the East squad, put in a running play designed to spring Brown for a long gain. He took the fullback aside and showed Jimmy how the blocking was set up on both the linebacker and the defensive back to guide him once he got into the secondary.

"Don't bother with those guys, Coach," scoffed Brown. "Just give me this much room through the line." Brown held his hands 18 inches apart.

"Who's this ————," thought Howell, "telling me how to coach?" And vocally repeated his thoughts. "But, Coach," insisted Brown seriously, "I can handle those other two guys myself."

"You know," said Howell, after Brown's rushes had helped the East team to a 28–21 victory, "he wasn't bragging. He could."

Nevertheless, the implementation of the run as the ultimate force in football was achieved by Brown when he worked within the total concept of an offense. His most glorious moment came in the 1964 championship game when the Cleveland Browns met the Baltimore Colts, who were favored by two touchdowns. In the third quarter, the Browns held a precarious 3–0 lead as they put the ball in play on their own 36-yard line.

When they broke the huddle, halfback Ernie Green, who normally lined up at arm's length from the fullback, shifted over to the left flank, outside the end, in a double wing formation, leaving Brown alone in the backfield. On the Baltimore side of the ball, Don Shinnick, the corner linebacker, started to cheat a little to the inside. The ball was on the left hash mark, and the Colts' defense was zoned to the wide side of the field, anticipating a pass.

Instead, quarterback Frank Ryan called a quick count, scooped the snap from center and quickly shoveled the ball out to Brown, who was already in full flight to his left, or the short side of the field. Halfback Green slanted in from his flanker position and nudged Shinnick off his feet with a perfectly timed block. Guard Gene Hickerson pulled and cut down cornerback Lenny Lyles, opening an alley for the Cleveland fullback down the left sideline. The Baltimore safety, Jim Welch, couldn't come over fast enough to cover. And Brown was gone. He hurtled through Lyles' desperate grab. At midfield, he cut back to his right, across the grain of pursuit and glided down the middle of the field. He wasn't caught until three Colts jumped him at the 25 and finally dragged him down at the 18, after a 46-yard gain. The Browns lined up in the same double wing formation on the next play against the unsettled Colts, and Ryan passed for a touchdown to blow the game open and lead to a 27–0 victory, the first and last championship thrill of Brown's career.

The search in pro football is endless for the Brown type of runner. It accounts for the fabulous buildup given to O. J. Simpson of Southern California after he made the Trojans the national collegiate champions in his first varsity season and then swept the board on all records as a senior in 1968. It also accounts for the $600,000 contract he sought from the Buffalo Bills, who drafted him No. 1 among all prospects. "He's worth as much as Donny Anderson," said O. J.'s agents. At the peak of the NFL-AFL recruiting war, halfback Donny Anderson of Texas Tech set the all-time record for a rookie's services when the Green Bay Packers tendered him a $600,000 deal.

A quarterback just out of college is a tenuous pro commodity since he needs a minimum three years of schooling to master his trade. Even an acknowledged artisan like Joe Namath of the New York Jets had his troubles. A running back can step right in and do the job. A rookie, Paul Robinson of the newly organized Cincinnati Bengals, led the American Football League in rushing in 1968, and the runner-up was Robert Holmes of Kansas City, also a first-year man. Since the National Football League started keeping official statistics in 1932, nine rookie runners have been annual ground-gaining pacesetters, and the total would have been even higher if Jim Brown (one of those nine rookies) hadn't dominated the rushing list for eight of the nine seasons he played with Cleveland. The rushing leaders in their professional debuts were: Brown, Cleveland, 1957; Alan Ameche, Baltimore, 1955; Bill Paschal, New York, 1943; Bill Dudley, Pittsburgh, 1942; Bill Osmanski, Chicago, 1939; Byron "Whizzer" White, Pittsburgh, 1938;

8

Alphonse "Tuffy" Leemans, New York, 1936; Beattie Feathers, Chicago Bears, 1934; Bob Campiglio, Stapleton, 1932. Marion Motley of Cleveland also led the league in his first season, but he was not a rookie, having torn apart the old All-America Conference for four years previously.

The first man ever chosen in a National Football League college player draft was a running back. On February 8, 1936, the Philadelphia Eagles selected Jay Berwanger of the University of Chicago, winner of the Heisman Award as the outstanding player in the nation. In the 1969 draft of college talent, five running backs were chosen in the first round: Simpson, Leroy Keyes of Purdue, Larry Smith of Florida, Ron Johnson of Michigan, and Calvin Hill of Yale. They and their ball-carrying brethren were by far the most precious species of draft material—sixteen runners were picked in the first three rounds, thirty-five in the first seven rounds. The desire by all teams to enhance their running games was also reflected in the total of twenty-four tight ends tabbed in the draft, since they're valued primarily as blockers in a ground attack.

Carrying a football is the intrinsic challenge to anyone first exposed to the contact of football. Steve Owen, the old Giant coach and a fine tackle in his playing days, used to tell about his introduction to the game on a ranch in Oklahoma Indian territory.

"I rode up on my pony one day and saw twenty boys or so in an old pasture near the school house having some kind of a war," spieled Steve, a delightful raconteur. "I always liked a good fight, so I stopped to watch and see if maybe I couldn't join in with the losing side. Man watching nearby asked me, 'How much you weigh, son?' I told him about 212 and then wondered what the chances were of joining into that fight.

" 'It's a game, son,' he said to me. 'It's called football. You want to play?' I told him sure, so he took me over to another man called 'Coach.' The coach looked me over real good, then handed me a ball and asked me to run with it down to the other end of that pasture.

"Well, I took off and started running. About twenty-one guys all started diving at me and grabbing at me, trying to knock me down. Finally I made it to the other end of the pasture—the fence stopped me. The coach just stood back there looking at me hard, so I figured I'd done something wrong and felt real dejected like. I went back and asked him, 'Did I do something wrong, Mister?'

" 'No, son,' the coach said, 'you did fine.

" 'But now let's see if you can do that again—this time with your spurs off.' "

The tough running back has a pervasive influence. In the mid-1940's Army crushed all opposition with the inside-outside attacking thrust of Felix "Doc" Blanchard and Glenn Davis. Blanchard was 208 pounds of explosive energy, battering anyone in his line of fire. After he had rammed the middle a few times in one game, the Army guard said to his opposite number on the line of scrimmage: "You might as well know, Mac, that on this play Blanchard's going to carry the ball right over me. I'd like to save my neck as well as yours, so let's both of us get the hell out of the way." Blanchard breezed through the vacated area for a touchdown.

In 1964, an organization was formed to eternalize the outstanding feats of the running back in the National Football League. It was called The 1,000 Yard Club, spon-

9

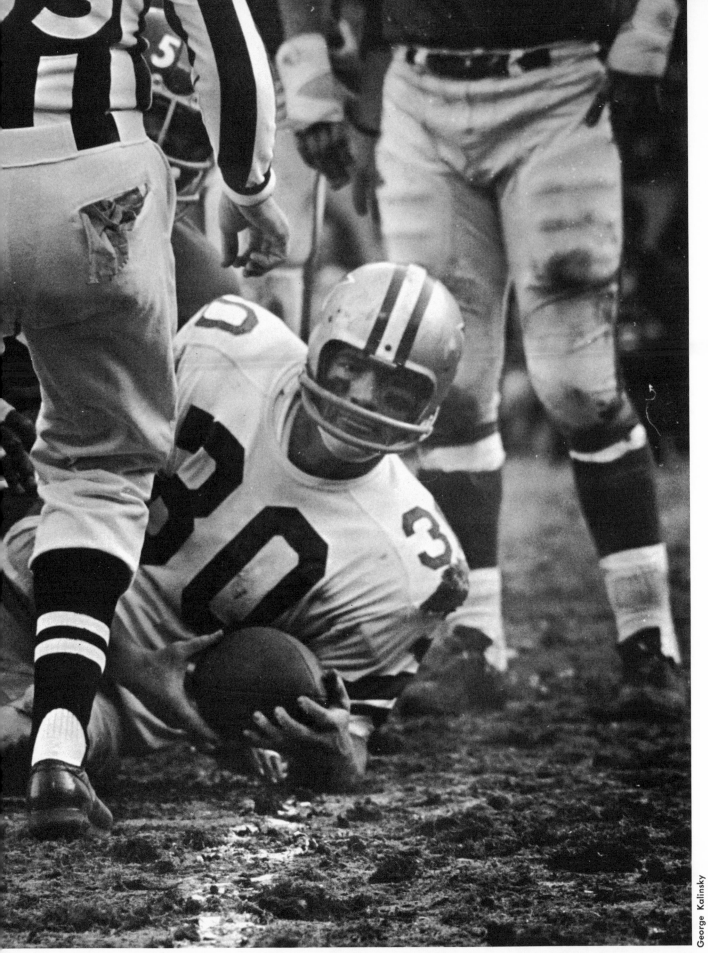

He's down, but the yard stripe has been crossed and the ball is still securely in the possession of halfback Dan Reeves of the Dallas Cowboys after plunging into the ranks of the enemy.

sored by a group of citizens in the Wisconsin Fox Valley area of the Green Bay Packers. Qualification for membership was simple: any man who gained 1,000 or more yards rushing in a single season. The first annual banquet was held in Neenah-Menasha, Wisconsin, and there were eleven charter inductees. They read like a sample Who's Who of the modern pro sport:

Beattie Feathers, Chicago Bears (the Roger Bannister of his time when he broke the 1,000-yard barrier in 1934)

>Steven Van Buren, Philadelphia Eagles
>Tony Canadeo, Green Bay Packers
>Joe Perry, San Francisco 49ers
>Rick Casares, Chicago Bears
>Jim Brown, Cleveland Browns
>J. D. Smith, San Francisco 49ers
>Jim Taylor, Green Bay Packers
>John Crow, St. Louis Cardinals
>John Henry Johnson, Pittsburgh Steelers
>Dick Bass, Los Angeles Rams

The roster has since been expanded to thirteen with the addition of Gale Sayers of the Chicago Bears and Leroy Kelly of the Cleveland Browns.

The American Football League, approaching the end of a decade of play, has its own 1,000 Yard Club. It's composed of the following men:

>Cookie Gilchrist, Buffalo Bills
>Abner Haynes, Dallas Texans
>Charley Tolar, Houston Oilers
>Clem Daniels, Oakland Raiders
>Paul Lowe, San Diego Chargers
>Jim Nance, Boston Patriots
>Hoyle Granger, Houston Oilers
>Mike Garrett, Kansas City Chiefs
>Paul Robinson, Cincinnati Bengals

The prowess of the running back has also been perpetuated in the Pro Football Hall of Fame at Canton, Ohio. Of the first forty men voted into the Hall for their performances as players, sixteen were noted chiefly as ball carriers. There are other evidences of esteem for the man who butts his head against enemy lines. Eleven running backs have had their jersey numbers retired by the clubs for whom they played.

And in the philosophy of the game of football, there has been an increasing awareness of the value of the running attack. It has been fashionable for critics of the pro brand of play to ridicule it as "basketball in shoulder pads" because of the overemphasis, they claim, on the passing attack. Throwing the ball is important. Technically, it's the easiest method to pick up a lot of yards in a short time. But by itself it doesn't win football games.

The statistics are revealing in this area. The number of passes attempted in any one year has never exceeded the number of rushes in NFL annals. The following are the figures since 1960:

NATIONAL FOOTBALL LEAGUE

	Rushing Attempts	Passing Attempts
1960*	5091	4114
1961	6106	5292
1962	6064	5356
1963	6112	5415
1964	6080	5437
1965	6031	5407
1966	6509	6108
1967	6868	6451
1968	7059	5997

* Each team played only 12 games in 1960.

This balance between running and passing has not prevailed in the nine corresponding seasons of the younger AFL. The figures for that period:

AMERICAN FOOTBALL LEAGUE

	Rushing Attempts	Passing Attempts
1960	3657	3699
1961	3218	3630
1962	3285	3456
1963	3077	3540
1964	3113	3750
1965	3203	3652
1966	3648	3982
1967	3710	3878
1968	4435	4037

The dramatic aspect of the above chart is that in 1968, when the AFL popularly achieved parity by winning a majority of its pre-season games with NFL opponents and climaxed the year with the stunning upset of the Baltimore Colts by the New York Jets in the Super Bowl, the young league for the first time showed more running than passing plays. (The imbalance of passing had been narrowing progressively for five years.)

On a team basis, there are some interesting deductions, too. Only four of the sixteen NFL teams in 1968 threw more than they ran—Washington, Pittsburgh, New Orleans and Philadelphia. All had losing seasons, finishing at the bottoms of their divisions in the Eastern Conference. Four of the AFL teams also favored passing over running—Buffalo, Denver, Miami and San Diego. Only San Diego had a successful season. Buffalo had the worst record in football.

The Minnesota Vikings, keeping the ball on the ground 64 percent of the time in 1968, the most run-conscious team in both leagues, also won its first division championship. In 1967, the Washington Redskins set the NFL all-time records for the most passes completed in a season (301) and the most yards gained passing (3,730). They won only five games.

The exultation of having carried the ball into the end zone envelops Matt Snell of the New York Jets, who raises his right fist in a victory salute. He ran for the only touchdown in the Jets' historic 1969 Super Bowl triumph.

This doesn't ignore the obvious merits of a good passer and receivers who can catch the ball. The New York Jets wouldn't have defeated the Colts, 16–7, in their classic encounter on January 12, 1969, without the threat of Joe Namath throwing to George Sauer and Don Maynard. But they also wouldn't have accomplished the job without fullback Matt Snell carrying the ball thirty times (two more times than Namath put it in the air) and gaining 121 vital yards, including a short burst for the only New York touchdown of the game. The strategic buildup for that score will be reviewed in a later chapter. But as the game evolved, the Jets knew they could win because they controlled the ball on the ground. In the last eleven minutes and six seconds of the fourth quarter, Namath didn't go to the air at all.

The keynote, then, to winning football is balance. And that extends to personnel as well as strategy. For every Namath who can throw the ball with flair, you need a Snell who can run it in style. He's a swift, hard-hitting fullback, a fine blocker, a good receiver, a pretty fair all round example of what a coach looks for in a running back. The NFL office catalogued the vital statistics of the average running back in a study made a couple of years ago. He is 6-1, weighs 212 pounds, is twenty-six years old and has been in professional football 3.6 years. Snell is a little bigger than that, a shade older and more experienced. Gale Sayers, on the other hand, is a trifle smaller, but no less effective. He is the most spectacular of all runners ever to play pro football, and the Chicago Bears have been in the doldrums because they had no passing game as a counterbalance.

The reference frame is, of course, the modern evolution of offensive football as a scientifically intricate mechanism in which all the little wheels must mesh. It was a lot simpler in the old days when the legendary Jim Thorpe pioneered the pro game.

When Thorpe was at his peak, his services were for hire to anyone who would fill his money pouch. Two towns in the Missouri valley had a bitter rivalry which carried over into all phases of the sports calendar but reached a particular pitch on the football field each Thanksgiving Day. A wealthy resident of one of the towns, with a big bet riding on the game, hired Thorpe as a "ringer" to get a little gilt-edged security on his wager. The Indian arrived in town on Thanksgiving morning. Just before the game was to start, he realized he didn't know his team's signals. In those days they didn't bother to huddle. So he told the quarterback, "Just wink at me when you want me to carry the ball."

After the kickoff, Thorpe's team put the ball in play deep in its own territory. On the first play, the quarterback winked at him, gave him the ball, but as he advanced, his own blockers piled him up. Another wink, and Thorpe was stymied again by his own interference. After it happened the third play, the Indian called time out and got the team around him.

"From now on," he said, "no winks. I'm calling signals. When I clap my hands, the right end runs to the right, the left end runs to the left, the tackles and guards fall down and stay down, and the center passes the ball back to me and ducks."

"But what about the backfield?" asked the quarterback. "What do we do?"

Thorpe looked at the three other backs and without hesitation ordered:

"Backfield, follow me."

14

2. Running Attack: The Strategic Evolution

THERE IS NOTHING NEW IN FOOTBALL.

Bill Osmanski's 68-yard gallop for the Bears on the second play of the 1940 NFL title game brought in the T-formation era. He's chased by Ed Justice (13) and Jimmy Johnston (31) of the Redskins.

Coaches have been whistling that refrain since Amos Alonzo Stagg tinkered with the flea-flicker at the University of Chicago when Grover Cleveland Alexander was President, and Ray Morrison used the old Statue of Liberty play at McTyeire School for Boys even before the bronze lady from France was implanted in New York harbor. All the experimentation in football style and formation was done by such original thinkers as Stagg and Glenn S. "Pop" Warner at the college level.

The T-formation, the single wing, the double wing, the A-formation, the spread (or shotgun), the short punt and all the other ways devised to line up the seven offensive linemen and the four backs in the best attacking positions can be traced back to doodlings in their sketch pads at the turn of the century.

Professional football contributed very little to the early strategic development of the game. It borrowed everything from the academic tacticians except the granddaddy of all offensive tricks, the old Flying Wedge, which Princeton foisted on the campus heroes in 1884 and used successfully until one of the legendary old bruisers, Walter "Pudge" Heffelfinger of Yale, flung himself at the point of the V-shaped wedge like a bowling ball and bodies toppled in a chain reaction.

The most publicized innovation of the pros was the wearing of sneakers by the New York Giants on a frozen field to beat the Chicago Bears for the NFL championship in 1934.

There was a lot of tug and pull in the early days of pro ball—the 1920's and even the '30's. Photographs of the period show most of the men in an upright position, struggling against each other dispiritedly like a bunch of milling longhorns caught in a tight corral. College coaches dismissed their efforts disdainfully as post-graduate exercises by out-of-shape sandlotters. That's why the entry of Red Grange into the pro orbit was such an exciting thing in 1925, since he was the super-hero of the varsity set. The stigma of the pro-type game lasted well through the 1930's, and even after World War II, Earl "Red" Blaik, the staid old Army coach, ventured a published opinion in *Collier's* magazine that a pro team was no match for a highly trained, disciplined, spirited college team. He took his Army teams to pro games on Sundays as a sort of holiday and for the spectacle, but he winced at the sight of beefy linemen who weighed more than 200 pounds. "I know," said Blaik, "and other college coaches know, that an active, enthusiastic young fellow of 190 pounds can do everything better than an old pro who weighs 250 or '60."

Col. Blaik also said, "Football is a college game. It calls for these things: youth, condition, spirit, plus continual hard work by coaches as well as players. . . . A fiery team like Tennessee would cripple a pro club. . . . The truth is, the pros won't pay the price to develop a running attack."

The Colonel's statements, made in 1950, would sound vapid today, after Green Bay built a dynasty under the whiplash of Vince Lombardi, a Blaik disciple. But at the time

—*after* the pro careers of such runners as Bronko Nagurski, Clarke Hinkle, Cliff Battles, and George McAfee—they stirred serious comment. Which indicates that perhaps the greatest development of the science of pro football has taken place in the last twenty years.

Except for Beattie Feathers, who had only one big season as a pro, no runner ever gained more than 1,000 yards in a season until Steve Van Buren of the Philadelphia Eagles, in the post World War II period.

Hinkle, a contemporary of Nagurski in the 1930's, offered a few comments on this phenomenon:

"The offensive formations of our day spanned about 12 yards because we did not have flankers and split ends. In addition, our offensive linemen were not spaced as loose. Result: the defensive formations were tighter, so it was harder to find a hole.

"Today, the split end, the flanker, the wider spacing of the line has widened offensive formations the width of the field, which also spreads the defense. There are bound to be more gaps in the line and more open spaces in the defensive secondary.

"Passing is the big offensive weapon in pro football today. Result: the defenses have to play looser, the running game has a chance to function better.

"In my time we went more for the touchdown inside our opponents' 20-yard line. Field goals were a last resort from 25 yards out. We felt that a team which couldn't score a touchdown inside the opponents' 10-yard line was not a good team. Our game was more tiring because we stayed in there for sixty minutes. Our offense was only thirty minutes of the game. We also had to concentrate on defense. I backed up the line on defense, played fullback on offense, did the punting, kickoffs and long field goals, defended against the pass, blocked for the pass and led the ball carrier when I wasn't carrying the ball.

"Result: less long runs, less high scoring games, more defensive football."

(Hinkle also added: "Less cheap statistical records.")

Professional football started to come out of the dark ages as an action sport on the basis of one game, perhaps even one play in that game. It took place on December 8, 1940, in Washington's Griffith Stadium, the Chicago Bears meeting the hometown Redskins for the NFL championship. Three weeks earlier, the Redskins had defeated the Bears 7–3. On the season, the Redskins, champions of the Eastern division had a better record (9 wins, 2 losses) than the Bears, Western titlists (8 wins, 3 losses).

The Bears, however, were just getting accustomed to a new style of offense in which the quarterback lined up directly behind the center, the other backs in a horizontal line three yards to the rear. It was called the modern T-formation.

The basic deployment of the personnel was not new. Stagg had lined up his teams in the T-formation half a century earlier. But Dr. Ralph Jones of Lake Forest College, Clark Shaughnessy, then at the University of Chicago and later a pro head coach, and George Halas of the Bears had worked cooperatively a couple of years to revive the old formation and imbue it with a few new wrinkles. They put a halfback in motion frequently to the sidelines, pulling a defender with him. They split the ends a little way from the tackle to provide some maneuverability. The quarterback under the center

18

retreated to pass after faking handoffs to the fullback or halfback or both, which kept the defensive linemen immobilized against the threat of a run.

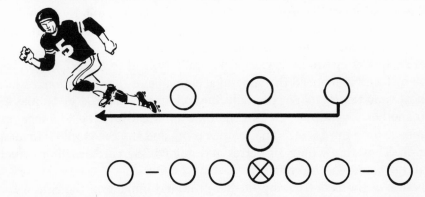

In 1940, Shaughnessy had gone west to Stanford University and introduced the modern T to college ball, displaying a young quarterback named Frank Albert. The effect was astounding. Stanford, which had won only one game the previous year, was undefeated and later beat Nebraska in the Rose Bowl.

Also in 1940, Halas of the Bears made prominent use of a young Columbia graduate named Sid Luckman in the new role of a T-formation quarterback after on-the-job training as a running back the year before. By the time of the December meeting with the Redskins, the Bears were thoroughly comfortable in their new system.

After receiving the kickoff to open the game, the Bears put the ball in play on their 25-yard line. On the first play, Luckman gave the ball to McAfee, the left halfback, on a straight dive over left guard. McAfee gained seven yards. The Bears were setting up the Redskins.

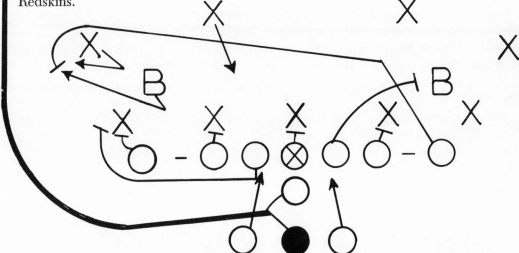

On the next play the action was exactly the same, except that the left guard pulled to his left and Luckman did *not* give the ball to McAfee. He handed it instead to fullback

Bill Osmanski, who turned wide around his left end. The Redskin linebacker, Jimmy Johnson, and the defensive back, Ed Justice, had been sucked in by the fake to McAfee, but now they recovered and pursued Osmanski down the left sideline. Meanwhile, George Wilson, the Bears' right end (later coach of the Detroit Lions and Miami Dolphins), came all the way across the field and levelled both Redskins with a tremendous "parlay" block. Osmanski romped 68 yards to a touchdown.

Luckman always insisted this Osmanski run, a typical "counter" action, was the crux of the modern T and influenced the general acceptance of the formation.

The next time the Bears got the ball they marched 80 yards in 17 plays, all on the ground, to another touchdown. Before the quarter was over, Joe Maniaci ran 42 yards from scrimmage for a third score. The romp was on, and the Bears rolled to an astounding 73–0 triumph. They threw only 10 passes and gained 382 yards rushing which, remarkably, is still the championship record.

The nature of the Bears' triumph had a profound impact on the rest of football. Not every team immediately abandoned its style of play. Generally forgotten is the fact that the Redskins, using Sammy Baugh out of a double wing and a short punt formation, revenged the 73–0 drubbing by beating the Bears for the NFL title just two years later. Detroit, coached by Gus Dorais, used the short punt with a lot of reverses through World War II. The Giants' Steve Owen stuck with his pet A-formation until 1953, when he was relieved as coach, though he mixed it with the T his last couple of seasons. The Pittsburgh Steelers, grounded in the traditional single wing by Dr. Jock Sutherland, held out the longest against the T-revolution but finally bowed to the new style of play after 1950.

In the All-American Conference, which was founded in 1946, the New York Yankees momentarily revived the glamor of the single wing because of the unique talents of Orben "Spec" Sanders, a triple threat who operated in the tailback position, and Claude "Buddy" Young, a sawed-off sprinter who lined up as his unlikely running mate at fullback. They used a lot of the modern trapping elements of the T to make it artistically successful for a couple of years and provide the Cleveland Browns with their major competition in the doomed league. Using the straight power off the single wing, Sanders set an AAC record by rushing for 1,432 yards in 1947. And Young augmented his mate by picking up 712 yards on such plays as this "wing trap" after spinning and faking a hand-off to Sanders:

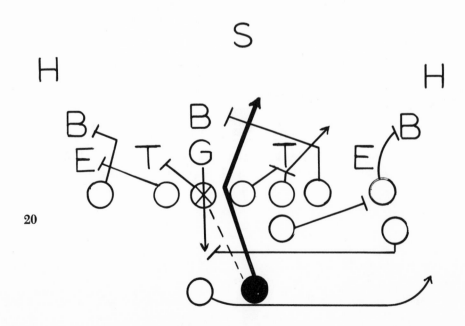

20

Buddy Young (22) was one of the last of the single wing flashes, but by the time he got to the Baltimore Colts, here in the final stages of his career on a sprint down the sidelines, all of pro football had converted to the T.

In his adaptation of the T-formation for Cleveland, Paul Brown quickly perfected a couple of important refinements that had dramatic effect on offensive thinking. The sideline pass (actually a square-out) with Otto Graham throwing to ends Mac Speedie and Dante Lavelli became a virtually unstoppable part of his offensive arsenal, and it was implemented by a delayed trap play in which Graham, simulating a pass, handed the ball to the fullback, Marion Motley, who ran through the drawn-in defense. Known popularly as the draw play, it is still widely used as an antidote to the overeager pass rush.

Brown's innovations opened up the game at a time when defenses were beginning to adjust to the Bears' T-formation. In the early years of the T, the dives and pitchouts were strange things to pro defenders who weren't used to plays that developed so quickly. But Greasy Neale's Eagle defense, a 5-4 with virtually nine men up on the line of scrimmage, plugged up the holes and contained the outside threat. However, it was vulnerable to the Cleveland style of attack, as the Browns showed in their NFL debut when they routed the defending champs, 35–10.

"The draw play was somewhat of an accident," Brown revealed. "The ball was handed off to Motley once in a delayed manner, on a broken play, and we were intrigued by the result when we saw the pictures. It was then refined—everything just like a pass. He'd fake blocking but be looking for the opening. Nature sometimes decided this, although we eventually set it up for a specific spot. The linemen invited their opponents to one side or the other, then bore them laterally, as though they were pass protecting. The fullback looked and picked the spot. Receivers actually ran patterns, the harder the better."

This is Brown's diagram of the original draw:

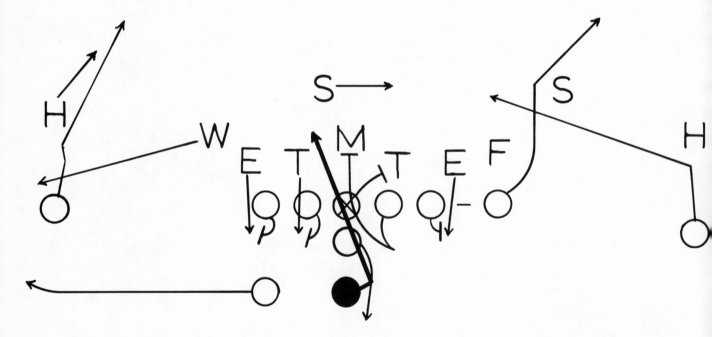

Brown also relied heavily on the quick pitchout, or the flip.

"It is the quickest end run we know of," he elaborated, and drew the play:

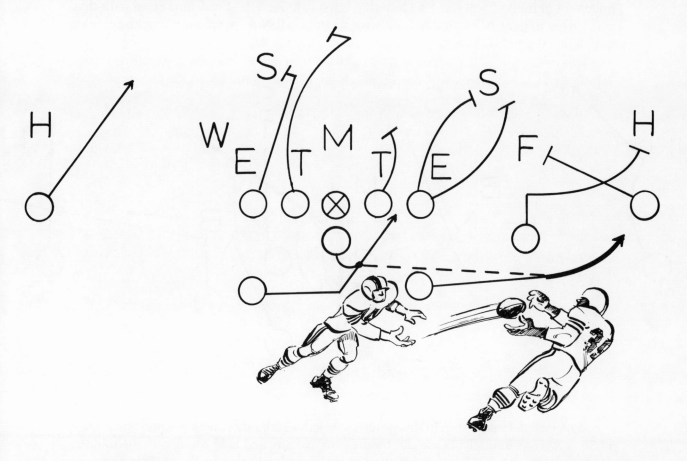

"Virtually the same play can go to the flexed, or weak side," he noted. The ball carrier and the slot man work on a checkoff automatic blocking play between the two of them, depending on where the opponents line up (signals are called). There are many ways to run the flip from all types of alignments. When a team has speed backs, and you know they'll run this play any time, it spreads things out.

"The two plays are still used very much as I've drawn them. Greasy Neale used to call us a pass and trap team, but really we used the draw more."

"Brown did a fine job of using the right people for the right formation," said Allie Sherman, a close student of offensive football. "He got Otto Graham to throw the ball to three exceptional receivers—Speedie, Lavelli, and Dub Jones. They could fly. And then he had Motley at fullback. The Brown offense, running-wise, was just about two plays: the quick pitchout to Motley or the draw. They used the draw like other teams use an off tackle play or a dive play. And they refined Motley's draw because they used it so much. He'd get the ball on a delay from the quarterback and run what we call a 'pick-'em' or what's known as running to daylight.

23

"But the thing that impressed me was design blocking for the draw. Besides picking the open hole, the Browns also used to trap on that draw with Motley. They'd pull a guard out in front of him and lead him through a definite hole. I was impressed with that and I went to pure holes on the draw after seeing that. Now people run it with more of a designated point of attack."

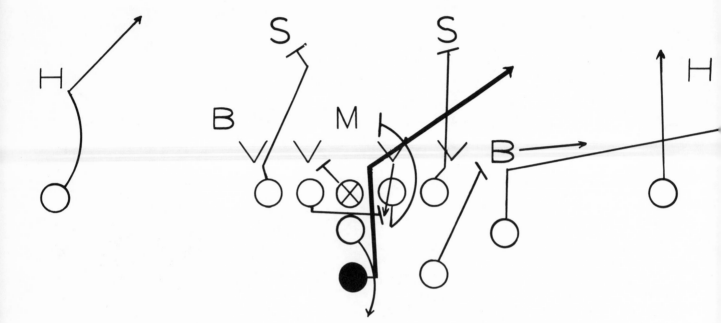

The next defensive step in this progressing game of human chess was the emergence of Steve Owen's umbrella to contain the Browns' passing and hold Motley up the middle. It started out as a 6-1-4 (six defensive linemen, one linebacker in the middle and four defensive backs spread out in an umbrella). Eventually, the two ends on the line dropped back a step and became corner linebackers for the final evolution to the 4-3-4 defense which remains the basic formation for every team in pro ball.

This took away, in large measure, the pitchout because the outside linebackers were conscious of protecting the flanks and the secondary was drilled to come up and meet the runner. "Actually," noted Sherman, "the only teams that use pure pitchouts now are those gifted with particular personnel, like Sayers of the Bears or Timmy Brown when he was running good with the Eagles. It's not as basic a part of the attack as it used to be."

The pro strategists started looking for little wrinkles to help the running backs squirm past the giants springing up on defensive lines. The Detroit Lions had a play called "26 cross-buck" in which the right halfback (or the "2" back) cut sharply to his left through the "6" hole between end and tackle. The No. 3 back, who happened to be Doak Walker, acted as a decoy on the play, faking a dive into the No. 3 hole, vacated by the right guard who pulled out of the line.

In a 1952 game against the Cleveland Browns, Doak noticed that every time the guard pulled on 26 cross-buck, the defensive left tackle, John Kissell, chased him, leaving Walker to fake into the No. 3 hole all by himself. "Kissell's not even touching me," Doak whispered to quarterback Bobby Layne in the huddle. "Give me the ball just once." So Layne called 26 cross-buck but varied the play by faking the handoff to the right half-back and slipping the ball to Walker. Kissell paid no attention to Doak, who burst through the line and went for a touchdown without a hand laid on him. That play became known as "33 take-off" and was widely used by all pro teams to keep defensive tackles honest.

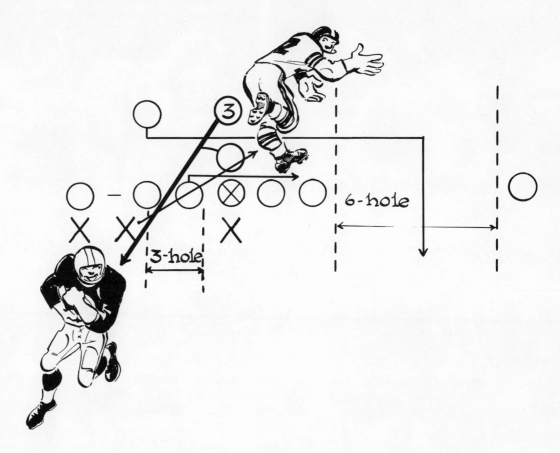

The brush blocking in the early days of the T, simply nudging a man who was already faked out of position by the action in the backfield, also became passé. Linemen were no longer suckered by quarterback fakes. They operated under a sophisticated system of "keys" pioneered by Tom Landry on the Giants, each defender reacting specifically (and in concert with the rest of the defense) to the movement of a designated offensive player—for example, the defensive tackle will "key" his reactions to the blocking of the guard opposite him, and the middle linebacker on certain plays will be guided by the fullback's movements. There was no guesswork. The result of this influenced a return to fundamental blocking principles. If you couldn't fool the defender, you

The quarterback, Len Dawson (16) of the Kansas City Chiefs, addresses an open huddle which might deploy the offense into one of a dozen different offensive formations.

had to knock him out of the way. Paul Brown, for instance, was more interested in execution than guile. He operated on the theory that even if you knew where his men were going, they were so well drilled they would make the play work anyhow. And Vince Lombardi came into the league with the idea he could run the ball down the opposition's throat, too, if necessary.

The immediate effect was a change in the type of running backs used. Backs like Bosh Prichard of the Philadelphia Eagles and Doak Walker of the Lions—quick 170-pounders—were out of business as ball carriers because when they weren't running they also had to bear the brunt of the blocking, and they just couldn't handle the 230-pound linebackers who were coming into vogue.

The Prichards and the Walkers were put out on the flank (Lance Alworth of San Diego and Johnny Morris of the Bears were later versions of them) and replaced by big men who were fast enough to run the ball. "If a back isn't big," said Sherman, "he darn well better be something else in his change of direction, acceleration, so they don't get a piece of him. Otherwise, a small back will give you three good games a year, but he wears down. Mostly, he's a spot player and supported by the rest of the club. You use him for certain things and special situations."

Steve Van Buren, the retired Eagle great, watched the evolution of this new style of running back with envy as the 1950's produced a wave of big 225-pound fullbacks who gained ground in large chunks—Jim Brown, Alan Ameche, Rick Casares, Deacon Dan Towler among them. "Running is easier nowadays," said Van Buren, "because of the diversification of offense. I never got to run such a thing as a draw play, for instance— just off-tackle plays and end runs. I'd also love to run against these four-man lines they have nowadays. One lineman can be blocked out and you have space to run."

In the 1958 championship game between the Giants and the Colts, which went into sudden-death overtime, Baltimore sprung Ameche loose for a 23-yard burst over the middle by trapping Dick Modzelewski, the defensive left tackle ("He was blowing in too fast to suit me," said quarterback John Unitas).

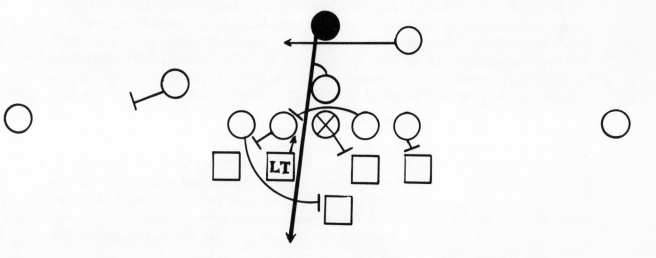

And then when they got down close to the goal line, Ameche barreled over tackle on a play which Coach Weeb Ewbank simply called "16 power." The Giants, backed up to the 1-yard line, were in a tight goal line defense, so the Colts double-teamed the tackle and got a good angle on the end and corner linebacker to spring Ameche for the winning touchdown.

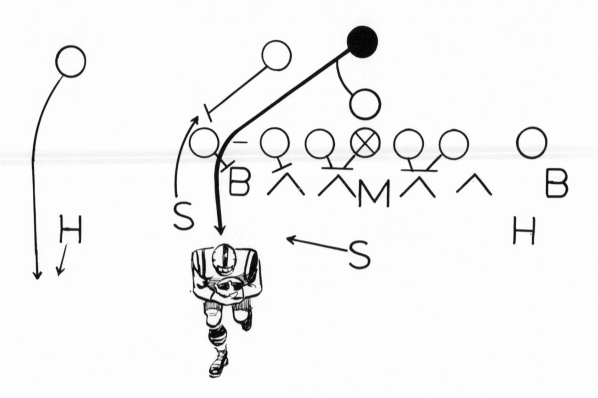

Incorporation of the old single wing concepts of double-team blocking, pulling guards and backs preceding the ball carrier into the hole was stimulated further by the great success of the Green Bay Packers after Vince Lombardi took them over in 1959. To him, running was a way of life—the only way to build a winning offense. And the Green Bay "49-sweep" was "our bread-and-butter, top-priority play, the one we have to make go and the one our opponents know they must stop." It was forged from the University of Pittsburgh single wing run by Dr. Jock Sutherland, from Lombardi's own experiences as a guard at Fordham, and reinforced by the slickness of the T-formation which did not tip off plays before they gathered steam.

"Everybody has to have a lead play," said Lombardi, "the play the team has confidence in because the coach has confidence in it. It's a hard-nosed play. It's got all the blocks that you teach. It's a teaching aid for me: the guards pulling, the tackles blocking down, the ends hooking, the backs blocking—everybody does something. In this one play, we can teach most every block we want. You call it the Green Bay sweep. The single wing off-tackle play is what it is."

28

The Green Bay Packers learned to combine the power of the old single wing with the finesse of the T to open up alleys for backs like Jimmy Taylor (31), squeezing between blocks by guard Jerry Kramer (64) and tackle Forrest Gregg (75). That's quarterback Bart Starr looking over Taylor's shoulder.

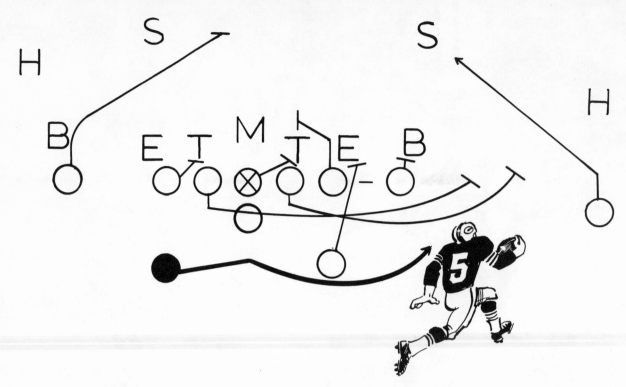

Other coaches periodically tried to break away from the orthodox alignment of the T which had two setbacks, a split end on the weak side of the line, a tight end on the strong side and a third back, the flanker, split outside the tight end. In 1958, Frank "Pop" Ivy borrowed from his experiences as a coach in Canada and evolved a triple wing-T for the Chicago Cardinals which he called the Jack-and-Jill formation. It had no running backs directly behind the quarterback. Both ends were split wide, right and left. Two backs were slotted outside the right tackle, the third back was in the gap between tackle and end on the left side. It was great for flooding the passing zones downfield with five eligible receivers, but it eventually had to be abandoned because a team couldn't develop a consistent running attack off it. It had no straight-ahead power.

The most radical departure from the T-formation was San Francisco's use of the "shotgun offense" for one exhilirating three-week period in 1961 when the 49ers beat the Detroit Lions 49–0, the Los Angeles Rams 35–0 and the Minnesota Vikings 38–24 on successive Sundays. Coach Red Hickey made his quarterback stop goosing the center and stand back five yards where everyone could see him take a direct snap. The left halfback and fullback lined up outside the tackles. The right halfback flanked wide to the right. It was actually a variation with modern spacing of the old spread used when the Southwest colleges put on aerial circuses in the 1930's.

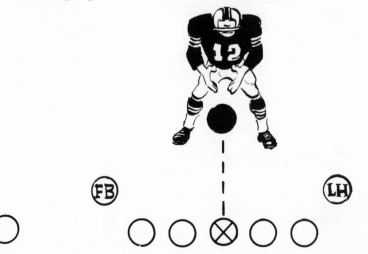

Even in the quick-hitting modern T, it's not uncommon to mass an escort of blockers in front of the ball carrier. Dickie Post of the San Diego Chargers, taking a handoff from John Hadl (21), finds no less than a five-man convoy—Brad Hubbert (26), guard Walt Sweeney (78), tight end Willie Frazier (83), guard Gary Kirner (72) and tackle Ron Mix (74)—in a foray against the Kansas City Chiefs.

Against the 4-3-4 defense the shotgun worked magnificently. Because the quarterback had to be a runner as well as a passer, in the manner of the traditional tailback, and T-quarterbacks weren't notably eager for that kind of contact, Hickey shuttled three different ones in and out of the game with spectacular success. Then they played the Chicago Bears. The Bears moved the middle linebacker, Bill George, into the line, right over the center. With the snap, he took off on a hell-bent charge directly for the quarterback. The Bear ends moved out to play head on the wingbacks and keep them from breaking over the middle for passes. The outside linebackers also made a beeline for the quarterback. The shotgun, under this kind of pressure, became a popgun, and the 49ers lost 31–0. The formation quickly disappeared, and stayed in limbo.

The ensuing entrenchment of the T-formation as the basic design for all the teams in pro football hasn't led to stagnation of offensive thinking, as some critics have claimed. Neither has the 4-3-4 defensive alignment meant that all teams play defense the same way. In fact, there is a schism in the philosophy of pro football right now.

Vince Lombardi was the great doctrinaire of the basic T-formation because he quickly found the horses to make it work. And since pro football is a business, and every businessman is impressed by success, other coaches quickly adopted his tack. The Los Angeles Rams play very much the same type of football as Green Bay.

But teams like the Dallas Cowboys have gone over to the multiple concept of offense. This means they try to present the defense with a different look on almost every play by varying their formations (i.e., the way they line up over the ball). The interior linemen and the quarterback remain constant, but in today's football you'll see teams shifting their backs around into the I-formation, the double wing, the triple wing, also sending a man in motion and frequently putting both of their wide receivers on the same side of the field.

The leading philosopher of the multiple concept is Tom Landry, the old defensive genius of the Giants who has been the only head coach in the history of the Cowboys (he was smart enough to start out with a ten-year contract, and the owners have had no reason to regret giving it to him). Landry started out coaching the Cowboys in 1960 with the knowledge that running the football was the foundation on which Dallas would build a representative team.

"When we started," he said, "the first thing we concentrated on was the development of a running attack. You must establish control by running action. Otherwise, the defensive linemen will ignore the running 'keys' and come strong on every play like it's going to be a pass. Then you're constantly under attack by the defense. You've simply got to establish a running threat on first and second downs.

"The defensive lineman keys mostly for traps. If he unloads on a passing game, he's vulnerable to trap or influence blocking. By establishing a run, you force him to hesitate mentally. Now your great defensive lineman like Deacon Jones of the Rams or our Bob Lilly can play every play for a pass and still have enough recovery to do his job if it's a run. But how many greats are there like them?

"Our philosophy of the running game has changed from the early days, however. We used an influence attack at first to mask our intentions from the defensive linemen.

32

[Note: what the Detroit Lions did to John Kissell of the Browns, described earlier in this chapter, is an example of influence blocking.]

"At the time [the height of the Lombardi era in Green Bay], the primary philosophy was run-to-daylight, with big linemen blocking for big backs. But on the Cowboys, an expansion team, we had ordinary linemen blocking for little backs. So we pulled our tackles to make the defensive end react, and then we ran inside the end. We'd throw a pitchout to look like a wide play, and then run inside. In influence blocking, you make a defensive man react according to his keys, and then you take it away from him.

"But with an attack like that, you end up in a situation where you're without bread-and-butter plays. Paul Brown at Cleveland and Lombardi had the personnel to make their types of offensive game go. We knew that when Green Bay got close or needed vital yardage, they would use the Jim Taylor slant to the weak side. But the Packers worked it anyhow.

"With our personnel, we couldn't afford to let the defense know where we were going. We started to change our attack, though, in 1965, when we got people like Ralph Neely and Tony Liscio [a pair of fine offensive tackles]. Now we have the horses up front, but we don't have the big backs. So we try to do different things. Our fullback, Don Perkins, doesn't have the tools for a basic concept of offense. We put in the multiple concept of offense. There are three teams that use the multiple concept—the Cowboys, the Bears, and Kansas City. Everybody else is basic, along the line of Los Angeles and Green Bay, although a team like Baltimore could be called in-between, using the basic formations but also some variations.

"You've got to have a philosophy. Ours is multiple formations. We might use ten to fourteen different formations in a game. We have twenty-five formations in our repertoire."

Landry argued that it doesn't put a big mental burden on the offensive back: "He doesn't care what ribbon the package is wrapped in; he just wants to keep the defense off balance."

Landry diagrammed the prevalent formations in pro football. First are the Basic Formations:

BALANCE

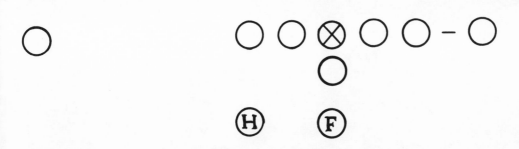

SPLIT

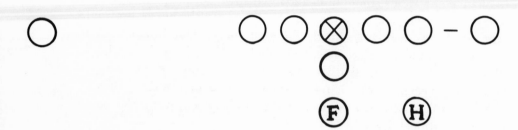

STRONG

Next, the multiple concept, or Variations, starting with (1) Double Wing:

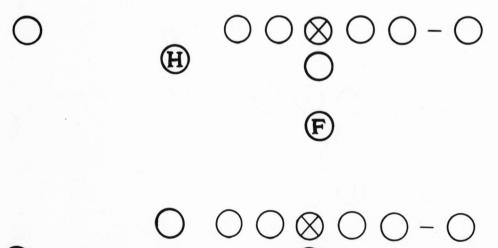

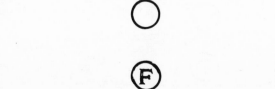

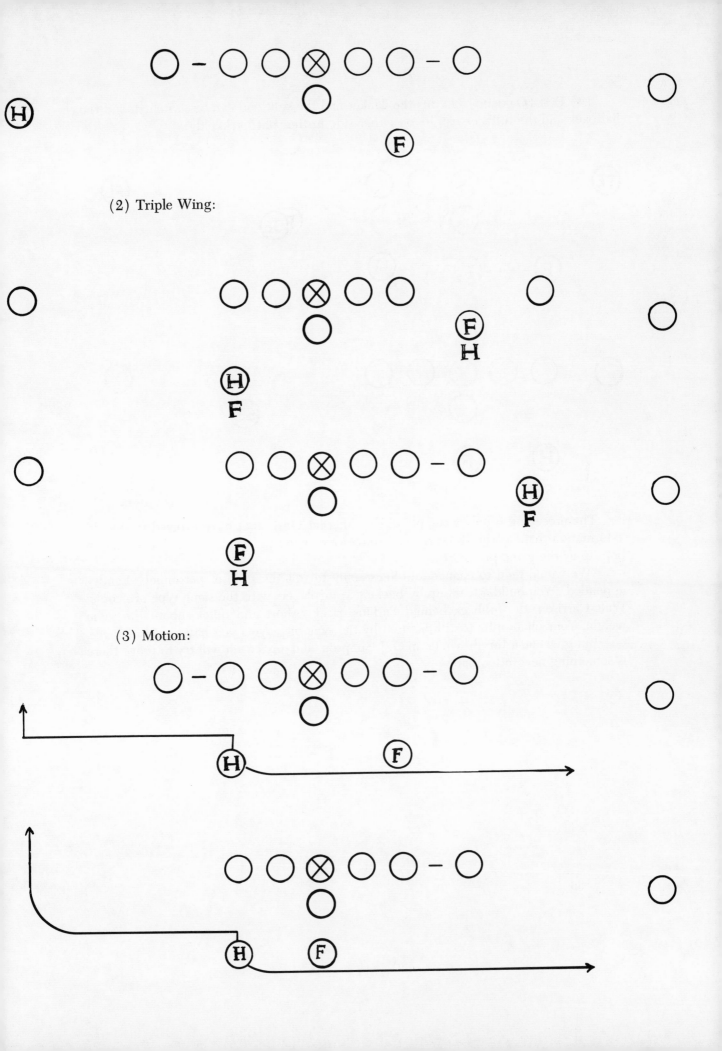

(2) Triple Wing:

(3) Motion:

(4) East (Oakland) (in this the flanker and the split end can be switched, and the halfback and the fullback can be on either side in the split backfield):

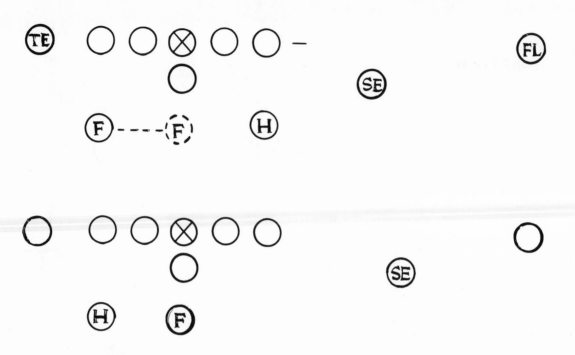

The preceding is only a sample of the different twists that have evolved in the old T-formation that George Halas revived thirty years ago. And new looks will continue to pop up as the game progresses.

"We would tend to change an offense only to suit the style of personnel," Landry appended. "You build a team up by backing your players with the same type of people. Walt Garrison, the fullback behind Perkins, is also short and quick, about the same weight. Your philosophy is still dictated by the type of players you have."

But give him a Jim Brown or an O. J. Simpson, and any coach will try to prove there is something new in football.

3. Run-to-Daylight Revolution

Vince Lombardi: "I think my great contribution, *the* contribution, was in the fact of the running game to start with. . . ."

From his office picture window on the second floor, overlooking the corner of Connecticut and L Streets in Washington, D. C., Vincent Thomas Lombardi could see spring winds swirl the government secretaries' skirts at the noon hour. But Vince wasn't looking. He was talking football, a passionate discourse that consumes him twelve months of the year. On this March afternoon in 1969, Vince Lombardi was back doing what he does best, coaching football. A one-year hiatus had worked fine for his golf game, but Vince was saying, "When football practice started last July 15, I realized the executive type of position or office type of position was not exactly my cup of tea. I felt at the time I had made a serious mistake."

Vince had resigned in 1968 from his active post as head coach of the Green Bay Packers with a nine-year record, excluding exhibition games, of 99 victories, 31 losses and four ties. That total included six Western division championships, five NFL titles and two Super Bowl victories. The Packers were the only team in modern pro history to win three league titles in a row. No one doubted that in his new stewardship with the Redskins, Vince would quickly achieve victory No. 100.

The record alone warrants inclusion of Mr. Lombardi's thoughts and philosophy in any study of the strategy of football. But particularly in a book devoted to the importance of running in football, the opinions of the emotional Italian from Brooklyn are as important as meat balls to spaghetti. Lombardi didn't, as they say, write the book. He merely underlined all the important phrases and changed a little bit of text, while adding an extra chapter to the art of running with a football.

Now, while he talked, Vince wheeled characteristically in his chair, turning profile to the visitor, drumming his fingers impatiently, a tight spring of energy repressed in his squat body.

"I think my great contribution, *the* contribution, was in the fact of the running game to start with," he said. "Well, they just didn't run in pro ball when I switched over from Army to the New York Giants in 1954 [as the chief assistant coach in charge of offense]. They just felt that they couldn't run. That was it, see? But everything is relative. They couldn't run because the people were too big or because of the defenses and so forth and so on. In the running game years ago, in professional football, the year I went with the Giants, they'd line up like this."

He sketched a bunch of circles hastily, impatiently on a lined yellow pad. "They'd split here and they'd split there."

Lombardi's diagram showed the left end moved away from the tackle and the right halfback moved outside the right end.

"Everything was so tight here," he continued, pointing to the circles which indicated the tightly bunched linemen, "the other team could line up opposite you on defense and, brother, they'd have you sandwiched in there, without any linebacker or anything else in there to help.

"Soon as we split the line [i.e., spaced the linemen with gaps between them], the linebacker couldn't stay inside to help jam up the play, and the man in the middle [the middle guard in the five-man line who played opposite the center] couldn't stay there because you'd isolate him and run all ways off him. They had to take him out and make him a middle linebacker. That's the evolution of the 4-3—the split line."

The split line gave his own men better blocking angles and also forced the defense to spread out. It was an invitation to the run, which is Lombardi's favorite play in football. He was a 180-pound guard at Fordham in the mid-1930's when the famous Seven Blocks of Granite evolved. Fordham and Pitt played 0–0 ties three years in a row, 1935–37, and Lombardi recalled that Pitt threw only one pass in two of the games—"In those days, everybody ran; nobody threw the ball." The doctrines of running and blocking which he applied at Green Bay were supposed to have been derived from his lessons at Fordham, and retained.

"No," he said, "none of that was retained. For example, the stance. We used to have kind of a sit down stance. We finally raised to a real sprinter's stance with the tail way the hell up in the air. We dropped it a little bit. But the tail is still higher than the shoulders. Years ago, you position-blocked more. You tried to get position on people. You don't do that any more. The change in blocking came when I was in high school. We always split the line wide. Take a look at all those high school pictures we had at St. Cecilia [in Englewood, New Jersey]—we split 'em. We always tried to isolate the defensive player. At coaching clinics, I always tell the high school coaches, 'You put the other fellow on an island by himself, with distance on either side of him, so the ball carrier working behind his blocker can cut either way.' That's the run-to-daylight style which we carry right today."

Run To Daylight! That's the Lombardi legacy to modern offense. It was the title of his book, published by Prentice-Hall in 1963.

"I've always used that term as long as I can remember," said Lombardi. "We used it when I was coaching high school. We'd block and say, 'Run to daylight.' The book gave it the publicity so that it became a cliché of football. I remember we were thinking about a title. Our first thought was something like Six Days to Sunday. And then we heard some guy in New York was using it on Allie Sherman's book. Then my wife, Marie, said, 'I don't know why you don't call it 'Run to Daylight.' That's all you ever talk about!'"

Weeb Ewbank, the veteran coach of the New York Jets, scoffed at all the credit going to Lombardi for the run-to-daylight principle. "Heck," said the coach of the 1969 Super Bowl champs, at sixty-two six years older than Lombardi, "my high school coach back in Richmond, Indiana, used to tell us to run to daylight." But the fact is that for as long as men run with the ball, the name of Lombardi will be associated with the phrase. He refined the strategy of a runner looking for the nearest shaft of light.

In putting it to work, Jimmy Taylor was Lombardi's original and best disciple. Taylor was a fullback built close to the ground, able to change direction quickly, and in 1962 he was the dominant runner in pro ball. One afternoon in a tavern in Green Bay, he explained what it was all about. He took four lumps of paper-wrapped sugar and placed them carefully on the polished mahogany that separated him from the guy in the black bow-tie and the rows of gleaming glasses.

40

The run-to-daylight concept perfected by the Packers finds Jimmy Taylor (31) breezing through a big hole against the Baltimore Colts and preparing to cut again off center Ken Bowman's (50) block. Taylor was the original disciple of the maneuver.

Rich Clarkson   Topeka *Capital-Journal*

The good runner, like Mike Garrett (21) of Kansas City, enhances the run-to-daylight philosophy by helping set up the blocks for his linemen. His fake here puts Ed Budde (71) in position to mow down San Diego's Rick Redman, as quarterback Len Dawson (16) watches.

"When I was in college at Louisiana State," he said deliberately, "there was no question where I was going when I carried the ball." He took lumps A and B, aligned them opposite lumps C and D. He moved his fingers so that A shoved C to the left, B shoved D to the right.

"And right through that empty space between them," said Taylor, "that was where I went."

But, the question was raised, supposing that the shoving was to no avail, that there was no hole? Jimmy shrugged as if to say he went there anyhow.

"Now," he grabbed a couple of lumps, "this is the way we do it in the pros. This here is [Packer offensive guard] Jerry Kramer. There," pointing to the second lump, "is the guy he's got to block. I come right in on Jerry's tail. I have an option. If I see Jerry's going to sting his man to the right, I go to the left around them. If I see he's going to block his man to the left, then I veer to the right. That's what you call running to daylight."

Taylor demonstrated the maneuver when he scored Green Bay's only touchdown in the 16–7 championship game victory over the New York Giants in '62. From the 7-yard line, late in the first half, he took a handoff and headed over the right side of the line. Middle linebacker Sam Huff and the other Giants slid over to meet him. The Packer blockers didn't try to deter them. They fired straight out at the Giant tacklers. But Taylor quickly turned from the pile looming in front of him and cut sharply left to daylight and a clear road to the goal line.

"We no longer teach backs to run solely to the hole," said Lombardi in his book. "They know, of course, where the hole is supposed to be, but we school them to run to the daylight . . . and when Jimmy Taylor doesn't predetermine where he is going, he is as good as they come at running inside or outside that block."

Although Lombardi as a coach espoused good old-fashioned hitting as the fundamental thesis of his system, he tempered it with realism. Running to daylight wasn't the magic formula for making other teams keel over. "All things being equal," he said, "a good offensive lineman cannot take a good defensive man in, out or straight ahead very often. That's why, at Green Bay, we used two-on-one line blocking for most of our running." He had been grounded in college football theory as an assistant under Red Blaik at Army, where the football infantry dominated all other branches, but he also understood how the pros related running to passing.

"The collegians use the pass to make the run go," he said. "The pros use the run to make the pass go. I think the pass is a very important part of the game. When two teams are evenly matched, I think it's the pass that wins the game. But I don't think you can just throw the ball. The running game makes your passing game, really. We never went into a game in which we said, 'We're going to throw the ball.' Or, 'We're going to run the hell out of the ball.' The trend of the game always dictates what you do. I realize there are some teams that are weak against the pass and some teams that are supposedly weak against the run. We may put a little more emphasis on the running game or on the passing for a particular opponent. But if we could run the ball and we could control the ball, that's what we would try to do. Against everybody."

43

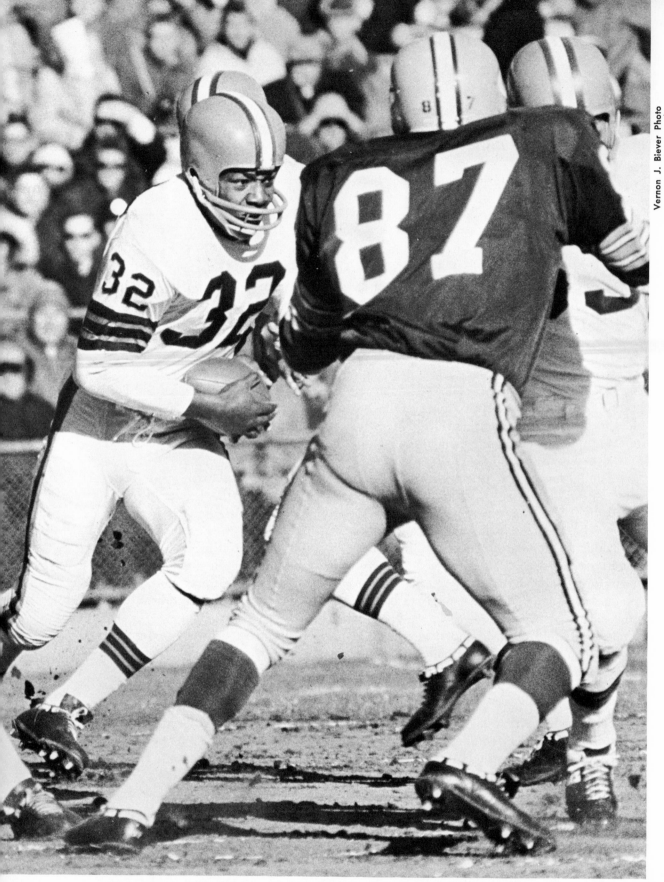

Jimmy Brown (32) felt a new running freedom when the Cleveland Browns installed an option type of offense, so that Jimmy, on his own initiative, could cut inside tacklers like Green Bay's Willie Davis (87) as a Brown blocker screens him off.

In the early years he was able to achieve control with the perfect execution the Packers gave to his favorite play, 49-sweep, described in the previous chapter. "Funny," mused Lombardi, "I used that same sweep in 1954 with the Giants, but it never got the publicity." Of course, Vince didn't get much publicity then either as an assistant coach. He came to the Giants virtually unknown outside the metropolitan area and a novice to pro ball.

"Some day," grinned Frank Gifford, who played halfback for him in New York, "I'll diagram the first play Lombardi put in. It was called 'Stutter Dive Lateral and Rollout.' Charley Conerly, our quarterback, practiced it for three years and never used it in a game. There was no way it would work."

(Gifford also added, "Lombardi's a great man. He learned from us, and then we learned from him.")

The Lombardi teachings are also tied in with his philosophy as a man. In August 1968, after he had stepped down as head coach of the Packers to concentrate on being general manager, he was invited to address the annual meeting of the Football Writers Association of America at the time of the College All-Star game in Chicago. It was a tough, cynical audience, the kind that you don't impress with clichés about the virtues of football. Yet Lombardi stood before them and delivered such homilies as: "I think football is a symbol of what this country's attributes are—courage, stamina, coordinated efficiency (or teamwork). . . . The great hope of this society is the character of a person in action. . . . Heart power is the strength of the Green Bay Packers. . . ." When he was done, the writers gave him a standing ovation, overwhelmed by the integrity of his feelings and the sincerity of his words. The force of his beliefs were transmitted to his team. A man who played for Lombardi had to "pay the price."

When he first came to Green Bay, he decided after studying movies of the previous season's games that the one ballplayer he really needed was Paul Hornung to play half-back and carry out another Lombardi strategem—the pass-option run off the sweep. Hornung was better known for his exploits off the field than on, but Lombardi investigated and found that a lot of it was exaggerated. He also found that Hornung would take direction. "Paul Hornung," he once wrote, "was the epitome of what you try to make every one of your players—a true believer."

Around the National Football League there were also other believers in the Lombardi cult after they saw the effectiveness of his methods at Green Bay. For one thing, throughout the NFL there was increased concentration on the development of a running attack, and there was better understanding of his basic principle of running to daylight. In pro ball, there are no secrets because teams make minute studies of each other's films and dissect a play into all its elements. Not everybody could adopt the Lombardi sweep and put it into perfect execution because not everybody had pulling guards like Jerry Kramer and Fuzzy Thurston and not everybody had a tailback like Paul Hornung. But they were impressed with the weakside slant, designated 36 off a Brown right formation, simple in its conception, easily adapted for any team that had a running back with the slightest imagination. On "Brown right 36," the fullback Jim Taylor slanted to the weak-side tackle and then exercised his options:

45

This was the essence of running to daylight, and it had a profound impression on Blanton Collier when he took over the direction of the Cleveland Browns in 1963. In Jimmy Brown, he had a perfect fullback to capitalize on the possibilities of option running. Brown was also temperamentally eager for something new after years of restraint under the rigid controls of Paul Brown, who sent in every play from the bench.

Halfway through the 1963 season, the Browns were engaged in a stubborn battle with the New York Giants. In the third quarter, holding a four-point lead, they recovered a fumble in New York territory. As they huddled on third down at the 32-yard line, Jimmy Brown nudged Frank Ryan, the quarterback, and said, "I think Option 7 would go good now."

On "Option 7" in the Cleveland play repertoire, the fullback moving to the left had three choices: he could hit between guard and tackle, drive over his left tackle or swing wide around the end. It was a replica of the Green Bay action. Brown also added a quick thought, "Let's use it with our old 3-and-2 formation instead of a 6-7."

This involved a subtle change and meant that Brown, instead of lining up directly behind Ryan, shifted over behind his left tackle, shading him closer to the outside. As the play broke, Sam Huff, the Giants' middle linebacker who frequently keyed on the fullback, blitzed up the middle, shutting off that alley. Brown took the ball from Ryan and swung immediately to the outside, shaking off Huff. He broke into the open along the sideline, saw a gang of Giants converging on him and cut across the grain (reversed his field) to sprint the distance of 32 yards and bust the Giant resistance for the rest of the afternoon. The Browns won, 35–24, and later the quarterback explained why it paid to let Brown have his head in the preceding situation: "You know he's going to carry the ball for you most of the time, so Jimmy's got to run plays he's going to have confidence in. He's a wonderful man to consult about running the ball, you know."

So was Vince Lombardi, who convinced the pros that the simple act of one man blocking and another man running could be highly successful in professional football.

46

4. Running Requisites and Styles

Vernon J. Biever Photo

"That's what running is all about—acceleration and cutting against the grain," and so Gale Sayers prepares to step out on one of his exciting gallops.

If every man who aspired to carry a football stood six feet two inches, weighed 228 pounds, ran 100 yards in slightly under 10 seconds, had the upper torso of a wrestler, the waist of an Egyptian belly dancer and the legs of Nijinsky (Nureyev, if you want to bring it up to date), every coach would still ask, "Yeah, but can he run?"

The amalgam of that specialized professional creature, the running back, can't be gauged for tensile strength on physical makeup alone, or pro scouts would stake out vantage points on Santa Monica's muscle beach to check prospects. There is no rigid code of anatomical specifications for the running back.

He has been as short as 5′ 4″ Buddy Young and as tall as 6′ 4″ Dub Jones. He has been as slender as 170-pound George McAfee and as bulky as 252-pound Cookie Gilchrist. He has been as fast as Joe Perry (a 9.5 sprinter) and as slow as Alex Webster, who barely broke five seconds for the 40. There have been runners such as Doak Walker and Bill Dudley who have been both relatively small and relatively slow. And there have been runners such as Hugh McElhenny and Ollie Matson who have been both big and fast. All have been highly successful ball carriers in the most strenuous competition.

There are, of course, ideals. When he is 6′ 2″, 228, V-shaped, with the highly developed thighs of a ballet dancer and answers to the name of Jim Brown, the coach doesn't ask any questions. When the coach has to settle for less than the ideal, there are still certain basic requisites he looks for.

"He's got to have size," noted Vince Lombardi, "for the physical punishment. And he's got to have quickness. I don't care how much speed he has. I never had a back in my life who could run, as far as pure speed is concerned. Not one. Paul Hornung had no speed. You'd see Jimmy Taylor get caught from behind. Elijah Pitts got caught from behind."

That word, "quickness," recurs every time football people start talking about the essential qualities of a great back. Red Grange had quickness. Steve Van Buren had quickness. Jimmy Taylor had quickness. Gale Sayers and Leroy Kelly have quickness.

Speed can't be dismissed glibly, however. There's no substitute for a back who can provide a long breakaway run at certain stages in a game, who tears loose periodically on 25-yard gallops. He opens up a game in the same way that a home run hitter like Mickey Mantle sparked the Yankees. Sayers has been that type of back. No one catches him from behind.

A couple of old campus greats who became silvery-tongued oracles of the sports microphone were talking about this relation of speed and quickness during a pause in the action of a game they were telecasting. Johnny Lujack, an All-American quarterback at Notre Dame and not a bad runner, noted that it was more vital for a back to have quickness than blazing speed. It suddenly occurred to Johnny that his partner at the mike, Tom Harmon, one of the all-time great college runners, qualified as a practiced authority on the subject. "Say, Tom," he asked, "in your running days, were you fast or quick?"

"Just scared," responded Harmon.

Along that line, A. S. "Jake" Gaither, the long-time coach at Florida A & M, an incubator of such pro running talent as the late Willie Galimore of the Chicago Bears and Hewritt Dixon of the Oakland Raiders, once said he preferred to have his halfbacks with a little streak of yellow showing up the middle of their backs—it didn't affect their quickness and certainly helped their speed. Jake also said he wanted his backs to be "a-gile, mo-bile and hos-tile." Speed is the plus item, if it can be harnessed.

Cactus Jack Curtice, a former president of the American Football Coaches Association, once had a fullback who started so fast the officials were always calling him for being in motion before the snap of the ball and penalizing the team five yards. "One day," Curtice related, "the referee was especially exasperating and I took him aside at the half and explained that my man was not really starting too soon. He was so fast it only looked that way. On the first play of the second half, my fullback takes off down the middle of the field for 40 yards and they call the play back. I'm out on the field before the ref can step off the first yard and complain to him, 'Didn't I already explain to you that my man is so fast it only looks like he's starting so soon?'

" 'I believe you,' the ref said. 'In fact, he's so fast, I'm penalizing the other 10 guys on your team for delaying the game.' "

In casting their backfields, coaches are cognizant of trying to fit the parts together —size, speed, quickness. "If you have a backfield with a Jimmy Brown and an Ernie Green, who had a lot of speed when he started at Cleveland, you have a good combination," said Allie Sherman. "But if you wind up with a big back who's got only power and a small back who doesn't have speed, you're not going to do much. You better go out and get yourself two big backs, regardless of speed. Then you have a chance of sustaining a running game. If you can average out to 4.2 yards a pop, though you like to do better, that's okay. But you also have to sustain the concept of offense—if you haven't got speed in the backfield, you better damn well make sure you have exceptional receivers and a good quarterback. Otherwise, with even the best power running backs, they're going to start taking that run away from you."

There are other qualities in the running back which can't be measured except under fire. There's a tangible gauge for quickness. How soon a back hits the hole, how swiftly he picks up his interference, how sharply he cuts to evade a tackle—his reaction time in all these instances is discernible. But you can't see such psychic attributes as toughness and instinct, which also are part of being a pro running back.

John Henry Johnson of the Pittsburgh Steelers and Jimmy Taylor were tough. A running back gets hit by 250-pound people. He must have a zest for contact. That means he must initiate it, get in the first lick, to overcome the disparity in size between him and the man trying to stop him. The Steelers were trying to groom a sturdy young ball carrier to be Johnson's running mate one year. He had an excellent college record, his school boasting that he had never been thrown behind the line of scrimmage. He weighed 230 pounds, was quick and strong, and from the back the slope of his neck almost obscured his ears. If ever a young prospect came prepared to earn a living, this kid was it. He also had the mental aptitude for the game, and for a while he fulfilled all expectations. Then a tough linebacker flattened him in an exhibition, stomped him and gloated, "I bet you

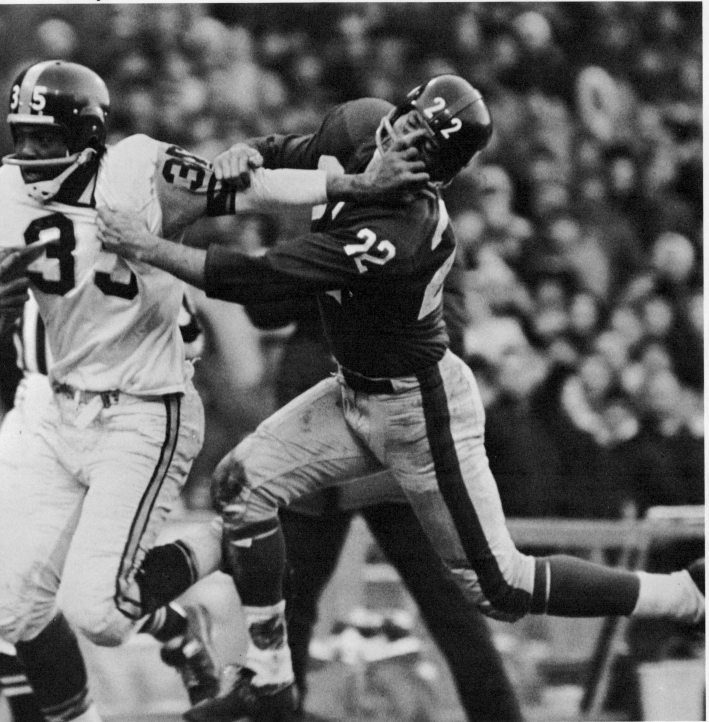

John Henry Johnson, shoving a hand against the face of Dick Lynch (22) of the New York Giants, was the prototype of the tough ball carrier.

never got hit like that before." The young husky quickly lost interest in his work and soon was out of pro football.

Paul "Tank" Younger of the Los Angeles Rams always made it a point to run over a tackler a time or two in the first quarter of a game. "It made it a lot easier for me when we met later in the game," said the big fullback. "It also had a psychological effect on our next opponent. He was going to see it in the films."

Instinct is a feel for the game. Good teaching can overcome some faults. When Eddie Price came to the Giants, he was a 190-pound bundle of toughness and getaway speed with one bad habit—he kept running into people. When Eddie learned to swerve, he became a league-leading rusher. But you can't teach a man to avoid the threat of a tackle reflexively. Nature has equipped him with a special antenna into his subconscious if he is a good running back. Harold "Red" Grange, the first and most renowned of the glamor backs, was very frank about his remarkable talent:

"I can't take much credit for what I did running because I don't know what I did. Nobody ever taught me, and I can't teach anyone. The ability to run with a ball is something you have or you haven't. They talk about the runs I made, but I can't tell you one thing I did on any run. The sports writers wrote that I had peripheral vision. I didn't even know what the word meant. I had to look it up. They asked me about my change of pace, and I didn't even know that I ran at different speeds. I had a cross-over step, but I couldn't spin away from a tackle. I'd have broken a leg."

Of the modern breed, Tommy Mason of the Minnesota Vikings and Los Angeles Rams said, "You can teach a man to pass or block or catch the ball, but running is instinct. You see a crease of daylight, and you go—sheer instinct."

Men like Frank Gifford and Paul Hornung applied their feel for the game to excel in allied roles of the running back—as option passers and pass receivers. Running the sweep, with an option of passing the ball or keeping it, they made their split-second decisions instinctively—there's no time for debate in a quickly developing play, when a wrong decision puts a 260-pound defensive end in the runner's lap. Frank and Paul were invariably right. When they went out of the backfield to catch the ball, that same feel was an asset in getting open. The good ones sense how a defender is going to react to their moves.

"Your reflexes," said Gifford, "are conditioned by what you're trying to do. I found that was true in carrying the ball also. When it was third down and one, I ran a lot different than when it was second and nine. Hitting into the line, I was never conscious of faces in front of me. I was never conscious of the fear of getting hit. I looked at belts and legs. They were my only guide."

Frank's style of running was search and slash, geared to his dimensions—he had average size and average speed for a pro back, but he had good elusiveness and drive. "The most important difference between college and pro ball," he said, "is that there is no room for dancing around in the pros. The only exceptions I know of are Hugh McElhenny and Sayers."

Gifford had it figured out that there's one major danger area where plays are stopped, where the pursuit catches up with the ball carrier, near the line of scrimmage, and his intention was always to spend as little time as he could in that area.

52

"I thought positively," he said. "I always felt the hole was going to open up the way the play was designed, but you have to be realistic. When there's a guard kicking out at the corner back, and another guard kicking out at the linebacker, you've got that little bit of space between, and you better get through there without any waste of time or it'll close up. There's little or no room for a guy dancing around. You have to accelerate at that one point."

Gifford was also helped in his running by being a diligent student of the game. "I tried to know where everyone was going to be," he said, "and what the assignments were. The right tackle on our team might be having a tough time with his man. If I was aware of it, it would force me wider on my sweeps to cut down the danger." And he also studied the opposing personnel. When Kyle Rote was the Giants' split end and a sweep was called with Gifford carrying the ball, Frank would advise Kyle on his spacing. If he wanted a "safety force" because he knew that the corner back was an excellent tackler, while the safety was just mediocre, Frank asked Kyle to line up wider than usual, keeping the corner back occupied and forcing the safety to come up to meet the run. If he felt the safety was a better tackler than the outside defender, Frank asked Kyle to line up tighter and keep the safety occupied, while he took his chances with the corner back. These nuances aren't visible to the average fan.

"There are four elements," Gifford pointed out, "in the making of a good running back besides the natural assets of size and speed. One is knowledge, being aware of what's going on. The second is confidence, thinking positive, and that takes in the courage to get hit and still keep going. Third is realism—not everything's going to work the way it's diagrammed in the play book, so you better be ready to adjust and improvise. Fourth is staying healthy, and that can be more than luck. Some guys like Tom Matte of Baltimore are always ready to play, no matter what's hurting."

Y. A. Tittle, who had a good observation post for seventeen years as a pro quarterback, felt there was a common characteristic in the way virtually all the great ones ran. "They don't," he said, "lift their feet off the ground as they're running. At least, not more than a few inches. Get 'em all in your mind. Brown, Taylor, Perry, John David Crow, Alex Webster, Don Perkins. They all look like they're riding low scooters. Even Lenny Moore, who's got that high knee action when he's out in the open, slides both feet close to the ground when he goes through the line.

"I think it's important. It gives them balance. If you're hit with one foot high in the air, it'll knock you right over. But if one foot's making contact with the ground and the other's only six inches away, you've got a chance to recover from the impact of a tackle and keep your feet."

Having both feet close to the ground also enabled the strong runners to drive quickly off either foot and kick through when they needed a little extra power. "I didn't try to run like Bobby Mitchell," Brown once said. "I couldn't skip over the grass. I had to pound into the turf."

Running style created a nickname in 1967 for rookie Travis Williams, a 9.3 sprinter who weighs 212 pounds, and provided a late season spurt to the Green Bay Packers' drive to the world championship. He returned four kickoffs for touchdowns and led them in rushing the last two games of the season and in the divisional playoff. To the

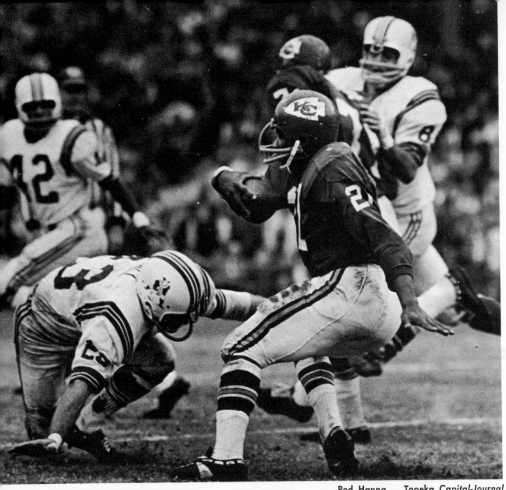

The "book" prescribes both feet close to the ground for running balance, and Mike Garrett, swerving from a Buffalo tackler, has his feet solidly under him.

Rod Hanna   Topeka *Capital-Journal*

Vernon J. Biever Photo

The ability to cut back, "against the grain," increased Jimmy Taylor's effectiveness as a Green Bay fullback. That's Alex Karras (71) of Detroit on the deck.

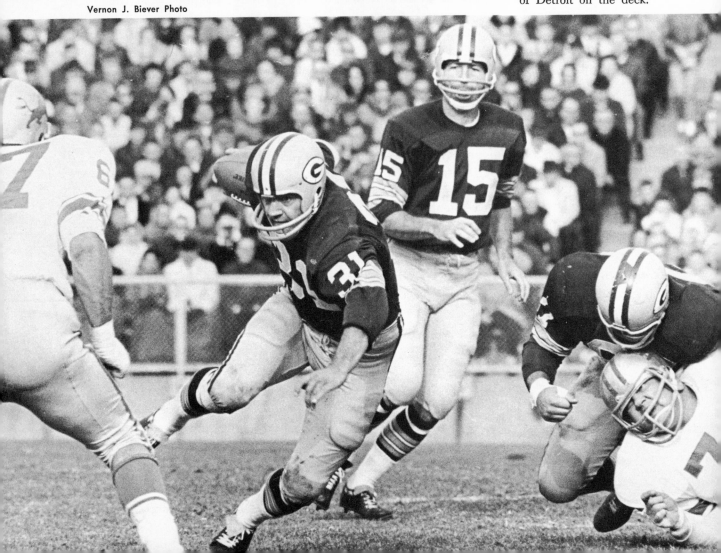

entire state of Wisconsin, he became The Road Runner, after a 20-inch bird whose real name is *Geococcyx Californianus,* who runs faster than a horse and makes incredibly fast turns. In the horse-and-buggy days, the feathered road runner got his name by whooshing out into the road ahead of a surrey and then pacing it down the road, clucking a challenge to the horse to catch up. None ever did. The Road Runner—latter day version—hasn't done much since that first spurt. He's still learning where the roads on a football field lead.

A runner has two main avenues of approach when he carries the ball. He can try to run around the crowd. He can try to run through it. The natural inclination would seem to be the detour, but curiously a majority of pro backs prefer to go inside. Although one of the NFL's smallest runners, the Rams' Dick Bass said, "I enjoy running up the middle because I have an advantage against a bigger man. I can duck under him or wiggle away from him. I have a tougher time outside where those defensive backs are more my size and can keep up with me."

Teammate Tommy Mason, rangier than Bass, also noted, "I'd much rather hit the 0-1-4-5 holes than go wide. If you get through the middle, you have the option of cutting in two directions. On a sweep, the defensive pursuit often won't allow you to cut back. Sweeps are harder, especially if you don't turn the corner right away. The defense begins to string out and it's waiting for you."

Eddie Price, another relatively little man, also ran inside all the time. The Giants used to call him "Popovich" because of the way he popped through the middle. The great inside runners, though, were men like Jim Brown and Alex Webster who added another dimension. The minute they hit the line of scrimmage they were looking for a way to "cut against the grain." Cutting against the grain is the simple description for a back reversing his field, which winds up with the pursuing tacklers (the grain) going one way and the runner going the other.

"That's what running is all about," said Gifford, "acceleration and cutting against the grain. My favorite play was the end run and the cutback. When you cut back, you decrease the amount of time you spend in the danger area. When you keep running wide, it becomes a footrace and you generally get caught. Of course, you also get hit a lot harder when you cut back and there's someone there to meet you. But if you do it consistently, it makes the pursuit a little more cautious. They don't come after you so fast, and that gives you a few more cutting angles to keep them off balance."

Gifford deplored the absence of outside runners in recent years and attributed it to the mania for big men in the backfield. The big backs generally don't have the agility to sweep right, plant the right foot and drive off it in a completely new direction.

"Teams started using such big backs," he explained, "to counteract the blitz which got popular after 1960. But I always felt that a 190-pound back can handle a linebacker. Now with big backs, who don't run good pass patterns, teams can also use bigger linebackers because they can cover those backs. I think in the future you might see more of those fast defensive back types shift over to the offense to carry the ball. They're also better receivers. Leroy Keyes is my prospect for a super type among all the young backs coming up because he already runs instinctively like he's been playing pro ball for ten years."

The good ones don't have to be told that when you run left, carry the ball in your left hand, and switch it when you run right, since 95 percent of the traffic comes from the inside, and it's good to have the inside arm free to ward it off. The old-fashioned straightarm is out. A good defensive player will grab it and spin the runner off his feet. But the free forearm has been used as a bludgeon very effectively by Jimmy Brown and John Henry Johnson. They intimidated tacklers. Someone like Gifford didn't have their strength, so he had another device. As a man came in to tackle him, he'd drop his left arm (he generally ran to the right) and let it take the initial blow, ride with it, then use the arm to shove off and break free of the tackle.

Not all runners have adhered to the orthodox methods. It didn't matter to Steve Van Buren which direction he ran in—he always carried the ball in his right arm, and no one complained at the results. Jim Crowley, a member of the famed Four Horsemen of Notre Dame, scored three touchdowns in the 1925 Rose Bowl game, two on long runs. After his second long run, Coach Knute Rockne took him out of the game, to a standing ovation. When Crowley, a droll character, got to the sidelines, he said to Rockne, "I know why you're taking me out, Coach. You saw it!"

"Saw what?" asked Rockne, who was known as a perfectionist.

"Why on that last run," said Sleepy Jim, "I carried the ball under the wrong arm."

The rules are flaunted by the exceptional talents. McElhenny might hit a line and turn his back. Sayers would leave his interference and start across the field in another direction. Both might look like they were off balance, one foot on the ground, another high in the air describing a pirouette. That kind you let alone.

For the others, there are basic prescriptions. The smart back in the open field will run straight at the defender to straighten him up before making his feints and fakes. Then, depending upon the reactions of the defender, he has three ways to go—right, left or straight. A good back will also set up his blocks by dipping one way or zigging another to make the defender hesitate and give the blockers a chance to move in and cut him down. In the swirl of action, backs are guided by the colors they pick up. They never see the men opposite them. "If I see a flash of color on my right," said Tommy Mason, "I know I'm about to be hit from that side and prepare for it. I spin and give them a limp leg and try to twist out and keep going."

For all his natural ability, no one analyzed his craft better than Jimmy Brown in the nine years he set every conceivable running record at Cleveland. In material prepared for *Sports Illustrated*, he broke down some of the essentials: "At the beginning of a play, I literally use a three-point stance. My right toe is on a line a bit behind the left heel. My head is up, I am balanced lightly by my right fingertips and I am in a position, coming out of the crouch, to look for my opening and blockers. For the hand-off, my hands are held palms up. . . . I cup a hand over one end of the ball and put the other end in the crook of my elbow. I still have one arm free to fight off tacklers. . . . When a tackler closes in, I counteract his force with two blows: one with my shoulder, the other with my free arm. I do not ram him with my head, but I do tuck my body lower to gather my strength. . . . I deliver a full, powerful blow with my forearm, aiming it for his chest or midsection. If I am hit low, I dip down to get a better blow with my forearm and pivot at the same time. . . . If I am hit high, I strike with my shoulder and swiftly

56

Running style can also be highly individualized, such as the high kick being displayed here by Keith Lincoln of San Diego.

Clemon Daniels gained more yards than any AFL back by occasionally vaulting over the enemy.

The feet of Donny Anderson (44), Green Bay's bonus baby, seem to be going in all directions.

Vernon J. Biever

Russ Reed

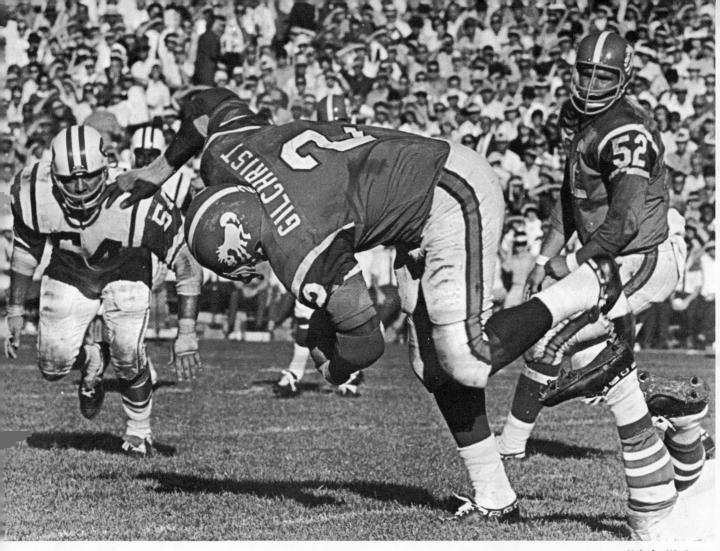

Malcolm W. Emmons

Cookie Gilchrist struggles manfully to keep his 252 pounds in an upright position as he advances against the New York Jets.

A tight cradle around the football keeps it secure in the grip of Earl Gros as he absorbs the jar of a tackle by defensive end Bill Glass of Cleveland.

The strength of Jimmy Brown was in his powerful glide, both feet in syncromesh, tacklers just along for the ride.

RECEIVING BACKS - 1959

A. <u>Stance</u> - Three Points

    1. Feet - Comfortable spread - under arm pits - toe to instep or parallel.
    2. Hips - Slightly lower than head - head up - eyes stright ahead.
    3. Keep weight balance on balls of both feet - hand touching ground - little weight on hands.
    4. Keep stance constant - no leaning.

B. <u>Start</u> - Start with the count every time.

    1. Your "down" hand should move with the starting number.
    2. Start fast and run hard.

C. <u>Hand-Off</u>

    1. Line yourself up with the defensive hold - there must be a definite point exchange for the hand-off - adjust to the five, six or seven man lines.
    2. Try to have the inside foot forward as the hand-off begins. Complete the hand-off while the outside foot is coming forward.
    3. Look straight ahead seeing both the ball and the defensive hole at the same time.
    4. As you receive the ball, have your body leaning forward but do not bend over - keep the pocket open.
    5. <u>Responsibility</u> - 2/3 is on the QB giving the ball - 1/3 is on the back taking the ball.
    6. <u>Inside Arm and Hand</u> - Palm up - Below and slightly in front of hip bone - elbow close to body - do not move hand until after ba is placed - this hand serves as a bottom to the pocke
    7. <u>Outside Arm and Hand</u> - Elbow close to body - arm extended forward - palm turned slightly upward - this serves as a front and side to the pocket.
    8. <u>Fold Outside Hand over Ball</u> - Be able to take the ball with this one hand.
    9. <u>Slide inside hand under ball</u> - <u>After</u> ball is placed, do not grab for the ball (if receiver grabs QB's hand he is wror
    10. <u>Put the ball away at once</u> - Get your hand over the point of the ball - do r shift the ball from arm to arm.

D. <u>Faking</u> - A definite assignment.

    1. Carry out all game fakes past the line of scrimmage - convince the defense you have the ball.
    2. <u>Point of Fake</u> - Fake through the correct hole every time - you are responsi for not bumping the QB or the ball.
    3. Use the same movement for faking as when receiving the ball.
    4. The best possible fake is hard running - buckle up and run hard - make the defense tackle you.
    5. After carrying out a fake, get ahead of the ball carrier as a blocker.

This is an actual page from the 1969 Cleveland play book
with specific instructions for running backs.

bring my forearm up at the tackler with a pendulum swing. . . . When I am hit squarely, I shake and move every muscle I have. Sometimes I manage to get loose."

Anybody who played for Paul Brown also came equipped with a full set of instructions, down to how his shoes were to be laced. A selection from the Cleveland play book is reproduced on the opposite page; it is taken from the 1959 edition when Jimmy was at his peak. It applied to all backs who got the ball from the quarterback.

Brown also learned as he went along. In the early years his biggest fault was hitting the line with his head down and his eyes closed. Against the Cardinals one afternoon, he drove forward on a dive play the Browns used in short yardage situations. He went into the middle with his head down, expecting to get hit hard. But it was one of those plays where every man did his job perfectly, and a clear field opened up in front of him. Nose downward, Brown lost his balance and fell, costing him an easy touchdown. After that, he hit the line with his head up and his eyes open.

"I like to come into the line in a semi-crouch," he said, "not too low, so that I'll be balanced if the hole jumps wide open. I like to grip the ball with one hand instead of two like a lot of fullbacks because I feel that you can't have much balance or make those quick veers with two hands over the ball. In the pros, it's very hard to open a large hole. So when a hole is open and you don't take advantage of it, you're really in trouble. You have to spot daylight and drive for it as hard as possible."

And the great Cleveland fullback borrowed from his contemporaries. "Don Bosseler, the Washington Redskins' fullback, was extremely successful in hurdling the enemy line in short-yardage situations," Brown noted. "I looked at films of him till I was groggy and finally got the answer. It was simple. When defensive linemen charged low, Bosseler hurdled over them. When they didn't submarine, he hit straight ahead. That's all there was to it."

And Brown went on to score more touchdowns than any runner in history. As he was ready to retire, he was asked to describe the qualifications for a good running back. His answer synopsized the subject:

"First, I think he should have quickness. This is very important in football. Speed is important but not as important as a lot of people think. Of course, he should have good speed but extreme speed isn't necessary. He should be powerful because he has to have the combination of quickness and power in pro football today. I think he should have good hands because then they pay attention to him when he flares. But most of all I think it is important that he is smart enough to be able to know the blocking of his linemen and to be able to make the cuts and make the adjustments that are necessary in running a pattern."

With all of those qualities, a man who was 6′ 2″, weighed 228 pounds and ran the 100 in slightly under 10 seconds set the style for all time in the ball carrying set.

5. Receiver and Thrower

One of the finest of all receivers to come out of the backfield has been Bill Brown (30) of Minnesota, in dark uniform, wrestling the ball away from Cleveland's Larry Benz.

The pressure was on Joe Willie Namath the first time he went back to pass in the Super Bowl game between the New York Jets and the Baltimore Colts in Miami's Orange Bowl on January 12, 1969. It was second and 14 early in the first quarter from his own 31-yard line, and 75,377 people watching the action live, plus eleven Baltimore Colts, knew he was going to put the ball in the air. In modern football, a theory has evolved that the best way to prevent a successful forward pass is to get to the quarterback before he can throw the ball. One of the ways to get to the quarterback is to send one or more linebackers or even a safety on a pell-mell charge through the massed forward walls with the single aim of shooting down the passer. This is known as blitzing, or red-dogging.

One of the ways for the offense to counter the effect of a blitz, or red-dog, is for the alert quarterback to dump the ball into the nearest friendly hands, which generally belong to one of his backfield mates. This is known as a safety valve or swing or flare control pass.

As Namath, schooled to recognize the blitz, dropped back to pass against the Colts in this situation, he immediately saw a flash of blue jersey out of the right corner of his eye, indicating to him that Mike Curtis, the left or strong side linebacker, would be breathing down his throat any split-second. It was just what Joe Willie, who is quick of mind and hand, wanted. He spun to his right an instant before Curtis could reach him and lobbed the ball in a soft arc behind the line of scrimmage. He put just enough on the pass so that Matt Snell, number 41, the fullback of the Jets, had to reach for the ball in full stride. Snell was a sometime end at Ohio State in his collegiate days. He has long, sure fingers. His hands cradled the football just as he reached the area outside his right end.

Normally, Mike Curtis would have confronted him. But the Colt linebacker was keeping Namath company in the backfield, so Matt had a clear road ahead of him. He chugged for nine yards beyond the line of scrimmage until defensive back Bobby Boyd of the Colts recovered to tackle him.

The gain was one classic example of how a running back is used to become a vital part of the passing game. Another classic example occurred in 1964 when the Baltimore Colts, this time the protagonists, unseated the Green Bay Packers as the NFL champions. The teams met in the second game of the season after the Colts had lost their opener. Another defeat, and Coach Don Shula confessed, "We had a feeling we would have blown it all." Green Bay was the team they had to beat.

In their planning for the Packers, the Colts spent a lot of time working on a flood play that had been devised to isolate Lenny Moore, their fast halfback, on a linebacker. In the flood, Moore moved from his normal setback position to a slot between the right tackle and tight end John Mackey. To his outside was flanked Jimmy Orr, which gave the Colts three fine receivers on that side of the field. Raymond Berry, their split end, was all alone by himself on the other side of the field. The strategy was that if the Packers rotated their defense to meet the triple threat on the strong side, Berry would be isolated in single coverage on the left side, an ideal situation for a receiver. If the Packers did not rotate, they had to pick up Lenny Moore with a linebacker, and there was no linebacker in football fast enough to match him step for step.

The Packers, as it turned out, did not rotate. They depended on Dan Currie, the strong side linebacker, to cover Moore as the Colts went into the flood formation at their 48-yard line early in the first quarter. Johnny Unitas, the quarterback, smartly saw this and called the play. Moore ran at Currie, side-stepped around him and then flew straight down the field, outrunning the linebacker. Unitas lofted the ball easily, and Moore caught it on the run to score the first touchdown.

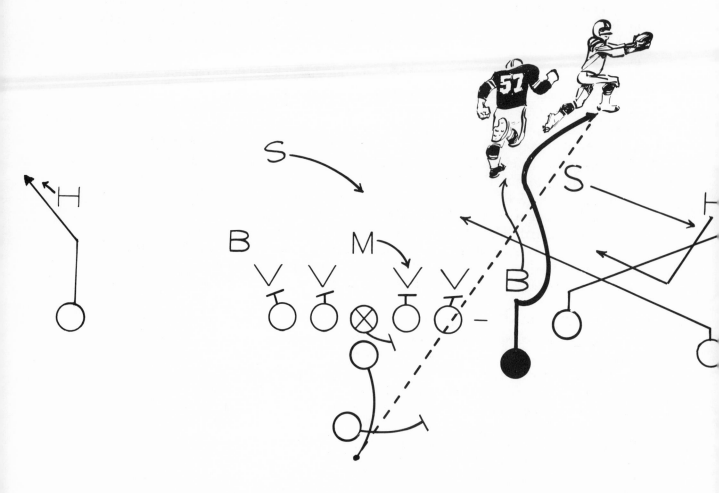

Ironically, the Colts protected their 21–20 victory over the Packers that day with a fortuitous defensive move on a pass play that was also designed to isolate a Green Bay halfback, Tom Moore, on a Colt linebacker. "Late in the fourth quarter," Shula reconstructed the situation, "the Packers had moved into our territory and were driving. They

Receiving ability is a prime requisite for young running backs in today's offense. Mel Farr of Detroit concentrates on the ball despite the threatening presence of Cleveland linebacker Jim Houston.

Malcolm W. Emmons

were within winning field goal range. Quarterback Bart Starr called the pattern we were afraid of—a pass to Moore against single coverage by Bill Pellington, our middle linebacker. Starr dropped back, and Moore circled out of the backfield and was all alone. Then Starr threw— but to the split end, Max McGee. Don Shinnick, our right linebacker, picked off the ball, and we ran out the clock. I don't know why Starr didn't throw to Moore. Probably the charge of the defensive line had shut off the passing lane so he couldn't see Moore."

The Packers got their chance to even the score a year later when both teams were still the primary contenders for the Western division title. They met in the thirteenth week of the season with the Colts a half-game in the lead. Paul Hornung was the whole show as he scored five touchdowns, one short of the NFL record. Two of the scores came when Paul circled out of the backfield, covered only by a linebacker, and caught passes which resulted in 50- and 65-yard touchdown plays.

The Minnesota Vikings scored twenty-five touchdowns in five years on passes to Bill Brown and Tommy Mason swinging out of the backfield. Both were fine receivers, too fast for linebackers to cover alone.

"In using running backs as pass receivers," noted Bobby Layne, the quarterback who guided the Detroit Lions to three world championships, "my main thought was working on linebackers. This became especially important about the time I retired after the 1962 season because of all the various red-dogging and blitzing that started to spread through professional football. All quarterbacks strive to have a 260-pound linebacker covering a fast halfback on pass patterns. But we also tried to draw the linebacker out of position some time—he did it himself when he blitzed—then have the back fake a block, delay and catch the ball in the area that the linebacker left."

Men coming out of the backfield run patterns with the same precision that split ends and flankers exercise. Many of their moves are the same. Layne produced diagrams of the pass patterns for the stationary backs when he was with the Pittsburgh Steelers:

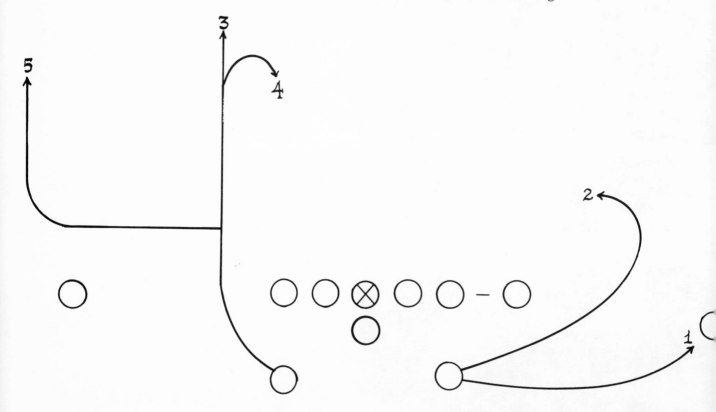

The numbers describe the following routes:

1. Divide
2. Trail
3. Flare
4. Turn
5. Cut Out and Down

(The terms used to describe pass patterns vary from team to team. The trail can also be a circle. A turn is the same as a button-hook. Cut Out and Down is also a Square-out and Takeoff.)

The following were some additional routes:

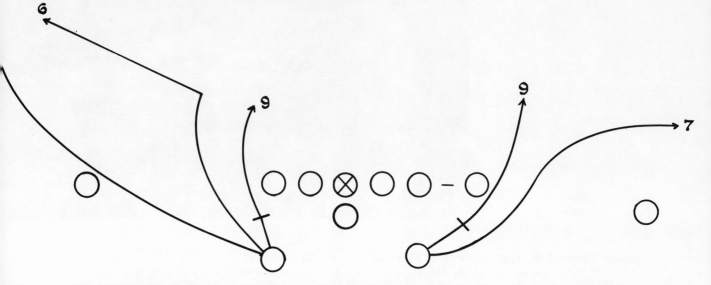

"I remember," said Layne, "on a pass that I threw deep to Tom Tracy, our fullback, we beat New York 14–9 in 1959, with time running out in the game. It went like this:

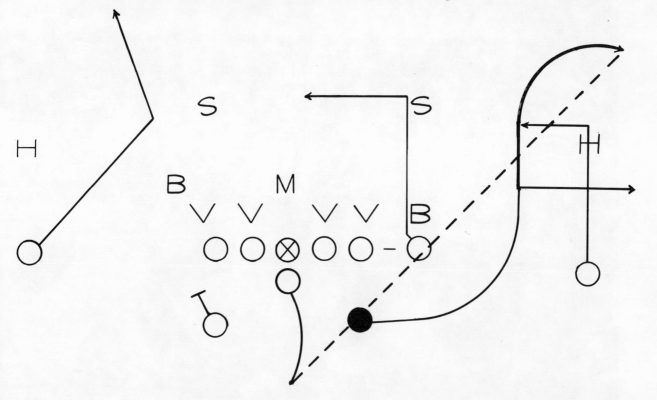

Frank Gifford (16) of the New York Giants was the first of the great modern left halfbacks to exploit the run-pass option on sweeps, the ball cradled expectantly in his poised right hand.

Daniel R. Rubin

Green Bay used the passing talents of Paul Hornung, an All-American quarterback in college, to increase the threat of its 49-sweep. He gets rid of the ball as New York's Andy Robustelli (81) starts to drag him down.

"As you can see, a lot of pressure is put on the left linebacker. Tracy could square out or run a flag pattern deep. He took the deep route to beat the Giants. On this same play, if the No. 4 back delays and goes out for a pass, the right linebacker would have to cover him.

"We had another pass play using the backs in which they both faked protection blocks and then slipped through. It forced the middle linebacker to decide which one he was going to cover. Also, both outside linebackers couldn't afford to drop back deep and help the coverage on the ends. And if the linebackers happened to red-dog, the '4' and '3' backs went out immediately for a pass.

"I thought the best receivers in my era were Doak Walker, Frank Gifford, Timmy Brown, and Hugh McElhenny. They were all great actors and could do great things after receiving the ball. Among those playing today, I would say Gale Sayers is tops because he's so dangerous after getting the ball and demands the constant attention of linebackers."

Vince Lombardi, who coached them both, admired Hornung and Gifford in his pass offense for a couple of other reasons. "They were excellent," he noted, "in coming back to the huddle after running a pass route and giving information to the quarterback. Both had been quarterbacks in college. They could read the pass defense pretty good when they went down the field. And they didn't have any reservations about coming back and telling the quarterback what they thought they could do to get open."

As ex-quarterbacks, Gifford and Hornung also worked the other end of the passing scale. They were effective throwers on the pass-run option developing off the sweep. In pro ball, the halfback with some experience as a signal caller has stood out as a combination runner-passer. Still working that double threat effectively are former college quarterbacks Dan Reeves of Dallas, Bobby Duhon of New York, and Tom Matte of Baltimore. "Reeves is the best option passer I've ever seen," claimed his coach, Tom Landry.

Coincidentally, all these former field generals are also excellent pass receivers. "Duhon," said Coach Allie Sherman of the Giants, "is the best rookie receiver we had for as long as I can remember. Gifford and Kyle Rote [another combination man] had to work like hell to get that instinctive feel for what Bobby was doing to defenders in his first year. Bobby has a balance and grasp of the situation we can't coach into him."

Bobby's 33-yard pass reception from Fran Tarkenton provided the only touchdown in a 7–6 win by New York over the Philadelphia Eagles in November 1968. "It was a play we put in for the game," explained the former southpaw Tulane quarterback. "We call it the 'X-and-A Fly.' Homer Jones [the split end] is X alone on the left side and I am A in the slot on the right side where we have tripled flanked with myself, Aaron Thomas, and Joe Morrison [note: the Giants' version of the Baltimore flood]. Fran keys on the free safety. If he moves toward Homer, I'm the primary receiver, which was what happened against the Eagles. I just took off and ran straight downfield, hoping to outrun the linebacker." And Bobby sprinted past the Eagles' linebacker and took the pass on a dead run in the end zone for his first scoring pass as a pro.

Dan Reeves of the Cowboys confirmed that this experience as a quarterback at the University of South Carolina helped him. "What Coach Landry teaches," he said, "is the

Malcolm W. Emmons

Coach Tom Landry of Dallas calls Danny R
(30), his running halfback, the best option
"I've ever seen."

Vernon J. Biever Photo

Hands outstretched, six points in sight, Hugh McElhenny
waits in the end zone, having outdistanced his defenders.

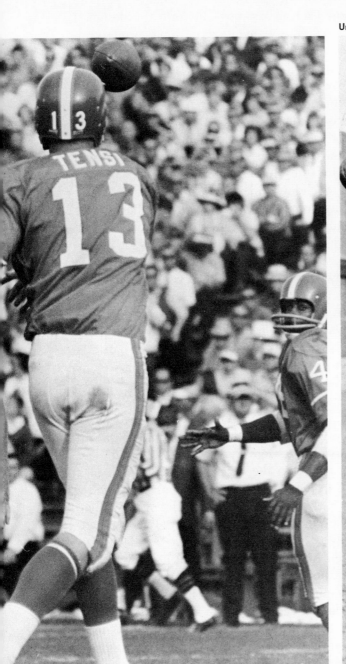

A quarterback under pressure, like Steve Tensi of Denver (here), will look to his running back—Floyd Little (44)—for a safety valve flip.

Bronko Nagurski was famed as the most bone-crushing of fullbacks, but also had throwing ability which the Chicago Bears exploited when defenses bunched too tightly to stop the Bronk.

meaning of a play, which fits in with how I feel about offense. He explains the purpose of the play, what it's designed to do and how each man's move fits into the design. I know if I'm running a pass route just to clear a defensive man away from a primary receiver, I run a better route if I know how my move fits in."

The idea of a halfback throwing the ball as well as catching it wasn't restricted to former quarterbacks. Keith Lincoln, a single wing tailback type, excelled as an option passer in his big years with the San Diego Chargers. In a five-year period, 1962–66, he completed eight of seventeen passes, and five of them went for touchdowns. As a receiver, he caught seven passes for 123 yards to set an AFL championship game record in the Chargers' 51–10 victory over the Boston Patriots in 1963. John David Crow was another who excelled throwing the ball on the run. He completed thirty-three out of seventy passes in his career, including five touchdown plays. Even the great Jimmy Brown kept the defense off balance by stopping occasionally on sweeps and flinging the ball. Defensive backs were so geared to coming up to meet him that out of the four passes he completed in his last five years with the Browns, three went deep for touchdowns.

There was a memorable 39-yard touchdown pass from Brown to flanker Gary Collins in 1965, his final pro campaign. It came in a victory over the Giants, and Coach Blanton Collier carefully explained that it was not an option pass: "It was pure pass all the way. We run Brown to the right on that play three different ways—pure run, option, and pure pass. The blocking varies on each. Of course, if he can't pass, his alternative is to run, but he's on his own then. We make no provision for the run on the pure pass as we do on the option play."

Lombardi has been a great believer in using the option to keep the defense off balance. It actually set up his wide running game at Green Bay. When Hornung was at his peak in 1962, he ran the option play seventy times during the season, but wound up passing the ball only fifteen times. The defensive backs were so wary they'd hold off and give Paul a chance to turn the corner on the run. (On the other hand, the threat of a run also helps set up a team's passing offense. In recent years, the play-pass, in which a quarterback simulates a handoff to one of the backs and all the men on the offensive line fire out on their blocking as if it's going to be a run, freezes the defense and gives downfield receivers a good chance to get open.)

The San Diego Chargers had a play, when Keith Lincoln and Paul Lowe were the setbacks, which beautifully took advantage of their dual abilities as runners and receivers. Lincoln was very effective on draw plays, and defenses were conscious of it. So as quarterback Tobin Rote backed up from the line of scrimmage, he simulated a handoff to Lincoln on a fake draw. As the defense reacted to chase down Keith, Rote spun around and passed the ball to Lowe on a screen play to the right, with the center, guard, and tackle drifting over to form a convoy.

The screen pass to a back was as effective a counter-measure to a hard-charging defensive team as the draw. The screen required even more acting by the principals. It was supposed to look like a regular drop-back pass that fell apart, the linemen acting like they were having a tough time holding off their opponents, the running back making a feint at blocking, then drifting off to the sideline, where he'd pick up his linemen again, as diagrammed:

74

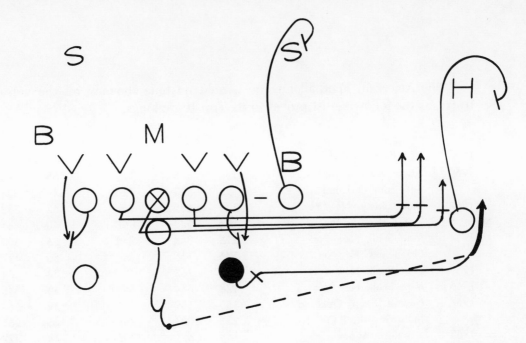

Y. A. Tittle of the 49ers was a master at throwing the screen to Joe Perry or Hugh McElhenny. The Cleveland Browns were another fine screen team. They perfected the quick screen to Bobby Mitchell, developing very quickly right after the penetration of the defense, and particularly effective against a slow defensive end. The Browns even had a double screen going to both sides of the field because all their backs were good receivers.

The record ledgers of both pro leagues bear out the effectiveness of good runners who can also catch the ball. Starting with Ernie Caddel, who played for the Detroit Lions in the 1930's, thirteen backs in the NFL have finished in the top ten statistically in both rushing and pass receiving. They are, by years:

Year	Player & Club	RUSHING			RECEIVING		
		Att.	Yds.	Stand.	Caught	Yds.	Stand.
1934	Ernie Caddel, Det.	101	428	10th	9	125	10th*
1936	Ernie Caddel, Det.	91	580	6th	19	150	3rd
1940	Dick Todd, Wash.	76	408	5th	20	402	8th*
1942	Dante Mangani, Clev.	59	344	8th	24	276	8th*
1943	Harry Clark, Bears	120	556	3rd	23	535	6th
	John Grigas, Cards.	105	333	8th	19	225	8th*
	Andy Farkas, Wash.	110	327	9th	19	202	8th*
1945	Henry Margarita, Bears	112	497	3rd	23	394	8th*
1949	Gene Roberts, N.Y.	152	634	4th	35	711	9th
	Charley Trippi, Cards.	112	553	7th	34	412	10th*
1956	Frank Gifford, N.Y.	159	819	5th	51	603	3rd
1957	Frank Gifford, N.Y.	136	528	10th	41	588	4th
1958	Lenny Moore, Balt.	82	598	8th	50	938	4th
1964	Charley Taylor, Wash.	199	755	8th	53	814	6th
1965	Timmy Brown, Phila.	158	861	3rd	50	682	10th*

Stand.—Standing in individual statistics.

* Tied for position.

The American Football League wasted no time showing off the versatility of its backs, as the following list proves in its Top 10 rankings:

Year	Player & Club	RUSHING			RECEIVING		
		Att.	Yds.	Stand.	Caught	Yds.	Stand.
1960	Abner Haynes, Dallas	156	875	1st	55	576	5th
	Billy Lott, Oakland	99	520	7th	49	524	6th*
1962	Dick Christy, New York	114	535	9th	62	538	3rd
	Ron Burton, Boston	134	548	8th	40	461	10th*
1964	Matt Snell, New York	215	948	2nd	56	393	7th*
	Sid Blanks, Houston	145	756	4th	56	497	7th*
1965	Matt Snell, New York	169	763	4th	38	264	10th*
1966	Matt Snell, New York	178	644	6th	48	346	9th*
1967	Hewitt Dixon, Oakland	153	559	8th	59	563	4th*
	Mike Garrett, K.C.	236	1087	3rd	46	261	8th*
1968	Jim Kiick, Miami	165	621	7th	44	422	10th

* Tied for position.

If the Baltimore Colts had paid close attention to the charts, they might have anticipated the use of Matt Snell as a safety valve receiver for Joe Namath's passes in the 1969 Super Bowl. Snell was in the top ten as a runner and receiver his first three years with the New York Jets. Other pro rookies who made the select list in both categories were Abner Haynes of the Dallas Texans in 1960, Jim Kiick of Miami in 1968 and, over in the NFL, Johnny Grigas of the Cardinals in 1943 and Charley Taylor of the Redskins in '64. The Skins were so enamored by Taylor's pass-catching abilities they transformed him to a fulltime flanker two years later, and he led the league in receptions. Charley's total of fifty-three in his rookie season is still the highest in NFL history for a man running out of the backfield.

There is a trend to converting running backs to receivers. Washington did it first with Bobby Mitchell, who was once Jim Brown's running mate at Cleveland. The Oakland Raiders revived the career of Billy Cannon by making him a tight end, where his speed and size gave them an extra deep threat. Cannon had already revealed his potential as a receiver back in 1960, in his rookie year as a halfback with the Houston Oilers, when he set a league record for a title game that still stands by gaining 128 yards on passes, including an 88-yard touchdown play, against the Los Angeles Chargers. The San Francisco 49ers tacked another year onto the career of John David Crow by shifting him to tight end in 1968. Lance Rentzel drifted aimlessly as a reserve back for a couple of years in Minnesota, before the Dallas Cowboys found a home for him as a flanker. Others who have made the transition successfully are Joe Morrison of the Giants and Gifford on the same club a few years earlier. The Chicago Bears have even talked wistfully of using Gale Sayers more as a flanker to lessen the danger of injury and to take advantage of his brilliant ability to elude tacklers once he catches the ball.

The running talent is what intrigues coaching about using backs primarily as receivers, to maximize their potential for long gains. The seven leading active pass receivers in the NFL at the end of the 1968 season were Bobby Mitchell, Tommy McDonald

A trend to converting small, swift running backs to flankers because of their receiving ability was pioneered by Buddy Young (22) with the Colts.

Long shadows drift across the turf as Elijah Pitts, isolated with a linebacker, clutches a Green Bay pass for vital yardage.

of Cleveland, Bobby Joe Conrad of St. Louis, Boyd Dowler of Green Bay, Jimmy Orr of Baltimore, Sonny Randle of Dallas, and Bernie Casey of Los Angeles, in that order. *All* of them had been backfield men in college football and switched after they became pros. Among the premier AFL receivers, Lance Alworth of the Chargers and Don Maynard of the Jets were first noted as college ball carriers, and Maynard even tried halfback with the Giants his first season as a pro.

"I think the wave of the future in offensive football will be greater use of backfield men as receivers," said Al Davis, managing general partner and former coach of the Oakland Raiders. He meant in their deployment as regular backs so that a quarterback might have five eligible receivers harrassing the defensive secondaries instead of three.

Never was the effectiveness of the backfield man as a double threat better demonstrated than on the afternoon of November 25, 1951, in Cleveland, Ohio. The home team Browns were hosts to the Chicago Bears, the first time the teams had ever met in a regular season game. The Browns had a halfback named William A. "Dub" Jones, whom they had secured from the Brooklyn Dodgers in 1948 for the draft rights to All-American tailback Bob Chappuis of Michigan. Paul Brown liked the way Jones had played on defense for the Dodgers. He was 6′ 4″, with a skinny neck and long legs, though he weighed a deceptive 205 pounds. The Browns called him "Six O'Clock" because of his long, lean look. In Cleveland, he became an offensive standout. On this day against the Bears, who came to town with the announced intention of "kicking the hell out of the bush Browns" from the defunct All-America Conference, Jones handled the ball an exact dozen times. He ran it on nine carries from scrimmage. He caught three passes from Otto Graham. On his first carry, he slanted off tackle for two yards and a touchdown. On three other occasions he swept end for 12, 27 and 42 yards, culminating each play in the end zone. To vary the routine, he then caught passes of 34 and 44 yards. They went for touchdowns, too. Altogether, Dub Jones crossed the goal line six times that afternoon.

No pro back in any one game has ever had better results in so varied a fashion.

6. Head and Shoulders to the Job

Paul Hornung insisted he could do "a few other things" besides block, and he could, but the Packers capitalized fully on Golden Boy's ability to clear a path for Jimmy Taylor (31).

It's the ditch-digger detail of pro football, the chain-gang chore. It's a lot of sweat with little reward. It's unnatural in execution and, in the physical matchup, unfair.

In Rule 3, Section 3 of the official code of professional football, it is defined:

"Blocking is the obstructing of an opponent, by the use of that part of the blocker's body above his knees. During a legal block, if a blocker uses his hand or arm to contact an opponent, such hand or the hand of such arm must be in contact with his own body." Of course, the "opponent" can use his hands and any other weapon he can lay hands on.

No back can claim to be a complete football player if he doesn't throw himself enthusiastically into this onerous duty. The stigma of the non-blocker was the only tarnish on the football reputation of Jim Brown. The old-timers have criticized the lack of zeal on the part of most moderns in their approach to the basic fundamentals of football like blocking.

"We blocked below the hips," said Ernie Nevers, the first of the great fullbacks in pro ball. "There was no just standing there brush blocking. Show me a good blocker, a man who doesn't flinch, who loves the game for itself and not only the money in it, and I'll show you a real football player who won't get hurt."

A generation later, a fullback named Marlin "Pat" Harder was a "real football player" —a good blocker who didn't flinch and in the years right after World War II helped both the Chicago Cardinals and Detroit Lions to world championships. Pat's forte was keeping the other side off the quarterback.

"I thoroughly enjoyed the blocking aspect of football," he said. "It gave me a chance to punish the other guy for what he did to me. I always lived under the philosophy that when two bodies collide, the one who recovered the fastest got the job done. You got to hit him again before he gets to you.

"You have to gear yourself mentally as well as physically. In high school, I had been primarily a running back. I did nothing else until my high school coach, Liz Blackbourne [later coach of the Green Bay Packers], took me aside and gave me a heart-to-heart talk, the gist of which was that if you want the other guy to work for you when you've got the ball, you also have to block for him."

When the single wing formation was prevalent, one of the backs was actually designated "blocking back" although nominally he was also called a quarterback because he lined up behind a guard, a fourth of the distance from line of scrimmage to the fullback. In those days, all backs had blocking responsibilities. As the T-formation evolved, the quick dives and pitchouts and men-in-motion, the halfbacks and the quarterback were generally absolved of blocking duties—the quarterback because of the nature of his job as the ball handler on every play, and the halfbacks because they were prized for their speed in getting through and around enemy lines. As the defense balanced out the scales, however (described in Chapter 2), the single wing principles were blended with the T, and now the halfbacks had to join in as blockers in the two principal areas of offense. On pass plays, they had to form a protective curtain around the quarterback, called the passing pocket; on running plays, they had to take on linebackers aggressively and, in some cases, even defensive linemen.

In his book, *Run to Daylight*, which revolved around a week's preparations by the Packers for a game with the Lions, Vince Lombardi decided that the first play his team would run in the game was "Brown Right-73." Outlined on paper, it looked like this:

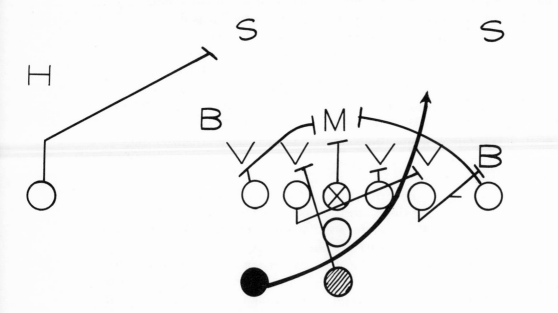

Note that Jimmy Taylor, the fullback, faked a dive up the middle and then put a block on Roger Brown, the defensive right tackle. Taylor weighed 212. Brown weighed 300 pounds and was one of the fastest defensive linemen in the game. It took a lot of confidence in the blocker to start a game with a play that had that kind of matchup. In Hornung, the Packers had another good blocker in the backfield. In fact, Paul's reputation as a man who could clear a path for Taylor received such publicity that Golden Boy, as he was called, began to resent mention of his blocking exploits—the ego of a runner still revolves around his exploits with the ball. "It tees me off," said Hornung heatedly one day. "You score 176 points in a season and all you hear is that blocking stuff. I can do a few other things."

But when Hornung's physical condition deteriorated, due to a pinched nerve in his neck, his manner of blocking was the tipoff to Lombardi that there was something wrong with his halfback. "A jamming blow on his head would give him excruciating pain," Lombardi noted. "In our game films, I saw too many pictures of Paul flinching on a block. This wasn't from lack of courage. Hornung possessed all the courage any ball-player needs. It was a natural protective reflex."

Techniques in blocking vary. Bill Austin, a Lombardi aide who went off to coach the Pittsburgh Steelers and then rejoined Vince in Washington, said, "There's only one way to block. Put the head in the other guy's belly." That's fine for a big offensive lineman, but how about a back who's giving away weight and strength to the defender and might never get to his belly? "Hit 'em across the thighs," Austin added. "They can't hit those 275-pound guys up high. They'd just bounce off."

Blocking seems like such a simple maneuver. Get in the way of the other guy and hit him—pass protection blocking, for instance, becomes a butting contest in which there may be three or four impacts as the pass protector tries to maintain a delicate balance against the charge of the defender. But there are subtleties in this continuous ramming and in other phases of blocking which call for detailed instruction. The following is a manual of instructions that the Cleveland Browns used to get a decade ago, and which still applies:

"The Shoulder Block—the most important technique in football.
1. Stance—comfortable but ready, eyes constant, keep *poise*.
2. Body dip—boom, uncoil into the man, *hit him*, no push or chest blocks.
3. Arm lift—make it an extension of your shoulder, but still block with your shoulder.
4. Follow-up—continue to raise up after you make contact.
5. Position follow-through—know the play, always be conscious of working for position follow-through.
"Long Body Block—use when you don't have position.
1. Uncoil across the man with force.
2. The quickness with which you throw the block is vital.
3. Force is a necessity in this block, same as for shoulder charge, break their defensive penetration.
4. Sustain it—keep after the man, working for position follow-through.
"Reverse Body Block—use when you have position.
1. Take short position step with foot closest to opponent, drive shoulder at far leg.
2. Break his charge, above all do not permit penetration.
3. Sustain it, keep after the man, the leg whip will be there by nature.
4. Follow through.
"Blocking for the Passer.
1. You will be rated on the percentage of times you got your man, regardless of technique. Our experience from movies has convinced us that to have a winner we must maintain a 'got man' percentage of 80 percent—this means four out of five times.
2. Approach—move with that ball and keep head-on position. Contact in the head-on position, aim for the middle. Don't think in terms of using a certain shoulder.
3. Accept the defensive charge, brace yourself, give ground very grudgingly, recover to fundamental position—the bigger the pocket, the better chance you have to complete the pass.
4. Follow through, hit and recover and maintain position between the man and the passer, go to the cutoff spot when necessary—foot movement is vital, keep a wide base, shuffle, never cross your feet or you are licked.
"Downfield Blocking—importance of blocking linebackers cannot be stressed too much; if they are blocked consistently, any defense will break down.

Malcolm W. Emmons

A quarterback fading to pass must keep his eyes on the receivers, confident that the fullback—here Clarence Peaks (26)—will pick up enemy blitzers. This was Sonny Jurgensen in his days as a Philadelphia Eagle.

Ernie Green (48) helped earn his keep as the "other man" in the Cleveland backfield by blocking first for Jimmy Brown and later Leroy Kelly (44).

Malcolm W. Emmons

1. Use the straight shoulder block, the long and the reverse body, but the important thing is to *him them*—any assignment on the linebacker is important.
2. Blocking in the deep secondary is almost entirely desire. You must know the play. Hitting the man is the basis of your grade. Above all, be sure you hit somebody."

Jimmy Brown used to rationalize his mediocre blocking by stating, "I don't concentrate on it because under Cleveland's offensive system I am called upon to block very seldom, and frankly, I like it that way. When a play calls for double protection for the passer, I have experienced satisfaction from throwing good blocks. But the pressure is on me to run. It constitutes my main value to the team. When I fail to gain 100 yards in a game, people say that I had a poor day."

But Tom Landry at Dallas stated, "Our fullback is the main blocker in the backfield. Don Perkins is an excellent blocker. And when he stays in most of the time, like Don does, he's dangerous for the screen passes. He's a blocker 75 percent of the time, and he goes out 25 percent of the time on pass plays." Size isn't the conclusive factor in good blocking by a back. The use of Jim Taylor on a defensive tackle is fairly rare. In today's game, most backs handle linebackers, and a 195-pounder like Perkins compensates for the missing pounds with explosive qualities.

Bill Koman, the erstwhile voluble linebacker of the St. Louis Cardinals, testified to the impression various backfield men made on him during the twelve years he tried to get around them. "The toughest guy I ever ran into," said Koman, "was Johnny Olszewski when he played with the Washington Redskins. He hit me with everything he had." Koman weighed 230 and Johnny O. barely scaled 200. "You know how you're young and foolish and think you can run over everybody in sight. We had a lot of success 'dogging.' The little guys used to hold back and throw themselves at me at the last minute. Well, I came in one time against Johnny O. He set up and played it perfectly, head for my belt buckle. I never got stuck so hard in my life. He hit me in the sternum and tore the cartilage loose around my chest. It took me ten weeks to get over it.

"Around 1959, when John Henry Johnson was with the Lions, I got blind-sided by him on a 'dog.' He was the 'near' back. I came across and thought I had the ball carrier for an eight-yard loss. I didn't even see John Henry. He got me right on the jaw and knocked nine fillings out of my mouth. I got up with a handful of silver."

On a 1968 day in which he ran for 162 yards against the Giants, fullback Willis Crenshaw of the Cardinals preferred to talk about his blocking: "I get a real kick out of knocking a linebacker on his back and seeing the surprised look on his face. There is nothing like the experience of throwing a good block to make a runner realize the value of the fellows who do the job on every play."

Abner Haynes, when he was running well for the Kansas City Chiefs, gave the perfect assent to that thought. He was asked if all his exploits made him subject to a swelled head. "No," he answered, "not once I talk it over with the blockers."

Of course, nobody appreciates the blockers more than the quarterback whom they protect. The backs form the final arc in the protective curtain that is drawn around the passer.

A couple of bull backs, like John Crow (44) and Ken Willard (40), can make John Brodie of San Francisco mighty comfortable setting up to pass in the pocket.

But if and when the backfield blocker falls down in his protective job (left foreground), the quarterback is susceptible to having his head taken off. Linebacker Mike Curtis (32) of Baltimore seems to be doing just that to Los Angeles quarterback Roman Gabriel (18), with the ball.

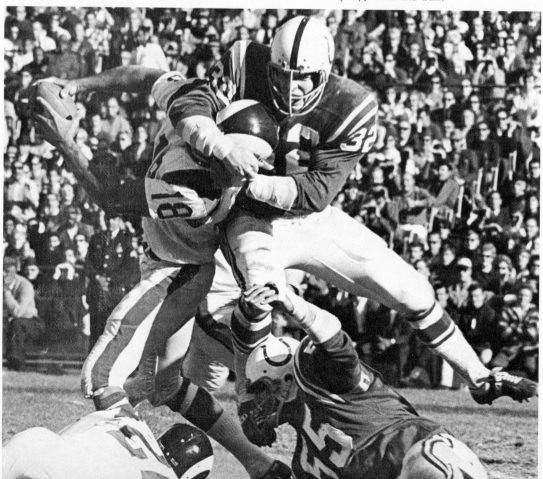

This is an example of how it works:

Breakdowns in the perimeter of protection leave quarterbacks vulnerable and coaches very unhappy. The Shea Stadium aficionados couldn't understand why Emerson Boozer had to sit on the bench so much as a rookie in 1966 when it was obvious he was a much better runner than Bill Mathis. But against Denver once on a pass play for the Jets, the Bronco whom Emerson was detailed to block lined up wider than usual, and Emerson forgot about him. The guy came in and knocked hell out of quarterback Joe Namath. So Emerson didn't play for a few games, while he brushed up on his assignments, because the Jets didn't want to risk losing $400,000 worth of quarterback.

"Give me guys like Jim Taylor and John David Crow and John Henry Johnson," said Layne, discussing the role of a back as a bodyguard. "They play even without the ball. Half of those good runners will get a quarterback killed if you keep them around long enough."

7. The Physical Risk

The mid-air flight of Gale Sayers is abruptly curtailed by a group of Pittsburgh Steelers. Already they've literally ripped the shirt from his back.

Begrimed and bespattered by the muck of battle, Tommy Mason was at least able to walk off the gladiators' turf under his own power.

But there have been times when Tommy Mason has clutched the turf in agony after his knees, the most vulnerable part of a football player's anatomy, have buckled.

Vernon J. Biever

The play started as a routine pitchout in the second quarter with Gale Sayers sweeping around his left end. Kermit Alexander, playing right cornerback for the San Francisco 49ers, "read" the action immediately and rushed up to meet the play.

It ended with Sayers sitting on the bench of the Chicago Bears, wadded towels holding his right knee in ice, tears rolling down the young halfback's face. His season was over abruptly in the eighth game of the 1968 schedule. And who could tell if Gale Sayers would ever carry a football again with inimitable greatness?

Alexander, angling toward the point where he figured Sayers would try to turn the corner and head up the field, had noted that Randy Jackson, the left tackle of the Bears, pulled out of the line and was running convoy for the halfback. Kermit thought quickly, "Gale likes to run behind his blocker and slip off when the defensive man comes up. I'll go for the blocker." That way he'd strip the interference and expose Sayers to a tackle by another 49er.

Alexander submarined on his charge to get under Jackson, who's 6'5". He went right through the blocker, and hit Sayers starting to cut back. His shoulder, on a descending arc, drove into Sayers' knee and crumpled the runner. A few hours later, Gale was on an operating table in a northside Chicago hospital for surgery to repair ruptured knee ligaments and torn cartilage.

"God," said Alexander disconsolately, "you never want to hurt a player, especially a great player like Gale."

But hurting players is tangentially a part of playing football. And the awareness has never been more acute than in the violent action of the 1960's. In the vortex of this surge of football injuries is the running back, the most vulnerable man on the field because at the moment of contact his guard is stripped. With the help of modern medicine, he has learned to live with the sudden yaws that his career can take.

Gale Sayers is expected to come back and function again as the most exciting sight on a football field. Right after the operation, surgeon Ted Fox predicted "100 percent recovery." Three days after the cast was removed on December 18 (the injury occurred November 10), Sayers walked without crutches. In three weeks he had full flexion in the knee. "The anatomical function is restored," said Dr. Fox after the three-hour surgery, "but whether something would happen to him because of the psychological effects, you don't know."

The year before, Johnny Roland, the leading runner of the St. Louis Cardinals, one of the brightest young backs in pro football, had suffered a torn right knee ligament in the thirteenth game of the season. A Pittsburgh linebacker hit him with a rolling block, the shoulder again doing the damage as it caught Roland's knee at the moment of full extension. Almost twelve months later, an operation behind him, he was a hesitant runner, unsure about cutting suddenly, unable to tear himself loose from tackles. His offensive production was cut virtually in half, to 455 yards for the 1968 season.

"I would try to push the knee to the back of my mind and not let it affect me," said Roland. "But when I'd run to the left and see a tackler pursuing along the line, I would instinctively drop my right shoulder to try to protect the knee. You can't do that and maintain the impetus you need. I think I got over it in our twelfth game of the season. I made a dive for third-down yardage and while I was in the air I got hit solidly on the knee. It stung, but when I got up it felt all right. I knew then that if I could get hit like that and still hold up, I'd be all right."

The New York Jets, world champions of pro football, went into their 1969 training with six veteran running backs. All of them could exhibit the scars of knee surgery. In fact, the Jets privately feel they would have made it to the top of the Super Bowl heap a year earlier than January 12, 1969, if a couple of hinges to their running backs hadn't been accidentally damaged.

For three periods of the 1967 season opener in Buffalo, fullback Matt Snell was a running terror. He gained 95 yards in nineteen carries, and he was on his way to increasing the total when he cut toward the left sideline. A cleat caught in the turf. He went down in a twisting scramble, tearing up his knee. An operation followed, and Matt's recovery was quick. He came back for the last six games of the season. But as a running threat he was a shell. "I was just there," he said. "I wasn't me. I was just somebody in a uniform." Meanwhile, in Snell's absence, Emerson Boozer, a fast, wide halfback, picked up the pace. After eight games, he had thirteen touchdowns, a phenomenal scoring spree for a running back. But in the eighth game, the Kansas City Chiefs caught him on a swing pass, threading down the sideline. He got hit from one side and from the other, high and low, and went directly from the field to the Hospital for Special Surgery in Kansas City.

"He's got the worst knee of all," said Dr. James Nicholas, the team physician, who had operated on Snell and also repaired both of quarterback Joe Namath's celebrated knees. "If he comes back all the way, it'll really be an achievement."

Well, Boozer did. It wasn't easy. He limped when the 1968 exhibition season started. He didn't put on a uniform the first four tuneup games when a back is supposed to get his timing and restore his feel for contact. Dr. Nicholas, whom the Jets sometimes refer to as Nick the Knife, finally braced Boozer two weeks before the start of the regular season and said, "I think we'll have you play tonight against Cincinnati."

"You got to be kidding, Doc."

"I mean it. You got to get hit a few times. The knee is sound. You got to test it in a game and find out for yourself."

"I don't know," said Boozer. "I broke my leg once in high school. When I came back and carried the ball, I was looking for a place to fall down before I got tackled."

"That's natural," said Dr. Nicholas. "You have to get over the fear."

The next week, Boozer played for the first time against the Lions in a big Cleveland doubleheader, was hit a couple of times, got up and kept running. He wasn't the same old Boozer in the regular season. Far from it. But his progress was steady, and in the Super Bowl game against the Colts he was an invaluable partner for Snell as a blocker, of all things.

94

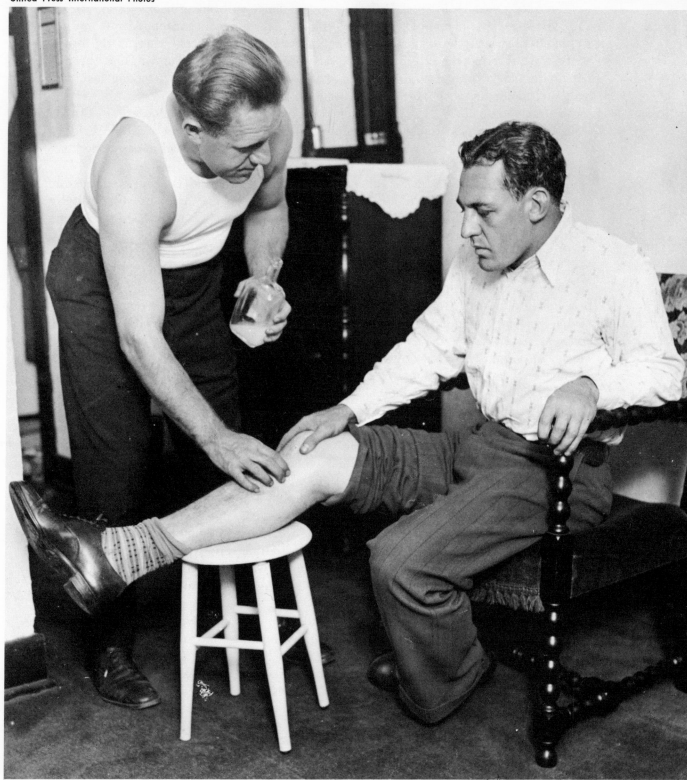

The risk of the knee injury is as old as football. Red Grange, the first of the glamor pros, missed the entire 1928 season because of a buckled right hinge. In his day, liniment in a hotel room was a prescribed treatment.

"It takes a year," said Snell, "to get your confidence and timing back."

"The knee," commented Dr. Anthony Pisani, "was not meant for football. Its motion is limited to straight knee bending—so-called extension inflexion—whereas the other joints, the ankle and the hip, have inversion and eversion, up and down, and the hip can rotate and go into several different planes of motion. The knee, having just two ranges of motion, is much more susceptible to injury."

The same year, 1967, that Dr. Nicholas was busy with Snell and Boozer, Dr. Pisani, an orthopedic surgeon, was equally occupied on the other side of the Tri-Boro Bridge, in the Bronx home of the New York Giants. By mid-November he had already operated on eight knees.

In the Giants' tenth game, at Yankee Stadium, fullback Tucker Frederickson dragged himself up from under a pile of Pittsburgh Steelers and limped a straight path across the field to the sidelines. Alex Webster, coaching the Giant backs, asked him, "You got a Charley horse?"

Tucker shook his head. He looked at linebacker Bill Swain, his buddy, and muttered, "The other one's gone." And Bill knew what he meant.

At 7 o'clock that night, Dr. Pisani had him in the operating room at St. Vincent's Hospital in mid-Manhattan and cut into Tucker's right knee to repair damage to the medial ligament and medial cartilage and, as he suspected, a tear in the anterior cruciate ligament. That was the medical part of it. There was no diagnosis for the way it tore Tucker up inside. He was just getting over fifteen months of pain and frustration and self-doubt, the post-operational effect of surgery on his other knee—the first serious injury in the glorious young football career of Tucker Frederickson, the first player drafted by the NFL in 1965.

At twenty-four, he lay in a hospital bed and didn't know if he'd ever again feel the elation of a football tucked tight against his elbow. But the second time around is easier than the first. He knew what he'd have to do to get in shape again, hours of rigorous special exercises to build strength in the atrophied muscles, days in the spring and summer when he'd have to go up to Yankee Stadium and work alone to get his body in shape. "Professional football," said Dr. James Nicholas, "gives the human body its supreme test. I've got the best laboratory in the world for studying how the body operates." Frederickson's case has turned out to be routine. His was the twentieth knee operation in the fall of 1967 in the NFL. And in between the operations, doctors draw countless ounces of fluid out of the puffed hinges. "Heck, I used to drain [fullback] Phil King's knee between halves," said Dr. Pisani.

Frederickson came back in 1968 and had a fairly productive season, leading the Giants on the ground with 486 yards and providing the kind of blocking that once prompted Mark Duncan, NFL head of officials, to call Tucker the best blocking back he had ever seen. He probably would not match the original talent the Giants signed, but late in the season, as his confidence grew, he was even cutting recklessly and playing football like he enjoyed it again.

The most remarkable recovery from knee surgery had to be Joe Perry, who at the age of thirty-five was ready to play for the Baltimore Colts a month after his incision in 1963. Knee repairs had come a long way in little more than a decade after Steve Van

Elbows, shoes, cleats and forearms mingle in a cacophony of violence, and in that maelstrom Tony Lorick tries to hang on to the football.

And sometimes the ball carrier—Mel Farr of Detroit—lies helpless in the face of the blow descending on him—by Lee Roy Caffey of Green Bay.

Buren had torn up his leg and was finished for always. In 1958, the Michigan state compensation department ruled that the Detroit Lions had to pay Gene Gedman, a former halfback, compensation for his services after a knee injury failed to heal properly and curtailed his career. "Gedman was a skilled employee," said the compensation referee. "As such, the law states that although he recovers from his injured knee, Gedman is legally disabled as long as he cannot return to his skilled profession—namely, football." He ruled Gedman was entitled to the difference between what he made at full physical capacity and what he made after his football career, as an insurance agent. It amounted to $33 a week.

It's a good thing the doctors are so skilled at rehabilitating the employees. The ranks of the running back in the NFL and AFL were sorely depleted in the fall of 1968. Besides Sayers, the following were knocked out of commission most of the season, for one ailment or another: Les Josephson of the Rams, Dave Osborn of the Vikings, Ernie Green of the Browns, Junior Coffey of the Atlanta Falcons, Dan Reeves of the Cowboys, Nick Eddy of the Lions, Mel Farr of the Lions, Jerry Hill of the Colts, Brad Hubbert and Keith Lincoln of the Chargers, Curtis McClinton of the Chiefs, and Jim Nance of the Patriots.

"Any team," said Fran Tarkenton, "needs five good running backs weighing at least 210 pounds each to get by in pro football. They must be able to run, block and catch passes, which means they are extremely hard to find. They must be tough, and even then they are going to get hurt. That's why I say a team needs five. A running back gets hit more times from more angles than any guy on the field."

"We don't get paid enough," Paul Hornung once said, "considering the energy we expend and the career risk of the violent sport we're in. You don't think about getting hurt when you're going good. A sprained ankle doesn't mean anything. In the pros, if you can walk, you play. They get their money's worth."

"Halfbacks," added Frank Gifford, when he was still in his prime, "take the most punishment. They are usually going full speed when they get hit. Players at other positions get hit, too, but not as often and certainly not as hard as the guy with the ball. An offensive halfback takes the opposition's haymakers. On the average, they're knocked out of the league in four or five years."

So how did Giff stay around for twelve years?

"Luck," he smiled. "Just plain luck."

The luck deserted him momentarily, though, one afternoon in 1960 when he went up to catch a pass and was hit in mid-air by Chuck Bednarik of the Eagles. The violent tackle left him unconscious. He didn't come back to football until a year and a half later. "He had a deep concussion," said the late Dr. Francis Sweeney, who okayed his return. "The brain is like a mass of jelly inside three coverings, all of this suspended in the skull like a player's head is suspended inside a helmet. There's the subdura, the dura and the meninges. A severe shock may start a hemorrhage which can seep down into the lower parts of the brain and affect motor areas and be very serious. This is what Frank had. But once that heals, it's completely healed and doesn't have a carryover effect."

In his career, which lasted through 1964, Gifford was able to avoid knee surgery. But he was laid out three different times in 1954, 1957 and 1958 with knee troubles.

"When I'm skiing," he said, "even now, going up on the lift line, I can sometimes feel that my right knee is a little loose."

As the longevity of pro players stretched out, due in part to the escalating salaries in the popularity splurge of the game, the veterans learned the rules of survival. "You can't be cautious up here," said Ollie Matson, who played until he was thirty-six years old. "The cautious ones get hurt because they try to evade the shock. What you have to do is keep running hard, then the man you hit will get more shock than you. And you got to know when to relax. I once went way up in the air to catch a pass and the halfback was under me and I came down on my neck. Many people thought I was seriously injured, but I wasn't hurt at all because I relaxed and I know how to fall and protect myself."

Jimmy Brown was a marvel at avoiding injury. He didn't miss a game in nine years. "It's how lucky you are with injuries that determines how long a player lasts," said Nick Pietrosante, who endured nine seasons as a fullback. "Especially to areas like the knee or the shoulder. John Crow was a great back, as good as anyone, but he had misfortunes with his knees."

A running back is most exposed on a delay play or on a counter when an ultra-fast lineman such as Henry Jordan of Green Bay gets a piece of him and holds him up to destroy the timing of the play. Before he can get going again, all the other defenders have time to come off their blocks and hit him from different angles. Sometimes, of course, a back can't protect himself. If he's swinging out of the backfield for a pass and has to turn to follow the ball, he can't very well keep his eyes on the defensive player thundering down on him from the blind side. Under those conditions, intimidated backs have been known to drop the ball, which is known in football as "hearing footsteps." Deacon Dan Towler, a league-leading rusher for the Rams in the 1950's, was very philosophical about footsteps. "Them that don't hear them," he said, "feel them."

Some injuries are aggravated and threaten careers because a running back is too conscious of his obligations as a player. The first time Tucker Frederickson hurt his knee, in a routine "nutcracker" drill at training camp, he was so important to the Giants' seasonal plans that surgery was delayed in the hope the injury would heal with rest. But when he tried out the knee in an exhibition game a few weeks later, he slipped trying to come back for a pass and the damage was complete. The modern trend is for immediate surgery, while the tissue is still viable, to increase the odds for complete recovery. In 1968, fullback Jim Nance, the most awesome rusher in the young history of the AFL, with two 1,000-yard seasons in a row, stepped in a rut at Harvard Stadium during a Labor Day exhibition game against the Eagles and twisted his ankle. Still hobbling, he tried to play in the second game of the season and caught a cleat in the turf, twisting the ankle again. What looked like a simple ankle sprain became a *cause célèbre* in Boston, with hints that big Jim was goofing off as he played sporadically all fall, missing five games completely. "I really don't know how the man ever ran on that ankle," said an examining physician during the winter. "It certainly had to kill him with every step. The ligament was completely torn loose at one end and had worked its way into the ankle joint. The cartilage was missing in some areas, so that it was bone crunching

100

There's nothing gentle in the way these Cleveland Brown tacklers (Jim Kanicki is number 69) embrace Jimmy Taylor.

Taylor struggles against the pain of the last blow, as the referee places the ball for the next play.

A hand reaches out rudely to intercept the progress of Chicago's Ronnie Bull. Sure, it's a 15-yard penalty for mask-grabbing, but only if the official sees it. And that doesn't ease the jolt.

"We don't get paid enough," said Paul Hornung, "considering . . . the career risk of the violent sport we're in."

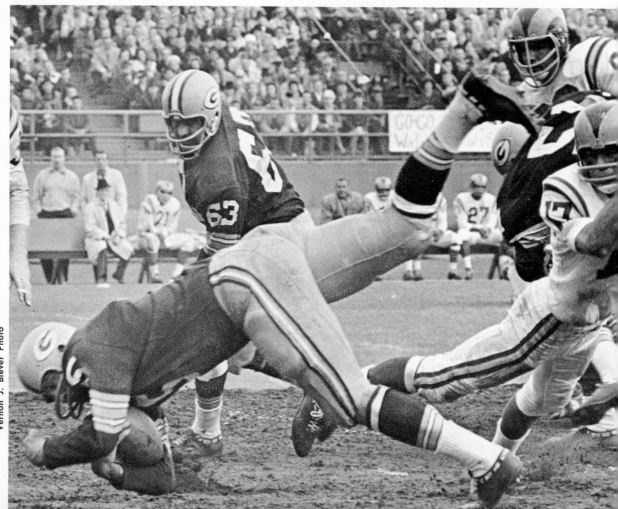

against bone." And the original ankle sprain evolved in an extensive three-hour surgical procedure to repair the ligament and cartilage and remove calcium chips. It left his future clouded.

The case of Mack Lee Hill was tragic. He was a robust runner who joined the Kansas City Chiefs in 1964 and had the best ground gaining average in the AFL as a rookie. He was 5′ 11″ and 235 pounds, low to the ground and hard to bring down. After a second successful season, he went into the hospital for a routine leg operation, but died from surgical complications not related to his original injury.

Most backs don't like to talk about injuries. But they think about them. "Sometimes I lay in bed at night and worry about getting hurt," admitted Leroy Kelly of the Browns. "I don't worry about the regular contact. I fear the freak plays, the plays that shouldn't happen but do. They ruin people.

"I try to stay relaxed, though. Nice and loose. When I get hit, I like to roll with the impact. A very bad habit is tightening up just before contact is made. That's a good way to get hurt. You've got to be loose to ride with the full force of a blow.

"Luck also plays its part. There have been times the last few years when I've had the hell scared out of me. Times I've been hit from the blind side and gone down with my knees and ankles twisting in all directions. There were times when I thought I'd never be able to get up. But luckily I did.

"I've run across only a couple of cheap shot artists who try to put me out of a game. Most defenses will hit hard in hopes of intimidating a running back and make him worry about the next time he has to go through the same hole. But very few try deliberately to hurt a running back. Sometimes, sure, in the heat of a game, somebody piles on, but that's only natural. Foul tactics, as a rule, are the least of my worries."

Football is a rugged sport, and physical risk is basic. It's even part of the challenge. The courage of the men who play it shouldn't be assailed. Nor should their tactics to protect themselves. There never was a tougher player than John Henry Johnson, the flailing fullback of the Pittsburgh Steelers. Once, seeing three tacklers about to hem him in against the sidelines, John Henry nimbly stepped out of bounds rather than butt his head against the trio. He was asked about it.

"I'd rather them say, 'There he went,'" explained John Henry, "instead of, 'There he lay.'"

8. Plotting a Running Attack

Hands apart, ready to embrace the football, the running back advances toward the quarterback, picking up speed with each stride. In this case, it's Charley Conerly of New York (42) preparing a handoff to Mel Triplett.

Wilbur "Weeb" Ewbank, the bustling little coach of the New York Jets, wouldn't say that his game plan for beating the Baltimore Colts was based on running over them because, like every member in good standing of the coaching fraternity, he insisted that the game situation dictated what plays would be called. Yet it was evident right from the start, when Weeb bundled his players on a Northeast charter from Kennedy Friday afternoon, January 3, for the trip to their pre-Super Bowl headquarters on the beach at Fort Lauderdale, that the Jets' coach was plotting to stick the ball up the nose of the Colts, who boasted the best defense statistically in football.

They had given up only 144 points during the regular season—the Jets had yielded 280. In the NFL title contest, the Colts had shut out the potent Cleveland Browns and limited Leroy Kelly, the leading runner in football, to 28 yards in thirty carries, the longest one 5 yards.

But Weeb bravely insisted, "We can run against them." And here's how he reconstructed his thinking: "In the first place, we were matching personnel against them. So-and-so of Baltimore is like this guy in our league, so here's how we work on him. There's Bubba Smith [at left defensive end] and here's a guard [Dave Herman] who was moved over to right tackle in front of him. We wouldn't expect Dave to do as well here. And Randy Rasmussen, the guard next to him, does a good job but he's still a kid. So we basically set our offense when we were in right formation, to run weakside to the left. And when we were in left formation, to go the other way. This was our best bet."

And here's how it went into operation when the Jets put the ball in play on their own 23-yard line after the opening kickoff. In the huddle, quarterback Joe Namath called the play: "19-straight."

On 19-straight, the execution was simple. Emerson Boozer, the halfback, lined up to the weakside, went straight at the linebacker, Don Shinnick. Winston Hill, the left tackle, fired out at Ordell Braase, the defensive right end, letting Braase influence the pressure. If Braase took an inside move, Hill blocked to the inside. If Braase tried to go outside, Hill went with him. Fullback Matt Snell, the ball carrier on the handoff from Namath, reacted to the direction of Hill's block. In application, but in different terminology, it's almost a replica of Green Bay's Brown Right 36 play in which Jimmy Taylor carried out the basic run-to-daylight principles.

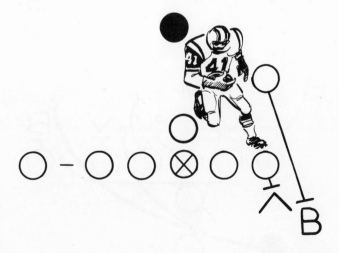

On that first play against Baltimore, Snell slanted in behind Hill. The defensive end was playing the inside, so Snell, taking the cue, veered to the outside. But Shinnick, the linebacker, fought off Boozer's block and stopped the runner on the 26-yard line. Three yard gain. Namath came right back with the same play. Braase, a canny thirty-six-year-old veteran, varied his charge by going outside, and Hill nudged him further in that direction. Boozer tied up Shinnick this time, and the fullback burst through a good hole for nine yards and a first down. The Jets had found out what they needed to know—they could run the ball against the Colts.

Namath is a smart quarterback. He saves his goodies for the appropriate spots. So he varied his attack the rest of the time. He ran Boozer off the right side just to keep Bubba occupied. It lost ground. When he called a pass on 2nd and 14, and the Colts blitzed, he dumped the ball to Snell flaring wide to the right. He probed with draw plays and squareouts. He tried 19-straight again, and Snell turned the end for nine yards. In the second quarter, the Jets got rolling on a long drive from their 20-yard line. On the first three plays, Snell took the ball on 19-straight—one yard, seven yards, six yards—and brought the ball to the 34. He ran a draw for 12 more yards, and now with the Colts squeezing up tight to meet the ground attack, Namath put the ball in the air five out of the next six plays for a first down on the Baltimore 9-yard line. He had been studiously avoiding tackle Fred Miller and 295-pound Bubba Smith on the right side with his running. Now he defied them, and Snell barged past Bubba on a power dive to the 4-yard line. In the clutch, at the 4-yard line, the Jets reverted to 19-straight. Snell slanted to his left, the hole closed and he bellied out behind Boozer's block on Shinnick to race into the end zone. An AFL team led for the first time in the history of the Super Bowl. It was the only Jet touchdown of the game—they added three field goals—but it established their superiority and led directly to the stunning 16–7 triumph over the Colts, who had been 17-point favorites.

In the last eleven minutes and six seconds of the game, the Jets almost flaunted their superiority by never passing again. They used four minutes and forty-six seconds in one drive which consisted of eight straight running plays. Altogether, Matt Snell carried the ball thirty times in the game. Halfbacks Emerson Boozer (ten carries) and Bill Mathis (three) rounded out the ground control game which worked perfectly according to plan. In the late stages of the fourth quarter, Boozer was driving over the Baltimore right side for vital yardage on this straight power play diagrammed by Ewbank, with an option of going inside or outside the tackle.

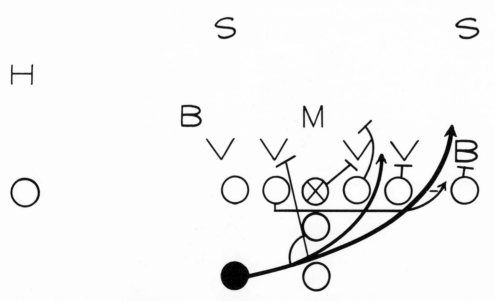

"A lot of people," said Ewbank after the game, "thought we were picking on Braase on that play to the left side. Not actually. We knew we had a good blocker there, and Boozer did a helluva job on Shinnick. We like to have our backs block. We don't like to have backs that you have to flare out of there and let somebody else do their work and hit 'em on rollouts because they won't block. Emerson was outstanding in the title game. And Matt did a good job of seeing the daylight."

The plotting of a running attack for an important game is a psychological thing. The first man who has to be convinced is the quarterback calling the signals.

"As a member in good standing of the quarterbacks' union," said Francis Tarkenton, "I've got to believe you don't win with a running game. Passing does it for you, in the final analysis. But I do believe you have to establish a running threat to make your whole offense go. Running with a football is a matter of attitude. Some teams don't even believe they can move the ball on the ground. It's a hard, trudging type of game, and you have to work for what you get.

"On first down, my play-calling frequency is divided 50-50 between running and passing plays. But when it's second down and seven yards to go, it becomes definitely a passing down. Yet there was one game we played against Green Bay when we twice had second-and-seven situations, and I knew their linemen were thinking 'pass' and their linebackers were thinking about taking their 'drops' [retreating to cover designated areas], so I crossed them up by sending Tucker Frederickson up the middle each time, and it worked. The Green Bay tackles, anticipating a pass, widened up to get a better rush on me, leaving a natural gap."

The New York Giants were helped to a division championship in 1962 by winning a key game against the Detroit Lions, who had the most vicious defense in football at the time. "Theoretically," said the Giants' coach, Allie Sherman, "you should have a balanced attack, but there are games in which, even if you have the best passing attack, you can't win with it because the pass rush line of the team you're going to play is going to beat you. So you damn well better run the football, at least until you dig them in. This was a game like that.

"We were going against Roger Brown and Alex Karras [defensive tackles] and Joe Schmidt [middle linebacker]. Every one an all-pro. Couple of games before they had torn up Green Bay's Bart Starr like I've never seen a team tear a passer up. And here our main strength was passing. We had the slowest backfield in the league.

"I don't think we ever delayed so long in the week putting a game plan together. It took a lot of soul-searching. We had to go away from our strength. There was no way we were going to block Brown and Karras much better than Green Bay did if we didn't get them dug in. We finally decided that to get a shot in this game, against the toughest defensive unit in the league, we were going to have to nullify Brown and Karras and make them run-conscious. Going into the game, they weren't going to be run-conscious because they knew our big threat was a great passer [Tittle] and good receivers [like Del Shofner].

"We used about four plays that we knew were not touchdown plays, with power blocking, direct hitting at Brown or Karras, knowing full well that if we could get six

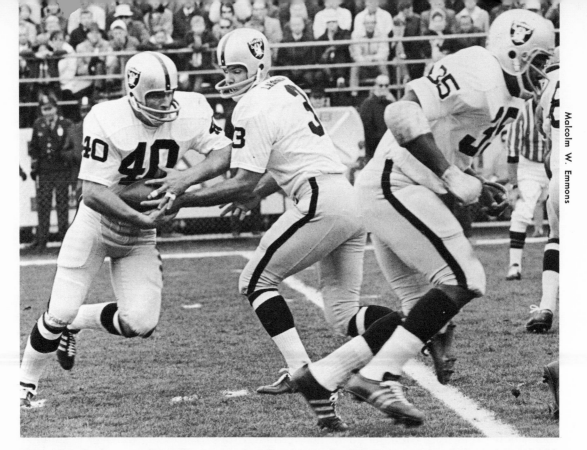

The quarterback, in traditionally approved style, shoves the ball into the pit of the running back's stomach. They're locked for only an instant and Daryle Lamonica of Oakland (3) makes a last second check to see that the ball is secure. Pete Banaszek (40), the runner, is already looking toward the hole as Hewritt Dixon blocks ahead of him.

The quick pitch to the fullback sometimes catches the defense off balance. The teamwork between Bart Starr (15) and Jimmy Taylor (31) must be perfect since the ball reaches him on the run. Note Taylor's hands cupped palms up.

yards out of the play, it would be a lot, but if we could get about three and a half, we would make them start honoring the run.

"There's a difference mentally in a defensive line about the run and the pass rush. When it's second and long yardage, the defensive lineman doesn't settle into the ground as solidly because he's ready to straighten up and rush. We were going to make them dig in, and if it didn't come off, we were licked. It took some talking to convince our kids."

One of the four plays was a halfback dive right at Brown, who weighed 300 pounds. They used double-team blocking on him. There was also a double pinch on Karras at the same time. And for Schmidt, the middle linebacker and the deadliest tackler in the league, they hoped the "wash" from the double team would get him. The Lions scored first, which could have made the Giants panic. But they stuck to their game plan, took the kickoff straight down the field on running plays to tie the score and then went on to triumph, 17–14, the start of a nine-game winning streak which closed out the season. Tittle said to Sherman after the game, "Brown and Karras stood there all day looking like they were saying, 'Hey, you're not supposed to do this to us!'"

A game plan in pro football isn't nearly as complicated as the mystique surrounding it. From the play book which is handed out at the beginning of the season and modified only for special circumstances, a team will select perhaps ten basic running plays which the coaches feel are particularly suited against the upcoming opponent. They will have a couple of draws and a couple of screens. There will be plays for short yardage defenses and for goal line defenses. The passing offense is even more limited in the number of plays. On this game plan, a running back might jot a few notes for himself. On 34, the fullback over left tackle from an SE formation, he'll remind himself to block the end. On 29 around right end, he'll write, "Follow guard." On Pitch 39, "Step laterally and up." They're just cues for himself. As the game evolves, the number of plays used is narrowed down, especially if those tried initially work well.

In the memories of all the New York Jets who played on January 12, 1969, 19-straight is firmly emblazoned. The following four pages are actual reproductions of sheets from a playbook of the Cleveland Browns when Jimmy Brown was playing fullback. They show the various offensive formations used by the team and some of the running plays designed to exploit the power (on traps and draws) and speed (on flips) of the great fullback. (They were graciously provided by Dick Gallagher, director of the Pro Football Hall of Fame, who was an assistant coach with the Browns.)

SPACING AND OFFENSIVE FORMATIONS

REGULAR "T"

06" 1' 1yd.

4-1/2 yds.

FB takes bearing on ball - HB's take bearing on ball and FB. Be absolutely constant in position or timing is impossible. The time to vary your position is when you are no factor. Line splits will constantly vary.

OPPOSITE LEFT
LH FB RH

OPPOSITE RIGHT
LH FB

SPLIT LEFT
LH FB RH

SPLIT RIGHT
LH FB

WING LEFT
RH LH FB

WING RIGHT
FB RH

DIVIDE LEFT
RH LH FB

DIVIDE RIGHT
FB RH

OPPOSITE LEFT "E"
LE vary LH FB RH

"E" means End is flexed wider than the flanking back

OPPOSITE RIGHT "E"
RH vary LH FB

SPLIT LEFT "B"
LH LE vary FB RH

"B" means Back is flanked wider than the flexed end

SPLIT RIGHT "B"
RE FB

FLOOD LEFT
RH LH FB

FLOOD RIGHT
FB RH

DOUBLE WING
LH 3yds. 3yds. RH FB

FLEX SIDE

Flex side indicates an end is flexed alone.

UNBALANCED LEFT

UNBALANCED RIGHT

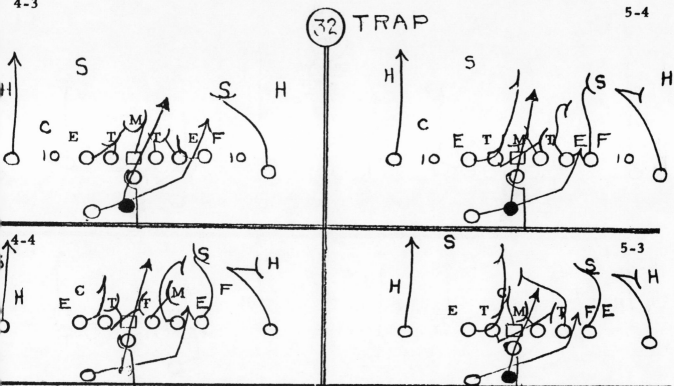

B - 3/8 Reverse pivot - Spin fast - Hold - Look the fake to the HB - Set up 76 Pass

I - Toes even with FB's insteps - Keep distance from FB constant - Run 36 - Drive

B - Right foot slightly left of ball - Hit close to power block on trap blocking.

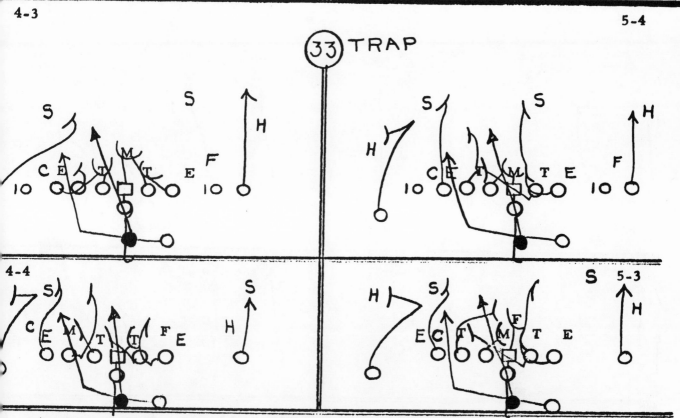

- 3/8 Reverse pivot - Spin fast - Hold - Look the fake to the HB - Set up 77 Pass

- Toes even with FB's insteps - Keep distance from FB constant - Run 37 - Drive

- Left foot slightly right of ball - Hit close to power block on trap blocking.

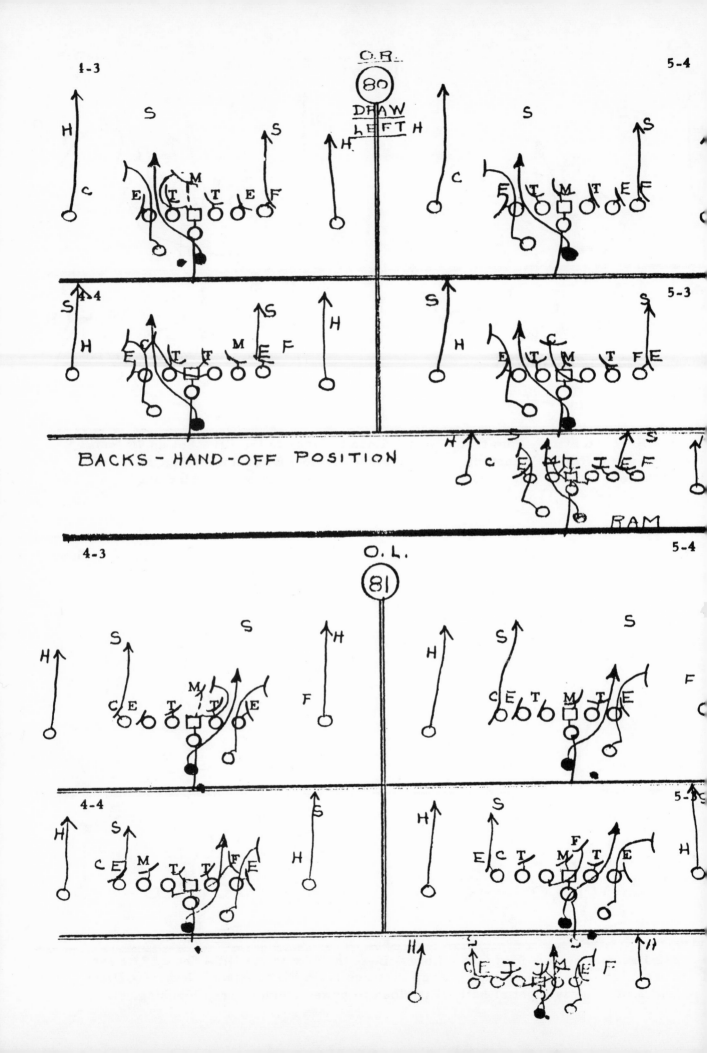

O.R.
(80)
DRAW LEFT

BACKS - HAND-OFF POSITION

O.L.
(81)

RAM

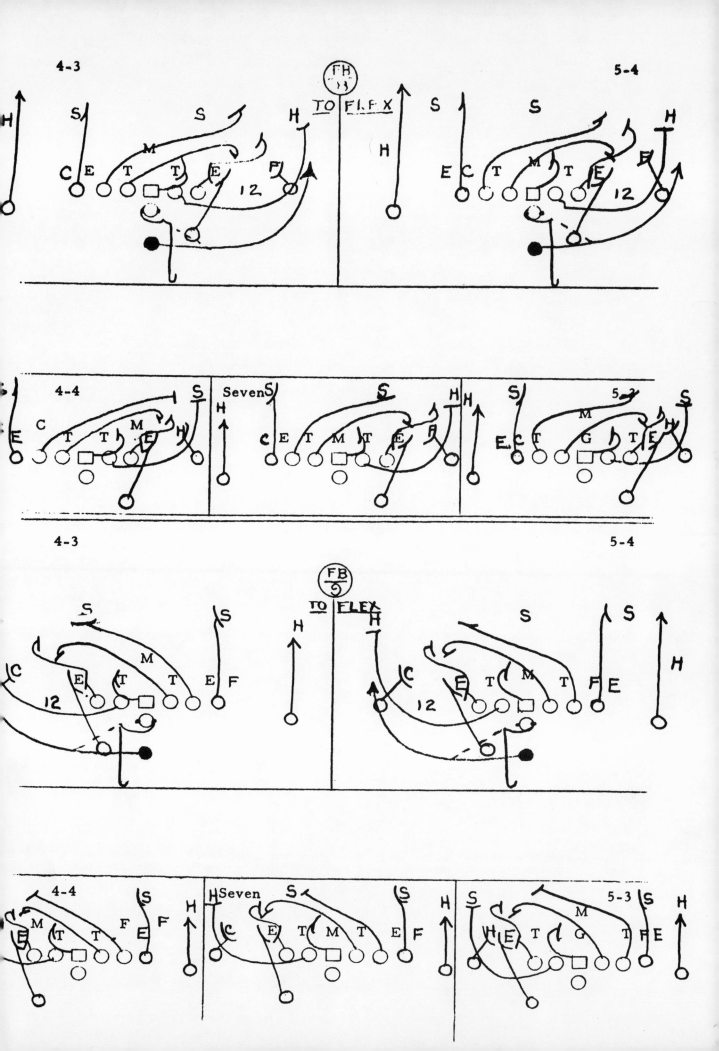

The fingers of the running back are stretched tautly, the hands in a cradled position as he drives forward to receive the football from the quarterback. Ahead lies his destination, enemy terrain, and his eyes are already scanning the scrimmage line for daylight. To his left, the fullback is also lunging forward, as a decoy and blocker. Donny Anderson (44) of Green Bay is the runner, preparing to take the handoff from Bart Starr (15), while Jim Grabowski (33) joins in the tableau of action.

The fake into the line, and Tony Lorick (33) hopes the opposition has been sucked into thinking he has the ball nestled in his arms, which he holds close to his midriff. John Unitas (19) still has the ball after the feint and will either fade to pass or shovel it to the other running back of the Baltimore Colts.

Gale Sayers (40) of the Chicago Bears follows close on the heels of his protective escort, Jim Cadile (72), with a couple of Washington Redskin tacklers trying to close in. The footrace between runner and defender is on, and Sayers is too quick for the Redskins to close the gap— he's already outdistanced one, and as he plants his left foot, he gets ready to turn the corner and whisk past the nearest pursuer.

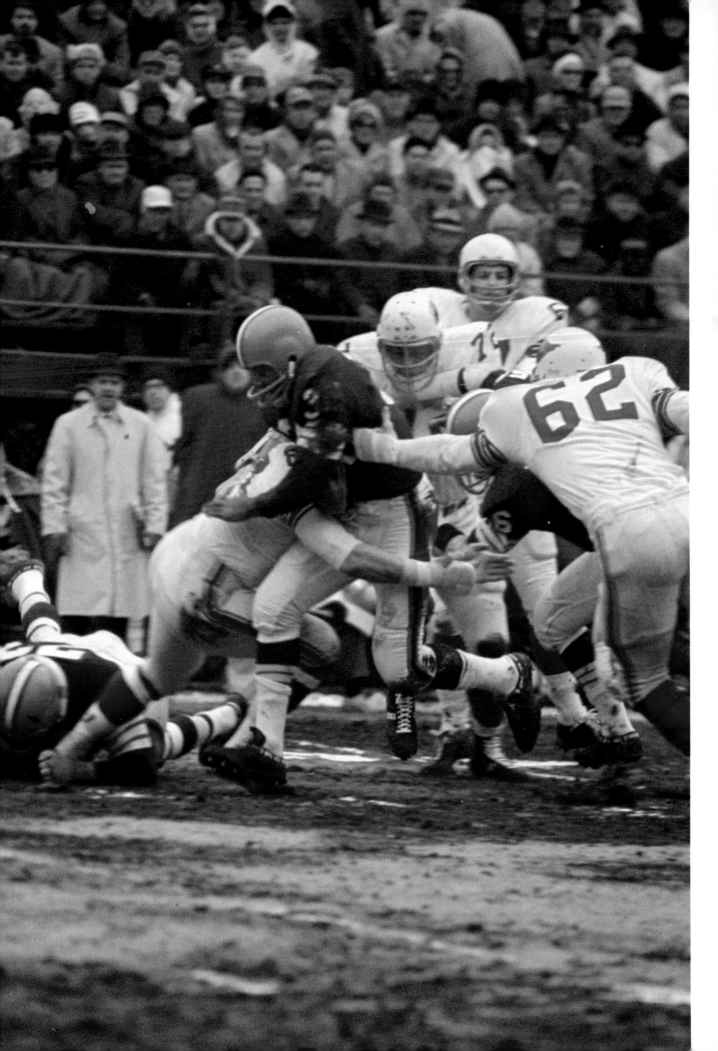

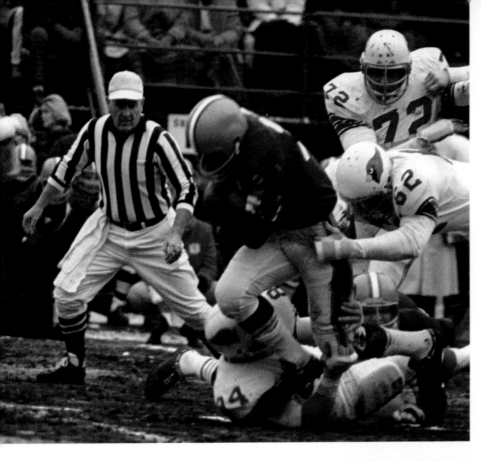

Arms reach out to impede the man with the football as he hurtles through a clump thick with white uniforms. But in full stride, pressing relentlessly straight ahead, he bursts through the alien grips. And with a forlorn fallen figure still on the ground behind him, he gallops into the open, exhilarated by the space to roam. This is Jim Brown of Cleveland at his best in busting tackles for a long gain.

The ball carrier, no matter how valiant, must work in unity with his blocker. Jim Taylor (31) cuts wide to allow guard Fuzzy Thurston (63) a good shot at the Kansas City tackler in the first Super Bowl game, played by Green Bay and the Chiefs.

The good ones stretch mightily for the extra yard. Lenny Moore, right, drives horizontally to maximize his gain for the Baltimore Colts. Below, Tom Matte, also of the Colts, adds the full length of his body to the yardage he has picked up before stopped by a prostrate Detroit Lion defender.

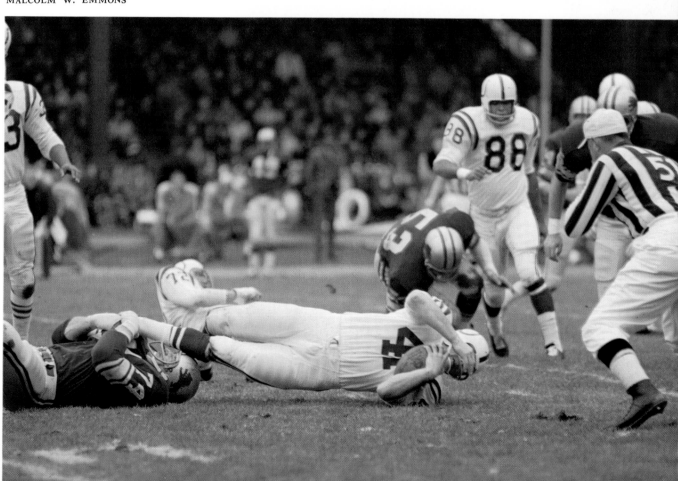

Jim Taylor is down, but those Cleveland Browns swarming over him aren't going to dislodge the Packer fullback from the ball.

Is Johnny Roland (23) of St. Louis going to pass, or is he going to tuck the ball under his arm and run? That's the beauty of the halfback pass option sweep in keeping a defense on edge.

The way it started out, Don Meredith (17), the Dallas quarterback, was fading to throw. But here's Don Perkins (43), left with the football and charging forward on a delay, or draw play.

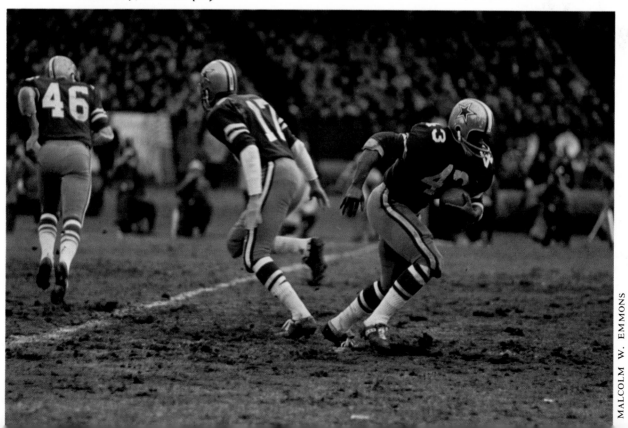

The pressure is heavy on Johnny Unitas of the Colts. The pass protector flinging himself in front of the Detroit rusher isn't going to keep him off interminably, but Johnny has already wheeled and spotted Lenny Moore (24), his halfback, alone in the right flat, in perfect position for a short flip on a screen, with Jim Parker (77) blocking.

The glamor is in the running, but Paul Hornung (5) also excelled in the rough guts of contact football by blocking with equal zeal.

A 230-pound fullback in full stride provides welcome security for a little man like Mike Garrett (21). That's Curtis McClinton of the Kansas City Chiefs out in front of him.

Inevitably, the man with the ball must prepare himself for the jar of contact. He meets it head-on, like Tom Woodeshick of the Philadelphia Eagles, in white uniform, top photo. Or he's caught from behind in mid-air, like Gale Sayers of the Bears (40), in the grasp of Washington's Rickie Harris.

There are also times when a friendly face is hard to find. In the pileup of running action, Bill Brown (30) of the Minnesota Vikings finds himself swirling in a sea of Dallas Cowboys.

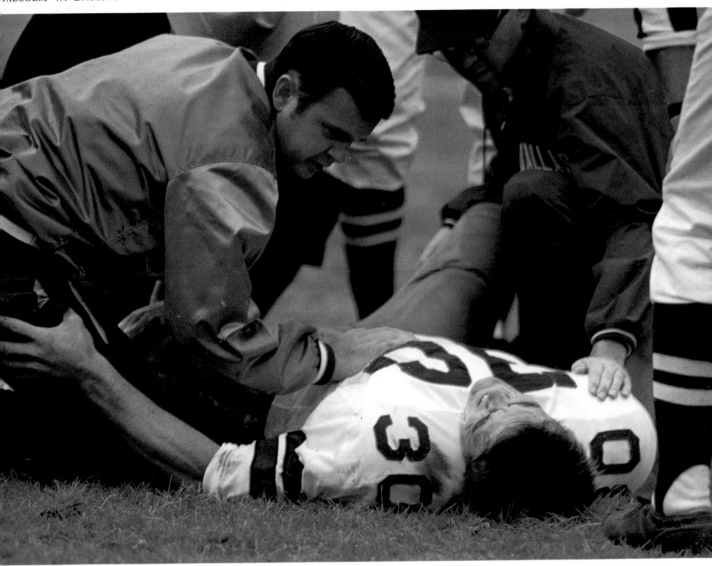

The jolt of violence has brought the runner to a complete stop. Danny Reeves of the Dallas Cowboys is down and out. Concerned faces hover over him. But he'll get up to run again.

PART II

9. To Start With...
Jim Thorpe

I WAS IN A LOT OF GAMES IN A LOT OF
PLACES.

—*Jim Thorpe, 1949.*

Murray Olderman

The legend obscures the man, fading the features like a frayed and weathered snapshot album.

Jim Thorpe was the greatest all-around athlete in the history of recorded sports, dating back to Coroebus of Elis in the eighth century before the birth of Christ. He was also the first president of the first nationally organized professional football league. He agreed to lead the National Professional Football Association into existence from the running board of a touring car outside an automobile agency in Canton, Ohio. The date was September 17, 1920, and two years later it became officially the National Football League.

Jim Thorpe himself was the first great performer of that league, its highest paid player, both the precursor and the prototype of the running back who has become the essential pawn in this violent game of human chess.

That is all part of the legend.

James Francis Thorpe was in reality a simple man who revelled in the playing of games, and when there were no games to play, his useful days as a man were over.

He was born to the great tradition of Black Hawk, a chief of the Sac and Fox tribe, who defeated the Osage and the Cherokee in battle. Chief Black Hawk's daughter was the maternal grandmother of the boy born in a tiny, two-room Oklahoma farmhouse in 1888. They first named him Wa-Tho-Huck, or Bright Path. The boy's father was Hiram Thorpe, half Sac and Fox, half Irish. The mother was three-quarters Sac and Fox, one-quarter French.

"I guess," said Jim Thorpe later in life, "that makes me an American airedale."

There were woods and open fields in Oklahoma for the Indian boy to roam in and develop a body as sturdy and swift as his black-maned ancestors. He tracked game and hunted deer and fished, and when they sent him to the school on the Indian reservation, he took up the white man's games and showed an instinctive, elastic skill that made him a superb performer in any sport he tried.

The country first became aware of Jim Thorpe in 1907 when he attended Carlisle Institute, an Indian school in western Pennsylvania, officially known as the United States Indian Industrial School. Ostensibly, he would study to become a carpenter or an electrician, but in fact he became an apprentice tailor. Athletically, however, Carlisle competed with the big colleges of the period, and in 1907, when Thorpe turned out for the varsity football team, Glenn Scobey "Pop" Warner had just come back to the little Indian school as coach. Warner was one of the great innovators and strategists in the early history of the game. He had coached at the Indian school once before and now on his return, the patterns of a new formation, called the single wing, were dancing around in his inventive fancies. To make it go, he needed a big, all-purpose threat in the tailback, or left halfback, role, a man who could sweep the ends, slash off tackle, punt and even throw the ball, since passing had just been legalized.

121

Pop didn't realize he had the man until he enforced a tackling drill one early fall afternoon to sharpen up the defense. Young Thorpe, fielding punts, was to play the part of the tackling dummy. He tucked the ball under his elbow and headed for the mass of tacklers. The first man hit him and bounced off. He gave the second a hip and withdrew it, and bludgeoned the third with his free hand.

"He had a way of running I never saw before," said Pete Calac, his teammate at Carlisle (and later in pro ball). "Jim would shift his hip toward the guy about to tackle him, then swing away and then, when the player moved in to hit him, he'd swing his hip back, hard, against the tackler's head and leave him in the dirt."

Thorpe pulled up at the end of the field, still standing and smiling.

"This is tackling practice," growled the coach. "Understand?"

"Nobody," said Thorpe deliberately, his eyes hooded, "tackles Jim."

When Albert Payne, the regular left halfback, got hurt in the Pennsylvania game, young Jim took over. Penn was undefeated and had three All-Americans in its lineup. Thorpe didn't even know his team's signals. Just the direction of the goal line. He grabbed a snap from center, didn't wait for his blockers to form and romped 65 yards to a touchdown.

"Hell," he said to his teammates, "that's fun. Give it to Jim again."

And he ran 85 yards to another touchdown. Penn suffered its only defeat in a twelve-game schedule to the Indian School, 26–6. Pete Hauser, who played fullback in the Carlisle single wing, made Walter Camp's All-American team.

"Hell's bells," recalled Pop Warner, "Jim was still a growing boy. He was lazy and didn't like to practice and he gave out his best effort only when he felt like it, which was about 40 percent of the time. He laughed and talked to the other team and enjoyed himself. But you couldn't keep him on the bench. Punishment didn't mean a thing to him. He was fearless and he hit so hard the other fellow got all the bruises."

Thorpe was blithe about his academics, too. He left Carlisle after another football tour de force in 1908 and wandered into the Carolinas and out to Arkansas for a couple of years, playing semi-pro baseball, then drifted back home to Oklahoma. That's where Warner contacted him again and persuaded him to return to Carlisle in 1911. "I wrote him," said Warner, "that he had a very good chance of making the American Olympic team."

By this time, Thorpe had reached full growth for football—six feet one and a half inches, solidly packed at 190 pounds. When Carlisle surged to victories over national powers like Harvard and Penn, Thorpe gained recognition as the greatest player of his day. Against Harvard, which had lost only one game in three years and was national champion in 1910, Thorpe played with bandaged legs and was used only as a decoy in the first half. He kicked three field goals to give Carlisle a 9–6 lead. When Harvard rushed out ahead, 15–9, Thorpe ignored the bandages and bulled 70 yards in nine carries for the tying touchdown. Then in the closing minutes he kicked a 50-yard field goal to give Carlisle an 18–15 victory.

"Jim Thorpe was usually quiet and reserved most of the time," said Joe Guyon, who played in the backfield with him for the first time that day. "But he was at home on a football field. There he had confidence in what he was doing. The modesty disappeared and aggressiveness came out. Jim liked a challenge."

The next summer he went to Sweden for the Olympic Games and won both the pentathlon and decathlon competition. And there is a story that Gustav V, King of Sweden, presented him with a bronze bust and a jeweled chalice to commemorate his feats, pronouncing solemnly, "You, sir, are the greatest athlete in the world." To which Thorpe replied succinctly, "Thanks, King."

Then he went back to playing football again for Carlisle and made the All-American team for the second straight year. But the medals and baubles from the Olympics never stayed with Thorpe because the purist AAU officials shortly discovered that during his two-year hiatus from school, the Indian had been collecting as much as $15 a week for his baseball excursion in North Carolina, thereby professionalizing himself. They took it all back and expunged his name from the record books.

At the time, however, Jim didn't care greatly. There were games to be played. It was only three decades later, when the vigor had gone out of his body and his personal life was a tangle, that Jim said ruefully, "I'd sure like to have those things I won. Haven't got much else any more."

Nothing remained from a major league baseball career that started in 1913 and lasted sporadically through seven seasons, or from professional football. Football—that was Jim's sport, his life and his plaything. The money wasn't big—he started out with the Canton Bulldogs at $250 a game, and he never made more than $500 a game. But it sustained him as an athlete until he was well into his forties.

"I'll tell you this," said Jack Cusack, an oilman who pioneered the team in Canton, Ohio, when pro football was regarded as a game for ruffians: "Jim didn't play for money; he played for the love of the game. He once showed me an offer to join the vaudeville circuit for $1,000 a week. He turned it down. Jim was really a reticent fellow."

Professional football had flourished earlier in eastern Ohio, then vanished for a decade because of a betting scandal. In 1915, Thorpe gave it new impetus as the most famous athlete of the time. Canton and Massillon were the great rivals, and kids like Paul Brown, growing up in that part of Ohio, rowed across the Tuscarawas River and wiggled under the fence to see them play.

The teams hired the best money could buy. The Massillon Tigers recruited the famous Notre Dame passing combination of Gus Dorais and Knute Rockne. Rockne lined up at end, determined to stop the legendary Indian. Rockne didn't have much size, but he was quick, and twice he crashed into the Canton backfield to nail Thorpe for losses.

"Hey, kid," said Thorpe reproachfully each time, "you shouldn't do that. The people paid to see old Jim run."

"Go ahead," said the fiery Rockne, "run—if you can."

On the next play, Thorpe swung wide around Rockne's end. Rockne tunneled in to meet him. Thorpe jolted him with a stiff arm, brought his knee up hard into Rockne's chest and whacked him with a hip, then straightened up and zipped 60 yards for a touchdown. Two men hovered over Rockne, dazed, as Thorpe trotted back to midfield.

In his prime, Jim Thorpe, the Sac and Fox Indian, was a fast, powerful man who could get off the mark with the speed of a sprinter.

"Good boy, Rock," said the Indian, "you let old Jim run for the people."

"Pro football in the days of Thorpe was a lot dirtier than college," said Pete Calac. "But the dirtier the football got, the meaner Jim got. He would stand there at halfback and yell across the line to tell them where he was going to run, and Jim would run over anyone who got in his way. He left a line of guys strung out from New York to Minnesota."

But that was only when the ire moved him.

"Jim didn't try to run down every man," said Guyon, who teamed with Thorpe, Calac, and Little Feather in an all-Indian backfield for the Bulldogs. "He used a technique Pop Warner taught his backs. Catch a man stopped when he's not charging you. Then, wham, hit him with the hip or stiff arm. Unexpected contact, Warner said."

The memory of Thorpe in Canton was deeply etched in the boyhood of Edgar "Rip" Miller, who was one of the famed Seven Mules (the line) under Rockne at Notre Dame and later became an assistant athletic director at the U. S. Naval Academy.

"I was going to high school," recalled Rip, "and we practiced on the same field. The pros would stay over and help us. Ol' Jim was the greatest I ever saw. He was a weaving type runner, heavy legged. He ran a lot like that guy from Michigan, [Tom] Harmon, weave and lean. He wasn't a dirty player, but he was rough.

"I'd go down to the McKinley Hotel to watch 'em dress for a game, and Jim would put on those hard hip pads, plaster of paris. It was like hitting a guy with plywood.

"He had one nemesis—Fritz Pollard. He never could get by him."

Pollard was the first great Negro back in professional football. He had been an All-American at Brown University and joined the Massillon Tigers. It was the day of the 60-minute player, and Pollard was stationed at safety on defense, in the seven-diamond formation which was prevalent.

"One day," said Rip, "I was giving Jim some heat about never getting past Pollard. He said, 'Don't worry. Ol' Jim'll get by him.'

"Next time they played, Thorpe broke through the line and only Pollard was in his way. Fritz kept giving ground and giving ground until he had him penned in around the 10-yard line. Suddenly Jim took the ball and shoveled it to Pollard, like a basketball pass. Fritz, surprised, reacted instinctively and caught it. Just about the time Thorpe hit him with everything he had and knocked his head off.

"The ball went in one direction, Pollard in another. And as they carried him off the field, Thorpe turned around and said, 'Now big Jim run.'"

Pro football was then a very informal operation. Players dressed at the hotel and ate in peoples' homes in town. The games were played in Myers Lake Park, and the fans rode out to it on the street car. Thorpe was both the star and the coach. The team played out of the double wing formation which Warner had taught them, and Jim handled the ball on almost every play ("I don't remember him blocking," said Rip Miller). Everybody in town loved old Jim, even if it was a well known fact that he hit the jug pretty hard. For six years, Thorpe and the Canton Bulldogs were a parlay as the best in professional football. So, when representatives from several cities (among them one George Halas of Chicago) met in Canton in September 1920, to form the American

Professional Football Association (later known as the National Football League), it was logical that Thorpe be named the first president.

It was an honorary gesture and, in the aftermath of history, had a touch of irony. Following that first season, Thorpe began his wanderings through professional sports on a declining graph of ability. Cusack, his original boss in Canton, put him in Cleveland for a year and from there he went to the Oorang Indians, the Toledo Maroons, the Rock Island Independents, the New York Giants, and eventually a final fadeout with the Chicago Cardinals in 1928, when he was forty-one years old.

Sporadically, a flash of the old fire possessed him. In 1924, Steve Owen (later the coach of the Giants) broke into pro football with the Kansas City Cowboys as a 260-pound tackle. By this time, Thorpe was putting on a belly and his jaw was sagging so that he was used primarily as a blocking back and kicker. Owen, respecting Thorpe's reputation, approached Jim warily as he charged across the line, then sidestepped Thorpe's block and dumped the ball carrier for a loss on the first play of the game.

Confidence building, Owen charged at a direct angle on the next play, brushed past Thorpe and tackled the ball carrier again.

"The old Indian doesn't have it any more," Steve chortled to himself as he dug in for the next down, focused only on the tailback getting the snap from center. He surged across the line and reached out. Steve never saw what hit him. The jolt and a shroud of blackness enveloped him simultaneously. From the ground, Steve looked back and saw the runner yards down the field. And over him stood Jim Thorpe.

"Never," said the old warrior, "take your eyes off an old Indian."

Pride motivated Thorpe when there was little else left.

"I got to know Jim pretty well," said Ernie Nevers, whom Pop Warner had called the greatest player he ever coached, better than Thorpe. "I played against him with the Duluth Eskimos, in Canton. He was in his forties, past his prime, so they played him at end. But this business about what Pop said nagged him.

"I remember it was a frozen field, and on punts I'd go back with the safety. I was just reaching for the ball when I got hit in the chest. I went down, and my head hit the ice. I was foggy when I saw the Indian standing over me. He said only one word: 'Awright.'

"He had to show the people who was best."

But the old Indian could never adjust himself to a life away from football when age forced him off the field. During the Depression, he was discovered digging ditches. He worked once in a while as a movie extra. He was a carpenter on a ship in World War II. He had a heart attack. He guarded a gate at an auto plant in Detroit. He was fined for drunk driving. He was a bouncer in a bar in Los Angeles.

In 1953, at the age of sixty-five, he died. He was living in a house trailer. But from a career standpoint, the epitaph had been written in a dispatch from Chicago on November 30, 1928:

"The Chicago Bears routed their ancient rivals, the Chicago Cardinals, 34–0, in the annual Thanksgiving Day game at Wrigley Field today. Jim Thorpe played a few minutes for the Cardinals but was unable to get anywhere. In his forties and muscle-bound, Thorpe was a mere shadow of his former self."

126

Harold E. "Red" Grange

THIS MAN RED GRANGE IS THREE OR FOUR MEN AND A HORSE ROLLED INTO ONE. HE IS JACK DEMPSEY, BABE RUTH, AL JOLSON, PAAVO NURMI AND MAN O' WAR.

—*Damon Runyon, 1925.*

With the snap of the ball, the big tackle, Steve Owen leaped across the line and hit the defensive end with the full force of his shoulder. The end fell, and Owen fell on top of him. Around the toppled bodies whirled a man with the ball, number 77 on his jersey.

"I lay there on top of this end," remembered Owen, "and watched him run. He was like two jack-rabbits. I've never seen hips switch as fast to the right, and then to the left. Seven hard-tackling pros had a clean shot at him. Not a one even laid a hand on him. He ran 68 yards for a touchdown."

And while Owen lay there, he heard a groan under him. "Listen, you big ————," the other guy yelled, "you going to spend the weekend on top of me?"

"Sorry," said Steve. "I was just watching a guy run."

In the 268 pages of the National Football League Record Manual, the name of the "guy" shows up in only two brief references.

Alphabetically, on the Roster of Members, under the section headed "Hall of Fame," it reads:

Red Grange (Illinois), Charter 1963, halfback, Chicago Bears (1925–37)

And again in "Chronology," at the bottom of the first page where it comes down to 1925, there is a simple statement:

Red Grange signed with Chicago Bears. (Nov. 22.)

He holds no records in the annals of the NFL or even of the Chicago Bears, for whom he played eight active seasons. He is not listed among the top twenty-five ground gainers in Bear history, but mainly because no accurate figures were kept in his early seasons. The fact is that in the cold light of achievement, Red Grange might have been neglected in the history of professional football.

Yet no man exerted a more profound influence over its destiny.

Red Grange, at the time he came into pro football in 1925, brought to the game in one valuable bundle two vital elements: magnetism and respectability. He showed that people who had no college alumni affiliations would come to see grown men play football. And he showed them a flair that would keep them coming.

The Golden Twenties were a dynamic period in American athletics—the decade of Dempsey and Ruth, Tilden and Jones, and a "handy guy named Sande." It was a period for romantics and F. Scott Fitzgerald novels. Red Grange belonged with all of them and in some ways superseded them as a glamorous figure.

That's the enigmatic part of it, because Grange as a pure personality couldn't have gotten a small squeal from a teeny-bopper. He wore no Fu Manchu mustaches or mink coats. He didn't smoke or drink. He spoke platitudes, and lived them. He was the nice guy next door, and he even worked in the summer time to pay his way through college. In fact, his red hair, neatly trimmed, was a myth, too. It wasn't red—more of a rusty brown.

Yet when he signed with the Chicago Bears and appeared with them in his debut on Thanksgiving Day of 1925, professional football became for the first time a sport that would appeal to urban centers of population. He made the pro game big-time as no other player could have.

"I wouldn't say he was the greatest back I've ever known," wrote Grantland Rice. "Not with Bronko Nagurski and Jim Thorpe around. But, in my opinion, Red had more influence on both the college and the pro game than any other player."

Put Grange's exploits in the context of the times, and you begin to understand the impact of his arrival as a football star. It was the aftermath of World War I austerity, and the country was in a hedonistic mood. People wanted their thrills vicariously. Dempsey gratified them by knocking out Willard at Toledo in 1919, and then had that sensational kayo of Luis Firpo, the Wild Bull of the Pampas, in September 1923. Ruth had hit 59 homers in 1921, and a year later the New York Yankees had moved into their new home, Yankee Stadium. Bobby Jones, at the age of twenty-one, won his first United States Open Championship in 1923. The United States won the Davis Cup in 1920 and was to keep it for seven straight years while Bill Tilden dominated tennis. Man o' War became the most famous thoroughbred of racing as a two- and three-year-old. Football needed hero imagery, too.

And in the fall of 1923, a sophomore named Harold Grange suited up for his first varsity game at the University of Illinois. He was twenty years old. Born in Forkville, Pennsylvania, he had moved to Wheaton, Illinois, where his father would eventually become the chief of police for twenty-three years. When he was eight years old, a doctor said he had a bad heart and shouldn't play sports. The kid didn't follow the recommendation and his heart never bothered him. He went out for the high school football team weighing 138 pounds and scored 75 touchdowns. He went to Illinois, however, expecting to play basketball and baseball. He didn't think there was room for a 166-pound halfback.

But he was fast—the state high school sprint and hurdles champ. And he was strong; in the summers he wrestled ice to pick up five bucks a day because colleges in those days didn't dispense athletic scholarships. He got the job on the ice truck because Luke Thompson, who owned the route, offered to give a dollar to any kid who could lift a 75-pound cake of ice on his shoulder. Red was the only one who could do it and Luke asked him to go to work. Red worked on the job every summer through high school and through college and even when he didn't need the money because lugging ice shaped him for football. It also gave him a nickname that was to be common—the Wheaton Iceman.

In 1922, the Illini, coached by Bob Zuppke, had won two games and lost five. Their opening game in '23 was against Nebraska, a national power which had lost only one game the previous season, and featured a fabulous sophomore of its own in Ed Weir, a tackle who would become a two-time All-American and eventually be elected to the College Hall of Fame.

Zuppke started the sophomore, Grange, at left halfback and pulled him out of the game after the first quarter. "You're tipping off all our plays, Red," he admonished the young back. "You're leaning in their direction."

"Strange," muttered Red to the guy sitting next to him on the bench. "I'm so excited out there I don't know where the plays are going myself."

130

Grange at Illinois was an elusive specter who captivated the nation in the Golden '20s with his brilliant open field feats against Michigan and Pennsylvania.

But he had run for 35 yards and one touchdown in that opening quarter. He went back in the game and rambled 65 yards through a broken field for another score, then added a 12-yard burst in the third period to account for all the Illinois touchdowns in a 24–7 victory over the Cornhuskers. Grange was on his way. Illinois went unbeaten in an eight-game schedule, and Red scored a touchdown against every opponent. Walter Camp broke procedure and put the sophomore on his All-American team. The pattern continued into Grange's junior year until the Illini faced mighty Michigan, at the zenith of its power under Athletic Director Fielding H. "Hurry Up" Yost. Both teams were unbeaten as they met on October 18 in the Illinois stadium before 67,000 fans.

Michigan, in fact, had not lost since midway through the 1921 season and had given up only three touchdowns in its last twenty games. "Mister Grange," warned Yost, "will be a carefully watched young man any time he takes the ball. There will be eleven clean, hard Michigan tacklers headed for him at the same time. I know he's a great runner, but great runners usually have the hardest time gaining ground when they are met by special preparation."

The Wolverines wasted no time throwing eleven tacklers at the wraith-like halfback who wore number 77 on his back—still the most famous number in the history of uniformed athletes. They kicked off straight down the middle to Grange, who stood at the 5-yard line. His running path carved an "S" on the turf as he reversed his field twice and sprinted 95 yards for a touchdown to open the game.

The next time Illinois got the ball, Red started around right end, changed pace momentarily to confuse his pursuers, then streaked 67 yards down the sidelines to another touchdown. Michigan punted after the ensuing kickoff, and Grange grabbed the ball in full flight on his 44-yard line and weaved through a broken field the remaining 56 yards to a third score. The first quarter still had more than three minutes to go when the Michigan punter kicked the ball out of bounds on his own 45. Red immediately circled his flank again and darted the full distance for a touchdown, his fourth in 12 minutes, and at that point in the game he had gained 303 yards.

Zuppke took him out for a breather, and in the second half he returned to throw another touchdown pass and spurt 12 yards for a sixth score as Illinois romped, 39–14. From scrimmage, he gained 402 yards in twenty-one carries for the afternoon, and Grantland Rice promptly dubbed him "The Galloping Ghost."

"All Grange can do is run," scoffed the Michigan school paper editorially.

"All Galli-Curci can do is sing," retorted Zuppke.

That was Grange at his greatest, though there were other memorable afternoons. In 1925, his senior year, the East wanted to be shown. Hurt by graduation losses, Illinois dropped three of its first four games and traveled to Franklin Field in Philadelphia to meet undefeated Pennsylvania. Rains had softened the turf, and cleats turned it into a muddy morass. But number 77 kept his balance before the critical Eastern audience. He scored three touchdowns and gained 363 yards on the ground to lead the Midwest invaders in a 24–2 upset.

Measure the impact of the great ones who followed him in college football—Tom Harmon of Michigan in the late '30's, Glenn Davis and Doc Blanchard of Army a

132

decade later, Doak Walker of SMU after them, and O. J. Simpson of recent vintage—together they don't total the force of Grange's national appeal as his career at Illinois came to its end in Columbus, Ohio, before a crowd of 85,500, the largest football audience ever congregated till that time.

The people of pro football were cued to Grange's importance. The National Football League was struggling as a cumbersome group of twenty disparate units operating in some towns which obviously couldn't support big league sports—Duluth, Frankford, Hammond, Pottsville, and Rock Island (at the time you would have included Green Bay, too). It badly needed a merchandising attraction like Grange.

"Football," growled Grange's own coach, Zuppke, "isn't meant to be played for money. Stay away from professionalism."

But Red was already hooked by the lure. A movie house operator in Champaign named C. C. Pyle had set the bait early by giving Red a pass that would get him in to see such matinee idols as Rudolph Valentino, and then he had contracted to become Red's agent. He was meeting with George Halas, the young impresario of the Chicago Bears, before Red played his last varsity game.

"You get paid for coaching," Red answered Zuppke's criticism softly. "Why is it wrong for me to get paid for playing?" And the morning after the Ohio State game, he signed with Pyle, who outlined prospects for a quick $100,000.

"I'm turning pro to make money," explained Red. "Unless I get the money now, I'll never get it because I'll soon be forgotten."

Forgotten? Not by men like Grantland Rice, who chronicled the exploits of the greatest: "Grange runs as Nurmi runs and Dempsey moves, with almost no effort, as a shadow flits and drifts and darts. There is no gathering of muscles for an extra lunge. There is only the effortless, ghostlike weave and glide upon effortless legs with a body that can detach itself from the hips, with a change of pace that comes to a dead stop and picks up instant speed, so perfect is the coordination of brain and sinew."

And for this kind of performance, C. C. (soon to stand for Cash and Carry) Pyle made the pros pay. In those days a collegian didn't have to wait to be drafted. He didn't have to wait until his class was graduated. On a Saturday, Grange intercepted an Ohio State pass in Columbus on the last play of the game to save a 14–9 victory (he had gained 235 yards). And on Sunday, he was on the bench of the Chicago Bears in Wrigley Field, signed to a contract which guaranteed him $3,000 a game against a 50 percent cut of the gate receipts. He didn't play that day because even a Grange needed time to learn a few plays. But he was unveiled as an active pro five days later, on Thanksgiving Day, against the Bears' south side rivals, the Chicago Cardinals.

More than 36,000 people, the largest crowd ever to see a professional football game until then, jammed Wrigley Field for the debut. Artistically, it was frustrating. Paddy Driscoll, the great halfback and kicker of the Cardinals (and later a coach of the Bears), punted twenty-five times, but Grange got his hands on the ball on only three of those kicks. "Kicking to Grange," shrugged Driscoll, "is like grooving one to Babe Ruth. It was a question which of us would look bad—Grange or Driscoll. I decided it would not be Paddy."

As a Chicago Bear favorite, Red Grange still wore number 77, but he was less a running threat than a defensive stalwart and pass receiver.

Schedules were also flexible in the pro game of that era. To capitalize on the lure of Grange, a barnstorming schedule was quickly arranged—a murderous slate of eight games in twelve days. Grange wasn't always at his best. And the Bears occasionally dragged their feet. But the money rolled in, from a crowd of 40,000 in Philadelphia, and 28,000 more again in Wrigley Field, despite a swirling snow storm—until the football caravan came to New York on December 5.

The Giants were a new franchise in pro ball, owned by a respectable bookie named Tim Mara (placing bets that way was legal then). He paid $5,000 for the franchise, but in the course of the season his losses totalled almost $200,000, and he was skeptical about the future of the pro game.

"I felt sure pro football ought to go," recalled Mara, "but it wasn't going any too fast. It wasn't going as fast as my money was.

"Then we met the Bears—with Red Grange. I would have been glad to see 25,000 people in the stands. Instead, the house was swamped. I knew that pro football had arrived, and my worries were over."

The 72,000 fans got what they paid to see—the sight of Grange weaving for a touchdown when he intercepted a pass and raced 35 yards. The New York showing put professional football in a new perspective. It took the game out of the cow pastures and the grimy steel and mining towns and endowed it with class. The game made the front page of *The New York Times*.

After a month's respite—Grange hurt his arm in Pittsburgh and couldn't play, and the other Bears weren't in any better shape—Cash and Carry Pyle took his troupe on the road again, to such diverse spots as Florida and the Pacific Coast, where 70,000 clustered to see Grange in Los Angeles. The money rolled in. Red Grange was also the first great sports athlete to be used in advertising on a large scale, the forerunner of entertainers and athletes who shunned greasy kid stuff. There was a Red Grange soft drink, Red Grange dolls, Red Grange shoes, Red Grange peanuts and Red Grange sports clothes. He made a movie called "One Minute to Play," followed by another, "The Racing Romeo." They've disintegrated peacefully in a can of celluloid, all traces vanished.

So did the shy small-town kid from Wheaton. He was even named the corespondent in a Beverly Hills divorce case—automatic qualification as a Flapper Age jet-setter. Grange grinned amiably, "I'm no love pirate. I'm in the ice business." He came home to Wheaton wearing a fashionable raccoon coat. He also had a bonanza of $100,000 for his share of that first exposure to professionalism.

Then Cash and Carry Pyle got hungry. For Red's return to the Bears in 1926, he demanded one-third of the franchise. Halas refused flatly, so Pyle and Grange went off and formed another league, with their own team based in New York, called the Yankees. The venture flopped and cost them most of the money they had accumulated. In 1927, the Yankees were welcomed into the National League, because the owners weren't stupid—Grange would still pull people into the parks.

And in the third game of the season, 30,000 scurried to Wrigley Field, plus a few thousand more who broke through the bleacher gates and clambered over the fences, to see Grange come back to Chicago, against the Bears. In the last minute of play, he ran out of the backfield as a pass receiver. George Trafton, the rugged center of the Bears, back-pedalled to cover him, and as Grange reached for the ball he was bumped hard by Trafton. The cleat of Grange's right shoe caught just as Trafton fell on him, and Red's knee popped.

Today they'd cart him off to the hospital immediately and remove a cartilage, and in two months he'd be ready to play. Then, knee surgery was primitive and meant an end to a career. So they packed the hinge in plaster of paris and put him on crutches, and sporadically he tried to play during the rest of the season. It was useless.

"After it happened," reminisced Red, "I was just another ordinary ball carrier. The accident took away most of my running ability."

He didn't play at all in 1928, but a year later, shorn of Pyle (they parted friends) and most of his money, Red made a comeback with the Bears. He carried the ball occasionally, in quick darts through the line from the T-formation, which the Bears used, but his lateral mobility was limited. Instead, Red perfected his other skills. He threw the ball, was a fine receiver, a competent blocker and became an excellent defensive back. Red played six seasons for George Halas and was a charter member of the Bear alumni club. He later coached a couple of years, became a successful insurance man and a football telecaster (the influence of Halas was evident there) before retiring to Florida.

The ghostlike rambles vanished with the knee injury, but the appreciation of Grange's contributions never faltered. In 1931, he was named to the first official all-league team ever selected. For company in the backfield, he had Earl "Dutch" Clark, Johnny "Blood" McNally, and a versatile, blond-haired giant named Ernie Nevers.

HAROLD "RED" GRANGE

BORN: June 13, 1903   Height: 5'11"   Weight: 175
University of Illinois

Chicago Bears, 1925, 1929–34
New York Yankees, 1926–27

Year	G.	Att.	Yds.	Avg.	TD.	P.C.	Yds.	Avg.	TD.	TD.	Pts.
			RUSHING				PASS RECEIVING			SCORING	
1925	17	204	1024	5.0							
1926	16	191	961	5.0							
1927	14	154	762	4.9							
1928		(inactive, injured)			unofficial						
1929	14	130	552	4.3							
1930	14	88	382	4.3							
1931	12	72	288	4.0							
1932	9	57	132	2.3	3	11	168	15.3	3	6	36
1933	13	81	277	3.4	1	3	74	24.7	0	1	6
1934	12	32	136	4.3	1	2	46	23.0	2	3	18
PRO TOTALS —3 YEARS	34	170	545	3.2	5	16	288	18.0	5	10	60

136

Ernie Nevers

ERNIE NEVERS WAS GREAT IN SPITE OF
THE FACT THAT HE WAS ALWAYS PLAY-
ING WITH LOUSY TEAMS. HE WAS ABLE
TO LIFT THEM BEYOND THEIR CAPACI-
TIES.
> —*Jimmy Conzelman, coach,*
> *Chicago Cardinals.*

Ernie Nevers was the most versatile of the original pro greats. He ran, passed, kicked, tackled and blocked with equal facility and ferocity.

A high threshold of pain is a coach's euphemism for guts. Some guys can't function with a torn hangnail. With Ernie Nevers, it didn't matter if he was knocked silly. He came to play. Right up until the last year he played as a professional.

It was 1931, and Ernie was the playing coach of the Chicago Cardinals. They used the old Pop Warner double wing formation in which Ernie had been indoctrinated as a collegian at Stanford. Ernie played fullback and handled the ball on every play. That season the Cardinals played nineteen games in the scrambled schedules then prevalent, a total of 1,140 minutes, and Ernie played 1,140 minutes, too.

The Brooklyn Dodgers almost snapped the string. Ernie butted through the line and went down under a load of tacklers. The whistle blew, but an enthusiastic Dodger, unable to curtail his momentum, landed on the pile, and his knees dug a crevice in Nevers' back. The Cardinal player-coach remained prone after everyone unpiled. He was unconscious, and the two minutes granted for a timeout didn't revive him. The referee graciously allotted the Cardinals a few more minutes to carry him off the field. Phil Handler, a guard (later a coach with the Cardinals and Bears), and the trainer propped him up and dragged the limp body toward the sidelines. They were almost there when Ernie hazily came to and mumbled, "What's going on? Where are we?"

"Easy, Ernie," Handler reassured him. "You were knocked out. We're taking you out of the game."

"You got to be kidding," Ernie protested and suddenly yanked himself free of his supports and wheeled around towards the field. "You're not taking me out." He took a rubbery step toward the cluster of Cardinals deep in their own territory, a firmer one next, and then broke into a trot. In the huddle which he rejoined, as the fullback and field general, he immediately called his own play on a straight smash to the short side between center and guard. He gained three yards and called the same play again. Five yards. He varied it with an off-tackle slant for the first down. And he kept calling his own signal for *sixteen* straight plays until the Cardinals had moved in for a touchdown. They won the game, 14–7.

Unusual? In his junior year at Stanford University, "Big Swede," as they called the burly guy with the unruly tousle of blond hair, broke his left ankle in a preseason scrimmage against a naval station team. Tiny Thornhill, an assistant coach, told all the Stanford players to tape their ankles, and Ernie had ignored his order. On crutches until early November, he found out that ". . . with the ankle heavily braced and taped, I could run better than I could walk, so I talked the Old Man (Coach Warner) into letting me start against Montana, the next-to-last game." After three minutes of play, he broke his right ankle.

But Stanford won the Pacific Coast Conference title and a bid to the Rose Bowl against fabulous Notre Dame, with its Four Horsemen in the backfield and the Seven Mules up front led by All-American center Adam Walsh. Ten days before the game, Nevers was still on crutches.

"The Old Man," he related, "got some aluminum, some shears and a hammer, and went to work. He pieced together what almost amounted to an artificial combination sole, heel, and ankle joint. Under this he wrapped a bandage and over it a layer of adhesive tape. Then he took the inner tube from an automobile tire and taped it to my heel, stretching it tightly up the back of my calf, and taped it in place just below the knee. It sounds like something out of a comic strip, but it worked. The rubber tube did what the injured tendon was supposed to do. With this on my right foot and a heavy coating of tape on my left, I went out on the field for practice four days before the game."

On New Year's day, the pain deadened by a shot of novocaine, Ernie went out to play against that dazzling Notre Dame team. He was on the field the entire sixty minutes, and those heavily encased legs ran for 114 yards in a one-man-gang performance that startled the country. Stanford also outgained the Irish, 391 yards to 192, but lost, 27–10, on five key pass interceptions. Years later, Nevers told Elmer Layden, the fullback of the Four Horsemen, "You were responsible for two of the longest runs of my football career that day."

"How do you figure that?" asked Elmer, puzzled.

"I was chasing you the length of the field, after a couple of those interceptions."

Walter Eckersall, an all-time great who was one of the game officials, wrote two days later in the *San Francisco Chronicle*, ". . . Nevers is about the best fullback who ever graced a gridiron . . . a terrific line smasher . . . an accurate forward passer and an excellent blocker."

Since Warner had also coached Thorpe at Carlisle, the comparisons were inevitable. Pop's assessment of the two was frank: "Nevers could do everything Thorpe could do, and he always tried harder than Thorpe ever did. Ernie gave 60 minutes of himself in every game. But I rarely could get more than 20 minutes out of the big Indian."

Any team Nevers ever played on got the full 60 minutes out of him. At Stanford, he had earned eleven letters in four sports. "And I hashed tables all my four years there," said Ernie, "and after my last football season I still owed the university $1,000. That's why I turned pro."

Grange and Cash and Carry Pyle were hauling in the loot on a barnstorming expedition in Florida. So a promoter put $25,000 in a bank in Ernie's home town, Santa Rosa, California, and said it was his if he'd organize a team to play Grange and the Bears in Jacksonville, Florida, then go barnstorming for $5,000 a game. Ernie arrived three days before the game. He had to assemble the players and practice. They lost to the Bears, 7–6, and the team disbanded. But Ernie still got his money: "I felt like a robber in collecting my $25,000."

At least, it was the start of his professional career.

In Duluth, Minnesota, a young football entrepreneur named Ole Haugsrud and his coach, Dewey Scanlon, bought the remnants of an NFL franchise for $1. They sold several players to National League clubs to pay the bills. They then signed the big, yellow-haired fullback from Stanford for a salary of $15,000, the highest ever paid in football at that time. It was a homecoming of sorts for Ernie. He was born in Willow River, Minnesota, not even big enough to be on the map, and went to school in Superior,

140

Wisconsin, just across the mouth of the St. Louis River from Duluth. His last year in high school, the family moved to Santa Rosa, California, but Ernie still returned that winter to play on the basketball team (where he invented the revolutionary hook shot).

He was a natural commodity for Duluth, but after the first game of the season, the townspeople never saw much more of the big blond, or his mates. Haugsrud (who is still in pro football as a board director of the Minnesota Vikings) promptly dubbed them Ernie Nevers' Eskimos and put them on the road to capitalize on the star's national reputation. They stayed on the road, from September until deep into February 1927. The Eskimos became instead Ernie Nevers and his Iron Men of the North. They played twenty-nine games, from Portland, Maine, to the Pacific Coast and in the process traveled 19,000 miles by train and bus. Out of a possible 1,740 minutes, Ernie played 1,713. He wasn't unique. The Duluth team went through that murderous schedule with a total squad of thirteen players, among them two future coaches of the Pittsburgh Steelers, the fabulous Johnny Blood and Walt "Butch" Kiesling.

When they came to New York in October, Tim Mara, the owner of the Giants, wanted to play gracious host. He brought a sight-seeing bus around to the team's hotel to show them the sights of Manhattan. The thirteen players and their manager, Haugsrud, climbed into the bus.

"Where are the rest of your players, Ole?" asked Mara. Not wanting the Giants to know that was the whole team, Haugsrud said airily, "Oh, the rest of the boys are still asleep in their rooms. Let's go without 'em."

Their game with the Giants was one of five played within eight days. And in the fifth, at Pottsville, Pennsylvania, Ernie first showed his versatility as a pro by completing seventeen passes in a row—a feat that isn't matched any place in the record book!

The twenty-seven minutes Ernie missed that season came in Milwaukee. "I was told by the doctor to stay out because of an appendicitis attack," he recalled. "But we were losing, 6–0, and I had to do something." So he put himself in the game and standing on his own 40-yard line threw a pass more than 60 yards in the air to Joe Rooney in the end zone. Ernie then kicked the extra point for a 7–6 victory.

After the five month expedition with the Eskimos, there was no respite. The last game ended a week before spring training began in the Florida baseball camps. Ernie had to report to the St. Louis Browns, for whom he had pitched the previous summer. They gave him a $10,000 bonus to sign right out of college and another $10,000 in salary (so that Ernie's money haul for 1926 amounted to $65,000, virtually tax-free).

"We were in West Palm Beach," remembered Ernie, "and Dan Howley was the manager. To him, I was just a college guy. They had a sand outfield, and they ran my tail off. I pitched a full game after I was there ten days."

Ernie never made it big in baseball, though he played both big league sports at the same time for three years. In 1927, he joined a select group as the pitcher for homers number 8 and 41 in Babe Ruth's binge of 60 round-trippers. A sore arm finally pushed him out of the majors in 1929. "I hurt it," he remembered, "throwing a pitchout to Lou Gehrig, high and outside." And years later, when a lady was introduced to him, she said, "Oh, yes, I heard of you. You were part of that Tinkers to Nevers to Chance team."

141

Football was really his bag. Ernie actually played only two varsity seasons at Stanford, and his pro career as a player covered but five full seasons; he missed all of 1928 with a broken transverse process and never revealed that he played later with what amounted to a broken neck. He never played on a pro team that won more than six games during the regular season. Yet he was a charter member of both the college and pro football Halls of Fame.

About the time he faded out of big league baseball, his football exploits came into sharper focus. The Duluth franchise faded from the NFL in 1929, and Nevers was one of a group of players sold to the Chicago Cardinals. At the age of twenty-six, he also became their head coach, their fullback, their signal caller, passer, punter, field goal kicker, and ace linebacker. On the field, he was surrounded by such top talent as Duke Slater, the great Negro tackle from Iowa, Kiesling and Doc Williams in the line, with Cuss Method and Roy Baker as his blocking backs, and Cobb Rooney, Chuck Kassel, and Milan Creighton among his receivers.

On Thanksgiving Day, 1929, Ernie Nevers left his monument for the record books. The Cardinals played their northside rivals, the Chicago Bears, at Comiskey Park. Earlier in the season the two teams had battled to a scoreless tie. But six minutes after the opening kickoff, Nevers banged across for a touchdown, and still in the first quarter he added another touchdown on a short plunge and kicked the extra point. He scored again in the second quarter and converted, to offset a long Bear touchdown pass to Garland Grange (Red's brother). In the second half, Nevers was consistent with three more touchdown bursts and two conversions. The final score was 40–6, and Ernie had scored all the points for the Cardinals!

The total points remain an NFL record. The six touchdowns by rushing are also a record. And Nevers is tied with Dub Jones of the Browns and Gale Sayers of the Bears for the most touchdowns scored in a game, rushing or passing. There is no category to show that in the previous Cardinal game, Ernie had also scored all 19 of his team's points against Dayton, so that he actually tallied 59 straight points for the Cardinals.

Under kicking exploits, Ernie is still listed for having booted five field goals in one game against Hartford, the only points his team scored in a 15–0 victory.

But the irrepressible running is what they really remember him for. He wasn't big by modern standards—a solid 210 pounds at his peak, about the same size as Jimmy Taylor. And he ran a 10.5 second 100-yard dash by his own estimate. He wasn't as elusive as Thorpe. But Ernie ran with a will. "If you know how to use your weight," he said, "you don't have to be a monster."

The Giants in 1927 were the roughest defensive team in the game when they faced Ernie and his Duluth Iron Men. Johnny Blood was calling the offensive signals for the club, which was bogged down on its own 45-yard line, trailing by 14 points.

"I'll start it off," said Nevers. "Give me the ball." He barged for a first down and turned to Blood.

"Let's try it again," he urged. He plugged for three yards.

"Again," he insisted, and went through the stacked defenses for four.

"They're ganging up the middle on you," said Blood.

142

"Give it to me anyhow," said Nevers. It went that way for nine straight plays, and on the ninth he scored, covering 55 yards, all the hard way, up the middle.

In 1931, when Bronko Nagurski was starting his rampage against pro lines, Ernie Nevers still made the first official all-league team as the fullback. It was his last season. He was twenty-eight, when most backs start to peak, but he wanted to try coaching and rejoined his old mentor, Pop Warner, at Stanford.

Nevers had a couple of abortive experiences in pro coaching later, with the Cardinals in 1939 and the Chicago Rockets of the defunct All-American Conference in 1946. But his post-football years were spent passively for the most part as a public relations man in northern California, where he became an avid fan of the San Francisco 49ers and an amateur critic of modern football.

"There's no variation in offense any more," he complained. "They don't have the running they used to have because the teams are so equal physically, and they play the same formation, so the defense knows exactly the way the plays are coming."

On December 12, 1965, he sat in his living room and watched the 49ers on TV playing in Chicago on a muddy field. A young back named Gale Sayers, in his second year of professional football, ran through and around the 49ers for six touchdowns and 36 points, and half the final quarter remained when he was pulled out of the game.

"I felt then, and I feel now," said Nevers, "that the Bears should have kept the boy in, to let him try to break that 40-point record with another touchdown."

ERNIE NEVERS' FAVORITE PLAY:

"I was the only back in pro football to use this formation. This is Pop Warner's double wing. The fullback handled the ball on every play. We also had many reverses and spinners.

"This play was my favorite because it presented four options. I could forward pass to the right end or quarterback in the flat; I could lateral to the left halfback coming around, or I could cut inside or outside the left tackle on defense, with my quarterback and left guard leading the play.

"We also trapped the left defensive tackle, making a great cutback play. I also ran straight smashes to the short side over center and between guard and tackle.

"I also ran this play and all our plays from left formation as well.

"It was most effective from our own 20-yard line to our opponents' 20. I used a pass pattern off it that looked the same as the running play."

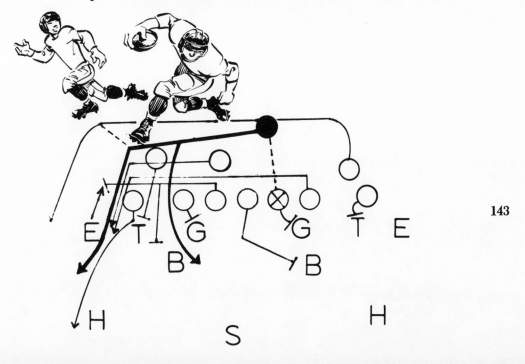

143

Johnny Blood

HE WAS A GREAT TEAMMATE. A CHEER-
FUL FELLOW, FRIENDLY OFF THE FIELD.
NOTHING FAZED HIM. SOMETIMES, AL-
THOUGH HE WAS PLAYER-COACH, HE
MIGHT MISS A PRACTICE AND EXPLAIN
NEXT DAY THAT HE HAD BEEN TO THE
LIBRARY.

—*Byron White, Justice,*
U. S. Supreme Court.

The pixieish character of Johnny Blood added to the early lore of pro ball but in no way diminished his effectiveness as a backfield talent.

Johnny Blood was an illusive figure, shifting across the scenario of his own life and building up the fable with such wild documentation until one couldn't even be sure he existed—unless he was there in the flesh.

And that's the way it was in this upstairs bar in Chicago in 1960 when a guy was having a drink with Bud Svendsen, the old Minnesota center. On the other side of him sat a guy with a thick mane of white hair, a thin, pointed nose and a ruggedly lined chin. He was well tanned and half crocked, and his deeply pooled eyes held a glint of wildness.

"This," pointed Svendsen, "is Johnny Blood." They had played together on the Green Bay Packers.

Johnny Blood was, at the time, running for sheriff of St. Croix County in Wisconsin. His platform for the electorate was honest wrestling. They did not vote him into office.

In the thirty years since he left the National Football League, Johnny Blood has left an improbable trail of identities. He'd vanish for a few years and show up as a candidate for a bachelor's degree at a little college in Minnesota (St. John's), twenty-six years after he'd originally enrolled as an undergraduate student. Into limbo he'd go again, and finally there'd be a report he was an economics professor somewhere in Illinois, researching the Malthusian theory for a book he eventually wrote. Then a 1958 news story had him running for sheriff. Four years later, Byron "Whizzer" White would be sworn in as a justice of the Supreme Court of the United States, and at his elbow would stand the hawklike, white-haired man known as Johnny Blood. The Green Bay Packers would embark on a championship reign which made professional football history, and in their victory celebration, the tall, improbable figure would show up.

A generation earlier, the meanderings of Johnny Blood were no less improbable. Johnny Blood was not his real name. He was christened John Victor McNally, the scion of a family of wealthy newspaper publishers and paper-mill owners. He was spindly and wrote poetry and was graduated from high school in New Richmond, Wisconsin, when he was fourteen years old. But a restless, inquisitive mind was soon supplemented by a lean body hardened by running off to work on a farm in North Dakota—just the first of many jobs. At one time or another, he was destined to be a stickman in a gambling house, a seaman, newspaper stereotyper, miner, feed salesman, floor waxer, hotel clerk, and ditch digger—when he wasn't playing football. Because in 1920, when he was barely seventeen, John McNally discovered his greatest talent when he enrolled at St. John's College. He was also an athlete.

Without any high school sports background, he pitched a one-hitter in his first game for the college baseball team, scored 53 points in a track meet, became captain of the basketball team and starred in football. In the school's yearbook, he wrote poignantly, "Dear God, how sweet it is in spring to be a boy."

He went off to play football at Notre Dame under Knute Rockne. In spring practice, the freshman coach put him at tackle. "A tackle's job," mused young Johnny, "is to make

147

body contact; a ball carrier's job is to avoid it. I was fast, and I wanted to be a halfback."

The solution—he took off from Notre Dame's classes on a motorcycle, met a young lady, put her on the back, wandered in the East from Newport to Newport News and eventually wended his way back to Minnesota, where he went to work for his uncle on the newspaper.

By now it was the fall of 1924, football season, and Johnny heard about the formation of a pro team called the East 26th Street Liberties. With a college friend, he started out for the ballpark where tryouts were held. They passed a theater marquee downtown blazoned with the name of Rudolph Valentino in his latest desert epic, "Blood and Sand."

"That's it," Johnny lit up. "I'm Blood, and you're Sand." He didn't want to use his real name. In the back of his mind lingered the idea he might want to go back to Notre Dame and he wanted to retain his amateur standing. It was an unnecessary worry. Johnny never went back.

For the next twenty-two years, in one form of football or another, he remained Johnny Blood. From the East 26th Liberties, he moved to a team in Ironwood, Michigan, then to Milwaukee, and in 1926 he joined the reorganized franchise in Duluth as a halfback with Ernie Nevers' Eskimos.

Blithe spirit Johnny Blood was already starting to create a legend. "The colorful character on the Eskimo squad was John Blood," wrote Ole Haugsrud, the team's owner and caretaker on the road (they played coast-to-coast for five straight months). "He was truly brilliant, both physically and mentally, but a trifle unpredictable. One night in San Francisco he and Cobb Rooney visited a Chinese museum. Blood came home with a wealth of material which he whipped into a story that sold for several hundred dollars.

"Another night he and Cobb had two girls out for dinner, then went to a cab stand. There was a taxi but no driver. Blood piled his party into the cab, delivered the girls to their homes and returned to the cab stand. He pinned a dollar to the steering wheel."

Johnny was one of the thirteen iron men who played a murderous 29-game schedule. With him, the danger in getting hurt was not on the field, but off it. During a romantic seance on the road, he cut his wrists to write his name in blood for his lady love. The blood spurted, the lady screamed, and several teammates rushed him to a doctor, who took a dozen stitches to seal the wounds.

"What'd you do that for?" demanded Nevers, the coach. "Now you won't be able to play tomorrow."

"Who said I won't?" scoffed Blood. He played his usual 60 minutes the next day.

When the other guys were sleeping, Johnny would be standing on a street corner reciting poetry. He was a striking figure six-feet-two, and a rangy 195 pounds, with the thick black hair of the Irish and penetrating blue eyes. They'd lock him in his hotel room, and he'd climb out the window and jump catlike to other buildings. It was fun as long as the Eskimos lasted.

They had no team in 1928, and Johnny was shipped to the Pottsville Maroons, who weren't quite geared to his antics. In 1929, he found his home base. Curly Lambeau brought him back to his native Wisconsin to play for the Green Bay Packers, and the move brought him the greatest period of stability of his life. Johnny Blood stayed with the Packers for eight lively years.

148

It was still fun, but it was professionally satisfying, too. The unique skills of the rangy halfback flourished, and he was a key figure on four world championship teams. The Packers were undefeated his first season and won their first title in pro football history. They repeated the next two years, a feat which would not be done again in the NFL until the Packers won three straight championships in 1965-66-67.

Blood was one of the fastest men in football, with the same swivel-hipped changes of direction that made Red Grange an electrifying runner. He was also a fine defensive back and became a brilliant pass receiver, the perfect foil for a strong-armed young thrower named Arnie Herber, who joined Green Bay in 1930.

"In my time," he admitted, "I guess I was as good a receiver as there was around —the best, maybe, until Don Hutson came along. I could carry weight—I mean the weight of equipment. Lots of great sprinters can't carry weight. I called signals for three championship teams. I always figured I was a pretty fair all-around back. I scored thirteen touchdowns for the Packers in 1931, and that was a record for the time."

Altogether, he scored thirty-seven touchdowns in his tenure with Green Bay. But the other Johnny Blood, the irrepressible character, was also in evidence, from the moment he arrived.

"I asked for $100 a game," he reminisced. "Coach Curly Lambeau came back with an offer of $110 a game, providing I would initial a clause in the contract forbidding any drinking after Tuesday of each week. I countered with an offer to take the $100 I had proposed and drink through Wednesday. Curly agreed."

Blood later claimed he never made more than $1,800 a year all the time he played for Lambeau. The team lived by one set of rules, Johnny Blood by another. The problem was making sure Johnny Blood was there at the appointed time when needed. So in Boston, once, Lambeau assigned a huge tackle the chore of making sure Johnny was on the train when the team left town. Failure would cost the tackle $250.

The tackle got Blood as far as the train station without trouble, but then unpredictable Johnny decided he preferred to remain in Boston. The huge tackle saw his $250 vanishing, too, so he swung a beautiful right haymaker flush on Blood's jaw. Then, helped by the equipment manager, he carted Blood onto the train and into Lambeau's compartment.

"Here he is," grunted the tackle, and dumped the limp body of Blood into Curly's lap.

In Los Angeles, once, Johnny was fresh out of funds and braced Curly for an advance. Lambeau refused and said he was going to his room on the eighth floor, lock himself in for the night, and wouldn't open the door for anyone. Blood circled the lobby, pondering the emergency, and took an elevator to the eighth floor. The door was locked, but Curly said nothing about the window. So Johnny found a door to the fire escape and inched out on a ledge toward Lambeau's room.

A teammate two floors below looked out and saw the figure balancing himself precariously.

"Is that you up there, Johnny Blood?" he asked anxiously.

"The same," answered Johnny.

"What the hell are you doing?"

"Coach wants to see me. Told me to drop in and talk over a matter of business." With that, he leaped the remaining six feet to Lambeau's room, landed nimbly on the window ledge, threw open the window and jumped in.

Lambeau turned around, startled. "Now about that advance, Coach . . ." Lambeau grabbed his trousers on a chair, thrust his hand into a pocket, and came out with a fist of bills. "Here," he said weakly. "Take it, take it. And go."

"Thanks, Coach," said Johnny Blood, "I knew we could come to a reasonable agreement after proper discussion." He walked softly out of the room, paused to close the door. "And have a good night's sleep, Coach."

When Ollie Kuechle, the sports editor of the *Milwaukee Journal,* heard that Blood rode a freight train to camp from his home in New Richmond, Wisconsin, he wanted to do a story about the Hobo Halfback. The Packers persuaded him to soften the title to Vagabond Halfback, and that became a part of the Blood image. He went ten days with a ruptured kidney, played a whole game and then collapsed. Red Dunn, the quarterback on the championship teams, threw him a long pass, and Blood had an open field to a score. Johnny turned around, laughed and threw the ball back to the surprised Dunn.

But he was also a winner when it counted. "I never saw a fellow who could turn a ball game around as quickly as Johnny Blood," said Don Hutson, the great receiver who joined the Packers in 1935. "When he came into a game, the whole attitude of the players changed. He had complete confidence in himself and a tremendous football sense."

In 1936, the Packers were locked in a crucial battle for the Western Division title with the Detroit Lions. Johnny was calling the signals for the Packers, and Lambeau instructed him not to pass. Green Bay got a 10–0 lead; Blood called a pass which failed. The Lions started to roll, and took a 16–10 lead into the last quarter. With five minutes to play, Lambeau put Blood back in the game.

Green Bay at its own 49-yard line huddled for Blood's call. He looked at Herber, the passer, and said, "Zoom it, Arnie. Number 3—as far as you can!"

With the snap of the ball, Blood took off straight down the field. He was thirty-three years old, but only Hutson could run faster. Herber dropped back 12 yards and threw the length of the field. Three men from the Lions' defensive secondary converged on Blood, and in one scrambling group they all went up in the air, groping for the ball. They fell in a tangle over the goal line. When the referee unpiled them, Blood on the bottom had the ball and the Packers had the game and eventually an NFL title.

"For 67 yards there," he grinned, "I guess I was unemployed."

The next year, the Packers let him go to the Pittsburgh Steelers as a player-coach for $3,000 a year. In the opening game of the season, on the opening kickoff, he ran 100 yards for a touchdown. But from there it was all downhill. It was tough enough for Johnny Blood to manage Johnny Blood, without the added responsibility of a whole team. The Steelers came to New York, played the Giants and left town, without their coach. He showed up in Giant offices two days later, disheveled and broke. He'd been rolled. But Whizzer White, whom he'd signed to play pro ball, said, "If it were not for Johnny Blood's persuasiveness, I would not have played professional football. I value him as a friend as much as I admired him as a player."

He was let go as the coach of the team after three games of the 1939 season. He drifted back to Wisconsin and played for a team in Kenosha. On December 7, 1941, he enlisted in the air force and served as a cryptographer in China and India. When he returned in 1945, he heard his old coach, Curly Lambeau, might need a halfback. He showed up in uniform for an exhibition game. Johnny Blood, at the age of forty-two, went back to field a punt and two huskies converged on him and knocked him flat.

"When I took too long getting up," he shrugged, "life and limb suddenly became important to me." And Johnny Blood bowed out of athletics. He could have done it with a poem.

> I have pondered oft of late
> The frigid, cold and dusty state
> The world has come to . . .
> . . . And though I've a flair
> For atmosphere that's clean and fresh—
> But there's that all-too-solid flesh.

It was written by John Victor McNally at St. John's College, in 1921.

JOHNNY BLOOD'S FAVORITE PLAY:

"I was a good running back, I believe, but I won my jewelled spurs at what's now called a flanker back. My career was quite similar to Elroy Hirsch, another northern Wisconsin boy. Only he 'Crazy Legs' and me 'Crazy Horse.' So I give you a pass play for a running back.

"We called the play 'Zoom It' because Herber could throw very far and high. You could judge your pace and fake as soon as he released the ball.

"The numbers here told him the target area he threw to, no matter where I appeared to be going. From this play I could go beyond 5 and return to it or even start down and return to 'B,' my departure point, where I could catch a lateral and throw downfield to Hutson if he got open.

"The key to its success was the variety of options which could be chosen. The opposition's scouts had seen options 1-2-3-4-5 and the lateral tried and executed more than once. Hutson, of course, was not only the top catcher but also a great decoy.

"I believe this setup is the original use of split end and flanker back from a running formation, a credit to Coach Curly Lambeau.

"In October 1936, we played Detroit at Green Bay. They had nosed us out in 1935 for the NFL championship. This game we had to win if we were to win the bunting, for they were already ahead of us in the standings. We were behind 16-10 and got the ball on our 49 after a punt. I was on the bench with five minutes left to play. Curly turned to me and told me to go in but did not say what to do. I was right half and signalcaller. It was first and 10. I crossed myself and said, 'Zoom It! No. 3. Pass as far as you can.' Herber ran back 12 yards, bent backwards and zoomed it 67 yards. Three Lions and a Packer went up for it. The Packer got lucky. It won that '36 championship."

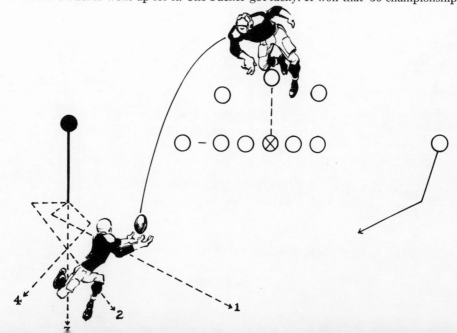

JOHN VICTOR "BLOOD" MCNALLY

BORN: Nov. 27, 1904   Height: 6'1"   Weight: 195
University of Notre Dame

Milwaukee Badgers, 1925–26
Duluth Eskimos, 1926–27
Pottsville Maroons, 1928
Green Bay, 1929–33, 1935–36
Pittsburgh, 1934, 1937–39

		RUSHING					PASS RECEIVING				SCORING	
Year	G.	Att.	Yds.	Avg.	TD.	P.C.	Yds.	Avg.	TD.		TD.	Pts.
1925–31		(statistics unavailable)										
1932	..	27	130	4.8	2	14	168	12.0	0		2	13
1933	..	14	41	2.9	0	7	214	30.6	3		3	18
1934		(no statistics available)										
1935	..	42	115	2.7	1	25	404	16.2	3		4	24
1936	..	13	65	5.0	0	7	147	21.0	3		3	19
1937	..	9	37	4.1	1	10	168	16.8	4		5	30
1938	..	2	—5	—2.5	0	2	8	4.0	0		0	0
PRO TOTALS —7 YEARS	..	107	383	3.6	4	65	1109	17.1	13		17	104

10. The Bronk's Era
Bronko Nagurski

THERE'S ONLY ONE DEFENSE THAT CAN STOP BRONKO NAGURSKI. SHOOT HIM BEFORE HE LEAVES THE DRESSING ROOM. HE'S THE ONLY BACK I EVER SAW WHO RUNS HIS OWN INTERFERENCE.
—*Steve Owen, coach,*
New York Giants, 1931–53.

The story is apocryphal, the kind you hear at high school football banquets. The coach, scouring the farm country on a recruiting trip, comes to a kid working behind a plow in the fields. He stops and asks the directions to town. If the kid simply points the way, the coach keeps going. But if the kid picks up the plow and points, the coach stops and signs him to a college football scholarship.

In the case of Bronko Nagurski, the late Herman Hickman embellished the story. He told it to Bronko, so he said, and then came to the punch line: ". . . but he's my boy if he picks up the plow and points." A faint frown creased Bronko's brow as he listened with interest. Then he asked mildly, "Without horses?"

Of all the players who have played football in the century since the men of Rutgers first clashed with the scholars of Princeton by the banks of the Raritan, no one better embodies the symbol of strength than Bronislau Nagurski, the son of Ukrainian immigrants.

He became "Bronko" officially and for always when his mother first took him to school in International Falls, a little community in the northern lake country of Minnesota on the border of Canada. Mrs. Nagurski told the teacher her boy's name was Bronislau, but in her accent it came out Bronko. And that was good enough. It's his legal name.

No one who ever saw Bronko Nagurski run with a football would question his power. He was awesome. "There was something strange about tackling Nagurski," said Red Grange, who was his teammate on the Chicago Bears and therefore thankful that their only contact came in brief preseason scrimmages. "When you hit him, it was almost like getting an electric shock. If you hit him above the ankles, you were likely to get killed."

"I tried to stop him in an open field," said Harry Newman, a quarterback for the New York Giants. "I hit him as hard as I could and all it did was throw him off pace a little."

"I was at safety," said Benny Friedman, also a Giant quarterback, "when the Bronk broke through with only me between him and the goal. My first impulse was to duck and run. It was like ordering a switchman to stop a locomotive with his bare hands." Benny tackled him on the 12-yard line. The Bronk was finally stopped and the ball put down on the one-yard line.

The Giants also had a tough linebacker named Johnny Dell Isola, a former All-American center at Fordham. On first down, he faced Nagurski and filled a gap in the middle. He met Bronko head-on at the line of scrimmage. "It was the hardest tackle I ever made," said Dell Isola. "I figured maybe he might have made a yard at most and I was congratulating myself pretty good. Then I heard the referee saying, 'Second down and two.'"

In his prime as a fullback for the Chicago Bears, he stood six feet two inches and weighed 230 pounds. Even his clefted, heavy jaw denoted power. Bronk took the direct

Moving toward a massed line, or even just holding the ball, Bronko Nagurski was a formidable sight as the Chicago Bears became known as the Monsters of the Midway.

Seldom did Bronko Nagurski go down from the tackle of one man. Here a couple of New York Giants ride piggyback on the fullback of the Bears.

route over tacklers, for a total of 4,031 yards in eight full seasons. He played a ninth as a tackle. While the figures may not be impressive in relation to the more than 12,000 yards totalled by Jimmy Brown in nine campaigns of a later era, the net effect was just as awesome. When Bronk ran the ball, the modern T-formation had not been perfected. There were no such subtleties as "influence" blocking and quick traps to spring the runner loose. He didn't rest up between series of downs. When the Bears relinquished the ball, Bronko moved over to linebacker and became a devastating tackler.

You can measure the Bronk's impact by the way defenses of the day (1931 to 1937) massed to meet his lunges. One tackler, two tacklers were never sufficient to drag him down. A picture of Nagurski running always shows three and four men hanging on as Bronko drags them a few extra yards.

"He was 75 percent of an opposing team's worry," said quarterback Newman.

"Here's a check for $10,000," owner G. A. Richards of the Detroit Lions once said, only half kidding. "Not for playing with the Lions, but just to quit and get the hell out of the league. You're ruining my team."

And yet there was nothing mean about the man.

Dick Cullum, the veteran sports columnist of the *Minneapolis Tribune*, followed Nagurski's exploits from the time he appeared in a varsity uniform for the University of Minnesota in 1927 through his last fling as a wartime player with the Bears in 1943. Years later, he wrote, "Bronko is still a loved figure in sports." And he summed up his personality:

> He's a *sweet* person. Yes, he is.
> He's a *boyish* person, battered and bruised though he is.
> He's a *wholesome* person who immediately wins, and holds, the trust of everyone who deals with him.
> He's a humble person who gladly by-passes the opportunity to capture more wealth and glory for a summer's fishing with his sons.

"Some of the words," admitted Cullum, "seem strangely sissified. But there has never been a teammate, coach, employer, opponent, or spectator through this full generation of activity who has seen Bronko do a petty thing."

The name had just the right ring. More than a quarter of a century after he played his last game, the presence of Bronko Nagurski was still electrical. In February 1969, the main ballroom of New York's Americana Hotel was filled with the greatest figures in baseball for the annual baseball writers dinner, and there was polite applause at the introduction of the diamond celebrities on the floor. Then the man on the dais said, ". . . and let's pay tribute to a visitor from another sport—Bronko Nagurski." Every man was on his feet, necks craned for a glimpse of the burly man with the size nineteen collar and the slightly cauliflowered ears, and an applause meter would have given Bronko the unanimous decision for the night.

The men who played against him retained the experience. After a particularly bruising day in Chicago trying to stop the line smashes of Nagurski, the Pittsburgh Steelers dragged themselves onto a train for the return trip home. An hour out of the city, the train came to a jolting halt, throwing the Steelers out of their seats and into the aisles.

"Run for your lives, men," yelled a Steeler. "That guy Nagurski is still after us."

He was the irresistible force. Steve Owen, the defensive genius of the Giants, experimented with a five-man line against Bronko, moving one of his linemen off the front wall and into a linebacker spot to give the defense more flexibility in meeting the big fullback's charge. The game started, and Nagurski came ramming through the middle on the first play. The converted lineman, anticipating the point of attack, was right there to meet him.

"Only two things happened that we hadn't counted on," said Owen later. "One, Nagurski made eight yards. Two, the linebacker had to be carted off the field. So we got back into our six-man line in a hurry."

Old buffs maintained the only thing that could stop him was a concrete wall. Wrigley Field, the home of the Bears, has an end zone practically tucked into the baseball dugout on the south end. Down by the goal line, one afternoon, Nagurski took a direct pass from center, lowered his head and bolted for the end zone. He knocked over his own center, barged past a defensive tackle, trampled a linebacker and was confronted only by the safety. He lowered his head, tucked the ball securely in the pit of his stomach, and simply ran him down. Under a full head of steam now, helmet down like a battering ram, he slammed into the goal post, careened off and crashed into the cement wall of the dugout. Bronko wobbled out moments later, still clutching the football, and mumbled, "Who was that last guy? He sure hit me hard."

Yet Bronko could finesse the enemy, too. The man who more than anybody in the history of football symbolized the brute power of running was ironically responsible for the modern era of the forward pass which has dominated offense. In 1932, the Bears broke the three-year title reign of the Green Bay Packers with Nagurski, in his third season, leading the way. They had tied in the league standings with the Portsmouth Spartans, so a playoff was arranged. But Chicago that December was in one of its severe winter spells, and the game was shifted indoors to the Chicago Stadium, with six inches of dirt covering the floor. The field measured only 80 yards long. Running room was restricted, and the teams battled into the fourth quarter, scoreless. A pass interception put the Bears in touchdown range at the 7-yard line, but three plunges by Nagurski left them a yard short. Fourth and one. The Spartans braced for another smash. Nagurski started forward with the snap, then suddenly braked himself, backed up a couple of steps and flipped the ball to Red Grange for the decisive touchdown.

Potsy Clark, the Portsmouth coach, claimed it was an illegal play because the rules at that time stipulated a forward pass had to be launched from at least five yards behind the line of scrimmage. The officials sided with the Bears and ruled the play legal, though the dispute lingered after the game.

It gave a laundryman named George Marshall, who had taken over the Boston franchise that year, a bright idea. Why not, he reasoned, settle all arguments and open up the game at the same time by letting a back pass from any spot behind the line of scrimmage? He found a ready ally in George Halas, Nagurski's coach, who sensed immediately the extra threat Bronko would pose if the defense had to be wary of a pass as he hit the line. They pushed the new rule through, and it eventually led to the T-formation revolution.

158

Bronko put the new rule to good use immediately. In 1933, the Bears met the New York Giants for the NFL title in the first modern divisional playoff (another Marshall idea). In the third quarter, with Chicago trailing 14–9, Nagurski bluffed a plunge into the line, jumped and flipped a 6-yard pass to end Bill Karr for a go-ahead score. The Giants rallied to take the lead again in the final period. Back came the Bears, to the New York 36, sticking to a ground attack. Bronko started another smash up the middle, then straightened up and lobbed the ball over the line to end Bill Hewitt, breaking over the middle. The Giant secondary converged on Hewitt, who turned and lateralled to Karr, cutting behind him, and the latter raced the remaining 33 yards for the touchdown. The Bears won, 23–21.

The other irony of Nagurski's career is that he never led the NFL in ground-gaining. He wasn't a player who insisted on monopolizing the ball. He was well established as the Bears' top threat in 1934 when a young All-American halfback out of Tennessee named Beattie Feathers joined the club. Until then, no man in history had ever gained 1,000 yards in a single season. Beattie changed all that. He carried the ball only 101 times during the course of the thirteen-game regular season (the Bears were undefeated and untied), but he gained 1,004 yards, and his average of 9.9 yards per carry remains the all-time NFL record. Beattie was smart. He'd get the ball and stay behind the inside shoulder of Nagurski, and daylight would follow automatically.

There was almost as much awe for Nagurski the blocker as Nagurski the runner. Cal Hubbard, a 270-pound giant of a tackle for the Green Bay Packers (and a Hall of Fame charter member), had heard a lot of stories about the big kid from Minnesota who had just joined the Bears—this was 1931. So the first time he faced him, Cal wanted to see for himself how tough the Bronk was. On a Chicago punt formation, Red Grange lined up in front of Hubbard.

"Let me through Red," whispered Cal. "I won't block the kick. I just want a crack at Nagurski."

Grange was curious, too, and he trusted Cal. So he let him go by and turned around, an interested spectator. The giant tackle dipped down and hit Nagurski with his shoulder. He bounced off like an over-sized yo-yo back toward the line of scrimmage, picked himself up and caught up with Grange downfield.

"Don't do me any more favors like that, Red," he said.

The one person who could never understand the fuss made over Bronko's prowess was his mother. His college coach, Dr. Clarence "Doc" Spears, the man who had discovered him, once went up to Bronko's home town of International Falls for a testimonial. Mrs. Nagurski had never seen her boy play. She didn't have the vaguest notion what the game was about.

"Do they run in football?" she asked Spears.

"Yes," he answered.

"And Bronko is good at it?"

"He's the best."

Mama Nagurski shook her head. "I don't understand," she said. "Bronko always was the laziest boy in International Falls."

Spears said later, "I think she thought the whole thing was a gag of some kind."

When Bronko first showed up at Minnesota and turned out for football, he tore a tackling dummy loose from its moorings. Spears asked him what position he played.

"Fullback, I guess," answered Bronko, "and tackle, and guard. Wherever they needed me." Spears put him at end, then shifted him to tackle, and in his sophomore season Nagurski blocked a punt against unbeaten Notre Dame to give Minnesota a 7–7 tie. As a junior in 1928, he carried the ball a few times, and in 1929 he was an All-American fullback. He was also an All-American tackle because he played that position when he was needed up front, and the selectors weren't sure where he was best.

After graduation, the Bears signed him for $5,000 a year. It wasn't the big money era for the pros. In the winter of 1933, he started another career as a wrestler. A couple of years later, the battering of football began to show. He had an operation for a bone spur in his hip. By 1937, he wasn't carrying the load alone for the Bears. They had a fine young fullback from Nebraska named Sam Francis. Jack Manders, a great place-kicker, also was a strong runner and the heavy duty ball carrier in the championship game, which the Bears lost to the Redskins, 28–21. The wrestling was getting so lucrative Bronko couldn't afford to pass it up in the fall. So after eight rugged seasons, he made a decision, reported in a Chicago paper: "The Bears' fullback, perhaps the greatest figure in the records of the National Football League, has decided to forego another season."

He was only twenty-nine years old, and he went back to the shores of his native Rainy Lake to fish for walleyed pike and be with his family. He emerged sporadically for the next sixteen years to fill wrestling engagements. And there was one last shot at football.

The year was 1943, a war year when even Coach George Halas of the Bears was away in the Navy. The Bears needed bodies. Bronko was thirty-four years old and still looked formidable. "They needed me, I guess," he said simply, "and I thought it would be fun." But the need was for a tackle, and so Bronko reverted to his old college position.

"I played in the line for nine games," he reminisced, "and enjoyed it. But I had played fullback all my earlier years with the Bears and I missed the thrill of carrying the ball. I was watching movies of a game we lost to Washington and noticed our blockers were having trouble with the Redskin ends. I told one of our quarterbacks, 'I wish they'd give me a chance at fullback. I'd take those ends out.'

"He must have repeated what I said to the coaches. Because the week before the last game of the season, against the Cardinals, I worked out in the backfield. We needed a win to qualify for the championship game against the Redskins."

Big No. 3, rolling from his familiar fullback spot, rallied the Bears from a 24–14 deficit in the fourth quarter to a three-touchdown spurt and a 35–24 victory. He scored the first one himself and altogether picked up 84 yards in sixteen carries. "That game," said Bronko, "gave me my greatest kick out of football."

Bronko bowed out a champion because the Bears also beat the Redskins for the NFL title. The big show was quarterback Sid Luckman, on weekend leave from the Merchant Marine, throwing five touchdown passes. But Bronko provided something special for the sentimentalists among the 34,000 who squeezed into Wrigley Field—a final tour de force.

160

Late in the second quarter, with the score tied 7–7, he crashed into the end zone from the three-yard line, a power thrust that revived for one last moment the glory of Bronko Nagurski.

BRONKO NAGURSKI'S FAVORITE PLAY:

"This play was off the T-formation with the man-in-motion, which the Chicago Bears pioneered.

"The left halfback was the man in motion, with the right guard pulling. The halfback would pull the opposition's outside defensive back with him. As the fullback, I faked a step to the outside, then cut on a direct line between the tackle and end.

"A good block by the right guard on the defensive left tackle was very important. The right end would also pick up the linebacker.

"This play worked very well for me most of the time. At least for short gains if nothing else.

"It was also a good scoring play which was used often, with a little variation in assignments to throw the defense off occasionally."

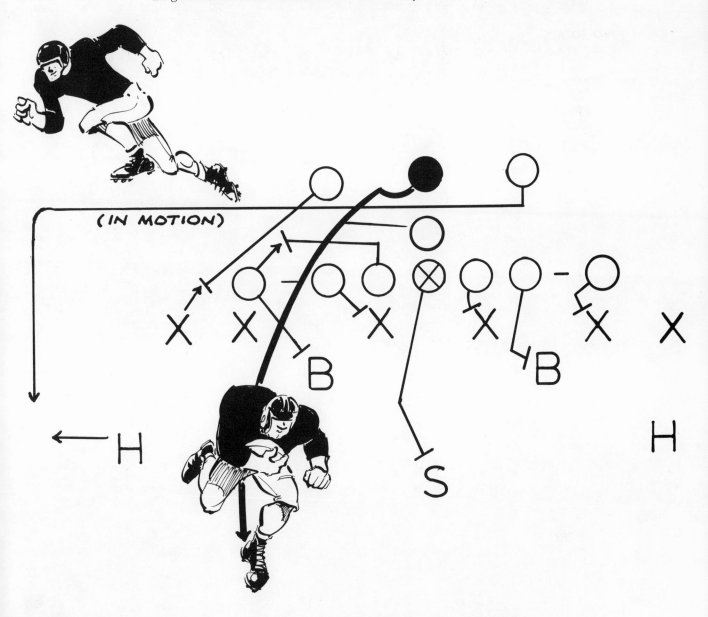

(IN MOTION)

BRONKO NAGURSKI

BORN: Nov. 3, 1908   Height: 6'2''   Weight: 230

University of Minnesota

Chicago Bears, 1930–37, 1943

Year	G.	RUSHING Att.	Yds.	Avg.	TD.	PASS RECEIVING P.C.	Yds.	Avg.	TD.	SCORING TD.	Pts.
1930	(no records available)										
1931	(no records available)										
1932	..	111	496	4.5	4	6	67	11.2	0	4	24
1933	..	128	533	4.2	1	1	23	23.0	0	1	7
1934	..	123	586	4.8	0	3	32	10.7	0	0	0
1935	..	50	170	3.4	1	0	0	0.0	0	1	6
1936	..	122	529	4.3	3	1	12	12.0	0	3	19
1937	..	73	343	4.7	1	0	0	0.0	0	1	6
1943	8	16	84	5.3	1	0	0	0.0	0	1	6
PRO TOTALS —7 YEARS	..	623	2741	4.4	11	11	134	12.2	0	11	68

Clarke Hinkle

HE'D GET SO FIRED UP BEFORE A GAME,
HE'D BE GLASSY EYED. IF WE LOST, HE
WEPT. CLARKE HINKLE DIDN'T KNOW
HOW TO LOSE.

—*Cecil Isbell, Green
Bay Packers.*

There was a tigerish vitality in the ball carrying of Clarke Hinkle, whose exploits for the Packers over a decade's time merited his election to the Hall of Fame.

Clarke Hinkle's first impression of pro football was physical. He crouched behind the defensive line of the Green Bay Packers, a rookie linebacker getting his first taste of action against the Chicago Bears. Straight at him roared Bronko Nagurski, the great fullback of the Bears, and Hinkle braced himself. When they picked him up a split second later, blood was spurting from a deep gash in his face.

"They took seven stitches," Hinkle ruminated, "and I learned something. Not to wait for the action to come at you. I never stood still again in a football game."

And so for ten years, from that start in 1932 through the 1941 season, Clarke Hinkle was a whirlwind of motion in the backfield of the Green Bay Packers, playing 90 percent of every game, fourteen games a year. "The greatest all around fullback ever to play in the National Football League," his coach, Curly Lambeau, proclaimed.

Some guys were bigger; Bronko Nagurski outweighed him by 30 pounds. And faster —someone like Bill Osmanski could outrun him. But none was more durable and none enjoyed the primitive contact of football more.

"He was one of the greatest competitors I ever saw," said George Sauer, Sr., who played in the same backfield with Hinkle for three years in Green Bay and is now the general manager of the Boston Patriots. "He shut out everything else. And he was so tough. He got such a kick out of hitting people, and getting hit, too.

"I remember one game he was really decked. Knocked out. And when he woke up, the first thing he said was, 'Boy, that sonuvabitch can really hit.' He laughed about it."

For perpetuity as one of the giants of football history, Hinkle had two important drawbacks. He was not a giant to start with; he stood a shade under six feet, and though he was well-bunched physically at 207 pounds, there was none of the awe-inspiring presence of a Nagurski. And he played most of his career as a contemporary of Nagurski, which limited the attention he got. A latter-day analogy was Jimmy Taylor, another great Green Bay fullback, who resembled Hinkle physically and esthetically, being over-shadowed by the magical prowess of Jimmy Brown.

Hinkle, however, could ease his frustration by confronting his rival directly, because in his day a man played both offense and defense. "He loved to go against Bronko," said Sauer. "Everything shook when they collided."

"I caught him in '34," said Hinkle, a touch of the old zest still in his voice as he spoke about it thirty-five years later. In a head-on collision, Hinkle shattered the myth of Nagurski's indestructibility, and his helmet splattered Bronko's nose. "I never," he added, "had any trouble getting up for the Chicago Bears."

Hinkle once busted through the Bear forward wall, past George Musso, a tough, 260-pound guard, and bounded into Nagurski. Bronko, on defense, often used a body block to level ball carriers instead of grabbing them with his arms. On this play, the Packer fullback rebounded like a carom off the backboard, right by Musso again and back to his starting point. Hinkle landed upright, with his legs still churning like the

165

sliding wheels of a locomotive seeking traction, and then he took off in a forward motion again, passing Musso once more and every other Bear, running 53 yards for a touchdown.

"That's the first time," Musso shook his head, "I ever saw a back go past me three times on the same play."

In his decade of pro ball, Hinkle did a lot more than run. He was a devastating blocker. He caught passes. And he played defensive linebacker with such agility and range that his old teammate, Sauer, the man who scouted most of the 1968 Super Bowl champion New York Jets, said Hinkle would have been a great middle linebacker in today's brand of platoon football. He was also Green Bay's ace placement booter, with nine field goals one season, including an official 47-yarder that could have been longer because Clarke suspected they only counted the distance of kicks from the line of scrimmage in his time.

In addition, he handled the punting for the Packers and averaged 43.4 yards a kick for the ten years. One off-season, the Packers were brought out to Hollywood to do a film short on their football specialties. Hinkle went on camera to demonstrate his punting skill by trying to angle a kick out of bounds on the 1-yard line, where a camera was set up behind a glass shield. On his first boot, he spiralled the ball high and accurately. It shattered the glass on the fly. The photographers didn't have the cameras grinding. They figured Clarke would need a few warm-up punts.

"I had great pride in my ability," he admitted candidly after he was inducted into the Pro Football Hall of Fame in Canton, Ohio. There was also that fervor for the game. In his own mind, the high spot of his career came in 1941, his last season as a pro, when he was thirty-two years old, and faced the Chicago Bears late in the season. This was the same Chicago Bear team which had devastated the Washington Redskins, 73–0, in the 1940 championship game and still hadn't lost a game. The Packers were included among the victims in an early fall encounter, their only defeat of the season.

On the third play of the rematch, the filed cleats of a Bear lineman tore a seven-inch gash in Hinkle's right leg, baring the shinbone.

"I called time out," he remembered, "and went over to the sidelines for a bandage. Curly gave me hell. So I went back and played 58 minutes, kicked a field goal, scored a touchdown and we won, 16–14. After the game, I walked fifteen blocks back to the hotel, still without a bandage. I couldn't get a cab."

Still active as a manufacturer's representative and sports telecaster in eastern Ohio, Clarke recently volunteered a comparison of the pro football then and now.

"The guys in newspapers and television are making supermen of today's players," he said. "But I wonder. Where would you play a Joe Namath in my day? We got in shape for 60 minutes of football. There were no specialists. I believe I still hold the record for most ball-carrying attempts for '60-minute players in the one-platoon era of pro football.' I carried the ball 1,171 times."

Carl Snavely, who discovered him, said, "Clarke certainly was one of the greatest football players I ever have coached or seen. He was great in every phase of the game . . . Curly Lambeau told me one time he thought Clarke was the greatest football player in the history of the game."

166

Snavely first saw him on the front porch of the Hinkle home in Toronto, Ohio, in that rugged part of the state where the Ohio River separates it from West Virginia. Actually, Snavely had come to see Clarke's older brother Gordon, who had played for him at Bellefonte Academy in western Pennsylvania and whom he now wanted to recruit for his team at Bucknell. But Gordon had just signed a professional baseball contract (he later caught part of one season with the Boston Red Sox) and said to Snavely, "Take Clarke instead. He's better than I am anyhow."

The boy's full name was William Clark Hinkle, but no one called him Bill. (In the third grade his teacher spelled his middle name with an "e" at the end—"I liked it better that way so it's been Clarke ever since.") He weighed 165 pounds. Snavely was skeptical but took him anyhow. By his sophomore year at college, he weighed 207 pounds. As a senior, he led Bucknell to an unbeaten season and a victory over Fordham which knocked the vaunted Rams out of a bowl bid. Clarke received a bid to the East-West Shrine game in San Francisco and was named its most valuable player. That's where Lambeau of the Packers first noticed him.

"I really met him once before, but he didn't remember me," mused Hinkle. "My Bucknell line coach took me to New York to meet the Giants and sit on their bench. They were playing the Packers, and at halftime the coach said, 'Let's go over to the Green Bay side. Maybe we can get more money there.' But Lambeau didn't pay much attention to me. The Packers were losing.

"When I signed with him the next year, I got $125 a game. It was the height of the Depression, and I didn't have a job. Besides, I didn't have all the football out of my system yet."

His last year, 1941, he held out for two weeks and signed for $10,000, a princely sum for that period. In that respect, he beat Nagurski. Bronko told Hinkle that in his prime years with the Bears he never collected more than a $5,000 salary.

Because he came into pro ball at a time Bronko was stampeding every tackler in sight, Hinkle's early exploits didn't attract much notice. Bronko made the all-pro teams, which were officially picked by the coaches, in 1932-33-34. Both of them were hurt in '35 and missed a lot of action (Hinkle had a bad back). But the next three years, Hinkle was voted to the all-pro teams, and he finished his career with a flourish by being selected again in 1941.

He was also a winner. The Packers won three division championships and two world titles during his tenure and had only one losing season. The needed men like Hinkle (and Don Hutson) as the talent core of a franchise which was struggling to stay alive during the Depression, when Green Bay was already an anachronism in big league sports, a city then under 50,000 population which only kept its identification with pro football with an outpouring of dollars and dimes from every economic level of its citizens.

Yet what a fullback like Hinkle meant doesn't show up in a retrospective study of the cold statistics. His records are being slowly obliterated from even the team record book, though he still stands third to Taylor and Tony Canadeo on the all-time roster of Packer ground gainers. His career average of 3.29 yards a carry is modest. He never gained more than 552 yards in a single season. But it was a different era in Green Bay.

The Packers emphasized the pass with Arnie Herber and later Cecil Isbell throwing to Hutson. The tempo of the game was slower, because men played 60 minutes and didn't try to rush through as many plays as there are in a game today. The yardage was harder to accumulate because the lines, both offense and defense, were massed in a closer knot on the field—line splits and fancy blocking angles were unknown; it was all power football, with double-team blocking and two or three men leading a back through the hole. The physical attrition was great. Hinkle remembered losing 25 pounds in the 1937 College All-Star game on a 100-degree September night in Chicago.

Still, he revelled in the physical aspects, the associations of pro football. "He loved people," said George Sauer. "He was a very congenial, fun-loving, guy. Life was wonderful."

Even when it came to butting heads with Bronko Nagurski.

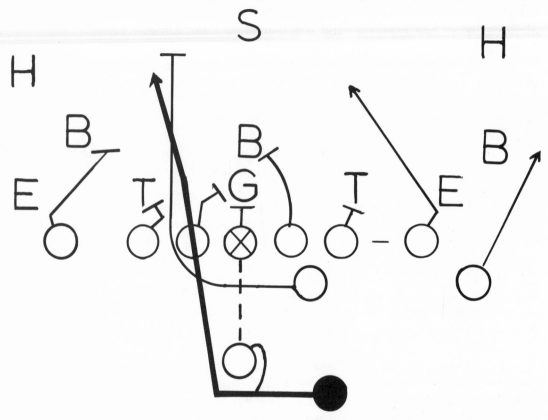

CLARKE HINKLE'S FAVORITE PLAY:

"Green Bay used the Notre Dame box on this play, with the backfield shifted right. Cecil Isbell, our tailback, took a direct pass from center, spun and handed off to me coming back to the weak side into the '3' hole, as we called it.

"Our blocking back, Larry Craig, led me through the hole. Key blocks were made by our center and left guard on the defensive middle guard. Craig would help block the middle linebacker if needed. Isbell, after handing off, faked a pass.

168

"This play got wide publicity against the Chicago Bears in Wrigley Field in 1936. Nagurski, the middle linebacker, hit me just as I arrived at the hole, knocked me back but not off my feet, and I came back through the same hole and ran 56 yards for a TD. The score was a big factor in the win over the Bears.

"It was after the game that George Musso, the Bear middle guard, said it was the only time in his career that a back passed him three times on the same play."

W. CLARKE HINKLE

BORN: April 10, 1910   Height: 6'0"   Weight: 200
                              Bucknell College

Green Bay, 1932–41

| Year | G. | RUSHING | | | | PASS RECEIVING | | | | SCORING | |
		Att.	Yds.	Avg.	TD.	P.C.	Yds.	Avg.	TD.	TD.	Pts.
1932	11	95	331	3.5	2	..	..	..	..	2	13
1933	13	139	413	2.9	4	6	48	8.0	0	4	30
1934	..	144	359	2.5	0	10	110	11.0	0	0	21
1935	..	77	273	3.5	2	1	4	4.0	0	2	18
1936	..	100	476	4.8	4	0	0	0.0	0	4	31
1937	..	129	552	4.3	5	8	116	14.5	2	7	57
1938	..	114	299	2.6	3	7	98	14.0	4	7	58
1939	..	135	381	2.8	5	4	70	17.5	0	5	35
1940	..	109	383	3.5	2	4	28	7.0	1	3	48
1941	..	129	393	3.0	5	8	78	9.8	1	6	56
PRO TOTALS —10 YEARS	..	1171	3860	3.3	32	48	552	11.5	8	40	367

Cliff Battles

I THOUGHT RED GRANGE WAS A RUNNER
UNTIL I SAW CLIFF BATTLES. RED WASN'T
EVEN IN BATTLES' CLASS.
  —*Benny Friedman, quarterback,*
  New York Giants.

In the spring of 1938, Clifford Franklyn Battles was indisputably the greatest running halfback in the world. He had the credentials to prove it. The Washington Redskins, for whom he played, were the world professional football champions. Cliff had led the NFL in ball carrying for the third time in six years and was a unanimous selection to the league all-pro team. He was twenty-eight years old, in perfect condition, at the peak of his career, marvelously tailored for his job at six feet, one inches and 200 pounds. He wanted to play more.

But Cliff Battles never carried a football again for money.

Playing professional football—grueling, arduous, even dangerous because of the rigorous demands of being a 60-minute performer—wasn't worth it to him. Not for $3,000 a year. And George Marshall, the colorful, truculent, laundryman who owned the Redskins, was adamant. He wouldn't pay Battles a dollar more. With Roosevelt in the White House, taxes were already going up.

But what nettled Battles even more than the money was Marshall's attitude.

"Sammy Baugh was holding out, too," recalled Battles, "and Marshall spent all his time wrestling with him. He ignored me. That was when Sammy was threatening to quit football (after a glorious rookie season in '37) to play shortstop for the St. Louis Cardinals. All he had to do was beat out Marty Marion, one of the all-time greats. Only Marshall didn't know that and chased after him. It hurt my feelings. So I went off in a huff and played no more."

He took a job as an assistant coach under Lou Little at Columbia, for $4,000 a year, a hefty raise, and that was the end of his active career. Considering what Baugh, the all-time great passer, meant to the Redskins then and later, you couldn't really fault Marshall's judgment. However, a man like Battles only comes along once in an era. The Redskins have never had another runner like him. For the half dozen years he played, the impression was indelible.

"Battles had the long stride," remembered Jim Lee Howell, who played against him as a defensive end for the New York Giants. "And he had the change of pace. He was fast, too. Maybe not like the sprinters of today. But he could turn it on."

And he specialized in turning it on against the Giants. There was, for instance, his last game in New York in 1937, his last season, when the teams played for the Eastern division title. Going into it, the Giants had given up only 60 points in ten games.

Early in the game, Battles carried the ball 37 yards in five straight slants off tackle into the Giant end zone for a quick Redskin lead. Later, after Baugh opened up the New York defense with his bullet passes, Cliff broke through the Giant forward wall at his own 23, cut to the right, reversed his field to the left, jiggered his direction, and wound up going to the right again, altogether zig-zagging an estimated 200 yards before he planted the ball over the goal line for an official 73-yard gallop. Then he intercepted a Giant pass from his safety position and sprinted 76 yards for another score. The Redskins routed the Giants, 49–14.

A week later, in the NFL championship game against the Chicago Bears, he got the Redskins off and running to a 28–21 victory with a 10-yard burst for a touchdown early in the first quarter, after he took his team out of a hole by catching a pass thrown by Baugh from the Redskin end zone. Cliff threaded through the open field into Chicago territory to turn the momentum of the game around.

The long run was a Battles specialty. In one game against Pittsburgh that season, he raced 71, 65, and 60 yards on individual touchdown sprints. "I chased him up and down the field many a time," said Al Slick, a referee in the Pittsburgh zone. So did many a tackler.

And yet he never intended to be a football player. He came from the part of Ohio that was the cradle of professional football. "But as a kid," said Cliff, "I never even knew the game existed. I was too small. Other kids chased after Jim Thorpe. I was taking apples to the teacher."

His father wanted him to be a violinist, and football was taboo. Gip Battles, as they called him at Kenmore High School in Akron, didn't go out for the team until he was a junior, when he sprouted to 175 pounds. Basketball was more his sport anyhow, and after gradution he went off to little West Virginia Wesleyan on a cage scholarship to major in English.

During his college years, however, Cliff filled out into a legitimate 195-pounder. He played basketball and was captain of the team. He ran the sprints in track and was captain of the team. He played baseball—of course, he was the captain. He even starred as a tennis player at the same time. And finally he developed an absorption for football. Again he was made captain.

In his four years at the little Methodist school in Buckhannon, West Virginia, from 1927 to 1931, he received fifteen letters in five sports. He also taught swimming, and his classwork was on a Phi Beta Kappa level.

But football really distinguished him. West Virginia Wesleyan was not the kind of school that produced All-American football players. Its scores made only an agate line in the Sunday papers. No metropolitan writers ever saw the Bobcats, as they were called. But word of a halfback named Cliff Battles did get around the hill country, particularly after one game against Salem College in which he ran for more than 400 yards and scored seven touchdowns. That was in 1930, his junior season, and against Waynesburg College, he also reeled off touchdown runs of 98, 96, and 82 yards. He penetrated Allegheny for 320 yards in 31 rushes. His season's total yardage was 2,186 and his 15 touchdowns made him the country's leading scorer.

But when Wesleyan stepped out of its class to play Georgetown, it got clobbered 76–12. The game in Washington, D. C., against Georgetown turned out to have special significance. That ebullient laundryman, George Marshall, was among the spectators and saw the great halfback from the little backwoods college run. He had a dream. He dreamed that Battles was running in the backfield of a new professional football team he would organize in 1932, the Boston Braves.

Cliff really wanted to study law. He also wanted to compete for a coveted Rhodes scholarship. The Braves weren't the only pro team that knew about him. The Giants and

174

Tape bridged across his nose, Cliff Battles (20) was a flashing figure for the early Redskin teams. In this action, he is taking off on a 75-yard touchdown run behind the blocking of Sammy Baugh (33).

the Portsmouth Spartans also sent him queries because in 1931, Battles-led Wesleyan played Navy to a scoreless tie. But Marshall was smart. He sent a special envoy with orders not to come back until he had signed Battles.

"They were the only team to send a personal agent to see me," noted Battles. "That flattered me. They also offered me $175 a game. I was a star."

He was a star for real. He came into the pro league as a rookie on a new team in 1932 and finished second in rushing. It was the first time official statistics were kept for league play. In 1933—with such runners as Nagurski, Hinkle, Ken Strong, and Ace Gutowsky at their peaks, and even Grange still active—Cliff Battles led professional football in rushing with a phenomenal (for the time) 5.0 yard average and a total of 737 yards gained. He was also named to the all-league team in a backfield with Nagurski, Harry Newman of the Giants, and Glen Presnell of Portsmouth.

The Redskins (a name they adopted in '33) played five seasons in Boston with desultory support from the fans, but Battles, running at left halfback, behind Ernie Pinckert and later Riley Smith, two of the greatest blocking backs in football history, was consistently brilliant. In 1936, he again topped the league in rushing and made the all-pro team as Boston finished first in the Eastern division. The Redskin press book described him like this: "A rampaging, untamed mustang when he breaks loose for one of his gallops. Rated as the best ball carrier in the National League. Established as the darling of Boston fans because of his brilliant playing. Plays football because he loves it and the rougher the going the wider his smile. A fast, elusive, brainy player."

There were not enough Boston fans for their "darling." By this time, Marshall was fed up with sparse crowds and deficits, and even shifted the 1936 title game against the Green Bay Packers to neutral territory, New York's Polo Grounds. After only three minutes of play, Battles was hurt and sidelined for the day. Without their chief threat, the Redskins lost, 21–6.

The next season, the franchise was moved to Washington and stabilized. To augment the threat of Battles' runs, Marshall signed a lanky passer from Texas Christian, Sammy Baugh as quarterback. The combination was devastating. Baugh, the rookie, led the league in passing, with such receivers as Wayne Millner, Charley Malone, Ed Justice, and that galloping halfback, Battles. Running on his own, Cliff also led the NFL in rushing with a career high of 874 yards.

Washington dovetailed its talents beautifully in the 1937 championship game against the Chicago Bears in Wrigley Field. On Washington's first play from scrimmage, deep in its own territory, Baugh faked a punt and threw to Battles in the flat. Cliff raced 42 yards to put the 'Skins in threatening position. Then from the 10-yard line, he took the ball on a reverse and swept the left end for 10 yards and a touchdown to get the 'Skins on the board first. After the Bears rallied for a pair of scores, but still were massed for Battles' thrusts through the line, Baugh unlimbered his passing arm and threw three touchdown passes to win Washington's first pro football championship, 28–21.

In those days, pro football players weren't capitalizing on their reputations between seasons. They took whatever jobs they could get. Battles, a good basketball player, played one winter as a pro with the Wheeling Steel team against such fancy opposition as the original Celtics. Another time he toured the East with Clarke Hinkle and a couple of other players in a training program for the Fisher auto body company. He also worked as a time study man. Battles, a bright man, brooded about his future, and when Marshall ignored his request for a raise after his greatest campaign in '37, he started looking around.

At the same time, Coach Lou Little needed an assistant at Columbia, which was big time then, playing schools like Michigan, Syracuse, Army, Navy, and Stanford, in addition to its traditional Ivy League opponents. Lou had a young tailback named Sid Luckman and wanted a backfield coach to work with him. The job was offered first to Hinkle, then at the peak of his career with the Packers. When Clarke turned it down, Lou enlisted Battles, at $1,000 more than he was making in Washington.

It was like Gale Sayers deciding the Chicago Bears weren't paying him enough and taking an assistant's job at some Big Eight school. In matching Battles against the great runners of history, there has been a tendency to downgrade him because he quit at the top. Yet with a full six years in pro ball, he played longer than Ernie Nevers, as long as Red Grange and George McAfee, and only a couple of seasons fewer than such redoubtable bulls as Bronko Nagurski, Marion Motley, and Steve Van Buren.

As a coach, Battles stayed at Columbia six years, turning out such All-Americans as Luckman and Paul Governali. He went into service and coached the famous El Toro Marines in California, and then returned to pro ball for a year and a half as the head coach of the Brooklyn Dodgers in the old All-America Conference.

In 1955, he was the first man from a small school to be voted into the collegiate Hall of Fame, and in 1968 he was voted into the Professional Football Hall of Fame. By this time, he had returned to Washington as a businessman and became a devout Redskin fan. He even did a TV sports show, delivering critiques on the Redskins.

"It wasn't until I got on the air," grinned Battles, rubbing his hand over a now glistening dome, "that they realized who my sponsor was, a hair restorer."

CLIFF BATTLES' FAVORITE PLAY:

"A weak side fullback reverse or off-tackle play worked very well in my days with the Redskins. It was a counter play against an overshifted defense, which was used against the more popular strong side plays. By faking across on some of Sammy Baugh's pass plays, we put additional pressure on the defense and were able to catch the other team by surprise.

"The play was our most effective ground gainer against the New York Giants in 1937, although Jim Lee Howell, their right defensive end, forced me outside by crashing in tight. I also scored our first touchdown in the 1937 championship game against the Chicago Bears on this play."

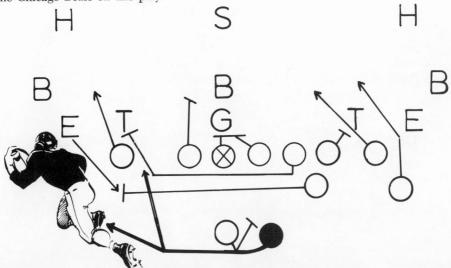

CLIFFORD "CLIFF" BATTLES

BORN: May 1, 1910   Height: 6'1"   Weight: 195
West Virginia Wesleyan College

Boston Redskins, 1932–36
Washington, 1937

Year	G.	Att.	Yds.	Avg.	TD.	P.C.	Yds.	Avg.	TD.	TD.	Pts.
			RUSHING				PASS RECEIVING			SCORING	
1932	8	148	576	3.9	3	4	60	15.0	1	4	24
1933	12	146	*737	5.0	4	11	185	16.8	0	4	27
1934	12	93	511	5.5	6	5	95	19.0	1	7	43
1935	6	67	230	3.4	2	2	22	11.0	0	2	12
1936	11	176	614	3.5	6	6	103	17.2	1	7	42
1937	10	216	*874	4.0	6	9	81	9.0	1	7	42

PRO TOTALS
—6 YEARS   59   846   3542   4.2   27   37   546   14.8   4   31   190

* Led NFL.

Earl "Dutch" Clark

HE LOOKED LIKE THE EASIEST MAN IN
THE WORLD TO TACKLE. THE FIRST
TIME I TRIED, I THOUGHT I'D BREAK HIM
IN TWO. BUT WHEN I CLOSED MY ARMS,
ALL I WAS HOLDING WAS AIR.
—*Bronko Nagurski, fullback,*
Chicago Bears.

Earl "Dutch" Clark was normally a quarterback, but his duties at tailback for Detroit called for triple threat action. And he was, above all, a leader by example.

Some men come so close to the ideal of perfection in sports that their lack of human fallibility, and the excitement it generates, makes them dull for historians. Earl "Dutch" Clark is an example.

Ted Williams had that irascible temper and a nonchalance about fielding, but they never detracted from his epic image as a hitter. So he was something to write about. So was Bobby Layne, in the same era, when he railed at mate and foe, didn't throw a classic pass, carried a pot belly, but won championships for Detroit. Wilt Chamberlain, Pancho Gonzalez, Joe Namath—they grab you for their eccentricities as characters as much as for their heroism as sports figures.

Then there are the Charley Gehringers of this world. He played seventeen full seasons for the Detroit Tigers, hit for a career average of .320, fielded flawlessly all that time at second base, was duly elected to the Hall of Fame and remained vital to Detroit baseball for years after he stopped playing. But ten Charley Gehringers around Tiger Stadium (formerly Briggs Stadium) won't get you one Dennis McLain—autographs, of course. Charley was so efficiently good and calmly controlled that he was unexciting as a personality.

In that same stadium, Dutch Clark was a contemporary of Gehringer, playing for the Lions every fall. In each of his six full seasons in the National Football League, he was named to the official all-pro team as quarterback. He was the last great bona fide triple threat in football, bowing out just before the T-formation revolution. He was a legendary runner, a good passer, a superb field general, a fine punter, and the final practitioner of that vanished art, the drop-kick. When the Pro Football Hall of Fame was established in Canton, Ohio, Dutch Clark was elected as a charter member.

Even in Detroit, Earl "Dutch" Clark is not a household name. In fact, however, Dutch was the one man responsible for modern professional football in Detroit, which had been represented briefly in the NFL in 1921 and again in 1928, when Benny Friedman, the All-American quarterback from Michigan, was the temporary attraction for a team called the Detroit Wolverines. Friedman's departure for New York in 1929 left the Motor City out of action until 1934.

A radio man named G. A. "Dick" Richards was interested in bringing football back to Detroit. The franchise of the Portsmouth Spartans was in shaky shape. Young Dutch Clark had joined the Spartans in 1931 and made All-NFL quarterback as a rookie. He was chosen again the next year and led the league in scoring. But pro football with the Portsmouth Spartans at the height of the Depression was a tenuous proposition, so he went back to his native Colorado as football coach at the Colorado School of Mines. Now in the winter of 1933–34, Richards had a chance to shift the Spartans to Detroit and asked George "Potsy" Clark, their coach, what he needed to make it go in the new locale.

"A winner," said Potsy bluntly.

"How do you get that?" Richards wanted to know.

"By getting Dutch Clark to come back."

"Do that," said Richards, "and I'll buy the club."

Potsy Clark (no relation) went out to Colorado and persuaded Dutch to return, and that's how the Detroit Lions began. He was the guts of the club, the man who called the signals and ran from the tailback position (his designation as a quarterback was actually a misnomer) on a team that was probably the most devastating ground-attacking force of all time. In their first year, the Lions gained 2,763 yards on the ground in a thirteen-game schedule. In 1936, playing only twelve games, they set an all-time NFL record of 2,885 yards running.

By way of comparison, the Green Bay Packers didn't gain 2,000 yards rushing in any of their three straight world championship years, 1965–66–67. And yet they were known primarily for their running attack.

Every year Dutch Clark's selection as all-pro was automatic. In 1935, the Lions won the NFL title by beating the New York Giants in grinding out 235 yards on the ground, but throwing only five passes, an historic low. The high point was a 40-yard run for a touchdown by Clark in the first quarter, a typical ramble in which he slanted off tackle behind double-team power blocking, then cut against the grain (i.e., the flow of the play) and used improvisations to cover the rest of the distance.

"No back ever followed interference better than Dutch," said his coach, Potsy Clark. "But when his interference gets him into the secondary, he begins his own dervish dance. He'll get out of more holes than anybody you ever saw, and just about the time you expect to see him smothered, he's free of tacklers and gone. He's like a rabbit in a brush heap. That's the best description of his way of running. He has no plan, no definite direction. He doesn't run better in one direction than another. He's a purely instinctive runner who cuts, pivots, slants and reverses by instinct."

"Running is like driving a car," Clark once reminisced. "When you drive, you're looking quite a ways down the street. The things that are close you take care of automatically, with reflex action."

In a Lion-Bear game, Dutch followed a tackle into the Chicago secondary. The tackle levelled a rookie linebacker with a block and then sat on the rookie as Clark accelerated and moved to another part of the field.

"I hate to hold you down like this," the Lion tackle explained to the squashed Bear, "but we gotta stick around. Dutch'll be breezing back this way again."

Spectacular as he was in action, Dutch lacked the color that Detroit had associated with another great performer in baseball, Ty Cobb. After Dutch had led the NFL in scoring for the fourth time in 1936, owner Richards wanted to stimulate his image as a personality. Dutch had gained 628 yards on the ground and completed 53.5 percent of his passes (at a time when the league average was 36.5 percent). Dutch's own team instincts inhibited personal glory, and the Lion's backfield, having three other excellent runners—Ace Gutowsky, Glenn Presnell and Ernie Caddel—made it that much more difficult for any player to stand out as a personality.

Potsy Clark left the Lions in 1937 to head the Brooklyn Dodgers, and Richards replaced him with the other Clark, Dutch, as the playing coach. Richards had also signed Steve Hannagan, a nationally known publicist, to glamorize the Lions' leader. Dutch wanted nothing to do with it. He was a handsome guy—six feet, a sculptured 185 pounds, with a strong face, and a firm jaw and wavy brown hair. He should have

Though not an overpowering runner, Dutch Clark's slashing style cut through arm tackles such as these by a couple of New York Giants.

been a natural for exploitation by a man who reshaped Ann Sheridan into the "Oomph" Girl, transformed a remote outpost in the Sawtooth Mountains of Idaho into famous Sun Valley, and brought out the sunshine of Miami Beach for the world to notice.

"You can't," said Dutch, "make me into the No. 1 man in football because Nagurski's better, and Hinkle might be, too."

The self-effacement was no act with Dutch. They once put together a "Dutch Clark Day" to commemorate a meeting with the Chicago Bears, who were the Lions' toughest opponents in those days. They got Dutch out of the game in the second half and then contrived to put him back in the final minutes for a game-ending ovation.

"Nope," Dutch shook his head, "I'm not going back in. Those guys out there been knocking their brains all afternoon, so why should I go in there and get all the credit?"

And yet he was a tremendous competitor under fire. He is still known as the greatest all-around athlete the state of Colorado ever produced. At Pueblo Central, he was a high school All-American basketball player. At little Colorado College, with an enrollment of less than 1,000, and playing an obscure schedule, he achieved national recognition by being named to the 1928 Associated Press All-American team. Dutch set the hammer-throw record for the Rocky Mountain Conference, and he later pitched in the Colorado State League.

He had gone to Colorado College, after first enrolling at Northwestern, because he was homesick and somebody had stolen his trunk off the porch of the fraternity house when he first arrived in Evanston, Illinois. He achieved his peak as a college football player when he scored all the points in a 3–2 battle with Denver University, a power in the Rockies. First, on the bad pass from center, he had been trapped in the end zone for a safety. Then, with time running out, he led a desperation rush into Denver territory and on fourth down, from the 25-yard line, drop-kicked the winning field goal. At first, the referee declared the kick no good because it went over an upright instead of the cross bar.

"That makes it good," argued Dutch. The referee shook his head. "Look it up in the rule book," Dutch insisted. The referee did and found out the young back was right. All hell broke loose when he reversed the decision and made Colorado College a winner.

The game was played in Denver's stadium, and Jeff Cravath, the Denver coach, had to rescue the official from the mob and sneak him to the dressing room.

In 1928, he gained 1,349 in 135 carries, a phenomenal average of 10 yards per carry in a period when line spacing was unknown and power, rather than finesse, was the mode, so that defenses were stacked against the ground game. After graduation, Dutch stayed at his school for a year as an assistant coach before the chance to play pro ball enticed him East.

And in his rookie season of 1931, with the Portsmouth Spartans, he was named to the first official all-pro team with such select backfield mates as Nevers, Grange, and Blood. He showed the veteran Johnny Blood his ability in a game against the Green Bay Packers. Clark's team, ahead of the Pack by a slim point, was backed up against its 1-yard line. Green Bay massed for an off-tackle smash by Clark to the strong side because that was his bread-and-butter play. In those days, the goal posts were two yards inside the end zone, though the cross bar hung over the goal line. The Packer line-

184

backers shot through with the snap of the ball to the tailback and had Dutch trapped for a safety behind his own line. It would mean the ball game.

"I still find it hard to believe what happened," mused Blood. "Dutch saw he was dead and, with the ball tucked under his left arm, hooked his right arm around the goal post as he shot ahead on the dead run. It had to be pure instinct."

The effect was that of a catapult, a human shotput, as he whirled and flew over the tacklers, landing past the goal line to avert the safety.

There is a championship psyche which comes out in great athletes under stress and handicaps. Dutch Clark played almost all of his career with limited vision in one eye, and no one realized it until the College All-Star game of 1936, for which the Lions had qualified by winning the NFL crown the previous December. Then, as now, it was played under lights in Soldier Field. The disparity between the pros and the collegians at that time wasn't great because of two factors—the pros weren't as well organized as they were to become, and they didn't have the overwhelming talent, since a lot of collegians still skipped professional careers after their eligibility ran out.

Available to the college stars were such renowned collegians as Wayne Millner, Gaynell Tinsley, Monk Moscrip, Ed Widseth, Bobby Grayson, Riley Smith, and Tuffy Leemans. In this, the third annual game, the All-Stars stunned the pros by scoring in the second period and leading at halftime, 7–0. It was the first time the pros had ever been scored upon in the series.

Clark was useless. "The lights glaring down on the chalk-lined battlefield had partially blinded him," a report of the game read, "and it was necessary to administer to him between the halves. As the Lions, battered and bruised, sauntered into the dressing room at intermission, low in spirit because of their failure to hold the onrush of the Stars, they were greeted with the words: 'Dutch is going blind!' "

An old college teammate, Bill Hinkley, recalled, "We played basketball together, and I know how much it bothered him. I used to literally lead him home after a game because his eyes hurt him so. I'd actually take him up and down curbings. . . ."

But in the fourth quarter, under the Soldier Field lights, Dutch came off the bench and rallied the still scoreless Lions. They recovered a fumble by the Stars, and Clark hit twice into the line for no appreciable gain. But he was setting the collegians up. He faked a buck into the line again, spun, and handed the ball to Ernie Caddel coming around on a reverse. The suckered college kids never touched Caddel, who raced for a touchdown. The Lions still needed the extra point to salvage a tie. Clark couldn't see the goal posts clearly in the glare, but he lined himself up, blinked hard to grab the snap from center, and booted a drop-kick for the final 7–7 score.

Long after his athletic career was over, Dutch admitted, "I know now that I needed glasses. But I wasn't blind in my left eye as they rumored. I didn't wear glasses because I didn't want to depend on them."

He was literally a coach on the field. "He is one of the most intelligent men who ever played football," said Potsy Clark. "He knows the game thoroughly. But his main asset is an ability to gain the confidence of players. He makes them absolutely believe in him. They never question any play he calls. And I have never known Dutch to criticize any player. Any time a play goes wrong he takes the entire blame."

185

Clark Shaughnessy, a football genius himself who coached the Bears and Rams and introduced the T-formation, said, "If Clark stepped on the field with Grange, Thorpe, and Gipp, he would be the general."

But ironically, as the head man, Clark was without his most valuable asset—himself as a player. After the 1937 season, when he coached and played full time, he retired to the sidelines. It was different being a coach. As a personality, he was reticent. "Five sentences from the Dutchman is a sermon," said an old friend, Aid Kushner, who was a trainer for the Lions. "Dutch feels that three people in one room is a crowd if one of them is Dutch."

Under Clark, the Lions missed out on the western division championship by one game in 1938. That was the year Byron "Whizzer" White, another legendary athlete to come out of Colorado, broke in with the Pittsburgh Pirates, as they were known then, and led the NFL in rushing. Halfway through the campaign, owner Dick Richards, always trying to generate a spark, told Clark he thought "this White kid" was available if he wanted him. "We just beat the Bears with the backfield we have," said Dutch coolly. "It's a good backfield. We don't need White."

A couple of weeks later, the Packers walloped the Lions, 28–7, and won the division crown. The next season, Dutch was coaching the Cleveland Rams. In four years, they never had a winning season and finally suspended operations after the '42 campaign. Dutch drifted on to a couple of other pro jobs on the west coast and then went back to familiar ground as the head coach at the University of Detroit in 1949. He later was the director of athletics and then got out of sports to work as a sales representative.

In the Lions' individual records, there is almost nothing to show that Earl Clark, the man who got them started in 1934, once passed through wearing the powder blue jersey and the silver helmet. However, George Christiansen, who was an all-pro tackle that inaugural year, defended Clark's achievements:

"I figure Dutch did everything with a football twice as good as any other player I ever saw. It's not his fault there isn't a page in the league record book where they measure a man's abilities in terms of his braininess on the field. Dutch's name would be all over it, just like he was all over a football field."

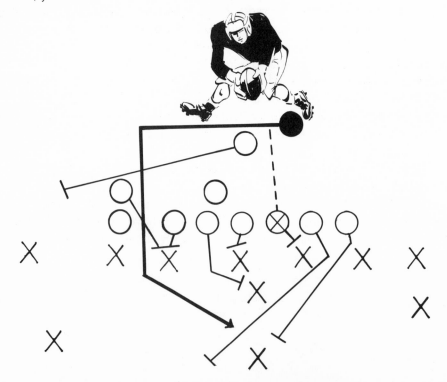

DUTCH CLARK'S FAVORITE PLAY:

"The off-tackle series was our bread-and-butter play when we needed the important yardage. We had spinners in off our single wing formation and good wide plays, but when the going got tough, we dropped back to the off-tackle play.

"I've shown it against a seven-man defensive line which was predominant at that time. Its success depended upon hours of practice for timing and good, crisp blocking.

"The ball carrier, as illustrated here, had to show a step to the outside of the de-fensive [left] tackle to make the block on him successful. If the tackle was charging to the inside, however, we would vary our blocking to go outside of him.

"We had a dedicated group of players that really loved to block, which was neces-sary for the type of game we played."

EARL "DUTCH" CLARK

BORN: Oct. 11, 1906   Height: 6'0''   Weight: 185

Colorado College

Portsmouth Spartans, 1931–32
Detroit, 1934–38

		RUSHING				PASS RECEIVING				SCORING	
Year	G.	Att.	Yds.	Avg.	TD.	P.C.	Yds.	Avg.	TD.	TD.	Pts.
1932	..	111	461	4.2	2	10	107	10.7	2	4	*38
1933	(inactive, coaching)										
1934	..	123	763	6.2	6	7	72	10.3	2	8	73
1935	..	120	412	3.4	4	9	124	13.8	2	6	*55
1936	..	123	628	5.1	6	1	5	5.0	1	7	*73
1937	..	96	468	4.9	5	2	33	16.5	1	6	45
1938	..	7	25	3.6	0	0	0	0.0	0	0	8
PRO TOTALS —6 YEARS	..	580	2757	4.8	23	29	341	11.8	8	31	292

		PASSING				
Year	G.	Att.	Comp.	Pct.	Yds.	TD.P.
1932	..	52	17	32.7	272	..
1933		(inactive)				
1934	..	45	21	46.7	366	..
1935	..	26	11	42.3	133	..
1936	..	71	38	53.5	467	..
1937	..	39	19	48.7	202	..
1938	..	12	6	50.0	50	..
PRO TOTALS —6 YEARS	..	245	112	45.7	1490	..

* Led NFL.

. . . And There Were More

At the age of 41, Ken Strong was still on the active roster of the New York Giants—as a place-kicker. But in his earlier days, he was also a fine all around running back whose versatility later merited election to the Hall of Fame.

KEN STRONG IS THE GREATEST FOOT-
BALL PLAYER I EVER SAW.
　　　　　　　　—*Judge Wally Steffen,*
　　　　　　　　Carnegie Tech coach.

A man is labelled by his most apparent skill, and so Elmer Kenneth Strong can't escape the tag that he was a kicker. When he was thirty-seven years old, he was still kicking a football, and twenty years later, the snap still in his right leg, he was showing guys on the New York Giants, like Don Chandler, how to kick a football.

But once in a while, a man is privileged to revert. In the late fall of 1943, a war year, the Giants were pushing the Washington Redskins around by a 31–7 score. Ken Strong, at thirty-seven, brought out of retirement because of the manpower shortage, and because his toe was still strong, was in the game to kick.

"Hey," he turned to Tuffy Leemans, calling the signals in the A-formation, "how about letting the old man run with the ball?"

"You must be off your rocker," said Leemans.

"It's like this," Strong explained. "Ken, Jr., is here, and he never saw me carry the ball."

Leemans agreed. Strong carried; he was piled up. He tried it again and was belted. He turned to Leemans and said, "Thanks, Tuffy. I just ended my career as a running back."

A decade earlier he had been an excellent ball carrier. That, and not just the fact he was a fine punter and place-kicker, put him in the pro Hall of Fame. From a pure running standpoint, Ken is not one of the glorified ones. He didn't stay still long enough, as a salaried employee, that is. In 1928, starring for NYU, he gained a record 2,100 yards from scrimmage and was a unanimous All-American choice. After a brilliant performance against Carnegie Tech, Grantland Rice rhapsodized, ". . . he was George Gipp, Red Grange and Chris Cagle rolled into one human form . . ." And the Carnegie Tech coach, Judge Steffen, called him the greatest ever.

But Ken Strong, versatile and magnificently put together at 201 pounds (big for that era), couldn't ever roost long enough to be appreciated as a pro. As a New Yorker, it was logical for him to play with the Giants, but they offered him only $3,000, and the Stapletons, a team on Staten Island, got him for a thousand more. He played with the Stapletons until 1932. Ken also wanted to be a baseball player—that was the big payoff in sports. After he hit .343 and 14 home runs at Toronto in 1931, he was sold to the Detroit Tigers for $40,000 and five players. But that same summer, he also hurt his wrist chasing a fly ball in the outfield. A doctor operated after the season and removed the wrong bone. His wrist permanently stiff, Strong was through as a baseball player. His only choice—back to football. But the Stapletons folded, and he had to sign with the Giants, for what they offered him originally.

He played three years in the Polo Grounds, 1933–35, at the time Coach Steve Owen was building the first pro football dynasty in New York. His first season, with Harry Newman, a rookie quarterback from Michigan, leading the league in passing and Ken carrying the heavy load on the ground, the Giants won their first division title and were barely nosed out by the Bears in the championship playoff. The same teams met again the next year, and Strong had his most notable day as a pro.

The temperature was nine degrees in the Polo Grounds. A sheet of ice covered the field. Both teams slid all over it, but the Bears were heavier sliders and built a 10–3 halftime lead. Meanwhile, a Giant agent had been dispatched to Manhattan College for a supply of basketball shoes. At halftime, they put on sneakers and George Halas, the Bears' coach, said, "Step on their toes."

In the fourth quarter, the Giants went on a 27-point tear to break open the game. Strong, who had kicked the first-half field goal, supplied two touchdowns on romps of 42 and 11 yards.

Ken was the spearhead of a third straight divisional championship in '35, but after the season, lured by an offer of $5,000 a year, he jumped the NFL to play with the New York entry in a new American league. Strong was suspended by the NFL for five years. The new league disbanded after little more than a season of play, and that was the end of Ken Strong as an all-purpose football player. He came back to the Giants, twice, in later years, but only as a kicker.

KENNETH "KEN" STRONG

BORN: Aug. 6, 1906   Height: 6'1"   Weight: 201
                          New York University
Staten Island Stapletons, 1929–32
New York Giants, 1933–35, 1939, 1944–47
New York Yanks, 1936–37

Year	G.	RUSHING Att.	Yds.	Avg.	TD.	PASS RECEIVING P.C.	Yds.	Avg.	TD.	SCORING TD.	Pts.
1929–31		(no records available)									
1932	10	96	375	3.9	1	5	56	11.2	0	1	9
1933	14	108	286	2.6	4	7	146	20.9	2	6	64
1934	13	135	431	3.2	1	7	52	7.4	0	1	25
1935	10	46	151	3.3	1	0	0	0.0	0	1	29
1936–38	(banned from NFL for jumping leagues)										
1939	7	1	1	1.0	0	0	0	0.0	0	0	19
1940–43		(retired)									
1944	10	2	−2	−1.0	0	..	..	..	..	0	41
1945	9	..	..	..	..	..	..	..	..	..	41
1946	11	..	..	..	..	..	..	..	..	..	44
1947	11	..	..	..	..	..	..	..	..	..	30
PRO TOTALS —12 YEARS	95	388	1242	3.2	7	19	254	13.4	2	9	302

I CAN HONESTLY SAY THAT FOOTBALL
KEPT ME IN SCHOOL—RIGHT THROUGH
COLLEGE—BECAUSE I KNEW I HAD TO
PASS TO PLAY.

—*Beattie Feathers, halfback,
Chicago Bears.*

Beattie Feathers wasn't the usual run of rookie when he showed up to play with the Chicago Bears in 1934. He was twenty-five years old and out of the tough Tennessee school of football coached by General Bob Neyland. As the tailback in the General's precision single wing, he was an All-American in 1933—a strong running back and a punter who could average 48 yards a kick, as he once did against Alabama.

By the time he got to the Chicago Bears, he was mature and hardened. "I was older than the usual rookie because I quit school three or four times in the grammer grades," he explained.

Herman Hickman, who had played guard at Tennessee, said, "Beattie Feathers was one of the greatest runners of all time—he could do it all, and well."

Blocking for Feathers, Hickman got a first hand view of his potency. Against Alabama in 1932, the Vols were trailing by a 3–0 score and bogged down on the Crimson 9-yard line, fourth down and goal to go. The Vol quarterback called for a single wing power play off tackle, with Feathers carrying. Both guards were to pull and lead the play. The wingback and right end were supposed to double-team the defensive left tackle; the blocking back and fullback, shoulder to shoulder, were assigned to wipe out the left end. Behind this phalanx of blocking might, Feathers was to take the pass from center, leading him by a yard, move three steps to the right, then cut through the wide swath behind the guards.

As the play unrolled, the Alabama defensive left tackle leap-frogged over his two blockers, who missed him completely. The blocking back and fullback tripped over each other going for the defensive end and didn't even touch him. The right guard pulled to his left, and the left guard pulled to his right—they met head-on and knocked themselves out cold. The center, jittery, didn't lead Feathers with the ball, but snapped it back over his left shoulder, away from the direction of the play.

Beattie reached back and made a one-handed grab of the ball. He faked the Alabama tackle with a head movement, ducked inside the end, ran over a linebacker and straight-armed the defensive back, squirmed and broke through a couple of other tacklers and darted into the end zone for the 7–3 victory that secured an unbeaten season for Tennessee. Before the extra point, he trotted back to the huddle, slapped every player on the rump and said enthusiastically, "Nice blocking, fellas. Nice blocking. Give me blocking like that and I'll go all the way every time."

With the Chicago Bears, he got the kind of blocking that, in his '34 rookie season, made him the first running back in pro history to gain officially more than 1,000 yards in a season. (The NFL started to keep statistics in an orderly fashion in 1932.)

Beattie carried the ball only 101 times, but he averaged 9.9 yards each carry for a total of 1,004 yards. Thirty-five years later, that 9.9 average is still the all-time record, exceeding the next best mark by more than three yards (Dan Towler of the Rams had

Beattie Feathers poses pretty as a passer, but he gained his niche in football's gallery of stars by becoming the first runner to gain more than 1,000 yards in a single season.

a 6.8 yard figure in 1951). In fact, thirteen seasons passed after Beattie's debut before another running back, Steve Van Buren of the Eagles, again cracked the magic barrier of 1,000 yards a season.

"It takes two things to make a 1,000-yarder," noted Feathers years later. "He's got to be lucky to avoid injuries, and he's got to be lucky enough to get good blocking. In 1934, I was healthy all the way and had the greatest blocker who ever lived, Bronko Nagurski.

"Whichever way Nagurski knocked them, I cut into the opening."

This technique presaged the run-to-daylight fad a quarter century after Feathers. Beattie came to the Bears about the same time Red Grange was fading out. And Beattie's first extensive use, ironically, was as a defensive replacement for Grange.

"Ol' Red wanted me to play all I could," mused Beattie. "He'd come in the dressing room and make believe he was helping the trainer give me a rubdown. 'Stay healthy, kid,' Red would laugh. 'You're looking great out there.'"

But Beattie had his one big season, and that was it. He dislocated his shoulder the next fall and played the rest of his career with his right arm immobilized by a shoulder brace. In a half dozen succeeding seasons as a pro, Beattie didn't even match the total yardage of his inaugural year. The Bears traded him to the Brooklyn Dodgers in 1938, and two years later he bowed out of pro ball from the Green Bay Packers to go into college coaching.

But just as Roger Bannister created his claim to fame by running the first mile under four minutes, Beattie left a legacy to pro football when he cracked the 1,000-yard barrier and led the NFL in running as a rookie.

BEATTIE FEATHERS

BORN: Aug. 20, 1909   Height: 5'11"   Weight: 188
University of Tennessee

Chicago Bears, 1934–37
Brooklyn, 1938–39
Green Bay, 1940

| Year | G. | RUSHING | | | | PASS RECEIVING | | | | SCORING | |
		Att.	Yds.	Avg.	TD.	P.C.	Yds.	Avg.	TD.	TD.	Pts.
1934	11	101	*1004	*9.9	8	5	174	34.8	1	9	54
1935	..	56	281	5.0	3	3	18	6.0	0	3	18
1936	..	97	350	3.6	2	2	5	2.5	0	2	12
1937	..	66	211	3.2	1	0	0	0.0	0	1	6
1938	..	28	94	3.4	2	3	34	11.3	0	2	12
1939	..	8	21	2.6	0	1	12	12.0	0	0	0
1940	..	4	19	4.8	0	0	0	0.0	0	0	0
PRO TOTALS —7 YEARS	..	360	1980	5.5	16	14	243	17.4	1	17	102

* Led NFL.

The next rookie after Feathers to lead the NFL in rushing was Alphonse "Tuffy" Leemans of the New York Giants. He was built along the same lines, a shade under six feet, a compact 190 pounds. Tuffy didn't have the speed of legendary ball carriers or the finesse. He didn't have the reputation, either. But to Wellington Mara, the president of the Giants, Tuffy was something special.

"He was," said Mara, "exactly what his name implied. And he was the first player I ever signed for the Giants."

In 1935, Ned Irish, a New York sports writer, was moonlighting as a publicity man for the Giants. This same Ned Irish also had an idea for making basketball big time by putting it into Madison Square Garden. So he bought out-of-town newspapers to line up teams. In the Washington papers, Ned kept noticing the name of a halfback from George Washington—somebody called Tuffy Leemans, from Superior, Wisconsin. Ned mentioned him to Wellington, whose father founded the Giants and was now breaking him in, at twenty-years old as a football man.

Scouting then was not the computerized, elaborate science of today—players were drafted by their clippings and on hearsay. The Giants went for Leemans, in the first pro football draft ever held, on the second round. Mara went to Washington and signed him, for $2,000 a year and no bonus.

Reporting to the Giants in 1936, Tuffy carried the ball a record 206 times, gained 830 yards to top the NFL, and made the all-league team. Like Feathers, he never matched those figures again in eight professional seasons. But he was always a productive back who led the Giants to three Eastern division titles and one NFL championship and repeated as an all-pro in 1939.

"Tuffy would bump tacklers with his hips to get them off stride," recalled Jim Lee Howell, his Giant teammate. "He had balance and great moves, but no speed. He was an Alex Webster type [a Giant running back in the Howell coaching era of the 1950's]. Maybe not as strong, though he was big enough, but quicker."

And very determined. Every season, when the rookie running backs reported to New York's training camp, Tuffy assembled them for a lecture on the difference between college and pro running tactics. In college ball then, as now, the ball was dead once a runner's knees touched the ground. But in the pro ball of Leemans' time, a back could be knocked down, then get up and run again or even crawl if he weren't pinned by the tackler.

196

Tuffy Leemans answered at home to the name of Alphonse, but his nickname accurately described his running for the New York Giants.

Tuffy would demonstrate, then caution the neophytes, "But don't you guys ever try it in a game or you'll get killed."

But Tuffy did it and added multiple yards in his running ledger after being tackled. He was tough enough to get away with it.

ALPHONSE "TUFFY" LEEMANS

BORN: Nov. 12, 1912   Height: 6'0"   Weight: 200

George Washington University

New York Giants, 1937–43

| Year | G. | RUSHING | | | | | PASS RECEIVING | | | | SCORING | |
		Att.	Yds.	Avg.	TD.	P.C.	Yds.	Avg.	TD.	TD.	Pts.
1936	11	*206	*830	4.0	..	4	22	5.5	..	2	12
1937	9	144	429	3.0	..	11	157	14.3	1	1	6
1938	11	121	463	3.8	..	4	68	17.0	0	4	24
1939	11	128	429	3.4	..	8	185	23.1	2	5	30
1940	9	132	474	3.6	..	None				1	6
1941	11	100	332	3.3	..	None				4	24
1942	8	51	116	2.3	..	1	—10	—10.0	0	3	18
1943	10	37	69	1.9	..	None				0	0

PRO TOTALS

| —8 YEARS | 80 | 919 | 3142 | 3.4 | .. | 28 | 422 | 15.1 | 3 | 20 | 120 |

PASSING

Year	Att.	Cmp.	Pct.	Gain	T.P.	P.I.	Avg.
1936	42	13	31.0	258	..	6	6.14
1937	20	5	25.0	64	..	1	3.20
1938	42	19	45.2	249	..	6	5.93
1939	26	12	46.2	198	0	2	7.62
1940	31	15	48.4	159	..	3	5.13
1941	66	31	46.9	475	4	5	7.20
1942	69	35	50.7	555	7	4	8.04
1943	87	37	42.5	366	5	5	4.21

PRO
TOTALS—

| 8 YRS. | 383 | 167 | 43.6 | 2324 | 16 | 32 | 6.07 |

* Led NFL.

198

I'VE SEEN PLAYERS WITH GREATER ABIL-
ITY BUT NONE WHO TRIED HARDER AND
GAVE 100 PERCENT EFFORT AT ALL
TIMES.

—*Art Rooney, owner,
Pittsburgh Steelers.*

In the 1930's, the dominant rookie runners were coming along every two years. In '34 it was Feathers; in '36, Leemans. And in the fall of 1938, Byron "Whizzer" White consented to play pro football for the Pittsburgh Pirates (they became the Steelers officially a year later).

It meant another profound escalation of respectability for the pro game because the lure of playing for pay didn't suck up all the great All-Americans of that generation. Jay Berwanger of Chicago, the first man ever to be chosen in the pro draft (instituted in 1935), spurned a contract and never did play again. Bobby Grayson of Stanford, a two-time All-American, also nixed the pros. And so did such other illustrious backs of the 1930's as Clint Frank of Yale, Sam Chapman of California, and Eric Tipton of Duke.

But Whizzer White; he was something else. They don't hardly make them like the Whizzer any more. In the august black robes of a justice of the United States Supreme Court, appointed by President John F. Kennedy in 1962, he was still known affectionately as the Whizzer.

Byron Raymond White was a small-town Colorado youth with waves of brown hair and a bump on his nose. At the age of eight, he was working the beet fields around Wellington, population 350—"all God-fearing souls," White described them. He got a dollar a day, sometimes $2. As he got bigger, he worked on the railroad through town, on the way to Cheyenne, as a section hand. But sports were also a big part of the community life, and Byron played them all ("Whizzer" didn't become part of his name until he got to college, when a Denver sportswriter tagged him).

"Sports," he later reflected, "is the one way to get some absolute experience. . . . You are constantly being exposed to critical situations which require performance under pressure, and you have to respond."

However, he went to the University of Colorado on an academic scholarship. In four years at the Boulder school, he got two B's—all the rest A's. He was elected to Phi Beta Kappa. He was first in the graduating class of 267 and was president of the student body. And he waited tables in a fraternity house for his room and board.

Oh yes, in his spare time he won three varsity letters in football, three in baseball and four in basketball. The basketball got him to Madison Square Garden, then the mecca of the college game. The football made him a national celebrity. The baseball kept him busy in the spring. "You study on weekends," said Whizzer, "so your social life is sacrificed."

Colorado wasn't big time then on the gridiron. Little Colorado College (which had produced Dutch Clark a few years before) and Colorado Mines were on the schedule.

199

Byron "Whizzer" White, right, didn't linger long on the pro scene. But the future Supreme Court justice led the league as a rookie with Pittsburgh in 1938.

But Whizzer, operating as the deep man in the short punt formation, could run in any company, as he proved then and later. In 1937, his senior season, he led the nation in rushing, with 1,121 yards; in scoring, with sixteen touchdowns, twenty-three extra points and a field goal to boot; and in punt returns, with 731 yards in 36 chances. He completed 22 of 48 passes and punted for an average of 43.3 yards. He also was selected unanimously on the All-American teams which flourished at season's end, and Colorado, unbeaten and untied in eight games, was picked to play Rice in the Cotton Bowl, the first time a Rocky Mountain school was ever invited to a postseason classic.

While the team left for Texas to practice for the game, White went to San Francisco and won a Rhodes scholarship for studies at Oxford after graduation. He rejoined his teammates a week later and in the opening minutes of play electrified the Cotton Bowl crowd by taking the underdog Buffaloes to a quick touchdown, then intercepting a pass and running 50 yards to another score and a quick 14–0 lead. But as a team, little Colorado wasn't in the same class with Rice and was finally worn down to a 20–14 defeat. Whizzer was the best man on the field, though, and the Pittsburgh Pirates drafted him despite his announced intention to skip the pros and go to Oxford on his Rhodes grant.

Art Rooney, the Pittsburgh owner, sent colorful Johnny Blood west to give White a sales pitch. Blood, unpredictable and zany, was the coach and hardly a model of stability for a solid character like White. But Whizzer was impressed by Blood's erudition and sincerity. He still preferred the Rhodes scholarship, but Johnny had a persuasive point—Pittsburgh would pay him $15,000 a year, a record salary for professional football, more than any practicing star of the game was making. The final argument was the best. "You can play with us in the fall," said Blood, "and start on your Rhodes scholarship in January. We found out they'll wait."

So Whizzer White became a pro for a season, and the eastern skeptics waited to be shown he was worth that kind of money. They didn't wait long. In his first league game against the New York Giants, a model for pro defenses, Whizzer accounted for 191 yards. The Pirates weren't much of a team, winning only two of eleven games, yet the rookie from the wild West led the NFL in rushing with 567 yards. They were gained the hard way, since the high-priced whiz from the cow country was a target for tough old pros making half his salary, and less. Tuffy Leemans, in the defensive backfield of the Giants, stretched him out with a vicious tackle on one play and chortled, "I always wondered how it would feel to get my hands on a $15,000 player."

There were rumors the other Pittsburgh players didn't block for him because they resented his salary and his reclusive tendencies off the field. "Not so," said Izzy Weinstock, a Pitt All-American fullback who played on the same team. "Byron was liked by the players, but he was a loner. He'd disappear after practice. He had already disciplined himself. He had academic goals in mind, and he was home hitting the books."

In January 1939, he was on the boat to England and settled down behind the stone walls of Hertford College, Oxford. Ostensibly, his football career was over. Whizzer was scarcely acclimated to the Oxford scene, however, before Germany invaded Poland on September 1 to precipitate World War II. The scholarships were cut short, and the Americans at Oxford were hustled back home because the United States was neutral.

Still, Whizzer had no thoughts of football. He enrolled at Yale Law School in the fall, after his return, and devoted himself to the books for the rest of '39.

Pittsburgh, meanwhile, had dealt the right to negotiate with him to the Detroit Lions. Whizzer was not a rich kid. The itch to play football hadn't completely subsided, and again he was sold on the idea of coming back to the pros and studying law between seasons. He reported to the Lions in 1940, and stepped right in as the regular tailback and signal-caller, a guy who didn't join in the gin rummy games on road trips, but curled up with a law book and puffed contemplatively on a pipe.

Although he had been away a year, he led the NFL in rushing again and was picked on the official all-league team. As a runner, he was a slasher, a man who wasn't afraid to stick his 195 pounds into the whirlpool of the action. He was quietly tough and dedicated, and under normal circumstances might have had a long and illustrious career because he earnestly liked what he was doing.

"I liked professional football better than the college game," he said. "I enjoyed it, and I might have played more if the war hadn't broken out."

After the '41 season, and Pearl Harbor, he enlisted in the Navy and served with distinction in the South Pacific as an intelligence officer. There he renewed a friendship with another young officer he had met in London during his Rhodes scholarship days—John F. Kennedy. His football career was truly over. After the war, he was a law clerk for the Supreme Court, then went back to legal practice in his native Colorado. He was politically involved when Kennedy ran for president in 1960, and two years later was appointed an Associate Justice of the Supreme Court.

More than a quarter of a century after his last game, he still carried his playing weight. His face was strong, but the hair was graying and vanishing, and the half-shell glasses were a constant part of him. But even past fifty, he retained an athletic uniqueness.

Whizzer White was the only Associate Justice of the Supreme Court who used the gym in the building to play basketball with the young clerks and pages.

BYRON "WHIZZER" WHITE

BORN: June 18, 1917   Height: 6'1"   Weight: 195

University of Colorado

Pittsburgh, 1938
Detroit, 1940–41

| Year | G. | RUSHING | | | | PASS RECEIVING | | | | SCORING | |
		Att.	Yds.	Avg.	TD.	P.C.	Yds.	Avg.	TD.	TD.	Pts.
1938	11	152	*567	3.6	4	7	88	12.6	0	4	24
1939			(did not play)								
1940	11	146	*514	3.5	5	4	55	13.8	0	5	32
1941	11	89	238	2.7	3	5	158	31.6	1	4	24

PRO TOTALS

—3 YEARS	33	387	1319	3.4	12	16	301	18.8	1	13	80

PASSING

Year	G.	Att.	Comp.	Pct.	Yds.	TD.P.
1938	11	73	29	39.7	393	1
1939			(inactive)			
1940	11	80	35	43.8	461	1
1941	11	62	22	35.5	338	2

PRO TOTALS
—3 YEARS   33   215   86   40.0   1192   4

11. The T-Totalizers

Steve Van Buren

HE WAS THE JIMMY BROWN OF HIS
TIME; PEOPLE DON'T APPRECIATE WHAT
STEVE VAN BUREN DID.
   —*Allie Sherman, former teammate,
   Philadelphia Eagles.*

The rain sloshed down through the canyons of the Coliseum, that cavernous temple of sports in Los Angeles, with its main floor below the level of Figueroa Street. The ground soaked up the torrents like a sponge and then when it could hold no more, threw it off like a squeezed squeegee so that when a man stepped on it, he felt like a barefoot grape trampler. And when he ran on it, he looked like a cop slipping on a banana in a Mack Sennett comedy.

This was the kind of surface they asked Steve Van Buren to run on that wet day in December 1949, when the Philadelphia Eagles met the Los Angeles Rams for the championship of the National Football League. And run he did, though Dan Reeves, the owner of the Rams, tried to get Commissioner Bert Bell to postpone the game. Bell was back in Philadelphia by his radio set. "The commissioner, who is 3,000 miles away," reported Reeves acidly, "informed us that radio commitments make a postponement impossible."

Van Buren was the kind of ball carrier who leaned at a 45-degree angle tilt when he turned the corner on his favorite slash inside or outside right tackle. The move required innate balance and, presumably, good footing. On this rainy day, in a quagmire of spongy grass and pure mud, Van Buren slithered through the Rams, over them, around them and past them thirty-one times for a total of 196 yards—more than nine times as much as the entire Ram backfield gained on the ground. Ironically, he never scored during the game, but his consistent charges backed the Rams repeatedly against their goal line. The Eagles tallied first on a Tommy Thompson-to-Pete Pihos pass for 31 yards against a Ram defense bunched for Van Buren's runs. And when the Rams were backed against their goal line in the third quarter, a punt by Bob Waterfield was blocked and scooped up in the end zone by the Eagles for a second touchdown. That was it for the day, a 14–0 victory, and the second straight world championship for the Philadelphia Eagles.

At that moment, Steve Van Buren was at a peak he'd never again achieve in his lifetime. He had led the NFL in rushing for the third straight year (and the fourth time in all) with a career high of 1,146 yards. He was on the edge of his twenty-ninth birthday, and it looked like nothing could stop him. He was making big money for those days, in the $15,000 range, so that he could indulge in his favorite diversion—curling up in the sack after a tough practice session, pulling on a big cigar and studying the *Morning Telegraph* to pick out his favorite ponies.

Steve wasn't the kind of guy who bothered anybody. He was quiet but not aloof—droll when he was with his buddies and not on public display. Football was his métier, and he worked at it. When the Eagles' defensive unit took over a practice drill (this was after he ceased being a two-way player to concentrate on his running), Steve didn't loaf. He'd sprint 100 yards the length of the field—at LSU he had been on the track team and for the first 50 yards nobody could beat him. He'd sprint 100 yards again, and walk back again. He'd repeat this routine ten times, and he did it every day.

Steve Van Buren ushered in the era of the speedy big back who could take advantage of the quick-hitting T-formation.

A broad-shouldered six-footer, deep-chested, with good legs and a wasp waist that limited his weight to 208 pounds, Steve was perfectly equipped for his job. He was the first of the modern era of speed backs with driving power who tore up pro defenses from the quick-hitting T-formation and set the trend for the same types who would come later —Jimmy Brown, Hugh McElhenny, Ollie Matson, Leroy Kelly, and O. J. Simpson.

And he was undone by a broken toe. It came early in the 1950 season, but Van insisted on playing, even after an operation failed to heal it properly. Missing two games, he still led the NFL in ball-carrying attempts, but his yardage was drastically reduced. Before every game, he'd have the toe jabbed with a shot of novocain so he could resist the pain. In 1951, his problems were complicated by bruised ribs, and he became a part-time player as the Eagles dipped to their first losing season since he joined them in 1944. In 1952, the toe started to heal. The ribs were all in place. And Van Buren, although he was thirty-one years old, announced on the eve of training camp, "I'm in great shape. I've been working out for a month and never felt better in my life. I'm ready."

On August 3, the Eagles held their first scrimmage of the year. On the second play, Van Buren took a handoff from quarterback Adrian Burk and slanted into the line. An ordinary play. An ordinary pileup as the defense reacted to meet him. But a rookie guard, who got his assignment mixed up, pulled out of the line and turned the wrong way. He collided with Van Buren on Steve's blind side. The runner got sandwiched between two tackles, and his left knee took the full impact of the rookie guard's blow. The knee ligaments were badly torn, and Van Buren's active career as a ball carrier was over. He tried to come back, but the knee had calcified after an operation and he lost the ability to pivot. He worked so hard he developed a spur on the inside of his big toe, and that really finished him. He never again carried the ball from scrimmage after his accident.

At the end, Van Buren held the following records for running in the National Football League:

Most rushing attempts, lifetime.
Most yards gained rushing, lifetime.
Most touchdowns rushing, lifetime.
Most yards gained rushing, season.
Most touchdowns rushing, season.
Most rushing attempts, championship game.
Most yards gained rushing, championship game.

Only the last two records, from that 1949 game in Los Angeles, remain on the books. All the rest have been exceeded by Jimmy Brown. But in the club annals of the Philadelphia Eagles, seventeen years after his retirement, Steve Van Buren retained the record for every category of ground gaining—a remarkable testimonial to his perpetuity as the greatest player in the team's history.

Van Buren came to the Eagles almost by accident. He scarcely heard of Philadelphia when the Eagles drafted him first after the 1943 season. On the train going north from Baton Rouge, Louisiana, he went right past the North Philadelphia station and wound up in New York. "We didn't pay much attention to pro football in those days," he reminisced. "The Bears and the Redskins were the only teams I knew about."

And if the Eagles were strange to him when he finally showed up at their training camp in Hershey, he looked only slightly less garish to them. The kid from Louisiana had on an open-necked shirt, no coat, carried a battered suitcase and had taken the trouble to wear a pair of shoes—but the feet inside them were bare, no socks.

"Take this kid," whispered Coach Earle "Greasy" Neale to Allie Sherman, a reserve quarterback out of Brooklyn College, "and get him some clothes." But otherwise, Greasy liked what he saw—a strong neck, firm jaw, a handsome, snub-nosed face with a deep tan and dark curly hair. In those days, that kind of specimen was rare in pro football camps. It was the middle of World War II, and all the prime guys were going off to the Army, Navy, and Marines. Van Buren was excepted because a childhood accident had left him with scarred vision in one eye.

The Eagles heard about him first through Bernie Moore, the coach at Louisiana State, who called Greasy, an old pal, and said, "This kid can make it for you. Give him as much as he wants." Steve wanted $10,000 but settled for less than half of that—he just wanted to play.

"I was an engineering student," he said, "when the Eagles offered me a job. I didn't even finish my course. I pulled out in the early spring of my senior year. I couldn't keep my mind on my books any longer. I had a job that suited me. I was going to run with the ball and get paid for it." Later in his career, Steve was called the Flying Dutchman, but it was a misnomer. He was born in Honduras and was of Spanish-English descent. His parents died when he was ten, and Steve, along with his brother Ebert, four years younger, came to New Orleans to live with his grandmother.

"I had no interest in football until I was fifteen," he said. "In Honduras, we'd never heard of it. We played simple running games. But in high school, I started to watch other guys playing football, and it seemed like a good game. But I weighed only 125 pounds, and when I went out for the team, the coach said, 'Forget it. You'll get hurt.'

"I left school after my first year and went to work in an iron foundry. It was hard work but I liked it, and it built me up. After two years, I thought I wouldn't get far without an education, so I went back to school."

This time the football coach put him on the squad, as an end. It wasn't the only time he was miscast in football uniform. When he went on to LSU, on a football scholarship, Coach Bernie Moore made him a blocking back. Bernie already had a fine tailback named Alvin Dark, a triple-threat from Lake Charles who was also making a fine reputation for himself every spring as a shortstop on the baseball team—he now manages the Cleveland Indians after a fine major league career. For two years, chunky Van Buren wiped out tacklers for Dark, but Alvin went into the service before the 1943 season, and Moore started looking around for a running replacement. Up stepped Van Buren to fill the breach. He gained 832 yards as a senior, and in the Orange Bowl game against Texas A&M, he scored all three touchdowns in a 19–14 victory, running 35 and 55 yards for two of the touchdowns and catching a pass for the other. "I think I made a mistake with you," Moore told Van Buren years later, when Steve had achieved prominence as the greatest runner of his time.

Under Neale, there was no question about what Van Buren was going to be. "A running back," said Greasy. "That's all he wants to do, run. He's a fair kicker, but he

210

could be better. He's a pretty good pass catcher, but he could improve himself. When he gets out to practice, all he wants to do is run."

Van Buren, geared to running, had a unique philosophy about the passing game which eventually dominated the pros. "The guy who threw the first forward pass must have been through as a football player," he said, "or just too tired that day to run with the ball."

Greasy Neale was smart enough to capitalize on Van Buren's desire to run. He never babied him. Against the New York Bulldogs in 1949, the Flying Dutchman carried the ball thirty-five times in one afternoon. As a rookie in 1944, he missed several games because of an appendectomy but nevertheless was chosen on the AP all-pro team. The next year, he moved into high gear and led the NFL in ground gaining while setting a league record of fifteen touchdowns rushing.

"He made me a great coach," said Neale. "There never was a player quite like him. He had the greatest head and shoulder fakes I've ever seen. He was better than Grange because Grange needed a blocker. This boy didn't. He could run away from tacklers like Red, or over them like Nagurski."

Van Buren was distinctive. He always carried the ball in his right hand, a trait that was the legacy of an old shoulder injury. Neale tried to get him to run with his head up. Van Buren preferred to duck his helmet and burrow through tacklers. He tried the straight-up style once at Greasy's behest and came back to the bench, reeling, his eye puffed up. "Now I know why I've been keeping my head down all these years," he groused.

He played with a fever of 103 degrees in an exhibition game against the Detroit Lions. "Van was sick all week," recalled Sonny Karnofsky, a young back who joined the Eagles in '45. "He wasn't supposed to play, and he had this fever, but he insisted on sitting on the bench. Then he jumped into the game. We were about midfield when he got the ball. He must have crisscrossed half a dozen times, with tacklers bouncing off him. He easily covered 100 yards before he finally shook loose. He ran full speed into the end zone and then passed out."

When Van Buren hit a man, the shock lingered. It didn't matter which team the victim was on, the Eagles or the opposition. On one of his patented swings around the flank, he cut a little sharper than normal and ran up the back of Jack Ferrante, an Eagle end. Ferrante dropped like a triphammer and shook his head woozily. The other team's tackle bent over him and said, "Hurts, doesn't it? Now you know what it's like for us when we try to tackle him."

The Green Bay Packers had a big linebacker, Dick Wildung, who was congratulating himself one afternoon for stopping Van Buren cold on successive plays: "Better tell your quarterback to stop calling those plays," Wildung taunted him, "or you're going to get killed in front of all these people." Back to the huddle, Van Buren dragged himself, and told Tommy Thompson, the quarterback, "Gimme the ball again." He took the handoff and ran straight at Wildung, hit him with a shoulder, trampled him and kept going.

Behind that quietness was a tough guy. The Steelers had a lineman who was roughing Van up on every play—gouging him after the whistle, shoving an elbow in his stomach, bringing his knee up when they were on ground, even a fist under his chin.

It was dirty stuff camouflaged in pileups. It was a playoff game in 1947 for the Eastern title, and Van kept himself in check. But after the Eagles had piled up a 21–0 lead, he turned to the quarterback and ordered, "Lefty, call '39' on the next play." Then he turned to a couple of the Eagle linemen responsible for double-teaming the Steeler and said, "You guys get out of the way. I want that Steeler all to myself."

Allie Sherman, now the Giant coach, was "Lefty" and recreated the situation: "I hated to call the play because, like the other Eagles, I idolized Steve and didn't want to see him get hurt, though I knew he'd take care of himself. But what could I do? I slipped him the ball on '39' and went through my fake, then turned around to look. Well, Steve was 20 yards down the field and this Steeler was flat on his back at the line of scrimmage. I'll never forget it. His eyes were rolling around in his head, spinning like pinwheels."

That year, Steve gained 1,008 yards from scrimmage, the second man in pro history to top the grand mark, and beat Beattie Feathers' record by four yards. He also scored touchdowns in eight consecutive games, something that even Jimmy Brown never did. The Eagles won their first division title in history but succumbed to the Chicago Cardinals in the championship game when Elmer Angsman and Charley Trippi broke loose for four long touchdown runs while the Cardinal defense bottled up Van Buren and held him to 26 yards in eighteen carries on a frozen field.

The two teams met again for the title in 1948 under the most abominable conditions in history. The biggest blizzard in Philadelphia weather records obliterated everything but the outlines of old Shibe Park, where the game was to be played. The snow came down so heavy that the tarpaulin covering the field couldn't be raised. It didn't matter. The snow was so deep, nothing would have been visible anyhow. Commissioner Bell got the players from both teams together at noon and asked them if they wanted to play. They nodded, and the game went on. Officials had to guess at the yard markers as the flakes kept piling up in white drifts. And yet 36,000 people squeezed into the old baseball park.

Early in the game, quarterback Tommy Thompson called an "81 special" to end Jack Ferrante, a straight "fly" pass which no one expected in this kind of weather. Ferrante mushed past the Cardinal secondary and caught the ball in full stride to complete a 65-yard maneuver. But outlined against the white December turf lay the head linesman's red flag.

"Offsides, Eagles," he signalled bravely.

And Ferrante, heated by his exertions, asked in a rage, "Who? Who was offsides?"

"You," said the official succinctly. The score was disallowed, and the teams wallowed through a standoff into the second half.

Two plays before the end of the third quarter, Bucko Kilroy forced the break; the Eagle guard plopped on a fumble at the Cardinal 17-yard line after a mixup in the Chicago backfield. Bosh Prichard skidded six yards for the Eagles on the last play of the period.

Fullback Joe Muha picked up three; Thompson sneaked for three more. And through the softly falling flakes came the din of the stands, "Give it to Steve! Give it to Steve!"

Thompson heeded the clamor. He handed off to Van Buren, who moved toward the left side. He saw a hole open up briefly between tackle and end. Like a Yukon trapper, he

212

Blasting straight ahead through the Washington Redskins for the 1948 Eastern Division title, Steve Van Buren raised clouds of dust for the Philadelphia Eagles.

Tackling Steve Van Buren was a gang effort, as shown here by the Pittsburgh Steelers.

cut surely on the snow and dove through the opening five yards into the end zone. The Eagles won, 7–0.

It was strange that Thompson took so long to call Van Buren's number. Allie Sherman recalled one game in which, as a third string quarterback, he had marched the Eagles down to the other team's four-yard line, first and goal to go. On first down, he handed off to Van Buren, who picked up a yard and a half. "On second down," Sherman said, "I thought I'd cross them up. I gave the ball to our fullback, Joe Muha, who was stopped cold. So I went back to Van Buren, and he scored. I was feeling pretty good about it when we're coming off the field, and all of a sudden Greasy's standing in front of my nose giving me hell.

" 'What's the matter?' I asked him.

" 'What the hell you trying to do out there?' Greasy roared.

"So I told him, 'We scored six points, didn't we?'

" 'Sure,' he said, 'but what happened on second down?' I explained that I thought they were laying for Van Buren and I'd try to cross them.

" 'Listen,' he said, 'any time you got the ball on the four-yard line, don't get fancy. Not with Van Buren around. I want him to get the ball every time, see!' "

But Supersonic Steve (another of his names) was not just an automaton as a football player. "He was smart," noted Sherman. "I remember during the war we had to work in the Philadelphia shipyards. I got all A's in college. I got a job loading cargo on the docks. Steve, he worked in the engineering office."

But he was also complacent and he liked the good times, and when his football career was done, Steve couldn't get motivated toward a new life. He had some business failures; he worked in public relations for the Eagles a while; he finally ended up coaching at the minor league level.

But of his playing days, he could say with pride, "I set a record every year I wasn't hurt." And the Eagles realized better than anyone else what he meant to them. Philadelphia never had a winning season until Steve Van Buren showed up, without socks, in 1944. When he hurt his big toe and faltered, after the 1949 title game in the Los Angeles rain, the Eagles went into a decline for the next decade.

STEPHEN "STEVE" VAN BUREN

BORN: Dec. 28, 1920   Height: 6'0"   Weight: 200

Louisiana State University

Philadelphia Eagles, 1944–51

Year	G.	Att.	Yds.	Avg.	TD.	P.C.	Yds.	Avg.	TD.	TD.	Pts.
			RUSHING				PASS RECEIVING			SCORING	
1944	9	80	444	5.5	5		(None)			7	42
1945	10	143	*832	5.8	*15	10	123	12.3	2	*18	*110
1946	9	116	529	4.6	5	6	55	9.1	0	6	36
1947	12	*217	*1008	4.6	*13	9	79	8.7	0	*14	84
1948	11	*201	*945	4.7	*10	10	96	9.6	0	10	60
1949	12	*263	*1146	4.4	*11	4	88	22.0	1	12	72
1950	10	*188	629	3.3	4	2	34	17.0	0	4	24
1951	10	112	327	2.9	6	4	28	7.0	0	6	36

PRO TOTALS

| —8 YEARS | 83 | 1320 | 5860 | 4.4 | 69 | 45 | 503 | 11.2 | 3 | 77 | 464 |

* Led NFL.

George McAfee

THE HIGHEST COMPLIMENT YOU CAN
PAY A BALL CARRIER IS JUST TO COM-
PARE HIM WITH GEORGE MCAFEE.
—*George Halas, coach,*
Chicago Bears.

The speed of George McAfee made the Chicago Bears' halfback a difficult man to drag down in the open field.

In the projection room on the eighteenth floor of the Coliseum Tower offices at Columbus Circle, Ken Kavanaugh was threading a roll of film. The New York Giants' coaches were in session, reviewing the plays of the 1968 season. And Kavanaugh, an assistant coach, who handled the ends, was asked by an intruder, "What would you do with George McAfee if you had him today? Where would he play?"

"Play?" responded Kavanaugh incredulously. "Any place you wanted him!"

"But he'd have to be a flanker. He couldn't be a running back."

"Why not?" challenged Kavanaugh. He had been McAfee's teammate on the Chicago Bears when George played halfback and Ken was an all-pro end.

"Well, he weighed only 175. He couldn't take the punishment of a running back today."

"They'd have to tackle him first," shrugged Ken. "No one touched George."

"Get him for us," urged Coach Allie Sherman, walking by. "We'd put in a couple of running plays for him."

George McAfee was a fleeting spectre in the panorama of pro football—his tenure was interrupted by a four-year stint in the Navy—but the few glimpses of him at his peak insured his stature as one of the most elusive runners in history.

"He was the first man," said Kavanaugh, "I ever saw who could run off balance. One leg would be one way, and the other leg would be the other way high off the ground, and his body going a third way, and he still wouldn't go down."

Even the statistics for McAfee are illusory. His heaviest duty as a ball carrier came in 1948, when he was thirty years old and rushed 92 times from scrimmage. He never gained more than 474 yards on the ground in a single season, and his biggest year as a pass receiver netted thirty-two catches, which would hardly keep company with a good tight end these days. He generally played no more than 30 minutes a game.

What was there about George McAfee that elicited the following raves?

Clark Shaughnessy: ". . . the greatest all-around back I have ever seen."

Curly Lambeau: ". . . the best and most dangerous man the Packers have ever faced."

Greasy Neale: ". . . the greatest plunging and quick opening back I have ever seen."

Jock Sutherland: ". . . Frank Merriwell come to life."

Hunk Anderson: "I played with Gipp and I saw plenty of Grange, but McAfee is better than either one of them."

He was human, too. A rather scrawny looking man who was listed at 180 pounds in the program sometimes, but probably never weighed more than 170. He had sandy hair that waved left and right from a part in the middle, a thin nose, gaunt cheeks and a little quizzical frown. His shanks were lean and slightly bowlegged. But George McAfee had one big physical attribute; from the back of the neck, he looked like a football player.

"He was," said Wallace Wade, his coach at Duke University, "really a one-man offense and practically unstoppable. He was a great kicker, great runner, great passer and one of the best receivers I've ever seen. He was a terrific safety man, too."

This was while George was in college (and although he was on the Duke varsity from 1937 to 1939, he really played full time only as a senior). Two years later, when McAfee was a fully-fledged pro, Wade wrote George Halas of the Bears: "I was amazed at the improvement in McAfee. He was a great player when I had him. Now he's the finest back I've ever seen anywhere, any time."

But for Dick Gallagher, the memories were different. Dick is the director of Pro Football's Hall of Fame (into which George was inducted in 1966). Before that, he was the general manager of the Buffalo Bills and a long-time college and pro coach—he helped organize the Cleveland Browns. And even before that, he was the high school coach in Ironton, Ohio, a smoky little town of 15,000 on the southernmost bend of the Ohio River, where the hills rising on either side spew out iron ore and coal. The McAfee brothers were already an athletic legend in Ironton when Gallagher was there in the early 1930's. Their dad was a secretary for the YMCA set up by the Chesapeake and Ohio Railroad in Russell, Kentucky, on the other side of the bridge from Ironton. They were clean-living, disciplined, dedicated boys—all eight of them. George was fifth in the line of succession. (There were three sisters, too.)

"First I remember of him," said Gallagher, "was this little spindle-legged kid, thirteen years old, always knocking on the window to get a ball. The McAfees only lived two blocks from me. I was the recreation director of the city, too. So George always wanted a ball, any kind—football, basketball, baseball. He was just one of those naturals—like Otto Graham and Wes Fesler. He could play anything. He had a tryout with the Reds in baseball. He scored eleven points in about five different events in the state track meet."

When he came under Gallagher's tutelage in high school, George led Ironton to an undefeated football season and was the all-state quarterback. He weighed 152 pounds. "But I was never conscious of the size," noted Gallagher. "He never got hurt. And you just knew he was going to be great."

His older brother John had played at Ohio State with Sid Gillman under Francis X. Schmidt, but George leaned toward a southern school because of his interest in track and baseball, especially after a visit to Columbus, where Schmidt snubbed him and George had to hop a ride home on a coal truck. A Duke University recruiter happened to be admiring the scenery in Ironton and marched young McAfee off to Durham, North Carolina, for the next four years. They were not especially noteworthy years for George. Wade, building one of the college football dynasties in the nation, didn't believe in playing his sophomores too much, so George was the second string wingback in 1937. He played only five minutes in 1938 because of a troublesome callous on the sole of his foot which refused to heal and eventually required surgery.

That was the year Duke, led by All-Americans Eric Tipton and Dan Hill, went through the season unbeaten, untied and unscored upon to win a Rose Bowl invitation. Duke went unscored upon for 59 minutes against mighty Southern California, too, until a third string tailback threw a last-minute touchdown pass to upset the Blue Devils, 7–3.

220

McAfee's contribution to all this, while minimal, was important: Duke was locked in a tough battle with North Carolina, which had George Stirnweiss (later a Yankee infielder) at tailback, when McAfee made a brief appearance and climbed the back of a Carolina defender to catch a long pass down by the goal line and set up a vital touchdown.

During his senior year, in which Duke lost only to Pittsburgh, 14–13, George's talents finally flourished and attracted the pros. The Bears, after a trade for Philadelphia's first draft choice, picked McAfee because Halas was always intrigued by speed, and George had been timed in 9.7 for the 100-yard dash. Mrs. Halas liked him, too. She picked George up in Chicago the next summer and drove him to the Bears' camp in Delafield, Wisconsin, and always thereafter considered him her discovery.

"We arrived at noon on a Sunday," McAfee recalled, "and the Bears were having their first scrimmage. I never had seen so many big men in my life. The first play, Bill Osmanski, the big fullback, broke through the line and Harry Clark, another rookie half-back (and later an all-league choice), came up fast to make the tackle. He was knocked cold, and I had something that stayed with me the rest of the time I was a pro—a picture of Harry there on the ground, cold as a stone. I made up my mind to run as fast as I could if there was any kind of daylight."

The Bears put him in a scrimmage, and Sid Luckman, who had just been converted to quarterback in the newly designed T-formation of the Bears, called for the 170-pound halfback to dart straight ahead on a dive play.

On the sidelines, Coach Halas turned to an aide and muttered, "The linebacker's smelled what's coming. The kid'll get killed."

The linebacker's intuition was good. McAfee did come straight at him. But when he charged ahead to devour him, he grasped only air. George gave him a leg and pulled it away. Balancing delicately and turning on a burst of motion at the same time, he squeezed through the hole and was gone.

"I think," said Halas softly, "we've got something there."

In a preseason night game at Ebbets Field against the Brooklyn Dodgers, who were coming under the spartan whip of Dr. Jock Sutherland, the Bears were trailing 9–7 with 25 seconds remaining for an incipient stunning upset. The Dodgers, on fourth down, felt safe in kicking deep to the Bears, confident they'd hold them long enough to run out the clock. They didn't know McAfee. He caught the punt on his own 25-yard line, darted one way, cut the other, weaved down the middle, eluded half a dozen clutches and ran the 75 yards for the winning touchdown. The McAfee legend was beginning, and eventually he would be called "One-Play" McAfee, for his ability to break open a game.

Sid Luckman, usually soft-spoken, got up on a bench in the dressing room and barked, like a sideshow spieler, "Ladies and gentlemen, you've heard about it. You've read about it. You've seen it in the movies. But here it is—in person—the one, the only, the original *Gone with the Wind*." He pointed to the thin man wearing No. 5. McAfee blushed.

George was embarrassed by exaggerated publicity. In one of his first Bear scrimmages, he carried the ball three times with negligible results, and a Chicago paper headlined him as the star of the session.

"He went to Halas, fuming," recalled Ken Kavanaugh, "the only time I ever saw him mad. He said, 'I won't have this. I won't put up with this. If you can't get those writers to tell it right, I'm leaving. I don't need it.'"

A little literary license in describing McAfee was understandable. The Bears unveiled him in Green Bay the opening game of the 1940 season after the Packers took the lead with a field goal. McAfee raced the kickoff back 93 yards to a touchdown and the start of a 41–10 rout. He later passed left-handed to Kavanaugh for a touchdown.

That Bear squad was one of the greatest in history, with three full sets of great backs. Even McAfee's use was rationed as he shared a halfback assignment with Hugh Gallarneau. The Bears won their division title and met the Washington Redskins for the championship. On Chicago's first play from scrimmage, Luckman handed off to George, who picked up eight yards on a dive play. The Redskins were alerted to his threat. When the next play started with the same action, they bunched to head him off. Luckman faked the handoff to McAfee and gave the ball instead to fullback Bill Osmanski, who went wide around left end for a 68-yard scoring gallop. They were off to the races in that fantastic 73–0 victory, to which McAfee later contributed a 34-yard touchdown dash with an intercepted pass.

Yes, he played defense, too, a brilliant safety who made teeth-jarring tackles and in 1941 picked off a record number of six interceptions. That 1941 season was, in his own opinion, the best of his pro career.

"I played a lot," said George modestly. And ran a lot—on kickoffs, punts, interceptions, and pass receptions, as well as from scrimmage. He scored twelve touchdowns to lead the NFL and was a unanimous all-pro selection. Jimmy Conzelman, the coach of the rival Chicago Cardinals, rhapsodized, "McAfee is a sprinter, and yet he has in addition to the cross step, which most great runners possess, a hip shift. That's something few fast men ever develop. He puts the defense off balance and fakes you with his head, as well as his legs and body." His average of 7.3 yards per carry in 1941 led the league, and the Bears powered to their second straight world championship with McAfee and Norm Standlee, a 230-pound rookie fullback from Stanford, giving them an unstoppable inside-outside thrust.

Then George went off to war, serving most of the next four seasons in the Navy. He rejoined the Bears in time to play three games in December, 1945. McAfee could have jumped for bigger money to the All-American Conference. His old high school coach, Dick Gallagher, was signing talent for the Cleveland Browns. Gallagher was also the best man at McAfee's wedding. But Dick didn't want to trample in Halas' territory. Just to secure his chattel, Halas then made the unprecedented move of giving McAfee a three-year contract. He also endorsed it, as follows: "McAfee is the greatest back of all time. He's in a class by himself as a runner, and he can block, tackle, pass and kick with the best."

If there was any doubt that George still had his old zip, he quickly dispelled it against the Pittsburgh Steelers. Halas told him he'd only play a few minutes because he wasn't in shape.

"It's okay, Coach," nodded McAfee. "I understand."

222

He played twelve minutes and carried the ball only five times. He gained 105 yards and scored three touchdowns. That was the old McAfee. An injury limited his work the following season, but from 1947 through 1949, he was a heavy duty performer on both offense and defense. And in 1950, fading gracefully at the age of thirty-two, he returned 33 punts, top total in the league, after which he retired.

His association with football remained through 1966, however. Every weekend he'd commute from home in Durham, North Carolina, where he ran the McAfee Brothers Oil Company, to work as a head linesman in NFL games.

As a football official, he was respected for his alertness and judgment. But one Sunday in 1961, the Detroit Lions accomplished what every team in the NFL had failed to do during the eight seasons in which George McAfee participated as an active player. In a game against the Baltimore Colts, Lion defensive players, following the flow of action, levelled every man in sight. And that included head linesman George McAfee on two occasions.

They never did it when George McAfee as a player had a ball tucked in his arms.

GEORGE MCAFEE'S FAVORITE PLAY:

"My favorite running play was the quick opener, run from the T-formation with the left halfback going in motion to the right. It was called '43B-26' in the Bear terminology.

"The play was designed to get the right halfback through the line and into the open with a chance to go all the way for a touchdown.

"Its success depended on the center blocking their right linebacker in the 6-2-2-1 defense, with the right guard and tackle blocking their counterparts on the other side of the line. The left halfback in motion hopefully pulls the left linebacker with him. The fullback also fakes to the right, and the quarterback hands off to the right half on a quick opener.

"This play was used against the Pittsburgh Steelers in December, 1945, when I went 47 yards for a score. It was my second game after coming back from service, and I was concerned whether or not I could run on an injured foot, hurt while I was in the Navy."

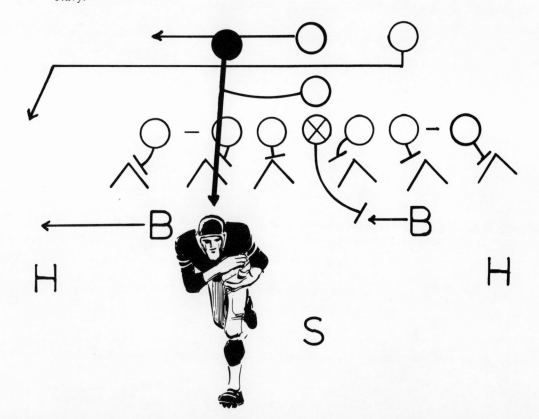

GEORGE ANDERSON MCAFEE

BORN: March 13, 1918   Height: 6'0''   Weight: 170

Duke University

Chicago Bears, 1940–41, 1945–50

Year	G.	RUSHING				PASS RECEIVING				SCORING	
		Att.	Yds.	Avg.	TD.	P.C.	Yds.	Avg.	TD.	TD.	Pts.
1940	10	47	253	5.4	..	7	117	16.7	0	3	18
1941	10	65	474	*7.3	..	7	144	20.6	3	*12	72
1942–43–44					(In Military Service)						
1945	3	16	139	8.6	3	3	85	28.3	1	4	24
1946	3	14	53	3.8	0	10	137	13.7	3	3	18
1947	12	63	209	3.3	3	32	490	15.3	1	4	24
1948	12	92	392	4.3	5	17	227	13.4	1	8	48
1949	12	42	161	3.8	3	9	157	17.4	1	5	30
1950	12	2	4	2.0	0	(None)				0	0

PRO TOTALS
—8 YEARS 74 341 1685 4.9 14   85 1357 16.0 10   39 234

* Led NFL.

Bill Dudley

HE RAN LIKE HE WAS STAGGERING,
THREW THE BALL LIKE IT WAS A LOAF
OF BREAD AND KICKED IT CLUMSIER
THAN ANYBODY I'VE EVER SEEN. ALL HE
COULD DO WAS BEAT YOU.
—*Paul Christman, quarterback
and commentator.*

What he lacked in size and speed, Bullet Bill Dudley made up in determination and dedication.

Bullet Bill Dudley was not a picture book athlete. He got short-changed when mother nature carved her little sculpture to produce an imperfect halfback from the Blue Ridge Mountains of Virginia. He was too young, too short, too light and too slow—debits that would have resigned any other human being to a seat in the stands instead of out on the field where the action was.

It is the destiny of men like William M. Dudley to have their credentials challenged at every stage of their athletic lives.

In fiction it reads great. Hero struggles against adversity. Hero conquers obstacles. Hero reaps the reward. Horatio Alger patented the formula, and the rags-to-riches syndrome became a part of the American dream.

In real life, it can be damn discouraging, as Bill Dudley can tell you. He was the twelve-year-old kid who entered high school in Bluefield, Virginia, and wanted to go out for the football team. But the coach asked him what he weighed, and when little Bill said 110, the coach didn't even have a uniform that would fit him.

But our Bill was determined. He had bought books by Knute Rockne and other experts of the gridiron telling him how to play football, and he pored over them. He also practiced drop-kicking by himself until he scuffed his toes through. Then he went out for football again the next year. Weight: 115. The coach let him on the squad but wouldn't let him play. He walked a two-mile paper route at 5 o'clock every morning, and he practiced football until dusk. He had the American dream. That's all it was. A dream. Until Bill turned sixteen and stayed in high school an extra year. He finally played.

He was the squad punter, had learned to place-kick, was tenacious on defense, and a baffling, determined runner. In the last game of his last year, little Bluefield played big Princeton from across the state line in West Virginia. The young tailback of the Virginia team stunned Princeton with a quick touchdown. Princeton tied the game in the second half. But with little more than a minute to play, Dudley drove his team to the enemy 20-yard line, stepped back and calmly kicked a 37-yard field goal for the victory. Maybe Horatio Alger knew what he was writing about.

That kind of performance should have brought the colleges running after him. He wanted to go either to Virginia Tech or Washington and Lee. Neither was interested in a 150-pound tailback. However, the University of Virginia, which had won just five games in three years, over such schools as St. John's and Hampton-Sydney, would take a chance on him. It offered him a scholarship of $500, to cover everything—but it figured on Bill only as a kicking specialist. He had never missed an extra point in high school.

In Dudley's first varsity season with Virginia in 1939, when he was seventeen years old, Bill was installed as the regular tailback on offense, the safety on defense, and the Cavaliers won five games. They almost upset Navy, losing 14–12. In his senior year, they lost only one game, a 21–19 thriller to Yale.

Dudley had already acquired a nickname—Bullet Bill. He finished his career with a brilliant flourish against arch-rival North Carolina. First, he threw a pass for a 67-yard touchdown play. Then he circled end and ran 60 yards to the end zone. Next, he dropped back to punt from his 11-yard line but took off instead and twisted 89 yards for a score. And he closed out the afternoon by bulling three yards up the middle for a fourth touchdown. He kicked all the extra points as Virginia won, 28–7. Bill was chosen on the major all-American teams. He was nineteen years old, and the good things were still to come.

In succession, he became a professional football star, made the all-league team his first two seasons in the NFL, married a beautiful blonde campus queen, became the highest paid player since Red Grange, was a highly respected pro for more than a decade, retired to become the most successful insurance man in western Virginia, was elected to the pro Hall of Fame and ultimately was elected to the state legislature. Perserverance, hard work, and dedication had made little Bill Dudley of Bluefield, Virginia, an American success.

But the carping critics—in football, at least—looked at him, 5'10" and 182 pounds at his best, and said, "It can't be." So Bill had to go out and show them.

He joined an All-Star team for a game against the Washington Redskins in 1943. In practice, the fifteen backs chosen ran 100-yard sprints for time. Bill finished fifteenth. But during the game, he intercepted a pass and ran 98 yards for a touchdown.

A Steeler assistant coach said after one game, "Dudley did a good job out there, but he didn't hit the right holes."

"Lucky for us," retorted owner Art Rooney. "If he ever starts hitting the right holes, the other team will never be able to stop us. We'd score so easily the games would get boring and the fans would probably stop coming to see us."

The Steelers were in their tenth year of existence when Bullet Bill joined them in 1942. He had sprained both ankles in All-Star games. The Steelers, coming off a 1-9-1 record in '41, had never had a winning season and had finished last five times.

On the second play of the opening game against the Philadelphia Eagles, Bill lined up at left halfback in the Steeler single wing and took the direct snap from center moving a step to his right. But he veered suddenly and cut back between center and left guard as Vern Martin, playing quarterback (or blocking back in that formation) moved across and cut down the Eagle right tackle. Bullet Bill burst through the hole, faked the safety out of position and raced 56 yards for a touchdown.

It was the start of a big year. He led the NFL in rushing as a rookie with 696 yards, which was to be his career high. He handled the passing, the punting, the place-kicking, and played a tremendous brand of defense. He also led the league in punt returns and was a unanimous all-league choice as the Steelers finished second with a 7–4 record, their most successful season in history.

Then Bullet Bill went off to serve in the Air Force most of the next three years in which he also made All-Service playing for the star-packed teams of Randolph and March Fields and then took part in the air offensive against Japan. He returned to Pittsburgh in late 1945 just in time to play the last four games of the season. The Steelers were winless when he joined them. He scored two touchdowns to pace a 23–0 victory over the Chicago Cardinals.

"That Man Is Back!" a Pittsburgh paper trumpeted in headlines.

228

"That Man" was really an ebullient boy parading around in a man's body. He was unabashedly rah-rah in his approach to the pros. To those tough, sometimes cynical veterans, he preached the homilies of the good life—no drinking, no smoking, no cussing. He could have been resented. But Bill made his brand of leadership stick because he was a practicing example of what the virtues would get you.

He was also a frank guy who spoke his mind. Dr. Jock Sutherland—austere, aloof, severe—came in to coach the Steelers in '46. Dudley was good-neighborly, amiable, and informal. Their personalities didn't mix. After he had trouble hitting his receivers in a team practice drill, Dudley suggested, "I think we'd do better if you used different colored jerseys so we could tell the receivers from the defenders."

Sutherland stared at him icily. "Are you coaching this team?" he asked. There was a strained silence on the practice field.

"No, sir," said Bill politely, "I am not."

"Then you take orders like anyone else."

Bill was no problem that way. He again led the NFL in rushing. He also led it in pass interceptions, with ten returned for a total of 242 yards, and Steve Owen, that master defensive strategist of the New York Giants, called him ". . . the best defensive back in football." He averaged between 52 and 56 minutes a game. And it was tough on a guy who only weighed 182 pounds.

"He used to get creamed so bad playing that old Steeler single wing, we called him Flat Top," recalled Paul Christman, then the quarterback of the Cardinals. "He was also the only breakaway runner I know who could get you that yard when you needed it. He punted well enough [40-yard average on 60 punts in 1946], kicked off, kicked field goals, extra points, threw passes, fielded punts [led the league in that department, too, with 27 for 385 yards], returned kickoffs, and tackled with more guts than brains."

But he was also smart enough to know he couldn't keep it up. He wasn't getting along with Sutherland, either. The chirpy little man from Virginia was unhappy and reacted in the only way he knew. After the season he got married and took a job as an assistant coach at his alma mater, Virginia. "I'm too small for pro football," he announced.

What he meant was that he was too small to play football for the Pittsburgh Steelers the way Sutherland ran the show. The Detroit Lions didn't take his retirement seriously. They traded two good backs, Bobby Cifers and Paul White, plus the draft rights to touted All-Americans Bob Chappuis and Bobby Layne, for Dudley. They paid for his honeymoon and they gave him a $25,000 no-cut contract, a sum unmatched since the Bears had enticed Red Grange off the Illinois campus in 1926. This was enough to persuade Bill that maybe he was big enough for pro football, and vice versa.

He reported to the Lions, who were coached by Gus Dorais. Dorais told him he didn't have to take part in the first scrimmage. Bill insisted and suffered a deeply gashed lip. He trotted to the sidelines, got it stitched quickly and then insisted on going back in. When the Lions met to elect a captain before the start of the season, Dudley got every vote but one—his own. In much the same way, Dudley did for the Lions what he had done for the Steelers. He was used for every facet of the game, though the load was lightened when Bo McMillin took over as coach in 1948 and installed the T-formation, with Dudley playing halfback and the man in motion, which took him out of the heavy contact. He had three good years in Detroit, but the Lions weren't yet a good team. In 1950, they traded him to the Washington Redskins. He rounded out his career with three seasons in Washington. The long, spectacular play remained a specialty with him until the end.

On December 3, 1950, he retreated to deep safety in a punt situation against Pittsburgh. Joe Geri of the Steelers angled a kick 60 yards towards the proverbial coffin corner of the Redskins. Dudley raced over to the sidelines, nimbly kept both feet in bounds with a semblance of an entrechat and reached out over the chalk stripe for the ball. The Steelers, figuring it was going out of bounds for sure, relaxed a second. Dudley looked quickly at the referee, who nodded. The ball was still in play. He pivoted abruptly and set off straight down the side of the field. Nobody touched him. He went 96 yards for the score, the second longest punt return in pro football history.

After his football days, Bill settled in Lynchburg, Virginia, and became a successful insurance magnate, a life member of the Million Dollar Round Table. He scouted college talent for the Lions on the side and appreciated the contact with the game. Also his experiences derived from it.

"Being small and playing both ways," he noted, "I needed a lot of help, got it from every member on every club I ever played for. It would be impossible for me to remember all of them, but I did then and do now express my sincere thanks and appreciation for the help all the boys gave me during my nine years in professional football."

When he was well past forty, however, and looked ten years younger, Bill Dudley still thought he could go out and do a job on the gridiron. In fact, he tried to prove it every spring when he went back to the old campus at Charlottesville and played in the annual alumni-varsity game. His final appearance, in 1962, was memorable. He was forty-one years old. He carried the ball a dozen times and gained 126 yards against the college huskies.

Of course, he also punted, passed, blocked, and tackled.

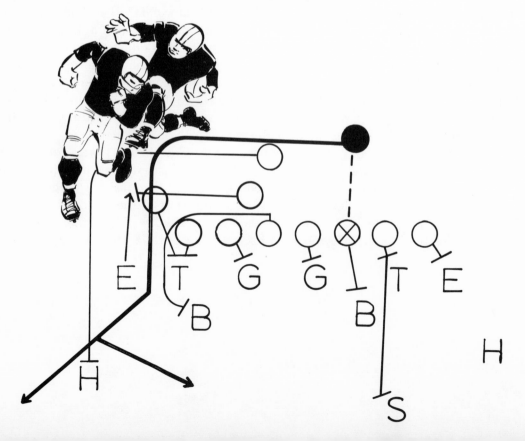

"The off-tackle play from the balanced and unbalanced line and the trap were all basic plays in the single wing. We ran it 60 percent of the time. The first two steps were always identical. You always looked to the sidelines before making a cut to go off tackle, off guard or to the weak side on the trap, as shown here.

"The tailback can help set up the block on the linebacker by making sure his cut is square. That block is the difference between a good gain or none at all.

"I recall that on the trap play from the balanced line, I went 56 yards for a touchdown against the Philadelphia Eagles in my first professional football game played in 1942. I also ran it 50 yards against the New York Giants the same season.

"Most of the blocking at the hole in the single wing was a double team. The center quite often was given key assignments, and in this respect Chuck Cherundolo at Pittsburgh did an outstanding job. The blocking backs also had to make key blocks just about every time. Vern Martin and Russ Cotton did their jobs well in 1942, and in 1946 it was Charlie Seabright."

WILLIAM M. "BULLET BILL" DUDLEY

BORN: Dec. 24, 1921   Height: 5'10"   Weight: 182
University of Virginia

Pittsburgh, 1942, 1945–46
Detroit, 1947–49
Washington, 1950–51, 1953

| | | RUSHING | | | | PASS RECEIVING | | | | SCORING | |
Year	G.	Att.	Yds.	Avg.	TD.	P.C.	Yds.	Avg.	TD.	TD.	Pts.
1942	11	*162	*696	4.3	..	1	24	24.0	0	6	36
1943–44					(In Military Service)						
1945	4	57	204	3.5	3		(None)			3	20
1946	11	*146	*604	4.1	3	4	109	27.2	1	5	48
1947	9	80	302	3.8	2	27	375	13.9	7	11	66
1948	7	33	97	2.9	0	20	210	10.5	6	7	42
1949	12	125	402	3.2	4	27	190	7.0	2	6	81
1950	12	66	339	5.1	1	22	172	7.8	1	3	64
1951	12	91	398	4.4	2	22	303	13.8	1	3	69
1952					(Did Not Play)						
1953	12	5	15	3.0	0		(None)			0	58
PRO TOTALS —9 YEARS	90	765	3057	4.0	15	123	1383	11.2	18	44	484

* Led NFL.

Year	G.	Att.	Cmp.	Pct.	Gain	T.P.	P.I.	Avg.	No.	Avg.
					PASSING				PUNTING	
1942	11	94	35	37.2	438	2	5	4.66	18	32.0
1943–44					(In Military Service)					
1945	4	32	10	31.3	58	0	2	1.81	2	18.0
1946	11	90	32	35.5	452	2	9	5.02	60	40.0
1947	9	4	3	75.0	24	2	0	6.00	15	43.8
1948	7	1	0	00.0	0	0	1	0.00	23	35.9
1949	12				(None)				32	39.9
1950	12				(None)				14	41.8
1951	12	1	1	100.0	13	0	0	13.00	27	34.9
1952					(Did Not Play)					

PRO TOTALS

—9 YEARS 90 222 81 36.5 985 6 17 4.44 191 38.2

* Led NFL.

Marion Motley

HE WAS ONE HELLUVA UNSELFISH
PLAYER; MARION MOTLEY NEVER
THOUGHT ABOUT MARION MOTLEY—
ONLY THE TEAM.
  —*Tony Adamle, former captain,*
  Cleveland Browns.

On the exterior, people saw only the coldly efficient, robot-like way that a professional football dynasty was built in Cleveland from the moment Paul Brown arrived in 1946 to assemble his new team. Messenger guards ran in and out of the lineup between plays, delivering orders from the bench. The passes were precision pieces of timework between the quarterback and the ends hugging the sidelines, catching the ball a split-second before their feet crossed the boundary. For variation in the relentless attack, the quarterback hesitated as if to pass and then gave the ball to the fullback, who pushed past the sucked-in defenses. It was called a draw play. Pass and trap, pass and trap—that was the simplicity of the Cleveland offense. And the maestro, Paul Brown, had just the right players to put it all together. Swift ends in Mac Speedie and Dante Lavelli who could cut on a dime; a gifted thrower in Otto Graham; a 238-pound bundle of muscle in Marion Motley to split the enemy lines.

It was so beautifully synchronized and meshed that the Browns never faltered from the moment they showed up on the pro football scene through the next five years of uninterrupted triumph. And if there was a mechanical, almost ruthless and relentless efficacy about them—well, they were only reflecting the personality of their mentor.

That was, of course, on the outside. On the inside, there were situations like this:

It was just before the Browns were to play the New York Yankees for the championship of the old All-America Conference in 1947. Coached by dynamic Ray Flaherty, the Yankees were pretty exciting stuff. They had tied the Browns, 28–28, in a game played three weeks earlier before a sellout crowd in Yankee Stadium. Spec Sanders, their tailback, was the only unanimous choice on the all-league team, and at fullback was a little explosive barrel named Claude "Buddy" Young, the most spectacular player in the new circuit. Just before the game, Coach Paul Brown drew his fullback, Marion Motley, aside and pointed to the 61,000 people crammed into Yankee Stadium.

"Marion," he said, "you see all those people out there? Guess what they're here for."

"I s'pose,' Marion mumbled, "they come to see a good game."

"No, Marion," said Brown, gently. "The thing they want to know is whether you or Buddy Young is the better man." And he turned and walked to the bench.

The second time the Browns got the ball, after an exchange of punts, with both teams still feeling each other out, Motley took a handoff from Graham. This was no draw off a pass-action play. It was a straight run, with the guards pulling and Motley swinging wide around his right end. A 238-pound fullback isn't supposed to run that fast. But by the time he rounded the corner, Motley had lost his cortege of blockers. He stampeded through the New York secondary, and from his own 36-yard line ran all the way to the Yankee 13 before they rode him to the ground. In four more plays, the Browns scored.

Motley's 51-yard burst was the longest run of the day and set the tempo for a 14–3 championship victory. He got the second touchdown march going, too, with a 16-yard plunge deep into Yankee territory. Altogether he dominated the field of play with 109 yards in 13 carries. And the Cleveland Browns of those early days were primarily a passing team.

Championship games always brought out the best in the burly fullback. In the first title game the Browns ever won—by defeating the Yankees, 14–9, in 1946—he bulldozed 98 yards in thirteen carries and scored the vital opening touchdown. In 1948, he ran wild for three scores and picked up 133 yards in fourteen rushes during a stampede of the old Buffalo Bills.

Yes, the Browns passed first and then turned Motley loose up the middle just enough to keep defenses honest. Nevertheless, he was the leading ground gainer in the four-year history of the old All-American Conference.

"But," pooh-poohed the staid artisans of the National Football League, "look at the humpty-dumpties he's been running against." So in 1950, Marion Motley, age thirty, was graduated to the "big leagues" along with all the other Cleveland Browns. The NFL was in for a revelation. What worked in the old AAC was just as effective against the Philadelphia Eagles, champions of the football world.

"Just think," Coach Paul Brown told his players before they went out to play the Eagles in the opening game of the season, their debut in the NFL, "tonight you fellows will have a chance to touch the great Steve Van Buren."

They touched him and toppled him and meanwhile the Browns startled the champs and brought in a whole new concept of offensive football by submerging the Eagles, 35–10. They went on to win the Eastern division title and defeat the Los Angeles Rams for the NFL crown. Van Buren, who had led the NFL in rushing for three straight years, was supplanted by big Marion Motley, who gained 810 yards in 140 carries for a striking average of 5.8 yards every time quarterback Otto Graham nestled the ball in his ample middle.

"I think," said Graham reflectively, "Motley was the best fullback I ever saw. He was a better all-around player than Jimmy Brown. Of course, there never was a better runner than Jimmy, and maybe he didn't have to block. But Marion was a great blocker, especially for the passer. I don't think anybody actually ever knocked him over. Maybe they got around him once in a while. Everybody's going to get beaten some time. But when they came straight at him, Marion just stopped 'em on a dime."

And Motley was a good guy to have on the club, aside from his obvious physical assets.

The other Browns called him "Mariooch" fondly—a big, good-natured guy, even-tempered, diligent, hard-working. In his early years he played both offense and defense, as a tough linebacker. Marion liked to stick his nose, sans face mask, up front where the action was. But as a linebacker, he also had some pass coverage responsibilities. In one game, Coach Brown on the sidelines was in a frenzy because Marion kept edging up into the middle of the line, oblivious to the threat of a pass.

"Loosen up, Marion," he screamed.

Marion was still inching toward the line so that he was almost nose to nose with the offensive tackle.

"For pete's sakes, Marion," yelled Brown, "loosen up!" And his screech reached the middle of the field. Motley looked over to the sidelines, a puzzled look on his face.

236

The surprising quickness of 235-pound Marion Motley made the pitchout a basic attacking weapon of the Cleveland Browns.

"Loosen up!" He stood up and shook his body like a shimmy dancer. That was what the boss wanted. The other Browns roared.

"He was a wonderful team man," said Graham. "He never said boo. He never complained. He was basically a happy guy. Only one time in my life did I ever get mad at him. I wasn't the kind of guy who got on my teammates. I minded my own business pretty much. But in our first year in the NFL we were playing the Redskins and not doing too good in the first half. On the last play of the half, Marion ran a draw some 20 or 30 yards and was knocked out of bounds. One of the Redskins hit him on the blind side—really whacked him with his fist. Marion went after him and swung back, just about the time the referee turned around and saw it. He threw Marion out of the game.

"When we got back to the dressing room at half time, I really lit into him. I chewed him out and told him he was too valuable a player to be thrown out of a game. He just sat there and took it, quiet. He never was thrown out of a game again."

Despite that great first year in the NFL, the string was beginning to run out for Motley. He had been playing more than fifteen years of organized football, going back to the high school days at Canton, Ohio, McKinley, which is where Paul Brown first saw him. Brown was coaching Massillon High, the rival school, and kept a memory file on a big kid fullback who kept tearing up his lines. Motley, after graduation, went out west with his high school coach, Jim Aiken, to Nevada, where he played three years before going into the Navy. That's where he caught up with Brown again, as the fullback on Paul's 1945 Great Lakes Naval Training Station team which ripped apart a fine Notre Dame team, 39–7, in the last game of the season.

Also on Brown's staff at Great Lakes was Petty Officer 2nd Class Blanton Collier, who eventually succeeded Maestro Paul as the head coach of the Cleveland team in 1964. "Marion Motley was the greatest all-around football player I ever saw," said Collier, who moved from Great Lakes into pro ball with Brown. "He had no equal as a blocker. He could run with anybody for 30 yards or so. And this man was a great, great line-backer."

When Motley got out of the Navy and the All-American Conference was being formed, he wrote to the Browns asking for a tryout. It should have been a cinch. But the AAC teams were, frankly, not being encouraged to sign Negro players. Not one of the other seven teams in the league had a Negro player on the roster. The NFL wasn't much more exemplary in this regard. Only the Los Angeles Rams, with veteran half-back Kenny Washington and end Woody Strode, made a token effort at providing equal opportunity.

And, according to Motley, the Browns first told him they had enough backs. Later, however, he received a phone call asking him to report to their training camp in Bowling Green. "You know why I think they called me?" he shrugged. "Bill Willis had come in for a tryout and he needed a roommate." Willis was a brilliant Negro guard from Ohio State who was destined to become an all-league selection for every one of the eight seasons he split between the AAC and NFL. And when Marion Motley was inducted into the pros' Hall of Fame at Canton, Ohio, his home town, in 1968, Bill Willis made the introduction of his old teammate.

238

There aren't many traces of Motley's name in the record book. His eventual successor as the Cleveland fullback, Jim Brown, took care of that. He never made Jimmy's big money. Motley started at $4,000 a year and worked himself up to $12,000 a year at his peak.

But he gave pro football a couple of tangible things to remember him by. His career average of 5.7 yards per carry was half a yard higher than Brown's. And his 17.1 average per carry against Pittsburgh on October 29, 1950 (he gained 188 yards in eleven tries), is still the best single game effort in NFL history.

Marion's effectiveness was limited after that by knee trouble and he faded from the pro scene after 1953 (though he tried to make an abortive comeback with the Steelers as a linebacker two years later). He wanted to coach, but the barriers were still up when he tried to get a job. He helped Otto Graham with the College All-Stars one summer, tutoring the backs in pass protection. And when Otto coached the Redskins, Marion did some part-time scouting.

But the only extensive use of his football background came in the fall of 1967 when Marion Motley coached a girls' football team in Cleveland. It was a hell of a note. He had to knock on the door—to make sure everyone was presentable—before he could come into the team's dressing room.

MARION MOTLEY

BORN: June 5, 1920   Height: 6'1"   Weight: 238
University of Nevada

Cleveland Browns, 1946–53
Pittsburgh, 1955

Year	G.	Att.	Yds.	Avg.	TD.	P.C.	Yds.	Avg.	TD.	TD.	Pts.
			RUSHING				PASS RECEIVING			SCORING	
1946	13	73	601	8.2	5	10	188	18.8	1	6	36
1947	14	146	889	6.1	8	7	73	10.4	1	10	60
1948	14	157	*964	6.1	5	13	192	14.8	2	7	42
1949	12	113	570	5.0	8	15	191	12.7	0	8	48
1950	12	140	*810	5.8	3	11	151	13.7	1	4	24
1951	11	61	273	4.5	1	10	52	5.2	0	1	6
1952	12	104	444	4.3	1	13	213	16.4	2	3	18
1953	12	32	161	5.0	0	6	47	7.8	0	0	0
1955	7	2	8	4.0	0		(None)			0	0
AAC TOTALS —4 YEARS	53	489	3024	6.2	26	45	644	14.3	4	31	186
NFL TOTALS —5 YEARS	54	339	1696	5.0	5	40	463	11.6	3	8	48
PRO TOTALS —9 YEARS	107	828	4720	5.7	31	85	1107	13.0	7	39	234

* Led NFL.

Charley Trippi

CHARLEY TRIPPI HAD TREMENDOUS
COURAGE AND A LOT OF DIGNITY. HE
NEVER FELT SORRY FOR HIMSELF, THE
WAY SOME BACKS DO WHEN THEY
AREN'T GETTING A LOT OF HELP.
—*George Connor, linebacker,
Chicago Bears.*

Neither mud nor rain nor enemy tacklers deterred Charley Trippi from his appointed task of running the ball for the Chicago Cardinals.

There is such a thing as a man being too good for his own place in posterity. In the case of Charles Lou Trippi, versatility was a drag. It despoiled his niche among the great running backs of history and eventually blotted his career.

Running is what Charley did best, with a jittery-legged gait that made it look like steel springs were suspended from his body and veered suddenly in all directions. He began the entire modern era of great bidding for college talent when both the National Football League and the All-America Conference pursued him ardently in the early months of 1947. Charley was the classiest senior back in the country available to the pros (Doc Blanchard and Glenn Davis of Army would have to stay in uniform) and he had made every one of the proliferating All-American teams.

The New York Yankees of the AAC, working together with their baseball brethren, were so confident that they'd landed Charley to play for both of them (he was also a talented outfield slugger) that they scheduled a noon press conference in New York to announce it. And Trippi showed up with Charley Bidwell, the owner of the Chicago Cardinals, to tell Larry MacPhail, the boss of the joint Yankee teams, that he was already committed to the Cardinals—on a four-year deal at something like $100,000, a fantastic contract at that time.

"I thought it was ridiculous to see MacPhail," admitted Trippi, "since I was already signed with the Cards. But Bidwell wanted it. He was a showman and wanted recognition for the Cards. I would do anything for him."

And Trippi did—everything. This was before the era of specialization had computerized the players so that a man now makes a 10-year career out of doing nothing but guarding split ends and flankers on defense. Charley Trippi had a nine-year career. But in it, he played halfback and flanker, quarterback and defensive safety. He punted and passed and returned kicks. Wherever the Cards needed him, he played.

After the Cardinals had finished last with a 1-10-1 record in 1953 and had given up 337 points, Earle "Greasy" Neale was brought to their next training camp as a special assistant to install the famous Eagle defense he had perfected in his coaching years at Philadelphia. Greasy took one look at the talent available to him and said, "There's only one guy here who can keep it together—Charley Trippi." So at thirty-one, the long-time ace of the Cardinal attack changed gears and became a defensive specialist, as the free safety.

In the exhibition season of 1955, still on the job, Charley was tracking a play run by the San Francisco 49ers. When the whistle blew, he relaxed. And Charley woke up many hours later with a new face. Unrecognizable. "I was blindsided," he said, years later. "I don't know what hit me, an elbow or a fist." John Henry Johnson, a back for the San Francisco 49ers, penetrated Charley's face mask and left him unconscious. Eventually, there was plastic surgery, but Charley never again had the acquiline nose that was a prominent part of his features when he was the most sensational running back

243

in football. Although he came back later in the 1955 season to play parts of five games, that was the end of his career.

It had started back in Pittston, Pennsylvania, on the banks of the Susquehanna River, smack in the middle of the hard coal region that has always been a favorite recruiting territory for the football factories of the east and southeast. But ironcially, neither Penn State or West Virginia wanted him after graduation from high school, though he hitch-hiked on his own to both campuses. "I weighed only 155 and had played in the backfield only one season."

A year at a prep school in New York fleshed him out and brought all the big schools after him. He chose Georgia and in 1942 turned out for the varsity as a tailback. The Bulldogs already had Frank Sinkwich playing that spot, and he was a celebrated All-American the year before on a fine Orange Bowl team. Coach Wally Butts did the obviously smart thing during the season and moved Sinkwich to fullback so he could have Trippi the sophomore and Frankie the senior as a twin threat in the same backfield. Georgia won ten games and lost one, crushing unbeaten Georgia Tech in the finale, 34–0, then shut out UCLA in the Rose Bowl, 9–0, when Charley carried the offensive load alone because Sinkwich was hurt.

Charley went off to the Air Corps the following spring and didn't return to the Georgia campus until the 1945 football season was already under way. He was married and had a daughter, and both the football and baseball pros were already after him. But Charley had promised Butts he'd come back and finish school. He did, with an athletic flourish. He exchanged his sergeant's uniform for the bright red jersey of the Bulldogs, with number 62 on the front, and racked up more than 500 yards offensively against archrival Georgia Tech. After he led Georgia to a postseason Sun Bowl victory over Tulsa, Houston humorist Morris Frank said, "I'm going home and turn Sammy Baugh's picture to the wall."

Trippi, still spurning the pros in '46, was even more brilliant as a senior, leading Georgia to its first undefeated season since 1896 and then out-dueling North Carolina's fabulous Charley Justice in the Sugar Bowl. Though the Bulldogs in the post-war period had converted to the T from the single wing in which Trippi had started, they still made use of his multiple talent as a punter and passer, as well as a runner. "And he was a great safety on defense," added Wally Butts. Years later, when Charley rejoined Butts as an assistant coach on the Georgia staff, Wally called all his players together before a practice session and said, "I want to introduce you boys to the greatest all-around football player I have seen."

And when Trippi started his pro career with the Cardinals in 1947, the immortal Jim Thorpe called him "the greatest football player I ever saw." Charley stepped into a beautiful situation at first with the Cards, who had just rehired colorful Jimmy Conzelman as head coach. They were coming out of the doldrums of ten straight losing seasons. A brilliant backfield was taking shape, with Paul Christman at quarterback, Pat Harder at fullback, and Marshall Goldberg alternating with young Elmer Angsman at right halfback. Trippi at left half was the final touch in what would become known shortly as "The Dream Backfield" (Angsman finally displaced veteran Goldberg, who

244

became a defensive specialist). "It was the type of football team," said Charley, "where the pressure wasn't only on one man."

Charley was their clutch performer, but he didn't have to do it all. He reported with a bad ankle after spending the whole summer with the Atlanta Crackers of the Southern Association and batting .334 in his only fling at pro baseball. He injured his big toe after that. But Christman's passes, Harder's extraordinary blocking and Angsman's breakaway dashes let Charley ease into his job gently. The Cards won their first division championship in history and then met the Philadelphia Eagles for the NFL championship—the Eagles of Greasy Neale, who, as a Cardinal consultant in later years, would eventually recommend Trippi for the defense.

Comiskey Park, the home field of the Cardinals, was frozen and icy, and the home team wore sneakers on the skidding surface. Trippi and Angsman took turns racing through the Eagle defense. In the first quarter, Charley slipped through the middle on a quick opener after only six minutes of play and scooted 44 yards for the touchdown that broke the ice. In the second quarter, Angsman shot through a big hole and raced 70 yards for a score. It was Trippi's turn after the halftime intermission. He grabbed a punt on his own 25-yard line and started down the right sideline. At the Eagles' 30, he skidded, staggered like a tightrope walker, then slipped again 10 yards further down but regained his balance and sprinted into the end zone for a 75-yard run, longest of the day. Angsman reeled off another 70-yarder from scrimmage in the final period to secure a 28–21 world championship victory.

Charley came back a year later and had his greatest pro season as the Cardinals powered to a second straight Western title, losing only once in 12 games. Charley's 5.4 yards per carry was the best in the NFL, and his 690 yards rushing represented a career high. But the championship rematch with the Eagles was played under impossible conditions, in the midst of one of the most severe blizzards ever to hit Philadelphia. Runners like Trippi and Angsman needed traction, and a foot of snow isn't the place to get it. "It was a disgrace," said Trippi, "and a disservice to pro football to play the game." The Cardinals lost, 7–0, after a fumble gave the Eagles the big break of the day.

For the future career of Charley Trippi, it was an omen. The breaks all started to go the other way. Conzelman quit coaching after 1948. The Dream Backfield started breaking up after the 1949 campaign. Harder was traded to Detroit, and Christman went to Green Bay. In another couple of years, Angsman would retire. The Cardinals became a hopeless team and would remain that way through the rest of Trippi's career, with a succession of coaches trying to salvage them. Altogether, Charley played through six coaching regimes.

By 1951, the Cardinals found themselves without a competent T-quarterback. Charley had been a single wing tailback passer back in his early days at Georgia. Coach Curly Lambeau recognized that Trippi was his best thrower—his best football player, in fact—and moved him into the signal caller's post, in a job completely new to him in his fifteenth year of organized football. On a team with competent talent, it might have worked. Charley was a tremendous threat rolling out with the snap of the ball. In fact, he gained 501 yards on the ground that year, an average of 6.4 yards per rollout. His passing was merely adequate.

The Cardinal coaches could have shown more confidence in his signal calling. There was one game against the Redskins in which Charley repeatedly took the team on his own inside the Washington 10-yard line. "Then," he said, "the substitutes would come in on every play with instructions from the bench on what to call. The confusion was worse than Grand Central. They even sent in the wrong substitutes. Now who do you suppose was to blame because the plays didn't score?"

The Cardinals were a last place team when they met the Bears in their traditional joust at the end of the season. The Bears had a shot at the Western division title. It was one of those typical near-zero encounters.

"While working out at the University of Chicago field house because it was too cold to practice outside," Trippi recounted, "I suggested to Lambeau we might surprise the Bears with a spread formation. I had been a tailback at Georgia. And the Packers had used the spread.

"The Bears led at the half, 7–0. In the second half, Curly gave us the go-ahead to use what was popularized by the 49ers as the shotgun offense. I believe I threw for two touchdowns and scored once. We won, 24–14, and knocked them out of the playoffs."

"He was at his best," said George Connor, the rugged linebacker of the Bears (later a prominent telecaster), "when all the other big names were gone and he was standing back there all by himself in that direct pass offense they were running then."

Charley stayed at quarterback one more year, 1952. The following season, with Joe Stydahar taking over as coach, he was moved back to a running slot, filling in only sporadically as the signal caller. Nothing helped. The Cardinals were the worst team in the NFL, winning only one game. Charley, at thirty, already felt himself getting a step slower, but he led the league in punt returns. He didn't object when it was suggested he switch to defense. When he first came up with the Cardinals in their glory years, he'd had a slight taste of it as the backup man to Biggie Goldberg, one time intercepting a pass and running 59 yards for a touchdown.

After the Johnson accident, on Labor Day of 1955, crushed his face, Trippi was ready for another career anyhow. He was an assistant coach with the Cardinals for a couple of years, then switched to Georgia to work under his old college mentor. He had always made his home in Athens. He returned to the Cardinals, in St. Louis, for another coaching hitch under Wally Lemm. But when they changed regimes in 1966, Charley was out and quit coaching to become a real estate man.

The years of frustration also had their balm. Charley is still the all-time leading ground gainer of the Cardinals. He even holds their record for punt returns. He was named to both the college and pro Halls of Fame.

"There's nothing more I can get out of football," he said, "a game that's given me so much."

CHARLEY TRIPPI'S FAVORITE PLAY:

"From the T-formation, it was a simple dive play we called '24 Dive.' When I received the ball from the quarterback, I would key on the line blocking and run for

246

daylight. Linemen would block any way the defensive man wanted to go, and this type of blocking took care of any defensive stunts.

"In the championship game against the Eagles in 1947, I broke one off for 44 yards on this play. And in the same type of action on the other side, Elmer Angsman, our other halfback, had a pair of 70-yard runs. This particular play was our bread-and-butter device."

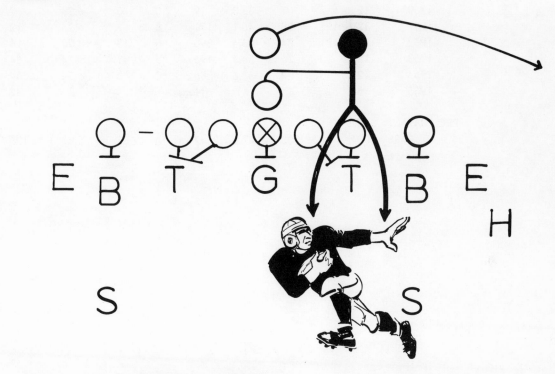

CHARLES LOU TRIPPI

BORN: Dec. 14, 1922   Height: 6'0''   Weight: 185
University of Georgia

Chicago Cardinals, 1947–55

			RUSHING				PASS RECEIVING				SCORING	
Year	G.	Att.	Yds.	Avg.	TD.	P.C.	Yds.	Avg.	TD.		TD.	Pts.
1947	11	83	401	4.8	2	23	240	10.4	0		3	18
1948	12	128	690	*5.4	6	22	228	10.4	2		10	60
1949	12	112	553	4.9	2	34	412	12.1	6		9	54
1950	12	99	426	4.3	3	32	270	8.4	1		4	24
1951	12	78	501	6.4	4		(None)				4	24
1952	12	72	350	4.9	4	5	66	13.2	0		4	24
1953	12	97	433	4.5	0	11	87	7.9	2		2	12
1954	12	18	152	8.4	1	3	18	6.0	0		1	6
1955	5		(None)				(None)				0	0
PRO TOTALS —9 YEARS	100	687	3506	5.1	22	130	1321	10.2	11		37	222

				PASSING					PUNTING	
Year	G.	Att.	Cmp.	Pct.	Gain	T.P.	P.I.	Avg.	No.	Avg.
1947	11	2	1	50.0	49	0	1	24.50	(None)	
1948	12	8	4	50.0	118	1	0	14.75	13	43.4
1949	12	2	0	00.0	0	0	0	0.00	8	36.5
1950	12	3	1	33.3	19	0	0	6.33	2	47.0
1951	12	191	88	46.1	1191	8	13	6.24	12	37.2
1952	12	181	84	46.4	890	5	13	4.92	16	36.8
1953	12	34	20	58.8	195	2	1	5.74	54	42.9
1954	12	13	7	53.8	85	0	3	6.54	59	39.1
1955	5			(None)					32	40.7

PRO TOTALS
—9 YEARS 100 434 205 47.2 2547 16 31 5.87 196 40.4

* Led NFL.

And, in Addition . . .

IF YOU DON'T LIKE BUDDY YOUNG, THEN
YOU DON'T LIKE PEOPLE.
        —*Cecil Isbell, former coach,*
        Baltimore Colts.

Buddy Young, eluding Rex Berry of San Francisco, was a forerunner of the Negro running back in pro football—all five feet four inches of him.

Claude "Buddy" Young of the southside of Chicago was the precursor of the great modern Negro running back. He opened the road for Ollie Matson and Jimmy Brown and O. J. Simpson. And he did it as an eighteen-year-old freshman at the University of Illinois. The year was 1944, and in another time Buddy Young wouldn't have been playing varsity football. But this was World War II, and Coach Ray Eliot of the Illini was taking anybody who walked. Little Buddy ran, maybe faster than anybody in the entire world, because he was a sprinter.

He stood only five feet four and a half inches tall and never grew even a fraction of an inch more. But Buddy was fully packed, like a container of ice cream that's squashed until you think it can't hold any more. They got 170 pounds of him into that frame, and it got down into the legs, tree trunk in circumference, and into a barrel chest. And still there was that speed which enabled him to win twenty-four out of twenty-seven sprints his first year in college, including the national 100-yard title.

However, he had something else to prove. "The theory until then," said Buddy, "was that track men couldn't make football players. Also, 1944 meant the emergence of schools looking at Negro football players with some depth."

There had been some isolated examples before him, like Ozzie Simmons at Iowa, and Kenny Washington and Jackie Robinson at UCLA. But somehow Buddy captivated the imagination and, unlike them, was an All-American. As a freshman, he equalled Red Grange's scoring record of thirteen touchdowns in one season. Then he went into the Maritime service and starred on the pro-laden Fleet City team, scoring four times against the famed El Toro Marines. He returned to Illinois in 1946 and was the pacesetter in the first Rose Bowl game ever played by a Big Ten team, as the Illini crushed UCLA.

The New York Yankees signed him in 1947, and he played fullback in a single wing attack that featured Spec Sanders of Texas as his running mate. Buddy gained 712 yards rushing his rookie year and was the most spectacular player in the All-America Conference, doubling as a pass receiving threat. Altogether, he lasted nine years among the pros, finishing up his career with the Baltimore Colts in 1955, still a flashy and dangerous breakaway threat.

But Buddy's influence and merit as a football immortal transcend the statement of career statistics and records. He led the league in humanitarianism. In 1947, Buddy played in the College All-Star game with Doc Blanchard, Glenn Davis, and Charley Trippi. The college stars were quartered in a dormitory at Northwestern.

"I went to my room," recalled Buddy, "and put on my pajamas, house shoes, and bathrobe. Then I went out to the lobby where the guys were playing cards. A couple of guys from the South laughed. You know, they had never before seen a Negro in pajamas."

On Buddy's first visit to Baltimore as a pro, racists with lamp black on their faces waited outside the locker room. "I didn't know whether I was there to play a football game or be in a minstrel show," said Buddy. But eight years later, the Colts officially retired his jersey number (22).

"Football," he said, "is a great market place to weed out the bigotry and prejudice in life. I always made sure I roomed with a white boy from the South so that he would know me."

Young's youngest son was named Zollie. The boy's godfather was Zollie Toth, a hard-nosed fullback on the Yanks and Colts, a blond giant from Louisiana State who made his home in Baton Rouge.

After his active career was over, Buddy stayed close to football as a scout and broadcaster, and eventually became an administrative assistant to NFL Commissioner Pete Rozelle, concentrating on job opportunities for black athletes. He was also responsible for signing such brilliant players as Gale Sayers and Jim Parker, the Colts' all-pro offensive lineman.

"The only thing I'm really proud of from my football days," said Buddy, "was the fact that I could knock people down. You ask Lenny Ford. You ask Ed Sprinkle."

They were a couple of all-pro defensive ends with reputations for meanness. They towered a couple of heads over chunky Buddy—literally, but not figuratively.

BUDDY YOUNG'S FAVORITE PLAY:

"When I was at Illinois, in 1944, eight of the 13 touchdowns I scored [to equal Red Grange's record] came on a '22 Slant' from the Oklahoma T with three setbacks and splits in the line. Among them were runs for 76, 85, 62, 55, 73, and 46 yards. I had a good game against Notre Dame in '44, although we lost, 13–7, in the last two minutes. They got to me after the touchdown run, and I didn't play any more.

"The success of this play resulted from the quickness of the back diving for the 2-hole between left guard and left tackle, setting up the tackle's block on the defensive tackle. Then the back veered off to the left. The fullback had a key block on the defensive end. There was a lot of pressure on the end, for he had to look out for the quarterback option in the split-T attack.

"The play was designed for a back with a quick start and quick feet who could veer suddenly, since, as you can see, no guards pulled on the play."

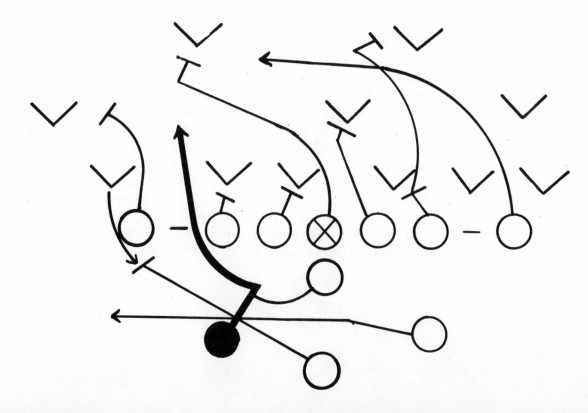

CLAUDE H. "BUDDY" YOUNG

BORN: Jan. 5, 1926   Height: 5'4"   Weight: 170
University of Illinois

New York Yanks, 1947–51
Dallas Texans (NFL), 1952
Baltimore, 1953–55

Year	G.	Att.	RUSHING Yds.	Avg.	TD.	P.C.	PASS RECEIVING Yds.	Avg.	TD.	SCORING TD.	Pts.
1947	14	116	712	6.1	3	27	303	11.2	2	7	42
1948	12	70	245	3.5	1	21	259	12.3	4	5	30
1949	12	76	495	6.5	5	12	171	14.3	2	8	48
1950	12	76	334	4.6	1	20	302	15.1	1	2	12
1951	12	46	165	3.6	1	31	508	16.4	3	6	36
1952	12	71	243	3.4	3	22	269	12.2	2	5	30
1953	10	40	135	3.4	0	12	201	16.8	3	4	24
1954	10	70	311	4.4	2	15	272	18.1	3	5	30
1955	11	32	87	2.7	1	19	426	22.4	1	2	12
AAC TOTALS —3 YEARS	38	262	1452	5.5	9	60	733	12.2	8	20	120
NFL TOTALS —6 YEARS	67	335	1275	3.8	8	119	1978	16.6	13	24	144
PRO TOTALS —9 YEARS	105	597	2727	4.6	17	179	2711	15.1	21	44	264

Marlin M. "Pat" Harder was also a man who knocked people down. Pat was better equipped for it than Buddy Young since he weighed a solid 205 pounds. But even that wasn't big for the job he held, as fullback and premier blocker in the "Dream Backfield" of the Chicago Cardinals when they led the NFL Western division in 1947–48.

A native of Milwaukee, Pat had first played on the strongest varsity team in Wisconsin football history—the 1942 aggregation coached by Harry Stuldreher which featured All-American Elroy Hirsch at halfback and All-American end Dave Schreiner.

Pat came to the Cardinals in 1946 after a service hitch and immediately stepped into a regular job as their fullback. There was nothing fancy about his running. He was a straight ahead power plunger who consistently picked up his four yards a carry and was particularly effective inside the 10-yard line.

The Cardinals became champions of the NFL in 1947 and won their division again in 1948. When he threatened to retire after 1950—in fact, he had announced his retirement because he was unhappy with the Cardinal organization—he was traded to the Detroit Lions. Buddy Parker, their coach, had been Pat's head man with the Cardinals in '49 and knew what he meant to a club. Pat could keep tacklers off a quarterback because he excelled in pass protection. He could lead the other backs on running plays.

He could go on his own; he recalled one 85-yard scamper against the New York Giants. And when Pat was on the field, the other team didn't take liberties. He was tough and he thrived on contact. He didn't like to be pushed around.

Len Ford, a punishing defensive end for the Cleveland Browns, found it out in a game against the Cardinals in 1950. "He was the kind of guy who wanted to hurt somebody," said Pat. "He ran over Fred Gehrke a couple of times when he was holding the ball on placements. Banged him up when he wasn't looking. Ed Bagdon, a little guard for us, got his face cut up. Mine was starting to get it, too. I got a tooth clipped. So with a minute and a half to play, I went looking for him."

Ford, a 240-pounder, came in high. Harder came up with his shoulder. Ford was carried off with a fractured jaw, a broken nose, crushed cheekbone, and a couple of teeth missing. The irony was that the Browns got penalized for roughness.

After Pat joined the Lions, who hadn't had a winning season in five years, they came within a half game of taking the Western title in '51. In 1952, they won it all, the division and the NFL crown. And they repeated in '53. Besides his fullback chores, Pat was also a valuable place-kicker throughout his career, and in the '52 campaign he contributed ten field goals, plus one which helped beat the Browns for the championship.

But the next year his legs started going bad; the cartilage in both knees was gone after two operations. And when he contributed very little to the Lions in 1953, he retired abruptly, without any commotion.

He kept active as a football official, and in 1966 was added to the NFL officiating teams as an umpire. "I get knocked down occasionally," he said, "but that elbow comes up to protect me, too. I guess it's instinctive."

MARLIN M. "PAT" HARDER

BORN: May 6, 1922   Height: 5'11"   Weight: 205
University of Wisconsin

Chicago Cardinals, 1946–50
Detroit, 1951–53

Year	G.	RUSHING Att.	Yds.	Avg.	TD.	PASS RECEIVING P.C.	Yds.	Avg.	TD.	SCORING TD.	Pts.
1946	11	106	545	5.1	4	11	128	11.6	1	5	35
1947	12	113	371	3.3	7	9	78	8.6	0	7	*102
1948	12	126	554	4.4	6	13	93	7.2	0	6	*110
1949	11	106	447	4.2	7	12	100	8.3	1	8	*102
1950	12	99	454	4.6	1	15	111	7.4	0	1	40
1951	12	101	380	3.8	6	17	193	11.4	2	8	57
1952	11	81	244	3.0	2	14	142	10.1	1	3	85
1953	5	8	21	2.6	0	1	19	19.0	0	0	0

PRO TOTALS
—8 YEARS 86 740 3016 4.1 33 92 864 9.4 5 38 531
* Led NFL.

PLACE KICKING

Year	G.	XP.	XPM.	FG.	FGA.
1946	11	5	0	0	0
1947	12	39	1	*7	10
1948	12	*53	0	7	*17
1949	11	*45	2	3	5
1950	12	22	2	4	9
1951	12	0	0	3	5
1952	11	34	1	11	23
1953	5		(None)		

PRO TOTALS					
—8 YEARS	86	198	6	35	69

* Led NFL.

Every year, when the members of the 1,000-Yard Club officially convene in Menasha, Wisconsin, just down the road from Green Bay, to celebrate their enrollment among the premier runners of pro football history, one man seems out of place. He's just a slight bit overweight, and not very tall by football standards. His hair—what there is of it—is silvery white.

Of course, he's almost a generation removed from playing football. But Anthony Robert Canadeo looked almost the same as when he was in the backfield of the Green Bay Packers over a period that stretched from 1941 through 1952.

In 1949, when he was thirty years old, on a team that won only two games out of twelve and was last in the NFL, Tony Canadeo gained 1,052 yards to ensure his niche among the great ones. He was called the Gray Ghost, a durable, dedicated halfback of flaming spirit.

That year, he was playing against the New York Yankees in the Polo Grounds and was buried under a swarm of tacklers on a sweep that went no place. As the players dragged themselves off inert Tony, an official waltzed over and magnanimously grabbed the Packer runner's arm and helped him to his feet. Then, as Tony's helmet fell off, exposing the silvery thatch, the official said, "Aren't you a little old to be fooling around like this?"

Canadeo whirled on him and barked, "I may be a little old, but I can see what's going on better than some people on this field."

In the long history of the Packers, only one man, Jimmy Taylor, gained more yards than Canadeo, the Gray Ghost of Gonzaga. A former Packer teammate said, "He looked less like a football player than any other man on the team. He wasn't fast. He wasn't big. He wasn't elusive like a lot of runners. But when Tony put the ball under his arm, he was all man."

He was a Chicago boy whose first exposure to Green Bay came when he went to visit his older brother going to school in the area. Tony, just graduated from high school but without a scholarship offer, met some kids going to school at Gonzaga in the state

Tony Canadeo was called "The Gray Ghost." The fiery Packer back is a member of the 1,000-Yard Club.

of Washington, and he tagged along. He made the team and got a scholarship, and the Packers eventually drafted him. He never left Green Bay thereafter.

After his playing days, he remained an official part of the family and became a member of the board of directors. He also helped telecast the Packer games. His enthusiasm for the team, and football, remained secure.

TONY CANADEO'S FAVORITE PLAY:

"The key block on this sweep was by the tight end on the left linebacker. In addition, a good fake to the fullback kept the defense in tight and made the play go.

"I used this sweep, with both guards pulling against all teams in my time, and it worked even against an overshifted defense.

"It was my favorite play during my 11 years with Green Bay. The year I made over a thousand yards, in 1949, I think 900 of those yards came on the sweep."

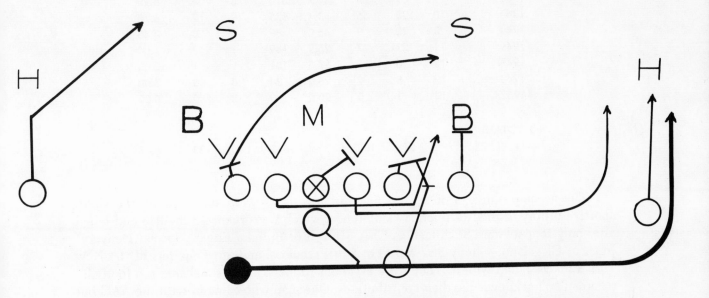

ANTHONY ROBERT "TONY" CANADEO

BORN: May 5, 1919   Height: 5'11"   Weight: 195
                          Gonzaga University

Green Bay, 1941–52

		RUSHING				PASS RECEIVING				SCORING	
Year	G.	Att.	Yds.	Avg.	TD.	P.C.	Yds.	Avg.	TD.	TD.	Pts.
1941	9	43	137	3.2	..		(None)			3	18
1942	11	89	272	3.1	..	10	66	6.6	0	3	18
1943	10	94	489	5.2	..	3	31	10.3	2	5	30
1944	3	31	149	4.8	0	1	12	12.0	0	0	0
1945					(In Military Service)						
1946	11	122	476	3.9	0	2	25	12.5	0	0	0

Year	G	Att	Yds	Avg	TD	No.	Yds	Avg			
1947	12	103	464	4.5	2	(None)				2	12
1948	12	123	589	4.8	4	9	81	9.0	0	4	24
1949	12	208	1052	5.1	4	3	—2	—0.7	0	4	24
1950	12	93	247	2.6	4	10	54	5.4	0	4	24
1951	12	54	131	2.4	1	22	226	10.3	2	3	18
1952	12	65	191	2.9	2	9	86	9.6	1	3	18
PRO TOTALS —11 YEARS	116	1025	4197	4.1	17	69	579	8.4	5	31	186

PASSING

Year	G.	Att.	Cmp.	Pct.	Gain	T.P.	P.I.	Avg.
1941	9	16	4	25.0	54	2	0	3.38
1942	11	59	24	40.7	310	3	4	5.25
1943	10	129	56	43.4	875	9	12	6.78
1944	3	20	9	45.0	89	0	0	4.45
1946	11	27	7	25.9	189	1	3	7.00
1947	12	8	3	37.5	101	1	1	12.63
1948	12	8	2	25.0	24	0	0	3.00
1952	12	1	0	00.0	0	0	0	0.00
PRO TOTALS —11 YEARS	70	268	105	39.2	1642	16	20	6.13

The accomplishments of several fine running backs were shrouded by the short, abortive history of the All-America Conference, which was organized in 1946 and faded after only four seasons. Such men as Chet Mutryn of Buffalo, Edgar "Special Delivery" Jones of Cleveland, Johnny Strzykalski of San Francisco, and Spec Sanders of the New York Yankees faded with it. They were excellent runners, and it's a shame pro football's records don't acknowledge their contributions. One man who came in with the AAC but went out with the NFL, and gave the game a chance to see him at his best in both arenas was Bob Hoernschemeyer. Bob was one of those war-time phenoms at Indiana. He started in the AAC with the Chicago Rockets, a terrible team, and played briefly with the Brooklyn Dodgers, who were equally bad. They were single wing teams, and Hunchy, as they called him, was a heavy-duty tailback who did the bulk of the running, all the passing and some of the kicking. He was, as a matter of fact, an excellent passer in the old triple-threat vein. In 1950, with the dissolution of the AAC, he was picked up by the Detroit Lions and tacked six more seasons onto his career. He came in with the young blood—Bobby Layne, Doak Walker and company—which was to produce Detroit's best teams. Playing in the T-formation gave the old tailback a new perspective. Hunchy was an important facet of their attack as the left halfback and as an option passer, the fore-runner of the Frank Gifford–Paul Hornung types. And as a ball carrier, he is still listed among the twenty most productive pros in history, with 4,548 yards as his career figure.

258

ROBERT J. "HUNCHY" HOERNSCHEMEYER

BORN: Sept. 24, 1925   Height: 5'11"   Weight: 192

Indiana University

Chicago Rockets, AAC, 1946–47, 1949
Brooklyn, AAC, 1947–48
Detroit, 1950–55

Year	G.	Att.	Yds.	Avg.	TD.	P.C.	Yds.	Avg.	TD.	TD.	Pts.
		RUSHING					PASS RECEIVING			SCORING	
1946	14	111	375	3.4	0	1	11	11.0	0	0	0
1947	14	152	704	4.6	5	1	4	4.0	1	6	36
1948	14	110	574	5.2	3	11	173	15.7	3	7	42
1949	12	*133	456	3.4	2		(None)			2	12
1950	10	84	471	5.6	1	8	78	9.8	1	2	12
1951	11	132	678	5.1	2	23	263	11.4	3	5	30
1952	10	106	457	4.3	4	17	139	8.2	0	4	24
1953	12	101	482	4.8	7	23	282	12.3	2	9	54
1954	11	94	242	2.6	2	20	153	7.7	1	3	18
1955	5	36	109	3.0	1	5	36	7.2	0	1	6

AAC TOTALS
—4 YEARS

	54	506	2109	4.2	10	13	188	14.5	4	15	90

NFL TOTALS
—6 YEARS

	59	553	2439	4.4	17	96	951	9.9	7	24	144

PRO TOTALS
—10 YEARS

	113	1059	4548	4.3	27	109	1139	10.4	11	39	234

* Led AAC.

Year	G.	Att.	Cmp.	Pct.	Gain	T.P.	P.I.	Avg.
				PASSING				
1946	14	193	95	49.2	1266	14	14	6.56
1947	14	173	73	42.2	926	4	11	5.35
1948	14	155	71	45.8	854	8	15	5.51
1949	12	167	69	41.3	1063	6	11	6.37
1950	10	4	1	25.0	19	1	1	4.75
1951	11	4	2	50.0	46	2	0	11.50

PRO TOTALS
—6 YEARS

	75	696	311	44.7	4174	35	52	6.00

The era of the 1940's needs a reference to the what-might-have-been school of ball carriers for an historically complete appraisal. Because World War II cut across the

In a different era, Tom Harmon might have duplicated his running feats as number 98 of Michigan. His pro career was curtailed for a longer run as a nationally known sportscaster.

grain of many promising football careers, several of the prospectively greaters runners of all time didn't achieve fruition in their pro endeavors.

You can start with old "98" of Michigan, Tom Harmon, the man who came closest to rivalling Red Grange as a Big Ten legend. Harmon of Michigan was as euphonious to the world of rah-rah as Merriwell of Yale, and just as heroic in an age when the campus star was still glorified as the epitome of athletic achievement. He played in the three years before our involvement in World War II, escapist years in a sense; and Tom was a fantasy in action, a brilliant, versatile player who could do everything. He had speed and size; he passed and kicked, and he ran—for thirty-three touchdowns in three varsity campaigns—and along the way he picked up every honor that comes to a collegian. They even made a movie, simply, "Harmon of Michigan."

After graduation, the Chicago Bears drafted him. Said Tommy, "What else was there for me to prove in football in those days? I turned George Halas down. I guess now I'm sorry I didn't play with the Chicago Bears in 1941. They were a great team." Instead, he made his movie, played one game with the New York Yankees of the short-lived American league and then went into the Air Force, surviving two plane crashes.

When he got out of the service in 1945, he was greeted with a bill of $7,000 from Internal Revenue for his movie earnings. Tom wanted to be an announcer, but the only way he could get money quickly was football. He signed a two-year, no-cut contract at $20,000 annually with the Los Angeles Rams, who got his rights from the Bears in a trade. His two years were undistinguished. He was a relatively old rookie and used only in spots, although one day in Wrigley Field he ran 85 yards from scrimmage against the Bears. "I didn't feel I was a T-formation man," said Tom simply. "It might have been different if they used the pass-run option that came in later." Ironically, his greatest achievement was on defense, where he intercepted eight passes in 1947. Then he quit to become one of the most prominent sports announcers in the country.

Fame, of a sort, followed him. He was on a plane years later with Vince Scully, who announces the Dodger baseball games in Los Angeles. "Aren't you on television?" the stewardess asked Tom.

"He is," said Harmon, pointing to Scully.

"Aw, go ahead," said Scully. "Tell her who you are."

"I," said Harmon importantly, "am Ricky Nelson's father-in-law."

Like Harmon, Glenn Davis only had two years with the Rams, also as the extent of his pro career. There were extenuating reasons. One of the greatest athletes ever to come out of southern California, Glenn gained his greatest renown at West Point at the height of World War II when he teamed with Felix "Doc" Blanchard as the invincible "Mr. Inside and Mr. Outside." Glenn was Mr. Outside, a tricky-gaited sprinter who won the Heisman Trophy in 1946 as the country's No. 1 football player, capping three undefeated years for Army. Davis spurred one of football's favorite after-dinner yarns when he was a plebe at the Point, and Coach Red Blaik ran him against the varsity first string. Davis skittered 87 yards to a touchdown.

Blaik didn't want to let it go to Glenn's head. "Maybe," said Red, "you thought that run was good. But you tipped off the way you were going by looking to your right. You didn't cut back like you should. When you got near the goal line, you let up. What have you got to say for yourself?"

Davis pawed the ground bashfully with a toe, then looked up from the corners of his eyes, blushed slightly and murmured, "But how was it for distance, Coach?"

After graduation, the West Point cadet had a service obligation which kept him busy until 1950, when the Rams signed him. He operated best as a flanker on a team that was one of the greatest offensive machines of all time, scoring a record total of 466 points in twelve games. The Rams won the Western division title in both of Glenn's seasons. In the 1950 championship game against the Cleveland Browns, only 28 seconds had elapsed when Glenn spurted 82 yards for a touchdown with a pass from Bob Water-field. But that was only a flash of what might have been with an uninterrupted career.

And finally there was Norm Standlee, who got the chance to show the pros what he could do, in his prime, and then had it taken away from him. Norm was the fullback in the original modern T-formation unveiled by Clark Shaughnessy at Stanford in 1940, with Frankie Albert at quarterback and Hugh Gallarneau and Pete Kmetovic at the halfbacks. All were destined to be pros. Physically, Standlee was the most awesome. "He was gifted by the gods with a terrific physique," Shaughnessy rhapsodized, "and remarkable speed for so large a man (6'1", 230). I think he had the most drive of any plunger in football history."

The Chicago Bears thought so, too, when he joined them in 1941 and became the fullback on an NFL title team, scoring two touchdowns in a rout of the New York Giants for the championship. "Standlee was the hardest runner in the league for me to bring down," said Buddy Parker, then with the Cardinals. "He was the toughest of them all, and we had some great backs in those days." He was their new "Nagurski." But after the '41 season, big Norm went off to war, and he never came back to Chicago, at least in a Bear uniform. In 1946, he joined the San Francisco 49ers of the new All-America Conference. He was still an imposing fullback, but something of the rampaging fire had vanished in the four years he was away in the Navy. Norm played with the 49ers until a polio attack curtailed his career in 1952, a respected pro who became the team captain, but from 1949 on, he became a linebacker, leaving the running to young bucks of a new era, like Joe Perry and Hugh McElhenny.

12. The Fabulous Fifties

Frank Gifford

HELL, I GET MORE EXCITEMENT IN ONE
DAY PLAYING FOOTBALL THAN MOST
PEOPLE GET IN A LIFETIME.
—*Frank Gifford, halfback,*
New York Giants.

Vince Lombardi, the man with the teeth a writer once said resembled a tank trap on the Maginot Line, flashed the full beam of his molars on the tanned, handsome young man at the bottom of the dormitory steps.

Lombardi, new to professional football in the summer of 1954, was greeting Frank Gifford at the training camp of the New York Giants on the campus of Willamette College in Salem, Oregon.

"You're my halfback," he said, in welcome.

Lombardi had never before met the supple yet intense Californian who stood there with his leather bag. But he knew him.

He knew him from hours of watching him in movie clips that spring in New York, after Jim Lee Howell had hired Lombardi from West Point to coach the Giants' offense. ("He had those 16 millimeter eyeballs," Gifford was to say years later, praising Lombardi's diligence.) And from studying Gifford on film, Lombardi had mapped out an offense built around Frank's versatility. (It was a pattern Lombardi repeated in a subsequent segment of his coaching career when he took over Green Bay and made Paul Hornung his left halfback.)

He first learned with Gifford, and in the process Frank also matured into the most versatile player in professional football, a man who stuck around by his wits as well as his physical abilities for a dozen brilliant, exciting years in a period when New York became the professional football capital of the world. In his time, pro football also became the sociologically attuned sport that meshed with a burgeoning medium, television, to pervade the national scene with a brand of action that captivated a whole new breed of fans. And thanks in part to the role in which Lombardi put him, Frank Gifford was the first great hero of TV-age football.

He was beautifully cast for the part, one of those golden kids from southern California with the sculptured body and the dazzling (if shy) smile. He was an All-American at the University of Southern California who married the campus beauty queen. And he even acted in the movies when he wasn't playing football. However, Frank wasn't one of those supercilious pretty boys. For one thing, his nose was a little flat and just enough out of line for an interesting flaw in the features. And a personality that seemed haughty was really withdrawn and a trifle insecure, the psyche marred by transient early years in the oil fields of the southwest that finally led to a more or less permanent home in the southern end of California's San Joaquin Valley, where he had to work for whatever he got.

Frank Gifford the All-American, the All-Pro, the phenomenally successful television personality after his playing days, never got a free ride to any of the success points in his career. The way he made it in professional football was typical. In that summer of 1954, when he was first exposed to Lombardi, Frank was theoretically established as a pro. He was a defensive back!

Of course, he was good enough to be chosen to play in the Pro Bowl game after the 1953 season, his second with the Giants. But the new Giant coaching staff assembled by Jim Lee Howell felt there was intrinsic waste of talent in using Gifford with the defensive unit. He was the most elusive runner on the team, a strong blocker, a threat as a passer and a fine receiver—all abilities which could be used to move the ball, and which he had displayed in the last five games of the '53 season when they played him fifty-five minutes a game on both defense and offense.

Gifford was destined to play the next five years under Lombardi on offense, and they were the wonderful years when the Giants built the nucleus of a dynasty which was to remain a force in the NFL through 1963. Gifford was lucky, too, because in their system it was inevitable that he would become the glamor guy, and even today an examination of the team records reveals that he still holds the following Giant career marks for:

Most points scored (484).

Most touchdowns (78).

Most passes caught (367).

Most yards gained, passes (5,434).

He is also second to Alex Webster for the club ground gaining record and for the number of touchdowns scored rushing.

Right from the start of his concentration on offense, Frank was one of those rare species who could finish in the league's top ten in both running and receiving. But figures never accurately measured his contributions, at any stage of his career.

Let's take 1963, when Frank was thirty-three years old, playing his eleventh year in the league. To get him out of the heavy action, in deference to his age, they had made him a flanker. He didn't have the speed of the fly boys who began to show up in the wide receiving spots—Bobby Mitchell, recently switched from halfback, too, Del Shofner, Sonny Randle, Gail Cogdill. Guys who could turn it on and run past a defender. Frank had, instead, the "smarts"—the experience and the tricks to get open.

The Giants went into the last game of the season, against the Pittsburgh Steelers, with the Eastern Conference title at stake, winner take all. Y. A. Tittle was at his best in pitching them to a 16–3 lead at halftime. But in pro ball, you never rest on any lead. Coming out for the second half, Tittle and Gifford jostled shoulder pads in the narrow tunnel that led from the Giant dressing room through the dugout and onto the frozen turf of Yankee Stadium that mid-December day.

"What's doing on your side of the field?" the thirty-seven-year-old quarterback asked the thirty-three-year-old flanker.

"I can beat my man with a zig-in or zig-out," answered Gifford.

"I'll remember that," nodded Tittle.

Five minutes into the third quarter, the Steelers scored, shaving the Giant lead to 16–10. One more score would put them in control, and after the kickoff, they had the Giants bottled up, third down and eight, on the New York 23.

In the huddle, Tittle started to call a squareout pass to Gifford. It was Frank's pet route on the forty-two passes he caught that season. But he nudged Y. A. and said, "Naw, let's do a zig-out."

266

Delicate timing, anticipation and quick cutting featured Frank Gifford's pirouettes as a running back for the New York Giants. He evades Don Shula (26), who later became the coach of the Baltimore Colts.

His ability to run tricky routes and catch the football forged a new career for Frank Gifford as a flanker when he returned to the Giants in 1962 after a year's retirement.

Tittle, with the final say, called a zig-in pass which required Gifford to run eight yards straight down the field from his position wide on the right flank, then cut in to the middle at a 45-degree angle. As the play unwound, Frank faked a step to the outside before making his cut. That threw the defender off and gave him a little opening as he broke towards the center of the gridiron. But Tittle, under a severe rush from the Steeler front line, had to release the ball prematurely on a low, hard trajectory—a tough pass to catch under any circumstances.

It looked out of Frank's reach as he lunged for it at midfield. He left his feet entirely in a horizontal dive, with his right hand reaching out at the same time. The ball hit his fingers and stuck, with Frank tucking it into his stomach, one-handed, at the same instant the Steeler defensive back crashed down on top of him. He held on to the ball to give the Giants a life, and two plays later they went in for the touchdown and had the game under control again. They won, 33–17.

"Gifford's fantastic catch," said Steeler Coach Buddy Parker, "was the big play."

Coach Allie Sherman of the Giants had his own tribute:

"The guy had a bad muscle pull. His timing was off. They said we played him for sentiment. There ain't no sentiment in this game. The guy happens to be one helluva pro."

The best years, esthetically, were the early ones, particularly after Alex Webster joined the club in 1955 to play the other halfback post. That was the first time Frank made all-pro. He and Alex had a knack of picking up the vital two or three yards necessary for ball control after they were ostensibly stopped at the line of scrimmage. It wasn't power in Gifford's case because he never weighed more than 205 pounds at any point in his career and he frequently wore down to 190 during the course of a season. He had balance and a knack for twisting his hips just before contact so the tackler never got a good shot at him.

The Giants also made full use of his versatility. He caught thirty-three passes in 1955, and he was a dangerous threat on the pass-run option play that developed out of an end sweep and forced the defensive halfback to commit himself. He didn't overdo the passing bit, but he got plenty of mileage out of it. From 1954 through 1959, he completed a total of twenty passes. A dozen of them went for touchdowns.

The big year of his career was 1956 as the Giants swept to their first division title in eleven years, breaking the monopoly of the Cleveland Browns, who had won six straight after their entry into the NFL. Then, on the frozen turf of Yankee Stadium, wearing sneakers, the Giants annihilated the Bears, 47–7, for the NFL championship.

Gifford was their nonpareil offensive weapon. He gained 819 yards rushing, No. 5 on the NFL lists; he caught fifty-one passes, third best in the league, a fantastic feat for a regular back; he threw two touchdown passes; he kicked eight extra points and one field goal; he was the tenth leading scorer. But to be among the top five in pro football in both running and receiving—that was the *pièce de resistance*.

And one morning at the Hotel Excelsior in mid-Manhattan, where he and Maxine lived during the season with their kids, he was awakened and told he had been named the winner of the Jim Thorpe Trophy as the most valuable player in the National Football League. It had special significance for him because the vote included all the players in the NFL, in a poll conducted by Newspaper Enterprise Association, and is considered the most prestigious trophy in the game.

"All the good things," said Frank, "started happening to me after that."

He meant endorsements, the opportunity to act in films, the start of a television and radio career that put his annual earnings in the six-figure bracket and kept them there long after he had finished playing football.

The ruggedness of the game began to get to Frank the minute he reached his peak. In 1956, he already talked wistfully of retiring if he could get a coaching job at his alma mater, Southern California. But he kept coming back because, simply, he couldn't stay away.

"When I came up in '52, Maxine and I talked it over," he mused, "and decided we'd get a few bucks together, pay back the money I borrowed from Wellington Mara [owner of the Giants] to meet the expenses for Jeff's birth that June, and then call it a career after one season."

"The next thing we knew it was 1960."

The elemental pull of the game kept him going.

"I'll be honest with you," he told Jimmy Cannon, a New York columnist. "It's sort of an ego thing. The good ones kind of like it. Hell, I get more excitement in one day playing football than most people get in a lifetime. You prepare for a week to play a game. You play it and then for two or three days you replay it."

So, though he kept trying to phase himself out each year, July would find him back in training with a new challenge. The Gifford-Webster entente continued to be the most imposing in the game, with veteran Charley Conerly providing the right amount of leverage as a passer. In one stretch covering the 1957–58 seasons, Gifford set an NFL record by scoring touchdowns in ten straight games. The Giants won the Eastern division titles in 1958 and '59, though the Colts nosed them out both years for the NFL title. After the famous 1958 sudden-death overtime loss, Gifford again seriously contemplated retirement because 20 pounds had peeled off his already lean frame, and he had already made a pilot for a television series.

But the next May he was titillated by a new opportunity—he would become a quarterback. In his school days, Frank had shown ability as a passer. At Bakersfield Junior College, and then for two big years at Southern California, he had played both T-quarterback and tailback in the single wing, as the Trojans used a multiple offense. Now Charley Conerly was thirty-eight years old and becoming a physical risk; Don Heinrich couldn't pass well enough to take over fulltime; and the No. 1 draft choice, Lee Grosscup of Utah, obviously wouldn't be ready. So Frank was lured back to the ranks by the chance of being a field general and out of the main stream of fire.

It didn't work—not because Gifford wasn't capable, but because there was no one good enough to replace him at halfback. So he had another typically big Gifford year, leading the club in rushing and receiving, being named to the All-Pro team for the fifth straight season. At 29, however, there were slight signs of deterioration. Until then, Gifford was the kind of guy who never got hurt. The worst injury he could recall was

270

an appearance on TV's Masquerade Party, when he twisted an ankle ducking a hurled pie and then had two inches of skin peeled from his face while pulling the makeup off.

In late October, he played in Pittsburgh against the Steelers and on the first play of the game swooshed past defensive back Dick Alban to catch a long Conerly pass for a touchdown. Seconds later, the Giants recovered a fumble on the Steeler 28. Same play, with Gifford flanked out to his left, and Conerly hit him behind Alban for a second touchdown. But before halftime, he fell down catching a pass on the 6-yard line. He fell on the ball and tore a cartilage shielding his tenth rib. He tried to get up and fainted. They took him back to the hotel on a stretcher, and he was still on the same stretcher when he boarded the team plane back to New York.

"Just my luck," muttered Frank. "I could have beaten Alban long all day, maybe caught a dozen."

A year later one quick blow finished him, temporarily. The Giants were playing the Eagles, their chief rivals for Eastern honors. Trailing by a touchdown in the fourth quarter, they penetrated deep into Philadelphia territory. Gifford went up for a pass, concentrating entirely on the ball. From the blind side, Chuck Bednarik hit him full force, and Frank landed on his head. The ball spilled out of his arms, recovered by an Eagle, and Bednarik, waving both fists in the air, jumped up and down exultantly over Frank's prone body. Gifford had suffered a deep brain concussion, and in the clubhouse, Maxine, his wife, blanched when a cop walked to a phone, dialed headquarters and said, "I want to report a D.O.A. in the Giant dressing room." Then he added it was a special policeman who had died of a heart attack.

But Frank played no more football in 1960, and after the season he announced his retirement. Bednarik came in for a lot of heat because of his tackle, but Gifford said, "He was just doing his job. I ran into him later and we sat down and had a beer. The thing never came up. We didn't mention it. We talked about his kids."

Gifford turned to fulltime sportscasting and also scouted for the Giants to stay close to the scene. Yet it wasn't enough. Football wasn't out of his system. "You walk into the locker room and talk to the guys," he said, "but when they go out on the field, you go upstairs. I miss the feeling of belonging."

And so in 1962, at the age of thirty-two, well-fixed financially, secure in his future, with a wife and three growing children, Frank Gifford came back—in a strange position. Allie Sherman, who had taken over as head coach, made him a flanker. And Frank was happy.

"I made a lot of money in the year I stayed out," he said, "but I missed pro football. I missed it like hell. If you're lucky enough to be able to do this for a living, I think you should do it as long as you can. I'm as fast as I ever was. I've got better reflexes.

"You've got to be in top shape to be a flanker. I figure he logs 30 to 50 yards on every pass pattern. That's a lot of running when you consider we average 35 to 40 pass patterns a game. Sometimes it's pretty tough just to hustle out of the huddle."

Frank, in his comeback, hustled to his most productive year as a receiving threat, gaining a career high of 796 yards, average 20.4 yards per catch, scoring seven touchdowns on passes and adding another on a surprise end-around that recaptured for a moment his old running skills. In the second phase of his career, he tacked on three more productive seasons as the old pro who didn't go by the book—he cut on the wrong foot, his hands were up in an unorthodox position when he caught the ball—but provided a winning attitude to the Giants.

"Our game is 30 to 40 percent emotion," he said. "I always get the butterflies before every kickoff. Lack of mental effort makes more guys quit than losing a step. You get smart, you can pick up the step by thinking. When it's a drag, quit."

After the 1964 season, with the Giants in a tailspin and Frank realizing he could no longer help them, he quit. He was already the sports director of a New York television station and hosted a network radio show, plus a 15-minute pre-game TV show. He also became a prominent analyst of NFL games, a familiar figure around the nation. He had started this auxiliary career as a timorous, not particularly articulate speaker, a little ill at ease. But he tackled it with the same intensity he brought to sports and eventually acquired a fluency and poise that got him big national commercial accounts.

"I think pro football is perfectly in keeping with the times in which we live," he extemporized. "We live in a violent world, at a very fast pace. There's a relationship between society today and the game of pro football."

Frank never forgot his origins and always thought of himself as an athlete first.

On a Florida trip, he relaxed one evening at the Racquet Club in Miami, a hangout for buddies like Paul Hornung (the night Hornung found out he would be suspended by the NFL for gambling, he sought out Gifford and walked the streets of New York with him). Frank was minding his own business when a commotion broke out on the second level of the club.

Eva Gabor, also visiting there, rushed to the top of the stairs and screamed, "Help me! I've been robbed!"

Frank looked up at her casually.

"Well, do something," she spluttered, "you, you, you—halfwit!"

"I'm sorry, ma'am," said Frank, and he swears this is true. "I'm not a halfwit. I'm a halfback."

FRANK GIFFORD'S FAVORITE PLAY:

"I would have to say the run-pass option was my pet play because it gave me a chance to do what I could do best. We called it '49-option' on the Giants, which may sound familiar because it was the same as the famous Green Bay sweep which Paul Hornung ran for the Packers. The same man, Vince Lombardi, coached it in both places.

"The key to its success, I felt, was to convince the guards to make it look like a run. They both pulled out of the line. The left halfback either threw right away or tucked the ball under his arm and ran. But I remember I had to remind our guards, Jack Stroud and Bill Austin, to keep their blocks flat, not to stop and set up like it'd be a pass, otherwise they'd tip off the option.

"A time I used it to good advantage was in the final game of the 1958 season, when we had to beat the Cleveland Browns to win the Eastern title. We won the game, 13–10,

272

on Pat Summerall's fantastic 50-yard field goal in the snow. But before that our only touchdown came on a 49-option pass to end Bob Schnelker."

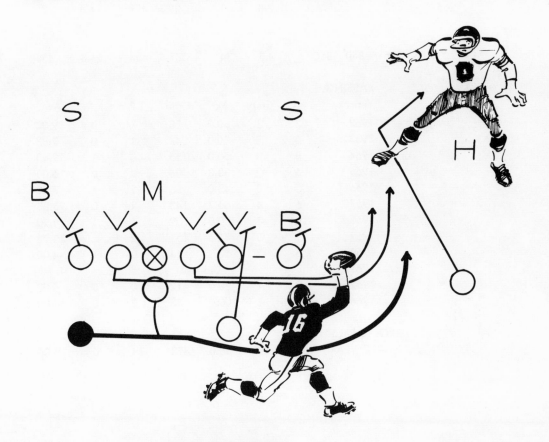

FRANK N. GIFFORD

BORN: Aug. 16, 1930   Height: 6'1"   Weight: 195

University of Southern California

New York Giants, 1952–60, 1962–64

		RUSHING				PASS RECEIVING				SCORING	
Year	G.	Att.	Yds.	Avg.	TD.	P.C.	Yds.	Avg.	TD.	TD.	Pts.
1952	10	38	116	3.1	0	5	36	7.2	0	0	0
1953	12	50	157	3.1	2	18	292	16.2	4	7	47
1954	9	66	368	5.6	2	14	154	11.0	1	3	18
1955	11	86	351	4.1	3	33	437	13.2	4	7	42
1956	12	159	819	5.2	5	51	603	11.8	4	9	65
1957	12	136	528	3.9	5	41	588	14.3	4	9	54
1958	10	115	468	4.1	8	29	330	11.4	2	10	60
1959	11	106	540	5.1	3	42	768	18.3	4	7	42
1960	8	77	232	3.0	4	24	344	14.3	3	7	42
1961					(Did not play)						

Year										
1962	14	2	18	9.0	1	39	796	20.4	7	8	48
1963	14	4	10	2.5	0	42	657	15.6	7	7	42
1964	13	1	2	2.0	1	29	429	14.8	3	4	24

PRO TOTALS
—12 YEARS 136 840 3609 4.3 34 367 5434 14.8 43 78 484

PASSING:

Year	Att.	Cmp.	Pct.	Gain	T.P.	P.I.	Avg.
1952	2	1	50.0	18	1	0	9.00
1953	6	3	50.0	47	1	0	7.83
1954	8	4	50.0	155	3	1	19.40
1955	6	2	33.3	96	2	0	16.00
1956	5	2	40.0	35	2	1	7.00
1957	6	4	66.7	143	2	0	23.83
1958	10	3	30.0	109	1	1	10.90
1959	11	5	45.5	151	2	2	13.73
1960	6	3	50.0	24	0	1	4.00
1961			(Did not play)				
1962	2	1	50.0	12	0	0	6.00
1964	1	1	100.0	33	0	0	33.00

PRO TOTALS
—12 YEARS 63 29 46.0 823 14 6 13.06

Hugh McElhenny

THE KING RAN SEVEN FEET TALL, BOTH
ELBOWS OVER HIS HEAD AND ONE KNEE
UNDER HIS CHIN. LORD, HOW HE RAISED
BUMPS ON THOSE TACKLERS.
—*a loyal San Francisco
49er fan.*

Hugh Edward McElhenny, called "The King," had a perfectly plausible explanation for his genius at running with a football. When he was a six-year-old kid playing on a Los Angeles sandlot marked "No Trespassing," the owner of the lot arrived suddenly, with a shotgun. The kids scattered, McElhenny in the forefront. "When I carried the ball," he said, "I thought of that man and his shotgun."

He also thought of a dark alley he used to have to cut through to get home at night.

"I was always scared," he recalled. "There was a light at the end of the alley and dark doorways on both sides of the street. So I wouldn't walk on either side. I'd run down the middle straight towards that light, and along the way, I'd sense a telephone pole which I couldn't see and duck away from it. And I'd have the feeling there was someone in each of those doorways trying to get at me.

"It was the same in football. I could just feel them coming for me. I could hear their footsteps."

Those footsteps, real and imagined, spurred him to some of the greatest open field running in the history of football.

Hugh McElhenny was a rookie pro halfback with the San Francisco 49ers in the fall of 1952 when the National Football League began to get an idea of his genius. He joined the club straight from the College All-Star game (where he had played with a couple of other West Coast collegiate progeny, Frank Gifford and Ollie Matson), arriving just in time for an exhibition game.

Frankie Albert, getting ready to call a play at midfield, yelled over to Coach Buck Shaw, "Send in McElhenny."

"He doesn't know the plays," Shaw shook his head.

"Since when did a little thing like that bother us?" flipped Frankie. In came McElhenny, and Albert in the huddle spread out his palm and improvised a play, noting the individual assignments.

"We'll call it a '27 toss,'" he said to McElhenny. "I'll pitch the ball out to you, and you take it from there."

McElhenny, unrehearsed, took it from there 40 yards to a touchdown.

Against the Los Angeles Rams, defending champions of the NFL, he ran back the opening kickoff of a preseason game for 62 yards. He was fidgety. An hour before the game, he got a wire saying his wife had given birth to their first child, a daughter.

In the second game of the regular schedule, he ran 89 yards from scrimmage through the whole Dallas Texan team. The 49ers started calling him "Nine Yard" McElhenny.

On October 19, in Chicago's Wrigley Field, he was really unveiled. Playing only half the time when the 49ers had the ball on offense, Mac collected 103 yards in twelve carries from scrimmage to set up four touchdowns. He ran a punt back 94 yards for a fifth as the Bears suffered a 40–16 defeat, their worst since Ernie Nevers had scored all the points in a 40–6 drubbing by the Chicago Cardinals in 1929.

For spectacular open field scampers, Hugh McElhenny was peerless. He was known as "The King."

"He's a combination of George McAfee and Bronko Nagurski," said Bernie Masterson, an assistant coach of the Bears. The 49ers gave him the ball and decided he needed a name more appropriate than "Nine Yard."

"The King" is what they come up with, and the nickname stuck throughout a career that spanned thirteen mercurial seasons.

His style was as unpredictable and eye-catching as the man. Hugh McElhenny, born the son of a successful vending company owner, had a flair for the unusual. When he was seven, he stepped on a broken bottle and ripped open his foot, severing the tendons. He was on crutches for seven months, and the doctors said his foot might be permanently deformed. But Hugh became a brilliant track man at George Washington High School in Los Angeles. In 1947, he was unbeaten in the broad jump and both the high and low hurdles, right through the California state championship meet. He tied the existing world prep record for the 120-yard high hurdles at 14 seconds flat. He also ran the 100-yard dash in 9.7 seconds.

Standing 6'1", filling out a limber frame to an eventual 205 pounds, he was ideally equipped to run with a football. But his father didn't care for the sport and wanted him to concentrate on track. He refused to sign the card which would let Hugh go out for football. His mother had to sign it.

After high school, Hugh signed on for an extension course at Southern California, with a side job of watering the gardens. Annoyed because he didn't get paid, he took off on a three-month bumming trip with a buddy through the midwest, picking strawberries and washing cars, with the idea they'd hop a cattle boat to Europe.

Instead, he realized he wanted to be closer to Peggy Ogston, whom he'd first met in the seventh grade in Los Angeles. He enrolled at Compton Junior College in the Los Angeles area and scored twenty-three touchdowns, a dozen of them on runs of more than 30 yards, while Compton breezed through twelve games undefeated and the national junior college championship. In the spring, he quit school, married Peggy four days later and magically showed up on the University of Washington campus in a recruiting *cause célèbre*.

With his curly black hair, puckish eyes and an easy grin, Hugh revelled in the life of a twenty-year-old college hero, even with the swirls of rumors about alumni gratuities that supported the McElhenny menage. "I've got three cars," he said in a beautiful put-on, "$30,000 in the bank, the promise of a lifetime job from four companies and two pro teams are paying my way through school. Every time I score a touchdown, a wealthy guy puts 10 bucks under my pillow. Hell, I can't afford to graduate."

For whatever he was getting, "Hurryin' Hugh," as they called him, delivered. In his first varsity game, against Utah, he broke the school rushing record. A week later, he ran the opening kickoff back 98 yards against a good Minnesota team. As a junior, he gained 296 yards in a game against Washington State. He also scored five touchdowns in that contest. Late in the game, a message came in from the bench. "Give it to McElhenny!" the substitute panted. "He's got a record coming up."

"Yeah?" said McElhenny. "What do I need?"

"Six yards."

Hugh ripped off tackle and made it with 7 yards to spare, also setting a new Pacific Coast ground-gaining mark for one season. Except for the pattern of Mac's scampers, there was really nothing fancy about the Washington attack. "We let him do what he does best," said Coach Howie Odell. "We just give him the ball."

His senior year, he was an All-American on a losing team and scored 20 points in a 20–20 tie with UCLA. "He is the darndest animal," said Uclan Coach Red Sanders. "He can run around you, through you and, if the situation demands it, right over you."

As a student, Hugh made no bones about his major at Washington.

"Why should I kid people?" he said. "I'm not a top student, and I'm not crazy about school. Football is my life, and that's where I'm going to make my money."

The San Francisco 49ers picked him first in a pro draft of such availables as Gifford, Les Richter of California, and Bill McColl of Stanford. Coach Buck Shaw had seen him score 22 points in a great game against California. McElhenny told owner Vic Morabito he wanted $30,000. "He looked at me," recalled McElhenny, "like I was some kind of nut. We 'compromised' at $7,000. That included bonus, salary, everything. My wife and I made more working at Washington." He grinned impishly.

"Men," Frankie Albert introduced him to the other 49ers, "meet the only college star who took a cut in salary to play pro football."

But right with his first year, McElhenny paid off for the 49ers. "When Hugh joined the 49ers," said Lou Spadia, who became the club president after the Morabito brothers died, "it was questionable whether our franchise could survive. He removed all doubt. That's why we regard him as our franchise saver."

His rookie year, McElhenny made the wire services' all-pro teams. He accounted for a fantastic total of 1,731 yards rushing, receiving, and returning punts and kickoffs. And he continued to be sensational as the 49ers built a reputation for potent offense. They came close to winning several times but never quite made it. At one time, they had a backfield of McElhenny and John Henry Johnson at the halfbacks, with Joe Perry at fullback—all three among the top ten leading ground gainers in history. And their quarterback was Y. A. Tittle, second only to John Unitas as the most effective passer in history. They came closest in 1957 when they tied the Lions for the Western crown and met in a playoff.

"It was heartbreaking," said Hugh. "I ran the opening kickoff back more than 50 yards, zig-zagged from one side of the field to the other until I covered at least 100, and then was brought down on the 9-yard line. We didn't score and lost the game, 31–27."

In the 1953 season alone, he had seven touchdown runs of 50 yards or more called back because of penalties.

Those years with the 49ers were bruising, too. In 1954, he sustained a shoulder separation and played the last half of the season with a special harness. In 1955, he injured his foot in the last exhibition game, sustaining a planetory neuroma which required surgery. Every Sunday he got two shots of novocaine before he suited up, another sustaining jolt at half time, and he played all twelve games on the schedule.

When Red Hickey became the 49ers coach in 1959, things started to turn sour for McElhenny. He was used less as a runner and more as a flanker. And after he showed the old running brilliance in the first part of the 1960 campaign, he wasn't used at all

The San Francisco 49ers in the mid-1950's put together one of the most talented backfields in history: left to right, halfback Hugh McElhenny, fullback Joe Perry, quarterback Y. A. Tittle, halfback John Henry Johnson.

With his "lived-in" face, McElhenny still retained enough youthful verve to contribute a couple of fine seasons to the Minnesota Vikings as an expansion draftee.

His elusiveness also made McElhenny a difficult man to cover as a pass receiver. He skips past Terry Barr of Detroit here to snatch a touchdown pass.

the last month of the season. "Hickey," said the veteran back, "thinks nobody over thirty can play this game." Mac was thirty-one.

The National Football League was expanding into Minnesota and stocking the new franchise with players made expendable by the other teams. When the new Vikings started to cull the 49er leftovers, there was McElhenny's name right on the top of the list. There was no sentiment left in football. The old warhorse had to whip himself into shape again to start a new career. Retirement was out of the question. A supermarket venture in which he had invested heavily on the Peninsula south of San Francisco was draining him. He needed the money.

And so he came in with the rest of the pickups, augmented by a couple of exciting young draftees like Fran Tarkenton and Tommy Mason, and showed the pros something all over again. "He's running harder and stronger now than he ever has," said Norm Van Brocklin, the new coach of the Vikings. "Maybe because he's lost a little of his speed, he's now running into people instead of around them. And he really lets them have it. Yet he can still go in an open field."

"You run with your head as much as your legs," said the veteran. "Your moves may depend on position on the field, the down, the yardage, your knowledge of the defensive man you're trying to beat. But there are times when all the moves in the world won't help you, and the only way you can help your team is with a couple of yards you can only get by driving straight ahead."

In Mac's comeback, he did everything he used to do in his coltish years, even returning kickoffs and punts, and he provided the Vikings with more than 1,000 yards of offense. "He helped us build a respectable team out of a group of displaced persons," said Van Brocklin, "and the inspiration and schooling he gave to Tommy Mason will be part of the record for as long as Tommy plays." Mason was the young halfback who was being groomed by Mac, selflessly, to take over the same position he played. And that happened quick enough, in 1962, as the old back's knees started to go.

Nineteen years of organized football had taken their physical toll. The cartilage in his left knee had literally worn out and snapped into three pieces. "Most guys plant their right foot when they cut," Hugh explained. "When I'm running and have to cut, instead of planting the right foot, I dip the left knee and cross over the right."

An operation put him into a semblance of working shape, but he was like the old fighter who's become a trial horse and hangs on pathetically to pick up another paycheck. McElhenny's outside business was completely busted now, and this was the only way he knew how to make a living for Peggy and the two girls.

There were flitting glimpses of the old McElhenny style. And there were small gratifications. The Vikings had elected him the captain of their offensive unit, and this was the first symbol of leadership in his entire career. "You've got to play in this game a long time to realize what that means to a man," he said emotionally.

"He had a Charlie Conerly type face," wrote Lee Grosscup, who had a brief spin with the Vikings in their '62 training camp, "full of lines and scars, each telling a story."

The Giants, having remarkably revived the career of his old backfield mate, Tittle, took a gamble and traded for McElhenny in '63. Hugh was so keyed up joining this new club, one that would give him the chance to savor the pride of contributing to a championship, that in an exhibition game with the Packers, he sneaked into the lineup four different times.

"He's still an artist at his job," said Coach Allie Sherman, and before the first Giant scrimmage of the year he asked McElhenny if he felt ready to participate.

The veteran back looked at him incredulously.

"Anything wrong?" wondered Allie.

"No, it's wonderful," grinned Hugh. "I've been playing football for close to twenty years, and this is the first time a coach ever asked me if I wanted to scrimmage. The others just told me what to do."

But McElhenny's bad knee filled with water after every exercise, and he was hardly able to practice between games. Still, he gave the Giants a lift. He made the key play in a game with Cleveland, catching a short swing pass and faking two Browns off their feet—they never touched him—to score a touchdown. He played in the NFL title game against the Bears and almost broke all the way with the second half kickoff. He was caught from behind after he ran out of gas.

The young McElhenny would have made it and won the game. The old McElhenny was barely hanging on. The Giants released him the next summer, and he dawdled through a final campaign with the Detroit Lions, who signed him as a free agent, before he realized the string had run out and it was time to go back to northern California and settle down to a new living.

One winter day Frank Gifford mused, "We called him 'The King.' Yet his retirement has gone unnoticed. It's a shame."

So Frank arranged a black-tie dinner in New York for him, and such distinguished guests as the late Senator Robert F. Kennedy turned out. Gifford remembered a college game when he played for Southern California against Washington and McElhenny.

"I punted from midfield," he said, "and The King caught the ball exactly on the goal line. He started to zig down the field, and suddenly there was only one man between him and the goal—me. He left me flat on my face and ran 100 yards for the touchdown."

And at other football gatherings, the image of McElhenny wasn't forgotten either.

"He would have been a sensation in any era," said Hall-of-Famer Ernie Nevers at a McElhenny tribute. "The only guy who has come close to his speed, balance, and elusiveness in recent years is Gale Sayers of the Chicago Bears."

"Mac was a better receiver than Sayers," noted Billy Wilson, a fine end for the 49ers and their assistant coach. "He also could cut a lot sharper. He would change his course two and three times in one run. He was the only 200-pounder I ever saw who could outmaneuver a 140-pounder."

"Mac," says Y. A. Tittle with some finality, "was the best broken-field runner pro football has ever seen."

"Mac's big outside play for San Francisco was '49 quick toss,'" said Coach Buck Shaw. "This play is still being run in pretty much the same form by a lot of clubs.

"It worked off a reverse turn by the quarterback and a direct pitch to the halfback. In my 38 years of coaching college and pro football, McElhenny was the greatest open field runner I ever coached or saw in action.

"When the wide defensive men on the strong side began playing to the outside, anticipating the wide play, the blocking would be changed and the quarterback would fake the pitch with a strong motion, then hand to the fullback driving over tackle. This kept defenses from overshifting on McElhenny."

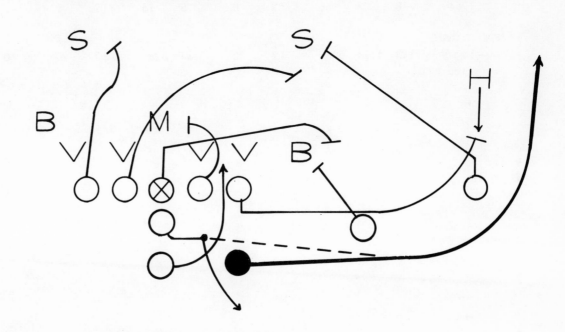

HUGH EDWARD "KING" MCELHENNY

BORN: Dec. 31, 1928   Height: 6'1"   Weight: 205
University of Washington

San Francisco, 1952–60
Minnesota, 1961–62
New York Giants, 1963
Detroit, 1964

Year	G.	Att.	RUSHING Yds.	Avg.	TD.	P.C.	PASS RECEIVING Yds.	Avg.	TD.	SCORING TD.	Pts.
1952	12	98	684	*7.0	6	26	367	14.1	3	10	60
1953	12	112	503	4.5	3	30	474	15.8	2	5	30

Year											
1954	6	64	515	*8.0	6	8	162	20.3	0	6	36
1955	12	90	327	3.6	4	11	203	18.5	2	6	36
1956	12	185	916	5.0	8	16	193	12.1	0	8	48
1957	12	102	478	4.7	1	37	458	12.4	2	3	18
1958	12	113	451	4.0	6	31	366	11.8	2	8	48
1959	10	18	67	3.7	1	22	329	15.0	3	4	24
1960	9	95	347	3.7	0	14	114	8.1	1	1	6
1961	13	120	570	4.8	3	37	283	7.6	3	7	42
1962	11	50	200	4.0	0	16	191	11.9	0	0	0
1963	14	55	175	3.2	0	11	91	8.3	2	2	12
1964	8	22	48	2.2	0	5	16	3.2	0	0	0

PRO TOTALS
| —13 YEARS | 143 | 1124 | 5281 | 4.7 | 38 | 264 | 3247 | 12.3 | 20 | 60 | 360 |

* Led NFL.

Ollie Matson

HE IS NOT MR. OUTSIDE OR MR. INSIDE.
HE IS MR. ALLSIDE AND MR. EVERY-
WHERE.

—Joe Kuharich, coach,
Chicago Cardinals.

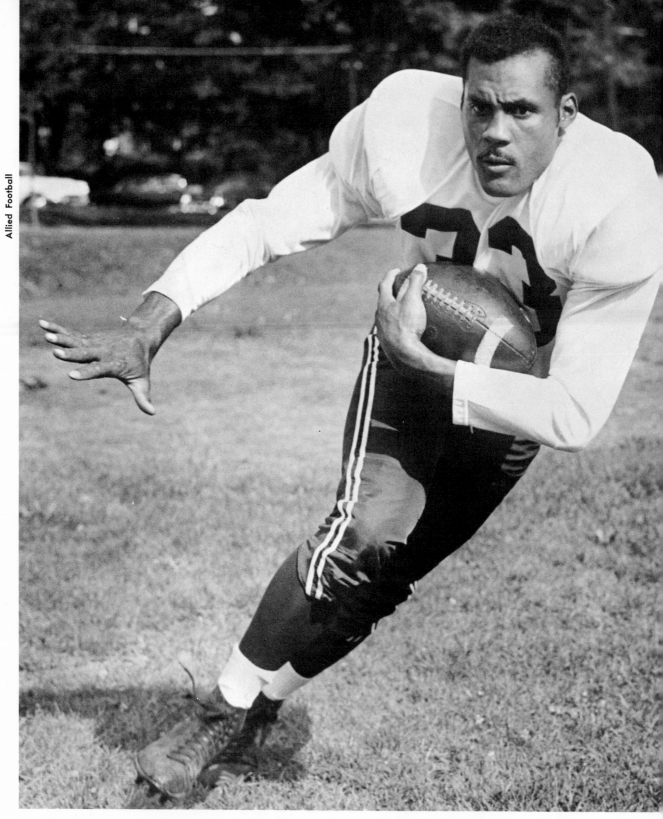

Ollie Matson brought an Olympic sprinter's speed to pro football, and eventually the Chicago Cardinals traded him to Los Angeles for 10 players.

The hypothesis is an indulgence of logic that lends itself amiably to sports. How many homers would Ted Williams have hit if he had played half his games aiming at the short right field porch in Yankee Stadium? Likewise, what would Joe DiMaggio have accomplished against the friendly left field barrier in Fenway Park? How many yards would Oliver Genoa Matson have gained if he played his career behind those great Green Bay lines of the 1960's?

The Matson thesis is peculiarly interesting because time shreds a man's reputation once the talent erodes and he becomes just another ballplayer, which Ollie Matson was the last half of his career. And yet there was a period in professional football when Ollie Matson was the top man in the game, a lone star in a sea of mediocrity that called itself the Chicago Cardinals. In fact, during the fourteen full seasons Ollie Matson played in the NFL, only twice did the teams on which he played win more games than they lost. Generally, they were hopeless and apathetic, and eventually they dragged him down to their level so that at the end Ollie was sort of an old handyman pro picking up a paycheck for filling in wherever it was most convenient. That's not to intimate he ever stopped trying. But the system licked him. The old football cliché that a man's only as good as the guys he's playing with applied to Matson just as it had to another Cardinal great before him, Charley Trippi.

And it was Ollie's bad luck that when he finally escaped from the Cardinals, just before the midpoint of his career, the teams he wound up with were no better.

There was a natural dichotomy in his tenure as a pro. For seven years, there was no better all around back in the league, every facet of offensive play considered. That was the real Ollie Matson, the one that got such tributes as: ". . . I have never seen anything like him in pro ball." That was from Charley Trippi, whose career with the Cardinals was fading just as Ollie's was coming on.

Matson bore the test of comparison with his contemporaries. He was bigger and stronger than Gifford; he was faster than McElhenny; he was more versatile than Jimmy Brown. In all the history of pro football, only one man, Brown, ever accounted for more than the 12,799 yards that Matson had accumulated when his pro career was done. But Ollie had one basic handicap in relation to the competition—he never played on a really good team with a finely balanced attack, which meant he was seldom in a position to gain maximum attention.

In retrospect, it seemed like Ollie was always destined for that kind of negative position, starting with his college days at the University of San Francisco. Their coach was Joe Kuharich, whose career was destined to be intertwined with Matson. Their publicity man was a young, bright fellow named Alvin "Pete" Rozelle. Their talent was absolutely great. Their linemen included Dick Stanfel, Gino Marchetti, and Bob St. Clair, each of them a future all-pro. Other USF players of the Matson era who went into pro ball were guard Red Stephens, end Ralph Thomas, quarterback Ed Brown, and halfbacks Roy Barni and Joe Scudero.

289

But the Dons, as USF was called, had trouble putting together a good schedule. None of the big schools on the West Coast wanted to risk their reputations against them. The writer saw Matson's debut as a college player against little College of the Pacific, which featured a dervish quarterback named Eddie LeBaron. In the game program, Pete Rozelle wrote, "The most widely known Don is the one who has not played a minute of varsity ball, sophomore Ollie Matson. USF supporters would be very satisfied if the 9.6 sprinter could utilize his 207 pounds in accounting for even half of the nineteen touchdowns he scored last fall as an All-American Junior College halfback at San Francisco City College."

The COP Bengals, who were loaded with a host of future pros themselves, stopped Matson cold. But you could tell he was going to be a great one. He would glide along behind the line of scrimmage, as if he were loafing, then suddenly hit a quick opening with a boom. The combination of speed and power was evident. Now all Ollie needed to do was to apply it, and that came in a game against St. Bonaventure, which was coached by Hughie Devore.

"Get that quitter!" yelled Devore the first time Matson ran near the Bonnie bench in Kezar Stadium.

Matson flushed.

"Hit him!" Devore railed. "He can't take it!"

Ollie was disturbed.

"He can't play football!" Devore continued his torment. And for three quarters, as Matson's play lagged, the teams were locked in a 21–21 tie.

"Then," said Ollie, "something happened inside of me. I can't explain it. But some mysterious force gave me a power I never had before. I suddenly seemed able to do the things I wanted to do and answer Devore in exactly the way I wanted to."

He raced for two touchdowns in five minutes of the last quarter—the first on a 92-yard gallop, the other measuring 42 yards. And after the game, Devore made it a point to find Ollie and tell him: "You bounced back. You showed me something. You've got it. Never let it get away from you."

Ollie's talents crested in 1951 when the Dons romped through a nine-game schedule undefeated. Matson, fulfilling Rozelle's early hopes more than twice over, scored twenty-one touchdowns and gained 1,566 yards for a new collegiate career record of 3,166 yards. The peak moment was in a game against Fordham in the Polo Grounds before the critical New York press. Despite their great individual talents, the Dons were thin in depth. They were wearing out in the fourth quarter when Fordham tied the score at 19–19. Matson, playing both ways, had already run one kickoff back 94 yards. He was dragging. On the sidelines, his backfield partner, Scudero, was hurt. "One more time, Ollie," pleaded Joey, as Matson took a deep breath. "Don't let us down now."

Ollie trotted out for the kickoff, lined up deep, caught the ball on the 10-yard line and threaded through the Fordham team 90 yards for a score. It was a reflex application of a drill that Joe Kuharich had used in practice sessions all through Ollie's varsity career. He'd line up eleven defensive players the length of the field. One behind the other. Matson would start at the goal line and try to run through them, with no blocking help. If he got past the first, the second would take a crack at him and so on down the line. Ollie had to stick to a course only five yards wide. "Maybe," said Kuharich, "someone would bring him down once every four times." After the Fordham exhibition, Kuharich said, with some exasperation: "If Ollie were with California or Notre Dame or Michigan he'd be hailed as another Jim Thorpe or Red Grange. He's a great runner. . . . He can also block, tackle, receive and hawk passes.

"I've seen all the great backs since 1926 when I was a kid—Marchy Schwartz, Joe Savoldi, Marty Brill, Marshall Goldberg, Bill Dudley. Some of them might have been able to do one thing better than Ollie. None could do everything as well.

"And I don't think he's reached his full potential. He should make a tremendous pro."

With Ollie's graduation, the University of San Francisco dropped football from its intercollegiate program and never picked it up again as a major sport. Kuharich was hired to coach the Chicago Cardinals. The first man they drafted was Ollie Matson.

He had a previous personal commitment, however. Ollie wanted to compete in the 1952 Olympic Games at Helsinki, Finland. He had been a fine high school track man. When he was seventeen, he had chased Herb McKenley of Jamaica to a world record time of 46 seconds flat in the 440-yard run. Dink Templeton, the venerable Stanford track coach, told him he was wasting his time. The varsity football interlude had shortened his stride. He'd have to learn to run all over again. But Ollie told him that when the boat left for Helsinki, he'd be on it. And he was. He barely qualified for the 400-meters.

The great quarter-milers of that era were Herb McKenley and George Rhoden of Jamaica, and Mal Whitfield of the United States. Ollie was sitting around playing cards with them the day before the race, and he told them quietly, "Fellers, there are three places on that stand, and I'm going to be on one of them." He finished third behind the Jamaicans to win a bronze medal, shutting out Whitfield (who later won the 800 meters). Ollie also picked up a gold medal running on the victorious 1600-meter relay team.

Then he came back to play professional football. In his first game, he was kicked out for fighting with veteran Sammy Baugh in the old quarterback's last appearance as a pro. In his second regular season game as a Cardinal, he returned a kickoff 100 yards against the Chicago Bears, and Ollie was well on his way to fulfilling Kuharich's prediction that he'd be a "tremendous pro."

"We played him both ways with a broken wrist against the Eagles," recalled Kuharich, "and he scored two touchdowns and intercepted a pass in the end zone." He also scored four touchdowns in the final period against the Steelers.

Matson went into the service and missed the 1953 season but returned in 1954 without a hitch in stride. Kuharich by then had moved over to the Washington Redskins and got a good view of Ollie from the other side of the field. Matson ripped off a 79-yard touchdown run, one of four he scored in the course of a one-man spree. He staked out a position on the all-pro teams for four straight years.

The only year the Cardinals came close to having a representative team in Matson's time was 1956 when they won 7 and lost 5, four of those games by a margin of a touchdown or less, and finished second to the New York Giants. Matson had backfield help

With mediocre support during most of his career with the Cards, Matson found most teams keying on his runs.

from Johnny Olszewski, a rugged blocker who was also a tough inside runner and gained 598 yards; Dave Mann, a fleet wingback and outside threat; and Lamar McHan, an adequate passer and dangerous running threat in the split-T which the Cards used. Ollie had his greatest rushing season, gaining 924 yards, and that doesn't include 232 yards which were called back because of penalties in the last two games.

By now he was a serene, pipe-smoking veteran (at the age of twenty-six) who could speak with authority on the art of running, and these were his thoughts, catalogued by Tex Maule in *Sports Illustrated:*

"You have to know how to use your speed. You have to use your head to some extent to use your speed to its fullest capacity. You have to set up the defense for the benefit of your blockers. You got to use your speed to get to the hole as soon as the blocker makes contact. When the defense man puts his hand out to ward off the blocker, you got to be there going fast to go by. You got to go right at the hole to do that; you can't square the route. By that I mean you can't run to the side and then cut in at the hole—you got to go right at it."

He also had a limp leg action which enhanced his open field capabilities.

"I've found it more beneficial to go right at a defensive halfback at slow speed," he said. "He can't judge your speed when you're coming straight at him, then you can pivot and put on that burst of speed and he'll miss you just a little bit. That's all you need—that little bit of speed."

Out in Los Angeles, the Rams slavered for that speed. They could see it teamed with that of Jaguar Jon Arnett, a young halfback from the University of Southern California who usurped Ollie's spot in the all-pro selections for 1958. Particularly anxious for Matson was their general manager, still youthful Pete Rozelle, who had come up the ladder from the University of San Francisco. The frustrations were building up in Ollie. He told Walter Wolfner, the managing director of the Cardinals, to go ahead when the idea of a trade was broached. The Rams were a force in the Western Conference, having finished only one game behind the world championship Colts, and Ollie preferred living on the West Coast.

On March 23, 1959, one of the most startling and drastic deals in the history of pro football was effected. Ollie Matson was traded to the Los Angeles Rams for *nine* players. Among them were such regular offensive and defensive linemen as Ken Panfil, Frank Fuller, Glenn Holtzmann, and Art Hauser. The Rams gambled that a twenty-nine-year-old back would compensate for the decimation of their roster. They lost.

The trade generally is noted as the initial step in the collapse of the Rams, which lasted for the next seven years and cost Coach Sid Gillman his job (Rozelle, of course, went on to bigger and better things as the commissioner of pro football). Los Angeles dropped from a contender to last place in the West. And poor Ollie—the change in scenery didn't pan out for him either, though he waged a valiant foray against the opposition in 1959, his first year with the Rams, to gain 863 yards.

"Somehow," he said philosophically, years later, "it was forgotten that I was the third leading ground gainer in the NFL. I think it is unfair for outsiders to criticize a trade. Only the people close to it know what they need and want. And often the outcome of a trade depends on how the player is used and handled."

It was a cinch that Ollie didn't think they handled him right. First, Gillman, who only lasted through the 1959 season, was a precision coach who wanted his runs and pass routes to adhere to a set pattern, and Ollie had spent all his years with the Cardinals as an individualist. Then Bob Waterfield, the old Ram hero, came in as the coach and began to see Ollie as the savior of his defense, after which he had visions of Ollie as a slotback, calling him the best in the league at that position. Finally, Ollie decided to play out his option—"I've been very disillusioned since I joined the Rams; I never felt I was given the opportunity to perform as I had in Chicago"—and the Rams decided not to play him at all.

After the 1962 season, he was traded to the Detroit Lions for a second string guard, Harley Sewell, who never even showed up with the Rams. The Lions figured Ollie, at thirty-three, would be the spur to make their fullback incumbent, Nick Pietrosante, hustle more. The Lions didn't use him any more than the Rams. Ollie hurt his foot early in the season and carried the ball exactly thirteen times (the year before for the Rams, he had carried it exactly three times). Matson didn't have the familiar number 33 on his uniform. That belonged to Pietrosante. After one year in Detroit, he moved on again. Matson was virtually a throw-in on a deal which sent defensive tackle Floyd Peters to the Eagles for offensive tackle J. D. Smith.

What did the Eagles want with a thirty-four-year-old running back, rusty from disuse, certainly a step or two slower and more brittle? For that, you had to ask their coach, none other than Joe Kuharich, who had started Ollie off fifteen years earlier at USF.

"Ollie," said Joe positively, "could be as good as ever. He's picked up speed [note: Kuharich has always worn rose-tinted glasses], and he weighs 215 pounds, which is what he should always have weighed instead of five pounds lighter."

And what did Ollie think about it?

"I'm home again," he said succinctly. He also got number 33 back. Amazingly, there was a revival of the old Matson form in 1964. He filled in for hobbled Timmy Brown at halfback; he played next to him at fullback. He carried the ball ninety-six times in a dozen games and gained 404 yards, plus another 242 on seventeen pass receptions. For two more seasons after that, Ollie continued to do spot duty in a thoroughly professional manner. At the age of thirty-six, he carried twenty-six kickoffs back for 544 yards in a job that most backs disdain because it's rigorous and it's dangerous.

And after he formally retired in 1967, to scout for the Eagles, he was prepared to play again if Kuharich had needed him. "Age," he said, "is compounded of a lot of things. There's the difference in body structures between one man and another. There's the difference in antecedents. There's the difference in the way men live."

And Ollie Matson liked to live easily. He was a quiet man whose personality radiated calmness and friendliness. He never grew old in looks. He never picked up weight. A pencil-thin mustache was the only distinctive feature in a handsome olive-skinned face. He had always been quiet, from the time his mother, a school teacher, moved him from his native Texas to San Francisco in his teens. But Ollie was also a competitor always, from his first contact with football.

294

"I loved to play," Ollie once reminisced. "I used to go out on Sunday and play in my Sunday clothes and get them all dirty, but my mother never became angry with me at all. She encouraged me to play if I loved it."

Considering the frustrations of fourteen years as a pro, Ollie had to love it. There was only one regret. "I came along too early," he said. "You ever read that old comic strip, 'Born 30 Years Too Soon'—I think that's what it was. If I was coming up now, I'd get so much money I'd have to carry it in shopping bags."

OLIVER GENOA "OLLIE" MATSON

BORN: May 1, 1930   Height: 6'2"   Weight: 220
University of San Francisco

Chicago Cardinals, 1952–58
Los Angeles Rams, 1959–62
Detroit, 1963
Philadelphia, 1964–66

Year	G.	Att.	RUSHING Yds.	Avg.	TD.	P.C.	PASS RECEIVING Yds.	Avg.	TD.	SCORING TD.	Pts.
1952	11	96	344	3.6	3	11	187	17.0	3	9	54
1953					(In Military Service)						
1954	12	101	506	5.0	4	34	611	18.0	3	9	54
1955	12	109	475	4.4	1	17	237	13.9	2	5	30
1956	12	192	924	4.8	5	15	199	13.3	2	8	48
1957	12	134	577	4.3	6	20	451	22.6	3	9	54
1958	12	129	505	3.9	4	33	465	14.1	3	10	60
1959	12	161	863	5.4	6	18	130	7.2	0	6	36
1960	12	61	170	2.9	1	15	98	6.5	0	1	6
1961	14	24	181	7.5	2	29	537	18.5	3	5	30
1962	13	3	0	0.0	0	3	49	16.3	1	1	6
1963	8	13	20	1.5	0	2	20	10.0	0	0	0
1964	12	96	404	4.2	4	17	242	14.2	1	5	30
1965	14	22	103	4.7	2	2	29	14.5	1	3	18
1966	14	29	101	3.5	1	6	30	5.0	1	2	12

PRO TOTALS

	G.	Att.	Yds.	Avg.	TD.	P.C.	Yds.	Avg.	TD.	TD.	Pts.
—14 YEARS	170	1170	5173	4.4	39	222	3285	14.8	23	73	438

Joe Perry

WHEN THAT GUY COMES BY TO TAKE
A HANDOFF, HIS SLIP-STREAM DARN
NEAR KNOCKS YOU OVER. HE'S STRICTLY
JET-PROPELLED.
—*Frank Albert, quarterback,*
San Francisco 49ers.

Cal-Pictures

They called Joe Perry "The Jet" because of his fast takeoff for the 49ers.

A quarterback had to get used to Joe Perry. Approaching a line of scrimmage, Joe had only one gait. Faster. So there was havoc when the greatest players in the Western Conference of the National Football League gathered to practice for the Pro Bowl game in January 1952. Bobby Layne of the Detroit Lions, seeing Perry on his side of the line of scrimmage for the first time, shook his head dolefully.

"None of us quarterbacks," admitted Bobby, "could hand the ball off to him fast enough. He disrupted all our practice sessions. He'd be past us in a flash before we could reach out and hand him the ball."

Eventually, quarterbacks adjusted to Joe Perry's speed because the compactly bundled fullback of the San Francisco 49ers lasted sixteen years in pro football and never let up. It was the key to his longevity.

Joe Jet, a title endowed upon him by Frankie Albert, the first of many quarterbacks who had to adjust to his takeoff launch, played over a stretch of years when the 230-pound defensive lineman became archaic—a 275-pounder emerged as the ideal—and the 230-pound fullback became the norm. Joe Jet started out in 1948 playing fullback at 200 pounds, and he finished in 1963 at 195 pounds, a marvel of his age.

His blazing propulsion eventually justified a docking platform for Fletcher Joseph Perry in Pro Football's Hall of Fame in Canton, Ohio. The scientific facts were unalterable: 1,737 rushing attempts for 8,378 yards and an NFL career average of 4.82 yards, which placed him third on the all-time list in each category for as far back as pro football was played.

He was miscast for greatness—an in-between type of runner who didn't have the natural power of the traditional fullback or the instinctive moves of the slippery halfback. He just had that speed and the will to use it. And he was smart. Buck Shaw, his coach on the 49ers, said, "He was the only man who could sit down after a game and diagram the opponents' defense on every play." Bobby Layne, who once played with him in a Hula Bowl game, marveled at Perry's acuity. In practice sessions, when Bobby wanted a breather, Perry stepped in at quarterback and knew all the assignments and all the plays and all the mechanics of running them.

Yet his football beginnings were most humble, with none of the sophisticated trappings of the big time college background. Joe didn't make a reputation for himself before he entered professional football. He was born in Stevens, Arkansas, but grew up in Los Angeles. At Jordan High School, which produced many fine Negro track stars, Joe was an outstanding sprinter (9.7 for the 100), broadjumper (23'5"), high jumper (6'3") and even a shot-putter (55' with the light shot). His mother wouldn't permit him to play football, so he went out for the team on the sly, broke a bone in his ankle and walked home five blocks with the injury to keep from revealing it. It swelled up, and he had to tell his mother. "If you want to play that bad," said Mrs. Perry, "you have my blessings." In normal times, he would have been an outstanding college prospect, but this was World War II, and Joe put in hitches with the Maritime Service while going off and on to Compton Junior College. It was the same school which later produced Hugh McElhenny, his longtime running mate on the 49ers. In 1944 Joe scored twenty-two touchdowns. After his second season at Compton, Joe went into the Navy and was stationed at the Alameda Naval Air Station in the San Francisco area.

His coach was John Woudenberg, a tackle with the newly organized 49ers who coached the Navy team in his spare time, and he kept urging Buck Shaw to come out and watch "this kid fullback I got." "When we need a touchdown," said Woudenberg, "we hand the ball to Perry, point him in the right direction and step aside." Before his own teammates were run over. Talk about speed—in the spring of 1947, Joe went over to the West Coast Relays in Fresno and raced against Mel Patton, the reigning "fastest human in the world." Perry ran a 9.5 second 100-yard dash and lost to Patton by a foot. In the fall of 1947, Shaw and owner Tony Morabito took a Saturday afternoon off and went out to watch the Alameda sailors play San Francisco State. Running from tailback in the single wing, Perry ran 75 yards on the first play of the game. He went 85 yards the second time. Then 60 and finally 52, before the coach took him out of the game.

Shaw looked at Morabito. Tony winked. This was the boy who'd take over for Norm Standlee when the veteran 49er fullback needed a replacement. But Joe wasn't a complete secret to football people. Because he had college eligibility, several big schools went after him. "Some of them," revealed Joe with a smile, "offered me more than Morabito did." The Los Angeles Rams almost doubled the 49er offer. Joe preferred dealing with Morabito. On a foggy San Francisco morning, at the polo field in Golden Gate park where the 49ers then practiced, he shook Morabito's hand and said he'd play for him. Then he borrowed five bucks from the 49ers' owner.

In 1948, when he reported, he shared the fullback's job with Standlee. His 7.3 yards per carry was the best average in the All-America Conference, and he scored a league-leading total of ten touchdowns on the ground. The 49ers really had something if they could harness it.

"His tremendous speed posed the only problem I ever had with him," said Shaw. "When he first joined us, he ran like a sprinter, straight ahead. When he got open, if a man was in his way, all he had to do was stand there to bring Joe down. We had to convince him to veer, to shift the ball from one arm to the other, to use his free arm as a lever."

Perry learned fast. In 1949, he shoved Standlee to the defensive unit, led the AAC in ground-gaining with 783 yards and displaced famed Marion Motley of the Browns as the official all-league fullback. His career was fully launched as the 49ers switched over the National Football League.

In 1952, after Hugh McElhenny joined the team, adding another dimension to the 49ers' offensive threat, Perry thrived as a productive runner. He became a member of the very exclusive 1,000-yard club in 1953, the fourth man in history to top that figure for rushing. And he reached his all-time high of 1,049 yards the next season. He led the NFL in rushing both years. The Perry-McElhenny double-pronged threat gave the 49ers the most potent offense in the game.

"Perry is like a bowling ball fired from a howitzer," said Frankie Albert. "It whistles straight down the middle and sends pins flying in every direction. McElhenny is like

300

a bowling ball thrown with 'body english.' It slides crazily down the alley, curls around the pins and scatters them gently. The net result is the same—a strike in both cases."

For constant productivity, there was never anyone to match Joe Jet until Jimmy Brown came along. For eleven straight years, Perry was the spearhead of the 49ers' offense. They did everything but win. It was galling to Joe, intense on the inside and mild in manner on the outside. The criticism burned him. "For two years," he noted, "I never read the newspapers."

And it was gruelling. He once slammed through the middle, head down, going full speed, unable to brake himself as he hurtled into the end zone and crashed into a goal post. Perry bounced off, staggered and wobbled back to the huddle, not realizing he'd scored. "Let's try it again," he muttered. "Somebody missed a block on that linebacker."

Over the years in San Francisco, he had thirty stitches taken in his face, broke ten ribs, suffered two shoulder separations, a fractured cheekbone, sprained his ankle some fifteen times and frequently strained ligaments in his knee. But he always carried the ball an average of anywhere from ten to fifteen times a game on a team that had a throwing quarterback like Y. A. Tittle.

Joe was one of the first backs to wear a plastic face guard on his helmet and made the mistake of discarding it for one game against the Rams in 1953 because it was hot in Kezar Stadium. After a 45-yard patented Perry burst, he was hemmed in against the sidelines, where a gang of Rams fell all over him. One of them led with his elbows, and Perry got up spitting out teeth. Four of them were his own; four were on a smashed bridge. He stayed in the game, gained 108 yards in 14 carries and scored three of the four touchdowns in a 31–30 thriller won by the 49ers. His dentist bill totalled $320.

"The work wasn't too costly," shrugged Joe. "After all, there were no extractions."

Joe didn't duck any brawls, although after he joined the team, the only Negro on the 49ers, at a time when Jackie Robinson was also pioneering the advent of the black man in major league baseball, owner Tony Morabito cautioned him, "Never, regardless of what happens, put up your dukes." There was plenty of provocation in the early days as players baited him with ethnic slurs—"I didn't expect anything like the nasty names I'd hear as a Negro."

A few years later, he let loose when he saw a couple of Philadelphia Eagles giving young Charley Powell a rough time. Powell was a defensive end who came to the 49ers straight out of high school, and Perry, knowing what it was like to be an unknown among the pros, looked after him. Joe was sitting on the bench, as he recalled, when the two Eagles ganged up on Powell (who later became a professional boxer). "I was so mad," said Joe, "I jumped up without my helmet and sprinted over to join in. I could have been killed. I hit one of the Eagles in the belly and the other one on the chin. Someone started hitting me in the head with the helmet. Then just about everybody got in the fight, even guys in the band."

Joe never became a militant. It wasn't his nature. He showed a smile with a lot of gold in his teeth. And he did his job, without regard for the risk. "There's no room in this game for caution," he said. "Once you get cautious you're through."

Even the best of them, though, wear out—at least that was Red Hickey's philosophy when he took over the coaching of the 49ers. In 1960, he sat Perry on the bench more than half the season—next to McElhenny and Tittle—while a new young fullback, J. D. Smith, carried the ball. The next year Red got rid of all the old-timers. Joe Perry, after all those years of service, was traded to the Baltimore Colts for a nondescript draft choice. Perry, at thirty-four, might have considered retirement, but there were two dissuading arguments. A service station business in downtown San Francisco turned out to be a loser, so he needed the money. And he wasn't ready to quit.

"Football is my life," he said. "I've given it everything I've had and I'll continue to do so as long as I can do the job. I just try to stay in good physical condition, working out with weights during the off-season, and when it's time to start playing, I don't seem to have trouble."

The Colts were in desperate need of a fullback after Alan Ameche snapped his Achilles tendon, forcing his premature retirement. Their running game had disappeared. Now they were putting it in the hands of a thirty-four-year-old fullback who weighed 195 pounds. The result was fairly amazing. In the opening game of the 1961 season, against the Los Angeles Rams, the Colts found themselves on the short end of a 24–10 score late in the second period. The expected tactic was a barrage of passes by the incomparable Johnny Unitas, especially since their key runner, Lenny Moore, was injured in the second quarter. But Unitas turned to Perry and started feeding him the ball. Altogether, the quick-starting fullback carried eighteen times for a total of 108 yards and turned the game around into a 27–24 victory. He became their old reliable, just as he had been for the 49ers those many years. He returned to the top ten among the league's runners and led the Colts with a season total of 675 yards. His durability gave them a balanced attack again. His enthusiasm flabbergasted them.

"Every Sunday offers a new adventure," said the veteran. "I don't suppose anyone who plays this game really expects to come out of the battle in one piece. I'm not crazy about the contact. How can anyone be? Who likes to get beat up every week? I'd rather go all the way on every play without a hand laid on me. But it doesn't work out that way."

On August 16th, 1962, preparing for his second season with the Colts, Perry carried the ball on a routine play in a preseason game with the Washington Redskins. He was sandwiched by two tacklers and couldn't get up. The ligaments in his right knee were torn, and that same night he was on the operating table for repairs. Of course, the Colts didn't expect to see him again the rest of the season. And a man who depends on his legs for a living and has a knee operation at thirty-five should start looking around quickly for another career.

A month later, when the Colts opened the regular season with the Rams again, Perry was on the sidelines—in uniform! He didn't play. They held him out until the next week, when he carried eight times against Minnesota. In mid-October, when the Colts played the Cleveland Browns, Perry ripped off 57 yards in eight carries for his contribution in a 36–14 rout. The great Jim Brown, at fullback for Cleveland, was held to 11 yards. Perry still ranked as the starting fullback through most of the season.

302

Perry's roommate on the road for the two years he played in Baltimore was Lenny Moore, a ranking star in the league. Said Lenny, "I was overwhelmed by the guy. I didn't know what to say, I was so much in awe of him. Joe was the best conditioned athlete I ever saw. And he was first class all the way in everything he did—in the way he dressed, the way he took care of himself, the way he played."

He even came back to the 1963 Baltimore training camp, determined he'd be the Colts' starter. However, the jet burners were starting to clog. He was released on the eve of the season. His old team, the 49ers, then made the grand gesture and picked him up for one final fling so he could qualify for the players' pension. There was no embarrassment for Joe, coming back to play for Red Hickey again. "You know me," he shrugged. "I've never been angry with anyone. San Francisco is a nice place to end it up. I have no intention of playing beyond this season."

He stuck to his word and quit. The 49ers made room for him in their organization, first as a scout for a few years, later as a fulltime member of their coaching staff. In 1969, he was selected for the Hall of Fame. Perhaps Joe Perry didn't receive the high acclaim that was given to many of the runners who played during his tenure. But he passed a lot of them along the way.

FLETCHER JOSEPH "JOE" PERRY

BORN: Jan. 27, 1927   Height: 6'0''   Weight: 197
Compton Junior College

San Francisco, 1948–60
Baltimore, 1961–62
San Francisco, 1963

Year	G.	Att.	Yds.	Avg.	TD.	P.C.	Yds.	Avg.	TD.	TD.	Pts.
		RUSHING				PASS RECEIVING				SCORING	
1948	14	77	562	*7.3	*10	8	79	9.9	1	12	72
1949	12	115	*783	6.8	*8	11	146	13.3	3	11	66
1950	12	124	647	5.2	5	13	69	5.3	1	6	36
1951	11	136	677	5.0	3	18	167	9.3	1	4	24
1952	12	158	725	4.6	8	15	81	5.4	0	8	48
1953	12	*192	*1018	5.3	*10	19	191	10.1	3	*13	78
1954	12	*173	*1049	6.1	8	26	203	7.8	0	8	57
1955	11	156	701	4.5	2	19	55	2.9	1	3	18
1956	12	115	520	4.5	3	18	104	5.8	0	3	18
1957	8	97	454	4.7	3	15	130	8.7	0	3	18
1958	12	125	758	6.1	4	23	218	9.5	1	5	30
1959	10	139	602	4.4	3	12	53	4.4	0	3	18
1960	8	36	95	2.6	1	3	—3	—1.0	0	1	6
1961	13	168	675	4.0	3	34	322	9.5	1	4	24
1962	11	94	359	3.8	0	22	194	8.8	0	0	0
1963	9	24	98	4.1	0	4	12	3.0	0	0	0

* Led the league.

AAC TOTALS										
—2 YEARS	26	192	1345	7.0	18	19	225	11.8	4	23	138
NFL TOTALS										
—14 YEARS	153	1737	8378	4.8	53	241	1796	7.5	8	61	375
PRO TOTALS										
—16 YEARS	179	1929	9723	5.0	71	260	2021	7.8	12	84	513

JOE PERRY'S FAVORITE PLAY:

A play on which Joe Perry ran for a great deal of yardage at the peak of his career with the 49ers was called "31 F trap."

"We designed plays to take advantage of Perry's terrific takeoff speed," said Coach Buck Shaw. "The line blocking did not have to be better than average since the linemen merely formed a screen for Perry's speed. The supremely important block was by the right tackle on the middle linebacker. The speed of Perry and the maneuvering in the backfield kept the corner linebackers pretty well out of the play, since they were lined up wide.

"This play put Perry in the open quickly, and although he was not as maneuverable as Hugh McElhenny, the halfback, he went for great yardage and often all the way. Perry was a great sprint star before he played football and developed a rather long stride after takeoff."

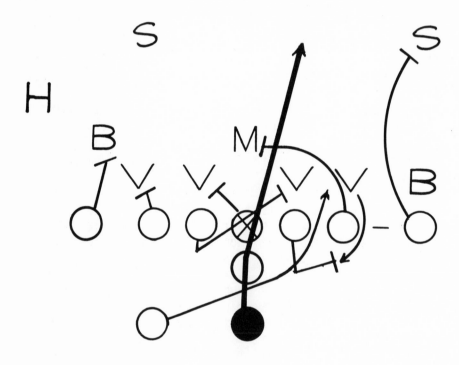

...But Don't Forget

I REMEMBER A WHITE MAN CAME INTO
THE DRESSING ROOM AND ASKED ME
WAS I INTERESTED IN PLAYING PROFES-
SIONAL FOOTBALL. THAT WAS THE FIRST
TIME IT EVER CAME INTO MY MIND.
—*Paul "Tank" Younger,*
Grambling College and
the Los Angeles Rams.

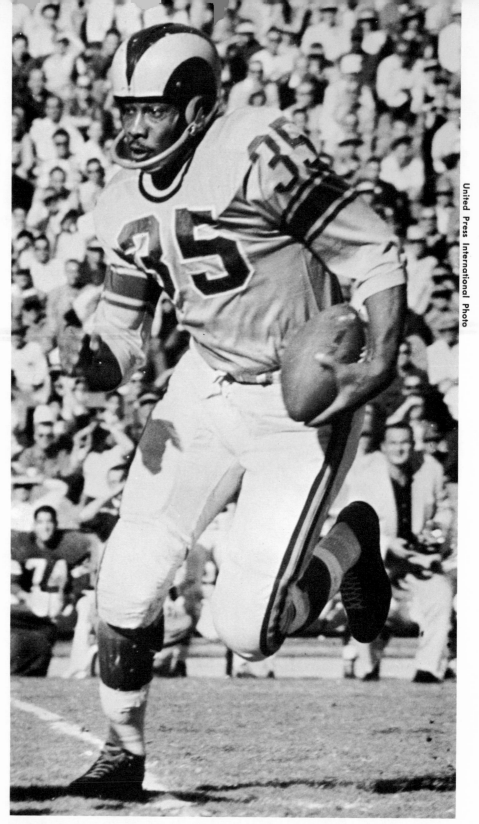

Paul "Tank" Younger was the first major NFL star recruited from the small Negro colleges by the Los Angeles Rams.

In the year 1949, no player from Grambling College, Florida A & M, Texas Southern, Jackson State, Maryland State, not to mention Philander Smith College, was on the roster of a National Football League team. To put it more bluntly, pro football wasn't signing players from the Negro colleges around the country.

Twenty years later, if you emptied the rosters of players from the Negro schools, there'd be virtually nobody to carry the ball or catch it, or play defensive halfback, and the ranks of great defensive linemen would be sorely depleted. In the 1968 season, there were twenty-two men from Grambling College alone employed on fourteen teams in the pro leagues! The New York Giants had three regulars from Grambling in their lineup.

The pioneer of them all was a helluva football player named Paul "Tank" Younger, who stood 6′3″ and weighed anywhere up to 230 pounds.

The Los Angeles Rams brought him into their camp as a free agent in the summer of '49, and on the second day, Clark Shaughnessy, the coach, ordained that he'd be tried at fullback. "He really put me in shock," remembered Tank. The Rams already had three veteran fullbacks in camp and six other rookies trying for jobs at that position. In those days, there were only thirty-two men on the roster, and taxi squads were unknown.

Tank went up to Tom Fears, the fine receiver of the Rams, after practice and asked, "Can this club keep four fullbacks during the season?"

"No way," answered Tom.

"Too bad," said Tank, "because one of them vets is going to have to go."

In an exhibition game against the New York Giants in Omaha, Nebraska, Tank broke loose on a trap up the middle and rambled 50 yards until Emlen Tunnell, an all-pro Negro defensive back, nailed him on the 5-yard line. Tank turned around to Emlen and wailed, "Why'd you want to do that for? I'm just a young guy trying to make good my first year."

"Up here," said Tunnell, "you have to make it every year."

Well, Tank started ten games for the Rams that rookie season, and he played an even decade of pro ball. The Rams had signed him for $6,000, and the most he ever made was $16,000. But there were no regrets that he didn't come along later when the O. J. Simpsons were starting out as millionaires. "I could have been born 10 years sooner," he said. "I could have come along in 1939 when there was no shot at all of making the club."

At the time he broke in, there were only three Negroes playing in the NFL. Kenny Washington had retired from the Rams, and Tank was going to be his replacement. He roomed alone and didn't mind it—"it was more conducive for my social life."

"Eddie Robinson, the Grambling coach, gave me the best advice a man could get going into pro ball," said Tank. "He told me in dummy drills to run the ball 25 to 30 yards down the field, not 10 yards and turn around.

" 'The longer you have the ball under your arm,' said Eddie, 'the longer the man is watching you.' "

With Tank's arrival, the Rams won three Western division championships in a row and capped the third one by defeating the Cleveland Browns for the NFL title.

Against the Bears in 1951, Tank played sixty minutes on offense and defense, scored two touchdowns, had another one of 73 yards called back, gained 73 yards in eight carries and caught two passes for 75 yards. He also played on all the special teams.

Tank's all-around utility on offense and as a linebacker was one of the reasons he never tore the league apart as a runner. And yet when his career was over after having gone to Pittsburgh for a final season in 1958, Tank had gained more than two miles on the ground.

TANK YOUNGER'S FAVORITE PLAY:

"A play we called '31 Mike Trap' on the Rams was designed against a hard-charging middle guard, since the five-man line was still in use when I started out. The right tackle was the key blocker, getting that middle guard. The rest of the blocks were more or less turn-outs, which are rather easy. Once the ball carrier was in the secondary, he had a clear field because there was no middle linebacker. So once this happened, you had a 230-pound fullback running against 185-pound defensive backs.

"But it was only effective against a 5-4 defense.

"I remember in a November game against the 49ers at Kezar Stadium, we had the ball on our 3-yard line. I ran this play for 97 yards and an apparent touchdown. But it was called back, and we were penalized for backfield in motion.

"I have been a fan of the 'Kill the Ref Club' ever since."

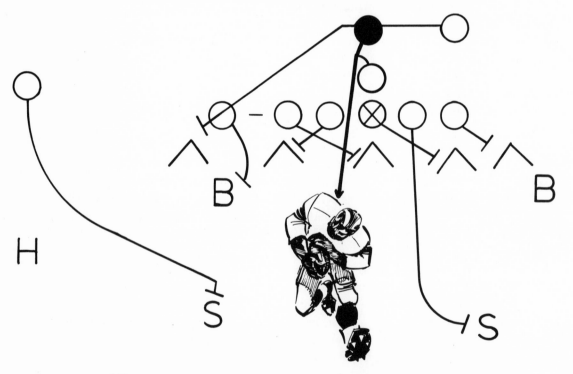

PAUL "TANK" YOUNGER

BORN: June 25, 1928   Height: 6'3"   Weight: 216
                    Grambling College

Los Angeles Rams, 1949–57
Pittsburgs Steelers, 1958

Year	G.	Att.	RUSHING Yds.	Avg.	TD.	PASS RECEIVING P.C.	Yds.	Avg.	TD.	SCORING TD.	Pts.
1949	12	52	191	3.7	0	7	119	17.0	0	0	0
1950	12	8	28	3.5	2		(None)			2	12
1951	12	36	223	6.2	1	5	72	14.4	0	1	6
1952	12	63	331	5.3	1	12	73	6.1	0	1	6
1953	12	84	350	4.2	8	20	259	13.0	1	9	54
1954	8	91	610	6.7	8	8	76	9.5	0	8	48
1955	8	138	644	4.7	5	6	51	8.5	0	5	30
1956	12	114	518	4.5	3	18	268	14.9	0	3	18
1957	12	96	401	4.2	3	8	61	7.6	0	3	18
1958	12	88	344	3.9	3	16	188	11.8	0	3	18
PRO TOTALS —10 YEARS	112	770	3640	4.7	34	100	1167	11.7	1	35	210

A year after Younger became a Ram, Los Angeles acquired a playmate for him—also a man who could lead them in prayer. He was the Reverend Daniel Lee Towler, called Deacon Dan by the players, and he studied for his master's degree in theology at the University of Southern California while he busted open enemy lines for the Rams.

Deacon Dan was from Donora, Pennsylvania, the hometown of Stan Musial, and had played football at Washington & Jefferson, leading the nation in scoring and gaining Little All-American acclaim. Towler was an inch shorter than Tank, but broader and a shade faster.

During the 1951 season, it suddenly occurred to Hamp Pool, who was designing the offense, that he wasn't getting maximum mileage out of his fullbacks. In addition to Towler and Younger, he also had another fine one in veteran Dick Hoerner. He couldn't play them all at the same time at fullback, so Younger was being diverted to the defense, which seemed like a waste of talent. All three were fast—only a shade behind the little speed-burners on the team, Vitamin Smith, Tommy Kalmanir and Glenn Davis.

After the 49ers whipped Los Angeles, 44–17, in the fifth game of the season, their second loss, and the Rams were confronted by the same team in the sixth game, Pool tried something new. He played all three fullbacks in the same unit. They scored 45 points against the Cardinals, 48 against the New York Giants. In beating the Bears in the key game of the season 42–17, the three bulls gained 205 yards on the ground and caught passes for 133.

United Press International Photo

With Tank Younger, Deacon Dan Towler (32) formed a Bull Backfield for the Rams. He also led the NFL in rushing.

A new concept of offensive football was created—the Bull Backfield—and its success set a style trend for big backs that still prevails. Towler was the sparkplug, the chief ground gainer, and led the team in rushing with 854 yards. The next year he led the whole league in rushing, with 894 yards. In fact, he was the Rams' top ground gainer for four straight years. He was voted the outstanding player in the Pro Bowl game of 1952, shortly after the formation of the Bulls. And he was voted to the all-pro teams three years in a row against the competition of people like Joe Perry and Marion Motley.

Before a playoff game for the division championship his rookie year, Deacon Dan had asked Coach Joe Stydahar if he might offer a prayer. Joe thought it was a good idea. The Rams won, and Towler's pre-game prayer became a club ritual for as long as he was with it.

During his playing days, he explained, "It's no longer just what I want. It's what the whole team wants. It's just an inspirational prayer for remembrance—that before we go out on the field of play we acknowledge the presence of God and thank Him for the opportunity of being able to play. It is a prayer for courage, for strength, for guidance. In some way I saw that in our play we want to represent the Christian ideals of clean, fair play, and we ask for victory if it is the will of God. I always close with a scriptural reference, 'Help us to run and not be weary, to walk and not faint.'"

Deacon Dan played an abbreviated career. He quit when he was twenty-seven years old, after five and a half seasons, firm in his belief that his life's work was in the church.

After finishing his studies, he took over a Methodist congregation in Pasadena, California, and became a pillar of the southern California community. He was active in the Fellowship of Christian Athletes, an impressive lecturer, and in 1968 he was named president of the Los Angeles County Board of Education (at Washington & Jefferson, he was a straight "A" student and cum laude graduate).

But his football background patterned him for the future, and the Rev. Towler appreciated it.

"But for football," he once said, "I probably would have gotten a job in a mill and become a little-educated pastor of some small church on Sundays while working in the mills all week.

"A football player's greatest asset is to make his ability fit into a team effort. And this includes the ability to get along. All those boys in the pros have great ability, but it is those who can make it fit into the team effort, who don't try to be stars themselves, who make it. There's no place for prima donnas."

DANIEL LEE "DEACON DAN" TOWLER

BORN: March 6, 1928   Height: 6'2"   Weight: 226

Washington & Jefferson College

Los Angeles Rams, 1950–55

Year	G.	Att.	Yds.	Avg.	TD.	P.C.	Yds.	Avg.	TD.	TD.	Pts.
		RUSHING					**PASS RECEIVING**			**SCORING**	
1950	12	46	130	2.8	6	8	63	7.9	0	6	36
1951	12	126	854	6.8	6	16	257	16.1	0	6	36

311

1952	12	156	*894	5.7	*10	11	68	6.2	0	10	60
1953	12	152	879	5.8	7	11	125	11.4	1	8	48
1954	12	149	599	4.0	*11	10	127	12.7	0	11	66
1955	7	43	137	3.2	3	6	25	4.2	0	3	18

PRO TOTALS

| —6 YEARS | 67 | 672 | 3493 | 5.2 | 43 | 62 | 665 | 10.7 | 1 | 44 | 264 |

* Led NFL.

Eddie Price was no prima donna. Any fullback who stood 5'10" and weighed 190 pounds couldn't afford to be. Eddie's career with the New York Giants covered exactly the same span of time as that of Towler, 1950–55. And he was a marvel. While coaches scoured the bushes for big bruisers who could carry a football, Eddie carefully kept his weight down to svelte size because there was only one way he could exist in the NFL: he had to get off the mark faster than anyone else. In this respect, he was a lot like Joe Perry, but smaller.

Eddie was a bubbly, emotional guy who came up to the Giants in 1950 after a distinguished college career at Tulane. At twenty-three, he was a little older than the average rookie because he had spent two and a half years in the Navy, piloting landing barges in South Pacific island invasions, under heavy fire. He was also tougher.

The compact little fullback stepped right into a regular job in Steve Owen's A-formation (though he had played only in the T during college), and clicked off 703 yards on the ground for a team that won ten games, lost two and tied the Cleveland Browns for the Eastern title before losing in a playoff. During his second year as a pro he really showed his stuff. He set a record for heavy duty work by carrying the ball 271 times. His net of 971 yards topped the NFL. He would have become the fourth 1,000-yard man in history if a 70-yard touchdown run hadn't been nullified by a penalty.

Eddie operated on that quick initial burst and sheer audacity. "When you face two pros," he said, "there's not much use in trying to fake or sidestep them. It won't work like it does in college. The only way is to buck right at 'em. Accelerate and shoot the works. You might split 'em."

Coach Steve Owen saw his little battering ram hitting repeatedly at the heart of the defense, and he developed a compassion for Eddie. Towards the end of the 1951 campaign, when he felt Eddie needed the rest, he ordered him to sit out a practice session. As Owen recalled it, the workout was interrupted because the players kept looking over to a corner of the Polo Grounds—Price was sitting there, sobbing. Owen went over and asked him what the trouble was.

"I have a lot of pride in my job," said Eddie, "and I can't understand why I'm not doing well enough to hold onto it."

Steve tried to reassure him the rest was only for Price's benefit. "But the way he saw it," explained Owen, "the job was his not only on Sunday afternoon, when we played, but every day of the week. He got it. He could have anything he wanted."

After three big seasons by Price, the Giants as a team started to falter. The extra pounding that Eddie took had its effect, though he never let up. "There's no such thing

312

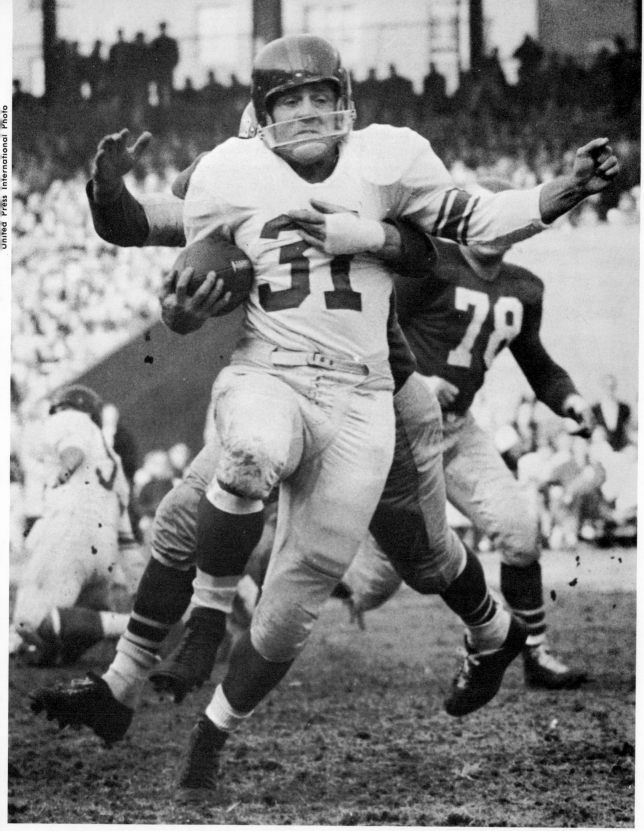

Quickness made Eddie Price of the Giants a tough man to drag down, though he weighed only 190 pounds, light for a fullback.

as running easy in the pros," said Eddie. "I did that once when I might have gained two or three more yards, and Owen told me I ought to quit football if I ever did it again. I never have." A sprained ankle and foot adhesions limited him severely in '53, a losing season. At the same time, Eddie had also developed into a competent receiver, a talent which was used when Jim Lee Howell succeeded Owen in '54. He played two years for Howell, then quit abruptly.

"I never really knew why," said Jim Lee. "Of course, we weren't too good then, and he was taking a beating. I thought he could have played several more good years."

Instead, Eddie went back to his native New Orleans, where he had a radio show, a restaurant, and assorted interests. The timing was too bad. The Giants won a world championship the year he quit.

EDDIE J. PRICE

BORN: Sept. 2, 1925   Height: 5'10"   Weight: 190

Tulane University

New York Giants, 1950–55

		RUSHING				PASS RECEIVING				SCORING	
Year	G.	Att.	Yds.	Avg.	TD.	P.C.	Yds.	Avg.	TD.	TD.	Pts.
1950	10	126	703	5.6	4	4	30	7.5	0	4	24
1951	12	*271	*971	3.6	7	5	19	3.8	0	7	42
1952	11	183	748	4.1	5	11	36	3.3	0	5	30
1953	12	101	206	2.0	2	26	233	9.0	1	3	18
1954	12	135	555	4.1	2	28	352	12.6	3	5	30
1955	6	30	109	3.6	0	1	2	2.0	0	0	0

PRO TOTALS

—6 YEARS	63	846	3292	3.9	20	75	672	9.0	4	24	144

* Led NFL.

There was another way, beside that of Eddie Price, for a little man to exist in the cauldron of pro football. Ewell Doak Walker II also came into the National Football League in 1950 scaling 173 pounds, if you didn't check for lead weights. And he ran the ball from left halfback in the offense of the Detroit Lions, shifting frequently to wingback to catch it. If he came along now, he'd probably be a flanker. But any place, he was a winner.

What was his formula? "You can sum up Doak Walker in just one word," said his coach, Buddy Parker. "The word is poise."

314

Doak Walker proved there was room for a 170-pound halfback in pro ball—he was a key offensive threat on a couple of Detroit championship teams.

Doak himself was dubious of his ability to survive. "Honestly," he said, "when I came into the Detroit training camp, I expected to be on the first shipment home. My weight, or lack of it, bothered me."

Normally, a man his size would compensate with speed or some special talent. For a back, Doak Walker had only average swiftness—he was timed in 10.2 for the 100 in high school. He had a good neck and strong legs—but so do some bank clerks.

No, what Doak had doesn't show up tangibly on paper.

"Uncanny ability to be in the right place at the right time," said Blair Cherry, a former Texas coach, "—that was Doak's strong point. And that, in my book, is the mark of a great athlete."

On December 28, 1952, the Detroit Lions met the Cleveland Browns for the NFL championship. On a cold day in the Cleveland arena, in sight of Lake Erie, Doak started at halfback for the Lions. He had missed half the season with a pulled hamstring muscle, incurred on a missed open field block. The game was a close 7–0 affair in the third quarter, with Detroit leading, tenuously. The Browns were a noted second-half team. Detroit put the ball in play on its own 33. Quarterback Bobby Layne dropped back as if to pass, then slipped the ball to Walker. A halfback draw. Doak cut sharply between right tackle and end, veered suddenly to his left to set up a block downfield and went 67 yards to score the crusher. It was his first and only touchdown of the year.

The next year, when the two teams met again, Doak scored the first touchdown, kicked a field goal and two extra points as the Lions won their second title, 17–16.

Four of the six years he played pro ball, Doak was selected to the all-pro team. But honors were an old habit for this quiet, self-effacing Texan. He played four varsity years at Southern Methodist, was All-American twice, won the Heisman Trophy as the nation's top collegian of 1949 and is still regarded as the greatest player in modern Southwest Conference history.

Doak Walker's kicking career started in college. The Mustangs were playing Baylor on a sloppy field, both teams scoreless in the fourth quarter, as SMU huddled for a fourth down play on the Baylor 20.

"Why don't you try a field goal, Doak?" someone suggested.

"Me?" answered Doak. "I never tried one in my life."

He kicked the three-pointer, the only one he ever attempted in college. And yet in pro ball, he became one of the fine field goal kickers in the league. He led the NFL in scoring his rookie year and again in 1955, his final season.

Doak and Bobby Layne were a contradictory and yet strangely complementary pair. They were high school teammates at Highland Park in Dallas, but their collegiate duels (Layne went to Texas) were among the most memorable in Southwest history. Layne was gregarious, aggressive, and he'd walk into the best joint in town. Walker was silent, almost shy and trained fastidiously. Like Layne, however, he was a competitor and took his losing hard. He surprised all the Lions by ordering a stinger after one galling defeat on the West Coast. "He didn't realize what he was drinking," cackled Bobby. "Thought they'd go down like soda pop."

Like a champion, Doak bowed out at the top, too. He was twenty-nine and still a fine player, but six years was tempting fate and the physical odds long enough.

316

EWELL DOAK WALKER

BORN: Jan. 1, 1927   Height: 5'11"   Weight: 173

Southern Methodist University

Deroit, 1950–55

| Year | G. | RUSHING | | | | PASS RECEIVING | | | | SCORING | |
		Att.	Yds.	Avg.	TD.	P.C.	Yds.	Avg.	TD.	TD.	Pts.
1950	12	83	386	4.7	5	35	534	15.3	6	11	*128
1951	12	79	356	4.5	2	22	421	19.1	4	6	97
1952	7	26	106	4.1	0	11	90	8.2	0	0	14
1953	12	66	337	5.1	2	30	502	16.7	3	5	93
1954	12	32	240	7.5	1	32	564	17.6	3	5	106
1955	12	23	95	4.1	2	22	428	19.5	5	7	*96
PRO TOTALS —6 YEARS	67	309	1520	4.9	12	152	2539	16.7	21	34	534

PLACE KICKING

Year	XP.	XPM.	FG.	FGA.
1950	38	3	8	18
1951	*43	1	6	12
1952	5	0	3	5
1953	27	2	12	19
1954	*43	0	11	17
1955	27	2	9	16
PRO TOTALS —6 YEARS	183	8	49	87

* Led NFL.

At Southern Methodist, when Walker left it, there was another legendary All-American in the making. Kyle Rote first sprang into national prominence in the last game of the 1949 season when Doak was sidelined by a leg injury, and Rote was shoved into the breach at tailback against a Notre Dame team that was undefeated for four years. The Mustangs were down by two touchdowns when Rote rallied them to tie the score, 20–20, in the fourth quarter. The Irish scored again, but young Kyle brought SMU deep into Notre Dame territory before he was hurt and the drive failed.

When they played together in the SMU backfield, Walker was frequently shifted to tailback to take advantage of Kyle's versatility as a runner and passer. He was an ideally sized halfback—six feet, 195, good speed, terrific moves. And after a fine All-American season all by himself in 1950, he was drafted by the New York Giants. He was going to tear up the pro ranks—until the Giants, on an exhibition tour, stopped in Ft. Smith, Arkansas, one day to work out. The practice field was lumpy. Rote, running

317

There's no telling how great a running back Kyle Rote might have been if he hadn't hurt his knees before his rookie season with New York. He converted to a valuable split receiver instead.

in a routine signal drill, stepped in a hole and collapsed. Nobody touched him. It was the same year Mickey Mantle stepped on a water nozzle in the World Series and his knee buckled.

Rote's knee, injured in the same manner, was never the same, even after an operation. "He was going to be the greatest," said Allie Sherman, the backfield coach at the time. "He had everything. No one could touch him." Eventually, Kyle's other knee went bad, too. His speed was affected, and his maneuverability, but not his instinct as an athlete. He stayed with the Giants eleven seasons. When it became apparent after the first four that his legs couldn't stand up to the pounding of a running position, he was shifted to end and began an amazing new phase of his career.

He helped the Giants to four division titles and one NFL crown. He ran the most adroit pass patterns in the league and had the surest hands. He was a smart old pro who lived by his head in a violent game. He also wrote songs, ad-libbed beautifully on a dais and started a separate career as a sport announcer.

In 1961, his last season, when he was thirty-three years old, he caught fifty-three passes, his best record ever. He coached for a while and then devoted himself fulltime to television sportcasting. Long forgotten was the fact that he might have been the unmatchable runner. He didn't do badly as it turned out.

KYLE ROTE

BORN: Oct. 27, 1928   Height: 6'0"   Weight: 190
                    Southern Methodist University

New York Giants, 1951–61

| | | RUSHING | | | | PASS RECEIVING | | | | SCORING | |
Year	G.	Att.	Yds.	Avg.	TD.	P.C.	Yds.	Avg.	TD.	TD.	Pts.
1951	5	21	114	5.4	1	8	62	7.8	0	1	6
1952	12	103	421	4.1	2	21	240	11.4	2	4	24
1953	9	63	213	3.4	1	26	440	16.9	5	6	36
1954	11	30	59	2.0	0	29	551	19.0	2	2	12
1955	12	10	46	4.6	0	31	580	18.7	8	8	48
1956	12	3	5	1.7	0	28	405	14.5	4	4	24
1957	12	1	13	13.0	0	25	358	14.3	3	3	18
1958	12		(None)			12	244	20.3	3	3	18
1959	10		(None)			25	362	14.5	4	4	24
1960	11		(None)			42	750	17.9	10	10	60
1961	14		(None)			53	805	15.2	7	7	42

PRO TOTALS
| —11 YEARS | 120 | 231 | 871 | 3.8 | 4 | 300 | 4797 | 16.0 | 48 | 52 | 312 |

13. Enter the Brown Period

Jim Brown

ALL YOU DO AGAINST JIM BROWN IS
GRAB HOLD, HANG ON, AND WAIT FOR
HELP.

*—Sam Huff, linebacker,
New York Giants.*

James Nathaniel Brown, the movie actor—not the football player—could have been playing a scene. He leaned across the table at the Metro-Goldwyn-Mayer commissary in Boreham Wood, Hertfordshire, a suburb of London. The dialogue concerned truth.

"I speak the truth," said Brown. "If you deny me, you're my enemy." The planes of his strong, dark face glinted like polished mahogany. The natural, downward curl of his lips—almost a smirk—accentuated the words. Suddenly, this was no play acting. This was Jimmy Brown, a man, who meant what he said.

"And just what," the writer asked, "is the truth?"

A half smile showed a trace of gleaming teeth. He leaned back reflectively, and he crooked his left elbow across the top of the chair to support his head. He was dressed in drab army fatigues, his uniform for a picture he was making called "The Dirty Dozen."

"Maybe," he suggested, "it's what Cassius Clay says when he calls all white men the devil. That could be the truth."

Then, caught up in the emotion of the subject, he leaned forward again, pointed a finger and said animatedly, "You're 'Charlie,' baby. I'm fighting you."

Brown wasn't playing this scene for mirth. "Charlie" was every white man. It was chilling to the listener, though there was no feeling of actual physical danger because this was a room full of professionals, and all were civilized and the intent was impersonal. But Brown had laid open the hostility and distrust which he couldn't always subdue if he sensed criticism.

After he wrote a book in which he took his first posture as a militant black man, there was negative reaction to his emergence as a philosopher of the socio-ethnic scene. "The white man," he wrote, "has forced me to be prejudiced against him." And he also noted, ". . . the Black Muslim's basic attitude toward whites is shared by almost 99 percent of the Negro population." So this writer mused about his qualifications as a spokesman for 99 percent of the black people in the U.S., especially since he made more than $50,000 a year for playing football and lived in a world in which he had a white guard from Mississippi to block for him and a tall Texan to call his signal and hand the ball to him.

"How can I talk to you," he said now, "and know that what I say won't be twisted? As a writer, you've got power that I can't answer. Prejudice isn't calling me a 'nigger.' That's stupidity—you can see the enemy and you got nothing to be afraid of. It's the others that I look out for, that aren't so obvious."

This *tête-à-tête* took place in July of 1966 when ostensibly he was still a professional football player, with another year to go on his contract with the Cleveland Browns, but was also getting into the business of movie-making as a serious vocation. The Browns, preparing to assemble in Hiram, Ohio, assumed that Brown would report for his tenth year of professional play. Physically, there was no reason he shouldn't. He was the finest offensive threat in the game. He was thirty years old, but there was no sign of debilitation. He weighed 228 pounds, exactly his size as a rookie in 1957. His capacity to excel was greater, if anything, because he had mastered the nuances of his trade, learned to apply his experiences and approached his job with an intelligence that wasn't visible behind his mask as a player who seldom showed emotion ("My public image," he once said, "is that of the strong, silent and even insensitive type").

Art Modell, the owner of the Browns, threatened to fine his star player $100 for every day he wasn't in camp. Modell knew the movie business. It was obvious the picture on which Jim Brown was working wouldn't be done until weeks after the July 17 reporting date. Modell issued an ultimatum which concluded: "If Jim were to show up in September, we would have to make an appraisal as to his physical condition, his ability to pick up quickly the new offense being prepared for the season plus the general personnel situation."

That was ridiculous and sophistical. It was like telling Raquel Welch she'd have to audition if she decided to do a brassiere commercial. Besides, Jimmy Brown in London made it quite clear that the football phase of his life was over—he soon formalized it with an announcement of retirement—and that acting had become his bag.

He left behind him a record of achievement which may never be equalled. To get the full impact of Jimmy Brown the football player, the records must be cited.

Over the course of nine full seasons, he set the existing standard for every career category in carrying a football:

Most seasons leading the league—8 (1957–61, 1963–65).

Most attempts, lifetime—2,359.

Most yards gained, lifetime—12,312 (eight yards shy of seven miles).

High average gain, lifetime—5.22 yards per carry.

Most touchdowns rushing, lifetime—106.

He also set the records for consecutive seasons as a league rushing leader, most attempts in a season, most yards gained in a season and most yards gained in a game. He went over the 1,000-mark seven different seasons. He gained over 100 yards in fifty-eight games, or almost half of the 118 regularly scheduled contests in his career (Jimmy Taylor, the next man on the list, had twenty-six games of more than 100 yards, also in nine seasons).

In the Brown period, Cleveland was essentially a running team because of him. The Browns ran 60 percent of their plays on the ground, and the indestructible full-back was their ball carrier on 62 percent of those plays. Over the span of his pro career, he averaged twenty rushes a game in a fantastic display of consistency and durability.

Now let's try to make those records and figures come alive. Every team playing the Browns keyed on the fullback as the man to stop. They gang-tackled him, jabbed at him with elbows, threw forearms at his head, tried to get under his face mask with their fists and otherwise aimed all their guns at him physically. Yet Jimmy Brown played in 118 straight games, plus one divisional playoff and three championship jousts, and only one time was he ever forced off the field of action because of an injury. In December 1959, he was hit in the head during a first quarter skirmish against the New

324

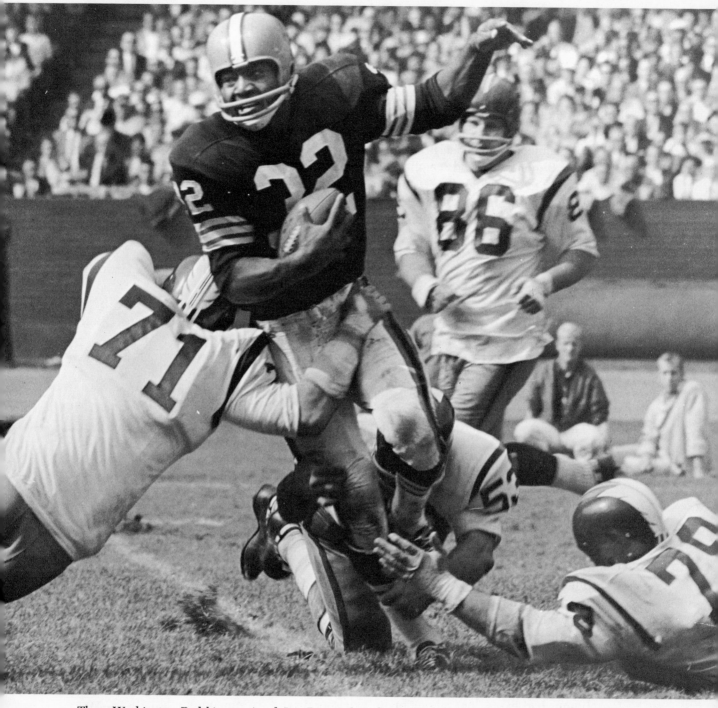

Three Washington Redskins surround Jim Brown, but the lunging Cleveland fullback is still a good bet to bust free for a long gain.

York Giants in Yankee Stadium and didn't even remember the play. Milt Plum, the quarterback, escorted him to the Cleveland bench when he was missing his assignments. He stayed out the second quarter, and then returned to play the entire second half, for which Coach Paul Brown was severely criticized since the Giants clobbered the Browns 48–7.

No football player was ever better equipped than Brown to withstand the punishment inherent to a fullback. He was a study in rippling, burnished bronze, and you had to see him in a locker room to appreciate it (of course, moviegoers later were privy in technicolor when the Brown muscles did a lot to sell him as a sex symbol). He was 6 feet 2 inches tall and weighed 228 pounds in or out of season, with no trace of flabby bulge ever visible. The chocolate skin sheathed pure muscle. The shoulders bunched like a torsion bar. The deep chest descended to a narow waist.

A theory has been promulgated that pro football became the *now* sport for women because the design of the uniform made the gladiator an erotic symbol in thigh-hugging pants. The mold belonged to Jim Brown. You could see the interaction of his leg muscles as he burst through enemy lines with his stylized glide, the feet scarcely inches off the ground, but the power pulsating with every step.

Henry Carr, an Olympic sprinter who caught on with the Giants as a defensive back, was privileged to see Brown up close in 1965, his final season. "He runs," said Henry, "like he has a halo over his head saying you can't touch."

Brown maximized his physical equipment with a finely honed instinct for self-preservation. Defensive tacklers never got a full, straight ahead shot at him. He was always positioning himself to absorb the impact, like a boxer rolling with a punch, and yet looking to spring himself free.

"The things you must avoid," said Jim, "are those shoulders in the mid-section and head-on collisions. You have to sense what's dangerous enough to put you out of business. Let's say, for example, two men grab you and are holding you tight. You're standing straight up. You know you can't get loose. If you remain standing and struggling, you're vulnerable to a third man sailing in and knocking your brains out. So you bend over, instead, and fall forward as far as you can. You also avoid untimely leaps over fallen players. Unless you see quickly that the path is clear, you don't go up in the air because while you're up there, somebody might blast you into the next county."

Jimmy only moved fast when he had to, and that was calculated, too. Nothing fires up a defender more than knowing he's bruised a runner. The guy who gets up slowly, shaking his head, is fair game to get clobbered again by an enemy which thinks it has softened him up. Jimmy countered that psychology. He got up slowly on *every* play and dragged himself leisurely back to the huddle. "I give all my energy when it's required," he reasoned, "and when it isn't, I move easily. But this is normal because I move that way when I'm not playing."

Jimmy had everything about his job reasoned out. "In one-on-one situations, you break tacklers into categories. A lineman who's four yards away, you figure to put a good move on him and run around. A linebacker is quicker and therefore harder to fake. If he's three yards or less away, you drop your shoulder and give it all you got. If he's a small defensive back, you just run right over him."

Some of his greatest jousts were with Sam Huff when that venerable West Virginian backed up the middle for the New York Giants. The Giants played a keying defense, and Huff generally was assigned to ride herd on Brown, renewing a rivalry that extended back to their college days when Jimmy played for Syracuse and Sam was a tackle at West Virginia. In one Cleveland-New York encounter, Huff anticipated a play perfectly and stopped Brown cold. As Jimmy got up, Sam exhorted the Giant defense, "C'mon, let's hit him harder."

Brown carried on the next down and only nudged forward a yard against the entire Giant line. Huff yelled impatiently, "We got to hit harder than that, you guys."

The Cleveland fullback attacked a third straight time and was stopped again. But Huff, fired up, shouted, "That's still not hard enough."

Brown pulled himself up slowly and laughed. "Hey, Sam," he said, holding his sore sides, "that's hard enough."

Another time, if you believe the story, Sam got so worked up after stopping the fullback for no gain on successive plays, he sneered impetuously, "Brown, you stink!" Then, on a trap play, Huff was suckered and number 32 burst right past him on a straight line to the end zone, 65 yards away. As he crossed the goal, he turned and yelled, "Hey, Sam, how do I smell from here?" It made a nice banquet anecdote, but Brown never talked much in those days.

A traumatic childhood left him withdrawn and a little sullen as he grew up. Brown was born on St. Simons Island off the southern coast of Georgia, a sleepy little place when he could go crabbing and play on the beaches and nobody gave him much mind. His mother had gone off to the north to work when he was two years old. His father, a blithe gambler called Sweet Sue, left even before that. Jim was called Nathaniel, his middle name, by his great-grandmother, with whom he lived in a neat, fading frame house, and Nate by the other kids. At seven, he was sent to rejoin his mother, who did housework with a family on Manhasset, L.I. Periodically, his mother and father reconciled, but it never lasted long. Once he lived in a foster home when his mother was squeezed for living quarters. He was a kid who could handle himself in the streets. In his teens, he became the warlord of a street gang named the Gaylords. Athletics veered him from what could have been trouble. It was obvious to the school coaches at all levels in Manhasset that Jim, as he was called up north, had extraordinary athletic talent, and he became a legendary prep star in every sport he tried, even lacrosse.

After high school, he could have gone to Ohio State, where Woody Hayes wanted him, but a group of local citizens, led by a lawyer named Ken Molloy, a Syracuse graduate and a lacrosse enthusiast, steered him to Syracuse. But not on a football scholarship. Unknown to Brown, the good citizens of Manhasset, proud of Brown's exploits and eager to see him get an education, chipped in to pay his way the first year. "Kenneth Molloy exerted the greatest influence on my life," said Brown, years after he had made it big as a pro. "He helped when I needed it most."

At Syracuse, it wasn't a breeze for him. He was the lone Negro on the squad at first. There had been a controversial Negro player in school before Brown, and the coaches were wary of more trouble. After his freshman year, they wanted to switch him to end. Brown balked. When he turned out for the varsity, he was listed as the fifth string left halfback. Coach Ben Schwartzwalder soon recognized his ability, however, and had him playing regular by the end of his sophomore year. Jimmy went on to a fine varsity tenure at Syracuse as the school burgeoned into a national power and was invited to play in the Cotton Bowl against Texas Christian after a 7–1 record in 1956, his senior year. Jimmy had gained 986 yards rushing and made the All-American teams. He was a one-man show against TCU, scoring 21 points as Syracuse was nosed out, 28–27.

At the same time, Jimmy was also an All-American in lacrosse, a high scorer on the basketball team, and competed in track.

In the pro football draft that spring, other running prospects like Paul Hornung of Notre Dame and Jon Arnett of Southern California were picked ahead of him. The Browns, after their first losing season in history, flipped a coin with the Pittsburgh Steelers for the fifth choice on the first round—they had tied in the 1956 standings at 5–7. Coach Paul Brown, desperate to get a new quarterback following the retirement of Otto Graham, was angling to select Len Dawson of Purdue. However, the Steelers won the toss and chose Dawson. That's how Cleveland settled for Jim Brown, and football history definitely was altered.

Although they gave him $15,000 his first year (which included a $3,000 bonus), the Browns really had no idea he'd be an instant sensation. Ed Modzelewski was the holdover fullback, a competent pro. When the rookie reported from the All-Star camp, the veterans on defense gave Brown their best shots in scrimmage. Big Mo was a favorite on the club. But Mo wasn't fighting the future. He could see the kid was going to be the fullback. If Jimmy got confused during drills, Mo would slip him the word on his assignment. When Jimmy showed up one day with a white Ivy League cap, Mo showed up the next day with one. Coach Brown asked him, "How come you're copying Jimmy?" Mo grinned and said, "If you can't beat 'em, join 'em." He said he felt like a stand-in for Babe Ruth.

Cleveland did an about-face that first year and regained the Eastern division championship, and its young fullback won his first rushing crown with 942 yards. Against the Los Angeles Rams, he carried the ball thirty-one times for 237 yards and an NFL single game mark that still stands (Brown tied that figure in 1961). Coach Sid Gillman of the Rams cautioned, "If he carries the ball that much in many more games, he's got to wind up either punch-drunk or a basket case."

Sid didn't know his Jimmy Brown. The years passed and Brown's rushing rate accelerated with no deleterious effects. In 1958, he was acclaimed the outstanding player of the year, winner of the Jim Thorpe Trophy in a poll of the players, and Brown always claimed it was his greatest tribute in football because it was recognition by his peers.

With success, Brown's salary mounted progressively until it reached more than $50,000 a season. He married a charming girl. They had twins, a boy and a girl, and then another boy. Jim and Sue Brown bought a home and settled into the Cleveland community life. In addition to football, he prepared himself for the future as a marketing representative for a national soft drink company. He dressed sedately in business suits with buttoned vest. He was impressive and articulate in speaking engagements. He became a golf enthusiast. Life should have been beautiful.

328

But Jim Brown was getting edgy. Despite his feats, the team wasn't winning titles any more after that initial success. The martinet rule of Paul Brown as the absolute boss of Cleveland's destiny became oppressive to him. "Although I was billed as Paul's star performer," Brown later wrote, "I had no relationship with him. I wanted to, but his aloofness put him beyond reproach. . . . It seemed to me that he thought of me as nothing more than a weapon. I felt he had no interest in me as an individual."

At the Pro Bowl in Los Angeles after the 1961 season, his busiest ever, Brown startled pro football by revealing to columnist Mel Durslag there was an even chance he would play no more football, that at the age of twenty-six ". . . I should start to think of something more substantial."

He catalogued publicly his complaint against Paul Brown: "It was my feeling last season that I was asked to do more than my share. I made more than 300 rushes and caught 46 passes. It was my roughest year in football."

He didn't retire, of course, but the first chinks in Jimmy Brown's armor as a man of steel began to show in 1962. He dipped under 1,000 yards in ground gaining. He lost the league rushing title for the only time in his career to Jimmy Taylor of the Green Bay Packers, who also grabbed off the all-pro honors at fullback. After the season it was revealed that he'd played all fourteen games with a badly sprained wrist. His left arm, the one he used to club tacklers, was useless.

Jim chafed under the thumb of Paul Brown's rigid control. "It became obvious," said the fullback, "that robots no longer would do. The Browns lacked spirit and they had become stereotyped. I am not built to be an automaton."

Art Modell had taken over control of the club, and Jimmy had established a strong relationship with him. The fullback made it clear to Modell that if the situation didn't change, he didn't care to play in Cleveland any longer. Modell took the precarious route in this dilemma and picked the player over the coach. He dumped Paul Brown, the founder of the team, the most successful coach in history, a genius at organization and innovation—and Paul owned a piece of the club, too. Modell elevated Blanton Collier, an original Paul Brown aide, to head coach in 1963. If the player-inspired switch failed, the franchise might be imperilled, too.

As it turned out, everybody subsequently thrived. Paul Brown had a few good years of retirement in La Jolla, California, was elected to the Hall of Fame and then came back to football as part owner and coach of the expansionist Cincinnati Bengals. Collier, a scholarly man who doesn't hear well (to tune out what he doesn't want to hear, some say), proved to be more than a tactician. The Browns responded to his easier style of handling men.

And Jim Brown—well, he had three straight years of individual achievement that were absolutely the best in the history of running a football. Remember, the pressure was on him, too, because he had precipitated the crisis and change at the top.

A tactical change in the Browns' offense helped him. Responding to the run-to-daylight syndrome that emanated from Green Bay and swept through football, Cleveland altered its running philosophy. The fullback no longer had to follow a specified route. On one play, Brown might run wide around end. On the same play, next time it was used, he was cracking inside guard.

"In rule blocking (the old way)," explained Collier, "you're wasting some of his talent. Jimmy does his best running in close quarters. In boxing, they'd say he was a natural infighter. With a back like Brown, you just don't tell him what to do."

He simply reacted to the blocking angles in choosing his course, and he must have been doing something right. In 1963, unfettered, he set an all-time rushing record of 1,863 yards. The Browns made a strong run at the Giants for Eastern honors and missed by one game, so Jimmy still had something to prove—that he could lead a winner. Otto Graham, their old quarterback, fanned the flames a little bit when he got up at a luncheon and suggested the Browns would be better off trading their fullback if they wanted to win because he wouldn't block or fake with the vigor of a Marion Motley, who had protected Otto's scalp. Blocking had always been pointed out as the glaring deficiency among Brown's skills. Not because he wasn't capable. A fine blocker like Pat Harder once pointed out that all blocking was balance, that a good runner had balance—ergo, a good runner should be a good blocker. It was largely a matter of enthusiasm and energy. Jim Brown saved his for running with the ball. "This is the day of the specialist," he explained. "The quarterback's job is throwing the ball. Mine is running with it."

Brown's lack of ardor for blocking certainly didn't bother Coach Collier. "You don't ask a thoroughbred," he said, "to pull a milk wagon." Instead of keeping Brown in the backfield to shield for the quarterback on passing situations, Collier frequently flared him out as an auxiliary receiver and achieved the same effect. A defender, generally a linebacker, had to go with him—the danger of Brown catching a pass in the open field was too much to ignore.

As a personality, Jimmy was getting a new exposure, too. His book, *Off My Chest*, written in collaboration with Myron Cope, was published in the summer of 1964 and revealed the sensitivities behind the brute force of his playing—his beefs with Paul Brown, his feelings as a black man. He was no longer the reserved young man who sat in a New York restaurant the year he was first acclaimed the outstanding player in pro football and said, "I admire Jackie Robinson for what he says, but I just couldn't say those things myself—it's not my way." Now it was his way.

He had more than his share of controversy and escapades. An assault charge involving a young girl in a motel made headlines. His private life was turbulent at times, but Brown blithely adhered to his own code of conduct. "They talk about a certain kind of life people are supposed to live in this country," he said, "but a lot of that is hypocrisy. We've got these tight rules that nobody abides by; it's just a game we're supposed to play."

Success finally feathered his niche in football and immunized him to the swirl of trouble. The Browns paraded through the National Football League in a victorious 1964 processional. They met the Baltimore Colts for the championship on a bleak day in Cleveland, given only a minor chance to win. Their defense harassed quarterback Johnny Unitas of the Colts into impotence. At halftime, the teams were scoreless. In the third quarter, Brown broke Cleveland out of its shell by circling left end on a tackle-tearing run that finally place them in Baltimore territory and set up a field goal by Lou Groza to break the deadlock. Frank Ryan picked up the spark and passed the

Ken Regan

The 1965 championship game was destined to be Jimmy Brown's last official appearance for Cleveland—mud-spattered but still resolutely moving forward.

Jim Brown in the latter part of his career was also a forthright player who didn't hesitate to speak his piece, to the referee or anybody else.

Browns to a 27–0 victory, and Brown augmented him by rampaging 114 yards on the ground. "It was the high point of my career," he noted. "We finally won the big one and mission was accomplished."

The Browns repeated as Eastern champions in 1965, and Brown won his third Jim Thorpe Trophy as the outstanding player in the NFL. But the Packers took advantage of a muddy field in Green Bay to win the league title. Brown went on to the Pro Bowl in Los Angeles and scored three touchdowns in a final burst of power. It was his last appearance as a professional football player.

The moguls of Hollywood had already been impressed by his physical presence, not to mention his exploitability as an athletic superman. In a time of increased racial enlightenment, vistas opened up for him as an actor, a Negro who could be a leading man. A minor part in a Western epic called "Rio Conchos" was followed by progressively more important roles.

"He has a tremendous opportunity," said Lee Marvin, who worked with him in "The Dirty Dozen." "He's the first Negro actor to come along that the average man in Watts or Harlem or the Detroit ghetto can identify with. He looks like them and slouches like them and talks like them. Not like Sidney Poitier, who goes around all day talking Shakespeare."

Brown himself dug the scene, the intellectualism of it. And the competition. "Actors like to zing you," he expounded. "They like to surprise you within the confines of a script. And they make you respond. They bring out real response in you. You have to meet these challenges by zinging back.

"Acting is more of a mental industry than football. It's like revealing yourself . . . it's almost like selling your emotions."

The easiest one for James Nathaniel Brown, actor, was the menacing look.

"I try to think mean," he explained. "I figure it will be in my face. I have a kind of frown anyway. It's easier for me to look mean than happy.

"I got that mean thing in me."

JIM BROWN'S FAVORITE PLAY:

"We called it an '18-sweep,' and I was lined up on the left side in our backfield set. The play went back to the strong side, with good blocking; both guards pulled out of the line ahead of me. The key to its success was the block by the halfback on the defensive end, and Ernie Green did a good job on it. Also vital were the blocks by the flanker coming back on the corner linebacker, and by the weakside guard taking out the outside halfback. "It was great for a breakaway when all the pieces fell in place."

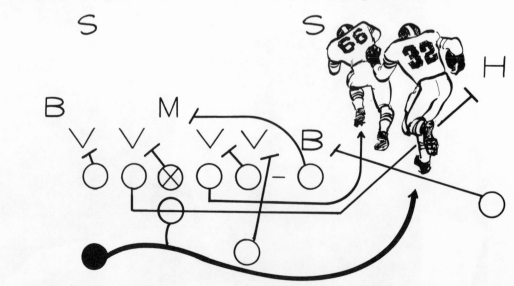

JAMES NATHANIEL "JIM" BROWN

BORN: Feb. 17, 1936   Height: 6'2"   Weight: 228

Syracuse University

Cleveland Browns, 1957–65

Year	G.	Att.	Yds.	Avg.	TD.	P.C.	Yds.	Avg.	TD.	TD.	Pts.
			RUSHING				PASS RECEIVING			SCORING	
1957	12	202	*942	4.7	*9	16	55	3.4	1	10	60
1958	12	*257	*1527	5.9	*17	16	138	8.6	1	*18	*108
1959	12	*290	*1329	4.6	*14	24	190	7.9	0	*14	84
1960	12	215	*1257	5.8	9	19	204	10.7	2	11	66
1961	14	*305	*1408	4.6	8	46	459	10.0	2	10	60
1962	14	230	996	4.3	13	47	517	11.0	5	18	108
1963	14	*291	*1863	*6.4	*12	24	268	11.2	3	*15	90
1964	14	*280	*1446	*5.2	7	36	340	9.4	2	9	54
1965	14	*289	*1544	5.3	*17	34	328	9.6	4	21	126

PRO TOTALS

—9 YEARS	118	2359	12312	5.2	106	262	2499	9.5	20	126	756

* Led NFL.

Paul Hornung

HIS PERSONALITY IS SUCH THAT HE HAS
TO BE THE CENTER OF ATTENTION AT
ALL TIMES.
> —*Vince Lombardi, coach,*
> *Green Bay Packers.*

The keepers of legends breathed a sigh of relief in the summer of 1967 when the doctor examining Paul Hornung told the new halfback of the new New Orleans Saints that he would never play football again. The pinched nerve condition in his neck, chronic for almost all of his pro career, had deteriorated to the point that Hornung would be risking his life if he exposed himself to the jolt of a tackle.

And so the football legend of Golden Boy from under the Golden Dome at Notre Dame was preserved from another chapter.

I mean, could you imagine Paul Hornung doing the New Orleans bit? The French Quarter, Brennan's for breakfast, the jazz joints, the dollies, the trumpet tootling of Al Hirt, the gambling spots across the river, the raucous hours, and the interminable quest for fun.

Why, Paul Hornung belonged to staid old Green Bay at the mouth of the Fox River in northern Wisconsin, where football on Sunday was a somber rite, where Bart Starr's name is listed in the phone book, where a haircut collects a crowd, where thirteen below zero is stadium weather. Where number 5 on the jersey was the most treasured numeral on the sandlots. It belonged, of course, to Paul Hornung. He felt at home in Green Bay.

Or did he?

The man they called Golden Boy, for the curly blond locks that hung high on his forehead like a tassel, was also very much at home in the Racquet Club, which was the swinging place of Miami Beach, and at the Kentucky Derby in his hometown of Louisville, or the bistros of New York and the discos of Los Angeles.

After one of his good seasons, he went out to the west coast to play in the Pro Bowl. Each member of the winning team collected $800. Paul's bill for his social activities during the week of preparation generally was double that amount. His first roommate was Bill George, an amiable linebacker for the Chicago Bears. "I roomed with Paul Hornung's suitcase all week," he said.

Every day was Derby Day in Paul Hornung's life of speckled excitement. It was an illusion he tried to purvey, the handsome bachelor All-American All-Pro football star with a good-looking "fiancee" on each arm, facial features lifted from Michelangelo's "David," flashy sports clothes, and a swift hand for picking up a check.

He was magnetic, in a literal sense. One night before a Packer game in Chicago, Paul took a pretty young thing dining and wining in one of the posh places on the near north side, the Red Carpet. Now the Packers had a standing rule that players were not to be seen at bars in public. The fine for any transgression was $500 automatically. The young lady, according to Paul, wanted to sit at the bar before dinner instead of in the lounge. It was early evening and uncrowded; Chicago was a big place with a lot of restaurants. So the chances of detection were slim. But no sooner had Paul ensconced himself at the polished oak counter than the girl said, "Oh, oh, look what we have here now."

Through the door at that moment, into the Red Carpet, of all the places in Chicago, walked head coach Vince Lombardi for dinner. "That," he greeted Hornung, "will cost you $500."

Among the legends that collected about his Golden Dome days (which also happens to be the central piece of architecture at his alma mater, Notre Dame) were (1) the stashing of an exotic dancer in his college dormitory—not true; (2) the sending of an engagement ring, tucked away in a football, to a Hollywood starlet—not true; (3) wild parties in the bachelors' pad that he and Max McGee, a Packer end, shared in Green Bay—could be true.

Yet fun and frolic weren't always the central themes in Hornung's football life. There was another side he kept well tucked away. For one thing, he was a mama's boy, and proudly so. Loretta Hornung raised him virtually alone in an Irish neighborhood of Louisville—his parents separated when he was four—and while there never was too much of anything, Paul always got a football or a glove when he needed it. After he signed his first pro contract, instead of buying the big Cadillac (that came later), the first thing he did was buy his mother a mink stole.

"People think, because of his flip attitude, that Paul doesn't care," said Frank Gifford, who became his good friend, "that he doesn't take things seriously. He covers up. He worries, like the everyday guy, about what's going to happen to him."

The apparent insouciance stemmed from the fact that everything in Hornung's life seemed to come so easy. He was a great schoolboy athlete with a flock of universities after his services. Paul "Bear" Bryant, then the coach at Kentucky, used to drink coffee in Mrs. Hornung's kitchen and charmed her with his folksiness. The governor of Kentucky visited the Hornungs, mother and son, to persuade Paul that his educational future was at the state university. But like every good Catholic boy, Paul also had a yen to play football at Notre Dame, where Frank Leahy was conquering the world on the gridiron. The dynamic personality of Leahy finally induced the Golden Boy to play his football in the shadow of the Golden Dome. "He was a helluva man," said Paul. "I wanted to play under him."

A shade of irreverence, however, was there from the start. He reported to the varsity in the spring of his freshman year, 1954. It was a warm and sunny day. "It looks like tough sledding, Coach," Hornung said to Blackie Johnson, for whom he'd played as quarterback on the frosh team.

"Tough sledding?" Blackie echoed. "Why, what's the trouble, Paul? Anything bothering you?" Leahy had resigned as head coach in January.

"Yep, tough sledding," Hornung repeated. He grinned slyly. "No snow."

His versatility showed up in his sophomore year. Ralph Guglielmi was the ranking quarterback, headed for unanimous All-American honors. Hornung spelled Ralph occasionally late in games, but Coach Terry Brennan wanted the young soph to get more battle time. So he switched him to fullback and played him on defense, too. Paul blossomed as an All-American quarterback his junior year. As a campus hero, he was irrepressible, with a dimpled chin, sparkling blue eyes, and the cascade of golden hair. Brennan chipped in one bit of criticism: "Paul's got to learn to pass better."

338

His senior year he repeated as an All-American and won the Heisman Award as the outstanding player in the country, against impossible odds. Notre Dame had its worst record in history, winning two, losing eight.

The bonus pick in the college draft that year fell to either Green Bay or the Chicago Cardinals. They flipped a coin, and the Packers won. They picked Hornung and signed him to a three-year contract at $16,000 annually. The money was pretty good, but Hornung, who'd already acquired the taste and habits of a boulevardier, wasn't enamored with the prospect of life in a smalltown goldfish bowl.

In the College All-Star game camp at Evanston, Illinois, on the north fringe of Chicago, he set an all-time record for absence without leave. One morning he reported for practice with the Stars and asked a coach, "What's the record for the numbers of hours being out after curfew?"

"I don't know," shrugged the coach. "Why?"

"I just think I set it." He had arrived straight from an evening on the town— it seemed he knew an exotic dancer, and she didn't get off work till 5 A.M., which rearranged his social schedule.

Paul's reputation preceded him to Green Bay. The Packers hadn't enjoyed a winning season since the end of World War II and desperately needed a quarterback, having just traded Tobin Rote to the Detroit Lions. Obviously, they counted on Hornung being it. That was asking a lot of a rookie, and his problem was compounded by a quickly obvious fact—he didn't throw with enough accuracy to be a pro quarterback. The Packers gamely tried to work him as a signal-caller but also used him as a spare fullback. His repertoire at quarterback was limited. When he entered a game against the Bears, middle linebacker George chortled, "Here comes ol' Rollout Right and Rollout Left."

The first two years in Green Bay were bitterly frustrating. Athletic failure was something he had never experienced. Definitely committed to a running role, he actually led the Packers in rushing in 1958, but there wasn't much fun playing for a team that won only one game the entire season. There was disorganization both on the field and in the front office.

That was all changed abruptly. The good times were about to start. Vince Lombardi was hired as coach and general manager. Bert Bell, the reigning NFL commissioner, used to have a standing proposition to all players that if they had any questions or problems, they could call him directly. This was when pro football was still considered a nice, homey sport. Bert gave all players his personal phone number. Hornung immediately called Bell and asked, "What kind of coach is this guy Lombardi?"

It was a legitimate question, at the time, and Paul got a legitimate answer his first day of practice in July. "This year," Vince told him, "you're going to sink or swim at left halfback." With the New York Giants, Lombardi had used Gifford as a multiple threat in that position. He saw Hornung fulfilling the same role. "Gifford may have been a little faster," Lombardi assessed them, "but Paul is stronger. Frank was excellent as a receiver and could run the patterns very well, but Paul is improving there.

Paul Hornung's destiny in Green Bay was intertwined with that of Vince Lombardi, whose first move as boss of the Packers was to install "Golden Boy" as his left halfback.

"He smells the goal line anywhere within the 10-yard line," said Lombardi. And Paul Hornung proves the point by vaulting into the end zone.

Hornung's place-kicking ability, with Bart Starr (15) holding, was also a prime part of the Packer scoring threat.

Paul is pretty nifty for his size. He's got good broken-field ability, and he's improving all the time on the option pass."

Lombardi also told Hornung and the Packers, "I've never been with a losing team, and I don't intend to start here." Every team has to have a soul leader. On the Packers, Hornung just naturally gravitated into the job. Lombardi was stern, excitable and an absolute disciplinarian. Hornung was relaxed, glib and cocky. Yet Vince detected a tough streak in him. For one thing, Paul never doubted who was the boss. He played it Lombardi's way all the time, and football became fun again. A bridge of genuine fondness connected them.

"Vince Lombardi, without a doubt, exerted the greatest influence on my life," said Paul. "If it were not for him, I doubt if I would be in the league."

Just to prove he hadn't basically changed, Paul didn't mind twitting the boss. "We came home from a trip one frigid night," related Paul. "Below zero, and those Green Bay fans kept us outside. Finally, Vince broke away and went home to sleep. It was late. He was freezing. Marie was already in bed. Vince climbed in, and his cold feet touched her. 'Jesus Christ!' she yelled.

"'That's all right, Marie,' said the Coach. 'At home you can call me Vince.'" Hornung grinned puckishly.

There was no kidding around on the field. The Packers became a good team almost immediately. Halfway through the first year under Lombardi, Bart Starr emerged as a competent quarterback. They had their best record in fourteen years and might have done even better if a young fullback named Jimmy Taylor hadn't burned his hand in a household accident and missed several games. Hornung and Taylor, thriving under Lombardi's emphasis on the running game, became the strongest pair of setbacks in football. Paul was the Packers' ground-gaining leader in 1959, Taylor thereafter. Paul also did the place kicking and led the NFL in scoring.

In 1960, Green Bay drove to the Western division title, and Hornung set an all-time scoring record of 176 points which still stands. He scored thirteen touchdowns on the ground, which prompted Lombardi to declare, "Any time he gets within the 10-yard line, he smells the goal line.

"Success brought confidence to Paul, and since he possesses great pride in performance, he played with greater effort as the season progressed."

A new vista and a new set of values had opened up for him in the pro game. "Pro football means first of all a way of life," he told the writer. "Of course, I realize that this is only for a short time. It affords all the players many opportunities to progress further in life with business contacts. Presently more football players are recognizing this fact and are readying themselves for the day they will retire.

"Pro football also gives me the chance to play the game I love, to associate with the best people in the world—people who have, for the most part, terrific ideals and have both feet on the ground."

The Packers called him "Goat" affectionately because Hornung had sloped shoulders hidden by big shoulder pads. The rest of him, however, was impressive physically. Now in his prime, he stood 6'2" and weighed 220—a mighty big halfback. "He has a 43-inch chest," said his buddy, McGee, "and a 36-inch head."

"Paul never plays the big shot with us," said one of his mates. "He takes kidding well, and we have more nicknames for him than anyone else. He's got a good sense of humor. And he's the greatest clutch player I've ever seen."

The Packers lost the 1960 championship game to the Philadelphia Eagles. Hornung's pinched nerve left him with a paralyzed shoulder and he had to be helped off the field in the first half when the Packers were leading. A year later they were on top of the football world, and Hornung again led the NFL in scoring, was named the top player in the league by the wire services and topped off the season by scoring 19 points (including three field goals) in the 37–0 title game rout of the New York Giants.

He had gone into the Army by the time the teams met on a cold day in Green Bay, but he was given a special leave, along with linebacker Ray Nitschke, to play in the championship game. His point production set a new NFL playoff record on a day when players wore gloves and scarves and even tennis shoes on the frozen turf. Then he went back to his Army base, where he served as a clerk-typist, and wrote, "I have never seen any part of the country with as poor a climate as Kansas." Paul was still in service for most of the next season as the Packers paraded to another championship, but true to his creed as an action man, he commuted to Green Bay games whenever he could get a weekend pass and managed to play in nine of them.

His value was recognized outside Green Bay. An American Football League team offered him $250,000 over three years to play out his option and jump to the new circuit. "When they start throwing that kind of money around," admitted Paul, "you've got to think about it." But he remained firmly committed to the Packers. "It would be like going from the New York Yankees (then champs of the baseball world) to the Louisville Colonels," he added. "But Green Bay has treated me good. And it's fun playing here because we're such a close club."

As a national celebrity, Paul also had his friends from coast to coast. One of them used to call weekly and ask how he thought the Packers would do. Paul knew his friend bet heavily on games. He'd tell him he thought the Packers would win. During one call, the halfback said, "Put $100 on the game for me, too." The bets became a habit—he got as high as $500 on a game—though it said specifically in Paragraph 11 of the player contract: "Player acknowledges the right and power of the commissioner of the National Football League (a) to fine and suspend (b) to fine and suspend for life, indefinitely and/or (c) to cancel the contract of, any player who accepts a bribe or who agrees to throw or fix a game or who, having knowledge of the same, fails to report an offered bribe . . . or *who bets on a game*. . . ."

In January of 1963, Pete Rozelle called Hornung on the west coast and asked him to come to New York. The previous August he had already questioned him about associations with gamblers. Now he confronted him directly with questions about his betting and asked him to submit to a lie detector test. Hornung didn't hold back. He confessed his violations. The investigations, of Hornung and other players, continued. On April 17, Rozelle announced that Paul Hornung and Alex Karras, the all-league defensive tackle for the Detroit Lions, had been suspended indefinitely. His case would be reviewed in 1964.

Hornung called Lombardi, who said, "I'm hoping you get reinstated next year. I don't want you reporting at any 250 pounds. So stay in shape and keep your nose clean." Hornung spent the year making appearances before youth groups, handled a radio show in Louisville and was scrupulously correct in his behavior, even subdued—that is, as much as Mrs. Hornung's boy could escape attention.

He showed up at the Pro Bowl after the 1963 season, and eyes started to turn. "Let's get out of here," said Paul to the writer, "before they recognize me." He had on a brilliant red sports jacket with mod sun glasses that curved around his eyes, and every blond curl on his head was in place. He was supposed to check into Rozelle's office in the winter without anybody seeing him, then duck out of town. Again, the red blazer.

The Packers obviously missed him, as a player and as a person. "You have to go over films," said Coach Lombardi, "to appreciate the blocking he gave us."

"Paul was missed more as a man than as a football player," said center Jim Ringo. "Tom Moore had the ability to take over for Paul. But Hornung is a leader. He's symbolic of something everybody wants to be—the world he lives in is a lot different. It isn't for me, but it fits him."

The Packers lost only two games in 1963, the year Hornung was away, but both were to the Chicago Bears and cost them the division championship. He was reinstated for the 1964 season, and the Packers finished second again. Tom Moore split the time with Hornung equally at halfback, but that was more because of Tom's ability than any perceptible slowing up by Golden Boy. Mysteriously, however, he had lost his rhythm and touch as a placekicker, and this cost the Packers several games during the season. A missed extra point was the margin of defeat against Minnesota. Then against Baltimore he missed five field goal attempts in a game lost by three points. He missed twenty-six field goal attempts during the season.

Paul was puzzled, but he didn't lose his humor. "After that Baltimore game," he related, tongue-in-check, "somebody slipped a gun into my helmet on the way to the dressing room. I wasn't really aware of it until we got inside. Then I saw it was a gun and it was loaded. Somebody was trying to give me a message. I put the muzzle up to my head, and Bart Starr got excited and came running over, yelling, 'Put that gun down, Paul. You crazy?'

"And from across the room, Jimmy Taylor looked up from his locker, surprised.

"'Don't worry, Bart,' he said, 'He'll miss.'"

The night before the Baltimore game, Paul had dinner with Al Silverman, his collaborator on an autobiography called appropriately, *Football and the Single Man*. (In the modern era of football, you're not successful until you publish your memoirs.) They were going over the chapter on his suspension when a friend of Silverman brought his wife over. The introductions were made, Hornung was most impressive in a blue blazer, immaculately groomed. The little lady was no sports fan. "And just what do you do, Mr. Hornung?" she asked.

"I'm a gambler, ma'am."

For a couple of years, rumors had been circulating that Hornung would be traded to New York. After all, he was a back-slapping buddy of restaurateur Toots Shor. The latest one hinted there would be an even-up swap, Hornung for split end Del Shofner. Allie Sherman called the Giants together in a clubhouse meeting and said, "I want you to know, Del, I wouldn't trade you for Hornung and all his girls." A player piped up, "Just a minute, Coach. Let's take a vote on that."

Hornung played out his career in Green Bay and had one last fling of glory. Moore and the fast-developing Elijah Pitts were shuttling in and out of the lineup with him in 1965. Elijah was a thirteenth round draft choice from little Philander Smith who came into the Packer camp in 1961. He was bashful and unsure of himself and didn't know anybody, a lonely Negro boy in a strange environment. Hornung was the big star, the natural leader. One night he said, "Elijah, you're coming with me." And took him out on the town. Pitts fitted in after that and eventually took Hornung's job away. On December 12, 1965, Green Bay, trailing by one game in the standings, invaded Baltimore. A loss would eliminate the Packers. To escape the Green Bay cold, they worked on a makeshift field outside a motel in Rockville, Maryland. Hornung had lost his starting job, but Lombardi called him aside early in the week and told him he'd be in the opening lineup again. Every day before practice, the offensive line serenaded him with an old, amended ditty: "We thought he was a goner, but The Goat came back."

Indeed he did. A dense fog shrouded Baltimore's Memorial Stadium on that Sunday. It was difficult seeing across the field. To the Colts, Hornung looked like a ghost drifting in and out among them. He cracked over them for a touchdown early, then sneaked behind them to complete a 50-yard touchdown pass from Starr, still in the first quarter. In the third quarter, he ran for two scores from within the 10-yard line. ("He smells the goal line," Lombardi reiterated). And in the fourth quarter, he caught another bomb from Starr for 65 yards and his fifth touchdown of the game. The Packers won to tie the Colts for first place, beat them in a division playoff and won the NFL title game from Cleveland, with Paul gaining 105 yards to lead all the running backs on the field (Brown and Taylor among them). It was his final flourish.

The Packers repeated as champions in 1966 and then defeated Kansas City in the first Super Bowl game ever played, but Hornung was just a spectator in uniform. Pitts was the starter. Paul's pinched nerve made him useless the last part of the season and his football future doubtful. He wasn't used for a single play in the NFL title game or the Super Bowl. The Packers put his name on the list available for drafting by New Orleans, an expansion team. The Saints gambled that he'd make a comeback. Bourbon Street awaited him eagerly. Hornung didn't pass the physical.

And all of Green Bay heaved a sigh of relief.

PAUL HORNUNG'S FAVORITE PLAY:

"My favorite play was anything close to the goal line!

"Actually, there were two I preferred: the Lombardi Sweep, called '49' in our playbook, and the goal line '41-trap.'

"Lombardi's whole offense was predicated on the sweep. This play must work in order for the offense to be successful. The following items were the key to its success:

"1) The tight end's block on the linebacker—he could block him either out or in.

344

"2) The fullback's block on the defensive end. He must knock him down.

"3) The halfback, carrying the ball, must decide whether to cut in or out depending on how the tight end was blocked.

"4) The guards pulling must watch the fullback's block also and help if it's needed there.

"The sweep has gained more yardage than any other play in the Green Bay offense since the arrival of Lombardi—an average of over 6½ yards each time. I used the sweep left (48) for the touchdown that clinched our championship game win over Cleveland in 1965."

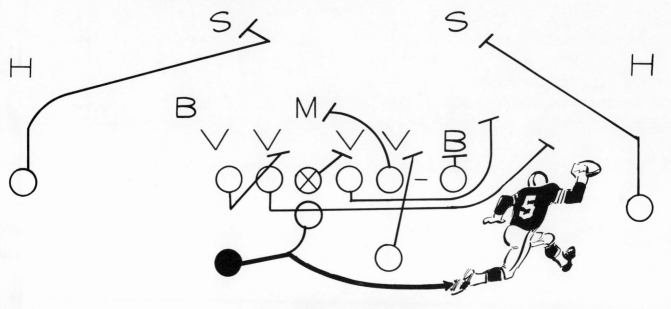

PAUL VERNON HORNUNG

BORN: Dec. 23, 1935   Height: 6'2"   Weight: 220

University of Notre Dame

Green Bay, 1957–62, 1964–66

| Year | G. | RUSHING | | | | PASS RECEIVING | | | | SCORING | |
		Att.	Yds.	Avg.	TD.	P.C.	Yds.	Avg.	TD.	TD.	Pts.
1957	12	60	319	5.3	3	6	34	5.7	0	3	18
1958	12	69	310	4.5	2	15	137	9.1	0	2	67
1959	12	152	681	4.5	7	15	113	7.5	0	7	*94
1960	12	160	671	4.2	*13	28	257	9.2	2	*15	*176
1961	12	127	597	4.7	8	15	145	9.7	2	10	*146
1962	9	57	219	3.8	5	9	168	18.7	2	7	74
1963					(Suspended for entire year)						
1964	14	103	415	4.0	5	9	98	10.9	0	5	107
1965	12	89	299	3.4	5	19	336	17.7	3	8	48
1966	9	76	200	2.6	2	14	192	13.7	3	5	30
PRO TOTALS —9 YEARS	104	893	3711	4.2	50	130	1480	11.4	12	62	760

		PLACE KICKING						PASSING				
Year	G.	XP.	XPM.	FG.	FGA.	Att.	Cmp.	Pct.	Gain	T.P.	P.I.	Avg.
1957	12	0	0	0	4	6	1	16.7	—1	0	0	—0.17
1958	12	22	1	11	21	1	0	00.0	0	0	0	0.00
1959	12	31	1	7	17	8	5	62.5	95	2	0	11.88
1960	12	41	0	15	28	16	6	37.5	118	2	0	7.38
1961	12	41	0	15	22	5	3	60.0	42	1	0	8.40
1962	9	14	0	6	10	6	4	66.7	80	0	2	13.33
1963					(Suspended for entire year)							
1964	14	41	2	12	*38	10	3	30.0	25	0	1	2.50
1965	12		(None)			2	1	50.0	19	0	1	9.50
1966	9		(None)			1	1	100.0	5	0	0	5.00

PRO TOTALS

—9 YEARS	104	190	4	66	140	55	24	43.6	383	5	4	6.96

* Led NFL.

Jim Taylor

JIM TAYLOR HAS A GREAT APPETITE FOR
CARRYING THE FOOTBALL. IT'S SORT OF
A CRAVING, A HUNGER—THE MOST UN-
USUAL THING I'VE EVER SEEN IN FOOT-
BALL.

> —*Bart Starr, quarterback,*
> *Green Bay Packers.*

Just as the man who fights the bull must inevitably face up to the moment of truth, when the din of the crowd becomes an indistinct hum, and he is confronted by his peril, so must the man who carries a football for gain face a similar moment of truth.

There isn't the same mortal danger for the ball carrier, but the test of courage and will and indomitability is analogous.

Jimmy Taylor of the Green Bay Packers approached every carry of the football as a moment of truth, when the enemy opposite him must be worn down, jabbed into frustration and destroyed.

True, he looked more like the bull in action than the exquisitely positioned matador who, having dominated the bull with his muleta, approaches him warily and then delivers a final, quick thrust of death. Taylor pawed the ground, snorted, tossed his head angrily when impeded and otherwise bounded wildly like somebody had tossed a dart in his back and he was going to take it out on anything that was in his way. This rage that came from within was awesome when Taylor attacked a defensive line because he literally ripped through the grasps of men who outweighed him by fifty pounds and were skilled in containing the run. He bounced, he squirmed, he bolted, and it was rare when he didn't wrench free to add a few more yards to his initial charge.

As an athlete, he could be compared to Rocky Marciano, the only heavyweight champion in history who voluntarily retired undefeated in his professional career. They were both relatively short—5'11"—and fanatics about conditioning their bodies for the tough course they plotted. Both realized early they didn't have the natural grace and fluidity of motion that would help them avoid contact—in other words, they'd have to take a blow to deliver a blow. Both developed a craftiness and professionalism that later spared them unnecessary punishment.

Their bodies were their weapons, providing simple brute strength as the source of their very physical approach to their jobs. Rocky developed his digging ditches in Brockton, Massachusetts. Right until the end of his playing days, Taylor worked incessantly at special exercises to pile up layers of muscle for a cushion against the punishment of physical contact and to provide the force with which to hit others.

He devoted himself to weight-lifting as a strength-builder. "I consider it a very important part of an athlete's conditioning and training," he said. "That is, if he wants to sacrifice. Weight-lifting gives you the endurance and stamina that pays off in the third and fourth quarter."

"He's not really a 212-pounder," said George Allen, the coach of the Los Angeles Rams, whose first contact with him up close was at a Pro Bowl. "He's the equivalent in muscle structure, of a 230-pounder, and he hits like that. He built himself up to the extent he can take it. It's not like Jimmy Brown, who has that size naturally."

349

Taylor's fetish for developing the upper part of his body gave him the effect of a head stuck straight on a set of shoulders, nothing in between. He got so insulated that his head movement was restricted—he'd rotate from the waist to change his line of sight. And all this body culture was necessary to fit his philosophy of playing football.

"I like to hit a man," he said. "I love the game; I love the contact of it. It's not that I want to hurt anybody. But if I have the ball running around end and the linebacker comes at me, and I try to finesse him out of the way, and he won't finesse, then I must run into him, over him, through him."

But Taylor once had an opportunity to go around a tackler and yet ignored the open way and hurtled through him to blast his way into the end zone. "Why did you hit him?" Coach Lombardi asked. "You had a clear path."

"You got to sting 'em, Coach," said Taylor. "I figure if you give a guy a little blast, maybe the next time he won't be so eager."

He elucidated: "Football is a game of contact. You've got to make them respect you. You've got to punish them before they hurt you. You try to give more than you take. It's either them or you."

And you were reminded of Rocky Marciano taking time out from a training day for the defense of his heavyweight title to talk to a group of prisoners at a nearby penitentiary. Rock stood in the middle of them and said, "You guys think you got it tough? Listen, once you get inside that ring, there's nobody to help you. It's either them or you." And the prisoners were impressed by that blunt talk.

Football did a lot for Jimmy Taylor, a poor boy from Louisiana whose father died when he was ten. He'd deliver papers at four in the morning on the streets of Baton Rouge. In high school, he swung a heavy sledge hammer for an oil company. And while he was at Louisiana State, he worked as a roughneck on offshore oil rigs. "Toughest job in the world," he said. But he was also an excellent basketball and football player, with the distinction of playing in North-South high school all-star games in both sports. At LSU, which had also produced Steve Van Buren as a fullback for the pros, Taylor was a consistent, solid player who led the Southeastern Conference in scoring his last two years but certainly was no prize attraction for the pros. His career overlapped that of Billy Cannon, who made his varsity debut as a glamorized sophomore when Jimmy was a senior. Taylor blocked for him. It was his first experience at playing in the shadow of a flashier performer, and it became a habit the rest of his career—there was always the spectre of Jimmy Brown during his pro days, and even on his own team, Taylor's efforts were frequently played down in the publicity glare spotlighting Paul Hornung.

The Packers chose him on the second round of the 1958 draft. In camp, with a last place team, he was a marginal player who had to sweat out the last cut. He was shy— he never did become much of an off-the-field talker—and his irrepressible drive hadn't picked up steam yet. "When he first came up," said Jerry Kramer, a rookie the same year who became an all-pro guard and best-selling author, "he hardly said anything to anybody, and when he did say something you couldn't understand half of what it meant

The Jimmy Taylor with the crew cut and the shy smile didn't jibe with the rugged, truculent fullback whose creed was to "sting 'em."

But Taylor was happiest when grime splotched his face and the juices of football combat pumped him up to greater effort.

because he talked so fast. Nobody around here really knew whether he could play football or not. Then in the last two games of the season they let him play, and he gained almost 250 yards on a team that didn't have much of anything."

Enter the Lombardi era in 1959, and everything changed—except for one mishap. Jimmy's wife was frying potatoes in their Green Bay apartment when the grease caught fire. Shoeless, Jimmy grabbed the pan handle and started to back out of the kitchen. The pan tipped, the boiling grease spilled on his right hand and wrist and burned the sock off his right foot. Jimmy spent four games in the hospital during the middle of the season.

But as it turned out, the tacklers in the NFL were just getting a temporary reprieve. In 1960, the real Taylor emerged in full, battering flight as a premier fullback in the NFL. He gained more than 1,000 yards to set a standard for the next five years. He never went under that figure. No other man in the game's history, not even Jimmy Brown, matched Taylor's feat of gaining more than 1,000 yards five consecutive seasons. And people began to appreciate that he was more than just a human battering ram throwing himself recklessly into enemy lines.

"Jim's main attribute as a ball carrier," said guard Jerry Kramer, "is his ability to adapt himself to the situation. The defense may be stacked at a hole, but if something opens up two or three holes away, Jim will find it." This was the crux of the run-to-daylight philosophy that soon swept over football, and Taylor was its chief guru.

"Don't ever get the idea that it's all legs and power," added Lombardi. "Sure, Jim blasts past linebackers and crashes through defensive backs, but he'd never get those opportunities if he wasn't moving in the right direction and using his blockers the way he should. He hits the right hole at the right time. He follows the right blocker. And he doesn't blow assignments. You only have to tell Taylor something once, whether it's running or blocking."

At the same time, a new Taylor personality was taking shape on the field. He was no strong, silent type. He snarled at tacklers, taunted them, jabbed them verbally as well as physically. After a particularly rough game, Dick Modzelewski, the defensive tackle of the Giants, came off the field and laid bare an arm that was bloody from wrist to elbow. "Taylor," said Little Mo, "he bit me like a dog."

"He ain't human," said Sam Huff.

Paul Hornung peeled off his uniform gingerly because of the welts and bruises on his body, suffered in the line of duty as Taylor's running mate. "The other team always hits hard if you're in the same backfield with Taylor," he said grimly. "He antagonizes everybody."

"If I didn't have that competitive drive," Taylor mused, "get so keyed up to get all the yards I can, I suppose if some guy popped me, I'd just get up and walk away and let them beat the hell out of me."

The gremlins of pride nettled the combative Green Bay fullback because, despite his exhaustive efforts, he really wasn't recognized as the best runner in the land. This was the era of Jim Brown dominance. Whatever Taylor did, Brown generally exceeded. For instance, in all those 1,000-yard years, he only led the NFL in rushing one time. He only made the all-pro team one time. Jimmy didn't take the inevitable comparisons with Brown gracefully. His natural aggressions brought to the surface a shade of resentment over the top billing that went to the Cleveland fullback. Brown was primarily a runner. Taylor forced himself to become a top-notch blocker, in addition to his ball carrying. "Lombardi got me down on all fours," he said, "in a crab block, so that every bit of yourself gets around the man you're taking out. Mr. Brown doesn't know anything about crab blocking. It's all news to him."

There is a general spirit of camaraderie among football players that transcends the hostility of the playing field. They share the fact of their violent game in an exclusive brotherhood. Brown had a fine rapport with Hornung that dated back to their first contact in the College All-Star game. But he was stumped by Taylor's apparent dislike for him. It was an impersonal dislike. They didn't know each other. "I don't understand why he seems to feel that he has to resent me to secure his place as one of football's top fullbacks," said Brown. "I think he's a great back and wish he wouldn't put down my abilities because it's really unnecessary and doesn't benefit either of us. Jim Brown doesn't have to be a bum in order for Jim Taylor to be a star."

One year, though, it helped. Brown, hampered by his sprained wrist and at the climax of his woes with Paul Brown, dipped as an effective player in 1962. Coincidentally, Taylor had the biggest year of his career. He outgained his Cleveland rival by almost 500 yards on the ground, achieving a peak total of 1,474 and setting a new league record of nineteen touchdowns scored rushing—Brown held the old record of seventeen. He was a brutal force in the champion game against the Giants, carrying the ball thirty-one times for 85 yards. He ripped through Sam Huff on a seven-yard burst for the only Green Bay touchdown of the game, and his gains set up the three field goals which Jerry Kramer kicked in a 16–7 triumph. The players of the NFL crowned his year by voting him the Jim Thorpe Trophy as the top man in the league.

In his home town of Baton Rouge, where he continued to live between seasons, the Green Bay fullback was accorded a "Jimmy Taylor Day" with tribute delivered by everyone from the governor of Louisiana to Vince Lombardi.

"He is not only a great football player," said Lombardi, "but he has many other attributes which make him a fine man as well. One of these is humility. Jim has always been humble. Sometimes he's so humble, he's reckless. And you've seen what he can do on a football field when he's reckless."

In Taylor's entire career, he revealed only one moment of weakness. When his wife gave birth to a daughter, JoBeth, Jimmy insisted on being in the delivery room. He fainted before the baby was born.

Taylor was a gentle, good-natured man when you caught him out of uniform, the face heavy in the jaw and a little battered, hair always cropped Prussian-close to his head, the thick neck the only give-away to his profession because the clothes hid that torso into which nature had poured concrete.

"The little extra things are what characterize Jimmy Taylor," said Hornung, his running partner. "Playing beside him has been a big help to me. I score a lot of points, but I have the percentages with me. Taylor takes the ball down to the one, and I have four chances from there."

354

For several years, though, pro players and coaches had been speculating that Taylor's reckless self-abandon on the football field would wear him out. "I definitely think he's shortening his career by playing the way he does," said Bill George of the Bears. "I'll hit him every chance I get because I know he wants that extra yard. He brings his troubles on himself."

And early in the 1963 season, it looked like the physical pounding was beginning to take its toll, though Jimmy was 28, an age at which George Allen said an athlete should be at his peak. An attack of hepatitis brought him down to around 200 pounds, dangerous weight for his type of play. Occasionally, during the season, Lombardi spotted a young husky named Earl Gros, also out of LSU, at fullback. "I don't think Jimmy'll ever have that physical drive again, ever be as strong again," noted Lombardi.

In the College All-Star game, Taylor swept around right end and was separated from his interference. As he turned the corner, only one man stood in his way—Lee Roy Jordan, the middle linebacker. Taylor hunched his shoulders and drove off his left foot to "sting" the tackler. Jordan weighed only 205 pounds, a rare luxury matchup for Taylor, who was used to 230-pound linebackers. Jordan drove in low and knocked the Green Bay fullback into the air and backward on his rear end for a two-yard loss. "It was embarrassing," admitted Jimmy, "Lee Roy tackling me by himself. I had no second effort."

"Is Jim Taylor Through?" That was the proposition examined by this writer for *Sport Magazine.* The Green Bay fullback provided the microcosm of answer in one play at the Pro Bowl game of 1964. He was playing for the West team the fourth year in a row, having recovered from his All-Star embarrassment and the hepatitis to gain 1,018 yards during the regular season. This is the descriptive passage of Taylor's response to the question:

"Baltimore's John Unitas is at quarterback for the West, which trails 3–0 in the first quarter and has trouble moving the ball, though it has penetrated to the East 37. Unitas fakes a give to halfback Tommy Mason and hands off to Taylor, running to his left. Jimmy is off the mark so fast that he has stripped past Jerry Kramer, who is supposed to lead the play. Maxie Baughan, the corner linebacker for the East, rushes across to meet the ball carrier. Jimmy turns on another jet of speed and runs around Baughan.

"Meanwhile, Galen Fiss, another linebacker for the East, converges on Jimmy from the side and safety Clendon Thomas rushes up to meet him head-on. Taylor looks trapped against the sideline by the three-man triangle formed by Baughan, Fiss, and Thomas. Without hesitation, he fakes Thomas off balance and cuts past him to the inside. He outruns Baughan. And Fiss? Galen is hit broadside by Jimmy's right shoulder and sent sprawling as the fullback heads for the goal line on a 37-yard run which starts the West to a 31–17 victory.

"This is the Taylor that is."

And continued to be for three more years. "He's got the greatest desire of anybody I ever saw running the ball," said the Bears' Bill George. "Last year he was hurt a little bit, and it's a helluva lot harder to play when you're hurt. Him slow up? Not at all. Listen, I can't even walk 1,000 yards."

The wisdom of an elder also came to Taylor. "I'm getting a little smarter," he volunteered. "When you're young, there's a different outlook. Then you're coming and you want respect so you got to hit 'em. There are certain times you got to lower the boom, but I know I can last a little longer by avoiding them."

In 1966, he was still making fantastic plays for the Packers. He started the year, on January 2, by being awarded a sports car as the outstanding player in Green Bay's NFL championship victory over the Cleveland Browns. This was his last direct confrontation with Jimmy Brown. Over the years, Taylor had generally fared better when both of them played on the same field, though you can argue Green Bay provided a better offensive line in front of him.

The same teams met in the second week of the regular '66 campaign. With two minutes to play, the Packers, trailing 20–14, were on the Cleveland 9-yard line, fourth down and goal to go. A field goal wouldn't be much use with time running out. Quarterback Bart Starr called a pass pattern which had the tight end and flanker, lined up left, as the primary receivers. As Bart faded to throw, he couldn't pick them out from the Brown secondary men clustered around. Taylor, from his fullback post, had flared right. Bart turned and dumped a little pass to him in the flat. Taylor caught it on the 7-yard line. Staring him in the face was Jim Houston, the strong side linebacker, a good one. Two defensive backs rushed up to help. Houston moved in to nail him. Taylor stopped and squirted to the left, the Brown linebacker overshot him and fell behind the Packer fullback. A defensive back got a hand on him but Taylor dragged free at the three. The other one tackled him, but Taylor was already in the end zone. "I've never seen a play like it," said veteran end Max McGee. "That was the greatest."

The Packers eventually moved on to the first Super Bowl game ever staged, in Los Angeles, with Kansas City representing the AFL. The final score was 35–10, Green Bay, a rout. But people forget that for one half the Chiefs hung right in there with the Packers and even scared the padding out of them. After Green Bay tallied first, the Chiefs drove immediately back for an equalizer. Then the Packers moved to the Chief 14. Taylor started to run a sweep around left end, but a Kansas City linebacker shot through and almost nailed him. Taylor yanked free and continued almost to the sideline. He cut sharply toward the goal line, broke through another tackle, stumbled, regained his balance, eluded a pursuing lineman and dove headlong into the end zone with two more Chiefs clinging to him. The Packers had the lead for keeps.

When Jimmy finally was stopped as a Packer, it wasn't by any tackler. Money did it. He had played the 1966 season without signing a new contract. The Packers had signed fullback Jim Grabowski of Illinois and halfback Donnie Anderson of Texas Tech to huge contracts. Grabowski, who would be groomed to replace Taylor, was reported to have a $400,000 deal. "Did you get a five-figure bonus when you started?" Taylor was asked. "Yes," he answered, "if you're including dollars and cents."

In professional football, a player who doesn't renew a contract plays out the option on his services and is theoretically a free agent, to deal with whichever team he chooses, the following May 1. Lombardi, a traditionalist, considered Taylor's action a breach of loyalty. When a wire service writer reported Taylor's impending free agent status,

356

Lombardi banned the newsman from the dressing room (the Commissioner's office intervened to rescind the ban). Taylor said that not once during the season did Lombardi refer to him by name.

An expansion team was already ticketed for New Orleans in 1967. Playing in Louisiana, where he had business interests, appealed to the thirty-two-year-old veteran. He signed a big personal services contract with the Saints after he became a free agent, and the Packers received a first draft choice and an unnamed player as compensation for his loss. On a newly organized team, especially weak in offensive linemen, with his legs starting to show the effects of nine bruising seasons, Taylor had a mediocre year. "Jim is trying to be our leader," said Coach Tom Fears of the Saints. "He's not a real leader type; he's always been more of a follower. But he's trying to be helpful with the kids. Some of them call him Coach."

Taylor was committed to playing again in 1968. He went through training camp. But the night before a September exhibition in Shreveport, Louisiana, Taylor was assigned to play with the special teams, hustling down on punts and kickoffs. It's the kind of duty that's relegated to marginal players, and it was a direct affront to one of the long-time stars of pro football. He dressed for the game, but left the field half an hour before it started, without consulting Fears, and later announced his retirement. He continued with the Saints organizations as a public relations man.

In this job, he wasn't required to run over people.

JIM TAYLOR'S FAVORITE PLAY:

"My best play was coming back to the weak side, called 'Brown Right 36' at Green Bay. It was an off-tackle play and it could go either off the left tackle's block on the defensive end or the halfback's block on the weakside linebacker. It features option running by the back and depends on strong blocking.

"We found it very successful at Green Bay in our games against the Browns and Giants because of the types of defenses they used. They were conscious of our sweep to the strong side, and this was a weak side driving play. The linebacker had to be up on the line and play it real tough to stop it. It was good on short yardage situations, particularly, when the linebacker edges up on the line of scrimmage and the halfback, Paul Hornung, generally, could cut him in, giving me a quick alley outside."

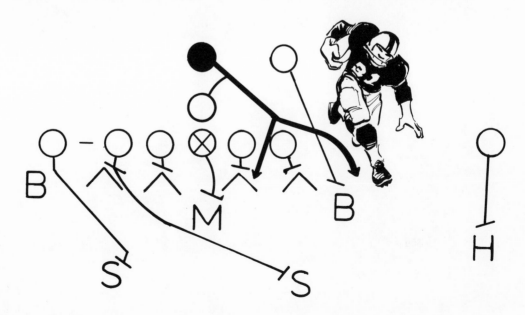

JAMES CHARLES "JIMMY" TAYLOR

BORN: Sept. 20, 1935   Height: 5'11"   Weight: 212
Louisiana State University

Green Bay, 1958–66
New Orleans, 1967

Year	G.	Att.	RUSHING Yds.	Avg.	TD.	P.C.	PASS RECEIVING Yds.	Avg.	TD.	SCORING TD.	Pts.
1958	12	52	247	4.8	1	4	72	18.0	1	2	12
1959	12	120	452	3.8	6	9	71	7.9	2	8	48
1960	12	*230	1101	4.8	11	15	121	8.1	0	11	66
1961	14	243	1307	5.4	*15	25	175	7.0	1	*16	96
1962	14	*272	*1474	5.4	*19	22	106	4.8	0	*19	*114
1963	14	248	1018	4.1	9	13	68	5.2	1	10	60
1964	13	235	1169	5.0	12	38	354	9.3	3	15	90
1965	13	207	734	3.5	4	20	207	10.4	0	4	24
1966	14	204	705	3.5	4	41	331	8.1	2	6	36
1967	14	130	390	3.0	2	38	251	6.6	0	2	12

PRO TOTALS
—10 YEARS 132 1941 8597 4.4 83 225 1756 7.8 10 93 558
* Led NFL.

Lenny Moore

LENNY IS SO GOOD HE GIVES BACKS
LIKE ME AN INFERIORITY COMPLEX.
—*Alex Hawkins,*
Baltimore Colts.

His shoes encased in tape which made them look like spats, Lenny Moore was a blur of forward motion for the Baltimore Colts.

Like, man, the oofuses who zanied after the Colts dug Spats the most. He three-cented a lick to his soul brother, Rosey Grier, jiving: "Man, they really love this cat in Baltimore." And why not? When Spats did his thing, the padded squares grabbed for oxygen.

"Spats" was Lenny Moore, a cool cat who flipped for the progressive jazz of Miles Davis, John Coltrane, Cannonball and Nat Adderley, Jimmy Smith, Sonny Rollins, ad infinitum. "His thing" was running and catching the football for the Baltimore Colts. And the "padded squares" were tacklers who grabbed for him and came away with air.

For a dozen seasons, from 1956 through 1967, Leonard Edward Moore was the most spectacular single force in the history of the Baltimore Colts, a franchise which had some spectacular success and failure. Guys like Johnny Unitas and Raymond Berry, Gino Marchetti and Jim Parker—all-time all-pros at their positions—also played for the Colts in his time. But they were more devastatingly efficient and scientifically competent than vividly colorful. Lenny had a flair for stirring the emotion with the staccato movement of his feet, a blur of white because of the tape wound tightly over the shoes (hence the nickname, "Spats"). He spoiled the Colts' enthusiasts, too. He did so much, they always expected more. So Lenny's career rode the yo-yo, from some of the most scintillating single plays in the history of football to abject periods of frustration.

He was the advance echelon in the Colts' first breakthrough to championship glory. An athlete of matchless grace, trim as a greyhound but surprisingly strong enough to run inside, he had been NFL rookie of the year in 1956 and then proceeded to rip off five straight all-pro campaigns. "Lenny," said the other Colts, "has more natural ability than any man in football. He's just as good as he wants to be. If he ever used 100 percent of it, no one would ever come close to him."

Maybe, temperamentally, Lenny wasn't geared to be a 100 percenter. As a professional football star, the living was good. And you had to understand something about where Lenny Moore came from to appreciate that good living could be an end in itself.

There were eight kids in the Moore house in Reading, Pennsylvania, a modest frame home on Poplar Lane. Lenny was the youngest of the four boys. "We were a poor family," he said. "One time I remember we were on relief." The father was always a steel mill worker. The mother died before Lenny hit it real big.

"The biggest dream I had," recalled Lenny, "was to excel in some sport professionally so I could help my parents. I had some little odd jobs, at a store, but nothing very much because the old man was always interested in us getting our schooling."

The three older Moore boys were good athletes, too. But they couldn't afford to go to college—that was a luxury. And the next best thing was to enlist in the Army. All three went into the service, and Lenny was headed that way also. "You couldn't get a decent job," said Lenny, "and you didn't want to be a burden at home. College scholarships? I was turned down by most of the schools that were interested in me because of the scholastic thing."

Not that Lenny lacked brightness. He was sharp and a smooth talker, a good-looking kid who carried himself well. But with baseball and football, basketball and track, that "scholastic thing" had to suffer. His high school coach, Andy Stopper, was the man who steered him right, who got the youngest of the Moore boys into Penn State. "He was the biggest plus in my life," was how Lenny put it. And at Penn State, Lenny became the best back in the distinguished coaching career of Rip Engle. He was a brilliant offensive threat, and equally capable as a safety on defense. A ball carrier thrives on gaining yardage, and egotistically Lenny was no exception. He was used to picking up more than 100 yards every Saturday. Before a Pitt game, Joe Paterno, the offensive coach who eventually succeeded Engle, plotted a different course for Moore. He decided to use him as a decoy. The strategy worked for a Penn State victory, though Lenny's role didn't show much in the game statistics. Afterward, Paterno pulled him aside and said, "Lenny, you understand why you didn't get to carry the ball much today. You were our faker—and it paid off."

And Lenny said, "Coach, it's lots of fun just faking. I had the easiest afternoon I've had all season. Couldn't we arrange a little more of the same?"

Years later, with the Colts, there would be insinuations that Lenny was a little too interested in taking it easy. But that's jumping too far ahead in the football life of Lenny Moore. First, there were the good years when, as he wrote his pen pal, Rosey Grier, a defensive tackle with the Giants, "they really love this cat in Baltimore."

He was the Colts' top draft pick for 1956, though he hadn't been an All-American—they seldom make selections from teams that win five and lose four, as Penn State did his senior year. The adjustment from Pennsylvania living to a border state like Maryland was a new experience. "Reading had no ghetto," said Lenny "It was integrated all the way through. I knew nothing about these racial things really until I came to Baltimore. I didn't know how to take the people. I stayed in my place and played it by ear to learn where I could go and where I couldn't go. Sports was a tremendous thing in opening up the gates."

It seems sociologically unsound, but acceptance in the general community comes easier for a Negro back who gains 7.5 yards each time he carries the ball, as Lenny did in his rookie year. It was the best average in the NFL. Lenny arrived on the scene the same year Johnny Unitas emerged as a quarterback and Big Daddy Lipscomb was picked up as a free agent to bolster the defense. And within three seasons the Colts had their first NFL title in history, winning the 1958 sudden death overtime playoff from the New York Giants. Lenny continued to be the most effective runner in the game, based on yards per carry. But he set no records for total distance because his use was controlled. In the offense devised by Weeb Ewbank, Lenny was as much a flanker as a running back; his pass receiving yardage generally exceeded what he picked up on the ground. He'd line up wide on one play, as a receiving threat, then be brought in to set up beside fullback Alan Ameche and slash through the line as a ball carrier. Lenny never carried the ball as much as 100 times a season in his first six years in the league, yet he soon built a reputation as the most dangerous offensive player in football because of his dual threat in the air or on the ground.

362

"He gives you the toughest tackling target of any man in the league," said Ben Scotti, a defensive back with the Redskins. "Lenny dips his shoulders, bobs, weaves, and doesn't give you much to shoot at. When you try to hit him, you only get about half of what you thought you were going to get."

"Lenny's the best offensive back in the league," declared Unitas. "Whether we play him in tight or out on the flank, the opposition has to play him tough. They know that he's a constant threat to go the distance and generally play two men on him. I know that I've always had the greatest confidence in his ability to make a play go."

"Lenny Moore has got to be the greatest athlete I've ever seen," said Raymond Berry, the spindly split end of the Colts. "He's got all the natural ability anyone could desire." Berry, with limited natural resources, drove himself to become the most prolific pass receiver in history. He worked to get open, where Lenny simply turned on the afterburner and took off.

His speed led to last second heroics because when the Colts trailed in closing moments and needed a touchdown fast, Unitas always looked to the only long range threat on the club, Spats. After Yuri Gagarin of Russia orbited in space, Big Daddy started calling him Sputnik, too.

In the 1959 championship game with the New York Giants, Moore got the Colts rocketing on a play which had Berry as the primary receiver. With Raymond covered, Moore broke down the middle of the field and burst between two Giant defenders to catch Unitas' pass and complete a 59-yard touchdown play. The Colts were off and winging to their second straight world championship.

A year later, the Colts found themselves one Sunday afternoon in Chicago, trailing 20–17, with 17 seconds left to play. Moore, flanked out to the right, hurtled straight down the field, a couple of Bears dogging him. Unitas threw the ball as high and as far as he could. Approaching the end zone, Lenny left his feet, dove horizontally, clutched the ball as he belly-slid into the end zone and hung on for the winning touchdown. A couple of weeks later, in the same situation, with 14 seconds to play and Detroit leading 13–8, the same battery made connections again in the end zone on a similarly spectacular fly pattern to climax what looked like another Colt victory. But this time there was a post-climax. On the last play of the game, with the clock run out, the Lions hit on a 75-yard touchdown play to upset the league leaders. And then the Colts went West and lost their last two games of the 1960 season to ruin their bid for an unprecedented third straight title. For the next couple of years, they were on the skids. By 1963, Weeb Ewbank was gone and Lenny Moore was virtually through.

In 1961, the Colts sent Big Daddy Lipscomb to the Pittsburgh Steelers in a trade that brought them Jimmy Orr. Now they had another established wide receiver to complement Raymond Berry, the split end. Ewbank, seeking to use Moore and Orr in the same lineup, decided to shift Lenny inside as a halfback permanently, making Orr the full-time flanker. The move was an abrupt change for Lenny after six years as a combination flanker-runner. He would be subject to a lot more pounding. As a 190-pound halfback, he'd have to take on 250-pound defensive ends when he was held inside to block on pass plays. Moore always looked deceptively frail since his thin shanks were no bigger in circumference than a cotton tail. And his style of running, with a high lifting of the knee and a long stride in full flight, was tailored more to wide open spaces. At the same time, he wasn't a weakling. He had the upper torso of a wrestler and he had that great quickness and a sliding technique to slip through the heavy traffic in the middle of the line.

"I really wish," he said later, "I could have spent my whole career as a flanker. I wish I might have said no when Weeb came to me and asked to make the change. But the way it was put to me, for the good of the team, I couldn't say no."

Then personal troubles for Lenny started. In 1961, he complained of a head injury and missed the last game, his first absenteeism as a Colt. In 1962, in the Colts' final preseason game, against the Pittsburgh Steelers, he circled left end and raced 43 yards before he was jolted out of bounds. His knee, hitting the ground, bumped a first base peg still left in the infield of Forbes Field—"It felt like hitting an end table in the house" —and Lenny couldn't flex his leg when he came back to the huddle. He left the field and played a little later in the game. The next day, x-rays revealed a fractured kneecap. Lenny didn't get back until the fifth game of the season; ironically, that year he carried the ball a new high, 106 times. But the effect of his heavier duty was negative in another area—his pass receptions dropped in one year from forty-nine to eighteen.

In 1963, at the age of thirty, he was a complete washout. He started with damaged ribs, and two days before the start of the season he had an appendectomy. When he came back, they played him—the most spectacular threat of the decade in pro football —at split end. Then they let him run again at halfback, briefly. In the ninth game, against the Detroit Lions, he was enmeshed in a pileup. His helmet was knocked off; an elbow clobbered him on the head. On Tuesday after the game he vomited. On Thursday he got dizzy spells trying to run in practice. He complained of a "buzzing" and a "funny feeling" in his head. The doctors examined him and could find no tangible injury. Lenny's use the rest of the season was negligible. Tom Matte, an all-purpose back, moved in as the starter at left half and did a solid job.

The Colt coaches—this was Don Shula's first year—were down on old Spats. So were his teammates. Other teams might want to take a chance on Lenny. They could have his headaches. A deal was even made to swap him even-up for Don Perkins, the mini-fullback of the Dallas Cowboys, but a last-minute decision by the Colts' front office vetoed it. There were other rumors: Moore to the Giants for Sam Huff, to the Packers for Tom Moore, to anybody that wanted him. It was no secret he could be had, for the right price, a halfback considered psychotic and controversial. But Carroll Rosenbloom, the Colts' owner, and Don Kellett, the general manager, retained an image of Lenny as the tie to their titular days. Moore was called in to huddle with Shula and the front office to resolve his future.

"I doubt if we ever would have traded Lenny," said Rosenbloom. "I just wanted to hear him say he wanted to play in Baltimore. He said it, and that was good enough for me."

"The controversy," said Lenny, "it burned the hell out of me. A lot of people said I was finished. I said to the Colts, 'I'm going to close the mouths of a helluva lot of these people.'"

364

Lenny was going to be just another guy trying to win a job on the club. Matte, the club rushing leader in '63 and an effective receiver coming out of the backfield, would come to camp as the starting halfback, deservedly. So when the Colts opened the 1964 season in Bloomington, Minnesota, against the Minnesota Vikings, Moore was not in the starting lineup. He played early and scored the Colts' first TD. He also caught a 70-yard touchdown pass as the Colts revealed a flood pattern in which Lenny was slotted outside the tight end to give them three deep receivers. But the Colts lost the opener.

Now the Colts were in Green Bay for the second game, facing the top team in football, winners of the Western division three years in a row and the NFL title the last two years. It was a game the Colts had to win. And it was also a game in which Lenny had to prove he could still produce under pressure. He started at halfback.

"You know he's your best runner," said Bill Pellington, the defensive captain, "but can you count on him?"

Halfway through the first quarter, Baltimore was on its own 48, and Unitas sent Moore out on a swing pattern to the right. The Packers, blitzing two of their linebackers, left Dan Currie on the strong side with the responsibility of picking up Moore. Lenny's fake drew Dan to the middle of the field, then the Colt back swung wide and down the right sideline. As Unitas released the pass, Currie wasn't within 10 yards of Moore.

"I said to myself," recounted Lenny, " 'Please don't drop it. Watch out. Don't drop this one.' " Moore clutched the ball and trotted into the end zone at half speed. It was the only pass he caught all day. In the second quarter, on a third down situation at the Green Bay 4, he dove through the middle on a trap play. He squirmed through tacklers. Linebacker Ray Nitschke met him at the goal line, and Lenny's lunge drove him into the end zone. "He ran," said Nitschke, "like he wanted it." And the Colts won a 21–20 cliffhanger.

It went that way all through the 1964 season, the Colts winning the crucial games, Moore scoring the big touchdowns, at a record pace. In mid-October, the Colts and Green Bay met again. A victory by the Packers would tie them with the Colts for the division lead. In the third period, the Colts trailing by four, Moore took a quick pitchout to the left and found Henry Jordan, the mobile Packer tackle, waiting for him. He blasted through Jordan's grip. Safety Hank Gremminger came up fast to meet him, and Lenny's legs cut through him like a scythe. Cornerback Jesse Whittenton jumped on his back, and Lenny carried him along for 10 yards. At the 2-yard line he unloaded Whittenton and galloped into the end zone to complete a 21-yard run.

With a minute to play in the game, Moore knifed through the left side of the line from five yards out for the winning touchdown after the Packers had regained the lead, 21–17. The Colts swept on to the championship of the West as Moore set a new NFL record of 20 touchdowns in a single season (since broken by Jimmy Brown and Gale Sayers). Lombardi once said Hornung smelled the goal line. So did Moore in that comeback year of 1964. "I think it's a sense all backs get inside that 5," said Lenny, "when they see that last stripe. Another instinct comes in them. You get extra drive, extra power from somewhere."

Lenny returned to all-pro status and was voted the most valuable player in the league. Teammate Jim Parker, the huge guard who led his sorties, filled out his ballot as

In 1964, Lenny Moore, as both the comeback player of the year and the NFL's most valuable player, receives the Jim Thorpe Trophy from the author.

follows: "1. Lenny Moore, 2. Lenny Moore, 3. Lenny Moore." Parker noted, "This is the only choice this year."

For dramatic purposes, Lenny should have quit right then, on top. But he played three more years. Every game, he carefully taped his ankles inside and outside the shoes, a habit he had picked up from a teammate at Penn State a dozen years before. When he was 34, he still ran a 4.6 second 40 yards.

Out of season, he was a disc jockey, making use of his love for cool jazz, and he operated Lenny Moore's Cocktail Lounge. He claimed he never made the big money— "My first three or four years in pro ball, I had to borrow ahead on my salary." But as he settled into the status of an elder statesman on the club, Lenny seemed contented. When he became a spot player in 1967, he was ready to bow out. He became the television color man on CBS for the Colts' games.

To the accusation that he had the ability to be the greatest back of all, but played only as well as he felt like playing, Lenny replied, without any bitterness, "I thought people expected more of me than I was able to give. You can only do what you can do."

What he did, in retrospect, wasn't bad. He played in seven Pro Bowls, made the All-NFL team five times, and scored more touchdowns (113) than any player in history except Jim Brown.

LENNY MOORE'S FAVORITE PLAY:

"It was called 'flow-38' or 'flow-39' when we ran it to the left, as here. The play was designed for me to cut anywhere I could hit the opening or carry it around the end. If the defense would overflow when they saw me swinging wide, I could cut back. Generally, I cut inside the linebacker after Alex Sandusky, our guard then, kicked him out.

"It was instrumental in the game that helped the Colts clinch their first division title and then win the world championship in 1958. We played the 49ers in Baltimore in 1958. I started around end, cut inside and then back out to the sidelines again, picking up a block by George Preas, our tackle, and going 73 yards for a touchdown.

"As a runner, I also liked the quick pitchout. If you could get around the end, with the flanker cracking back on the outside linebacker, you had good running room to pick up downfield blocks."

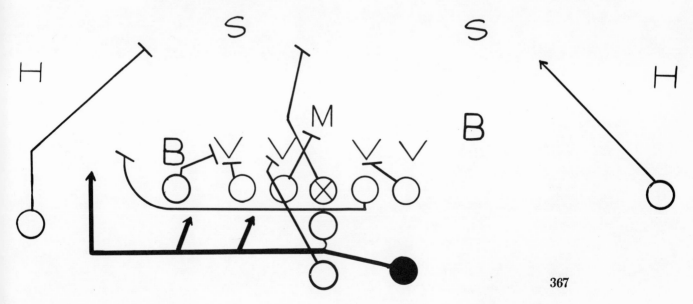

LEONARD EDWARD "LENNY" ("SPATS") MOORE

BORN: Nov. 25, 1933   Height: 6'1"   Weight: 195

Pennsylvania State University

Baltimore, 1956–67

Year	G.	RUSHING Att.	Yds.	Avg.	TD.	PASS RECEIVING P.C.	Yds.	Avg.	TD.	SCORING TD.	Pts.
1956	12	86	649	*7.5	8	11	102	9.3	1	9	54
1957	12	98	488	*5.0	3	40	687	17.2	7	*11	66
1958	12	82	598	*7.3	7	50	938	18.5	7	14	84
1959	12	92	422	4.6	2	47	846	18.0	6	8	48
1960	12	91	374	4.1	4	45	936	20.8	9	13	78
1961	13	92	648	*7.0	7	49	728	14.9	8	15	90
1962	10	106	470	4.4	2	18	215	11.9	2	4	24
1963	7	27	136	5.0	2	21	288	13.7	2	4	24
1964	14	157	584	3.7	*16	21	472	22.5	3	*20	*120
1965	12	133	464	3.5	5	27	414	15.3	3	8	48
1966	13	63	209	3.3	3	21	260	12.4	0	3	18
1967	14	42	132	3.1	4	13	153	11.8	0	4	24

PRO TOTALS
—12 YEARS	143	1069	5174	4.8	63	363	6039	16.6	48	113	678

* Led NFL.

John David Crow

WHAT JIMMY BROWN IS TO CLEVELAND,
WHAT PAUL HORNUNG IS TO GREEN BAY,
JOHN DAVID CROW IS TO US.
—Wally Lemm, coach,
St. Louis Cardinals.

Vernon J. Biever Photo

John David Crow was once regarded the equal of Jim Brown as a football property and served 11 years with distinction for both the Cardinals and the 49ers.

Bill Koman, in his first training camp as a young linebacker with the Chicago Cardinals, wasn't going to be late for a team meeting. John David Crow, already wise to the pro routine in his second season, said to Koman after lunch, "I'm going to get me a little shuteye. Come by my room on the way to the meeting and make sure you get me up."

At the appointed hour, Koman walked down the corridor of the dormitory at Lake Forest College, where the Cardinals trained that July day in 1959, and looked in at the open door to Crow's room. The big running back of the Cardinals was flat on his back. From where Koman stood, his left eye was open.

"Hell," thought Bill to himself, "he's awake. I'll go on to the meeting."

Half an hour later, with the coaches lecturing, no Crow. He slept right through the meeting. At practice in the afternoon, a few dollars lighter, John David collared Koman on the field: "Where in the —— were you? I thought I told you to come by and get me up."

"I did," pleaded Koman. "You were awake. I saw you."

"I was asleep," insisted Crow. And then it was explained to the new man on the team that John David Crow always slept with his left eye open. It never closed day or night because he was born with a partial paralysis of the left side of his face which prevented the lower lid of his left eye from meeting the upper lid.

John David (because of his Southern heritage the middle name was generally attached in referring to him) accepted the congenital disfigurement of his face—the left side of his mouth dropped slightly, too—early in life and adjusted to it. After a while, anybody who was around John David very much never thought about it because in his social attitude, he was as normal a man as ever was exposed to the public, and in his physical action as an athlete he was far better than most. Maybe he wasn't a cover boy and didn't get some of the endorsements which normally accrue to a football star of his stature, but he was never bitter. As long as he played football, he didn't want to risk plastic surgery. He planned to do something about his face when his playing days were over (and he did when he retired after the 1968 season).

"I was born out in the country, down in Marion, Louisiana," John David once explained to an interviewer. "The doctor didn't get there for my arrival. He came soon after, though, and found this trouble with my face. You know how little kids are. They're going to tease you about something like that when you're growing up. I had a few arguments and maybe a couple of fights. But after a while I got to be bigger than the other kids so nothing more was said."

Psychologists would have to probe for the inner motivation that derived from little John David Crow's physical flaw and drove him to sports—he became an All-American at Texas A & M, the winner of the Heisman Trophy as the outstanding college player in the country, an all-pro running back and a respected professional for eleven years—but to the layman, there were obvious reasons for his excellence. In his physical prime, Crow was 6'2", 220 pounds, quick and smart, and a guy that the other players on the team liked to be with, on or off the field.

He wasn't superman. His career was hampered by mechanical failures, like a proclivity at one point for fumbling a football. He didn't have the training zeal and the fanatic dedication of a Jim Taylor (who was a schoolboy rival in his native Louisiana— they played against each other in high school all-star football and basketball games). In the early years, when everything was going good for him with the Cardinals, he didn't make any special efforts to stay in shape between seasons. Nature, which quick-shuffled him on one count, compensated by giving him a strong body and the will to use it.

"I'm a poor kid from a small town," he said at the peak of his career. "If I hadn't been a good football player, I'd still be there, just beyond the Arkansas border.

"I love the atmosphere of football. I just don't think I'm cut out for the 9-to-5 hitch, though in some ways I envy the guys who can do it. The only thing I know is that I try to play hard. I'm not real fancy, but I know only one way to play this game, and that's as hard as I can."

Later on, when the hard way he played football inevitably led to a series of bumps and bruises which aborted his potential greatness as a player, and he was traded to the San Francisco 49ers, general manager Lou Spadia of that club said, "John has been hurt a great deal because he plays with such reckless abandon and doesn't run for the sidelines like some other backs."

Among the injuries that spotted his record were a knee bump which caused him to miss half his rookie year, a chest bone dislocation, a fractured leg which sidelined him after the greatest season of his career, severely sprained ankles and another knee injury, and an operation from which he never came back as a super star.

The term "super star" is used because there was one campaign in which John David Crow put all his abilities together and was a match for almost everyone who ever carried a football. The year was 1960, when the Cardinals had just been moved from Chicago to St. Louis. In the flush of enthusiasm in their new surroundings, they had their first winning record in five years, and Crow, in full prowess at the age of twenty-five, gained 1,021 yards running, with an average of 5.9 yards per carry which topped the NFL. He was also a good receiver in Frank "Pop" Ivy's version of the double wing T, and a rugged blocker.

"Crow can go inside or outside with as much power and speed combined as any back I've ever seen," said Ivy. "I believe he's at least the equal of Jimmy Brown of Cleveland as a running back, although Brown has the advantage of a better offensive line."

"He's the finest complete football player I've ever seen," said Buddy Young, scouting for the Baltimore Colts.

A St. Louis newspaper reported in January 1961 that Paul Brown of Cleveland had twice in ten days offered to trade Jimmy Brown for Crow, and that the Cardinals had refused the proposed swap. The report led to the big debate of the winter in pro football circles: Would you trade Brown, already regarded as the greatest runner in history, for Crow?

"I would go with John David," said outspoken Chuck Bednarik, the linebacker of the world champion Eagles. "They're almost equally hard to tackle. Crow can run almost —and I say 'almost'—as hard as Brown. He's a terrific passer and a better blocker. I like Crow better because of his versatility."

372

"Brown is the hardest runner in the league," said quarterback Ralph Guglielmi of Washington. "Crow can do more things. He's the best all-around back in the league. But I wouldn't trade. I'd keep what I have."

The debate might have lasted for at least a couple of winters if, fatefully, a Cardinal quarterback hadn't loused up a pitchout on August 18, 1961. The Cardinals were playing the suddenly potent Green Bay Packers in a Busch Stadium exhibition. It was the third quarter, and the play called for Crow to circle left end. The sloppy pitchout hit the ground, and Crow bent over on the run to retrieve it. He hadn't fully recovered his balance when a Packer linebacker hit him. The impact didn't knock the Cardinal back down. As he twisted to get free, unable to protect himself, two more Packers hit him broadside, and he went down in a tangle of limbs and bodies. Crow's left leg was broken a half inch above the ankle.

He was out until the fifth game of the season, got hurt again and wound up carrying the ball only 48 times in 1961.

Then a strange thing happened to John David Crow on the way to full recovery. He misplaced the handle on the football. Physically, there was nothing wrong with him when he returned to full duty in 1962. He ran from scrimmage 192 times and scored fourteen touchdowns on the ground. But for every touchdown, there was also a fumble to match. Against the Redskins one afternoon, he fumbled the ball four times. Against Dallas, a weak expansion team, he fumbled four times and dropped a couple of passes. "League statistics charge Crow with fourteen fumbles," said Wally Lemm, who succeeded Ivy as head coach, "but in our study of game movies we have found nineteen fumbles in which Crow could be charged with at least partial responsibility."

"I played bad in more ways than just fumbling," said Crow. "I got conscious of the ball. A good running back in this league can't be conscious of the ball. I wasn't going into the hole as hard as I could. I was thinking too much about having the ball and having it good."

By this time, the Cardinals were starting to load up with running backs and shopped around for a trade. They wouldn't get Jim Brown, but Crow was still valuable baggage for a lot of clubs. With Paul Hornung suspended on the gambling charge, Green Bay was interested, but Lemm's price was too high. Crow returned to the Cardinals and in an exhibition game against the Bears tore a ligament in his right knee. Young Bill Triplett, in his second year with the Cardinals, took over at halfback. When Crow was reported fit to play a month later, Triplett remained the regular, and John David's vanity was bruised. In late October, he reinjured the knee and submitted to surgery. His total output for 1963 was 34 yards on nine carries.

Crow, approaching 29, buckled down and trimmed his weight to 212 for the 1964 season. He reinjured the knee slightly in a workout, and his job passed on this time to Willis Crenshaw (Triplett was out for the year with tuberculosis). During the season he was even put on waivers, which were withdrawn when the Bears claimed him. Shuffling in and out of the lineup, Crow managed to lead the Cardinals in rushing as they came within half a game of winning the division title from Cleveland, but John David strained his knee in the final game and was ignored in the post-season Playoff Bowl at Miami.

Within a couple of weeks, he notified the Cardinals: "Trade me, or I quit."

"I didn't play as much as I should have," he explained, "to be of some value to the team. I'm not here just to draw pay. For sixteen years I've started every game I've been able to. Maybe they want to mature Crenshaw, or maybe they just thought he was a better football player. It's time for me to make a move." He was traded to the San Francisco 49ers for Abe Woodson, a defensive back. Crow said he had three or four good years to help another club, and his assessment was right on the button.

He didn't burn up the league when he came to the 49ers in 1965. He was a steady contributor who chipped in his 500 yards a season and provided the kind of blocking support that made John Brodie an all-pro quarterback. The 49ers roomed the veteran with Ken Willard, his partner in a "bull" backfield, and he tutored the young 230-pound rookie from North Carolina on the essential points of being a pro back. "John David is always around when the kid has a question," said Brodie. In 1966, Crow received the Len Eshmont Most Inspirational Player award for the 49ers.

"The guy," said Jack Christiansen, the 49ers coach, "is a results man. He gets the important yards, running or pass catching."

"He makes the plays that take 'feel,'" said Y. A. Tittle, handling the backs. "That comes from maturity. This man has gained 1,000 yards in a season."

"He also gives the club a big emotional and mental life," said Spadia. "He played his first three games as a 49er with his broken hand in a cast—a great competitor."

Another knee operation after the '66 campaign didn't slow him up. He still ran like a dachshund, both legs pattering along barely above the blades of grass. Strength was more important to him than speed. "Whether a tank is going fast or slow," he once smiled, "you can't really tell."

Crow was always a realist. "When I get to the point where I'm not a little nervous before a game, when my palms aren't damp from excitement," he said, "I'll know I've had it. The biggest thing about this silly kids' game is trying to find out when to quit. Some players have the philosophy that you should never quit—you should let them 'quit' you. Personally, I don't want them to tell me."

Before the 49ers were to play the Los Angeles Rams in the final tuneup for the 1968 season, they gave Crow a new job. Dick Nolan, taking over as head coach, told him he would play tight end. "Dick claimed it would mean a lot less wear on me because I wouldn't have to take the pounding of a back," said John David. "What he didn't tell me was that I'd have to face Deacon Jones." Deacon is the terror of an all-pro defensive end for the Rams.

Like a good pro, Crow accepted the challenge and played tight end the whole season. He caught thirty-one passes and scored five touchdowns. But if his palms were wet with anticipation each week, it wasn't from the excitement of the impending game, but the prospect of blocking Deacon Jones and company. In the early winter of 1969, John David Crow announced his retirement from football to devote himself to real estate and construction in Pine Bluff, Arkansas, where he lives with his wife and three children.

The injuries that had thwarted his chance for greatness as a runner he dismissed philosophically: "It's like getting on an airplane. If you worried about what might happen, it would ruin the trip." John David Crow had travelled long enough.

374

JOHN DAVID CROW'S FAVORITE PLAY:

"This play is known throughout the league as a late or a draw. Of course, it works only in a passing situation, when the defensive line is coming strong. The linemen have to do a little play acting to get the defense to think it is a pass, and the ends and backs have to make the linebackers think pass, too, with their initial moves.

"It is a very simple play using both strength and finesse, and this is what pro football has become. It is the ball carrier's responsibility to read the guard—in this case, the left guard—and break off his block. When he gets into the secondary, he should have lots of room, for the safeties and linebackers have retreated for a pass.

"We called it 'fake quick pass right 23 halfback draw.' In the last few years it has become a very important play for all teams. There may be different blocking patterns but the principle is the same.

"The best men I ever teamed with on this play were John Thomas, our left guard on the 49ers, and Bruce Bosley at center. And another man who would always get in the act eventually was David Parks, the split left end. He would run his fake pass pattern first and then come back and help out by blocking someone downfield."

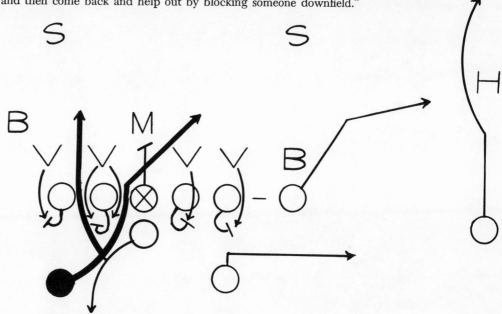

JOHN DAVID CROW

BORN: July 8, 1935   Height: 6'2"   Weight: 220

Texas A&M University

Chicago Cardinals, 1958–59
St. Louis Cardinals, 1960–64
San Francisco, 1965–68

Year	G.	Att.	RUSHING Yds.	Avg.	TD.	PASS RECEIVING P.C.	Yds.	Avg.	TD.	SCORING TD.	Pts.
1958	6	52	221	4.3	2	20	362	18.1	3	6	36
1959	12	140	666	4.8	3	27	328	12.1	4	7	42

1960	12	183	1071	*5.9	6	25	462	18.5	3	9	54
1961	8	48	192	4.0	1	20	306	15.3	3	4	24
1962	14	192	751	3.9	14	23	246	10.7	3	17	102
1963	3	9	34	3.8	0		(None)			0	0
1964	13	163	554	3.4	7	23	257	11.2	1	8	48
1965	14	132	514	3.9	2	28	493	17.6	7	9	54
1966	14	121	477	3.9	1	30	341	11.4	3	4	24
1967	14	113	479	4.2	2	31	373	12.0	3	5	30
1968	14	4	4	1.0	0	31	531	17.1	5	5	30

PRO TOTALS
—11 YEARS 124 1157 4963   4.3 38 258 3699   14.3 35   74 444

    * Led NFL.

John Henry Johnson

HE'S THE ONE MAN IN FOOTBALL I'D LEAST LIKE TO BE. THERE ARE SIMPLY TOO MANY MEN IN THE LEAGUE WHO WOULD LIKE TO SEE HIM CARRIED OFF ON A STRETCHER.

—Jim Brown, fullback,
Cleveland Browns.

Malcolm W. Emmons

For all his ruggedness, John Henry Johnson, shown here with the Pittsburgh Steelers, also found it prudent to stay out of tacklers' ways.

The mystery of modern football is how John Henry Johnson, a mortal man, survived two years of varsity football, one year of Canadian football, twelve years in the National Football League and one final season in the American Football League. And walked away from it all—not exactly with a smile, more of a grimace because pro football no longer had a spot for him.

John Henry Johnson was a most jovial man, if it had nothing to do with football. Put him in its working clothes, however, and he was transformed. Normally, it is the defensive player with the power to use his hands who wreaks the most damage. John Henry, for the most part, shunned the hands. To him, the elbow and the forearm and the shoulder were the bludgeons of his trade, and it really didn't make much difference which side of the line he stood on. In his time—sixteen years of organized pressure football—he played mostly offense, and in the NFL Record Manual he is listed No. 4 among the all-time ground gainers.

But John Henry perpetuated his reputation in another way. He broke heads and bones. He started when he was only a sophomore at St. Mary's College in California, in 1950, the last year that little school played big-time football. John Henry was a two-way performer. On defense he stationed himself immediately behind the line, though he was supposed to be a safety. St. Mary's entertained the University of Georgia when it was terribly progressive for a southern school to play a team which had a Negro in the lineup. Coach Wally Butts of Georgia cautioned his boys to avoid all incidents. One Georgia fullback was carried out twice after running into John Henry, who didn't bother to tackle people in the traditional way by wrapping his arms around them. He drove his forearm at the runner, generally penetrating to the jaw, stiffening the enemy and stretching him unconscious.

Georgia, favored by 24 points, was tied 7–7 by little St. Mary's, which won only two games all year. When the southern Bulldogs weren't ducking John Henry's forearm shiver, they were chasing after him. He took the opening kickoff 94 yards for St. Mary's only score. If a man like John Henry was going to live by the forearm shiver, he also had to risk the consequences.

The next week, the Gaels visited Hollywood's old Gillmore Field for a game against a strapping Loyola of Los Angeles team. Don Klosterman, the quarterback (now the general manager of the Houston Oilers), kept sending backs in John Henry's direction, and after every play, a new Loyola back would be in the lineup. They carried them out as fast as they could line up stretchers. Finally, the late Gene Brito (who graduated to all-pro defensive end for the Washington Redskins) spit on his hands, a characteristic gesture when he got angry, and asked Klosterman to call a play on which he was free to block anyone. When the play terminated, John Henry was the man carried out and played no more that afternoon as Loyola ran up a big score.

After college (he transferred to Arizona State when St. Mary's dropped football), John Henry ignored a bid by the Pittsburgh Steelers, who had drafted him on the second round, and went off to play for Calgary in the Canadian League. In an intra-squad scrimmage, a young halfback was running a kickoff down the sideline when John Henry came across to intercept him. John Henry let him have it with a flying block-tackle, his patented forearm leading. The halfback's jaw was broken in two places. "Was that really necessary?" the general manager of the team asked John Henry. He shrugged: "What did you want me to do—kiss the guy or tackle him?"

Advancing to the NFL, where a man might use some caution considering the size of the adversaries, John Henry was no less timid. He virtually ended the career of the great Charley Trippi when the latter, idly watching a play from his position in the Cardinal secondary, was felled by a Johnson blow which changed his face. Linebacker Les Richter of the Los Angeles Rams, regarded as a fairly menacing character himself, once tailed John Henry on a pass patern. The ball went to someone else, but Les decided to tackle John Henry anyhow. Result: one broken jaw—Richter's.

Through all this, there were some retaliatory attempts. For instance, John Henry was tackled once near the Rams' bench after the Richter episode. Lustily, the Rams cleared the bench and came charging at John Henry in a single body. They came up short—in a single body. John Henry had arisen from the tackle clutching a yard marker with which he slashed the air in warning.

And so the years passed, one after the other, and John Henry's survival was no longer a matter of conjecture. He began to threaten Satchel Paige as an antique of sports longevity, and miraculously he seemed to get better as he got older. "You get to be a smarter runner when you get older," said John Henry, by now entrenched as the fullback of the Pittsburgh Steelers. "I don't mind running inside because I know how to turn those young tigers around. I stay young myself by watching my diet. I load up on steak and skip the bread and potatoes. And I get lots of sleep."

At the age of thirty-three, he had his greatest year as a pro, gaining 1,141 yards in 251 carries, also catching thirty-two passes. Two seasons later, in 1964, he gained 1,048 yards, a truly remarkable feat for a thirty-five-year-old fullback who was still the target of every tackler in football. Just that summer, Brady Keys, a defensive back of the Steelers, had told him, "John Henry, you look like you can play another ten years."

"Oh, no," John Henry answered. "My time is coming, baby, just like your time is coming."

Sometimes the other guys on the team called him "Sweet"—no reference to his disposition. Every time John Henry delivered a knock, he punctuated it with a borrowed aphorism: "How sweet it is."

John Henry was in many ways a likeable guy, quick with a comeback. One day in the Steelers' training camp, he was reading a newspaper's sports pages closely. "Reading about yourself, John Henry?" a teammate asked. "Naw," the veteran fullback shook his head. "Don't have to read the paper to find out what I'm doing. I already know that. I read it to check upon how the rest of you are making out."

He was also a man who cared. "Main thing is," he said, "I love to play. I like to run with the ball, and when I don't have it I like to block. You have to like to block to do a good job. I like everything about football."

John Henry was one of the finest athletes ever produced in this country. He could have been great in any sport. Born in a little hamlet called Waterproof, Louisiana, he moved west with his family to Pittsburg, California, an industrial suburb east of the San Francisco bay area, and became a legendary high school track star. In 1948, California had produced Bob Mathias, an eighteen-year-old boy wonder from Tulane who won the decathlon competition at the summer Olympics in London. A year later, John Henry was topping or matching Mathias' best marks in almost all the events on the decathlon program. He was also an all-Northern California basketball player and batted .500 in baseball as a sophomore. He gave up playing the outfield, though. "Not enough action for me," he drawled. Of all his activities, football was the favorite because it meant knocking heads.

"He loves to hit somebody head-on," said Jim Cason, who played with him in pro ball at San Francisco, "just to find out who's the better man."

His NFL career started with the San Francisco 49ers in 1954. Originally, as noted, he had been drafted by the Steelers, who paid for a knee operation and then lost him to Canada. The 49ers swapped the draft rights to an obscure defensive halfback for Johnson and persuaded him to return to the States. He became a halfback in an attacking unit which had Y. A. Tittle at quarterback, Joe Perry at fullback, and Hugh McElhenny at left half—with John Henry, it had to be the most loaded backfield in history. The problem was how to get enough work for all of them. John Henry, as the junior member, was also used on defense. Perry, once timed in 9.5 for the 100, had been the fastest man on the team. Now John Henry led the practice sprints, so in "prevent" defenses he was stationed at the deep safety spot in his rookie year. One late afternoon against the Chicago Bears he was sent in to protect against the long pass in the fading seconds. Harlon Hill, a great receiver with the Bears, was out wide and John Henry's job was to stay in the shadows of the goal post. But the Bear quarterback faked a run, and John Henry, anxious for some action, moved up on the play. Before he could recover, Hill was already racing down the field, past the first 49er defensive back assigned to guard him, without John Henry as the "prevent" backstop. Hill caught the pass thrown through the murky sky and streaked for the winning touchdown. John Henry, trailing him too late, sat down in the end zone after the play and wept.

He had his light moments, too. In that same game with the Bears, he was on offense. The Bears had been doing a lot of stunting in the line, with men jumping around before the snap of the ball. Y. A. Tittle, calling the signals, turned around and yelled to John Henry, "If I say 'white,' run around end. If I say, 'black,' go off tackle." But with the crowd roaring, John Henry didn't hear Tittle's instructions. Y. A. whirled around with the ball, and John Henry was still down in his three-point stance, a few yards back.

"What'll I do now?" Tittle asked, as the Bears lunged for him.

"I don't know," said John Henry, "but get that ball away from me."

The 49ers never did get the full offensive value out of Johnson and traded him to the Detroit Lions in 1957. John Henry arrived just in time to take over as the fullback on a team moving to the NFL championship. After three average seasons with the Lions, John Henry was traded to Pittsburgh, rejoining an old Lion backfield mate, Bobby Layne. The quarterback appreciated John Henry's willingness to block for him. The Lions got rid of Johnson because he was already thirty years old, and they were grooming a fine young husky from Notre Dame, Nick Pietrosante, for the fullback post. In his new assignment with the Steelers, John Henry had to carry the main part of the ground attack for the first time in his NFL career, and he responded nobly. For five seasons, he was a steady, heavy-duty ball carrier. He never led the league because he was bucking the competition of Jim Brown and Jim Taylor, but he was never more than a stride behind.

In a big game against the championship Philadelphia Eagles of 1960, he picked up 187 yards rushing, including an 87-yard dash, the longest of the year in the NFL. The rangy veteran had a galloping style with all parts of him flailing—he described it as a combination jitterbug, Charleston, and twist, with a little rhumba thrown in. "When John Henry's only blocking," said Coach Buddy Parker, "he's a real football player. When he's blocking and running, too, there isn't a better one in the league."

John Henry had his moments of moodiness. After he peaked in 1962 with 1,141 yards, second to Taylor in the league, he began to feel his hurts. He was kicked in the ankle early the next season and removed himself from a couple of games. His absence on a couple of goal line drives hurt the Steelers badly. When Parker figured he was ready, John Henry announced he needed another week of rest. Buddy banned him from practice. On the eve of the '64 campaign, Parker announced that Johnson was no longer the starting fullback. But the old warhorse came on strong. Before the season was a month old, he carried thirty times one Sunday against Cleveland and gained 200 yards, including a couple of coltish 33 and 46-yard touchdown jaunts. It was his best game as a pro and spurred him to his second 1,000-yard season.

John Henry was still operating at the same old stand when the 1965 season started, but in the first quarter of the opener against Green Bay, the ligaments in his knee were badly torn and sidelined him for the entire schedule. Before the next training camp, he wrote the Steelers a letter, listing several complaints, chiefly money. The club promptly released him. As a free agent, Johnson jumped over to the Houston Oilers of the AFL, but the old boy had lost his effectiveness and vanished from pro ball before the '66 season ended.

He wanted to stay in the game as a coach, but no one hired him. "You should write about the sad plight of the black athlete," he noted with bitterness, "who can play in the league a dozen years, help to make it the type of game it is today and cannot get a job in all pro ball. I know the game and can coach it much better than some of the coaches that have tried."

JOHN HENRY JOHNSON'S FAVORITE PLAY:

"Our favorite play on the Pittsburgh Steelers was a '37-slant.' We ran it against every team every week. The key was my ability to pick the right hole. We got some very good blocking from Ray Lemek at right guard, Charley Bradshaw at right tackle, and Preston Carpenter at tight end.

"You take advantage of the movement of the defensive men. You go where 'they ain't.' If the defensive men got a stand-off on their blocks against them, it was just as good, because you went around the end.

"And if you were an outstanding runner, you ran like water to the area of least resistance.

"On October 15, 1965, we used this play about 15 times against the Browns, and I ran for over 200 yards. We also ran it very successfully against the Giants several weeks later, when I collected about 158 yards."

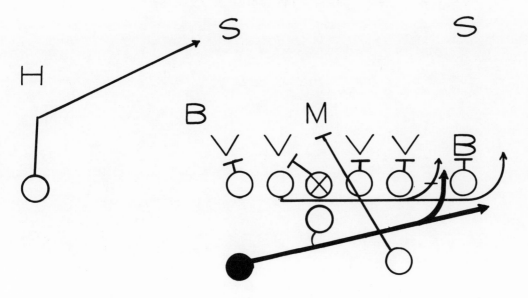

JOHN HENRY JOHNSON

BORN: Nov. 24, 1929   Height: 6'2"   Weight: 225

St. Mary's, Arizona State

San Francisco, 1954–56
Detroit, 1957–59
Pittsburgh, 1960–65
Houston, 1966

Year	G.	Att.	RUSHING Yds.	Avg.	TD.	P.C.	PASS RECEIVING Yds.	Avg.	TD.	SCORING TD.	Pts.
1954	12	129	681	5.3	9	28	183	6.5	0	9	54
1955	7	19	69	3.6	1	2	6	3.0	0	1	6
1956	12	80	301	3.8	2	8	90	11.3	0	2	12
1957	12	129	621	4.8	5	20	141	7.1	0	5	30
1958	9	56	254	4.5	0	7	60	8.6	0	0	0
1959	10	82	270	3.3	2	7	34	4.9	1	3	18
1960	12	118	621	5.3	2	12	112	9.3	1	3	18
1961	14	213	787	3.7	6	24	262	10.9	1	7	42
1962	14	251	1141	4.5	7	32	226	7.1	2	9	54
1963	12	186	773	4.2	4	21	145	6.9	1	5	30
1964	14	235	1048	4.5	7	17	69	4.1	1	8	48
1965	1	3	11	3.7	0		(None)			0	0
1966	14	70	226	3.2	3	8	150	18.8	0	3	18

NFL TOTALS
—12 YEARS 129 1501 6577 4.4 45 178 1328 7.5 7 52 312

PRO TOTALS
—13 YEARS 143 1571 6803 4.3 48 186 1478 7.9 7 55 340

... Also Noteworthy

WHEN YOU TAKE THE BALL, YOUR ONLY
IDEA IS TO RUN IT AS FAR AS YOU CAN,
AND IF YOU DON'T HAVE THAT IDEA, YOU
MAY NOT GET ANY YARDS.
—*Alex Webster, back,*
New York Giants.

"Big Red," Alex Webster, was a master at cutting behind blockers like Jack Stroud (66) of the New York Giants.

For all the years he played with the New York Giants, Alex Webster was a case. He couldn't walk on Tuesday; he jogged lightly on Wednesday; he trotted on Thursday; he ran half speed on Friday; he rested on Saturday—and he ran like hell on Sunday.

Without a ball tucked under his arm, Alex looked like an amiable soul who could be the big, friendly cop on the corner. Big jaw, reddish hair, broad Scottish face, ambling gait—a big guy, but not exactly what a pro coach envisions as a running back. Outwardly he lacked fire. And he couldn't run fast.

It took a while for Alex to overcome this prejudiced image. When he came out of North Carolina State in 1953, with a reputation as a hard-running halfback, the Washington Redskins, who had drafted him and brought him to camp in July, didn't even look at Webster as a running back. They tried him on defense and released him before they left camp.

Alex was broke and married and went home to Kearny, New Jersey, to ponder the future. He wrote a letter to "Peahead" Walker, the coach of the Montreal Alouettes. Peahead had coached at Wake Forest and remembered Alex had once run back a long punt against him for NC State. He phoned Webster and brought him up to play. Alex became the outstanding player in the Canadian League, and the Giants lured him away from the Alouettes in 1955.

"He came to camp," recalled Jim Lee Howell, building a new regime in New York, "and we wondered about him. The fire and zip didn't seem to be there, and when we realized how slow he was, we even thought of him as lazy. Then we put him in his first scrimmage. He bowled over everything standing. He put all his enthusiasm into action."

For most of his ten subsequent seasons with the Giants he was that type of player —dull during the week, animated on Sunday. His speed never dazzled anybody, but Alex had an instinct for cutting in the open field. Because of his size, 6'3" and 220, he was ideal for short yardage and a good blocker. He also became an excellent receiver, catching forty-seven passes one season. Webster never got a lot of national recognition, or even local, because he played at the same time as Frank Gifford, the other halfback on the team. But he was the bread-and-butter ball carrier of the Giants most of that decade, gaining 1,000 yards more than flashier Frank.

Alex was one of those players who was always coming off the sick list. He invariably was hampered by a muscle pull or a bruised shoulder or a sore neck. But it was never safe to count him out. The Giants figured after the 1960 season that Big Red, as they called him, was through, after a half dozen campaigns that had taken their physical toll. He was bothered by a sac of water on the left knee. His legs were weary from muscle pulls, his ribs were aching. He was thirty years old and had been reduced to carrying the ball twenty-two times the whole year. For a halfback who earned his keep on the ground, that was like Benny Goodman coming on without his clarinet. But in 1961, Allie Sherman took over as head coach and revised Alex's role—he made him a fullback. As a halfback in the old system, he had spent a lot of his time flanked out, running pass routes.

As fullback, he'd direct his energy to straight ahead plunging. He responded with the biggest season of his career, gaining 928 yards in 196 carries as the Giants regained their winning touch.

Alex went on to play through the 1964 season and then became a Giant backfield coach. In all, New York won six division championships and one world title during his career. He was the typical old pro who always showed up on Sunday, ready to play.

ALEXANDER "BIG RED" WEBSTER

BORN: April 19, 1931   Height: 6'3"   Weight: 225

North Carolina State University

New York Giants, 1955–64

Year	G.	Att.	Yds.	Avg.	TD.	P.C.	Yds.	Avg.	TD.	TD.	Pts.
		RUSHING				PASS RECEIVING				SCORING	
1955	12	128	634	5.0	5	22	269	12.2	1	6	36
1956	12	178	694	3.9	7	21	197	9.4	3	10	60
1957	11	135	478	3.5	5	30	330	11.0	1	6	36
1958	9	100	398	4.0	3	25	279	11.2	3	6	36
1959	10	79	250	3.2	5	27	381	14.1	2	7	42
1960	8	22	48	2.2	0	8	106	13.3	0	0	0
1961	14	196	928	4.7	2	26	313	12.0	3	5	30
1962	14	207	743	3.6	5	47	477	10.1	4	9	54
1963	7	75	255	3.4	4	15	128	8.5	0	4	24
1964	12	76	210	2.8	3	19	199	10.5	0	3	18
PRO TOTALS —10 YEARS	109	1196	4638	3.9	39	240	2679	11.2	17	56	336

When he was 28 years old, Alan Ameche retired to become a millionaire. Not one of those playboy heirs out of F. Scott Fitzgerald, but one of those honest-to-goodness self-made millionaires, the son of a mattress factory worker in Kenosha, Wisconsin.

Alan made his money in hamburgers, millions of them, sold at stands up and down the East coast through an enterprise originated by him and a couple of other players on the Baltimore Colts, Gino Marchetti, and the late Joe Campanella. They all became rich, Alan the richest, so that he could retire before he was forty years old.

The foundation of their success, and Ameche never kidded himself about it, was the football reputation he made as a fullback and Gino made as a defensive end. He didn't play long—exactly six seasons. On December 4, 1960, setting up to block for Johnny Unitas against the Detroit Lions, Ameche snapped the Achilles tendon in his right foot and that was the end of his career. But while he played, the squat, strong fullback, broad-beamed and broad-shouldered at 220 pounds, made some kind of dent.

They called him The Horse, the type that you hitched a plow behind rather than one of those skittish thoroughbreds. He was built for heavy duty and distance. The first time he carried the ball as a pro, when the Colts opened the 1955 season in Chicago

United Press International Photo

Alan Ameche came into the NFL with a boom in 1955, running for a touchdown on his first carry, leading the league in rushing. "The Horse" helped carry the Baltimore Colts to the top.

against the Bears, Ameche busted off tackle and drove down the middle of the field 79 yards for a touchdown. In that opening game, he carried twenty-one times for a total of 194 yards, a rushing figure which is still in the books as the Colts' record for one game. In that 1955 rookie season, he gained 961 yards to lead the NFL, and that also remains the team record.

A lot of people around Baltimore, remembering how The Horse was a consistent running threat for five years as the Colts rose to become consecutive world champions in 1958–59, think it's significant they collapsed as an NFL power after Ameche got hurt and retired. They didn't have the threat up the middle to keep the defenses honest and balance Unitas' passing prowess.

Alan was a second cousin of Don Ameche, who "invented" the telephone (on celluloid), but every achievement in his life he made on his own. He was born Lino Dante Ameche. When he was sixteen, he marched resolutely into city hall of Kenosha and officially changed his name to Alan—"Lino sounded so effeminate."

He entered a Golden Gloves boxing competition as a novice and won his class by default. All the other entries dropped out when they heard Ameche was in. A year later, he was the varsity fullback at Wisconsin as a freshman (eligible to play because of the Korean War manpower shortage on campus). On a frigid December day in Minneapolis, with straw banking the sidelines to protect the players from the piles of snow turned into ice, Alan put on sneakers and bulldozed through the Minnesota Gophers for 200 yards in 30 carries. He capped four great varsity seasons by making the All-American team and gaining the Heisman Trophy as the outstanding collegian in the country for 1954.

The Colts drafted him No. 1 (quarterback George Shaw was their bonus pick the same year), and there was never any question who their fullback would be. One pro scouting report on him at Wisconsin questioned his ability as a pass receiver because "his hands are too small." But The Horse caught 101 passes in his abbreviated career as a swing man out of the backfield. The Colts' own dossier on him said: "Great pro prospect. Has good speed and power. . . . Should be easily coached."

After his brilliant rookie season (with all-pro selection at the end), The Horse tailed off as a ground gainer because the Colts drafted Lenny Moore as an auxiliary threat. However, he gained esteem as one of the most forceful blockers in football. In 1958, he scored the winning touchdown in the famous sudden-death playoff for the NFL title at New York, called the greatest game ever played. He retired gracefully after his Achilles tendon injury with more than 4,000 yards gained. It was time to go on to capital gains.

ALAN D. "THE HORSE" AMECHE

BORN: June 1, 1933   Height: 6'1"   Weight: 217
University of Wisconsin

Baltimore, 1955–60

Year	G.	Att.	Yds.	Avg.	TD.	P.C.	Yds.	Avg.	TD.	TD.	Pts.
			RUSHING				PASS RECEIVING			SCORING	
1955	12	*213	*961	4.5	*9	27	141	5.2	0	*9	54
1956	12	178	858	4.8	8	26	189	7.3	0	8	48

1957	12	144	493	3.4	5	15	137	9.1	2	7	42
1958	12	171	791	4.6	8	13	81	6.2	1	9	54
1959	12	178	679	3.8	7	13	129	9.9	1	8	48
1960	10	80	263	3.3	3	7	56	8.0	0	3	18

PRO TOTALS
—6 YEARS 70 964 4045 4.2 40 101 733 7.3 4 44 264
* Led NFL.

When the definitive history of all pro football is written, the name of Richard Jose Casares, a ruggedly handsome man who lived in style, won't get much positive attention. Though Rick Casares lasted eleven hardy seasons in the NFL and rushed for 5,662 yards —which made him the sixth leading ground gainer in history when he left the league in 1966—athletic posterity will record him as the man who was incident-prone.

The exposure that football gave Rick turned him into a suave, urbane man of charm. But under the surface remained the scars of the tough life. At the age of fourteen, when he was still in the eighth grade, he fought on a phony birth certificate and won a New Jersey middleweight amateur championship. He was, self-admittedly, a roughneck: "I was chased out of Paterson. I'd already been put on probation as a truant. I wasn't going to school. I was more interested in fighting. They were going to send me to a disciplinary school. A policeman and a truant officer came to take me one day, and my mother pleaded with the policeman to let her send me to my father's people in Tampa." (His father had died when Rick was seven.)

The tough street kid discovered football in Tampa and progressed to the University of Florida. Rated a prospective All-American, he missed his senior year because he had a head-on auto collision. The woman in the car with him was killed. Rick suffered a broken nose, severed tendon in his right hand, and multiple lacerations. Then in a football scrimmage, he separated a shoulder.

In 1955, after Army service, he came into the NFL as the fullback of the Chicago Bears and led the league in rushing average, with a 5.4 mark. The next season, he became the running ace of pro football, gaining 1,126 yards to lead the league and pace the Bears to a Western division title. In seven years, he was the Bears' ground-gaining leader six times—a powerful 6'2", 225-pound line-crasher. "I wouldn't classify him as an elusive ball-carrier," said Charley Winner, then the defensive coach of the Colts. "He prefers stomping over a tackler to giving him the slip by hipper-dipper methods." He had a fast start and once into the secondry he ran with his shoulders, shoving people aside.

In the social life of Chicago, he also cut a wide figure. When rumors of gambling in pro football started passing around, investigators came to Rick. "I went in," he said later, "and told them everything I knew. I had nothing to hide." He also submitted to a lie detector test. And when the scandal finally broke, the one which eventually caused the indefinite suspension of Paul Hornung and Alex Karras, Casares' name was the first one mentioned publicly. Though he was never officially involved or reprimanded, he was branded through association with the scandal investigation. "I was a victim," he said, "of my willingness to cooperate."

Rick Casares fitted a tradition of powerful Chicago Bear fullbacks. He's the leading runner in that team's illustrious history.

On the field, injuries began to slow him up—among them a broken wrist and a broken ankle. After ten years, the Bears traded him to the Redskins, and in the first game of the 1965 season, trying to make a second block on the kickoff, he cracked two ribs. He carried the ball twice all year.

Casares made one final fling at playing the following fall, back in Florida with the Miami Dolphins. He was thirty-four years old, the zip gone out of his stride, and he soon faded from the scene. He took it, like most things in his life, stoically.

"I'm a football player first," he had said when the Bears got rid of him, "a sentimentalist second."

RICHARD JOSE "RICK" CASARES

BORN: July 4, 1931   Height: 6'2"   Weight: 225

University of Florida

Chicago Bears, 1955–64

Washington, 1965

Miami, 1966

Year	G.	RUSHING Att.	Yds.	Avg.	TD.	PASS RECEIVING P.C.	Yds.	Avg.	TD.	SCORING TD.	Pts.
1955	12	125	672	*5.4	4	16	136	8.5	1	5	30
1956	12	*234	*1126	4.8	*12	23	203	8.8	2	*14	84
1957	12	*204	700	3.4	6	25	225	9.0	0	6	36
1958	12	176	651	3.7	2	32	290	9.1	1	3	18
1959	12	177	699	3.9	10	27	273	10.1	2	12	72
1960	12	160	566	3.5	5	8	64	8.0	0	5	30
1961	13	135	588	4.4	8	8	69	8.6	0	8	48
1962	14	75	255	3.4	2	10	71	7.1	1	3	18
1963	10	65	277	4.3	0	19	94	4.9	1	1	6
1964	13	35	123	3.5	0	14	113	8.1	2	2	12
1965	3	2	5	2.5	0	1	5	5.0	0	0	0
1966	6	43	135	3.1	0	8	45	5.6	1	1	7

NFL TOTALS

—11 YEARS	125	1388	5662	4.1	49	183	1543	8.4	10	59	354

PRO TOTALS

—12 YEARS	131	1431	5797	4.1	49	192	1588	8.2	11	60	361

* Led NFL.

"You know when you give J. D. Smith the ball," said Coach Tom Landry of Dallas, "he's going to do something with it. He's a pro. He's durable. He's tough." Which explained why Landry had bothered to pick up a thirty-three-year-old battle-worn running back in 1965. And why Smith helped the Cowboys win a couple of big games in the first break-even season in their young history.

The initials, J. D., didn't stand for anything, so some of his old college teammates at North Carolina A&T started calling him John Duky and in pro ball he became Old Duke. He was the least recognized of that select number of men in pro ball who have gained 1,000 yards in a single season. And he did it in his first full year as a regular running back.

J. D. came into the NFL with the Chicago Bears in 1956, tabbed for the defensive secondary. The Bears released him after six games, and the San Francisco 49ers picked him up. They kept him in the secondary, too, as gross a job of miscasting as Shirley Temple playing Lady Godiva. This was the low part in the career of the phlegmatic old pro. When Lenny Moore of the Colts once got behind him to catch a 70-yard touchdown pass, the boos in Kezar Stadium shook the quiet Southerner, and he was booed steadily thereafter.

"He wasn't our worst defensive back," said Red Hickey, the 49ers' coach. "He could have been a good one if he had stayed with it. But those boos really shook him." So Red looked over Smith's assets reflectively—6'1", 210 pounds, good speed—and decided to shift him over to the offense. J. D. Smith sat around for one year waiting for a chance, though he reeled off an 80-yard run against Green Bay to support Hickey's hunch. Then in '59, Hugh McElhenny was shifted to flanker. Jim Pace, supposed to be the starting halfback, was hurt. Smith was moved in and gained 1,036 yards. He was no one-shot fluke. Over the next four years, he was consistently among the top five running backs in the league. In 1962, when he was thirty years old, Smith set a club record by carrying the ball 258 times.

"This is one hell of a football player," said Y. A. Tittle, the quarterback when Smith took over as a regular. "When I jam that ball in his belly, I've got confidence in him. He only knows one way to go—and that's toward the goal." There was nothing fancy about J. D. Smith as a runner.

He was tough, as Landry said. Big Daddy Lipscomb, the defensive tackle, was terrorizing the league in those days. Big Daddy had a habit of knocking the stuffing out of a runner, then magnanimously reaching down and helping him to his feet. When he reached down to help Smith, J. D. snarled, "Get your big fat hands off me. I can take care of myself." Not many people talked to Big Daddy that way.

And he was durable, as Landry said. The first injury of his career came in 1964, when he split a knee cartilage in the second game of the season. He was out for the year and never played a league game for the 49ers again. They traded him to Dallas, and Smith, at 33, came back to play. "He is," said Danny Villanueva, the placekicker on the club, "one of the few guys left who will come look you up to hit you."

The Cowboys, a young team on the rise, only needed Smith's services a couple of years. But at least he stayed around long enough to cash in on a division title in '66. And then he slipped away, inconspicuously, completely in character.

J. D. Smith was a bust as a defensive back but a surprisingly robust runner on offense when the 49ers gave him the chance.

J. D. SMITH, JR.

BORN: July 19, 1932   Height: 6'1"   Weight: 210

North Carolina A&T College

Chicago Bears, 1956
San Francisco, 1956–64
Dallas, 1965–66

Year	G.	Att.	RUSHING Yds.	Avg.	TD.	P.C.	PASS RECEIVING Yds.	Avg.	TD.	SCORING TD.	Pts.
1956	9		(None)				(None)			0	0
1957	12		(None)				(None)			0	0
1958	12	26	209	8.0	3	6	59	9.8	0	3	18
1959	12	207	1036	5.0	10	13	133	10.2	1	11	66
1960	12	174	780	4.5	5	36	181	5.0	1	6	36
1961	14	167	823	4.9	8	28	343	12.3	1	9	54
1962	14	258	907	3.5	6	21	197	9.4	1	7	42
1963	12	162	560	3.5	5	17	196	11.5	1	6	36
1964	2	13	55	4.2	0		(None)			0	0
1965	14	86	295	3.4	2	5	10	2.0	1	3	18
1966	14	7	7	1.0	1	1	3	3.0	0	1	6

PRO TOTALS
—11 YEARS | 127 | 1100 | 4672 | 4.2 | 40 | 127 | 1122 | 8.8 | 6 | 46 | 276

A sharp curve on a country road outside Rensselaer, Indiana, a skid, a car out of control—and the life of Willie Lee Galimore was tragically snuffed out. He was on his way to the training camp of the Chicago Bears with teammate Bo Farrington, also killed, that Sunday night in the summer of 1964. And to different people, the tragedy of Willie Galimore meant different things.

To Rick Casares, fullback, it meant the loss of a dear friend—"I loved to play alongside him because of his love for football."

To Audrey Galimore, who broke down at the funeral, it meant the greatest loss of all—he was the father of her three young children, a gentleman, a kind, thoughtful husband of good purpose.

To Bill Gleason, a sports writer in Chicago, it meant the loss "of a beautiful kid." He wrote, "Willie was one of those uncomplicated rarities. He loved everybody. Everybody loved him."

To the Chicago Bears, it meant the loss of speed in their offense. Willie was the only back who had it on a team that was coming back to defend its NFL title and desperately needed his threat in the lineup. "For the first time in years," he told everybody in camp, "I got two good legs under me."

And for the impersonal world of football, it meant the premature end of one of the most spectacular players in the game, a skinny-legged speedster who in action reminded everyone of another slender Bear great, George McAfee.

Until his tragic death in an auto accident, Willie Galimore was a sparkling breakaway threat for the Bears—and they missed him as a personality, too.

Willie Galimore was discovered at a race track, indirectly. Phil Handler, a Bear aide to Coach George Halas, was relaxing in Florida one winter and went out to Hialeah to do some research on the laws of probability. His research took him in the direction of a jockey named Willie Fronk. Willie couldn't define the probabilities of the third race that day, but he could tell Handler about a halfback up at Florida A&M who ran like Man o' War. The halfback was Willie Galimore. Handler checked him out, and the Bears drafted him.

Galimore, arriving in 1957, was an instant sensation. Today, they'd probably make him a flanker. Then he both ran and caught passes. Against the Los Angeles Rams, the 6'1", 190-pound wraith scored four touchdowns. "He was not hard to bring down," Lamar Lundy, a defensive end for the Rams, remembered, "once you got your hands on him. But getting your hands on Willie was unbelievably difficult."

What did stop Willie was a high incidence of injury. He played all or parts of seven seasons as a heavy-duty halfback. One year he carried the ball 153 times for 707 yards and caught thirty-three passes for 502 yards, ignoring pulled groined muscles and tender ankles. After the 1962 season he had both knees operated on and came back to help the Bears win a title. "Willie's greatest quality," said Paddy Driscoll of the Bears' staff, "is his courage. He'll always go for that extra half yard, and that's what puts him in a class above other scatbacks."

When Willie first joined the Bears and made them perk up to his abilities, he received a letter from his old college coach, A. S. "Jake" Gaither. It read, in part, ". . .You have so much to learn. You have a good start, but you haven't arrived. You won't arrive until about thirty."

Willie was twenty-nine years old the night his car didn't make that dangerous curve.

WILLIE LEE GALIMORE

BORN: March 30, 1935   Height: 6'1"   Weight: 190
DIED: July 26, 1964

Florida A&M University

Chicago Bears, 1957–63

Year	G.	RUSHING Att.	Yds.	Avg.	TD.	PASS RECEIVING P.C.	Yds.	Avg.	TD.	SCORING TD.	Pts.
1957	12	127	538	4.2	5	15	201	13.4	2	7	42
1958	12	130	619	4.8	8	8	151	18.9	3	12	72
1959	12	58	199	3.4	1	10	125	12.5	2	3	18
1960	12	74	368	5.0	1	3	35	11.7	0	1	6
1961	14	153	707	4.6	4	33	502	15.2	3	7	42
1962	7	43	233	5.4	2	5	56	11.2	0	2	12
1963	13	85	321	3.8	5	13	131	10.1	0	5	30
PRO TOTALS —7 YEARS	82	670	2985	4.5	26	87	1201	13.8	10	37	222

"Jaguar" Jon Arnett had the balance of a gymnast in his fancy stepping for the Los Angeles Rams.

When the Washington Redskins converted Bobby Mitchell to a wide receiver, they only gave him more running room. He once gained 232 yards rushing in one game for Cleveland.

The trouble with great talents like Jon Arnett and Bobby Mitchell was that none of the coaches who handled them through their long careers was quite sure how to use them, or that they were getting the maximum mileage out of them.

Jaguar Jon was a curly-haired blond from Southern California who had everything except a sense of career timing. He arrived on the USC campus touted as the greatest runner in thirty years and did nothing to dispel that notion. Red Sanders at crosstown UCLA said, "He's the greatest football animal I've ever seen." Arnett was an acrobatic tumbler with speed.

"You get out of the habit of moving in a straight line," he noted, "when you master such tumbling tricks as doubleback flips, back flips with a full twist, Arabian fronts and the like. They also give your legs additional spring."

So Jaguar Jon with catlike quickness sprang over and around tacklers but missed his chance at all-time college greatness because USC got hung up in a recruiting probation, and he was limited to five games his senior year.

He was drafted by the Rams, ahead of Jimmy Brown. He stayed with the Rams for seven seasons. The last five of these campaigns the Rams settled into a deep morass of losing. From one year to the other, Arnett wasn't quite sure whether he'd be a running back or a flanker. He shifted between the two jobs like a man on a see-saw. There were big days. For five straight years he was good enough to be chosen for the Pro Bowl. But there was a lot of frustration, too. And finally he was shipped to Chicago, the year *after* the Bears won a title. By this time, Arnett was twenty-nine, and a little of the bounce and the extra speed had gone out of his legs. He became a solid, workmanlike running back, sort of a semi-regular, and after he had rounded out a full decade of pro ball, Jaguar Jon retired. The Bears by then had a young gazelle named Gale Sayers, who had a lot of the moves of the young Jon Arnett, and a few extra.

Bobby Mitchell's time in pro football has also vacillated between running back and flanker. He came on the scene in 1958 as the running mate that Cleveland sought for Jimmy Brown, and he fulfilled that function for four seasons. As a member of the College All-Stars in 1958, he had virtually destroyed the champion Detroit Lions by streaking for two touchdowns, one on an 84-yard play, after catching short passes in a flanker role.

Playing the setback alongside Brown didn't seem to crimp Mitchell's style. In 1959, one November afternoon against the Washington Redskins, he carried the ball 232 yards on fourteen rushes, for an amazing 16.6 yards per carry. Coach Paul Brown, however, had the elusive sprinter from Illinois (where he had been a track star) tabbed as a fumbler and sometimes limited his usage in big games. In 1962, Bobby was traded to the Washington Redskins for the draft rights to the late Ernie Davis (who was stricken with leukemia and never played). Mitchell's acquisition broke the color line on the Redskins. Washington had never had a Negro player.

The Redskins immediately converted him into a fulltime receiver, and Bobby started out by leading the NFL with 72 catches. For five straight years he was among the premier pass receivers in football. But in 1967, Coach Otto Graham of Washington was running short of men who could carry a football from scrimmage and started working Bobby back into his old job. At thirty-two, he felt like a rookie again but didn't run like one. A year later he also lost his post as the starting flanker.

Despite the juggling of roles, Mitchell had passed such receiving greats as Don Hutson and Bill Howton and ranked second only to Raymond Berry of Baltimore in the number of passes he had caught during his career. Here was one case where perhaps a man did not have to run for his money.

JON DWANE "JAGUAR JON" ARNETT

BORN: April 20, 1935   Height: 5'11"   Weight: 200

University of Southern California

Los Angeles Rams, 1957–63
Chicago Bears, 1964–66

| Year | G. | RUSHING | | | | PASS RECEIVING | | | | SCORING | |
		Att.	Yds.	Avg.	TD.	P.C.	Yds.	Avg.	TD.	TD.	Pts.
1957	12	86	347	4.0	2	18	322	17.9	3	6	36
1958	12	133	683	5.1	6	35	494	14.1	1	7	42
1959	12	73	371	5.1	2	38	419	11.0	1	4	24
1960	12	104	436	4.2	2	29	226	7.8	2	4	24
1961	14	158	609	3.9	4	28	194	6.9	0	5	30
1962	10	76	238	3.1	2	12	137	11.4	0	2	12
1963	9	58	208	3.6	1	15	119	7.9	1	2	12
1964	14	119	400	3.4	1	25	223	8.9	2	3	18
1965	14	102	363	3.6	5	12	114	9.5	0	5	30
1966	14	55	178	3.2	1	10	42	4.2	0	1	6
PRO TOTALS —10 YEARS	123	964	3833	4.0	26	222	2290	10.3	10	39	234

ROBERT CORNELIUS "BOBBY" MITCHELL

BORN: June 6, 1935   Height: 6'0"   Weight: 195

University of Illinois

Cleveland Browns, 1958–61
Washington, 1962–68

| Year | G. | RUSHING | | | | PASS RECEIVING | | | | SCORING | |
		Att.	Yds.	Avg.	TD.	P.C.	Yds.	Avg.	TD.	TD.	Pts.
1958	12	80	500	6.3	1	16	131	8.2	3	6	36
1959	12	131	743	5.7	5	35	351	10.0	4	10	60
1960	12	111	506	4.6	5	45	612	13.6	6	12	72
1961	14	101	548	5.4	5	32	368	11.5	3	10	60
1962	14	1	5	5.0	0	*72	*1384	19.2	11	12	72
1963	14	3	24	8.0	0	69	*1436	20.8	7	8	48
1964	14	2	33	16.5	0	60	904	15.1	*10	10	60
1965	14		(None)			60	867	14.5	6	6	36
1966	14	13	141	10.8	1	58	905	15.6	9	10	60
1967	14	61	189	3.1	1	60	866	14.4	6	7	42
1968	14	10	46	4.6	0	14	130	9.3	0	0	0
PRO TOTALS —11 YEARS	148	513	2735	5.3	18	521	7954	15.3	65	91	546

* Led NFL.

14. The Swift Sixties

Don Perkins

IT'S FANTASTIC THE WAY HE BLOCKS A
240-POUND LINEBACKER WHO HAS A
SEVEN-YARD RUN AT HIM. HE UNCOILS
AND POW! THAT'S EXLOSION AND GUTS.
—*Ermal Allen, backfield coach,*
Dallas Cowboys.

The quiet dignity of Don Perkins was always hidden under the silver helmet with the dark blue lone star, the double bar faceguard shielding any emotion he might have, the bulky shoulder pads covered with the white jersey a barrier to the inner man. These physical trappings suited the nature of his job. He was a human battering ram, indistinguishable as a personality, a squat lump of motion fulfilling the duties of a fullback for the Dallas Cowboys.

And then, through the pervasive medium of television, came the exposure of Donald Anthony Perkins as a very special person. It was on Thanskgiving Day, 1966, the evening of a nationally televised game, after the turkey and cranberries were well digested, and a living room audience glutted with six hours of professional football (two games) looked for something besides square-outs and draws and audibles.

In his faceless role, Don Perkins had just rushed for 111 yards against the Cleveland Browns and scored the final touchdown to secure a 26–14 victory, the crucial milestone en route to the Cowboys' first Eastern division title ever. Jack Buck had the microphone on the field for the postgame interview, and Perkins came on camera. He was without his helmet. Grass stains smudged his jersey. The sweat of the game glistened on his dark face. His eyes gleamed softly in a pool of white, framed by the high cheekbones, the strong jaw. And Don Perkins spoke.

What he said wasn't important and is scarcely remembered. But the way he said it, in a deep, mellifluous voice (they once claimed he listened to Ronald Colman records) made a fantastic impression on the football-satiated television listeners. He was no longer that low slung number 43 who carried the ball and threw himself into blocks. He was an impressive, articulate spokesman for the sport of football—humble and appreciative but also full of the pride of accomplishment. Don Perkins had come a long way from Waterloo, Iowa, from the poor part of town—"sort of out in the country but not really on a farm"—where the social life was nonexistent, since his brothers and sisters were the only other Negroes around.

("He did a brave thing going to college," his wife, Virginia, once said. "All of his relatives—everyone—were against it. . . . They thought football and college were big wastes of time.")

Perk, as the Cowboys call him, has a fantastic quality of making people listen when he talks. He doesn't talk much. He's essentially a stoic. But he measures his words carefully and delivers them with such conviction that people react. Perk is not a militant. He played seven years in Dallas without speaking up about what it was like for him as a human being, specifically as a Negro, off the field. And then when he was getting ready to play his eighth and thinking of transplanting his family from their regular home in Albuquerque, New Mexico, to Dallas, a discouraging process which once led him to announce his retirement, he told an interviewer simply:

"Do you know my wife Virginia and I would be embarrassed to have you visit our home in Dallas? We'd have to take you to a nice restaurant. The Negroes on the Cowboys can only find roach-infested houses. The problem has improved very little in my seven years with the Cowboys. All I want is a place where my family can live happily and, I would say, comfortably for four months."

Tex Schramm, the Cowboys' president and general manager, acknowledged the validity of Perkins' complaint and added, "He is such an honest and forthright person that it would be difficult for him to look anybody in the eye and say something he did not really believe."

Perkins' statement came when there was much national publicity in the summer of 1968 about a series of articles in *Sports Illustrated* dealing with injustices to and exploitation of Negro athletes. Perkins said, "I honestly don't feel I've been exploited any more by the Cowboys than I've used them. I've been hired to play fullback, and I receive a good salary to do the job."

Then he went out and gained 836 yards in the 1968 season to brush past the great Steve Van Buren and become the fifth leading ground gainer in the history of football. It's startling to see Perkins' name up there. Even the men in the press box weren't aware, until it was brought to their attention, that Perkins, by 1968, had rushed for more yards than any active player in pro ball.

In style and in physical makeup, he doesn't look the part. He's an anachronism— a fullback who stands 5'10" and weighs, at his best, 197 pounds. He doesn't have the compensatory speed you'd expect—he never breaks loose for spectacular long gainers. He's just an average pass receiver coming out of the backfield. He's not even nifty, despite his lack of size, in his running style. He's the nitroglycerin kid, a back who has blasted his way to football prominence on sheer explosive force, with a mindless disregard for the physical consequences.

Perkins has been hurt. Injury was his constant running mate for the first five years he played pro ball, and Landry used to despair that he'd ever get a full season out of his mini-fullback. "He'll never play an entire 14-game NFL schedule," said Tom once. "He just can't bang around with those 260-pound linemen down after down and get by, but he goes as far with what he has as any man who ever played in this league."

In the normal sequence of events, Perkins would have started slowing up as he got older, the injuries would become more frequent and tougher to shake off. But he reversed the routine. In 1968, he passed his thirtieth birthday and celebrated his third straight season with virtually no mishap. And Landry reversed his field, too. "Don knows his job so well," he explained, "he seldom gets hurt."

Two Dons, Perkins and Meredith, were with the original Dallas Cowboys and have been linked in the team's rise to competitive respectability. They were drafted by other NFL teams and earmarked for Dallas before the expansion franchise went into operation in the summer of 1960. Perkins had been an excellent running back at the University of New Mexico, setting a conference rushing record, leading the nation in kickoff returns. But he weighed only 180 pounds. Reading about the bruising demands of pro ball, he spent the spring stoking up on biscuits and gravy and came into the early camp, at Pacific University in Oregon, weighing 215 pounds. A human butterball. Landry, in

The indomitability of Don Perkins is evident as he strains to break loose against the Cleveland Browns.

his first year as a head coach, wanted his guys in shape. He instituted what became known as the Landry mile.

"The first day we ran the mile," recalled general manager Schramm, "Perkins couldn't finish it. He would run a few steps, fall down, get up and run some more, and fall again. We didn't know what to think. Normally, when a guy does this, it's an indication he doesn't have a great deal of pride or courage and is taking the easy way out. We didn't realize it until later, but what we thought was lack of courage was in fact one of the greatest displays of courage any of us had ever witnessed. It's really ironic—the one thing we thought he lacked turned out to be his forte."

Perkins went from the Cowboys' camp to the College All-Stars, and in a scrimmage against the Chicago Bears broke the fifth metatarsal in his foot. He had first broken it in junior high and then in high school. The injury did not respond to treatment—the bone didn't reset properly. A piece of his hipbone was grafted to bridge the metatarsal break, and he missed the entire 1960 campaign.

He reported as a rookie again in '61, this time his weight down to 195, and beat out the veteran L. G. Dupre, an erstwhile regular on Baltimore championship teams, for a starting job. Despite a knee injury in mid-season, he gained 815 yards, and the Cowboys had the nucleus of a running game which would sustain them for years. They weren't much of a team in those early days, which didn't help Perkins, as Landry shuffled the deck to find adequate blocking on his offensive line. But Perk kept piling up the yardage. In 1962, he had a shoulder separation, a leg injury, and some more trouble with his broken foot. It caused him such pain that he told the Cowboys he was going to quit in training camp, but they convinced him it was just scar tissue pulling loose. He went on to gain 945 yards and achieve an historical first for the Cowboys, selection to the NEA All-Pro team chosen by the players.

Each year there was another injury. In '63, the bone graft had dissolved, and the doctors had to take another piece from his hip to put his foot in shape. He missed the first two games with a shoulder separation, hurt his knee and finished the season by separating his other shoulder. In 1964, he sustained badly bruised ribs and a sprained ankle.

Sandwiched by a couple of Cleveland tacklers in an October game, he ripped most of the ligaments from the back of his rib cage. "It only hurts when I breathe," he told the trainer, and then apologized that night for being injured. Out of the hospital on Tuesday, he managed a few steps walking on Thursday. With help, he laced on shoulder pads a couple of days later. And on Sunday, against the New York Giants, he gained 96 yards.

"He's awful long on guts," said Tommy McDonald, a veteran receiver who had joined the team. "He picks everyone up by just doing his job."

By this time, naturally shy Don was also showing a droll sense of humor. His short stature among the tall Cowboys was a speculative item for people who attended their workouts. On a typically hot Dallas day, in 90-degree heat and high humidity, with jerseys drenched, Perkins trotted past a knot of fans. "Do you think that kid'll make it?" one of the spectators asked his buddy in a loud whisper. Perkins did a stutter step, turned and smiled, "If you mean will I make it through the afternoon, the answer is no."

In his first two seasons as a pro, Don gained a total of 1,760 yards on the ground—exactly one mile. So he was asked facetiously if he thought he could cover the distance in four minutes instead of two years, *à la* Jim Ryun. "It all depends who's chasing you," he winked. "If those track stars had Roger Brown or Big Daddy Lipscomb chopping at their heels, they just might make it in three minutes."

Frank Clarke, a veteran receiver on the Cowboys, wasn't noted as a zealous blocker. But one day, he produced an action shot which showed him in the act of throwing his body at a tackler to clear a path for Perkins. He proudly taped it to Don's locker. Perkins studied the photograph a moment, then said softly, "Yes, Frank, you're really going after him . . . and it looks like you're not going to have time to change your mind."

In his own quiet way, he was becoming a leader of the team.

"He leads with his determination," said Landry. "Everyone on the club has this feeling about Perkins. He doesn't talk much and for that reason I guess nobody really knows him. You can't tell by his mood what he is feeling inside because his mood is always good. When he is depressed, he hides it."

Between seasons, he went back to New Mexico, grew a beard and blew off steam, and each summer he was back, ready for action, to make a living for Virginia and the three kids. There were moments of depression. He threatened to quit several times as his older boy, Tony (Don Anthony Perkins, Jr.), reached school age. He didn't like the idea of sending him to a segregated school, de facto, in Dallas, and finally decided to keep him at home in New Mexico. In Albuquerque, he was a folk hero, a supporter of Republican Governor David Cargo, who appointed him the State Director of Courtesy and Information for New Mexico. He even contemplated an active political career at one time. He loved Albuquerque, from the moment he came down out of Iowa to play football. He had never seen a mountain before, but his first day in New Mexico he climbed one in a snowstorm, wearing a T-shirt.

However, reality is a part of the Perkins psyche, too. Carrying a football for the Dallas Cowboys paid better than anything he knew, especially after they reached championship class in 1966. Although the Cowboys were nosed out for the NFL title by the Packers, 34–27, when a final drive petered out on the two-yard line, Perkins had a great game—"probably the best of his career," said Landry. Don gained 108 yards against the best defense in football.

That winter he announced his retirement, to concentrate on his state job at $11,400 a year. But the Cowboys came up with a two-year contract, close to the $100,000 range, and Perkins came back to carry the ball.

"Perkins is the real article," said quarterback Meredith. "He doesn't open his mouth in the huddle except sometimes when he has really been laid out on a play and I'm wondering if he can still go. He'll look up and say, 'Yeah, I can run.' That's all. He'll always run for you, no matter how he's hurting."

The Cowboys always know that when Perkins takes himself out of a game, he's really hurting. He's not an alibi man. Early in his career, when Eddie LeBaron was the quarterback of the Cowboys, an assistant coach jumped Perk for missing an assignment that cost them a chance to beat the St. Louis Cardinals. Trailing by four points, Dallas

He's not big, as fullbacks go, but what there is of Don Perkins is solidly put together.

had driven inside the Cardinal 10. LeBaron called a pass pattern on which Perkins' primary job was to pick up a blitzing linebacker. If there was no blitz, he would roll out of the backfield as a potential receiver.

With the snap of the ball, Perkins swung wide as a receiver. The linebacker came in unchallenged and creamed LeBaron from the blind side, killing the rally. In the dressing room, the coach berated Perkins, "I never saw you foul up like that before." Perkins shrugged, "Yeah, wasn't that something." And he went on to his shower. The coach consoled LeBaron, "Too bad, Eddie. That's the first time I've ever seen Perkins miss an assignment."

"What do you mean?" said Eddie. "I told Perk in the huddle to run the route no matter what the linebacker did." Perkins wasn't going to offer that as an excuse.

The Cowboys, like many other teams, have a locker room prayer session, led by Landry, a devoutly religious man. It isn't mandatory. "Some fellows who apparently do not believe just sit on their chairs instead of kneeling," said Perkins. "I don't know how many because I am busy kneeling.

"We just give thanks for where we are and who we are. Then we have to forget all about meekness and humility and love thy neighbor, and be prepared to hit as hard as possible."

Don's conviction carries over into his job, though.

"When it's third and one," he mused, "you've got to have faith. You've got to believe the play will be run just the way it was drawn up, and you give it everything."

With experience, Perkins has approached the flawless player. The Cowboys in 1965 started to put in their multiple offense, with its many formations. A simple foulup, like a back lined up wrong, could ruin the play before it got under way. Ermal Allen, the backfield coach, reviewed Perkins' performance after the season and noted that he had missed only three assignments in 649 plays, and that included the execution of the plays. "In the years I've coached him," said Allen, "I've never raised my voice because I know that on every play he will do the very best he can. He's the greatest pass blocker in the NFL by far. As a person, any superlative you want to use about him is deserved."

The blocking is a facet that doesn't show up in statistics and has been a distinguishing characteristic of Perkins' play from the time he came into the NFL. It typifies his courage and selflessness. It's not an easy thing to brace yourself against a man in full flight who outweighs you anywhere from 50 to 80 pounds. Perkins dismisses the problem typically: "Look at it this way. When I'm blocking, it's strictly one man against one man. When I'm carrying the ball, there are eleven guys after me."

Compared with the spectacular runners of his age, Perkins doesn't come through as a memorable performer. Limited as an open field runner, depending primarily on explosion to pick up yards, he put himself in the record book by force of will. But those who've seen him as a man as well as a football player have something to remember. Perkins finally decided to make his retirement stick on the eve of the 1969 season.

DON PERKINS' FAVORITE PLAY:

"It's run from the I-formation in which I'm the lead back. The play is 'Dive 37 Switch.' The tight end has the key block at the point of attack. There is no predetermined hole in the line which I must hit. The play anticipates the defensive reaction, and we hit any place on the line that opens up.

"The best shots I can recall from the '68 campaign came in our game with the Vikings, though it was one of our basic plays all year."

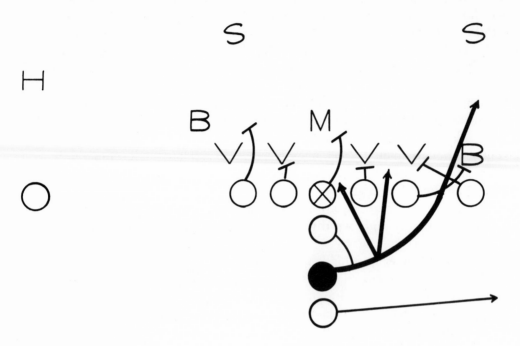

DONALD ANTHONY "DON" PERKINS

BORN: March 4, 1938   Height: 5'10"   Weight: 205

University of New Mexico

Dallas, 1961–68

Year	G.	Att.	RUSHING Yds.	Avg.	TD.	P.C.	PASS RECEIVING Yds.	Avg.	TD.	SCORING TD.	Pts.
1961	14	200	815	4.1	4	32	298	9.3	1	5	30
1962	14	222	945	4.3	7	13	104	8.0	0	7	42
1963	11	149	614	4.1	7	14	84	6.0	0	7	42
1964	13	174	768	4.4	6	15	155	10.3	0	6	36
1965	13	177	690	3.9	0	14	142	10.1	0	0	0
1966	14	186	726	3.9	8	23	231	10.0	0	8	48
1967	14	201	823	4.1	6	18	116	6.4	0	6	36
1968	14	191	836	4.4	4	17	180	10.6	2	6	36
PRO TOTALS —8 YEARS	107	1500	6217	4.1	42	146	1310	9.0	3	45	270

Dick Bass

THE BASS SECRET IS HIS LOW CENTER
OF GRAVITY. WHEN HE RUNS INTO BIG
MEN, IT IS ACTUALLY AN UNEVEN CON-
TEST IN WHICH THE ADVANTAGE IS WITH
BASS.

—Harland Svare, coach,
Los Angeles Rams.

Behind the charades of Dick Bass' off-field capers lurks the serious soul of a football artist—the little man of the Rams is all business at play.

Richard Lee Bass—fullback by vocation, dilettante by avocation—is some kind of character. One day he might stroll out of the dressing room of the Los Angeles Rams looking like a yeh-yeh boy heading for London's Kings Road on a Saturday afternoon to eye the "birds." The next day, spiffied up in bowler and walking cane, he'd be suitably dressed for an appointment at No. 10 Downing. He bridges the void between the Strip and Carnaby Street as easily as he went from the back streets of Vallejo, California, to the salons of Hollywood. Wherever Richard goes, it's with aplomb.

He lived in a Los Angeles apartment owned by Wilt Chamberlain. Wilt's mother and father managed it. Bass came home from a practice session with the Rams, marched through the foyer and out to the pool, jumped in with all his clothes on, swam the length of the pool, and then marched to his apartment, dripping wet. He came home the next day, said hello to Mom Chamberlain and ceremoniously dunked himself full dress again. He repeated this a couple more days, until Mrs. Chamberlain followed him to the apartment, unable to contain her curiousity. "Richard," she asked the bubbly football player, "haven't you got a bathing suit?"

Dick Bass looked at her seriously and said, "I thought you'd never ask." And started laughing.

His actions as a runner have been almost as unorthodox as his behavior off the field, and that partially explains how a sawed-off 5′9″ fullback has managed to have nine productive seasons in the NFL and become the biggest ground gainer in the history of the Rams (who have had plenty of literally big fullbacks like Tank Younger and Deacon Dan Towler).

In all the 45-year history of the NFL, only thirteen men have gained more than 1,000 yards rushing in a single season, and one of them is the sprite known as Scooter or Bull Mouse. He has done it twice—1,033 yards in 1962 with a team that won only one out of fourteen games, 1,090 yards in 1966, when he was approaching the ripe old age of thirty. "If you know how to follow blocks, size is immaterial," said Bass, a low-slung 200-pounder. "A runner is a runner. I know which side to run on in the event I get a good block.

"Now where the size comes in, I think, is in the image of the big man in the backfield and the little man. Since I'm labeled as a fullback, this doesn't look right because he's the one who's supposed to be big.

"This has caused a lot of discussion and problems. The only time I have a problem is in a third down situation because, being 5′10″ [note: he likes to fudge a little on his height], I can't lunge for the extra yard like a bigger man could."

This business of being a fullback or a halfback is slightly academic in the current alignments where both setbacks line up side by side and both run either through the line or around it. For a little man, however, Bass has had an amazing antipathy to the circle route around the enemy lines, and so he has been nominally the fullback for the Rams. He runs through the crush of 275-pound linemen by choice.

"Running inside," he said, "is like a cushion. I bounce around in there like a rubber ball. The only problem is that I'm short, and the linebackers hit the top of my helmet."

What effect does this have?

"I have a lot of headaches."

He has survived that minor inconvenience to take his rank as No. 8 among the Top Ten rushers of history, and second only to Don Perkins among the active players. When Dick plunged four yards through the Pittsburgh Steelers on a routine third-quarter play early in the 1968 season, the game officials stopped the clock and presented the ball to Bass as a memento. He had cracked the 5,000-yard barrier, and it would go on the big mantelpiece up in Vallejo, California, where his mother and father are keepers of the trophies, plaques, and other honors which Dick has accumulated in 15 years of organized football.

He was the most fabled high school football player ever to come out of northern California when he played for Vallejo High near the navy yards of Mare Island in San Pablo Bay, within sight of San Francisco on a clear day. Every college in the country was aware of him, since he scored 68 touchdowns in three years and had an average gain of 13.2 yards every time he carried the ball. Dick chose little College of the Pacific, virtually in his backyard, and in 1958 he became the NCAA's first triple crown winner since Byron "Whizzer" White by leading the country's colleges in rushing, scoring, and total offense. Six major league baseball teams were also after him (his younger brother, Norman, pitched briefly in the American League), but football was obviously his bag. He was a first round draft choice of the LA Rams as a "future" when he still had a year of varsity eligibility remaining.

Bass reported to the Rams in 1960 with Jon Arnett in full flower as a runner, Ollie Matson still considered a fullback, and such other assorted talents as Tom Wilson and Joe Marconi on hand. Dick was used sparingly. "I was too conservative," he said. "I ran by the book. If I was supposed to hit the four-hole, I did. If a 300-pound tackle was standing in the four-hole, I hit him."

But a year later he had perfected his pro style—"I veer"—and he had settled down as a fullback.

"Running from fullback," he said, "I've got a choice. There are more options to pick from. If I run inside, off tackle, and it's shut off, I can bounce to the outside. It's that way all along the line. Halfbacks running a sweep can't reverse their field any more because the defense protects the pursuit angle. They all take a lane, and you're dead if you cut back."

He had also developed a simple philosophy of forward progress which translated into yards gained:

"The first thing that comes to my mind is never to be tackled. The only way you can gain yards, even if you're tackled, is across the stripes. That means not to run laterally, but up the field. I use all means and methods to do this."

It was squirt and squirm, bounce and bound—a rabbity bundle of energy. In 1962, he broke away for gains of at least 20 yards or more in seven of the Rams' fourteen games, though they were a miserably inefficient team without another healthy threat

416

It looks as though Don Shinnick of the Colts has Dick Bass of the Rams nailed behind the line, with other Colts closing in . . . But wait, there's Shinnick (66) bouncing off and hitting the dust—the Colts still have Bass hemmed in, they think . . . Not quite, for here's Rapid Richard scooting free and on his way to a big gainer.

in the lineup. Against the Chicago Bears, he burrowed into the line on a play which started at the Bear 45. "There he is!" yelled Bill George, the rugged middle linebacker, as all hands reached out. A quick burst, and five seconds later Bass called out from the end zone, "Here I am!"

His entry into the 1,000 yard club was typical. He popped through left tackle against the Green Bay Packers, in a crouch, and slammed into the thighs of Ray Nitschke, a tough customer backing up the line. With no leverage, Nitschke hung on as the little fullback, 30 pounds lighter, dragged him along for eight yards.

"He carries his weight low," explained Swede Svare when he took over as coach of the Rams a year later. "They carry theirs high. They just can't get at him with power."

Blocking big men, an essential duty for a fullback, didn't bother him either. "You have to go back to the story about the little ball and the big ball," said Bass. "If the little ball gets there first, he can defeat the big ball. Now I'm involved in pass protection with linebackers. If I can get there first and cut him at the weakest part of his body, which is the knees or below the knees, it's to my advantage. When I get hurt, it's when I try to hit him in his strength, which is in his chest. Knowing my size, I try to hit a man low."

His size was a definite asset when the Rams practiced at an old ball park in downtown Burbank. A sign over the dugout door read, "Low Bridge." The doorway measured a scant six feet high and was often littered with the stunned bodies of Ram giants who forgot to duck going through. So they all learned to run like fullbacks, hunching forward —all except Dick Bass. He trotted erect and proud, all 5'9" of him.

Beautifully able to rationalize his job in the violent world, Dick blithely changed pace as an extroverted funny man when football didn't absorb him. Svare came in as coach full of stern intention. Practices were lengthened. Meetings were added. The film projector whirred incessantly. During a long film session, Swede suddenly became aware of someone moving around from player to player in the darkened room. He switched on the lights and barked, "Bass, what're you doing?"

Dick held up a bottle in his hand. It was half filled, labeled: "No-Doze Pills."

Even injuries didn't get him down. The Bears damaged his ribs once. Five days later, he was still sore and unable to work out. While the Rams were on the field, he sat in the dugout, writing on a long sheet of lined paper. Svare asked him what he was up to.

"Making out my last will and testament."

"Who're you leaving the body to?" asked Swede.

Dick's pencil-thin mustache curled in a grin on his coffee-colored face. "The Ku Klux Klan," he said. "Who else?"

His dress also broke the everyday tedium of playing football. "I never know how I'll cut on a football field," he said, "or how I'll dress off it. I wear what I think will make me the most comfortable each day. I'm always uncomfortable in a football suit."

He checked into a hotel with the club on a road trip, outfitted in a homburg, English cut suit, splendid vest, umbrella cane and attache case. "Name, please?" asked the clerk.

"Hobbes," said Dick, in clipped accent, "of British Intelligence."

418

Another day might find him in black boots, orange, ruffled shirt, and double-breasted, charcoal-gray, pin-striped coat. "My Al Capone threads," he winked.

After the duds were off, however, and the pads securely locked on his shoulders, he came to play. "I like to have a lot of people around me," he said, "especially when I'm carrying the ball. When one tackler hits me and I start to fall, I want another one there to fall on. That straightens me up. I can often keep going because I never stop running as long as my feet are under me."

And running into his tenth pro season in 1969, Dick was still a potent factor in the Rams' offense. The only concession to his age (thirty-two) was a rest through most of the exhibition campaign so that they'd have the full benefit of his services during the regular season. The Rams as a team offered him a lot more help than in the early days, so the job wasn't as demanding. And the records kept piling up for the little man who looked more like a bop musician than a rugged fullback, in his super-sharp pastel outfits.

"You only talk about records and stats," he shrugged, "after the game is over. The game is not over by any means."

He meant his career.

DICK BASS' FAVORITE RUNNING PLAY:

"In the playbook of the Los Angeles Rams, it's called '36 M Bob.' I'm '3,' and '6' is the hole I'm supposed to hit, although actually I have a lot of options. It's a weakside running play in which the ball can go inside or outside or straight ahead.

"It's designed to run at the defense's weak side or on an odd defense, away from their strength. Overall, it has been our biggest yardage producer in my years with the Rams, particularly during the 1966 season when I went over 1,000 yards for the second time in my career."

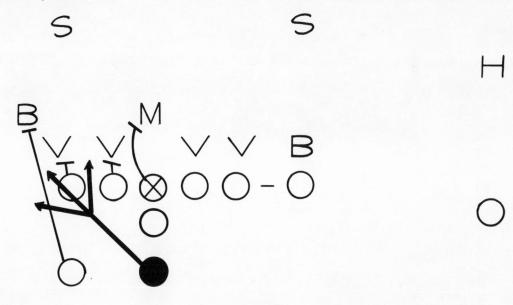

RICHARD LEE "DICK" BASS

BORN: March 15, 1937   Height: 5'10''   Weight: 200

University of the Pacific

Los Angeles Rams, 1960–68

Year	G.	Att.	Yds.	Avg.	TD.	P.C.	Yds.	Avg.	TD.	TD.	Pts.
			RUSHING				PASS RECEIVING			SCORING	
1960	12	31	153	4.9	0	13	92	7.1	0	0	0
1961	14	98	608	6.2	4	16	145	9.1	0	5	30
1962	14	196	1033	5.3	6	30	262	8.7	2	8	48
1963	12	143	520	3.6	5	30	348	11.6	0	5	30
1964	9	72	342	4.8	2	9	83	9.2	0	2	12
1965	12	121	549	4.5	2	21	230	11.0	2	4	24
1966	14	248	1090	4.4	8	31	274	8.8	0	8	48
1967	14	187	627	3.4	6	27	212	7.9	1	7	42
1968	14	121	494	4.1	1	27	195	7.2	2	3	18

PRO TOTALS

—9 YEARS 115 1217 5416   4.5   34   204 1841   9.0   7   42 252

Timmy Brown

THE GREATEST THING ABOUT TIMMY IS
THAT YOU HIT HIM WITH A SHORT ONE,
AND HE MAKES IT A LONG ONE.
—Norm Snead, quarterback,
Philadelphia Eagles.

Timmy Brown's forte was blazing speed around the flanks. The Philadelphia Eagle flyer had an instinct for the open field.

Timmy Brown had this kind of ability: he returned a kickoff against the St. Louis Cardinals 99 yards for a touchdown; he returned a kickoff against the Washington Redskins 99 yards for a touchdown; he returned a blocked field goal against the Cardinals 100 yards for a touchdown; and he returned a kickoff against the Cleveland Browns 105 yards for a touchdown.

In between these runs, spread over a three-year period from 1961–63, he also had such assorted items as a 61-yard touchdown run from scrimmage, an 82-yard touchdown run with a pass, an 80-yard touchdown pass reception, and a 66-yard punt return for a touchdown.

Thomas Allen "Tim" Brown was one helluva runner when there was an open field strewn with would-be tacklers whom he could dodge, feint and simply outsprint.

In 1966, he was already considered a battle-worn veteran of the football wars and prefaced his conversations with, "When I was a youngster—." He was twenty-nine, and the first weekend in November he took his place with the kickoff return unit of the Philadelphia Eagles after the Dallas Cowboys had opened the game with a touchdown. He trotted forward to meet the ball at the 7-yard line and ran. "It's been so long I wasn't sure I could make it all the way." Soon he was at midfield. "I wasn't warmed up and my thighs tightened up on me." And then he was past all the Cowboys with the goal line in sight. "I kept widening my legs, wider and wider, to keep my equilibrium." He staggered in with a 93-yard run. "I thought they had me."

In the second quarter, the Cowboys went ahead again and kicked off to the Eagles. Brown caught the ball at the 10, danced quickly through a covey of Cowboys and raced 90 yards for a touchdown. "They had the oxygen ready the second time," he smiled, "but I didn't need it. I wasn't even breathing." He was the first man in NFL history to return two kickoffs for touchdowns in the same game.

That was Timmy Brown's bit, eleven of the enemy spread out in front of him, converging on him, but with pockets of daylight so he could thread his way through them nimbly, looking for the final burst of freedom. It was dangerous duty, the kind that coaches are loathe to expose their top talent to. Tom Landry of Dallas let Bob Hayes return punts—if it got sticky, Bob raised his hands for a fair catch. But Landry withdrew him from the kickoff return unit. The danger of being "clotheslined" (running full tilt into an outstretched arm) wasn't worth the extra yards he might pick up. But Timmy accepted kickoffs stolidly as just another of his chores.

When he was going good in the big years with the Philadelphia Eagles, from 1961 through 1966, Timmy did it all. He carried the ball more than any man in the backfield. In a good year like '65 he picked up 861 yards from scrimmage. He caught as many as 52 passes a year (in '62), gaining 849 yards. He blocked for the passer, too. He returned punts and, of course, kickoffs. "Tim has been the most underrated back in the league," said Jim Brown of Cleveland. "He's the finest halfback around." This was just after Timmy had spent an afternoon rushing through the Browns for 186 yards.

The men who get their kicks from adding machines totalled up his production and figured that Timmy accounted for 2,428 yards from all sources in 1963, an all-time record.

However, the Timmy Brown who counts isn't a feeder for computers. He is a vibrant, hip guy to whom football has always been an accessory to the real life he wants to lead—that of an entertainer. He digs James Brown, the soul singer, as "the greatest." And he digs Jim Brown more for his success as a movie actor than for his fabulous running. He dated Diana Ross of the Supremes and he cut his own pop records. When he was with the Eagles, his alarm went off promptly at 8:30 on a Monday morning, his day off from football exercises, and he commuted by train to New York for a full program of singing and voice lessons, drama lessons, and acting bits until 11:30 at night.

"I've always wanted to be an entertainer," he said, "never a football player. I don't want to be known as the singing halfback. It chokes me up. I don't want the easy buck. I want to act because I can act."

He considered it tougher than lugging a football for a living.

"On the football field," he explained, "I have no control over most situations. If I'm hit right, I may fumble. Or if any of the other ten players fails to coordinate on a given play, I may be tossed for a loss. I can't always control things on my own. In acting it's different. I have control. If it doesn't come out the way I planned, I'm disappointed in myself. The criticism comes from within. There is more pressure in acting."

But there was more work to be had in football, and it gave him identification. Identification is something that Timmy Brown has sought desperately all his life. His parents separated when he was seven, and he found himself in a place called the Soldiers and Sailors Children's Home in Knightstown, Indiana. "I was always so lonely as a kid," he remembered. "Even now I'm lonely sometimes and I want to find someone I like to spend time with, someone special, but I usually can't find someone and so I spend a lot of time alone."

He went through high school at the orphanage and hadn't built up the confidence yet to try big time college athletics. In Indiana, every kid concentrates first on basketball, and Timmy was a good one, with seventeen scholarship offers. He could have gone to Michigan State. He chose little Ball State. "The idea of a big school scared me," he said. At Ball State, he doubled in football, which became his major sport. The Green Bay Packers drafted him in 1959, on the twenty-seventh round.

He survived the final cut in training camp, at the start of the Vince Lombardi era, but in the opening game of the season, he made a fatal error. He fumbled a punt. Lombardi released him. "I think you could play in the NFL," he told Timmy, "but you're too small to fit into our system." The young halfback caught on as a member of the Philadelphia Eagles' taxi squad, learning but not playing, building up his weight to a snug 198 pounds (he's 5'11"). In 1960, he made his debut in the NFL as a kick return specialist, and in 1961 they began to break him into the regular backfield. A year later he was a full-fledged starring halfback, and from time to time he would see Lombardi. "We talked about 1959," said Timmy, "and he said he was proud of what I'd done since. Coming from him, I considered it a real compliment."

In 1964, the New York Giants reportedly offered nine players to the Eagles for Timmy and were refused. The good years piled one on top of each other, and Timmy's elegant wardrobe expanded. In his pad at 62nd and Vine Streets, there were 25 suits and 25 sports coats, 75 dress shirts, 115 slacks, and 56 pairs of shoes, including 20 of the finest alligator. The boy from the orphanage was surrounded by 1,000 LP's and drove a gleaming white sports car.

With heavy duty performance on the field came some physical distress. A thigh injury knocked him out of four games in 1964 and recurred chronically. They'd drain a pint of blood off after a game and fitted him with special pads to keep Timmy running. He ran an inside trap through the champion Cleveland Browns for a 54-yard TD scamper in '65, and against the strong St. Louis Cardinal defense he gained 169 yards on the ground in the first two quarters before a helmet plunked him in the ribs and caused a hairline fracture.

Timmy's life with the Eagles was further complicated by a personality clash with his new coach, Joe Kuharich. The Eagles ordered new green blazers for all the players to wear around town and on trips. "This unit stuff is okay to a degree," said Timmy, "but I'm an individual guy. Besides, it was a lousy color. I couldn't match it up with anything."

There were other spats. The Eagles didn't like his side concentration on acting, the trips to New York, and needled him about it. They said he wasn't a good blocker. "I'm not the most genial player here," Timmy admitted. "I'm moody, kind of arrogant at times. At the last count, I had 107 different moods." But Timmy knuckled under and gave up the acting classes in New York. He stopped ordering snacks in his hotel room the night before a game. He stopped being a night man (though he was never a carouser). In 1966, the Eagles spurted to a fine second place finish, and Brown had one of his typically good years. After the Playoff Bowl in Miami, he took off for Hawaii to do some modeling assignments.

"Timmy was absolutely thrilled with the prospects for the future," said Ed Snider, a former vice-president of the club and a Brown booster. "He felt sure the Eagles could win the championship. Then he picks up a paper and reads a story quoting Kuharich as saying he had made his plans for the coming season and Timmy wasn't included in them. This completely demoralized the guy."

"The biggest blow," nodded Timmy, "was when I was in Hawaii and I read they said they didn't need me."

The next year was a nightmare. A pulled hamstring muscle sidelined him for the first half of the season. Some Eagle teammates criticized him publicly for malingering. Timmy was morose and resentful. "I'm fighting for something I didn't think I'd ever have to fight for again," he told Philadelphia columnist Sandy Padwe as he sat in his corner cubicle in the Eagles' locker room the day before Thanksgiving. "Respect. From my teammates first. From the people second. I resent that I have to fight for it." And then there was physical disaster. He was peeling back on a pass pattern against Dallas, looking up at the ball thrown high over his head, when linebacker Lee Roy Jordan's elbow smashed him in the jaw. Out came nine teeth, and Timmy was on a liquid diet.

425

He announced through clenched teeth that he wanted to be traded. The Eagles sent him to the Baltimore Colts for Alvin Haymond, a spare defensive back. "It's a travesty what Kuharich did to Timmy Brown," said Snider. "He beat him into the ground and then traded him for less than he was worth."

In the summer of 1968, Timmy announced his retirement to devote full time to show business, but the Colts finally persuaded him to come to camp. He felt he still had incentive at thirty-one. "Kuharich spent the last few years knocking me," he said. "I suppose I do have to prove to a lot of people I still have it. I want to be a champion. That's why I'm here. I've been a loser all my life."

Timmy was a minimal factor in Baltimore's 1968 parade to the NFL championship. Still hampered by muscle pulls, he was a spot performer behind regular Tom Matte at halfback. He got his chief exercise during the season returning kickoffs. Which was where Timmy Brown came in a decade ago.

THOMAS ALLEN "TIMMY" BROWN

BORN: May 24, 1937   Height: 5'11"   Weight: 198

Ball State Teachers College

Green Bay, 1959
Philadelphia, 1960–67
Baltimore, 1968

| Year | G. | RUSHING | | | | PASS RECEIVING | | | | SCORING | |
		Att.	Yds.	Avg.	TD.	P.C.	Yds.	Avg.	TD.	TD.	Pts.
1959	1	(None)				(None)				0	0
1960	12	9	35	3.9	2	9	247	27.4	2	4	24
1961	14	50	338	6.8	1	14	264	18.9	2	5	30
1962	14	137	545	4.0	5	52	849	16.3	6	13	78
1963	14	192	841	4.4	6	36	487	13.5	4	11	66
1964	10	90	356	4.0	5	15	244	16.3	5	10	60
1965	13	158	861	*5.4	6	50	682	13.6	3	9	54
1966	13	161	548	3.4	3	33	371	11.2	3	8	48
1967	7	53	179	3.4	1	22	202	9.2	1	2	12
1968	14	39	159	4.1	2	4	53	13.3	0	2	12
PRO TOTALS —10 YEARS	112	889	3862	4.3	31	235	3399	14.5	26	64	384

* Led NFL.

Tommy Mason and Bill Brown

TOMMY'S ONLY WEAKNESS IS BALANCE.
HE'S INCLINED TO BE A STUMBLER. BUT
HE'S THE KIND OF KID YOU'D LIKE TO
CLAIM AS YOUR OWN. HE DOESN'T DRINK
OR SMOKE, BUT HE DOESN'T MAKE IT
UNCOMFORTABLE FOR THOSE WHO DO.
—*Norm Van Brocklin, coach,*
Minnesota Vikings.

Tommy Mason, left, was the original Viking. And when he was healthy, the Vikings were a healthy team. He's struggling here against the grasp of Green Bay's Dave Robinson.

The flickering action on the home screen used by the Minnesota Vikings to review their games was isolated on a number 20 in a purple and white uniform trying to block a blitzing linebacker of the Green Bay Packers. As Norm Van Brocklin, the coach of the Vikings, slowed down the pace of the projector, number 20 slipped and sprawled ingloriously on the damp grass. The linebacker leaped over him and pounced on quarterback Fran Tarkenton.

"Gentlemen," announced Van Brocklin to the assembled Vikings, "that is how a guy blocks who has a Cadillac and a banjo."

Tommy Mason blushed. He had the banjo long before he got the Cadillac. And he got the Caddy because he rated the highest salary on the Vikings as their most proficient football player. "He is our best runner," Van Brocklin once said, "our best pass receiver, our best blocker and, if he was a defensive back, he'd be our best pass defender. He's the best football player in the National League."

So when Dutch Van Brocklin caustically pointed out the failure of number 20 (Mason) on the screen, Tommy was more embarrassed personally than resentful. Heck, Dutch had also called him a Hollywood beach bum because his hair was long. Tom was victimized on this one play and throughout his seven seasons with the Minnesota Vikings by his eagerness to excel.

He was the original Viking, the first player chosen in the NFL draft when the new team was franchised in 1961, and he felt a keen obligation for that honor. When the Vikings blew an exhibition game because of his fumble, he sat in the locker room of a high school stadium in Cedar Rapids, Iowa, and cried. "They picked me ahead of every other player in the country," he sobbed, "and I'm not doing a thing for them."

"Tommy," said an older guy on the Vikings, "you'll forget about this because you're going to be one of the best halfbacks who ever played pro football. In a year or two, you're going to have my job." The veteran was Hugh McElhenny, and for the first year of the Vikings he was Tommy's alter ego. In the second year, Mason displaced old Mac as the regular halfback on the new team.

Did he become "one of the best halfbacks who ever played pro football"? There's no definitive answer. If you take the 1963 season, when he was a unanimous all-pro, the first in the Vikings' short history, the answer might be yes. If you rate a man on cumulative effort, the response would have to be negative.

The fact is, Tommy Mason has had one of the most frustrating careers in football history. He never has played a full season at top speed. His injury log reads like a medical school text book. His manner of playing defeated him in the long run. "Football," he said, "is a game of hitting. I don't think of myself as a hard-nosed player. But I know you have to keep hitting and hitting until you make the other guy quit, and that's how you win."

It became an axiom of the Minnesota Vikings in the years he played with them that they never won a game without a healthy Mason in the lineup. He was that important. But a man's ability to hit tails off drastically when he is hobbled by a hyperextension of the right knee, then a hyperextension of the left knee, ultimately operations to both knees, chipped bones in his feet, hyperextension of the elbow—so that eventually he found himself playing wrapped in three pounds of gauze and tape and was known as "The Mummy in Cleats."

Tommy Mason laid himself bare to the inevitability of injury because of the way he plays. He's a slasher, a man who hurtles full speed into the action, depending largely upon his velocity to break tackles. There have been others like this in pro football, but they were generally built close to the ground, with thick necks and broad torsos to absorb the shock of impact. Tommy Mason's like a whippet. With weight lifting, he built himself into a 200-pounder, but the body-building doesn't shelter the streaky slenderness of a greyhound. A man proportioned on his scale, tapered to a 32-inch waist and trim legs, has no business being reckless in a sport populated by 250-pound antagonists.

"Nobody has to tell me," he said in the middle of his injury troubles, "that Tommy Mason still hasn't been able to go through a full season in one piece. I used to get mad when people said I was injury-prone. After a few years, I have to admit a running back in the NFL's going to get bumped around. But I have no thoughts about changing my running style. I don't think I'd be worth much to the team running pussyfoot."

In the early days, when he learned at McElhenny's knee, Tommy tried the style of the master, the prancing around looking for an opening, the delicate balance and footwork to spring free. "I tried to copy him," said Tommy. "I would be dancing around looking for holes and wham! While I was dancing, the hole closed and I was nowhere. I finally learned what I had to do was break for that hole and run as fast and as hard as I could. I'm no dancer."

The ultimate irony was that the injuries to the knees, the most damaging of all, occurred on plays on which he wasn't even hit. In successive years, he carried the ball against the Packers behind strong interference, cut sharply and collapsed without contact. The knees gave way from the strain of changing direction. Compounding the frustration was the fact that he had gone through his varsity career at Tulane virtually without mishap and the Vikings had chosen him as the first collegian in the draft because, in Van Brocklin's words, "we got the best football player in the country."

Mason is a native of Lake Charles, Louisiana, the home of another fine athlete (and halfback) named Alvin Dark. He played saxophone in the high school band and then put on a uniform to set district scoring records with a football. Music was a part of his life since he walked the banks of the Calcasieu River, harmonizing with his older brother Boo. He followed Boo, also a football star, to Tulane, and they played in the same backfield when Tommy was a sophomore.

At Tulane, Tommy's natural enthusiasm for people took him into the French Quarter and an absorbing friendship with Lily Christine, who was better known to the patrons of exotic salons as The Cat Girl. She had other interests besides stripping. She was a health faddist and got Tommy started lifting weights. She introduced him to romantic poetry—Byron, Shelley, Keats. Tommy also had a guitar and a taste for

430

country music, so one night after scoring a couple of touchdowns against Vanderbilt in Nashville, he went to the Grand Ole Opry and was persuaded to get on stage for a duet with Chet Atkins, a country music star. A yen to sing has persisted, and he has made some records.

The zest for varied activities made life around Tommy exciting. When he wasn't playing for the Vikings, he might be in Las Vegas or Los Angeles or New Orleans, and one winter he ventured into British Honduras to become part-owner of a sugar cane plantation. His exuberance made him one of the most popular men around Minneapolis, too. He took flying lessons, studied karate, and even cooked. He was a bachelor then. He had a pet monkey and an active social life, and if it weren't for that injury spectre, his years with the Vikings would have been glorious.

However, Tommy said, "I can't keep from thinking about tomorrow. Basically, I'm a worrier. I'm a very bad loser. I used to sulk when I lost at anything." After the 1966 season, when his knee miseries, culminated by an operation in November, caused him to miss half the games and curtailed his effectiveness in others, he seriously contemplated retirement. "I don't want to be a hanger-on," he said. "I want to contribute to the team. If I can't do the job the way I'd like to, I'll retire."

He had another reason for serious thought about his future. He was married that winter to the former Rita Ridinger, prominent in her own right as world champion in the five-gaited event at the American Saddlebred championships, a show horse rider since she was ten years old.

That March he was traded to the Los Angeles Rams. He heard about the switch from a hospital bed in Oklahoma City, where he had been sent to have cartilage removed from his left knee and his right kneecap scraped. "I feel," he said, "like a used car that is shined up before it is sold."

The first phase of professional football in Minnesota had ended with the departure of Mason, since in the same month quarterback Fran Tarkenton was unloaded to the New York Giants. Ostensibly, Tommy was going to step into a regular job with the Rams, the hot new team of the Western Conference, and his enthusiasm was spurred. To fortify his shaky hinges, the Ram trainers wrapped him in bandages daily. It was figured 12,000 feet of tape would hold him for the season. Unfortunately for Tommy, an obscure back named Les Josephson came on as a tremendous work-horse in 1967 and put Mason on the bench. Chafing from inactivity, urged by friends to retire, he even volunteered for special kicking teams. At the age of twenty-eight, he felt he had a lot of football left. He got a chance to play more in 1968, when Josephson was sidelined for the whole season by injury. But Tommy was resigned to the fact he'd never be more than a spot player again.

Meanwhile, in Minnesota, the Vikings still retained one vital plug in their backfield. Mason's old running mate, William Dorsey Brown, was uniquely healthy and effective and about to come out from under the shadow of Tarkenton and Mason. He has none of the personal color of the other two. As a runner, he doesn't have the knifing speed of Mason which got people up on their feet. The most eye-catching thing about Bill Brown

Bow-legged Bill Brown has finally come out of the shadows as one of the toughest backs to bring down. He originally teamed with Mason as Minnesota's one-two punch.

is the conformation of his legs. He's bow-legged enough to rival Utah's Natural Bridge as a structural wonder.

"He'd stand 6′5″ if he straightened out those legs," cracked Norm Van Brocklin at his first sight of Brown toddling into the Vikings' camp in 1962.

Probably the most identifying mark ever attached to Brown was his nickname, Boom Boom, created by Minneapolis writer Jim Klobuchar after he heard Brown hit a line, bounce off and hit it again.

As a fullback at Illinois, he was only second team all-conference. He was a good shotputter on the track, a sturdy specimen, 5′11″ and 230, but not an outstanding prospect. The Chicago Bears drafted him in 1961 and had him sitting around for a year. The Bears, who felt he was a slow learner, didn't have the patience to wait for him to come around. They were about to put Bill on waivers when the Vikings grabbed him for a draft choice. He showed little more at Minnesota the second year, playing third string fullback behind Doug Mayberry and Mel Triplett.

In 1963, he got the starting job almost by default. He was hesitant as a runner, a plugger who was going nowhere fast. The other teams were still keying heavily on Mason, the spectacular halfback. "He was too intense," said one of the Viking coaches. "He'd be trying so hard and worrying so much that he wasn't alert to the situation, and he'd make mental mistakes."

The shock that snapped Brown out of the doldrums came in the spring of '64 when he was visiting the team offices. A trade was announced bringing Ted Dean to the club from Philadelphia. Dean was a fullback. The Vikings had also drafted a couple of fullbacks. The message got through to Boom Boom. "They were asking me to put up or get lost, right there," he said. In training camp, he was a terror. Van Brocklin's camps were grueling ordeals. They were known as the stalags of the northwoods. But Brown exceeded the pace of training. When he was asked to run 15 yards, he'd run 30. He stayed after practice to work on his pass-catching routes. He had great hands. He needed technique. At Illinois, he had caught only three passes in three years.

In the 1964 season, Brown caught 48 passes, more than any fullback in history, and gained 866 yards on the ground, a new club record. He had arrived as a class player. "Previously," noted Van Brocklin, "he had been running with indecision, thinking his way along, and he looked slow. With experience, he could run with confidence. He knew where he wanted to go and how to get there. Then the speed, which must always have been there, asserted itself."

He was good. He knew it, the Vikings knew it, and the teams who played against them knew it. But hardly anyone else. "Part of it," said running mate Mason, "is that his name is Brown and he plays fullback." You see, there was a Jim Brown still active. And other Browns, like Roger and Robert, Timmy and Tom, plus Ed and Roosevelt, all established stars in the NFL.

"They try to fit him in with Fran Tarkenton and me," added Mason, "and since they think we're colorful, they figure he must be the strong, silent type. Actually, you can't shut him up. He has a special muscle in his mouth. The minute his eyes open in the morning he starts yapping."

Recognition came slow, though he played in the Pro Bowl after the '64 campaign and scored two touchdowns in a West team romp paced by Tarkenton, Mason and Brown. During the regular season, he had a spectacular game in the Vikings' first visit to New York, grabbing a pass deep down the middle with one hand for the winning touchdown in the fourth quarter. It was one of nine scoring passes he caught that year.

He quickly proved that he was as good a receiver as any man who ever came out of the backfield, primarily because he never dropped a ball thrown his way, and defenses couldn't believe that a stumpy bow-legged man could have his quickness at getting open.

In his primary job of carrying the ball inside, he was less showy. They called him "Second Effort" Brown. "When you hit," he explained, "you're always trying to get extra yardage. If something's not there, the best thing is to go somewhere else. There's no reason to just dive into the stack."

As injuries continued to plague Mason at halfback the next two years, the load shifted gradually to iron-man Bill. He led the NFL in rushing attempts with 251 in 1966. "There is one of my biggest mistakes," said George Halas, watching him bulldoze through the Bears.

With the exodus of 1967, when Mason and Tarkenton were gone, and Van Brocklin had also resigned as head coach, Brown's role didn't change. Bud Grant took over the strategy and used Brown's versatility as a foundation of his attack. "He's a complete football player in every way, in temperament as well as ability," said Grant. "A lot of other coaches tell me their top runners, after a tough game on Sunday, don't want to practice much until Thursday. They want to take it easy. Bill is just the opposite. You can't be a prima donna and play on the same team with Bill because he works that hard."

He emphasized another of his abilities, blocking, in '67. Dave Osborn succeeded Mason at halfback and piled up 972 yards rushing, in large measure because Brown was carrying out the linebackers or ends on most plays to give Osborn running room. When Osborn missed most of the '68 season with a knee injury, Brown took over the major part of the ground attack again and led the Vikings to a division title with 805 yards, scoring 11 touchdowns, most of them in that zone inside the 10-yard line. He also tallied three times on passes. With Jim Brown retired in 1966 and Jim Taylor fading out a year later, the Vikings claimed Bill Brown was the most complete fullback in the NFL. Brown wanted more tangible appreciation. He refused their salary offer and played out the option on his contract. He later signed for the '69 season at a healthy raise.

Exposure was no longer a problem for him—not after what happened on a trip to visit American troops in Vietnam. He checked into a room in a Saigon hotel with John David Crow of the 49ers when a Viet Cong terrorist raid struck in the middle of the night. An American officer ordered them to a nearby lounge with their mattresses. There was not time to get dressed. Crow ran to the lounge in his underwear. Brown walked in naked, holding the mattress over his head. He didn't know there'd be a dozen girls in the room, too. He gallantly wrapped the mattress around himself until help arrived.

TOMMY MASON'S FAVORITE PLAY:

"I like quick-hitting plays because they cut down on the pursuit of the defense. Also the runner, if he's quick reacting, can go either left or right of the hole if it closes up on him. My pet play is called '21 fast trap.' The runner *must* keep his head up so he can read the defense and make the cut. For instance, in an odd-man line where the tackle plays directly over the center, the hole will move about a half space to the 'on' side, in this case the right side.

"In Minnesota's opening game in 1964, against the Baltimore Colts, I scored the first Viking touchdown of the season by running 51 yards for a touchdown after I found a quick hole on this trap. You'll note the center and left guard play a switching game in their blocking assignments and get better angles. We went on to win the game."

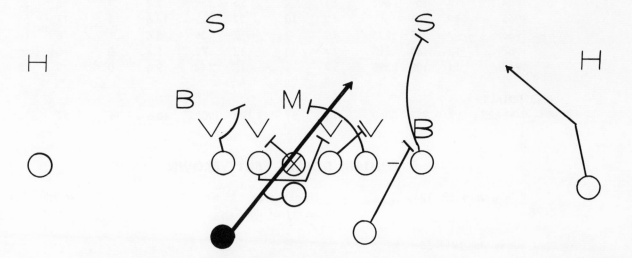

BILL BROWN'S FAVORITE PLAY:

"At Minnesota, we call this slant to the weakside '34.' It's an off-tackle power play which gives me the option to run to daylight and is used in similar form by a lot of teams. The key to its success is the ability of the running back to read the defensive tackle. Also Mick Tingelhoff at center has to cut off the middle linebacker. The guard, Jim Vellone, takes the defensive tackle in or out, depending on how he charges. Grady Alderman, the left tackle, takes the defensive end. And the halfback, Dave Osborn, then has to read the linebacker and block down on him.

"The beauty of it is that it can be run so many different ways, depending on the defensive line play. We've used the play in almost all games, successfully."

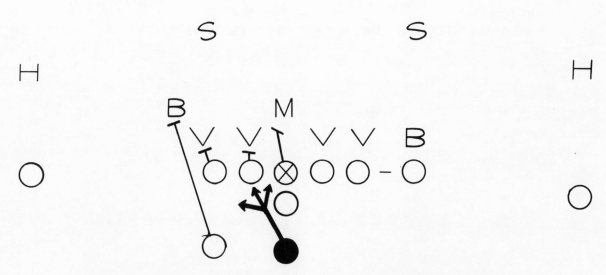

THOMAS CYRIL "TOMMY" MASON

BORN: July 8, 1939   Height: 6'2"   Weight: 200
Tulane University

Minnesota, 1961–66
Los Angeles Rams, 1967–68

Year	G.	RUSHING Att.	Yds.	Avg.	TD.	PASS RECEIVING P.C.	Yds.	Avg.	TD.	SCORING TD.	Pts.
1961	13	60	226	3.8	3	20	122	6.1	0	3	18
1962	14	167	740	4.4	2	36	603	16.8	6	8	48
1963	13	166	763	4.6	7	40	365	9.1	2	9	54
1964	13	169	691	4.1	4	26	239	9.2	1	5	30
1965	10	141	597	4.2	10	22	321	14.6	1	11	66
1966	7	58	235	4.1	2	7	39	5.6	1	3	18
1967	13	63	213	3.4	0	13	70	5.4	0	0	0
1968	14	108	395	3.7	3	15	144	9.6	0	3	18

PRO TOTALS
—8 YEARS

	G.	Att.	Yds.	Avg.	TD.	P.C.	Yds.	Avg.	TD.	TD.	Pts.
	97	932	3860	4.1	31	179	1903	10.6	11	42	252

WILLIAM DORSEY "BILL" BROWN

BORN: June 29, 1938   Height: 5'11"   Weight: 230
University of Illinois

Chicago, 1961
Minnesota, 1962–68

Year	G.	RUSHING Att.	Yds.	Avg.	TD.	PASS RECEIVING P.C.	Yds.	Avg.	TD.	SCORING TD.	Pts.
1961	14	22	81	3.7	0	2	6	3.0	0	0	0
1962	14	34	103	3.0	0	10	124	12.4	1	1	6
1963	14	128	445	3.5	5	17	109	6.4	2	8	48
1964	14	226	866	3.8	7	48	703	14.6	9	16	96
1965	14	160	699	4.4	6	41	503	12.3	1	7	42
1966	14	*251	829	3.3	6	37	359	9.7	0	6	36
1967	14	185	610	3.3	5	22	263	12.0	0	5	30
1968	14	222	805	3.6	11	31	329	10.6	3	14	84

PRO TOTALS
—8 YEARS

	G.	Att.	Yds.	Avg.	TD.	P.C.	Yds.	Avg.	TD.	TD.	Pts.
	112	1228	4438	3.6	40	208	2396	11.5	16	57	342

* Led NFL.

Steve Van Buren was a trailblazer as a T-formation back with the model combination of size and speed. He led the Philadelphia Eagles to consecutive NFL titles.

When Bill Dudley strapped his helmet on to play, it was for keeps. The little Virginian put out 110 percent in dedication and effort.

Frank Gifford in profile was a handsome halfback for the New York Giants and produced handsome results. The black smudge on his cheek is to dull the sun's rays on his face.

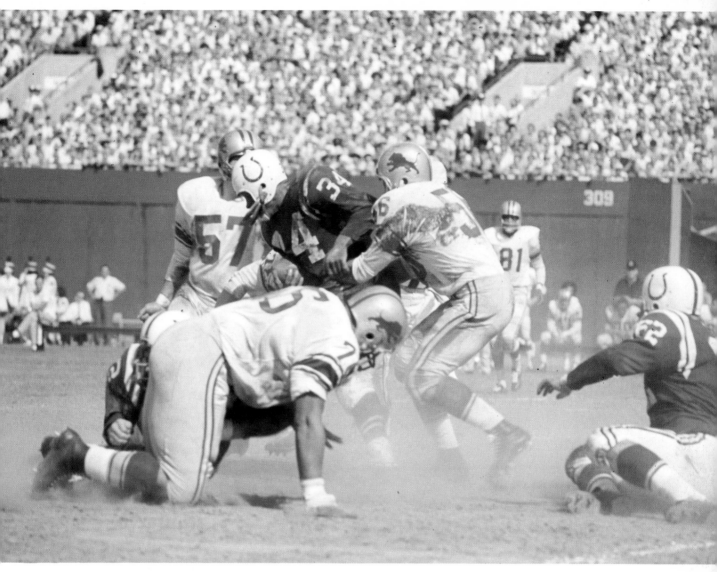

Joe Perry (34) matched his number in age but was still going strong as a ball carrier when he played with the Colts after long service with San Francisco.

The three backs shown here blended ruggedness, swiftness, durability and results. John Henry Johnson, top left, smashed wide open through defenses for 13 years. Lenny Moore, above, never slowed up in a dozen years for Baltimore. And the great Jimmy Brown, left, was indomitable as the all-time leading rusher.

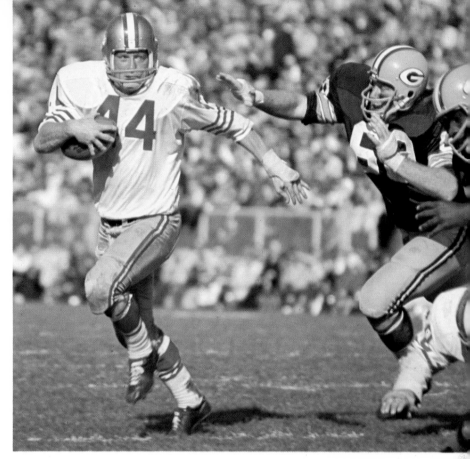

John David Crow, carrying the ball for the San Francisco 49ers, got by with guile even when his speed flagged after more than a decade of pounding enemy lines.

It took more than a casual grab to stop the ferocious plunging of Green Bay's Jimmy Taylor, who dragged tacklers along like accumulated debris.

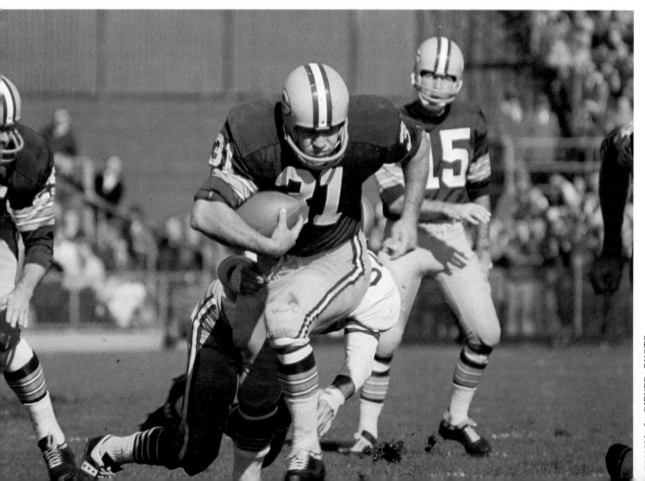

Paul Hornung, left, was more than a versatile, productive performer for the Green Bay championship dynasty. He was its soul leader as well.

Timmy Brown (22) was excitement in kinetic form when he zipped brilliantly through open fields in his great years with the Philadelphia Eagles.

Size was no deterrent to the rushing of Dick Bass, the colorful little fullback of the Los Angeles Rams. His low center of gravity has made him hard to knock off his feet.

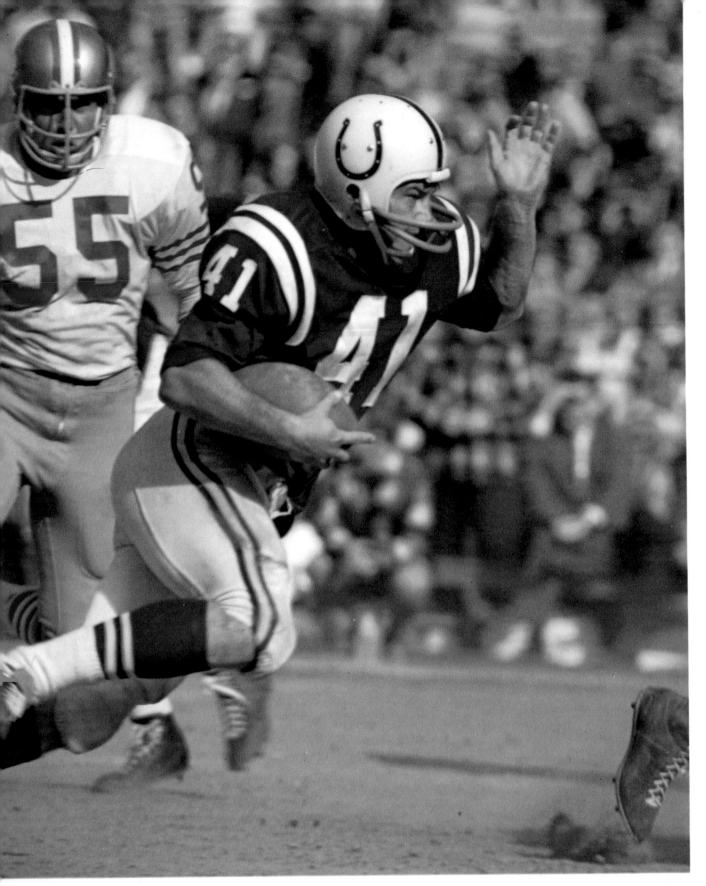

All Tom Matte ever needed was the opportunity to play to show he could be a progressive offensive force for the Baltimore Colts.

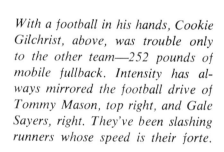

L. SMITH

With a football in his hands, Cookie Gilchrist, above, was trouble only to the other team—252 pounds of mobile fullback. Intensity has always mirrored the football drive of Tommy Mason, top right, and Gale Sayers, right. They've been slashing runners whose speed is their forte.

The New York Giants have made a fetish of "Baby Bulls" in their backfield in the mid-1960's. The prime specimens have been Ernie Koy (23) and Tucker Frederickson (24).

Cleveland hardly missed Jimmy Brown after his abrupt retirement because Leroy Kelly (44) took over immediately as a league-leading rusher.

W. EMMONS

MALCOLM W. EMMONS

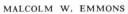

In his young career with the New York Jets, Emerson Boozer (32) has already shown a definite affinity for the end zone.

Jim Nance, left, is power personified as the fullback of the Boston Patriots.

Detroit's quest for a respectable running back was fulfilled when Mel Farr took his first handoff for the Lions.

Mike Garrett of Kansas City, right, was one Heisman Trophy winner who transferred his greatness as a collegiate runner to pro football.

The Oakland Raiders rose to championship status coincidental with the installment of Hewritt Dixon (35) as their fullback.

Matt Snell proved his merit as a running back to all of pro football when he blasted through the Baltimore Colts in the astounding victory of the New York Jets in the 1969 Super Bowl.

The Green Bay Packers have a million dollars invested in Jim Grabowski, top left, and Donny Anderson, lower left. The entire investment hasn't been paid off yet, but the Packers have seen enough to know the capital gains will keep rolling along.

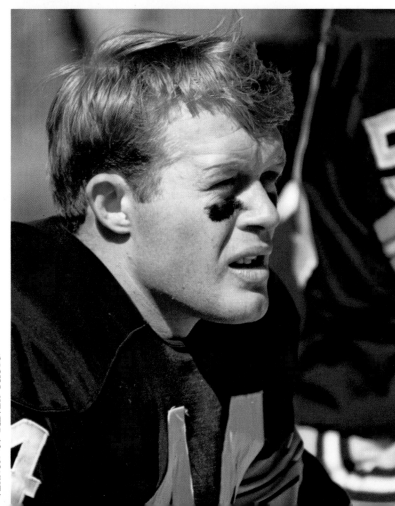

Almost from nowhere, the new Cincinnati Bengals produced a new running sensation in 1968, Paul Robinson (18). He cracked the 1,000-yard barrier and led the AFL in rushing as a rookie.

A new era of the running back is dawning with the coming out of O. J. Simpson, the most acclaimed ball carrier since Red Grange.

Tom Matte

THAT MATTE—HE'S A GARBAGE CAN
RUNNER.
　　　—*Alex Karras, defensive tackle,
　　　Detroit Lions.*

Tommy Matte waited patiently for years to show off his multiple skills as a halfback for the Baltimore Colts. He's shielding this handoff from John Unitas.

The little seed of Walter Mitty that lurks in all men was nurtured and exposed to full bloom for one exhilirating month in the life of Tom Matte. Matte-Mitty, in the month of December 1965, was the little boy whose finger held the dike; he was the hero swooping in to rescue Pearl White tied to the railroad tracks; he was Don Quixote fulfilling the impossible dream. Matte-Mitty came within one disputed field goal of guiding the Baltimore Colts to a championship.

You see, Tom Matte was a halfback, and not even a regular halfback. Every man on the club dreams at one time or another of taking charge of the team, which means playing quarterback. The Colts were faced with an implausible situation as they approached their last game of the season on December 18, needing a victory to stay alive. They had no qualified quarterback. John Unitas was in a cast from a knee operation. Their second string quarterback, Gary Cuozzo, was also in a cast with a shoulder separation. Ed Brown, a castoff passer, was signed during the week but had absolutely no knowledge of the Colts' system.

So there was Matte. He had played quarterback at Ohio State, which really meant he was an auxiliary halfback in Woody Hayes' "three-yards-and-a-cloud-of-dust" offense. In four seasons of professional football, he had never lined up directly behind the center, hands cupped for the snap. It was all new to him again. Coach Don Shula taped some elementary plays to his wrist, and Matte-Mitty strode forth to face the big, bad Rams in Los Angeles. With the help of Brown, who threw an important touchdown pass, Matte led the Colts to a stirring 20–17 victory, and when the weekend was over they were tied in the final standings with the Green Bay Packers. League rules eliminated the use of Brown in a playoff. Now the whole burden was on Matte, who had a few extra days to brush up. Shula taped a plastic band to Tom's wrist again, listing formations and plays. The inspired Colts built a 10–7 lead and held it until 1:58 remained in the fourth quarter. Don Chandler attempted a field goal from the 22-yard line and turned in disgust as the ball veered toward the right. But the official waved it good. In a sudden death overtime, Chandler kicked another to settle the conference title.

Matte had one final Mitty-like episode a couple of weeks later when he led the Colts to a Playoff Bowl victory over Philadelphia in Miami and was voted the outstanding player of the game. "We learned a lot," exulted Shula. "We can play Tom as quarterback but treat him as a halfback. We will probably keep the Matte offense as part of our system."

And that's when Tom Matte lost faith in Walter Mitty. The next season rolled around, and our hero was right back in the familiar spot which had bugged him ever since he had been a pro, which brought on ulcers, which made him act like a happy-go-lucky, irresponsible kid to cover his frustration—he sat and watched Lenny Moore play the position for which he was trained. In pro football, he had to be a halfback or nothing. He didn't throw well enough to be a quarterback. The Colts had picked him No. 1 in the

1961 draft because, as a solid 210-pounder, he looked like he could be converted easily into a runner.

In the early years, he had a reputation as a pussyfooter, a guy who wouldn't hit hard into the pile and knock people over. His rookie year was a virtual bust because he cracked a vertebrae and sprained an ankle. By his second year, the Colts had resolved that Lenny Moore would play inside all the time, so they tried Tom in the defensive backfield part of the season. In his third year, when Moore got kicked in the head and became a problem child, Matte finally got his chance and showed good promise as an all around back, a Paul Hornung type who could run, block, throw the option pass and catch the ball well.

But it turned out he was just holding the franchise for Moore, who made a sterling comeback as player of the year in 1964, leaving Matte right back on the bench to nurse his ulcers. One day in 1964, he lost four and a half pints of blood as the worries churned inside him.

The only time the ulcers didn't bother him was in that glorious one-month interlude when he stepped into the emergency breach at quarterback. "I had," said Tom, "no time to worry then."

Shula, as the coach, appreciated having him around. "He is a tremendous individual," said Don. "He'll do anything you ask him and never complain. He looks for challenges and thrives on pressure."

There was a point in the crucial Green Bay playoff of 1965, when Matte, calling the signals, looked at Raymond Berry, the veteran split end, and asked what he had open as a receiver. "I got nothing," said Raymond. So he turned to Jimmy Orr, the veteran flanker (and his roommate on the road) and asked him for a suggestion. Jimmy shook his head and mumbled, "Run it!" So Tom gulped, swallowed his nervousness, grabbed the ball and ran it around the Packer flank for a gain.

Matte saw some positive benefits from his brief fling at quarterback: "I learned total offense, the overall picture—what we're trying to accomplish as far as line play and pass protection and pass patterns. Every back should know these things."

All he wanted was an opportunity to apply that knowledge before his future receded into the past. He finally got it in 1966, when he had passed his twenty-seventh birthday. In the fourth game of the season, Lenny Moore pulled a leg muscle. Matte started against Detroit in the fifth game, rusty from disuse, and gained 73 in 13 carries. He's never relinquished the job since.

He was a busy boy. Against the Los Angeles Rams, with their front four averaging 275 pounds in weight, he carried the ball 10 times for 60 yards. When the Colts punted, he was the slot man in the backfield who blocked for the punter and then ran downfield to make the tackle. When the Colts received a punt, he was the short man who kept the wave of bodies off deep man Alvin Haymond. The day was just fine until he drank the bottle of soda pop after the game. He broke out in a cold sweat and his stomach flipped. He recognized the symptoms. Ulcers.

Yet this worry wart isn't the popular image of Matte because even at thirty he retains the round face of a little boy with an impish smile and a reckless nonchalance. It's

440

a cover. Take away the career frustrations, and he's still had his share of troubles. A highway head-on collision ("some cop cut me off") sent his wife through the windshield. Tom was dazed and woke up to find her inert and bloody. He thought Judy was dead and beat his fist on the trunk door, breaking his hand, until he heard her sigh, "Stop making a fool of yourself, Matte." One day he noticed a dark spot on the side of his nose. He ignored it for a few months, then casually asked a doctor to check it out. The doctor told him it was a malignancy. If it had gone a half inch further, it would have cut off his sweat glands and been fatal.

In 1967, a fully established regular, Tom reached football maturity as one of the class running backs in pro ball. He got a three-year contract that made him only the second man in Colt history to work on that kind of tenure—the other was John Unitas. And he started working it off on merit immediately as the point man in a revived Colt running attack. He showed the hardnosed resolve that Baltimore first looked for when it drafted him eight years earlier. As the Colts charged to a 13-1 record, Tom achieved a career high of 662 yards—not a fancy figure, not one run longer than 23 yards, but included were 9 touchdown spurts. The tougher the going, the better he played. In the division playoff win over Minnesota, he took a bad jolt to the head, suffered a concussion and a splitting headache the week before the title game with the Browns. Playing in Cleveland was a homecoming. It's where he was raised and where his father was a pro hockey star and coach. He rushed through the Browns for 88 yards and three touchdowns in a 34–0 waltz by the Colts. The scores tied an NFL title game record. He outgained Leroy Kelly, the NFL rushing leader, by 60 yards on a soggy field.

Matte shrugged off the post-game adulation. "I don't consider myself a super-star. I don't have speed. I only try to give 150 percent." If he was a garbage can runner, as Detroit's Alex Karras once described him, Shula noted, "It's gold-plated."

The happy ending for Matte, and the Colts, was spoiled in their upset by the New York Jets in the 1969 Super Bowl. "It was my best game of the season," he admitted, after he had gained 116 yards. In the second quarter, with the Jets holding a seven-point lead, he spun off tackle, broke through the grasp of a Jet safety and ran 58 yards deep into New York territory.

"I slipped when I went through the line of scrimmage," he said, "and went down to one hand. That slowed me up. But they still wouldn't have caught me if I had the speed of Gale Sayers. He's something else."

So, finally, is Tom Matte.

TOM MATTE'S FAVORITE PLAY:

"This play is called a 'halfback special option pass.' The key to its success is the fake of the halfback. He must make it look like a run to draw the defense up. Once he does this, he throws it back to the quarterback, and the quarterback picks out his best receiver downfield.

441

"The Colts worked it successfully against Atlanta in 1968. We scored on the last play before the half-time intermission to take the lead. It was the key to our victory that day. When I flipped the ball back to Earl Morrall, our quarterback, he found Jimmy Orr, our flanker, standing all alone in the end zone with no one within 10 yards of him."

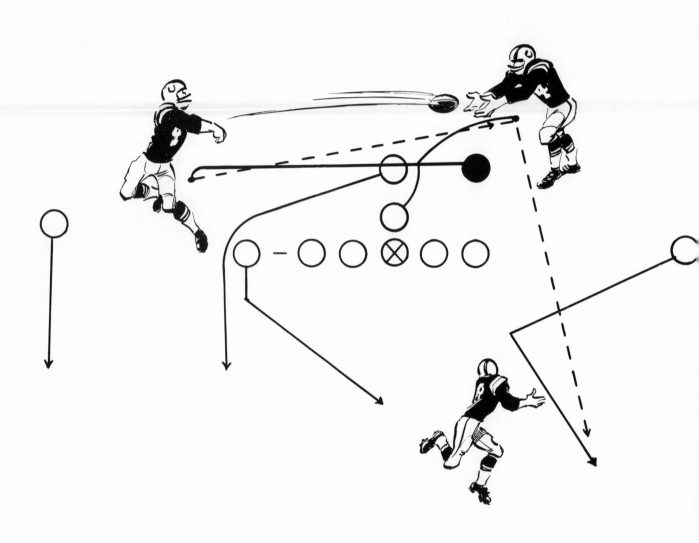

THOMAS ROLAND "TOM" MATTE

BORN: June 14, 1939   Height: 6'0"   Weight: 214

Ohio State University

Baltimore, 1961–68

Year	G.	RUSHING Att.	Yds.	Avg.	TD.	PASS RECEIVING P.C.	Yds.	Avg.	TD.	SCORING TD.	Pts.
1961	8	13	54	4.2	0	1	8	8.0	0	0	0
1962	14	74	226	3.1	2	8	81	10.1	1	3	18
1963	14	133	541	4.1	4	48	466	9.7	1	5	30
1964	14	42	215	5.1	1	10	169	16.9	0	1	6
1965	14	69	235	3.4	1	12	131	10.9	0	1	6
1966	14	86	381	4.4	0	23	307	13.3	3	3	18
1967	14	147	636	4.3	9	35	496	14.2	3	12	72
1968	14	183	662	3.6	9	25	275	11.0	1	10	60
PRO TOTALS —8 YEARS	106	747	2950	4.0	26	162	1933	11.9	9	35	210

In the parade of great runners who have sprinted across the pro football vista, a man can get lost in the crowd if there's nothing sensational in his record or he hasn't had the good fortune to play on a championship team. Such a man was the leading runner in the history of the Detroit Lions. In his career from 1959 through 1967, he gained more yards than Bronko Nagurski, Charley Trippi, Frank Gifford, or Paul Hornung. He was an ideal-sized fullback, 230 pounds, with good speed for a big man, and an outstanding blocker. Oh, yes, his name—Nick Pietrosante. He was personable, articulate, an All-American at Notre Dame. He was the work-horse of the Lions for seven seasons and finished his career as a backup fullback at Cleveland for two seasons. He rushed for 4,026 yards the hard way. His best season was 1960, when he gained 872 yards.

There were others like him—competent, plugging pros who peaked as pro football turned the corner into the spectacular Sixties—but they didn't have the glitter of a Hornung.

Some of them are, alphabetically:

Billy Ray Barnes, a hard-driving halfback on the championship Philadelphia Eagles of 1960. He played an even decade until his retirement in 1966, after additional service with Washington and the Minnesota Vikings.

Ronnie Bull, an in-between type of back, not quite big enough for fullback, not quite fast enough to sparkle at halfback, but a solid contributor to the Chicago Bears' title drive in '63. He joined them in 1962 and is still active.

Ernie Green was the "other" man in the backfield of the Cleveland Browns for seven years, first pairing with Jimmy Brown and then Leroy Kelly. He complemented them perfectly as a swift, good-blocking halfback and fine pass receiver. A knee injury forced his retirement after the '68 campaign.

As a durable plugger, Nick Pietrosante of the Detroit Lions piled up a lot more yardage than many more publicized backs.

Dick Hoak (42) of the Steelers has made a career of fighting off claimants to his halfback job, all the while forging consistent gains.

Dick Hoak was always "too small, too slow" and always about to be supplanted as the halfback of the Pittsburgh Steelers, but in 1968, in his eighth season, he gained 858 yards and was named to the Pro Bowl squad. Which proves again that looks don't mean everything.

Phil King (1958–66) was a great character in his half dozen years with the New York Giants and a frequently valuable contributor. But "the Chief" (1/32nd Indian blood) wasn't quite fast enough to be top caliber and not quite nifty enough to compensate. He was just rugged and a good guy to have around.

Danny Lewis was Nick Pietrosante's running mate in the Detroit backfield. He was a strong rather than shifty runner, too. They called him "Train." Like Nick, he plugged along for years and wound up with a career total of 3,205 yards, most of them unnoticed.

Amos Marsh had the size (6' 1", 225) and the speed (he was a college hurdler) to excite people, and every now and then in his four seasons with Dallas and three with Detroit (1961–67), he'd come up with a big game. In 1962, he led the NFL with 5.6 yards average per carry. But he was never consistent.

Clarence Peaks played nine years with the Philadelphia Eagles and Pittsburgh Steelers, always on the verge of a big season, never quite making it, although he was a strong runner and a fine blocker.

Elijah Pitts had to spend a few years getting over the fact he was an obscure kid from Philander Smith before the Green Bay Packers began to realize his talents. And then he had to get out from under the shadow of Hornung. He finally beat out Hornung and was headed for big things until he snapped an Achilles tendon.

NICHOLAS VINCENT "NICK" PIETROSANTE

BORN: Sept. 10, 1937   Height: 6'1"   Weight: 230

Notre Dame University

Detroit, 1959–65
Cleveland Browns, 1966–67

Year	G.	RUSHING Att.	Yds.	Avg.	TD.	PASS RECEIVING P.C.	Yds.	Avg.	TD.	SCORING TD.	Pts.
1959	10	76	447	5.9	3	16	140	8.8	0	3	18
1960	12	161	872	5.4	8	13	129	9.9	0	8	48
1961	14	201	841	4.2	5	26	315	12.1	0	5	30
1962	13	134	445	3.3	2	26	251	9.7	2	4	24
1963	12	112	418	3.7	5	16	173	10.8	0	5	30
1964	14	147	536	3.6	4	19	152	8.0	0	4	24
1965	14	107	374	3.5	1	18	163	9.1	0	1	6
1966	13	7	20	2.9	0	1	12	12.0	0	0	0
1967	14	10	73	7.3	0	6	56	9.3	0	0	0

PRO TOTALS

| —9 YEARS | 116 | 955 | 4026 | 4.2 | 28 | 141 | 1391 | 9.9 | 2 | 30 | 180 |

Elijah Pitts succeeded Paul Hornung as the regular halfback in the Green Bay backfield before Paul was really ready to give up his job. That's Detroit's fearsome Alex Karras (71) in vain pursuit.

Tom Woodeshick of the Eagles, undaunted by the prospect of running into Sam Huff (70), shows signs of having arrived as one of the solid backs in the NFL.

RICHARD JOHN "DICK" HOAK

BORN: Dec. 8, 1939   Height: 5'11"   Weight: 190

Pennsylvania State University

Pittsburgh, 1961–68

Year	G.	Att.	Yds.	Avg.	TD.	P.C.	Yds.	Avg.	TD.	TD.	Pts.
			RUSHING				PASS RECEIVING			SCORING	
1961	14	85	302	3.6	0	3	18	6.0	0	0	0
1962	14	117	442	3.8	4	9	133	14.8	0	4	24
1963	12	216	679	3.1	6	11	118	10.7	1	7	42
1964	14	84	258	3.1	2	12	137	11.4	3	5	30
1965	14	131	426	3.3	5	19	228	12.0	1	6	36
1966	13	81	212	2.6	1	23	239	10.4	0	1	6
1967	14	52	142	2.7	1	17	111	6.5	1	2	12
1968	14	175	858	4.9	3	28	253	9.0	1	4	24

PRO TOTALS

| —8 YEARS | 109 | 941 | 3319 | 3.5 | 22 | 122 | 1237 | 10.1 | 7 | 29 | 174 |

447

15. The AFL Joins In
Cookie Gilchrist

ON THE FIELD, HE'S NO PROBLEM, BUT
OFF IT ONE HEADACHE AFTER ANOTHER.
I TELL MYSELF I'M GOING TO GET RID OF
HIM, AND THEN I SEE THE BIG SON OF A
GUN CARRY THE BALL.
—*Ralph Wilson, owner,*
Buffalo Bills.

Carlton Chester Gilchrist is a monologue of life. He is in his own way a total experience, and the only way to fathom it is to listen to the rambling philosophy of the man. At various times in his career, the following dictums emerged:

"You've got to be more than a football player. You've got to be a person. You've got to have character, be colorful—*be* a character, if you want to put it that way. That draws fans. Maybe that's what's responsible for my reputation."

(Also responsible for his reputation was the fact that Cookie Gilchrist had as many varied stops in his ledger as a Caribbean cruise ship. He went from Sarnia and Kitchener in the Ontario Rugby Football Union to Hamilton, Saskatchewan, and Toronto in the Canadian Football League to Buffalo, Denver, Miami, and Denver again in the American Football League. He was a football vagabond. "Cookie's good," said one of his former employers, "if you can move him every two years.")

"I believe half of what I see and none of what I read and hear. There have been numerous stories about me over the years that are untrue. Well, I haven't been the run of the mill Negro athlete who accepts the crumbs offered. I felt that I produced better than the white athlete and I wanted to get paid better. Some people have been shocked at my extreme individuality and outspokenness. I never attended a college. Still, I was about the most rounded football player you'd find today."

(Cookie went from Har-Brack High School in Brackenridge, Pennsylvania, where he was a contemporary of Dick Modzelewski, a fine pro tackle, right into a tryout camp of the Cleveland Browns as an eighteen-year-old kid fullback. Cookie lasted until the last cut and went on up to Sarnia to begin a turbulent career in Canadian football. He began as a defensive tackle.)

"I think going from high school right into professional football, I didn't have discipline. I think trying to force discipline on me, I rebelled. I picked up $150 to $200 a week in high school playing football. Guy would come up and shake my hand and there'd be 50 bucks or 25 bucks in it. I've been independent from the age of twelve. I've always been a hustler. I've made my own decisions and never consulted anyone or confided in anyone."

(One afternoon in 1964, in his third productive season with the Buffalo Bills, the outstanding fullback in the AFL, Cookie decided he wasn't carrying the ball enough times against the Boston Patriots. Shortly before half time, he waved Willie Ross, a rookie back, into the game and summarily dispatched himself to the bench. The next day he was suspended and put on waivers. A couple of clubs claimed him, and the waivers were withdrawn. But Cookie wasn't reinstated until he had made a personal apology to Coach Lou Saban and a public apology to the Bills.)

"My mother called me Carlton most of the time. When she wanted something, she called me Cookie. I always resented the name, even up to 1957. I used to go to this old fellow's house back home in Brackenridge and ask for cookies every day—walk up the steps, like clockwork."

(In 1964, he was a special guest at the inauguration of President Lyndon B. Johnson. Cookie was invited by Senator Joseph Clark of Pennsylvania. When Cookie was a high school junior, he was walking home through the Natrona Heights section one early fall afternoon. An elderly, white-haired woman of 80 was mowing the spacious lawn of one of the homes. Young Cookie stopped and gently reproved her, then took over the mower himself and finished the job. Senator Clark sat on the Buffalo team bench one game, approached Cookie and said, "You don't remember me. But that little old lady whose lawn you once mowed in Natrona was my grandmother.")

"Canadian football gave me a chance to exercise my individualism, which I think this country was founded on. America was built on individualism. America needs more individuals like me. I was selling my body for X number of dollars and when I negotiated a contract I was negotiating my future. I had no education—I had nothing to fall back on after football. Every team I ever played for got their money's worth."

(There never was a more fabulous performer north of the border than C. C. Gilchrist. The Canadian game, because of the three-downs rule, is principally a passing game. In 1958, at Saskatchewan, he gained 1,254 yards rushing. In the six seasons he played in the Canadian Football League, he also doubled as a fulltime linebacker. He placekicked and blocked and played on special teams. When he came to the AFL, at the age of 27, he became the first back in league history to gain more than 1,000 yards rushing. He was over 900 each of the next three seasons. "They're not using me right," he moaned. "I'm a better linebacker.")

"I was at a disadvantage because of my image. I'm supposed to be a character. Very few people listen to me. Jimmy Brown was more respectable. All I could do was associate. I respected Brown, but I thought I was more the complete football player. His offense was set up so he didn't have to block. To me, blocking was just as important. I was 252 pounds. I moved well. I ran hard. Even big men feared me."

(There were valid arguments by the AFL people that Cookie was a more rounded fullback than Brown, because of his blocking prowess. He didn't run as fast as Brown, nor with the same uncanny balance, but he moved well for a big man and not always on a straight line. The blocking separated him, however. Wahoo McDaniel, a linebacker, once exhibited a chewed left ear as evidence of Cookie's blocking. Wahoo said Cookie hit him so hard he cracked Wahoo's helmet and impaired his hearing.)

"I'm the type of person who if I'm a friend, I'm a friend all the way. There's no such thing as if I don't like you, I'll tolerate you. If I don't like you, the hell with you; I don't want to have anything to do with you. I don't want to talk to you. I might say hello. That's all. If I had been a nice guy, and not created any fuss, I'd probably be one of the best liked guys in organized sports. But I preferred to speak out, to be myself. . . ."

(On January 10, 1965, Cookie Gilchrist arrived in New Orleans to play in an AFL All-Star game. That night, with Abner Haynes and some other Negro players, he went out on the town. The colored cabbie said, "You boys look like football players. Now that Abner Haynes, he's really something." Cookie said, "Naw, he's terrible. That Cookie Gilchrist, he's really great." The cabbie mulled this a moment and nodded, "You're right. Why, if I had him in my cab, I'd let him ride around all night and not charge anything." Cookie said quickly, "You start driving, man." The next morning, at 10:30, he was

awakened and told that the black contingent was meeting to vote on pulling out of the All-Star game because of racial incidents the night before. The vote was a unanimous 21–0 for leaving. A mayor's committee tried to dissuade them in the early afternoon. By this time, Cookie was the black contingent's spokesman. The players stuck to their original decision. They left town, and the game was cancelled in New Orleans.)

"I came from nothing. I've got nothing to lose. If some day I lost my bid for recognition and reward, I can always go to work pushing a wheelbarrow. And I'd do that before I'd compromise with the power structure and lose my self-respect as a man."

(Money was always the big hangup in Cookie's life. He was a poor businessman as a kid in Canada and lost a lot of money in a couple of business ventures. He was always getting tied up in exotic schemes, like searching for oil wells in the frozen north or mining copper in Zambia. His reputation was distorted. He was not a carouser, only a mild swinger. But he worked up such a distrust for football management—though he milked them for advances on his salary and loans—that he always felt he was being cheated. And this was always at the root of his trouble with the front office of every team he played for.)

"I don't believe in violence on or off the field. But if I felt a guy did something on the field he should be chastised for, I felt I should be the guy who chastised him. I was a policeman on football fields for a long time."

(His troubles as a football player in the States started in Buffalo one winter night when Cookie, after visiting the house of a University of Buffalo professor, allegedly ran a stop light. Cookie didn't like the way the cops interrogated him. They didn't like the way Cookie answered. One word led to another and led Cookie to the precinct station, where one shove led to another and Cookie was booked for disorderly conduct. The incident gave him a label as hard to handle.)

"There comes a time in every man's life when he must sacrifice fame and glory for a productive role in the business and social community."

In the early months of 1968, rather than add one more stop to his football itinerary by joining the newly organized Cincinnati Bengals, who had plucked him from Denver in the expansion draft, also dubious about a surgically repaired knee, Cookie sallied forth to "a productive role in the business and social community" of Denver. He passed out cards for a new business venture, C. G. (for Cookie Gilchrist) Mayd Services, Ltd.

Pro football was the poorer for his loss as a player and as a personality. You didn't have to like Cookie, although anybody who ever got behind the publicity barricade did, because he was always a most congenial social creature, invariably smiling, most amiable to kids, at home in any surroundings. You had to recognize his individuality. For fourteen tempestuous seasons he kept pro football lively wherever he happened to be on the North American continent.

Cookie was a fine performer—no one ever denied him those credentials. In the scrabbling struggle of the AFL for survival, in the early years, he had a role much more significant than that of merely carrying a ball. He was the young league's first colorful star on a national scale, before it started doling out $400,000 for young quarterbacks. When Cookie quit a team or wrote a letter to management or spoke his mind or simply sulked, it was news all over.

There was a brightness to the personality of Cookie Gilchrist, football player, that transcended his troubles with the front office on the many teams with which he performed.

He was a man built for fables. When the Buffalo Bills, casting around to find an offensive spark after two greatly disappointing seasons, heard that Cookie had worn out the patience of the Toronto owners and was available, they dispatched Harvey Johnson, their super scout, to sign him. This was in July 1962. Harvey had been his coach when he was a kid at Kitchener. So persuading Cookie his future fortunes lay in Buffalo wasn't difficult. He owed the Toronto club $5,000, a debt the Bills would wipe out. Johnson was accompanied on his foray north of the border by Jack Horrigan, then a newspaperman, now a vice-president of the team. They drove up in a car with the official Buffalo Bills' seal. Intelligence directives had gone out to the natives warning them that Harvey was about to bag one of their prime football species.

"Here come the carpetbaggers," a mob around the Toronto football stadium shouted. "They're coming to steal Cookie."

"Roll up the window," Horrigan said to Johnson.

"Don't be ridiculous," said Harvey. "This is Canada. They won't bother us. I know. I live here."

The heavy thud of blows reverberating off metal intruded on their debate. The natives were giving vent to their irateness by pounding on the car. "Hey, Jack," said Harvey. "Roll up the window."

So Cookie came back to his native land. They held Cookie out of action in the first half of a game played the day he joined Buffalo. Cookie was getting jittery because he wanted to get a taste of action, defense, anything. Coach Lou Saban let him kick off opening the second half. Cookie followed his boot by roaring straight down the middle of the field, jamming against the nose of the protective wedge. He knocked the first man unconscious, trampled two others and hurled the runner down on the 12-yard line.

That was his introduction to the American Football League. Warmed up, he pounded through the other seven teams in the league for 1,096 yards during the regular schedule, scoring 13 touchdowns on the ground. He caught 24 passes, two of them for scores, booted 14 extra points and eight field goals. "I find myself getting moody," he complained, "because I'm not playing defense. That's where you get even. I would prefer to play both ways. I get a little bored sitting on the sidelines." The Buffalo Bills had their first winning season ever in 1962, and things kept getting better, on the field, as Cookie continued to stampede the opposition for a couple more years. He was the work-horse ball carrier of the AFL, carrying 232 times in '63, 230 times in '64. And finally the Bills were respectable title challengers.

But by this time, it was getting so you had trouble separating fact from fiction in the private and public life of Carlton Chester Gilchrist. One fall day in 1963, he sat down in an attempt to get the record straight on his exploits. This is the way it went:

Fable: That the Canadian teams let him escape to the United States because Cookie was over the hill, football-wise, an old man, not born May 25, 1935, as the record book listed.

Fact (these and subsequent ones supplied by Cookie): "Nobody picked me up for the waiver price of $350. I was blackballed because I wanted to be treated like a man, and they wanted to treat me like a kid. I was too far advanced in performance for Canadian football. My true age is what the book says. I haven't reached my peak."

For a big man, Cookie Gilchrist could really dig as he pounded toward the enemy lines.

Fable: That in Canada he used to drive a big, white limousine with the legend, "Lookie, Lookie, Lookie, Here Comes Cookie," blazoned on the sides.

Fact: "I had an electrical business and a sedan delivery with that sign on it for advertising purposes. Buffalo publicity turned the sedan delivery into a Cadillac. I told them, 'Now that you started this, why don't you give me a Cadillac? And you can put any sign on it that you want.'"

Fable: That Cookie almost drowned falling overboard from his new cabin cruiser and cracked, "Fellow who sold me the boat couldn't afford to let me drown. I only made the first payment."

Fact: "I bought a 17-foot outboard and paid cash for it. At my place on the lake, I had a dinghy with a little motor and used to stand in front to get it out of the water, steering with an oar. Fellow called me from the shore, the paddle slipped and I was spun out of the boat. I can swim enough to save my life."

Fable: That Cookie in Canada once showed up late for a game, was cussed by Coach Jim Trimble, slugged him, was fined and traded.

Fact: "I never had a fight with the coach. I won't say I got along with him. My electrical truck once broke down the morning of a game, and I had to hitch a ride to town, missed the team bus, rented a car and got to the stadium just before the kickoff. I was traded a year later."

The legends continued to build up while he was in Buffalo. One off-season, Coach Lou Saban heard that Cookie was dropping out of a helicopter into northern Canada lakes, prospecting for minerals. "Isn't that dangerous?" Saban asked him. "I heard you can't swim." Cookie shrugged, "That's one of my problems."

Then there was the trouble with the Buffalo cops, and one of them claimed Cookie belted him. "If I did," said Cookie, "he wouldn't be here to tell the story." And looking at him, people were inclined to believe Cookie.

He was one impressive hunk of man. In a game against the New York Jets, he stampeded through the line for a record 243 yards, still the all-time AFL record. He did it essentially on brute power. "I'm not shifty," Cookie confessed. "I can't sidestep. If I run over a guy, maybe he won't be there next time and I won't have to deviate. But I don't get any real joy out of trampling someone. Most teams take away the inside from me, so I go outside more than up the middle. I try to get one-on-one with cornerbacks who're smaller than I am and make them hit me from the side. Then I can slide off or spin away. I'm as big as most defensive linemen and bigger than the backs, and I'm fast. That's my advantage. But I try to use my power wisely."

In 1964, he powered the Bills to the American Football League championship. In the title game against the San Diego Chargers, a 20–7 victory for the Bills, Cookie blasted the enemy line for 122 yards in 16 carries and blocked superbly as a pass protector. But that was also the year Cookie defied Saban's authority by yanking himself out of the game against Boston because he felt he wasn't carrying the ball enough. "I believe I have to carry a ball 25 or more times for it to mean anything," he said. "I have to be so tired I can't stand. That's when I'm best." Saban preferred to judge for himself. "No man," said Lou, "is bigger than the team. He's suspended." Lou took him back after Cookie apologized, but following the title showing he unloaded him to Denver for another fullback named Billy Joe who has never come within 400 yards of equalling Cookie's best output. Remembered were the words of the Toronto Argos' general manager when he wished Cookie on Buffalo: "Put up with him for a season or two, and he'll be great. But then get rid of him before you have a nervous breakdown."

Cookie wasn't very receptive to resuming his career in Denver. He was receptive to the $20,000 advance on his salary tendered by the Broncos, but then he refused to report. After a few days of public haggling, Cookie changed his mind and came to the training camp in Golden, Colorado. "My desire to win," he said, "is greater than ever, regardless of the inadequacy of the coaching." And what did he think of the training setup in the little college town (Colorado School of Mines), 14 miles from Denver? "It's got some good hamburger stands." Cookie was also very busy exercising his mind. "I'm reading Karl Menninger [an eminent psychiatrist]," he announced. "Some people pay 50 bucks an hour for this kind of stuff. I get it all for $3.25."

But on the field, as usual, Cookie performed valiantly. He carried the ball 252 times for 954 yards behind a weak offensive line on a team that won four and lost 10. Cookie despaired and refused to report the next year after disagreeing with management on his true worth and how the Broncos should be run. He announced his retirement and showed unprecedented resolve in staying away from football. In October, the Broncos gave up and shipped him to Miami. The Dolphins provided him, per a contractual agreement, a new car with seat warmer, twilight signal for headlights, pushbutton trunk lid, rear window defroster, four-speaker stereo, six-way seats, automatic light dimmer, adjustable steering wheel, rear vents, tinted glass, air conditioner, cruise control, front disc brakes and a few other extras. Cookie wasn't altogether happy. "It rattles," he said. Cookie was badly out of shape, having ballooned up to 265 pounds, and he had the most undistinguished season of his career. Then unbelievably, and this adheres to the Gilchrist pattern, the Dolphins traded him back to Denver, which was now under the coaching reins of Lou Saban, who had gotten rid of him at Buffalo in the first place.

With new determination, at the age of 32, Cookie whipped himself into shape and participated in a couple of startling exhibition performances by the Broncos against National Football League opponents. The Broncos upset both Detroit and Minnesota in the first inter-league competition in history. But Cookie was limping by the time the season started and, unlike the old Cookie, he wasn't saying much about it. He played the opener against Boston and was obviously hobbled. The Broncos needed one yard on fourth down at the Patriot 3-yard line. Cookie boomed into the pile, but nothing happened. He was held to no gain and limped off the field.

He never played another down of football. The next week he submitted to knee surgery to repair bone deterioration. He had some thoughts of playing again in 1968, but when the Broncos exposed him in the expansion draft, and Cincinnati claimed him, Cookie figured that was it. He was in no mood to start all over again in a new town. He became a local entrepreneur and was even engaged by the Broncos for part-time scouting and public relations. The old fires had simmered down.

"If it meant carrying the water bucket to win a football game," he said in one final burst of pride, "that's what I would do. I always felt that I had the respect of all the other ballplayers."

458

CARLTON CHESTER "COOKIE" GILCHRIST

BORN: May 25, 1935   Height: 6'2½"   Weight: 252

No College

Hamilton, Canadian Football League, 1956–57
Saskatchewan, CFL, 1958
Toronto, CFL, 1959–61
Buffalo, AFL, 1962–64
Denver, 1965, 1967
Miami, 1966

			RUSHING				PASS RECEIVING				SCORING	
Year	G.	Att.	Yds.	Avg.	TD.	P.C.	Yds.	Avg.	TD.	TD.	Pts.
1956	14	130	832	6.4	5	..	..	..	..	..	..
1957	14	*204	958	4.7	8	8	82	10.3	0	9	54
1958	16	235	1254	5.3	5	15	144	9.6	0	5	30
1959	14	87	496	5.7	4	5	70	14.0	1	5	75
1960	14	88	662	7.5	6	25	346	13.8	2	8	115
1961	14	105	709	6.8	3	15	147	9.8	0	3	41
1962	14	214	*1096	5.1	*13	24	319	13.3	2	15	128
1963	14	*232	979	4.2	*12	24	211	8.8	2	14	84
1964	14	*230	*981	4.3	*6	30	345	11.5	0	6	36
1965	14	*252	954	3.8	6	18	154	8.6	1	7	42
1966	8	72	262	3.6	0	13	110	8.5	1	1	6
1967	1	10	21	2.1	0	1	—4	—4.0	0	0	0

AFL TOTALS

—6 YEARS	65	1010	4293	4.3	37	110	1135	10.3	6	43	296

* Led the league.

Clem Daniels

I KEPT CLEM DANIELS ON DESPITE THE
FACT I DIDN'T THINK HE REALLY KNEW
MUCH ABOUT THE GAME OF FOOTBALL
. . . BUT HE SHOWED ME DESPERATE
DESIRE.

—Al Davis, coach,
Oakland Raiders.

When Clem Daniels (36), leading rusher in AFL history, got past a tackler, he was seldom caught.

This was one of those stories that didn't make the newspapers. The Oakland Raiders, champions of the AFL, were getting ready to play the Green Bay Packers, NFL champs, in the second annual Super Bowl in January, 1968. Clemon Daniels, the halfback of the Oakland Raiders, wasn't going to play. He had his right leg in a cast from above the knee to below the ankle. He had broken the leg in the third quarter of the Raiders' ninth game of the season. So, according to the rules set down by the bosses of pro football, Clemon was only going to get 9/14ths of a share of the Super Bowl booty.

And yet the league statistics showed that Clemon, despite the fact he had missed five and a half games, was Oakland's leading rusher for the season just past. In fact, he was [and still is] the leading rusher in the history of the American Football League, the only man in the history of the young circuit to exceed 5,000 yards. To a sizeable segment of his teammates it didn't seem right that after seven years of valiant service, through despairing periods when the Raiders were a pitiful team and Clemon was one of the few authentic big leaguers, he shouldn't get a full cut. They threatened mutinously to strike the Super Bowl game. The run-out was averted only because, secretly, the AFL decided to make up the missing 5/14ths of Clemons' share.

It wasn't great compensation for a career that was played mostly in the shadows of obscurity. Clem didn't come into pro football as a name player. He was sidetracked and fired and suffered through the patience-rending experience of being a taxi-squadder before he found his niche as a very fine running back. For all around ability, there weren't many better, although not many people outside of Oakland were aware of Clemon. He had his greatest moment of emergence in 1963 when he was voted the AFL's outstanding player and received a gleaming silver convertible right off the assembly line as the tangible reward. It was difficult to overlook Clem that year (though the wire services managed by naming a couple of other players as their MVP choices). He set a new AFL ground-gaining record of 1,099 yards. He caught five touchdown passes. Football has had mercurial halfbacks, but few who weighed 220 pounds and ran niftily in a ground-hugging style. "I don't classify him as a dynamic runner," said Al Davis, then the Raiders' head coach and now the managing general partner, "but rather as a very strong, durable and punishing runner."

Because he wasn't dynamic, Clem always had a recognition problem. Take his origins in pro ball. He signed with the Dallas Texans as a free agent in 1960, the year the AFL was organized, after playing at little Prairie View A&M in his native Texas and coaching high school ball in Dallas. All through his school and college days, Clem was hampered by a string of injuries and a chronic case of hemorrhoids (finally cured by an operation). His experiences gave him compassion. As a coach, he remembered taking his team to the state playoffs, where his kids were matched with the defending champs who outweighed them 30 pounds at each position. After a 155-pound guard was stretched out by a 240-pound defensive tackle, Clem motioned one of his reserves into the game. "Wait, coach," the kid cautioned, "I saw his leg move. He isn't dead yet."

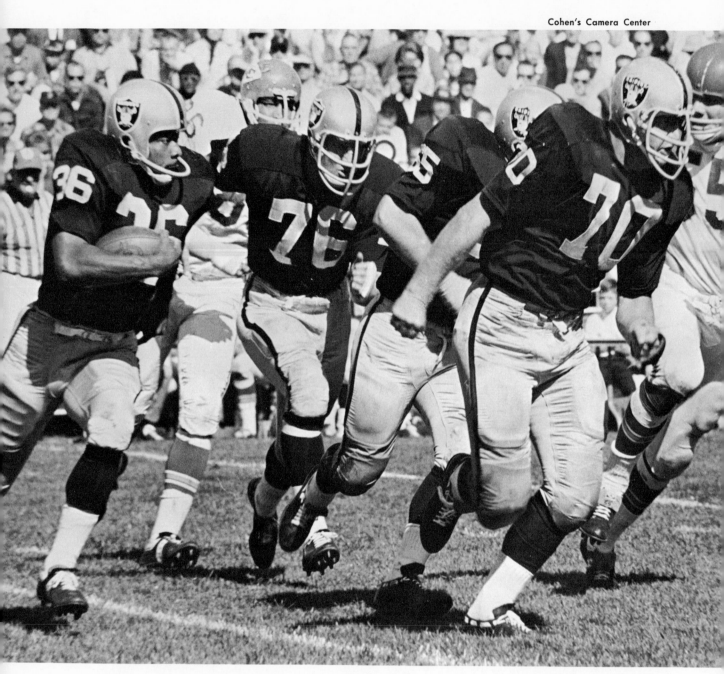

Clemon Daniels was a smart runner who used the protective curtain of such Oakland blockers as Jim Harvey (70) and Bob Svihus (76).

Well, when Clem joined the Texans ("for a handful of peanut shells") and saw the array of competing talent, he knew he was figuratively dead as a running back. He was up against Abner Haynes, Johnny Robinson, Jim Swink, Jack Spikes and Bo Dickinson. The Texans, forerunners of the Kansas City Chiefs, switched him to defensive back and Clem got a disconsolate view of the season's action from a seat on the bench. The Texans still didn't see any need for a 6'1", 220-pound back with a size 18 neck and a tapered waist, who ran like a sprinter, when they gathered again in 1961, and released him before the season started. Clem had damaged an ankle running back a kickoff and missed the exhibition campaign.

Nobody else in American football seemed interested, though Clem provided credentials which showed he could run the 100 in 9.8. Therefore, he responded to a phone call by Hamilton of the Canadian league. When he flew in, the team was on the verge of flying out for a couple of weeks and didn't plan to take Clem along. The coach told him to stick around until they got back. "Mister," said Clem, "I got to eat." Big shrug. And then a good twist of fate. The late Eddie Erdelatz, looking for anybody who could help the Oakland Raiders, located Clem in Hamilton and invited him to California. The morning Clem arrived in Oakland, Eddie was fired from his job, and the office secretary never even heard of Daniels. Neither had Erdelatz's successor, but he agreed to let Clem hang on as a member of the non-roster "taxi" squad.

The frustration gnawed at Clem so deeply that he even went to Coach Sammy Baugh when the New York Titans hit town and pleaded with him for a job. The Titans in those days were paid off a dining room table in Harry Wismer's Park Avenue apartment. A little backtracking into contextual history sharpens the floundering and humiliation of a man who still managed to believe in himself. The year 1961 doesn't seem so long ago, but in the AFL it was the dark ages. Of the 30 leading ground gainers in the league, only two are still active players—Billy Cannon and Johnny Robinson, college teammates at LSU—and neither has been a running back for years. Men were playing and starring who couldn't make the travelling squad of the Westchester Bulls. The threat of Daniels jumping over to the Titans finally prodded the Raiders into activating him. The Oakland team was nothing to brag about. It won two games out of 14. Clem started the last three, all losing efforts, and managed to look good. He averaged five yards a carry. He plugged through another season, this time as a regular performer, the fourth leading ground gainer in the AFL, with a 187-yard game against the hotshot Houston Oilers. And then came the surge of the Raiders to respectability. Al Davis, a young assistant coach at San Diego, was brought up to take over the Oakland organization.

He looked around for big league talent and saw a couple of offensive linemen, center Jim Otto and guard Wayne Hawkins. And then there was this halfback, Daniels, with the chest muscles chiseled from granite, and thick legs that zipped faster than a locomotive. He also had big hands with long fingers, the kind that looked like they could hold on to a football, and Davis, a former end tutor, believed in putting the ball in the air. That trio, and a lot of discards, was his nucleus for a refurbished offense. The Raiders astounded the AFL with a 10–4 record, and Daniels rushed to all kinds of new statistical heights, plus acclamation as the Player of the Year.

465

Besides his record-setting yardage on the ground, Clem showed tremendous talent as a receiving threat. In one two-game period, he hauled in five throws for 202 yards, an average of more than 40 yards per catch. "He's one of the quickest big men I've ever seen," said Coach Davis. "He's the finest receiving halfback in football. His great ability to catch the deep pass adds a scoring weapon which complements perfectly the threat of Art Powell at the flank."

The defensive terror of the AFL in those days was Ernie Ladd, 6'9" and 319 pounds, a tackle for the San Diego Chargers. Daniels, under a full head of confidence, slammed into Ladd during a game and smashed him five yards back. Ladd roared, "Come here, Home Boy!" (They were both from Texas.) Clem approached warily. "You're running the hell out of the ball, Home Boy," Ladd whispered to him.

The season would have been a triumphant processional for both Clem and the Raiders if there hadn't been a stretch in late September and early October when they lost four games in a row. Clem nursed a deep thigh bruise on the sidelines during this period. And there was some skepticism about Clem's willingness to perform.

"This is a very subtle, complicated, intelligent man," said Davis. "He needs careful handling. You don't jump him. You work to understand him." Clem came back against the New York Jets with a 200-yard game and the Raiders launched an eight-game winning streak that carried them within one game of the Western Division title.

Over the next four years, Clem proved he was no fluke. He didn't set any more rushing records because the Raiders improved as a team and brought in other backs to share the load (in his big '63 campaign, his rushing total of 1,099 yards more than doubled the output of all the other runners on the team, which had a rushing figure of 1,595 yards). Clem also thrived as a receiver, averaging 39 receptions a season, scoring seven touchdowns through the air in '65.

He also became a fixture in the Oakland community. In his early years, he was a substitute teacher in the school system, a job for which he was temperamentally suited. There is no abrasive flash to Clem Daniels, just a quiet, firm resolve to do his job as best he can. A thin mustache, a curious slash in an oval face which smiles easily, is the only ostentatious sign about him. He taught art and English, math and science, shop and physical education. "It was an education," he said. "You don't fool kids, you know. They read you like a book. You better level with them if you want the privilege of interesting their minds."

Eventually, he quit the teaching to become a business entrepreneur, opening his own liquor store in Oakland, branching into a real estate venture which even took him back to his home town of McKinney, Texas. He also re-evaluated his worth as a football player. In the summer of 1967, he was a serious holdout. "There isn't a back in all of pro football," said Clem, "who's been in the top four of rushing statistics for the last five seasons. If I'm No. 1 here, I expect to be treated like No. 1." He was back on the job when the season began. At the age of thirty, he was rolling along in peak style until a November tussle with the Miami Dolphins.

Clem was pass blocking in the third quarter. Just in front of him, tackle Bob Svihus was trying to hold off a charging Dolphin. Svihus fell back and landed on Clem's leg. The fibula bone was broken five inches above the ankle, and there were ligaments torn in the ankle. Clem was through for the year.

And, as it eventually turned out, he was through with the Raiders forever. He missed the thrill of participating in the first Raiders' championship victory. He missed the Super Bowl, too, though he collected his full share after the walkout threats by his teammates. When he reported to the Raiders' training camp in the summer of 1968, he had a career total of 5,101 yards rushing and 3,291 yards receiving (second only to Abner Haynes, who had seen some action as a flanker). At thirty-one, Clem thought he was 100 percent again and had all of his speed. He was ready to reclaim his starting job from Pete Banaszek, a good fill-in. But the Raider brass, with a half dozen other backs available, all of them younger, weren't convinced. They wanted Clem to retire gracefully. Clem, feeling he had some football left, refused. Regretfully, they put him on waivers September 10, and not a team in the AFL claimed him (his high salary could have been a factor). The Raiders released him. "Professional football is a cold-hearted business," said Clem realistically.

In a move motivated by public relations as much as expediency, the rival, cross-bay San Francisco 49ers of the NFL signed the veteran halfback, and everyone gave them a plus for sentimentality. It doesn't win football games, however, and the 49ers treated him as a stand-in for their other star performers. Ken Willard and Gary Lewis, a couple of "bull" types, were the regulars, with Willard finishing the '68 campaign as the second leading rusher in the NFL, only thirty-three yards shy of membership in the 1,000 Yard Club. Bill Tucker, a 232-pound sophomore, was on first call. Clem stuck out the schedule but carried the ball only twelve times for thirty-seven yards, and it was clear his future was in the past.

CLEM DANIELS' FAVORITE PLAY:

"In the Oakland Raider system, this play is called '16 Bob Trey O.' There are three important blocks necessary to make it work. First, the fullback must block the end man [linebacker] on the line of scrimmage. Second, the tight end must block down on the defensive end—the better his block, the more pressure is put on the linebacker. Third, it's good to have a big fast guard who can pull and go through the hole to lead the play. If the linebacker closes down at the point of attack, an experienced guard will step outside and lend more flexibility to the play, giving the back a chance to bust for long yardage.

"We used it very successfully several years against Houston because we felt their strong safety was not an exceptionally good tackler. If someone commits too early or is caught out of position, it can break for a long gainer. I remember particularly a game against New York in 1966 when I accounted for more than 100 yards, most of them on this play. Guards Wayne Hawkins and Jim Harvey did excellent jobs of blocking. And, of course, Hewritt Dixon at fullback always does an outstanding job."

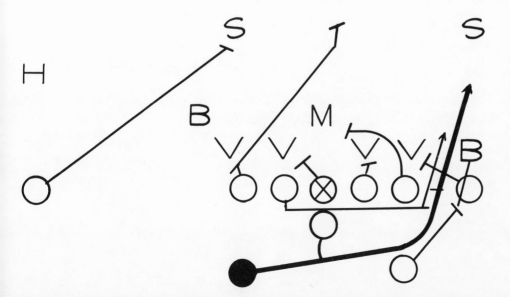

CLEMON DANIELS

BORN: July 9, 1937   Height: 6'1"   Weight: 220
Prairie View A&M College

Dallas Texans, 1960
Oakland, 1961–67
San Francisco, 1968

| Year | G. | RUSHING | | | | PASS RECEIVING | | | | SCORING | |
		Att.	Yds.	Avg.	TD.	P.C.	Yds.	Avg.	TD.	TD.	Pts.
1960	14	1	—2	—2.0	0		(None)			0	0
1961	8	31	154	5.0	2	13	150	11.5	0	2	12
1962	14	161	766	4.8	7	24	318	13.3	1	8	48
1963	14	215	*1099	5.1	3	30	685	22.8	5	8	48
1964	14	173	824	4.8	2	42	696	16.6	6	8	48
1965	14	219	884	4.0	5	36	568	15.8	7	12	72
1966	14	204	801	3.9	7	40	652	16.3	3	10	60
1967	9	130	575	4.4	4	16	222	13.9	2	6	36
1968	14	12	37	3.1	0	2	23	11.5	0	0	0

AFL TOTALS
—8 YEARS	101	1134	5101	4.5	30	201	3129	16.4	24	54	324

NFL TOTALS
—1 YEAR	14	12	37	3.1	0	2	23	11.5	0	0	0

PRO TOTALS
—9 YEARS	115	1144	5138	4.5	30	203	3314	16.3	24	54	324

* Led AFL.

Lincoln and Lowe

YOU KNOW, EVERYBODY WANTS TO PLAY
HALFBACK ON THIS TEAM, AND I THINK
IT'S MY JOB.
—*Paul Lowe, halfback,*
San Diego Chargers.

Lowe and behold, Paul Lowe of the San Diego Chargers also made a home for himself in the AFL after being cast off by the 49ers.

They didn't particularly like each other as people. They didn't even complement each other particularly as football players. And because of injury, truculence, and even a touch of individual petulance, they only really played together fulltime for a couple of years. But in the early years of the American Football League, Keith Lincoln and Paul Lowe of the San Diego Chargers were the best that young circuit had to offer as a backfield tandem.

The AFL couldn't claim parity as a league, but its partisans could hold their own in any barroom argument about the best set of running backs in pro ball by pointing to Lincoln and Lowe.

They were each brilliant runners, positive personalities, and mercurial performers. They were temperamental, disdainful of routine, possibly a bit arrogant but always delightful to watch in action. They didn't jibe completely because essentially both were equipped to do the same job—play halfback with all the breakaway excitement that position implies. At their best, they weighed around 200 pounds. Lincoln was a shade taller at 6'1". Lowe was faster. Lincoln was more versatile. Both were effective and frequently spectacular. But Lowe had first call at the halfback position—he was there a year earlier as a Charger original in 1960—and Lincoln, because he was so good at so many things, was the more adaptable for fullback, a position he never really liked but played for the major part of his pro career.

The years they thrived as a combination were 1963 and '64, when the Chargers started a three-year domination of the Western Division of the AFL, also winning the league championship in '63. Though Keith and Paul also had brilliant moments on their own, when one or the other was hurt, they'll be chiefly remembered for the luster of those big seasons because their double threat made defensing the Chargers a strategist's nightmare.

There were several points of similarity in their backgrounds. Both were schoolboy stars in southern California who emigrated to the Pacific Northwest to play college football, Lowe at Oregon State, Lincoln at Washington State.

But Paul Lowe, the older of the two, was already a professional football reject when the AFL started operations in 1960. He was a twenty-four-year-old rookie. The year before, he had skipped his senior season in college to try out with the San Francisco 49ers and in his first exhibition game he returned the opening kickoff 105 yards for a touchdown. He also carried three times as a wingback with sensational results. But the 49ers couldn't see much future for a runner who weighed only 170 pounds at the time, and released him. Paul went back to his native Los Angeles and worked for Barron Hilton in the Carte Blanche offices as a handyman. Hilton was also busy putting together the first edition of the Chargers in Los Angeles. Al Davis, a young assistant coach, was detailed to sign Lowe, who had several offers in the new league. Al got his signature one midnight for a $750 bonus. "I remembered," said Davis, "that no matter where he played, he always got in the end zone."

The development of Keith Lincoln, a pure-bred AFL product, was a symptom of the rising stature of the young league. The versatile San Diego back belonged on any football field.

True to form, Lowe grabbed the opening kickoff of the first game the Chargers ever played, an exhibition against the New York Titans in the Los Angeles Coliseum, and returned it 105 yards for a touchdown. By this time, he was also embarked on a weight-lifting program which had added twenty-five pounds without reducing his speed. But he was still inexperienced and started on the bench. He stayed there for five games while the Chargers faltered to three losses. After a 35–0 shutout by Boston, Coach Sid Gillman put him in at halfback against Denver, and the Chargers took off. So did Lowe. He ended his rookie year as an all-league choice, the second leading rusher in the AFL, with the best average per carry (6.3 yards), and the sparkplug of the drive to the Western Division title in which the Chargers won eight of their last nine games.

He said, meaningfully, "I love pro football because it is a sport, and sport is my hobby. I also look at pro football as a job, and I play it that way." Paul and Sophia Lowe had three little youngsters and were to have two more before he quit playing football.

After another fine season in 1961, when the Chargers were moved to San Diego, Lowe took an independent turn. By this time, the established National Football League was waking up to the fact that the AFL meant business in its determination to share the pro football market and was siphoning off a good portion of the upcoming collegiate talent. In '61, for instance, the Chargers' rookie crop yielded Lincoln, Ernie Ladd and Earl Faison, specimens who could help any team in football. There was little raiding across the borders of either league for established talent—until one morning in May came the disclosure that Paul Lowe had signed a contract to play for the Detroit Lions in 1963, after playing out the option on his contract in '62.

The Chargers reacted indignantly to Lowe's planned defection (Detroit's motive was clear—it had lost its top draft pick, John Hadl, to the Chargers, and the Lions' players had hung their club president, Edwin Anderson, in effigy).

"When we picked him up," Coach Sid Gillman said, bitterly, "Lowe was having trouble buying milk for his kids. I've never heard of such a thing in all my years in football. It's not only unethical and illegal but an invitation to anarchy. It could have terrible consequences for both leagues." (It had such "terrible consequences" a few years later when Pete Gogolak, a Buffalo placekicker, jumped to the New York Giants, that both leagues hastily negotiated a peace and effected a merger which would take effect in 1970.)

The Chargers eventually signed Paul to a new contract which voided his deal with Detroit, but the 1962 season turned out to be a complete bust. In training camp, Gillman had him running in drills with the kickoff coverage team, demeaning duty for a star. Paul slid on a patch of concrete and broke his wrist, missing the entire campaign.

That gave Lincoln his chance to emerge as an offensive star for the first time. Keith had joined the club the year before as a second round draft choice after establishing himself as one of the most versatile players in college football, a Frank Gifford type who could do everything. He had gone to Washington State as a quarterback. "After my freshman year," he said, "I broke my collarbone in a horseplay wrestling match with a buddy in my college fraternity house. He fell on me—and the shoulder went. The coach told me I could 'red-shirt' [stay out a year] as a quarterback or come out for the team as a running back. I've always been for playing—not watching." He became a running back.

Before he joined the Chargers, he played for the College All-Stars in the 1961 game against the Philadelphia Eagles. Otto Graham, the Stars' coach, said Lincoln wasn't cut out for offense and used him on defense as the strong safety. When Keith reported to the Chargers, he stayed on defense most of the time because the club had a good supply of running backs, led by Lowe. Keith had a few sporadic shots at carrying the ball and then got hurt. But with Lowe out of the picture in 1962, he stepped right in as a running star. Against Oakland, on September 30, he gained 168 yards. His 86-yard burst for a touchdown was the longest of the year in the AFL. But in mid-season, Lincoln joined Lowe on the sidelines with an injury, and the Chargers collapsed.

The two men returned in 1963 to compete for the left halfback job. "It's good for both of us," said Lincoln. "Keeps us on our toes in the game." Yet Sid Gillman was no dummy. If they were both good, and there was no fullback on the squad who measured up to either as a talent, why not play them in the same backfield? Lincoln, a more powerful runner at 205 pounds, was the fullback in this combination. The Chargers had a romp. From a 4–10 record in '62, they went to a division-winning 11–3. With Lincoln blocking, Lowe rushed past the 1,000 yard barrier. Keith himself picked up 826 yards, his career high, and his average gain of 6.4 was the best in the league and the best in AFL history. Lincoln was voted to the official All-AFL team in his first year as a fullback. Lowe made the second team. The Chargers had a season rushing average of 5.6 yards per ground play which remains the best in league history. They completed the regular schedule with a flourish by rolling up 58 points against Denver.

Then they met the Boston Patriots in the title playoff. This was Lincoln's show. On the first play from scrimmage, he caught a 12-yard pass from Tobin Rote. On the next play, he burst through middle of the line for 56 yards. A few minutes later he swept end for 67 yards and a touchdown. Lowe broke the routine momentarily by zig-zagging 58 yards to a score, the Chargers' third of the opening quarter. Lincoln dominated the rest of the action. Altogether, he ran for 206 yards, caught passes for 123, and even threw once for 20 to account for a grand total of 349 yards in the course of the game, the best one-man showing in pro championship history. The Chargers won, 51–10. Lincoln polled 38 out of 39 votes as the game's outstanding player. One writer turned in a ballot for the first three choices that read: "Lincoln, Washington and Jefferson."

In the AFL All-Star games which followed a couple of weeks later, Keith ran 64 yards from scrimmage, gained 121 yards in all and was again voted the outstanding player on the field. He was considered the AFL's new Super Star. "The closest comparison I can make for him is Frank Gifford," said Gillman, "and when I compare him to Frank, I'm comparing him to one of the great ones of all time." He matched Gifford in handsome good looks, too, but the young AFL wasn't graduating players to the world of heavy payoffs in endorsements and other merchandising. Sonny Werblin, putting the New York Jets together, offered Barron Hilton $100,000 cash for Lincoln, whom he could sell as a star in New York. "If Lincoln goes," Coach Gillman reportedly told his boss, "I go, too." Football was Keith's only bag, and he had some complaints to register. He

474

played the title game against Boston at 196 pounds and he said afterward, "I'm too darn small for a fullback. They knocked hell out of me on every play."

Gillman disagreed: "He's the perfect fullback. He has the speed to go outside, and he has the power to break tackles, which is the basic ingredient of an inside runner if the hole isn't big enough. He also has a tremendously quick start."

Weeb Ewbank of the Jets, with vast experience in the NFL, called the team of Lincoln and Lowe "the best two running backs on any one team in professional football." So much for barroom arguments. The entente continued strong through 1964 as the Chargers' domination of the West continued. Lincoln was again selected to the all-league team. Lowe's production fell off because of a torn thigh muscle, but he added place-kicking to his other accomplishments to fill an injury void. On one play the day after Christmas, 1964, it all turned into reverse gear for him.

The Chargers met the Buffalo Bills for the AFL championship. They scored first and were moving into position for another. Lincoln had been brilliant, reeling off 47 yards in three carries. He flared out for a pass from Rote, jumped to catch it, and at that instant linebacker Mike Stratton drove a shoulder into Keith's rib cage. Lincoln suffered a rib fracture and was lost for the game as the Bills rallied to upset San Diego.

The injury was portentous, the end of Lincoln-Lowe as the devastating combo of the AFL. Lincoln, who had always complained he wasn't big enough to take the gaff of a fullback's chores, finally got Gillman to take him seriously. When he wasn't hampered by muscle pulls, he had Gillman down on him for "blocking deficiencies." Midway through the next year, at a period when he was perfectly healthy, Sid even benched him, and Keith, not the bashful type, suggested that maybe it was time he played for some team other than San Diego. After another mediocre season in 1966, partly because of the chronic injury factor and partly because Gillman apparently had lost confidence in him, Keith was finally peddled to the Buffalo Bills.

Meanwhile, Lowe, who had pouted in the shadow of Lincoln's glamor-boy publicity, was revitalized and became the Super Charger again to take up the slack, especially in 1965. He set an AFL rushing record of 1,121 yards and was named the AFL Player of the Year. His weight had increased to 210 pounds, the better to hit people with. There had been a myth around the league that if a team gave Lowe a good shot the first time he carried the ball, he'd lose his zest for contact the rest of the afternoon. The myth vanished, and Paul got a substantial three-year contract at a reported $40,000 annually, a long way from the $7,500 salary he had played for in 1960. He was turned out as a cool cat in suedes and pastels with black horned-rim glasses for an astigmatism. That was also a long way from his beginnings as a rag-tag street kid in Los Angeles, where he first revealed his competitive instinct.

"As a kid," he once reminisced, "I was a Ram fan. They gave our playground tickets for the games, but there weren't enough to go around. So we chose up sides and the winners got the tickets. Those games were rugged. I've never played any harder than I played then. But I never missed a Ram game."

Lowe without Lincoln was an act that played San Diego only one year, however. He stayed through 1967, but it was a waste, except for the salary. Gillman dredged up a sawed-off 5′ 9″ rookie halfback named Dickie Post who got his chance when Lowe was limping with a leg injury. The rookie kept his job after Paul recovered. In mid-season, he was fined $1,000 and suspended for showing up late at a team meeting. His relations with Gillman, always touchy, deteriorated. Gillman challenged him as a bad influence on the team. Lowe ended the season squatting on his helmet near the Charger bench, peering detachedly through smoked glasses at the field action. He tried to come back in 1968 but was released after carrying the ball once for eight yards. The Kansas City Chiefs picked him up, and he carried the ball one more time. He lost 9 yards. The season's total showed Paul with two carries for minus one yard and left him 38 yards short of 5,000 for his career, a frustrating finality.

His old partner, Lincoln, experienced a revival in his Buffalo transplant. He found himself as a regular again, at fullback, and became the Bills' leading ground gainer. "I'd rather be a fullback," he said philosophically, "than sit on the bench. Not playing bothers me even more than trying to block those big defensive linemen." He gained 601 yards, No. 6 among AFL rushers. But the string was running out for a man whose body wasn't designed for his reckless style of running. The Bills let him go halfway through the '68 season, when all they had on hand were a bunch of rookie backs. Keith, like a homing pigeon, returned to San Diego. The Chargers used him a couple of times on kickoffs. On the second, he was hit by two players and didn't get up. With pain etched on his face, he pounded his helmet on the ground. His left leg was broken. And that wasn't too good a way for his career to end either.

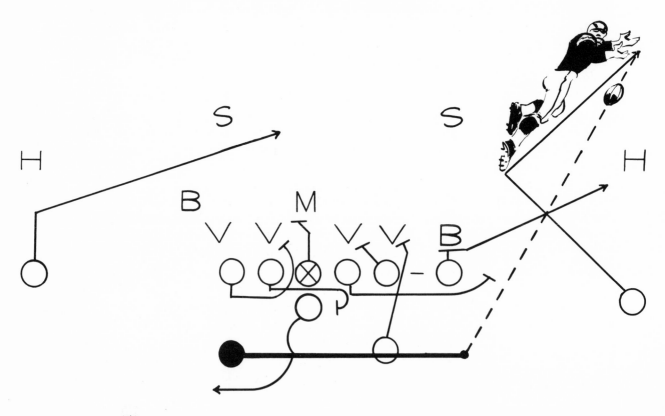

KEITH LINCOLN'S FAVORITE PLAY:

"A run-pass option type of play has been my favorite. In San Diego terminology, it's a '28 Bill Y Odd.' The halfback must fly to the sidelines, taking some depth after the handoff. He puts the ball away to give the play an honest sweep look. Then he turns towards the line for more accurate throwing. He looks for the deep receiver first, the flanker (or Z man). Then the tight end slanting towards the sideline (the Y man). If he decides not to throw, he yells 'fire' or some other oral signal to the blockers so they can help him downfield.

"I consider it a running play because 75 percent of the time, I did keep the ball. It causes many problems for the defense, which is forced to hold off to determine whether it's a run or a pass. The defense can't be sure it's a sweep, although it starts like one, because the guards hold up.

"My personal highlight in using it was in the 1963 championship game against the Boston Patriots, which the Chargers won, 51–10. I gained 206 yards in 13 carries and completed one pass for 20 on this play."

KEITH PAYSON LINCOLN

BORN: May 8, 1939   Height: 6'1"   Weight: 216
Washington State University

San Diego, 1961–66
Buffalo, 1967–68
San Diego, 1968

Year	G.	RUSHING Att.	Yds.	Avg.	TD.	PASS RECEIVING P.C.	Yds.	Avg.	TD.	SCORING TD.	Pts.
1961	14	41	150	3.7	0	12	208	17.3	2	3	18
1962	14	117	574	4.9	2	16	214	12.9	1	4	24
1963	14	128	826	*6.5	5	24	325	13.5	3	8	48
1964	14	155	632	4.1	4	34	302	8.9	2	6	67
1965	10	74	302	4.1	3	23	376	16.3	4	7	42
1966	14	58	214	3.7	1	14	264	18.9	2	3	18
1967	14	159	601	3.8	4	41	558	13.6	5	9	54
1968	10	26	84	3.2	0	1	3	3.0	0	0	0

PRO TOTALS
—8 YEARS

	G.	Att.	Yds.	Avg.	TD.	P.C.	Yds.	Avg.	TD.	TD.	Pts.
	104	758	3383	4.5	19	165	2250	13.6	19	40	271

* Led AFL.

PAUL EDWARD LOWE

BORN: Sept. 27, 1936   Height: 6'0''   Weight: 205
Oregon State University

Los Angeles Chargers, 1960
San Diego, 1961–67
Kansas City, 1968

Year	G.	Att.	RUSHING Yds.	Avg.	TD.	P.C.	PASS RECEIVING Yds.	Avg.	TD.	SCORING TD.	Pts.
1960	14	136	855	*6.3	8	23	377	16.4	2	10	60
1961	14	175	767	4.4	*9	17	103	6.1	0	9	54
1962				(Missed Entire Season Because of Injury)							
1963	14	177	1010	5.7	8	26	191	7.3	2	10	60
1964	14	130	496	3.8	3	14	182	13.0	2	5	30
1965	14	222	*1121	*5.1	*7	17	126	7.4	1	8	48
1966	14	146	643	4.4	3	12	41	3.4	0	3	18
1967	7	28	71	2.5	1	2	25	12.5	0	1	6
1968	3	2	—1	—0.5	0	0	0	0.0	0	0	0

PRO TOTALS
—8 YEARS   94   1016   4962   4.9   39   111   1045   9.4   7   46   276
* Led AFL.

Abner Haynes

IT DOESN'T LOOK AS IF I'LL EVER GET
IN A SUPER BOWL, AND I FEEL GOD SOME
KIND OF WAY SHOULD FIX IT AND TAKE
EVERY GUY WHO FIRST SAID, "I GO WITH
THESE DREAMERS," AND LET HIM BE IN
ONE.

—*Abner Hayes, halfback,*
1967.

Rich Clarkson   Topeka *Capital-Journal*

The first genuine hero grown by the AFL was Abner Haynes of the Dallas Texans, but his career slowed abruptly when they became the Kansas City Chiefs. The Denver Broncos have latched onto him here.

The rosters of the American Football League in 1960, the dawning of a new phase of the pro game, showed everything from thirty-year-old rookies to thirty-six-year-old hockey players. They had a 5'6", 162-pound halfback who played regular, and a 6'9", 300-pound tackle who couldn't make the team. They pulled in guys who hadn't played in a half dozen years, and they had some who had never played. And it showed.

Occasionally, there was a nugget like Abner Haynes, who was born in Denton, Texas, went to school in Dallas, then returned to Denton to play college football for North Texas State. He was the all-time greatest halfback in the history of North Texas State when the newly formed Dallas Texans, owned by Lamar Hunt, sought to sign him. The Pittsburgh Steelers also bid for his contract. They sent Mr. Buddy Parker, their coach, a native Texan, to visit the Haynes family. Buddy, a direct sort of man, "sort of scared" the Rev. F. L. Haynes, Abner's father. Winnipeg of the Canadian league offered young Abner more money than anybody. But the thought of playing in Dallas before the home folk was the most persuasive factor. Abner also knew that Lamar Hunt was unlikely to run out of money, and this transcended any pioneering feeling he might have had about starting with a new league.

"Everybody," he mused, "would ask me why I didn't go NFL. They said I'd have a lot more prestige. And I'd say that I wanted to play right away, which I could do in the AFL, and that I couldn't put prestige on my dinner table and eat it."

So Abner became the first pure-bred folk hero developed exclusively by the AFL. It can be argued that Billy Cannon with the Houston Oilers was also an AFL exclusive in that first year of operation, but Billy came with full-blown credentials as a unanimous All-American, the most famous college player in the country, the winner of the Heisman Award, so he wasn't exactly new to the public consciousness. Abner was. The fame of North Texas State might spread as far as Paris (Texas, that is) to the east and Muleshoe (Texas, of course) to the west, but Abner Haynes was not a household name. The American Football League made him one, or you could turn that phrase around because Abner did as much for the AFL in its infancy to stabilize it as a football entity.

In the early years, he was its best and most exciting player. Abner was oddly fitted for his assignment since he wasn't overpowering in size (6'0" and 185) nor particularly speedy. He had instinct. His runs seemed to materialize from nowhere. Abner would be drifting around behind the line of scrimmage, surrounded by clutching players, and suddenly the players would all be in a group and Abner would be off someplace else loping with that curious, long-gaited stride that resembled jerky stop-action. After watching Abner break loose on one of his patented runs, Blackie Sherrod of the Dallas *Times-Herald* noted, "He stopped, gave a guy change for a quarter, picked up a paper at the corner, dealt a hand of stud and ambled off to happy land."

The results were in the ledger. He led the AFL in rushing, was Rookie of the Year and Player of the Year in an across-the-board payoff. He had a little wisp of a goatee, a forehead that was always creased and a blasé attitude that helped him over the rough spots in a new situation. "Just a little wild kid," he said, "and I felt I could run by anybody." In that confidence, he reflected the chest-popping brashness of the young league which held up Abner as an example of the type of playing it could produce, then and in the future. The young AFL was emphatically a passing league, and in his rookie year Abner also caught 55 passes, led in punt returns and took his place under the goal posts for kickoffs.

For as long as he was in Dallas, Abner was comfortable and secure in his ability to evade tacklers. In their third season, the Texans uprooted the Chargers as champions of the Western Division and met the Oilers for the AFL crown. Abner was, as usual, the kingpin, gaining 1,049 yards and setting the existing league record for touchdowns, 13 by land and six by air.

The championship playoff was a storied encounter with suspense, big plays and a freak "boner" that almost put Abner alongside Fred Merkle and Roy "Wrong Way" Riegels as one of the great sports "goats" of all time. It was also the longest game in professional history. In a strategy switch, because of an injury to split end Chris Burford, Coach Hank Stram of the Texans moved Abner from running back to flanker, and he scored the first touchdown of the game on a 28-yard pass from quarterback Lenny Dawson. The Texans built a 17–0 lead with Abner scoring again late in the second quarter on a two-yard dive. He was returned to his regular post at halfback and kept there as Dallas tried to conserve its lead through the second half. But the Oilers rallied for 14 points to tie the game and produce an overtime. Now the team captains gathered at midfield for the coin toss before the start of the fifth quarter. The winner had the option of receiving or choosing which goal it would defend, an important factor because of the wind and the fact that a field goal would end the game. Abner was the Dallas delegate. In the excitement, he confused the instructions from Stram. The Texans won the toss, and Abner indicated they elected to kick, but neglected to indicate the direction. So the Oilers chose to receive, with the wind behind their backs and a tremendous field goal kicker in George Blanda.

Fortunately for Abner, the Dallas defense held in this crucial situation, and the fifth quarter was scoreless. In the sixth, the Texans sustained a drive and kicked a 25-yard field goal to win their first and last championship in Dallas. The nationally telecast game, which was officially played in 77 minutes and 54 seconds, was a promotional thrust for the league.

A championship team hadn't produced much support, however, in Dallas, where it competed directly with the Cowboys of the NFL. The Texans took their title and moved to Kansas City to become the Chiefs, and football was never the same for Abner. The Chiefs, in the off-season, drafted and signed Stone Johnson, a world class sprinter— largely, Abner felt, through his influence. In their final exhibition game, Johnson was fatally injured on a kickoff play, and Abner never fully recovered from the tragedy. "That was the worst thing I can ever remember happening during my football career,"

482

said Abner after he retired. "We were close friends. I'm not sure what effect it had on me, but it bothered me."

The dashing, insouciant verve which had characterized his play in Dallas wasn't evident in Kansas City. He brooded over the tragedy. His concentration was further disturbed by what he called a "personality conflict" with Stram. He played most of the season as a flanker, limiting his ball carrying to 99 tries, less than half his work of the previous year. There was no Haynes cult in Kansas City, like there had been in Dallas, to prod him with adulation. Willie Mays went through the same kind of transition when the baseball Giants moved from New York to San Francisco, but Willie stuck around long enough to win the Californians over, mainly because the caliber of his play never diminished in the change of cities. The Chiefs couldn't wait for Abner to bounce back. He improved some his second year, but in 1965 he was traded to Denver for Jim Fraser, a rather obscure linebacker. The market for Abner had gone way down. Or perhaps the league had started to catch up with and bypass some of its early stars. The little moves that compensated for lack of power and great speed no longer sufficed against the rabid young huskies crowding against him. At any rate, Abner Haynes was suddenly just another ball player fighting for a job.

Two more years in Denver were undistinguished except for the fact that he led the league in fumbles in 1966. Abner never did get over the habit of carrying the ball out where everybody could take a whack at it—college teammates had called him "Loaf of Bread." The Broncos unloaded him on Miami, an expansion team, before the 1967 season, and Abner, at the age of thirty, was making his last stand. Every once in a while, the old fire would flare into the open. When the Dolphins met the Broncos in their season opener, Abner carried the ball 12 times for 151 yards, scoring twice, and was picked as the AFL back of the week. "I got up for that one," he said. But the Dolphins were trying to build a team, and Abner wasn't building material. By December he was on waivers. "He's a real pro," said Coach George Wilson, "and you don't find many individuals of his caliber. But we've got to go with our young players and think of the future."

The New York Jets, jammed up by injuries, kept Abner around for a couple of weeks but never got around to using him. Abner saw the way it was going and gracefully retired after the season. He wasn't bitter. He'd seen the AFL come a long way in his eight years. In his brief stay in New York, he couldn't locate a place to live, so Joe Namath invited him to share his pad in the East 70's. That was a long way from Denton, Texas, too.

"Looking back," he said, "I think a running back loses a little every year. He loses something and learns something. My talent was finding the open spaces." And there were no more open spaces for him in this new football.

But Abner had explored a few in his time. In his career, he had gained more yards than anybody in the league—12,065 by running, catching passes, returning punts and kickoffs. No one else in AFL history has gained as much as 10,000 yards.

ABNER HAYNES

BORN: Sept. 19, 1937   Height: 6'0''   Weight: 198
North Texas State University

Dallas Texans, 1960–62
Kansas City, 1963–64
Denver, 1965–66
Miami, 1967
New York Jets, 1967

Year	G.	RUSHING Att.	Yds.	Avg.	TD.	PASS RECEIVING P.C.	Yds.	Avg.	TD.	SCORING TD.	Pts.
1960	14	*156	*875	5.6	*9	55	576	10.5	3	12	72
1961	14	179	841	4.7	*9	34	558	16.4	3	13	78
1962	14	221	1049	4.7	*13	39	573	14.7	6	*19	114
1963	14	99	352	3.6	4	33	470	14.2	2	6	36
1964	14	139	697	5.0	4	38	562	14.8	3	8	48
1965	14	41	166	4.1	3	26	216	8.3	2	6	36
1966	14	129	304	2.4	2	46	480	10.4	1	3	18
1967	14	72	346	4.8	2	16	100	6.3	0	2	12

PRO TOTALS
—8 YEARS

	G.	Att.	Yds.	Avg.	TD.	P.C.	Yds.	Avg.	TD.	TD.	Pts.
	112	1036	4630	4.5	46	287	3535	12.3	20	69	414

* Led AFL.

484

Other Pioneers

ONCE YOU PLAY RUNNING BACK, IT'S NOT
THE SAME GAME TO PLAY ANYWHERE
ELSE.

*—Billy Cannon, tight end,
Oakland Raiders.*

Billy Cannon was the most famous college player in the land when the Houston Oilers signed him in 1960. He ran them to a title but has since been converted to a tight end by Oakland.

Some mornings, when Billy Cannon got out of bed, it took him an hour and a half to straighten up so he could sit down for a cup of coffee. He slept on a board and applied heat, but there was no way Billy was going to get the stiffness out of his back.

And it wouldn't have mattered much if Billy had just stuck to studying dentistry, which he did every year from January to July at the University of Tennessee. But the rest of the time, Billy played football. And there it mattered, because Billy was the first showcase star of the American Football League before a ball was ever snapped from center.

He was the man who showed the country and Big Brother (the NFL) that the AFL meant business when eight millionaires banded together to form their own football playpen.

With television cameras focused on him, Billy signed a contract with Bud Adams, the ebullient owner of the Houston Oilers, under the goalposts of the Sugar Bowl on January 1, 1960, after Louisiana State had been blanked by Mississippi, 21–0. "Actually," said Billy later, "I had already signed a three-year personal services contract with Adams. The bit under the goalposts was just for show."

Actually, he had also signed a contract with Pete Rozelle in a Philadelphia hotel room even before that, to play football for the Los Angeles Rams of the NFL. The Rams' deal was $50,000 for three years. The Oilers' deal was $100,000 for three years, plus a $10,000 cash bonus, a new Cadillac for his father, who was a janitor at LSU, plus a Billy Cannon Oil Co. One guess as to which offer Billy preferred. But the Rams (Rozelle was then their general manager) took Billy to court, and the judge ruled against them on the grounds they had taken advantage of a 21-year-old country boy, after Billy had testified he wouldn't play for them even if awarded to Los Angeles.

It was an important decision for the AFL. Their teams now had the entire 1959 All-American backfield: Cannon, Charley Flowers of Ole Miss (Chargers), Richie Lucas of Penn State (Bills) and Ron Burton of Northwestern (Patriots). Cannon was the big boomer, though, the all-everything back who meant prestige.

For two years, Billy justified the money lavished on him by Adams as he led the Oilers to consecutive AFL championships. In the first title game, he clinched a 24–16 win by racing 88 yards for a touchdown with a pass from George Blanda. In the second title game, he caught a short jump pass from Blanda and bulldozed 35 yards to the end zone, the winning margin of a 10–3 game. He also led the league in rushing with 948 yards.

But after that, in the running annals of pro football, you can practically forget about William Abb Cannon. The detour to mediocrity started on a play so routine that Billy can't really figure why it happened.

"It was in my third season," he recounted. "We were playing San Diego, and I carried the ball into the line on a short yardage situation. There was no hole, so I tried to jump over the pile and was thrown back and fell flat. A linebacker playing the walk-

Charley Tolar was called the Human Bowling Ball when he rolled up more than 1,000 yards on the ground for the Houston Oilers.

away position came running over. He landed on me with both knees and tore the muscles loose in my back."

Result: one football player with a chronic bad back and a twisted career. Billy had been a 210-pound whirlwind who once was clocked in 9.4 for the 100. After the injury, he was never again an effective runner. "My lateral mobility was gone," he said. Only a man with a bad back knows the extent of his limitations. Cannon went through a miserable period in Houston when he was accused of being a malingerer. "It's a good thing I'm not a horse," he said. "They'd have shot me by now." The Oilers even put their No. 1 showcase on waivers. Ultimately, they unloaded him on the Oakland Raiders in 1964. The Raiders got some mileage out of him but discovered his greatest assets were his blocking ability and a good pair of receiving hands. They had an emergency at tight end, so one day Al Davis, the coach, moved him into the spot. "You sure you want me?" asked Billy. "I only weigh 205 now." Davis shrugged, "You're all I've got."

It saved his career. Billy built himself up to 228 pounds, became a solid blocker and a fine receiving threat with the vestiges of his old speed. In 1967, as the Raiders paraded to the championship and an appearance in the Super Bowl, Billy was named to the all-league team by the wire services. "As a tight end," said Johnny Robinson, a Kansas City safety and an old LSU teammate, "Billy's out of sight. He's a different dimension."

And what did Cannon have to say?

"The real fun of the game is running with the football. I'd still much rather be a back."

The Houston Oilers would have felt a lot worse about the de-fusing of Billy Cannon as their chief running threat if Charley Tolar hadn't picked that point to trigger one of the most unusual running mechanisms in pro football. There was nothing classical about Charley Tolar as a ball carrier. They called him "The Human Bowling Ball." Houston listed him at 5'7", but they were fudging by at least an inch. Charley didn't need a buildup or sympathy. He had the upper torso of a 250-pounder, he managed to squeeze almost 200 pounds into his 5 feet 6 inches, and his center of gravity was so low that tacklers had trouble pinning him down—if they could find him.

"Whenever I couldn't see where the ball went," said Tony Sardisco, a Boston linebacker, "I figured they gave it to Charley."

"He's so short," said E. J. Holub of the Chiefs, "that when he bends low you just can't get under him. When you tackle Tolar, you just butt helmets."

Tolar, who came out of Northwestern Louisiana State, had a trial with the Pittsburgh Steelers in 1959, but pro football wasn't mentally geared to the sight of a 5'6" fullback then. With the advent of AFL, a lot of psychological barriers were down. The Oilers took him on, and he played seven full seasons. When he finished, he was the fifth leading rusher in AFL history and is still in the top 10. In 1962, he took over for Cannon full time and gained 1,012 yards. Charley was also an effective receiver swinging out of the backfield (he caught 41 passes in '63), and despite his size he was a remarkably effective blocker on pass protection. He was called football's only "kneecap blocker."

Coach Pop Ivy explained, "Charley is exceptionally quick in his reactions and has great balance. Because of that balance, he's tough for a lineman or linebacker to bowl over when they charge."

He was fearless, too. Nothing could scare a man who spent his off seasons as an oil field fire fighter in such exotic places as Persia and Algeria, using dynamite as an everyday tool on his job.

Larry Garron got his first chance as a football player by answering an ad in a newspaper. Lou Saban had come to Western Illinois University to coach the football team. Larry was a student. To be able to attend school, he worked on three campus jobs to support his mother and eight younger brothers and sisters. He answered Saban's ad for football candidates and signed up. His first college game, he scored three touchdowns after spending the first half on the bench.

Saban moved on to coach the Boston Patriots in 1960 and took Garron along with him. In high school, he had started out as a 145-pound tackle. Now he was a 165-pound pro backfield aspirant. They tried him as a flanker, and he couldn't hold the ball. As a runner, he couldn't hang on to it. The other players needled him because he was a Saban project. He had bad tonsils and no confidence. The Patriots cut him early that first season. Larry got the tonsils out and embarked on a weight-lifting program in a Boston YMCA. The next year he was back to stay, filled out to 195 pounds. He played for the next eight years at that weight, and he played at fullback a good part of that time. In 1963, when the Patriots won their only Eastern Division crown, Larry was their leading ground gainer with 750 yards. Size was always a factor in his career, and occasionally the Patriots would think of making him a flanker. But when the Patriots needed the tough yards, and Larry was physically able to take his place in the lineup, he didn't flinch. And he didn't need Saban's protective wing to keep his job. When the Patriots played Buffalo for the division title, Saban had already moved over to the Bills, and Larry scored two touchdowns in Boston's 26–8 playoff victory.

Three stellar backs in the formative years of the AFL were Bill Mathis of the New York Titans (later Jets), Wray Carlton of Buffalo and Curtis McClinton of the Dallas Texans and Kansas City Chiefs. They all had good size. Mathis was the smallest at 6'1" and 220. McClinton was the biggest at 6'3" and 227. At one time, McClinton was rated by pro scouts as the best running prospect in the country, but he never quite fulfilled their promise. He was a good back. He joined the Texans their last year in Dallas and stepped right into a regular job at fullback. He sang pretty, made an impressive appearance, but he didn't have the extra burst of speed the great ones have. After an injury shelved him for the 1968 season, the Chiefs contemplated moving him to tight end. Mathis and Carlton who were AFL pioneers, also were held back by lack of speed. Mathis achieved a reputation as one of the finest blocking backs in football. Carlton, almost knocked out of the game by recurring muscle pulls in the middle years of his

490

An AFL original who suffered through the growing pains of the New York franchise was Bill Mathis (31). He lasted long enough to participate in a Super Bowl triumph.

career, lasted eight seasons with the Bills and was a steady contributor to their ground game after the turbulent Cookie Gilchrist departed from the Buffalo scene. All three, in their own plugging ways, ran up more than 3,000 yards apiece when the AFL was being ridiculed as a throwing league. Their kind was needed to give it stability. They all played on championship teams, and Mathis lasted long enough to participate in a Super Bowl triumph.

WILLIAM ABB "BILLY" CANNON

BORN: Aug. 2, 1937   Height: 6'1"   Weight: 220

Louisiana State University

Houston, 1960–63
Oakland, 1964–68

Year	G.	Att.	RUSHING Yds.	Avg.	TD.	P.C.	PASS RECEIVING Yds.	Avg.	TD.	SCORING TD.	Pts.
1960	14	152	644	4.2	1	15	187	12.5	5	7	42
1961	14	200	*948	4.7	6	43	586	13.6	9	15	90
1962	14	147	474	3.2	7	32	451	14.1	6	13	80
1963	6	13	45	3.5	0	5	39	7.8	0	0	0
1964	14	89	338	3.8	3	37	454	12.2	5	8	48
1965	10		(None)			7	127	18.1	0	0	0
1966	14		(None)			14	436	31.1	2	2	12
1967	14		(None)			32	629	19.7	10	10	60
1968	14		(None)			23	360	15.7	6	6	36
PRO TOTALS —9 YEARS	114	601	2449	4.1	17	208	3269	15.7	43	61	368

* Led AFL.

CHARLES GUY TOLAR

BORN: Sept. 5, 1937   Height: 5'6"   Weight: 195

Northwestern State (La.) College

Houston, 1960–66

Year	G.	Att.	RUSHING Yds.	Avg.	TD.	P.C.	PASS RECEIVING Yds.	Avg.	TD.	SCORING TD.	Pts.
1960	14	54	179	3.3	3	7	71	10.1	0	3	18
1961	14	157	577	3.7	4	24	219	9.1	1	5	30
1962	14	*244	1012	4.1	7	30	251	8.4	1	8	48
1963	14	194	659	3.4	3	41	275	6.7	0	3	18
1964	14	139	515	3.7	4	35	244	7.0	0	4	24
1965	11	73	230	3.2	0	25	138	5.5	0	0	0
1966	14	46	105	2.3	0	13	68	5.2	0	0	0

PRO TOTALS
—7 YEARS 95 907 3277 3.6 21 175 1266 7.2 2 23 138
* Led AFL.

LAWRENCE "LARRY" GARRON, JR.

BORN: May 23, 1937   Height: 6'0"   Weight: 195
Western Illinois University

Boston, 1960–68

Year	G.	Att.	Yds.	Avg.	TD.	P.C.	Yds.	Avg.	TD.	TD.	Pts.
		RUSHING					PASS RECEIVING				SCORING	
1960	3	8	27	3.4	0	1	8	8.0	0	0	0
1961	14	69	389	5.6	2	24	341	14.2	3	6	36
1962	11	67	392	5.8	2	18	236	13.1	3	6	36
1963	14	175	750	4.3	2	26	418	16.1	2	4	24
1964	14	183	585	3.2	2	40	350	8.8	7	9	54
1965	10	74	259	3.5	1	15	222	14.8	1	2	12
1966	14	101	319	3.2	4	30	416	13.9	5	9	54
1967	14	46	163	3.5	0	30	507	16.9	5	5	30
1968	14	36	97	2.7	1	1	4	4.0	0	1	6

PRO TOTALS
—9 YEARS 108 759 2981 3.9 14 185 2502 13.5 26 42 252

16. The Moderns

Gale Sayers

THE TRUE TEST OF GALE SAYERS WILL
BE WHEN HE HAS TO PLAY WHEN HURT.
THE TRULY GREAT ONES WILL GO ON
ANYTHING SHORT OF A BROKEN LEG. IT'S
ALL MENTAL. YOU HAVE TO SHUT OUT
ABSOLUTELY ANY FEAR OF PHYSICAL
INJURY YOU MIGHT HAVE. WHEN GALE
DOES THAT, I'LL KNOW HE'S GREAT. AND
I HAVE NO DOUBT THAT HE WILL.
—*Buddy Young, Office of
Commissioner,
Professional Football.*

When Gale Sayers was carried off the cleat-scarred turf of Wrigley Field, Chicago, in the chill of the late November afternoon, the feeling wasn't one of disaster. Maybe for the Bears, who still had hopes of winning a division championship, it was. But not for Gale. When a man is twenty-five years old, as Gale was on this date in 1968, the furies of competition override any thought of personal doom. Sure, his leg was a mess and any man close to football who has seen a knee dangling oddly like a tree branch ripped in a storm recognized immediately that this was an operative case. Yet it never occurred to Gale, the moments after it happened—when his knee collapsed from the impact of a shoulder tackle—that it would be anything more than a momentary interruption in his career.

"I was so mad that this should happen to me," he mused later, "that it never even crossed my mind I wouldn't come back, even when they were carrying me off the field. I was so disgusted, being laid up just when the team was starting to go good, I never felt the pain."

The operation was, technically, a success. Months later, except for a sliver of a scar where the doctors had stitched across the skin encasing his knee, there were no overt signs to reveal there had ever been an injury. Gale didn't limp. He was running and moving with all his old agility. And certainly there were no psychological scars if you talked to him. "I heard how other guys felt after knee operations," he said, "how shaky they were and all that, but I just don't feel that way. I'm ready to go."

A Sayers ready to go is just about the most glorious sight in football. Word descriptions don't portray the real thing. "He doesn't look any different than any other back coming at you," said George Donnelly, a San Francisco safety, "but when he gets there, he's gone." George Halas, the old pioneer of professional football, was always a conservative man when it came to dispensing Bears' money (since he was the controlling stockholder, as well as the coach), but he gambled $150,000 over a three-year period on the talents of Gale Sayers as a runner, after he was graduated from Kansas in 1964.

"He detects daylight," said Halas. "The average back, when he sees a hole, will try to bull his way through. But Gale, if the hole is even partly clogged, instinctively takes off in the opposite direction. And he does it so swiftly and surely that the defense is usually left frozen. He has wonderful speed. And he can lull you into thinking he is going all out, then he turns it up another notch and he's gone."

The Bears had their offensive destiny tied to his twisting feet. After four seasons of pro ball, he had already amassed the following honors: Rookie of the Year (1965), unanimous All-Pro (1965, '66, '67, '68), leading ground gainer in the NFL (1966). He set NFL records for most touchdowns in a season (22), for total offense in a season (2,440 yards), for most touchdowns on kickoff returns (6, on runs ranging from 90 to 103 yards). He had tied the pro record for most touchdowns in a single game (6). "He is the greatest football player I have ever seen," said Mike Ditka, a tight end with the Bears when Gale joined the club.

Vernon J. Biever Photo

A study in concentration is Gale Sayers of the Chicago Bears as he strides forward.

Over friend or foe, Gale Sayers steps with alacrity. That's Willie Wood (24) of the Green Bay he'll have to sidestep next.

Vernon J. Biever Photo

Perhaps the greatest tribute to Sayers was his selection to the all-pro squad in 1968 after he had hurt his knee in the ninth game of the season, missing five games completely. He had accomplished so much until then (856 yards rushing, a league-leading average of 6.2 yards per carry) that the players in the NFL just couldn't see picking anybody else as the running mate for Leroy Kelly of the Browns on the mythical team.

No back in the history of pro football, not even Jimmy Brown, has so awed his contemporaries. Coaches run and rerun reels of film on him and still can't believe him. How do you explain him? With Brown, you looked at his marvelous torso, gauged his remarkable speed, saw his balance and you knew what made him the greatest. With Gale, none of the qualities, except perhaps the speed, are so obvious. Gale himself can't explain it.

"I have no idea what I do," he said. "I hear people talk about dead leg, shake, change of pace and all that, but I do things without thinking about them."

For Gale Sayers, that was a big speech. Without a football under his arm, tucked in the crook of his elbow, Gale reverts. He's a mixture of introspection and shyness, and the words come hard. He is not by nature an articulate man. When the Chicago Bears travel, he takes along a tape recorder. Not for the usual reason, like digging the latest from Cannonball Adderley or Thelonius Monk. Gale uses it to practice enunciation and diction, to come out of his shell, to live up to his responsibilities as a public figure as well as player, to develop his personality so he can also function in his allied field as a strockbroker.

"Gale is very, very withdrawn," said his wife, Linda, herself outgoing. "And I think people like him have a tendency to be misunderstood. We were married more than a year before I understood him. Even his mother has told me she was never able to understand him. He was so quiet, I couldn't get him to talk on our first date. Most boy friends and girl friends spend hours on the phone, but with us it was at most a two or three minute conversation. He was terribly shy."

But put him in uniform—the deep navy blue jersey and helmet of the Bears, the number 40 in white, the silver pants with a sliver of orange and blue down the thigh—and Sayers takes on new dimension as a personality.

Gale looks almost lethargic until the ball is cradled in his arms. Then all parts begin to move in concert. He darts for daylight with a low, quick swoop into the line. If one avenue of traffic is blocked, he quickly changes gears and slides over to another. In the case of a football player, the pivotal point for changing direction is in the hips, and Gale can jiggle his with the fluid bounce of a go-go dancer, except that he's not rooted to one spot. With a quick burst of energy, he's past the main stream of traffic and reaching for distance. That's when another facet of his running technique takes over. With each step, the stride seems to lengthen until after a while it begins to seem like a series of long jumps. There's no illusion of furious energy. Gale merely seems to float away from all pursuers.

The classic execution of this technique was demonstrated on a damp December day in Wrigley Field, Chicago, during his rookie year of 1965, against the San Francisco 49ers. The turf was soft, the air was chill with winter. It was a good afternoon for television and a hot toddy—if you were outside the blacked-out area of Chicago. The first time the Bears got the ball, quarterback Rudy Bukich flipped a short screen pass to Sayers on his own 20-yard line. The 49ers reacted quickly, but Gale squirmed through a gap near the sidelines, wiggled once, twice and then lengthened out his stride to romp 80 yards for a touchdown. Late in the second quarter, he took a handoff and bolted around end for 21 yards and another touchdown. In the final minute of the half, he turned the corner again for a seven-yard scoring sprint. That made three touchdowns at intermission.

At midfield, early in the third quarter, he took a quick pitchout from Bukich and whisked through the San Francisco secondary without a hand touching him to put six more points on the board. The same period, he varied the routine by jolting into the middle of the line from one-yard out and landing in a pile of bodies across the goal line. That tied the club record for touchdowns in a single game.

In the final quarter, he broke it. A San Francisco punt floated down to the Chicago 15-yard line. Gale grabbed it and shot past two San Francisco tacklers right up the middle. When other 49ers coming downfield angled laterally to head him, Sayers cut quickly across the grain of traffic without breaking stride or losing acceleration. He was home free by the time he reached midfield, for his sixth touchdown of the day.

Gale allowed himself a rare relaxation of restraint. He flipped the ball into the air, clapped his hands once, hopped back gleefully toward his teammates and then sprinted to the Chicago bench, where he could be bashful again. Ronnie Bull, the fullback of the Bears, came over and said, "Gale, it's a pleasure to block for you."

Back in 1929, Ernie Nevers, calling his own signal in the backfield of the Chicago Cardinals, ran for six touchdowns against the rival Bears. Dub Jones matched that total in 1951, again with the Bears as victims. And now Sayers shared the distinction.

Gale isn't molded to the image of a record-breaking running back. He's a six-footer who keeps himself just a shade under 200 pounds because he "feels real good" at that weight. "I'm a little small to be a halfback," admitted Gale, "but I enjoy running the ball, and I think I can continue to run the ball."

Roosevelt Grier, a defensive tackle who weighed 300 pounds when in good shape, agreed. Big Rosey took a shot at Sayers when he caught a screen pass one afternoon against the Los Angeles Rams. He thought he had him securely nailed. "I not only laid an arm on this boy," said Grier, "but I thought I'd fractured him with my shoulder. As far as I was concerned, he was dead. When I heard a roar from the crowd, I figured he must have fumbled. So I started to look around for the ball. What I saw instead was Sayers 15 yards away and fast disappearing the full 80 yards for a touchdown. That boy is something else again."

After his rookie year, when he set the all-time NFL record for touchdowns scored, Sayers should have had it tougher. Certainly, every team in the league was alerted to the threat of Sayers running the ball and figured to key on him. Moreover, Rudy Bukich hit a disastrous slump as a passer, which meant increased concentration of Sayers as a ball carrier. Finally, the Bears lost the one man who could divert attention from Sayers and give him more running room, when Andy Livingston was hurt during the exhibition season and ruled out for the year. Livingston was a 243-pound fullback who could match Sayers in straightaway speed and, although a rookie with virtually no college experience, already rated critical appraisal as another Jimmy Brown. None of the other Chicago backs had the speed or size to be taken seriously when Sayers was lined up just an arm's length away. The Bears had a mediocre record in 1966, winning five games, losing seven and tying a pair. Sayers carried the ball 229 times, more than twice the number of rushes by any other back (Ronnie Bull had 100), and gained 1,231 yards. Only three other backs in the history of the NFL—Jimmy Brown, Jimmy Taylor and Leroy Kelly— have gained more ground in a single season!

Yet before Sayers got into pro ball, there were skeptics of his ability to stand the gaff. He had been a well-publicized prospect at the University of Kansas, a two-time All-American. As a little kid, Gale had lived on a farm near a small town in Kansas called, appropriately enough, Speed. His father had moved the family to Omaha, Nebraska, when Gale was nine. His older brother Roger was a sprinter who attended the University of Omaha. Gale went to Omaha Central High School and turned out for the football team as a linebacker. That's like casting Ursula Andress as Ma Kettle. But by his junior year, he was in his natural niche running the ball, and by his senior year there were 100 college scouts making calls on the Sayers family. He spurned Nebraska and chose Kansas for a simple reason—he liked Coach Jack Mitchell.

Gale's special talents were obvious. The writer recalls seeing a freshman football game between Kansas and Missouri, something to while away a Friday afternoon. The big attraction was a Missouri halfback named Johnny Roland, recruited from Corpus Christi, Texas, and notable as one of the first Negro football players on scholarship at that school. Roland was excellent (and became a strong ball carrier for the St. Louis Cardinals). Sayers was superb, dominating the field, breaking loose repeatedly for long gains.

By his senior year, Don Klosterman, chief talent scout for the Kansas City Chiefs (and later general manager of the Houston Oilers), noted, "The two best running backs in football, at any level, are Jim Brown and Gale Sayers. And I'm not sure which is number one."

The Chiefs then picked Sayers as their top draft choice for the 1965 season. So did the Bears. "I remember seeing him play one game against Oklahoma," said former backfield coach Chuck Mather of Chicago. "He took a kickoff near the goal line and at midfield he made a move that was out of this world. He actually faked an Oklahoma tackler to his knees. I'd never seen a college kid do that before."

The Chiefs were so eager to get him that Lamar Hunt, their owner, made the pursuit of Sayers a personal project. Gale, never showing a bit of emotion, picked the Bears. "I felt funny," he said, "having a millionaire open doors for me." That may be an apocryphal quote, but it suits the Sayers psyche.

After he'd made it big with the Bears, Gale was asked to address a high school assembly in Chicago. The school had a record of almost 50 percent dropouts among boys.

"I'm not going to take up too much of your time," he began, "because I know you want to get back to your school work."

The kids smiled and relaxed.

"I didn't think too much of education when I was your age, either," he continued.

"Sports helped keep me in school, and going to school was being 'in.'

"Now an older man I knew dropped out of high school when he was in the 10th grade. This man could have been a lawyer. He had an uncle who offered to send him to college and then to law school. But instead of being a lawyer, wearing nice clothes and working pleasant hours, this man works as a car polisher and washer in a used car lot."

The kids looked around at each other, there was nothing different about this story.

"The man I'm talking about," said Gale quietly, "is my father. He works long hours and comes home tired every night for not much money. He's been working that way for years. He gave me the incentive to get an education."

Gale has a depth as a person that's camouflaged by his lack of facial expressiveness. ("He never gets excited," said his wife, Linda, herself a bundle of vivacity. "He never gets upset, and anything he does feel he holds inside.") After his last football season at Kansas, when he was already signed by the Bears, he participated in a protest sit-in outside the office of the university chancellor and was among 110 students arrested. They protested against discriminatory housing of students. "I'm an athlete and so I have good housing," explained Sayers, "but my fraternity brothers and other Negroes do not have good housing."

He is not, however, a militant activist on civil rights or any other subject. He says his piece simply and succinctly on whatever absorbs him, and in this phase of his life he is absorbed with being a total football player. Gale wasn't always accepted as such.

Before reporting to the Bears, he had a chore with the College All-Stars in the summer of 1965. Gale didn't endear himself to Otto Graham, the coach of the Stars. Graham developed a notion that Gale wasn't putting out to get ready for the game. In a scrimmage against the Bears, the halfback ran off the field, claiming a leg injury. The doctors couldn't find it. Graham, convinced that Sayers was goofing off, warned that Sayers "wouldn't make it in pro ball unless he changes his attitude." Although he suited up for the College All-Stars against the Cleveland Browns, he never got in the game.

"I was hurt," said Sayers quietly. "That's all."

With doubt about his attitude and a natural skepticism over his size for the role of a running back, Gale had a lot to prove. He scarcely played in the first two regular season games. In the third, he scored two touchdowns against the championship-bound Green Bay Packers, and the pace never slackened.

George Halas, his boss and the Original Bear, quickly put him in a class with Red Grange and George McAfee, a pair of primary heroes in Chicago pro football. Rival players poured on the tributes, too. "I wish I had the vocabulary to describe Sayers," said John David Crow of the 49ers, a pro back with a decade of achievement. "He's a great, great football player, at a very young age. He's got quickness and speed, but he has something else that a great back must have. He has a sense of football, a feel for the game. It's easy for a coach to tell a back, 'Follow your guard around end and then make your move.' But there is more to it than that. You have to see downfield and Sayers must see an awful lot to make the runs he does."

"He's the toughest gosh-darn runner I ever saw," said Coach Charley Winner of the Cardinals. "He's the fastest thing in the league," added all-pro middle linebacker Ray Nitschke of the Packers.

502

All the gee-whiz raves tended to make Sayers noticed more than ever when he stepped into action. If you played the Bears, you defensed against Sayers. When Jim Dooley took over the coaching reins in 1968, he was cognizant of the concentration on Gale. He also worried about the exposure to traffic which would inevitably expose him to injury. A sprained ankle had limited his work in '67. Jim's idea was to use Gale part of the time out of backfield as a flanker, much as the Baltimore Colts had used Lenny Moore in his prime. "If I'm not injured," shrugged Gale, "I think my strongest spot is in the backfield. But Jim tells me, and I believe him, that under certain circumstances I can be of greater help to the team at flanker. Above all, I want to win, and if we can win with me on the flank, that's the way I want it, too."

In an exhibition game against the Dallas Cowboys, he was put out there and immediately raced downfield to catch a touchdown pass. But there was one hitch in Dooley's plans. When Gale wasn't in a setback position, the Bears had no comparable running threat. So during the regular season, until he got hurt, he was the target for all tacklers.

"They've keyed on me for so long, it doesn't bother me," said Gale. "I know I'm a marked man. I got to go into games with that attitude and do my best."

And the best, in his book, isn't only physical. "I'm not a great runner," he insisted. "I do not consider myself great. I just get paid to do a job and I'm doing it. The toughest part is picking up different defenses, learning the game. You can't be a dumb football player. You got to be pretty smart."

But it sure helps to be able to run—the way Gale Sayers can.

"I thought I coached the two greatest backfields of all time," said that veteran observer, Buddy Parker. "Charley Trippi, Elmer Angsman and Pat Harder with the Cardinals, and Doak Walker, Bob Hoernschemeyer and Harder with the Lions. But Sayers is the best backfield all by himself."

GALE SAYERS' FAVORITE PLAY:

"In the first Minnesota game of the 1968 season, in the first quarter, I bounced outside on an off-tackle trap play and went for about 35 yards.

"This type of play is a simple off-tackle power play. I like it so well because it gives me a great chance to use the blocking of our left guard. Also, I have the option of cutting in either of three directions. If the guard knocks his man inside, I can go outside. If he knocks him outside, I can go inside. And if we are going for the first down, I can always blast straight ahead."

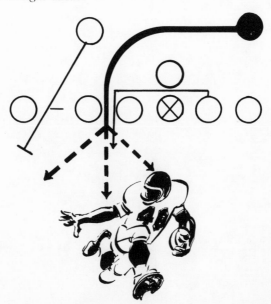

GALE EUGENE SAYERS

BORN: May 30, 1943   Height: 6'0''   Weight: 200

University of Kansas

Chicago Bears, 1965–68

| | | RUSHING | | | | | PASS RECEIVING | | | | SCORING | |
Year	G.	Att.	Yds.	Avg.	TD.	P.C.	Yds.	Avg.	TD.	TD.	Pts.
1965	14	166	867	5.2	14	29	507	17.5	6	*22	*132
1966	14	229	*1231	5.4	8	34	447	13.1	2	12	72
1967	13	186	880	4.7	7	16	126	7.9	1	12	72
1968	9	138	856	*6.2	2	15	117	7.8	0	2	12

PRO TOTALS

—4 YEARS	50	719	3834	5.3	31	94	1197	12.7	9	48	288

* Led NFL.

504

Leroy Kelly

LEROY IS LIKE A CAT. IT'S DIFFICULT TO KNOCK A CAT OFF HIS FEET. HE'S AGILE AND HAS BALANCE.
—*Ernie Green, halfback, Cleveland Browns.*

It is late December 1965, and Warren Lahr, who used to play defensive back for the Cleveland Browns, is looking into the future. He is standing on a practice field in Green Bay, Wisconsin, near Lombardi Avenue, watching the Cleveland Browns work out for their championship game with the Packers. Warren, retired a half dozen years, is there as a color announcer for the Browns, making sure he doesn't miss anything that will help him in the Sunday telecast. It is sub-zero weather, but Warren is intently watching the practice session.

A stocky kid with a familiar shuffle is fielding punts down at one end of the field, catching them snugly, briefly ducking to secure the ball in his arms, then sprinting straight ahead in a quick ramble, both legs barely skimming the surface of the ground. If you didn't see that the practice jersey carried the number 44, and if you didn't know that Jim Brown was over at the other end of the field running signal drills with the starting offensive unit of the Browns, you'd be confused and wonder what the heck the great fullback was doing catching and returning punts.

Already there have been reports that Brown, the greatest runner in history, is seriously contemplating retirement from football to concentrate on his movie assignments.

"They won't miss him," says Warren, watching the muscular kid smoothly sprint forward, cut suddenly to change direction, spin and shuffle slowly back in a halftrot. "That kid out there runs like he does."

"What's his name?" asked a man standing next to Warren.

"Kelly. Leroy Kelly. And wait'll you see him go. He's the second best runner in the league right now."

At the time Lahr would have been hard-pressed to prove his point. In the entire 1965 season, Leroy Kelly carried the ball just 37 times for a piddling 139 yards. He was known mainly as a specialist on punt and kickoff returns, and his sole recognition came from leading the league in average punt returns (15.6 yards). Moreover, Leroy didn't look like a guy who could be groomed to succeed Brown, no matter what his running style. A shade under six feet tall, 200 pounds after a heavy meal, he didn't seem geared for the heavy ball carrying traffic of the NFL, though pro football was belatedly getting used to the idea that such non-giants as Dick Bass and Mike Garrett could find their way through the crush of clashing lines.

But Warren Lahr got a lifetime membership in the Crystal Ball Gazers Union that afternoon in Green Bay. Brown did retire the following summer on movie location in London; Kelly did succeed him. He was, for the type of running Cleveland demanded, the second best in football behind Brown (for all around scampering, you couldn't beat Gale Sayers). And a check of the records for the next three years verifies the prediction that Cleveland never missed the man who wore number 32, Jimmy Brown.

In 1966, Leroy Kelly, unknown, slipped easily into his spot as the chief Cleveland ball carrier, led the league in rushing until the last Sunday of the season and finished up with 1,141 yards on the ground and an impressive total of 16 touchdowns. That was his first year on the job. Remember, only eleven players in NFL history had previously gained 1,000 yards in a single season. That initial performance was only the prelude. In 1967, he took over the league rushing leadership in every category—most attempts (235), most yards gained (1,205), best average (5.1), most touchdowns (11). And in 1968, he went a step further with 248 carries for 1,239 yards and 16 touchdowns rushing, each of those figures also topping the league.

So much for spotting talent. Kelly was one of those longshots who pop up once in a running generation, unexpectedly, making people wonder how he could ever have been overlooked, *after* he got a chance to show his stuff. Even the Browns couldn't have been that sure of him. He was an eighth draft choice in 1964, and he was completely ignored by every team in the AFL. A few teams in the younger league said later they were interested in signing him as a free agent—to play defense! The Browns gave him a bonus of $7,500 and a contract for $10,000, which was chicken feed at the height of the War between the Leagues.

Leroy had gone to school at little Morgan State in Baltimore, the school which once took Roosevelt Brown out of the band and introduced him to football—he eventually became an all-pro tackle with the Giants. Leroy went there because big schools, like big pro teams later, weren't interested in him. For one thing, he's not a talker. You don't find Leroy by listening for him. The Browns got on his trail by watching him play in the Orange Blossom Classic in Miami against Bob Hayes of Florida A&M. "I met Kelly a couple of times on the beach," recalled Hayes, the world's fastest human who put his speed to good use as a flanker for the Dallas Cowboys. "The cat was real quiet, never said a word. They said you could get up close to him and hear the ocean roar, like you do with a seashell."

Kelly was always a doer, not a talker. Sports were big in the Kelly family from the Nicetown ghetto of south Philadelphia. Pop had been a semi-pro ballplayer. Leroy was an all-city shortstop with major league potential, if he hadn't been diverted to football. His younger brother Harold has made the majors as an outfielder. Three brothers preceded Leroy as quarterbacks for Simon Gratz High School, and he played quarterback, too. He handled the ball first that way and ran with it. Once, his team was pinned on its own two-yard line, fourth down and 12 to go. The coach signalled Kelly to run for it. He went 98 yards for a touchdown.

But he wasn't big. When the Browns brought him to Cleveland in the spring of 1964 for a pre-camp look, Coach Blanton Collier checked him over closely and said, "I like the way you run. I'd like to see you on offense. But I wish you were bigger." Leroy weighed 188 pounds. "Next time you see me, Coach," he said, "I'll be bigger."

He returned in the fall as a 200-pounder. The Browns were set at the running spots, with Jimmy Brown and Ernie Green a finely-matched pair. The only way Leroy could justify a spot on the roster was to play with the special teams on punts and kickoffs. He showed immediately he was a good runner, with balance and speed. He also showed a streak of toughness. "He was a vicious tackler on kick coverage," remembered Collier. "I knew right away we had ourselves a good boy."

"I felt," said Leroy, glad to be of some service, "like I was an asset to the team."

508

The turf flies as Leroy Kelly of Cleveland moves on past a felled dark jersey in quest of another rushing title.

He was awed just being on the same field with the great Jimmy Brown. And he learned by watching. He copied Brown's mannerisms, right down to the slow way of dragging himself up after a tackle, hunched inside his shoulder pads, painfully deliberate but impassive. The first words Brown ever said to him were: "Hey, rookie, run over there and get us a couple of footballs from the bag." That time Leroy ran.

If there were frustrations, Leroy kept them to himself. Then came the sudden retirement of Brown, and he had his chance to play. Leroy adjusted to his new status quickly. Brown had let his hair grow out in a "natural" cut. So did Leroy. Brown was an elegantly conservative dresser. Leroy started getting his suits tailor-made, three at a time, and piling up so many alpaca sweaters he lost track of them. He was a bit more mod than his alter ego, but always tasteful. *Esquire* magazine picked him among the 10 best-dressed men in America. He got himself a swank pad in a high rise apartment building on Cleveland's East side, with a fine view of the city and Lake Erie. The only intruders were pals of the paper boy who came up to get Leroy's autograph.

It was, as owner Art Modell of the Browns soon found out, a not freely dispensed signature. After Leroy gained his first 1,000-yards plus in 1966, he refused to sign the Brown's proferred contract for 1967. Instead, taking their cue from the bloc negotiations once conducted by Sandy Koufax and Don Drysdale of the Los Angeles Dodgers, Leroy and three other black players insisted on presenting their contract demands as a group. They refused to report to training camp. Management was not in a conciliatory mood. Two of the players were immediately traded. A third, guard John Wooten, followed a year later. Kelly remained adamant. He had made $23,000 as Brown's untried successor. Now he wanted $40,000. Modell offered $35,000. Leroy said he'd play without a new contract, meaning he would have to stay at $23,000, minus an automatic cut of 10 percent, but on May 1, 1968, he would be a free agent.

It was a gamble with huge risk for the player. If he were hurt during the year he played out his option, the club would bear no future financial responsibility. If he had a bad season, his bargaining position went down. Leroy was betting his entire future on the '67 campaign.

Kelly reaped the payoff by leading the NFL in rushing as the Browns won their division title. They had to beat the Giants in a crucial December meeting. With a slim 3–0 lead, they took command on a drive from midfield which had Kelly carrying the ball four out of five times. On each carry a back with less agility might have been stopped for no gain. His smashes took them inches from the goal line. Then he slashed over right tackle and scored standing up. Two months later he signed a four-year contract at a figure "slightly in excess" of $250,000. Now he was shorn of two tensions: (1) he no longer had to prove himself as a runner, and (2) he was financially secure. With that aura of contentment over his work, Leroy in 1968 banged ahead to his third straight 1,000-yard season, a record achieved by only two others, Jimmy Brown and Jimmy Taylor. "He's a miniature Brown," said Buddy Young, who had originally recommended him to Cleveland. "He flies, cuts, never gives you a full piece of himself and keeps those feet close to the ground for balance."

"Leroy doesn't have Jim's strength," analyzed Ernie Green, his running mate, "so he has to compensate in other ways. Jim broke tackles. Leroy has to move about more, slide around, give head and shoulder fakes and sidestep to get around tacklers."

510

Leroy Kelly of the Browns has the quickness
to skirt danger as well as squirt through it.

Like Brown also, Leroy never got hurt. Part of Brown's durability lay in his tremendous physique. Leroy isn't puny—the thick neck and massive chest were smaller scale replicas of Brown. But he worked out his own scheme for survival:

"I watch some ball carriers fighting long after the issue is closed. That's how a back gets hurt. There is a time to give that second effort you read so much about, and there is a time to find yourself a soft spot."

As Leroy racked up the yardage consistently for three years, the comparisons with Brown were inevitable. Coach Collier stayed neutral. "It's like apples and oranges," he said. But some of the Cleveland players who had blocked for both were more positive in their preferences. "Kelly," said guard Gene Hickerson, "hits a hole a lot quicker. You really have to move to get out in front of him." From the other side of the line, veteran defensive star Jim Houston said simply, "Leroy's a better football player."

Any assessments were colored by current events. "What's he doing for me now?" means a lot more to the player than past achievements. Great as Brown was, he hadn't contributed to the Cleveland cause since 1965. Kelly, meanwhile, scored 20 touchdowns in 1968 to lead the National league in point-making. Four of those scores were on passes, indicating he matches Brown as a receiving threat. He was certainly a more capable blocker, if only for the fact he approaches that assignment with a lot more zeal than Brown displayed.

He did not have the leadership mystique of Brown, and he never will because he can't match Brown's symbolism as a leader. The response to Brown was automatic because the players reacted hypnotically to his physical stimulus. It was almost a privilege to be a part of his greatness, whatever his personal foibles.

Kelly doesn't convey Brown's personal intensity. He's quietly bland, a craftsman— "I don't think he has Jimmy's imagination," said one Brown veteran. But no one faults the results.

Leroy is starting to emerge as a more positive person as well as player, with a little twist of slyness to indicate the real Kelly is still to be seen. In January 1969, he was a prize recipient of his third straight trophy as a member of the NEA All-Players All-Pro team at a fete in Hollywood's Television City hosted by CBS. Most of the other honored players made the pat speeches—how thrilled they were to be chosen, what an honor it was to be paid this tribute by their fellow players, etc. Leroy, sedately splendid in a double-breasted, tapered black silk suit, a gleaming white tie against a white shirt, his eyes with their oriental cast slightly hooded to hide a twinkle, clutched the statuette symbolic of all-pro selection and said, very briefly:

"I'm honored to be part of this, too. I'll see you all here next year."

He smiled confidently.

LEROY KELLY

BORN: May 20, 1942   Height: 6'0''   Weight: 200

Morgan State College

Cleveland Browns, 1965–68

Year	G.	Att.	Yds.	Avg.	TD.	P.C.	Yds.	Avg.	TD.	TD.	Pts.
			RUSHING				PASS RECEIVING			SCORING	
1964	14	6	12	2.0	0		(None)			1	6
1965	13	37	139	3.8	0	9	122	13.6	0	2	12
1966	14	209	1141	*5.5	*15	32	366	11.4	1	*16	96
1967	14	*235	*1205	*5.1	*11	20	282	14.1	2	13	78
1968	14	*248	*1239	5.0	16	22	297	13.5	4	*20	*120

PRO TOTALS

	G.	Att.	Yds.	Avg.	TD.	P.C.	Yds.	Avg.	TD.	TD.	Pts.
—4 YEARS	69	735	3736	5.1	42	83	1067	12.9	7	52	312

* Led NFL.

Matt Snell

THEY LAUGHED AT ME ONCE WHEN I
SAID HE'D BECOME THE COMPLETE FOOT-
BALL PLAYER. BUT MATT SNELL HAS IT
ALL NOW.

> —*Weeb Ewbank, coach,*
> *New York Jets.*

Over the top goes Matt Snell of the New York Jets as linebacker Nick Buoniconti hangs on desperately.

The highlight film of the New York Jets' triumphant procession through 1968 caught number 41 in the green and white jersey, Matt Snell, in the act of falling down, with a tackler driving him towards the ground. But as Matt fell sideways on this attempted sweep around right end, he released the football from an almost horizontal position. And the pass blooped into the air, like the cork popping from a fizzed-out bottle. Somehow it got to the hands of the receiver 26 yards closer to the goal line. Coach Weeb Ewbank, watching the film, was enraptured. "Beautiful," he said, "beautiful."

That's not a word generally associated with Mathews Snell, fullback of the New York Jets. His first five years in football weren't altogether beautiful.

First of all, there had been a lot of physical frustration. Matt Snell was like a finely tuned, sleek Grand Prix racing prototype. If the engine timing was just a little off, he sputtered and stalled. There had been such earlier nagging malfunctions as a pulled hamstring muscle, a bad knee, a sprained ankle and finally the major breakdown—a knee operation which left him psychologically as well as physically scarred. Matt became morose and dissatisfied. He was sullen and withdrawn in his contact with outsiders. He brooded because Broadway Joe Namath was the gleaming model in the showcase of the Jets. He ultimately refused to sign his contract for the 1968 season, and after the first game on the schedule, against Kansas City, in which he made a minimal contribution of 20 yards in 10 carries and no pass receptions, he stated explicitly he would not play in the second game against Boston unless the club gave him a substantial pay raise. A couple of days later, he claimed the usual shelter—"I was misquoted." He did suit up against the Patriots, but he was not in the starting lineup, having lost his job to Bill Mathis. He also was reduced to scrub duty as a member of the suicide wedge on kickoff return teams, an assignment not relished by any man who wants to stay healthy. He got into the game at fullback only because Mathis was hurt in the third quarter. He wasn't a ball of fire, with 23 yards this time in 10 attempts.

But two days later, Snell capitulated and signed a multi-year contract. Simultaneously, he reclaimed his job on offense and the rest of the '68 campaign was notable for its results—both for Matt and the Jets—with the ultimate achievement of a Super Bowl victory in which Matt was a dominant force. So Ewbank could justifiably feel exultation over the performance of his fullback. It was something he had always expected.

Matt was the first symptom of the Jets' quest for respectability when David O. "Sonny" Werblin and his group bought the club and brought in Ewbank to remold the field image. Snell was their first coup in the warring scramble for talent which enveloped both leagues. Both New York teams had drafted him. The year before the AFL team had failed to sign a single one of its top twenty-five draft choices. But Sonny Werblin, the old talent hustler from show biz wasn't going to let this nugget, the No. 1 pick for 1964, elude him.

Matt had been a three-year varsity performer at Ohio State—a halfback his sophomore year, an end as a junior, a fullback as a senior, and linebacker on defense whenever the Buckeyes got in trouble. He was 6′2″, weighed 216, and looked like he could fill out. Clive Rush, a member of the Jets' coaching staff, had been an assistant to Woody Hayes at Ohio State. He went out to Columbus to study films of the kid and was satisfied that Matt would be an asset to the Jets. "He could help us in three positions," noted Ewbank. "He could play linebacker, defensive end—if he put on some weight—and fullback. He was also a Long Island boy." The Jets wanted a local name to sell, though Matt Snell's reputation was restricted. He made no All-American teams. He just was a guy who could help a team that needed it desperately.

Werblin cut short a Miami vacation to fly out to Columbus and personally sell Matt on the advantages of playing for the Jets. That pleased Matt because he needed some selling. He wasn't even convinced he could play pro ball. Bob Ferguson, his fullback predecessor at Ohio State, a unanimous All-American, had been a horrible flop in the NFL. "I thought to myself," Matt said later, " 'Bob Ferguson is one of the greatest players I've ever seen. If he couldn't make it, what's my chance?'

"I never looked at myself as being good enough to be a pro football player. I always looked at them as superhuman. Jimmy Brown, he's 230 and runs a 9.6 hundred. And that wasn't me."

And if some pro team was willing to gamble on him, he wasn't sure it should be in the "AF of L," as he called it then—"You have these little doubts about the league until someone explains it to you." Werblin's explanations were sugared by a $30,000 bonus and a $20,000 annual contract for three years. A smart bit of public relations didn't hurt. The week before the draft, Matt's parents had attended a Jets' game in Shea Stadium at Sonny's invitation. It was bitter cold. Werblin thoughtfully sent down some hot chocolate to them.

For one year, it looked as though Snell actually sold himself short. Despite a pulled hamstring muscle incurred in the College All-Star game, he took over immediately as a regular. He gained 948 yards, the all-time high of his career, and caught a phenomenal total of 56 passes, a tribute to his background as an end in college. He was a quick study, just as he had been at Ohio State. Woody Hayes once put in an off-tackle play, and seven straight times Matt ran into somebody before he got past the line of scrimmage. Hayes blew his whistle and lectured him, "The object of this game, Matt, is not to look for extra people to run into." On Matt's next carry, he ran 65 yards.

"He's the complete football player," Ewbank declared, "and has the necessary ability to be one of the great ones in pro history." Mike Holovak of Boston predicted, "He'll be the next Jimmy Brown." Which meant something special to Matt because he came out of the same Long Island high school area that produced Brown. Like Brown, he had spent his early years in Georgia, the son of a poor produce farmer, and even at the age of six he was already working in the fields. Like Brown, he moved north and discovered the world of sports. "He was the only Negro in school," said his high school coach at Carle Place, Long Island, "and the other kids idolized him. He was worth it, too." He resembled Brown in physique, the tawny skin drawn tight over impressively bunched muscles. Perhaps he wasn't as fast as Brown, but the difference wasn't discernible.

He did not, however, have Brown's tolerance for the bumps and bruises of football. Or maybe it was lack of luck. He hurt his knee in an exhibition game his second year with the Jets and his workload dropped off to 763 yards. Joe Namath had joined the club, so there was a greater emphasis on the passing game. Where Matt had been the big gun, now it was Broadway Joe's show. "Emotion," he said, "gnaws away at you inside, even though it may not show outwardly. We all have our emotional idiosyncracies." The progress in introspection and self-expression was admirable, but it was not doing anything for the Jets. The worst came in the opening game of the 1967 season when he skidded on a slippery field during the opening game in Buffalo and tore the ligaments in his knee. He tried playing a couple of weeks, then submitted to an operation. He returned in the fading weeks of the season but was a hesitant, ineffective player. He had no illusions. "I was thinking about that knee," he said. He was unsure about his future and unhappy with the Jets' salary offer in a new contract.

After the shock of the demotion to second-stringer and the subsequent settling of his differences with the front office, Snell came on fast. His running efforts weren't remarkable—747 yards in 179 attempts, sixth among AFL rushers. But they were solid enough to give some balance to the Jets' offense, which leaned heavily on the passing threat of Namath. Snell's part in the success of Namath is immeasurable. The colorful quarterback operates on the most precarious set of knees in sports. One hard, unanticipated whack, and his career could be over suddenly and tragically. The Jets as a team would suffer correspondingly. So there's a tremendous burden of responsibility on the pass blockers. The inside perimeter or protection is Snell's province. And he's one of the great ones.

"He's been a great blocker," claimed Ewbank, "from the day he came to us. Matt rates with Marion Motley and Alan Ameche as the three finest pass protectors I've ever seen. He has a knack of timing and the ability to pick up blitzers. He also makes less errors on his assignments than any player we have."

"Blocking's something I enjoy," said Matt, "because it doesn't hurt. And it's just as important a part of the game as running. The most important factor is discipline."

As he became more of a contributor to the Jets, his inner tensions eased. He relaxed to become a part of the social communion in the locker room and on the practice field that's so vital to team morale. "Life's proving one thing or another," he said philosophically, as he prepared to play in the Super Bowl game against the heavily favored Baltimore Colts. Three days before the game, he had his knee tapped and drained of excess fluid.

Then he went out and proved he was one of the class running backs in football.

MATT SNELL'S FAVORITE PLAY:

"My favorite in the Jets' offensive arsenal is called 'flank right 19 straight.' It consists of one-on-one blocking up and down the line, with the halfback taking on the outside linebacker and the split end either cracking back on the weak safety or running his corner back deep, depending on the coverage he reads after coming off the line.

"I've diagrammed it against a 4-3 defense which is basic throughout the league.

"The linemen have to fire straight into their opponent's middle, taking him wherever he wants to go. The running back works off the block, running to daylight.

519

"We have been using this play successfully ever since I came with the Jets five years ago. It made me rookie of the year in 1964, and we completely destroyed Baltimore with it in the recent Super Bowl. And would you believe Baltimore uses the very same play, from Coach Weeb Ewbank's old days with the Colts?

"Our motto is, against all defenses: whenever in doubt, call 19 straight!"

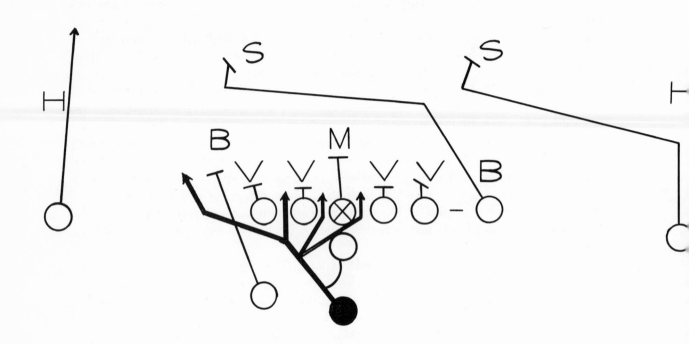

MATHEWS "MATT" SNELL

BORN: Aug. 18, 1941   Height: 6'2"   Weight: 219
                             Ohio State University

New York Jets, 1964–68

Year	G.	Att.	Yds.	Avg.	TD.	P.C.	Yds.	Avg.	TD.	TD.	Pts.
		RUSHING				**PASS RECEIVING**				**SCORING**	
1964	14	215	948	4.4	5	56	393	7.0	1	6	36
1965	14	169	763	4.5	4	38	264	6.9	0	4	24
1966	12	178	644	3.6	4	48	346	7.2	4	8	48
1967	7	61	207	3.4	0	11	54	4.9	0	0	0
1968	14	179	747	4.2	6	16	105	6.6	1	7	42
PRO TOTALS —5 YEARS	61	802	3309	4.1	19	169	1162	6.9	6	25	150

Ken Willard

I WANT TO BE THE BEST. I CAN'T IMAG-
INE ANYONE ENTERING ANY PROFESSION
WITHOUT WANTING TO BE THE BEST. I
WANT TO BE THE ABSOLUTE TOPS.
                    —*Ken Willard, fullback,*
                    San Francisco 49ers.

Eyes alert for the nearest opening, Ken Willard (40) of San Francisco cruises behind the 49er line before making his cut up-field.

Ken Willard doesn't fancy himself as a glamor boy. The actuarial tables which he has studied well as an insurance man between seasons in his home town of Richmond, Virginia, tell him a lot about his football probabilities. "I know," he said with some degree of firmness, "I'm not going to run all the way too often. The idea is to get 10 or 15 yards consistently." To be more precise, he should have said four yards since that is almost an exact average for the first four seasons he carried the ball in professional football, and the figure is consistent with his attributes as a fullback.

He is 6'2" and weighs 232 pounds. He will never outrun a fire engine down Market Street in San Francisco, but he is strong enough to push a cable car around the turntable. He is one of those big, tough, hard-running types whom almost every coach likes to see at fullback. He blocks and catches the ball acceptably. His attitude is serious, his enthusiasm consistent, his approach thoroughly professional.

But don't put him completely in a routine fullback mold. On December 15, 1968, for instance, he chose to break out. The 49ers, completing their first season under new head coach Dick Nolan, visited Atlanta for the finale. The Falcons, revitalized by Norm Van Brocklin's direction, were surprisingly stubborn against the high scoring 49ers. They took a 6–0 lead. Willard, on the next series, broke off tackle and sprinted 69 yards for a touchdown. The Falcons regained the lead, 12–7. Willard plunged over the line for a second touchdown and the margin of victory. In the course of the afternoon, he gained 162 yards and jacked his season total to 967 yards, which placed him just behind Leroy Kelly among the premier runners of the year.

"I want to be the best fullback in pro football," Ken stated as the thesis of his ambition when he first joined the 49ers in 1965, as a twenty-one-year-old honors graduate of the University of North Carolina, and he had taken a giant step towards its fulfillment.

He has light sandy hair, a perpetual squint and a heavy jaw that's completely in character with his image of strength. Ken speaks softly with a Virginia inflection in his voice but a special firmness that lets you know his ideas are positive. Sample: "I don't believe anybody 230 pounds meeting a defensive back who weighs 185 should get stopped. If he is, he hasn't put enough into it."

Ken has never lacked resolve or direction. He was gifted with the natural assets to be a professional athlete, and he took advantage of them the same way Denny McLain decided pitching was his game. Ken's only decision revolved around the choice of sports. Before he was graduated from high school, a scout from the Boston Red Sox sat in the Willard kitchen in Richmond and offered him $100,000 to sign a baseball contract. When he was 11, he hit 12 home runs in Little League competition and was banned because he made the other kids look too bad. At 14, he was already 6' 1", weighed 195 and he hit .480 for the state Legion champions. He could have used the bonus money. His father died of cancer when Ken was a high school freshman. But his mother told him that a college education was paramount, and Ken had some football scholarship offers.

"Talk the same money to me in a few years," Ken told the baseball scout, "and I'll think about it." He went off to North Carolina to play football and attain a B-average in his studies, making the Dean's list three times. He kept up with his baseball, as a slugging outfielder, but his chief athletic concentration was on football. A guy built like a tackle, who could run the 100 in a little over 10 seconds, and turn the corner like a tailback, was a rarity on the campus at Chapel Hill. He led the Tar Heels to a Gator Bowl engagement and a 35–0 thrashing of the Air Force Academy. He wanted to play pro ball for the Washington Redskins because of their proximity to Richmond (and, in fact, threatened to quit football in early 1968 unless he was traded to Washington). But in the 1965 college draft he was chosen by the San Francisco 49ers on the first round; the only player selected before him was Tucker Frederickson of Auburn by the Giants. Ken signed with the 49ers the night before the draft. He had been tapped by Buffalo in a secret draft of the AFL but with typical candor told Coach Lou Saban, "I don't want to take you for a ride. I prefer to play in the NFL."

His pro career has been a model of consistency. He finished among the top five rushers in the NFL three of his first four years. In his time with the 49ers, he has monopolized the ground gaining leadership of the club. He has been an excellent pass receiver, with a high of 42 catches his sophomore year, 1966. In '67, he was hampered severely by a foot injury and still managed to do the heavy work. "He's our first down runner," said John Brodie, the veteran quarterback of the club, meaning that when it was third-and-two or fourth-and-one the strategy was simplified: hand the ball to Willard and watch the Red jersey part the sea of linemen for the first down.

In his rookie year, the 49ers showed their faith in him when Jack Christiansen, then the head coach, sent in a substitute on fourth down, one yard to go, the 49ers leading the Los Angeles Rams, 14–7, the ball on the 31-yard line. The orthodox call would be a field goal. "Jack says to run 56," relayed the sub. On "56," Willard, the fullback, carried the ball on a slant over left tackle. Willard made it with a yard to spare. Three plays later, it was fourth and two on the 22. They gave him the ball again. Ken broke through the Ram wall, reputedly the best in football, for 10 yards.

"I want to stay in there and pound every play," he said. "I want them to leave me in there when nobody else is there."

Coming within 33 yards of the breaking the 1,000-yard barrier in 1968, at the age of twenty-five, he was the leader of the new class of power backs in pro ball. Not flashy, seldom spectacular, but productive. "I wondered," he said introspectively, "what type of personality I should have. Should I be colorful or controversial? But I soon discovered I was incapable of being either. I was capable of being consistent."

And, in San Francisco, very much appreciated.

524

KENNETH HENDERSON "KEN" WILLARD

BORN: July 14, 1943   Height: 6'2"   Weight: 230

University of North Carolina

San Francosco, 1965–68

Year	G.	RUSHING Att.	Yds.	Avg.	TD.	PASS RECEIVING P.C.	Yds.	Avg.	TD.	SCORING TD.	Pts.
1965	14	189	778	4.1	5	32	253	7.9	4	9	54
1966	14	191	763	4.0	5	42	351	8.4	2	7	42
1967	13	169	510	3.0	5	23	242	10.5	1	6	36
1968	14	227	967	4.3	7	36	232	6.4	0	7	42
PRO TOTALS —4 YEARS	55	776	3018	3.9	22	133	1078	8.1	7	29	174

Mike Garrett

THE NUMBER ONE THING THAT MIKE GARRETT HAS GOING FOR HIM IS THAT HE IS TOUGH. IF YOU HAD TO GO INTO AN ALLEY AND FIGHT, YOU'D WANT HIM TO COME WITH YOU. HE'D BE BACK-TO-BACK AS LONG AS YOU WERE THERE, AND IF YOU LEFT HE'D PROBABLY STAY.
—Curtis McClinton, fullback, Kansas City Chiefs.

The ability to change direction quickly and to hug close to the ground, out of sight of tacklers, is an asset to Mike Garrett in his sorties for the Kansas City Chiefs.

A man who carries an inflated oval ball into a pack of humanity, in defiance of the natural instinct to avoid contact, is not necessarily a mass of insensitivity. Or more bluntly, one of those animal brutes caricatured as the big, dumb football player.

Michael Lockett Garrett is neither big nor dumb. When he first came to the Kansas City Chiefs in the late summer of 1966, he was called variously "Stumpy," "Pygmy" or "Midget." He didn't like it and told them so. They started calling him "Elmer Fudd." They also put him through the physical wringer.

"They were knocking me down," he recalled, "hitting me with elbows, everything. They said it was an initiation, but they didn't do it to other rookies."

"Sure, we got on him," said Jerry Mays, the all-league defensive end and captain of the team. "We rode him pretty hard for a while, but he just kept working and pretty soon we realized we had a rare kind of individual in him."

"It was harder for Mike than most rookies," said Jim Tyrer, the all-league offensive tackle. "Acceptance in the pros is a strange thing. It's not where someone comes in and everyone says, 'We accept you.' One morning you wake up and it's there. With Mike, maybe the money and the publicity was in the back of our minds. But the kidding is just part of the maturing process of a rookie. We all had to go through it."

Finally, Mike Garrett—not big, not dumb—realized. "If you have a screwed-up personality," he said, "you won't get along with anyone. These guys accept you as a person first."

And Michael Lockett Garrett is his own person—sensitive, tuned in to the scene, complex. Football happens to be his bag and his escape route to individuality. He grew up in a Watts-like area of East Los Angeles, an ethnic ghetto with palm trees and no coconuts on the kitchen table. He was one of six kids. He stayed out of trouble, but it could have been the other way. He had sports and the ability to play them—football, baseball—and they ultimately channeled him to a productive life. They even took his hardworking mother and his understanding step-father (Mike's own father died when he was an infant) out of the ghetto and into the comfortable suburbancy of Altadena. Mike was not a good student, but when there was direction and purpose, he applied himself. This brought him to the University of Southern California, just on the fringe of Watts but light years away in terms of social and economic change. Mike felt the difference. "USC was too expensive for Negroes," he said. "Practically the only Negroes were athletes. The white students did not know or like Negroes. I got into a fraternity, and then I quit. I couldn't stand it."

But football was the leveller, the means to identity. To play football, Mike was motivated to improve himself scholastically, to remedy an early hangup about reading, to acquire diversified intellectual interests, to become articulate and expressive.

These facets of himself weren't always apparent behind the Mars-like plastic helmet with the bars and underneath the bulky shoulder pads, the satin knee pants with their bulging thigh pads, the cleated shoes. Frankly, the thousands who flocked to The Coliseum on Saturday afternoons weren't too interested anyhow. Their kick was watching Mike run. To Johnny McKay, the coach who had recruited Mike from Roosevelt High School in Los Angeles, Mike was a special talent. "Garrett is the greatest football player I have ever seen," he said. "And I didn't say just the greatest back, either." McKay used a good thing when he saw it, a pattern he repeated two years later when a back named O. J. Simpson enrolled at USC. "Give it to Garrett" was the standing order for the quarterbacks when he formulated his weekly game plans. In three years, Mike set a new NCAA rushing record of 3,221 yards. A game in which he carried the ball fewer than 30 times was considered a breather. In his senior year against Stanford, he rushed 40 times for 210 yards. At the end of the season, he was a unanimous All-American, named the winner of the Heisman Trophy as the outstanding college player of the 1965 season. He was the second Negro player so honored (the first was the late Ernie Davis of Syracuse).

The American and National football leagues were still jostling each other for talent at that time (peace didn't come until the summer of 1966), but Mike was undecided which way he was going to cash in on his athletic abilities. At USC, he had also kept up his baseball skills as a hard-hitting outfielder. The Pittsburgh Pirates offered him $100,000. The competition would make pro football go higher, but even the Los Angeles Rams, for whom Mike would be a natural, were wary.

You see, Garrett stands only 5 feet 8¾ inches tall in a pair of heavy wool socks. He has a size 17 neck and thick shoulders, but he'll never play effectively at more than 195 pounds. His toes turn out duck-like, almost in a waddle when he walks. The effect altogether doesn't stir up an image of a six-figure property. He wasn't even a first draft choice. The Pittsburgh Steelers tapped a fullback named Dick Leftridge of West Virginia whose entire pro career would consist of eight carries for 17 yards. The Rams, aware of fan reaction, finally picked Mike on the second round. In the AFL, he was almost totally ignored. The Oakland Raiders had wanted a commitment from him before the draft, and Mike didn't want to shut himself off that way. The Raiders snubbed him. On the 20th round, practically a throwaway, he was selected by the Kansas City Chiefs.

"Place your bids, gentlemen," said Mike. "Just one offer. I'll make my choice." Surprisingly, Kansas City came up with the right money, reliably reported to total $300,000 in bonus and salary over a five-year period. Thus fortified, he became a professional running back. And there was this immediate skepticism by the other Chiefs the first time Mike waddled onto a practice field. For one thing, the Chiefs have been for years one of the most physically awesome squads in football. The smallest man on their defensive line is Mays, who stands 6'4" and weighs 250. Buck Buchanan is 6'7", and Ernie Ladd is 6'9". The offensive line is populated by such people as Tyrer (6'6", 290) and Ed Budde (6'5", 260). Curtis McClinton, the incumbent fullback, was 6'3" and 227. Bert Coan, Mike's competition at halfback, checked in at 6'4" and 220. When they trailed through a hotel lobby, Mike looked like the little man who used to yell, "Philip Mor-r-r-is!"

"I had no confidence at the start," he admitted. "I didn't know the system and I wasn't absolutely certain I could play."

But in the opening game of the season, Mike gained his acceptance from the Chiefs with just one play. He fielded a Buffalo punt on his own 23-yard line and quickly fanned out to the right sideline. He had a narrow corridor down the field. He entered it and broke through one tackle. A shoulder move sent a Buffalo player sprawling in his wake. Mike never veered in his course. But with delicate balance and fakes, he sprinted the distance to a touchdown. By mid-season he had the starting job at halfback. As the Chiefs paraded to an AFL title and a date in the Super Bowl with Green Bay, he gained 801 yards and his 5.5 average was the best in the league.

"He's motivated by the fact that everybody thinks he's too small," said Coach Hank Stram. "Every time he runs, he's doing a selling job. I use a phrase—bleed yardage—and I think he 'bleeds' better than any runner I've ever seen. When he goes into a line, he comes out of it with some yards."

"A little guy always has to prove himself," agreed Garrett, with a wink. "I guess I've always been little. I walked out of the hospital this size."

He had some pungent thoughts on running in pro traffic:

"My style is to challenge the tackler, attack him, trying to make him tackle me, and then elude him. I am only effective if I keep people off balance.

"But the factor I'm most concerned with is how I'm running—am I attacking the hole, am I getting the most out of every play? Some of my best runs gain only two yards. It's harder to gain two sometimes on a play that could lose five than it is to go all the way. I could skip past defense men in college, but not here. You have to take what is there, and get it quick.

"What a guy my size isn't big enough to do is block. This doesn't mean that I can't knock a big man down. It's just that when I do, it hurts more."

The day the Chiefs clinched their division title his rookie year, Jerry Mays got up in the celebrating locker room and said, "The game ball goes to the little man they all said was too small to make it in pro ball, but who has been a giant on our team."

Bobby Burnett, a slender Buffalo halfback, was voted the rookie of the year, which Chiefs' owner Lamar Hunt grandiosely labeled "the greatest miscarriage of justice in history." "Mike has tremendous motivation," said running mate Curtis McClinton, as the Chiefs prepared to play the Bills for the AFL title. "When he gets to Buffalo, he's going to want to show some people they made a mistake." Garrett in the title game was the leading ball carrier on the field and scored two touchdowns. Burnett was limited to six yards for the game.

Even the Packers in the first Super Bowl didn't intimidate Garrett as a pro rookie. "Linebacker Dave Robinson—the best—laid back when I came at him," recalled Mike. "He kept his head up as if to say, 'It's your move.' So I ran away from him, laterally. I have great lateral movement. It's my forte."

In his second year with the Chiefs, Mike gained 1,087 yards and caught 46 passes. He felt he could have done better. "I didn't play too well," he said. But he played with confidence and reckless verve. In an exhibition game, a 270-pound Houston lineman bumped the Chiefs' quarterback. Little Mike popped the lineman in the teeth and started a general brawl on the field. "Really," said Mike, "I try not to get into fights. I once got into one with Willie Brown, a defensive back. He beat the hell out of me and I got fined 50 bucks. It just isn't worth $50 to get the hell beat out of you."

He always remains conscious of his size. When he first went into pro ball, he said, "I expect to play a total of five years, no more. I don't think I can last longer than five years."

Sore ribs and other assorted hurts limited his play drastically in 1968 and cut his yardage almost in half: 564. He wasn't able to break away for any long runs. But he was piqued that anybody would attribute his injuries to the old business about his being too small for pro ball. "Jim Nance has been hurt a lot," he said. "Why doesn't anybody say he was hurt because he's too big?"

If Mike Garrett were to quit pro football abruptly, it would not be due to the physical hazards of the trade. He resolved them a long time ago. He is, however, increasingly intent on being more than just a football player. Between seasons, he has studied for a master's degree in sociology. He has expressed a desire to return to his old section of Los Angeles some day and work on a poverty project. After his rookie year, and the Watts riots, he went into the ghetto to visit schools and talk to the kids. He called it Operation Cool-Head.

The theme of social work has been dominant in his adult life. In January 1969, he was involved in a tragic accident. An airline stewardess whom he'd been dating was killed when a car which Mike was driving skidded on wet pavement into the path of another car. Sensitive Mike, cut only slightly, was left in a state of shock and there was some speculation he might even quit football.

But there's a lot of resiliency in a twenty-five-year-old who still measures accomplishment by how far he carries a football. "There is room for the little man in this game," he said. "But the little man must work twice as hard as the big man to achieve success. Every time I carry the ball, I feel I'm running for every small guy who ever wanted to play the game of football."

MICHAEL LOCKETT "MIKE" GARRETT

BORN: April 12, 1944 Height: 5'9" Weight: 195

University of Southern California

Kansas City, 1966–68

Year	G.	RUSHING Att.	Yds.	Avg.	TD.	PASS RECEIVING P.C.	Yds.	Avg.	TD.	SCORING TD.	Pts.
1966	14	147	801	*5.5	6	15	175	11.7	1	8	48
1967	14	236	1087	4.6	9	46	261	5.7	1	10	60
1968	14	164	564	3.4	3	33	359	10.9	3	6	36
PRO TOTALS —3 YEARS	42	547	2452	4.5	18	94	795	8.5	5	24	144

* Led AFL.

Hewritt Dixon

HE'S THE GUY WE USE TO GET US OUT OF THE HOLE. HEWRITT DIXON'S THE BEST FULLBACK IN THE LEAGUE.
— *Daryle Lamonica, quarterback, Oakland Raiders.*

Hewritt Dixon takes a quick blow from his offensive chores as the fullback of the Oakland Raiders.

The Hewritt Dixons of Alachua, Florida, a little farm town north of Gainesville, just off U.S. 75 leading to Georgia, knew their first-born was someone special when he was twelve years old. Hewritt, Jr., was in the sixth grade, and his Uncle Rufus, eighteen, was a tackle on the high school team. Hewritt was a big kid for his age, 6 feet and 202 pounds. In little farm communities of 1,000 or so people, the school team will take all comers. Hewritt put on a uniform and beat out Uncle Rufus for the starting position.

"Poor Uncle Rufus," mused Hewritt, years later when he was established as a pro star, "his main interest was football. He quit school. Still lives in Alachua."

Hewritt's mother, a gentle soul, was opposed to the violent sport. Hewritt convinced her that he was merely staying late after school to watch practice as a spectator, not a participant. But Hewritt didn't reckon with the power of a loudspeaker. The Dixons lived only two blocks from the school. The opening game, the lineups were announced over the public address system. Mrs. Dixon, hanging clothes in the backyard for the eight little Dixons, heard Hewritt's name blared loud and clear.

"That was the first she knew what I'd been doing," said Hewritt. "But she let me stay with it." Hewritt played six years of high school football and went on to Florida A&M in Tallahassee. By then, he was fairly well filled out to his present 6'2" and 230 pounds. Since he also was able to run 100 yards in 9.9 seconds, he was placed at fullback. His teammates called him "Freight Train" because in the kind of company he was in, Hewritt was a chugger. Bob Paremore and Gene White, a couple of halfbacks who had shots in pro ball, each ran the 100 in 9.4. Bobby Hayes, who came along soon after, ran the 100 in 9.1.

Dixon didn't get much attention. The Denver Broncos drafted him on the eighth round in 1963, the Pittsburgh Steelers on the eleventh round. He signed with Denver, ripped a knee cartilage in his rookie season and got into only five games. The night before the opening game of the next season, Coach Jack Faulkner of the Broncos said, "Hewritt, you better study your play book real good tonight, especially the pass patterns. Tomorrow you're starting at tight end." Hewritt had never played the position. But in the course of the next two seasons, he settled down as a blocker and as a steady third down receiver.

Out in Oakland, California, meanwhile, Al Davis was studying game films one night to pass the time—that's what coaches do to relax—when he saw this big end from Denver take off with the ball after grabbing it with his long fingers. "Say," noted Davis, "there's a natural fullback if I ever saw one." In 1966, he shipped Archie Matsos, a traveled linebacker, to the Broncos for Dixon even up. Within one year, Matsos had retired, but Hewritt's career picked up momentum. Mac Speedie, the end coach, used to wave a branch in his face to make sure he concentrated on the ball. The experience as a receiver helped.

"Hew is a big problem to the defenses," said Johnny Rauch, who took over for Davis as coach. "He's got excellent speed for a big man, and he can run deep patterns as well

Determined running and sure hands for gripping the football feature Hewritt Dixon's fullback performance for the Raiders.

as short ones. When we need short rushing yardage, we call on him for that, too."

Cookie Gilchrist was always considered the toughest man to drag down by defensive linemen, but Gerry Philbin, the all-league end of the Jets said, "Dixon hits you as hard as anyone."

As the Raiders progressed to an AFL championship in 1967, Hewritt was their most versatile performer. He led them in both ground gaining and pass receiving. Until Clem Daniels got hurt in the ninth game, he threatened to set every record for passes caught by a back. But with Daniels out, Hew had to take over more of the ball carrying duties. He finished with 59 receptions.

"I've been around since the start of the AFL," said Don Webb of Boston to the big Raider fullback after tangling with him on the field, "but I've never seen a runner who hits as hard as you do." Dixon revelled in the work.

"My folks were laborers," said Dixon, "and they were barely making it when I was a kid. I would spend all day running in the potato fields. We were poor but happy. My father was a good sandlot ball player. When I was five, he started me out catching the ball and being proud to keep my body fit. After homework every day, he took us out to the potato patch to play ball. When I was in the tenth grade, I was offered a contract by the Milwaukee organization as a catcher."

Football has paid off for him, however. With the money he got for helping lead the Raiders to the Super Bowl, Hewritt built his parents and younger brothers and sisters a house in Alachua to replace the rented, weather-beaten clapboard place they had lived in for twenty years. This normal filial act is typical Dixon. He's a solid citizen of the Raiders. In 1968, he was elected the offensive team captain. "There are six blacks and sixteen whites on the offensive team," he said, "and I got a majority of the votes, so it wasn't just the blacks that put me in. That's very important. We have no racial divisions on this club."

His receding hairline has led to pet names around the clubhouse—Old Man, Gramps, Baldy—all of which he takes with good nature. He doesn't even resent being kidded about his frugality. He's almost as tough with a buck as with a football. Ike Lassiter, the huge defensive end, is a close friend. "Hewritt took his wife to a movie once," said Ike, smiling, "and they sat in the $2 seats. She said she couldn't see well. So Hewritt went to the box office and bought her a $2.50 ticket. He told her they'd meet after the show, and he went back to his seat."

Dixon, at twenty-eight, also became the elder statesman of the Raiders. "He's given me a lot of advice," said Carleton Oats, a defensive lineman who also went to Florida A&M, "and he's taken care of me financially to make sure I was all right. I know he's done the same for others."

And on the field, he did all that was required of him. In 1968, he was the AFL's third leading rusher with a personal peak of 865 yards, despite a twisted knee that slowed him up for three games. He ran for 187 yards in a 24–15 victory over Houston.

The juices of competition flowed in him. "I almost never sweat," said Hewritt, "but the day of a game, water just pours out of me. I feel like a rookie again."

HEWRITT FREDERICK DIXON, JR.

BORN: Jan. 8, 1940   Height: 6'2''   Weight: 230

Florida A&M University

Denver, 1963–65
Oakland, 1966–68

| Year | G. | RUSHING | | | | PASS RECEIVING | | | | SCORING | |
		Att.	Yds.	Avg.	TD.	P.C.	Yds.	Avg.	TD.	TD.	Pts.
1963	5	23	105	4.6	2	10	130	13.0	0	2	12
1964	14	18	25	1.4	0	38	585	15.4	1	1	6
1965	14		(None)			25	354	14.2	2	2	12
1966	14	68	277	4.1	5	29	345	11.9	4	9	54
1967	13	153	559	3.7	5	59	563	9.5	2	7	42
1968	14	206	865	4.2	7	38	360	9.5	2	9	54

PRO TOTALS
—6 YEARS   74   468   1831   3.9   19   199   2337   11.7   11   30   180

The Million Dollar Parlay

DONNY ANDERSON TALKS A LOT ABOUT
HAVING A GOOD TIME, BUT ACTUALLY
HE'S JUST A RED-BLOODED AMERICAN
BOY. WELL, MAYBE A LITTLE MORE RED-
BLOODED THAN MOST.
—*Jim Grabowski, fullback,*
Green Bay Packers.

There's a million dollars of backfield talent roosting here on helmets on the Packers' sideline. That's how much the Pack had to dole out for Donny Anderson (44) and Jim Grabowski (33).

As a community-owned matter of civic pride, the Green Bay Packers have certain legal advantages. When they really want something to enhance their product, they don't have to check their reserve of profits to see if they can afford it. The stockholders don't get dividends and don't expect them. The Packers plow all their profits back into the team. In the golden age of professional football reached in the 1960's, this turned out to be a terrific boon.

Because in 1966, coach and general manager Vince Lombardi looked around at his backfield talent and saw that Paul Hornung was thirty-one years and had a pinched neck nerve and Jimmy Taylor was thirty-one and beginning to show the effects of his bumping style of running. Then Vince looked around the country and saw a big thoroughbred type at Texas Tech named Donny Anderson and a standard bred at Illinois named Jim Grabowski.

And Vince said, as dryly as a stockholders' report, "I want them."

This meant, of course, a million dollar commitment by the Packers. Anderson, drafted No. 1 as a future in 1965, was highly coveted by the Houston Oilers in his native Texas. Grabowski, the No. 1 draftee of 1966, was being ardently wooed by the Miami Dolphins. But both boys were championship athletes, and those types like to be associated with winners. The Packers were winners, and in the due course of negotiations both committed their football futures to Green Bay. Figures are always open to speculation, but it was reliably reported that Anderson went for a total package of $600,000 spread over a period of years, and Grabowski was bagged for $400,000. A hundred thousand either way would still leave them comfortably settled for a long time.

In the summer of 1966, they checked into the training camp of the Packers at St. Norbert College, a short distance from Green Bay, ready to earn their riches. Grabowski already had a black, air-conditioned limousine to suit his conservative nature. Anderson (called the Golden Palomino) had a flashy wardrobe and an address book. He was going to be Hornung's social apprentice. The veterans on the team might have looked at them disdainfully and enviously because of all the money ballyhoo, but Captain Willie Davis, the defensive end, said, "There's no resentment. The bonuses may have been irritating in principle, but we don't resent the individuals for getting the best deal possible. We just came along a few years too soon ourselves." Hornung, in fact, had entertained Anderson regally, as only Hornung could, when the Packers visited Baltimore the previous seasons and Anderson had been brought in from school at Lubbock, Texas, to see what life on the Packers was like.

All that Grabowski and Anderson had to do was show the Packers they could make their contributions as football players. The first looks were quite impressive. After all, Anderson is a 6'3", 220-pounder with the stride of a whippet. Grabo is an inch shorter but the same weight, a little more compact in appearance, a shade more powerful in his running. Both had impressive college careers. Anderson, who stayed out of school one year because self-admittedly he was a bad student who didn't hit the books and "needed to grow up," was a two-time All-American, a great runner and receiver and punter. Seldom are men drafted on the first round as "futures" (the pros no longer can select collegians until all their eligibility has been completed). Grabowski had broken eleven of Red Grange's running records at Illinois, starred in the Rose Bowl as a sophomore and set a Big Ten mark by rushing for 237 yards in a single game.

Between the two, there never has been the slightest feeling of rivalry. They got acquainted playing in post-season college all-star games and developed a fine rapport, though they are dissimilar as personalities. Anderson is a flip bon vivant who's always looking for the action. Grabowski is pleasant but intense, a Polish butcher's son from Chicago who plots his course in life as steadfastly as he hits a hole in the line. Their personalities are reflected in their styles of play. Anderson is skittish, looking for the broad open spaces. Grabowski is a quick hitter, intent on forward motion. As backfield mates, they complement each other well.

Anderson is the glib one. He teased Grabowski about getting married right after he finished school. "Here we are havin' all this money," he said, "and he's gonna get hitched. We should be takin' advantage of it a little." But Grabowski was the man who came along faster as a contributor to the Packers. Donny had his troubles adjusting to the pro style of backfield play. His blocking was mediocre. His running lacked authority. After his rookie year, Lombardi spoke seriously about recasting him as a flanker back. Grabowski, the understudy to Taylor as a rookie fullback, grabbed off the starting job in 1967 when Taylor left the team. Grabo's running mate in the backfield was not Anderson, but Elijah Pitts.

However, when Pitts tore his Achilles tendon in the eighth game of the season, Donny drew his first starting assignment as a Packer, against the Cleveland Browns, and scored four touchdowns in the game. But his buddy Grabo wasn't Donny's backfield partner. In addition to Pitts, Grabo also went out for the year with a damaged knee and later had an operation. Despite his curtailed service, Grabo led the Packers in rushing.

But Anderson made the more vital contribution to the Packers' drive toward a second straight Super Bowl. Donny was one of the few healthy backs on the team as the Packers squared off with the Dallas Cowboys for the NFL title in 13-below zero weather. At fullback was Chuck Mercein, a New York Giant castoff. The week before, Travis Williams, called the Road Runner, had been the big gun in beating the Rams for the conference crown. But on the frigid turf of Lambeau Field, approaching New Year's eve, Donny shouldered the running load. Late in the fourth quarter, trailing 17–14, the Packers started a drive from deep in their own territory. Twice they were caught in third-down and long yardage situations. Both times, Bart Starr dumped the ball to Donny on safety-valve passes, and he skipped past the Cowboys' linebackers to pick up the first downs and sustain the drive. He also moved the ball up inches from the goal line in the last minute of play to set up Starr's winning quarterback sneak.

In 1968, they finally made it together as a starting unit, but the results were inconclusive. Grabo still wasn't 100 percent recovered from the knee operation during the first half of the season. Donny had to carry most of the load and suddenly thrived with the responsibility. He finished in the league's top ten as a runner and earned a bid to play in the Pro Bowl.

542

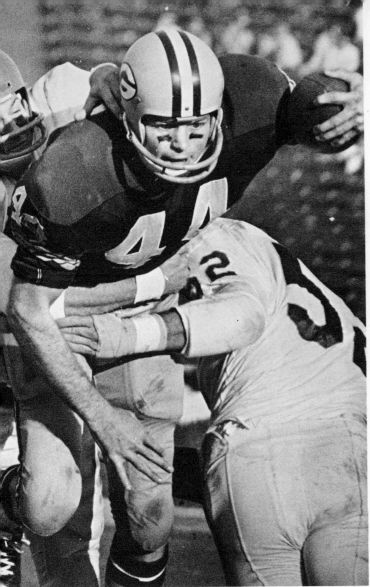

Vernon J. Biever Photo

Donny Anderson has begun to justify the $600,000 invested in him (as well as vested in him) by the Green Bay Packers. He struggles forward against the Chiefs.

Vernon J. Biever Photo

Jim Grabowski was the handpicked successor to Jim Taylor in the Green Bay backfield, a straight ahead runner with good initial burst.

Of course, the Packers, adjusting to life without Lombardi's whiplash (he had turned the coaching over to Phil Bengtson), had a bitterly disappointing season, their first losing record (6-7-1) since 1958. The huge investment in their set of running backs was producing only a relative dribble in capital gains. However, their full market value hadn't been realized yet. Donny Anderson, at the age of twenty-six, and Jim Grabowski, at twenty-five, still had a lot to gain.

JIM GRABOWSKI'S FAVORITE PLAY:

"The name of the play is a '36.' It's just a short off-tackle slant that everybody uses. It's been one of Green Bay's most successful plays over the years. It usually uses zone blocking—the center cutting off the middle linebacker, the guard on the defensive tackle and the tackle on the defensive end. The halfback tries to block the weakside linebacker out first. If he can't, then he takes him any way he can. The tackle tries to take the defensive end any way he can. The split end goes downfield a couple of steps, then goes at the weak safety. This often takes the defensive halfback inside with the split end.

"As the runner, you must read the blocks by the tackle and halfback. The play is designed to go between their blocks. But the runner can also dip around the halfback's block or inside that of the tackle, so he can actually hit at three different holes.

"In my rookie season, 1966, we were playing the Vikings. The situation was third down and 1. We ran this play, and I was hit on the line of scrimmage, but I dipped outside, broke a tackle by the corner back and ran 33 yards for a touchdown."

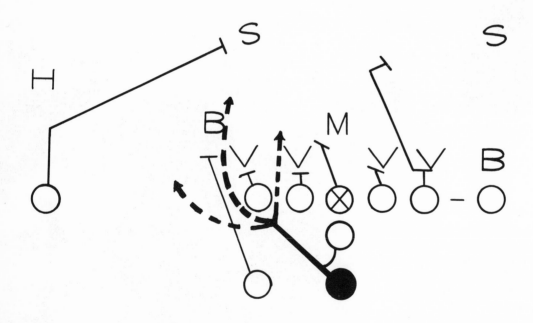

GARRY DONNY ANDERSON

BORN: May 16, 1943   Height: 6'3"   Weight: 220

Texas Tech

Green Bay, 1966–68

Year	G.	Att.	RUSHING Yds.	Avg.	TD.	P.C.	PASS RECEIVING Yds.	Avg.	TD.	SCORING TD.	Pts.
1966	14	25	104	4.2	2	2	33	16.5	0	3	18
1967	14	97	402	4.1	6	22	331	15.0	3	9	54
1968	14	170	761	4.5	5	25	333	13.3	1	6	36
PRO TOTALS —3 YEARS	42	292	1266	4.3	13	49	697	14.2	4	18	108

JAMES S. "GRABO" GRABOWSKI

BORN: Sept. 9, 1944   Height: 6'2"   Weight: 225

University of Illinois

Green Bay, 1966–68

Year	G.	Att.	RUSHING Yds.	Avg.	TD.	P.C.	PASS RECEIVING Yds.	Avg.	TD.	SCORING TD.	Pts.
1966	14	29	127	4.4	1	4	13	3.3	0	1	6
1967	9	120	466	3.9	2	12	171	14.3	1	3	18
1968	14	135	518	3.8	3	18	210	11.7	1	4	24
PRO TOTALS —3 YEARS	37	284	1111	3.9	6	34	394	11.6	2	8	48

The Hurt Ones

IF I AM GOING TO MAKE MY MILLION
DOLLARS, I HAVE TO BE A STARTER. ONLY
THE STARTERS GET THE BUSINESS BREAKS
WHICH GO WITH PROFESSIONAL FOOT-
BALL.

*—Mel Farr, running back,
Detroit Lions.*

Mel Farr carries the future of Detroit's running game in its capable hands. He was sensational for a year and a half until sidetracked by a knee operation.

As the 1969 season dawned in professional football, the state of Gale Sayers' knee evoked as many progress bulletins as a Paris peace conference. One would have thought the future of the professional running game hinged on his recovery to full flight. But there were at least five cities in the National league, outside Chicago, who were more preoccupied by their own health charts. As much as the Chicago Bears were dependent on Sayers, these cities were equally concerned with the recovery of running backs who displayed incisions from surgery within the past year. The list:

Detroit Lions—Mel Farr, knee operation

Dallas Cowboys—Danny Reeves, knee operation

Minnesota Vikings—Dave Osborn, knee operation

Los Angeles Rams—Les Josephson, Achilles tendon operation

Atlanta Falcons—Junior Coffey, knee operation

In every one of these cases, the destiny of the team for 1969 was linked directly to the availability of the above backs. Since all are young and vital (the oldest, at twenty-seven, is Coffey), their prospects are uniformly good to become again highly valued performers.

Mel Farr tore the cartilage in his left knee on the third play of a game against the San Francisco 49ers on October 27, 1968. At the time the Detroit Lions had lost only one game in the NFL season, and Marvelous Melvin was the league's leading rusher. Less than a month later, he was on the operating table. He had tried to come back but complicated his injury by spraining an ankle. The Lions won only one more game the rest of the season. Despite Farr's limited service, no other Lion back came within 200 yards of his rushing total of 597. If they can keep Melvin healthy for one full year, there's no telling what he can accomplish.

In 1967, he was the overwhelming choice of the NFL coaches for the Bert Bell Trophy as the rookie of the year. He suffered two broken noses, a broken toe, a twisted ankle and a pulled hamstring muscle, and still gained 860 yards to place in the Top Five for the season.

"I want to rush for a thousand yards, I want to be Rookie of the Year and I want to make All-Pro," announced Mel when the Lions made him their top draft choice after his college days at UCLA. Mel had gotten himself an agent, and the agent said his price tag to play for the pros was a million dollars. It was cut down to a more realistic $50,000 per annum by the time Mel signed his contract. That was still enough to keep him in a canary yellow Jaguar and enough soul food for his wife and two little babies.

"Farr is the best college halfback I've ever seen," said UCLA coach Tommy Prothro after the long-shanked slasher paced his team to a Rose Bowl triumph in his junior year at school. "Most people are aware of those long, explosive runs which showed his power and speed. What they may not realize is that he is outstanding as a blocker, pass re-

The San Diego Chargers feel Brad Hubbert (26) is as strong as any runner in the pro leagues.

Emerson Boozer, left, has an affinity for scoring territory. However, the psychological scars of a knee operation kept him below par in 1968.

Malcolm W. Emmons

ceiver and faker on plays where he doesn't carry the ball." Prothro used to call him All-Universe.

Truthfully, at 6'2" and 208, Mel was molded to be a running back. He came out of the famous incubator of football talent in Beaumont, Texas, which produced Bubba Smith and Gene Washington, who went to Michigan State, and Jerry Levias, a spectacular All-American at SMU.

In his first game as a pro, he ran through the world champion Green Bay Packers for 95 yards. "It was because I was a rookie," said Mel modestly. "They didn't know what I could do, so they played a normal defense."

Every Sunday night, he called his brother Miller, an all-league defensive back with the Houston Oilers, to compare notes. Miller answered the phone this one evening, after Mel played against Minnesota, and asked, "How'd you do today?"

"Ran for 197 yards," said Mel.

"I knew you were good," said Miller, "but not that good!"

He came within one yard of the club record for a single game, set by Bob Hoern-schemeyer in 1950. "My running can be improved a whole lot," said Mel critically. "I noticed several times I hit the wrong hole. I outran my guard on a trap block. I also fumbled three times and dropped a pass in the open to blow a sure touchdown that would have won the game for us. These are some things I have to learn."

He was also the team's leading pass receiver. "He's the best back to come into the NFL in 20 years," said Bill McPeak, the Lions' offensive coach. All that remained was for Mel, at twenty-four years of age, to stay in one piece long enough to prove it.

Danny Reeves is one of those intangible athletes, like Eddie Stanky was on a baseball field. Eddie couldn't hit, couldn't run, couldn't throw. All he could do was beat you. "He has the intangibles," said the venerable Branch Rickey, the Mahatma of baseball. Danny has them, too. Backs are supposed to have quick starts and blazing speed, up to the line and through before a linebacker can say, "Pete Rozelle." Dan Reeves approaches a hole warily, like a businessman over a lunch menu, then carefully charts his course.

"Guys like Jim Taylor, Jim Grabowski," said Ermal Allen, the Cowboys' backfield coach, "they have quick starts. They hit the hole so fast the linebacker can't react. But Dan's more of a picker. He picks his way until he can turn upfield. Then he's real good."

He's one of the most deceptive people ever to make good in pro ball. After the 1964 college football season, both the NFL and AFL went through more than 500 names in their annual college draft without picking him. The Los Angeles Rams thought about making him a late choice but were afraid they'd be accused of publicity seeking. Their owner's name is also Dan Reeves. "I should have changed *my* name," said Dan Reeves, the owner. Dan Reeves, the player, had been a quarterback at South Carolina. The Cowboys, who herd free agents like a rubber band collector, signed Dan on the long shot he might make it as a defensive safety. They kept him on the squad in 1965 because he showed he could catch a football.

Dan Reeves likes people to know he's "country." A big shot in Dallas, taking him out to dinner, asked Dan if he liked *escargot* (snails). Dan nodded. He thought the man said Chicago.

"He also asked me if I knew what caviar was," smiled Dan, "and I said, 'Sure.' But I didn't."

Danny lived six miles out in the country before he came to town to go to school in the ninth grade. He fed the hogs and cows, baled hay and plowed. "Town" was Americus, Georgia, where the epicurean taste leans strongly to grits.

The kids back in Americus hardly believe Reeves, the established pro who plays halfback for the Dallas Cowboys, one of the explosive offensive teams in football. When Dan turned out for football his sophomore year at Americus, the coach raced all the boys and Danny came in dead last—behind the tackles and guards.

He's faster than that now, doing the 40 in respectable 4.7, which is only two-tenths of a second behind Bullet Bob Hayes, his teammate. But Dan has long, loping strides that are as deceptive as a Texas millionaire wearing blue jeans. He slides and squirms and glides, always in a forward direction. In his first camp with the Cowboys, in 1965, he was put on offense in a rookie game against the Rams, because the Cowboys were out of bodies, and was a revelation.

"He showed the unusual faculty of being where the ball is, of making the big play," said Tom Landry, the coach, who kept Reeves on offense. "Every time we put him in a game he did something. But we still weren't sure he had what we wanted as a running back."

So Mel Renfro, an all-pro defensive safety, was shifted to offense and started the 1966 season at halfback against the New York Giants. He was injured in the first half. Reeves replaced him and caught three touchdown passes, carried the ball six times for 38 yards and made a home for himself. Renfro went back to defense. "Danny has a feel for football," said Don Meredith, the quarterback, "and instinct. Those are qualities you can't teach."

They worked like this:

In a game against Minnesota, Meredith called an "audible" at the line of scrimmage. He called out, "54!" Behind him, Reeves drawled, "You mean 55."

"Right," said Meredith, and threw a touchdown pass.

"Fifty-four is a right formation," explained Reeves, "and we were in a left formation, so the call was 55. Don was calling for a weakside pass to beat the blitz. The weak safety had moved up just a little, which told him the weakside linebacker would blitz, so the safety had come up to cover the halfback. This meant the left corner back was man-to-man on Bob Hayes [the split end] and this is what you want. With the safety up, Bob had the whole middle of the field to run in. The closest help was the strong safety, who had to cover the X-end [tight end]. So the call was for Hayes to run a post pattern and the halfback to run a shoot."

It was pointed out to him that he talked like a quarterback.

"I think like one," he said. "I was one for eight years, and it gets in your blood. Sure tough to shake."

With a warm grin, a handsome face and an ability to blush, Dan quickly became a favorite in Dallas. At a Cowboy luncheon, a fan sent up a question to Coach Landry: "My wife is in love with Dan Reeves, What is your advice?" Landry, fast on his feet, replied, "I have a lot of problems with Dan Reeves, but that isn't one of them."

552

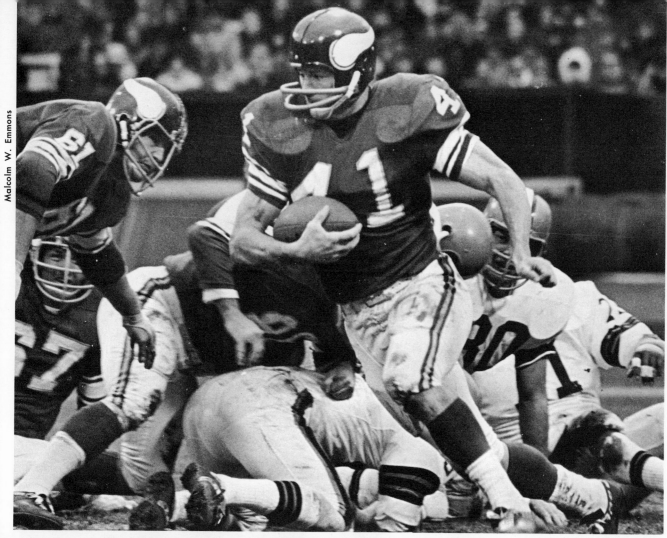

Dave Osborn (41) is the steady hard-hitter who's the staple of a ball control team. The Minnesota Vikings count on him.

The Los Angeles Rams found they couldn't move the ball consistently in 1968 without Les Joseph-son, their blond bull.

In his first full season as a running back, he led the Cowboys in rushing and was second in pass receptions. They won their first division title in history and battled the Packers valiantly in the championship game. The Cowboys were on the two-yard line late in the fourth quarter, needing a touchdown to tie the score. Meredith called a swing pass to Reeves. Danny had a lane to a score, but he dropped the ball. He was seeing double from having been hit hard on the previous play.

That was one of the rare times he didn't make the big play. He scored 16 touchdowns in '66 and continued as a productive clutch performer through '67. Against Washington, the Cowboys trailed 14–10 with 10 seconds to play. From the 36-yard line, Reeves flared out in the flat, the weakside linebacker failed to pick him up, and he caught a wobbly pass for the winning touchdown.

Something went out of the Cowboys when Danny's knee collapsed against the St. Louis Cardinals in mid-October 1968. He was trying to cut behind a Cowboy escort when a flying block-type tackle by Lonnie Sanders, a defensive back, hit him with his foot extended. The injury was the same suffered by Gale Sayers. The Cowboys had an adequate physical replacement in Craig Baynham, who is bigger and faster.

"But we missed his leadership," admitted Landry.

Those intangibles again.

Behind those faceless bar masks that are supposed to safeguard a football player's molars, Dave Osborn and Les Josephson—a pair of sturdy six-footers—are almost as indistinguishable as the Bobbsey Twins, except for their uniforms. Osborn plays for the Minnesota Vikings, which means he wears purple; Josephson performs in the royal blue of the Los Angeles Rams. Both are hard-running, straight ahead towhead types who were nicked by injuries in the 1968 exhibition season. Both are products of the Dakotas, with little fanfare preceding them into pro ball. Both have been active for four seasons.

Josephson, at twenty-seven, is a year older than Dave. He went to little Augustana College in South Dakota and was signed by the Cowboys as a free agent, then quickly traded to the Rams. He blossomed out three years later as the heavy duty ball carrier of the Rams, gaining 800 yards in their rush to a division title. He also caught 37 passes and was picked to play in the Pro Bowl game. "I'm not the breakaway type," said Josie. "I have only average speed. I must make up for it by staying in top condition."

But running on the field in a warm-up exercise for a preseason game against Cleveland, Josie tore a muscle in his calf, then later ripped his Achilles' tendon while undergoing rehabilitation for the original injury. He missed all of 1968.

Osborn, sometimes called "Rocky" by the Vikings, was a thirteenth round draft choice out of the University of North Dakota. After spot duty for a couple of years, he blasted out as the second leading runner in the NFL in 1967, gaining 972 yards. "The average football fan knows that Ozzie is a great runner," said Coach Bud Grant, "but what they don't realize is that he's an outstanding blocker. When Bill Brown made a good run, you could be sure Osborn had thrown an important block." Osborn kept highly publicized Clint Jones, the No. 1 draft choice, on the bench.

554

The little zing that was in the Atlanta ground attack disappeared when Junior Coffey (34), running behind Dan Grimm, hurt his knee in 1968 training camp.

But in a 1968 preseason game, he also was hurt, ripping a knee cartilage. The Vikings, hopeful he'd recover quickly after an operation, kept him on the active list. He returned to action as a regular in the final three games of the year.

At their best, Rocky and Josie are not stirring runners. But they're the kind a coach feels he can win with.

Junior Lee Coffey is his real name. He also hurt his knee before the 1968 regular season and sat out the fall. No one really claims the Atlanta Falcons' title chances were seriously damaged by his absence. With or without Junior, the Falcons were not an imposing team. But after he got hurt in an early camp scrimmage, they were definitely worse. Junior is a compact 6' 1", 215-pound fullback who was picked up by the Falcons from Green Bay in the 1966 expansion draft. He was expendable, since the Packers had just signed Donny Anderson and Jim Grabowski for their running corps.

In his only season with the Packers, Junior had carried the ball just three times. But with Atlanta, the University of Washington graduate got a chance to play regularly and was notable for his consistency. He gained 722 yards in 1966 and 722 yards in 1967. The figure was 0 for '68. It hurt the Falcons as much as it did Junior.

The recovery potential of running backs can be measured by the examples of Tucker Frederickson of the New York Giants and Johnny Roland of the St. Louis Cardinals. They came back from knee surgery to earn their salaries as running backs in 1968. Their level of production didn't measure up to their earlier efforts as pro stars. But at the end of the season both were running in the uninhibited style that had made them prized chattels when they first became pros.

Ivan Charles "Tucker" Frederickson was the first college player chosen by an NFL club in 1965. An All-American at Auburn, he was a kid who could be used at half a dozen different positions—linebacker, defensive back, safety, tight end, halfback, fullback. The New York Giants placed him at fullback because he stands 6' 2" and weighs 225 pounds, and for one year he justified all the confidence they had in him.

"He's the quickest big man I've ever seen," said Pop Ivy of the Giant coaching staff.

With his turned-up nose and his soft Florida accent, Tucker was a natural for popularity in the Big City. He lived in the East 60's, in an apartment building where his neighbors on all sides were 300 airline stewardesses. Less ostentatiously than Joe Namath, who came along at the same time and had a pad a few blocks north, Tucker enjoyed the benefits of being a big athletic hero in the big city. He didn't even mind not getting $400,000.

"I wouldn't have the nerve to ask for that kind of money," Tucker blushed. "I got what I wanted."

He instantly became the regular fullback, and a good one. He blocked as well as any back in football, showed ability as a receiver and gave every indication that he would become an all-pro in due course. New York was a fun city for Tucker Frederickson. "This is where I wanted to play," he said as a rookie. "This is the place to be. Who knows, I could be busted up next week and never play again."

556

With incisions on both knees, Tucker Frederickson (24) has been held back as a potent force for the New York Giants. But the young husky from Auburn has shown signs of a strong revival.

Johnny Roland of the St. Louis Cardinals, recovered from knee surgery, is what they need for championship aspirations.

He wore $150 alligator shoes (bought wholesale, of course). His second day in New York, someone stole his new Corvette. It was recovered sans top, steering wheel or hub caps. "Don't need it 'round here, anyhow," he said. With his buddies like Ernie Koy (his 6′3″, 230-pound partner in a backfield they called the Baby Bulls), Tucker made the night scene at Mr. Laffs and other "singles" places on the East side. The amiable fullback had a ball.

But life turned grim in the next training camp of the Giants when his knee was seriously damaged in a running-tackling exercise. He reinjured it in an exhibition game and missed the entire season. He came back to play in 1967, timidly, and then hurt the other knee.

"He is a twenty-five-year-old with the legs of a forty-five-year-old," said a Giant follower.

"Note quite true," retorted Tucker. "Sometimes I feel like a forty-five-year-old with sixty-five-year-old legs." And then he went on to tell the effects of injury.

"I've lost a step, at least, he admitted. "I don't come out of the backfield as quickly and I don't hit the line with as much power as I used to. The physical things can be overcome to an extent; it's the mental part that hangs you up. But I feel better.

"What made a big difference was passing the New York stockbroker's test. Before, all I had was football. I had to play. Now I know I can do something else, so I play with more abandon. If I play, I play. If don't—well, I don't."

Benched for a while, he got his job back as regular fullback and led the Giants in rushing again.

Johnny Roland went through almost the same experience, although his injury was less severe, in St. Louis. Johnny came into the NFL in 1966 as its brightest new offensive star. At the University of Missouri he had been, ironically, an All-American defensive back.

He was not the fastest man ever to hit the pros, but he had just enough speed to play halfback and qualify for end sweeps. At 6′2″ and 210 pounds, his power was obvious. He proved his dedication when he practiced with the College All-Stars in late July for six days of the week, and on the seventh traveled a few miles north to the Cardinals' camp at Lake Forest, Illinois, to participate in their workouts for a running start on his pro career (and also compensate for his lack of offensive work in college).

"He knows his assignments," said Bill Koman, the veteran linebacker, "makes no mistakes and never complains. He's a pro."

For most of two seasons, Johnny carried the ground attack of the Cardinals. But in the thirteenth game of his second year, as he got within reach of the magical 1,000-yard goal, Johnny's knee crumpled when a linebacker flattened him on an end sweep.

He was supposed to be physically sound again in 1968 after an operation, but the mental hangup that all running backs seem to have after surgery hounded Roland through most of the schedule. He had only flashes of his old form. At the age of twenty-six, however, Johnny Roland didn't despair. He'd be back to run another day.

MELVIN FARR

BORN: Nov. 3, 1944   Height: 6'2"   Weight: 208

University of California at Los Angeles

Detroit, 1967–68

Year	G.	Att.	RUSHING Yds.	Avg.	TD.	P.C.	PASS RECEIVING Yds.	Avg.	TD.	SCORING TD.	Pts.
1967	13	206	860	4.2	3	39	317	8.1	3	6	36
1968	10	128	597	4.7	3	24	375	15.6	4	7	42
PRO TOTALS —2 YEARS	23	324	1457	4.5	6	63	692	11.0	7	13	78

DANIEL EDWARD "DAN" REEVES

BORN: Jan. 19, 1944   Height: 6'1"   Weight: 205

University of South Carolina

Dallas Cowboys, 1965–68

Year	G.	Att.	RUSHING Yds.	Avg.	TD.	P.C.	PASS RECEIVING Yds.	Avg.	TD.	SCORING TD.	Pts.
1965	13	33	102	3.1	2	9	210	23.3	1	3	18
1966	14	175	757	4.3	8	41	557	13.6	8	*16	96
1967	14	173	603	3.5	5	39	490	12.6	6	11	66
1968	4	40	178	4.5	4	7	84	12.0	1	5	30
PRO TOTALS —4 YEARS	45	421	1640	3.9	19	96	1341	14.0	16	35	210

* Led NFL.

JUNIOR LEE COFFEY

BORN: March 21, 1942   Height: 6'1"   Weight: 215

University of Washington

Green Bay, 1965
Atlanta, 1966–68

Year	G.	Att.	RUSHING Yds.	Avg.	TD.	P.C.	PASS RECEIVING Yds.	Avg.	TD.	SCORING TD.	Pts.
1965	13	3	12	4.0	0		(None)			0	0
1966	14	199	722	3.6	4	15	182	12.1	1	5	30
1967	14	180	722	4.0	4	30	196	6.5	1	5	30
1968						(Injured)					
PRO TOTALS —3 YEARS	41	382	1456	3.8	8	45	378	8.4	2	10	60

560

IVAN CHARLES "TUCKER" FREDERICKSON

BORN: Jan. 12, 1943   Height: 6'2"   Weight: 225

Auburn University

New York Giants, 1965–68

Year	G.	Att.	Yds.	Avg.	TD.	P.C.	Yds.	Avg.	TD.	TD.	Pts.
			RUSHING				PASS RECEIVING			SCORING	
1965	13	195	659	3.4	5	24	177	7.4	1	6	36
1966	0				(Missed entire season with injury)						
1967	10	97	311	3.2	2	19	153	8.1	0	2	12
1968	14	142	486	3.4	1	10	64	6.4	2	3	18
PRO TOTALS —4 YEARS	37	434	1456	3.4	8	53	394	7.4	3	11	66

JOHNNY EARL ROLAND

BORN: May 21, 1943   Height: 6'2"   Weight: 210

University of Missouri

St. Louis, 1966–68

Year	G.	Att.	Yds.	Avg.	TD.	P.C.	Yds.	Avg.	TD.	TD.	Pts.
			RUSHING				PASS RECEIVING			SCORING	
1966	14	192	695	3.6	5	21	213	10.1	0	6	36
1967	13	234	876	3.7	10	20	269	13.5	1	11	66
1968	14	121	455	3.8	2	8	97	12.1	0	2	12
PRO TOTALS —3 YEARS	41	547	2026	3.7	17	49	579	11.8	1	19	114

Weighted Results

HOW LONG CAN JIM NANCE LAST?
WELL, HE'S BIG AND STRONG AND FAST
AND AGILE. HE'S GOING TO LAST A LOT
LONGER THAN THE GUYS WHO GET IN
HIS WAY.
>   —*Babe Parilli, quarterback,*
>   *Boston Patriots.*

For a couple of years, Jim "Bo" Nance of the Boston Patriots devastated defensive lines; he's still young enough to regain that form—if he can control his weight.

Malcolm W. Emmons

Syracuse University has a history of great running backs. Jimmy Brown, Ernie Davis and, most recently, Floyd Little (now of the Denver Broncos) etched a tradition. They all wore number 44 on their jerseys, a hallowed set of numerals in the annals of the Orange. In between Davis and Little, another runner matriculated on Piety Hill—Jim Nance of Indiana, Pennsylvania. He wore number 35.

"I didn't want to be compared to Brown or any of the others," he said. "I wanted my own identity."

He didn't achieve it at Syracuse, where he was a disappointment as a football player. He ate too much, got too fat, didn't exert himself. "I don't think I was prepared for such a big school," he said. "I wasn't grown up enough to accept the life and to discipline myself."

Pro scouts keep tab on a player's social as well as physical qualities. The reports on Nance weren't encouraging. The Boston Patriots ignored him until the 19th round of the 1965 college draft. Then Big Bo walked into camp weighing 260 pounds. They expected a fullback who weighed 225.

"The transition to the pros had me worried," claimed Nance. "I just kept eating because I was worried. I eat almost anything and it sticks to me. It's my metabolism."

Coach Mike Holovak didn't want to give up on any man over 200 pounds who could run a respectable 10-second 100. He threatened and cajoled and finally told Big Bo that if he didn't cut his weight down, he'd be making his living as an offensive guard. After limited, mediocre service his rookie year, Nance got the message.

He showed up in training camp for the 1966 season weighing 235 pounds, which is almost sylph-like for Big Bo. Within three months, Coach Holovak was telling the world, "Jim Nance can be the greatest fullback who ever lived." And the rest of the AFL wasn't in any position to dispute him. Big Bo was a rambling terror as he tore up defenses, good and bad, in the most devastating one-man parade in the history of the American Football League. When the regular season was over, he had set an all-time league rushing mark of 1,458 yards and, equally important, had put the stamp of Nance on every defensive player in the AFL.

"I've been noticing," said Bo, "that when a guy hits me head-on, he's not quite so quick to hit me the next time. So I keep running at him and pretty soon he starts to turn his shoulder and then I know I've got him. When a man turns his shoulder on me, I'm going to get past him before he turns back."

There was no finesse to Big Bo's style. He didn't run around the ends, though Holovak intended to drill him on that maneuver to provide a little more variety to the Patriot's ground attack. Nance took the handoff from quarterback Babe Parilli and barreled straight ahead or slanted slightly toward the tackles. It scarcely bothered him that he was bumping hordes of bodies on every play. He was built for the buffeting. This is how Tim Horgan of the *Boston Traveler* described him: "His shoulders are as broad as Charles Street, his chest as deep as the Frog Pond. And if he loiters on the Common, somebody will tack a sign on his thighs reading, '*Ulmus Americanus.*'"

The San Diego Chargers ganged up on him once, and an elbow clopped him on the head. Jim was seeing three of each Charger. That didn't deter him, either. He picked out the middle one and steamrollered him. "I want them to run into me every play," he gloated. "That's my job. Sure, it hurts sometimes, but I figure it hurts them more than it hurts me. I'm bigger than most of them and I've got momentum going."

The momentum carried him to all-league honors and designation as AFL Player of the Year. "He's the best fullback I've seen, next to Jimmy Brown," said quarterback Parilli, who admitted he was a little prejudiced in his view. "He's certainly the best I've ever played with. And he's only twenty-three years old."

Brute strength was Big Bo's tour de force, and yet enigmatically it didn't tally with his character. The Patriots called him "Odd Job" because he looked vaguely like the villain in the James Bond movie, "Goldfinger." But Bo proved to be a complex, sensitive man when he wasn't carrying a football.

He is from Indiana, Pennsylvania, in the western anthracite belt. He was always a big kid, which singled him out for such sports as football and wrestling (he became an intercollegiate champ in the latter). But his father didn't want his boy to play football. The Nance house was right next to a football field, and a kid in the neighborhood had been killed on it.

"My dad worked in the mines for forty years," said Jim. "He worked hard. His job was what they call a 'shot-fire.' That's the guy who plants the little sticks of dynamite that blast out the chunks of coal. He thought football was more dangerous. I didn't play until junior high. I played a whole year in the seventh grade without my dad knowing it. Everyone in the family knew, but they were afraid to tell him."

By the time he was sixteen, Jim weighed 216 pounds and was timed in 10.1 seconds for the 100-yard dash. A career in football was inevitable after he made the all-state team as a fullback. Watching Jimmy Brown run for Syracuse, on television, influenced his choice of university. He was not the college player his coaches expected. "To me, Jimmy Brown was up here," he said, reaching high over his head, "and Jim Nance was far below."

But that tremendous physique sustained him through three spotty varsity seasons and the initial disappointment as a pro. He matured enough to ignore the spectre of Brown and to override his phlegmatic nature with a sudden desire to excel. "I'm going to be the best back in the league," he said to himself before his second pro campaign, and he was.

Then he said with conviction, "If you want something, you go after it and get it. In this game you really should whack people. I enjoy knocking them out of the way. It's a feeling of accomplishment."

"When Jim hits people," said Holovak, "he not only stops them, he straightens them up."

He sustained his claim as pro football's most powerful runner with another strong performance in 1967, gaining 1,216 yards, though the Patriots slumped to last place in the Eastern Division. "I learned what it's like to be keyed on," said Nance, "to be a marked man." He also felt that he was getting a better concept of the game:

"The first year is like an introduction. You come in not knowing what pro football really is and you end the year not much smarter. I figured I could run over people. I found out I couldn't. I don't think any rookie learns a lot. All he gets is a little orientation.

"In the second year, you start to pick up things—how to cut away from tackles, how to choose the right holes. You learn who to look for on blitzes. But it still isn't a clear picture.

"Then comes the third year and you start adding everything up. You get to a point where you know when your quarterback is going to check off before he actually does. You can see when the other team is going to blitz and you don't have to wonder who you're going to block, but how."

He was the epitome of confidence as he looked ahead. "Before I'm finished," he announced, "there are a lot of records I'd like to put out of sight." He was candid about aiming at Jim Brown's record of 1,863 yards rushing in a single season. Nance's popularity in the Boston area was firm. He opened the Jim Nance Lounge in Roxbury. He spoke out firmly about his posture for civil rights, not as an extremist but as a pragmatist: "I believe you can't let people run over you, but by the same token I prefer non-violence. You can't get away from violence by causing it."

He also talked frankly about his marriage to the former Kathy O'Brien, a white girl: "We have the same problems that every young couple has but none concerning the fact that it is an interracial marriage."

And about himself: "I'm the type who doesn't like to have other people tell me what to do. I don't need their advice, and I don't mean this arrogantly. I have always been that way."

In 1968, however, playing on the second year of a reported $125,000 contract, Nance had a bad season—for him. He hurt his ankle in the Patriot's final pre-season game. He favored it and pulled a muscle in his other leg. The inactivity ballooned his weight to 247 pounds. He was used less as a runner and gained less—under 600 yards. After the season, doctors operated on his ankle. The Patriots had a new regime, led by Clive Rush, a former Jets' assistant. The status of Nance in the new setup was indeterminate. Big Bo, the AFL's strongest runner, would have to prove himself again.

For power imagery, the only current fullback in the AFL close to Nance is Hoyle Granger of the Houston Oilers. His legs are stanchions as thick as the cypress of his native Louisiana. Granger (pronounced grawn-jay) is the embodiment of the modern fullback. He's 6'1" and weighs 225 with those trunk-like legs and good straight-ahead speed. He blocks and catches and has a stoic attitude about the heavy physical demands of the job. He's used to work. He developed his physique toiling in the fields of his father's rice farm at Oberlin, Louisiana, forty miles northeast of Lake Charles. They measured the calves of his legs at 19½ inches when he was a junior in college.

567

Hoyle is a Cajun, a descendant of the early French settlers of Louisiana. He speaks French back home. Charley Tolar, his predecessor as a fullback of the Oilers, was a Cajun, too. Charley was 5′ 6″, which provides a gauge of progress in the AFL.

"The first time I saw him as a rookie," said Tolar, "I knew he had the size, speed, and ability to be a super star. What's more, he really wanted to be a football player. We didn't get many rookies like that in the old days."

And yet when the Oilers drafted and signed him out of Mississippi State University in 1966, Hoyle was cut from the active list just before the opening game because Coach Wally Lemm couldn't figure a rookie who didn't say anything, didn't seem to know anything and, in the Oilers' system, couldn't do anything. Apparently, he wasn't all dumb, however, since his safety deposit box contained a contract with an estimated value of $300,000—the Baltimore Colts had been after him, too—and a no-cut clause which insured he'd get the money.

When Hoyle was dropped and put on the taxi squad, the Oilers signed antiquated old John Henry Johnson. But in the first month of the season, they brought the kid back and revised their ideas about him. Every time he carried the ball, he gained seven yards. What the Oilers had mistaken for stupidity was reticence. Hoyle was confused. At Mississippi State, they handed him the ball and said, "Run." The pros did it a lot more complicated. They had audibles, an oral change of signals at the line of scrimmage to meet shifting defenses.

"I made a mistake," said Lemm. "It wasn't lack of intelligence by a long shot. Hoyle is a smart boy and was a good student in college. He memorized our play book in record time. It's just that he had no idea what audibles were and was too quiet to say anything about it."

"Once they explained what an audible was," nodded Hoyle, "I had no trouble."

Before the season was over, he had gained 178 yards in one game against the San Diego Chargers. He slithered through the Oakland line on a hopelessly muddy field, outran his blockers and required a three-man mugging to bring him down after a 69-yard sprint. The next year, as Houston rallied to Eastern Division title, Hoyle gained 1,194 yards and left no doubt about his force as a fullback. He also led the Oilers in pass receiving with 31 catches.

There was a slight tailoff in 1968, largely due to the fact that Hoyle didn't have consistent support in the backfield, with three or four different running mates. The twenty-five-year-old plunger wasn't discouraged, though. He has a simple philosophy of running:

"I just try to give them a good lick and bounce off."

568

JAMES SOLOMON "BO" NANCE

BORN: Dec. 30, 1942   Height: 6'1"   Weight: 240

Syracuse University

Boston, 1965–68

Year	G.	Att.	Yds.	Avg.	TD.	P.C.	Yds.	Avg.	TD.	TD.	Pts.
			RUSHING				PASS RECEIVING			SCORING	
1965	14	111	321	2.9	5	12	83	6.9	0	5	30
1966	14	*299	*1458	4.9	*11	8	103	12.9	0	11	66
1967	14	*269	*1216	4.5	7	22	196	8.9	1	8	48
1968	14	177	593	3.4	4	14	51	3.6	0	4	24
PRO TOTALS —4 YEARS	56	856	3588	4.2	27	56	430	7.7	1	28	168

* Led AFL.

HOYLE JOHN GRANGER

BORN: March 7, 1944   Height: 6'1"   Weight: 225

Mississippi State University

Houston, 1966–68

Year	G.	Att.	Yds.	Avg.	TD.	P.C.	Yds.	Avg.	TD.	TD.	Pts.
			RUSHING				PASS RECEIVING			SCORING	
1966	11	56	388	6.9	1	12	104	8.7	1	2	12
1967	14	236	1194	5.1	6	31	300	9.7	3	9	54
1968	14	202	848	4.2	7	26	361	13.9	0	7	42
PRO TOTALS —3 YEARS	39	494	2430	4.9	14	69	765	11.1	4	18	106

The New Breed

IN RECENT TIMES THERE HAVE BEEN
ONLY THREE TRULY GREAT BREAKAWAY
RUNNERS IN PROFESSIONAL FOOTBALL:
JIM BROWN, GALE SAYERS, AND LEROY
KELLY. THERE WILL SOON BE A FOURTH:
O. J. SIMPSON.
    —*Fran Tarkenton, quarterback,*
    New York Giants.

A virtual unknown, on an expansion team, Paul Robinson was a revelation as a rookie with the Cincinnati Bengals, pacing the AFL in rushing. Aaron Brown of the Kansas City Chiefs, in dark jersey, reaches for him over a block attempt.

For the young running back of the late 1960's, opportunity definitely sent a calling card with the letters "AFL" on it. The young, rising American League was led in ground-gaining for the 1968 season by two newcomers, Paul Robinson of the Cincinnati Bengals and Robert Holmes of the Kansas City Chiefs. Neither had any advance reputation. In 1969, there would be O. J. Simpson of the University of Southern California and the Buffalo Bills, and O. J. was the most heralded player to enter the pros since Harold "Red" Grange more than 40 years ago.

Meanwhile, back on the fields of the NFL, not a single rookie's name was spotted among the top 20 ground gainers of 1968.

Cincinnati's Robinson was the first rookie ever to gain 1,000 yards (the exact total was 1,023). No one in the world was more surprised than this son of a Tucson, Arizona, janitor that he was running for a living. Through two years of junior college and two years at the University of Arizona, he had been a track man, setting a school record in the hurdles. But he didn't have his degree. His track eligibility was gone. The only way he could stay on scholarship was to play another sport—like football. So he turned out in football togs for a fifth year of study at Arizona. Somebody noticed him. The newly organized Cincinnati Bengals made him their third draft choice in '68.

"Actually," said Robinson, "playing one year of college might have been a big break for me. I didn't have to unlearn anything."

When he reported to the Bengals in July, he was asked if he had any goals. A big grin split his face. "Yes," said the unknown, "I want to make rookie of the year." He laughed. "Anyway, rookie of the week." He laughed some more. "Maybe I better make the team first."

In one year of pro ball, the swift 198-pound halfback gained more yards than he had in three years of high school and one year of college ball—laughing all the way.

Robert Holmes, the second leading rusher in the AFL, startled the Kansas City Chiefs when he showed up. He was a vision of the past. A few years ago the Chiefs had a wonderful young man named Mack Lee Hill playing fullback for them. His death during the course of a routine leg operation shocked them. Mack was built like a fire-plug, under six feet, weighing 225 pounds. He had come to them, a virtual unknown, from Southern University, and worked himself into a starting job in 1964–65.

The Chiefs had no shortage of running backs when Holmes reported. He was a 14th draft choice, also from Southern University. He was 5′ 9″ and weighed 225 pounds. "That was the thing I remembered most in training camp," said Coach Hank Stram. "He had this remarkable resemblance to Mack Lee Hill."

It turned out that Holmes also ran like Hill, with good speed and balance and power. As injuries decimated the Chiefs' running corps, Holmes got his chance. He played one half in their third game, started the fourth, ran 76 yards for a touchdown and was a fixture thereafter. He gained 866 yards for the season.

No rookie runner has ever come into professional football with the fanfare of O. J. Simpson, the Southern California all-everything drafted by the Buffalo Bills.

The conversion from college to pro ball is no snap for the All-American running back. Floyd Little of the Denver Broncos uses the halftime intermission for a breather and some introspection.

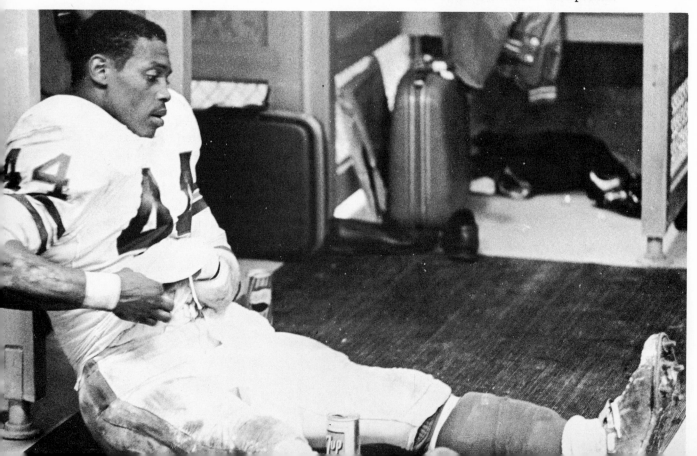

Of course, all figures become meaningless when the subject is O. J. Simpson.

In college football, there has never been a player to match Orenthal James Simpson of USC. He was bigger than Grange, quicker than Harmon, faster than Glenn Davis, more punishing than Blanchard, more durable than Nevers and more valuable than penicillin. In two years of college football (the first two were spent at junior college to build up a grades structure) he broke every existing record worth breaking. He carried the ball an average of 32 times for 162 yards per game. In style, he was a combination of Jim Brown and Gale Sayers. In results, he was uniquely O. J., and in southern California there's still an entire generation of youngsters which believes those initials stand for Orange Juice.

The diversion of the 1968 pro football season was the O. J. Simpson Sweepstakes, which team among four possibles—Buffalo, Pittsburgh, Philadelphia, Atlanta—would contrive to have the worst record so that it would have the honor of claiming Simpson in the draft. Coach Joe Kuharich was virtually burned at the stake when the Eagles, losers of their first eleven games, managed to win two straight and turn over O. J. to Buffalo as the prize.

If the two leagues were still warring, O. J. might have jacked his contract demands to a couple of million dollars. As it was, the owner of the Bills, Ralph Wilson, blanched when O. J. said he'd settle for $600,000 and an interest-free loan of half a million for his various business ventures. And they still call it a sport.

Yet almost any team in football would gladly have relieved the Bills of their financial problem. O. J. Simpson is a rare species, both as a football player and as a man. Let's take them in order.

Football—He's 6′ 1″, 207 with the prospect of filling out. He has run the 100 in 9.3. He has been unbelievably durable under the most severe pounding a college back ever endured. He responded to the pressure of championship games with his greatest runs. USC didn't emphasize his threat as a pass receiver, but he proved his talent in that phase of football as a junior college star. He has it all.

Man—He's a poised, gentle young man of twenty-two who worked himself out of the street corner gang gig to responsible citizenship. He is perceptive. He will not be used just because he is a Negro athlete. There was pressure on him to support the threatened boycott before the Olympic Games in Mexico City. Tommie Smith, a sprint champion, was a black leader and raised his fist in protest on the victory stand during the playing of the national anthem.

"I respect Tommie Smith because of his personal courage," said O. J., "But I don't admire him. I believe that as a Negro you prove yourself first, then go back to the kids in the ghetto and tell them, 'Here's what I did.' You can't change the world until you change yourself."

His wife, Marguerite, helped change him. He was a kid who roamed the streets of San Francisco, picking fights, looking for the action. He sneaked into 49er games. Later he scalped tickets. He had two overnight stays in juvenile hall. He met Marguerite Whitley when he was a high school junior at Galileo in San Francisco.

"At first," said Marguerite, "I hated O. J. He was a tough, always wanting to fight.

The Philadelphia Eagles, tapping Leroy Keyes for the 1969 season, expected the Purdue flash to fit easily into their concept of an all-around offensive threat.

Once I was at a party and he and his friends were not allowed in. So they broke windows to get in. It broke up a nice party.

"Well, we started dating anyhow, and my mother was not thrilled about it. He'd come over on Sundays dressed—uh, casually. Jeans and sandals. My mother is very religious and thinks you should wear a suit and tie on Sunday. O. J. started doing that. My mother also felt that any boy I went with should go to church. He started doing that, too."

"I came from an area," added O. J., "where kids would goof off. So I didn't have the grades for a four-year school. Then I saw some of the players I knew weren't as good as me get it, and I realized it was my own fault."

He went to the City College of San Francisco for two years, then transferred to USC as a junior.

"I wanted to major in sociology," he said, "but I didn't see eye to eye with my professors and the other students. They would read all the books and talk about what life was like in the underprivileged areas, the poverty areas. I would disagree—because I lived in those areas and I knew."

So he majored in public administration and planned a future career working with juveniles.

But first, for O. J. Simpson, there was a lot of running ahead with a football in his arms.

PAUL H. ROBINSON

BORN: Dec. 19, 1944   Height: 6'0"   Weight: 198
University of Arizona

Cincinnati, 1968

Year	G.	RUSHING Att.	Yds.	Avg.	TD.	PASS RECEIVING P.C.	Yds.	Avg.	TD.	SCORING TD.	Pts.
1968	14	*238	*1023	4.3	*8	24	128	5.3	1	9	54

* Led AFL.

ROBERT "JUNIOR" HOLMES

BORN: Oct. 5, 1945   Height: 5'9"   Weight: 225
Southern University

Kansas City, 1968

Year	G.	RUSHING Att.	Yds.	Avg.	TD.	PASS RECEIVING P.C.	Yds.	Avg.	TD.	SCORING TD.	Pts.
1968	14	174	866	5.0	7	19	201	10.6	0	7	42

Epilogue

The composite running back in football should have the supreme confidence of Jim Thorpe; the crowd appeal of Red Grange; the sheer strength of Bronko Nagurski; the dazzling speed of Gale Sayers; the breathtaking quickness of George McAfee or Joe Perry; the open field elusiveness of Hugh McElhenny; the blocking zeal of Marion Motley; the versatility of Frank Gifford; the incredible balance of Jim Brown; the cool smartness of Paul Hornung, and the mental toughness of Jim Taylor or Clark Hinkle.

But no one man has had all of these qualities in the ultimate.

The procession of pro football, however, has had a constant flow of great talents over the fifty years of its organized existence. And what follows is one man's way of rating them, numerically:

1. Jim Brown—It's all there in the record books. For moving a football closer to the goal line of the other team and across it, he was pro football's greatest. He also came closest to the ideal in size, speed and durability. He's the undisputed champ.

2. Steven Van Buren—He was, with no apologies needed, the Jim Brown of his time, the bridge from the pioneering days of the pros to the modern, a superb runner who showed present-day coaches how a running back could be utilized as the staple weapon of the offense.

3. Jim Thorpe—It's impossible to mix eras, but it's also impossible to ignore the fact that the Sac and Fox Indian was the greatest athletic talent this country has ever produced. Football was his best sport and running with the ball was his outstanding ploy.

4. Gale Sayers—The only thing that keeps him from moving up a notch or two or even three in these ratings is extended performance. He's still active as the most sensational running stylist of any period of the pro grame, and his playmates are as enthralled by his skills as the fans.

5. Bronko Nagurski—The moderns may snicker, but Bronko had to carry the ball the hard way, without the elements of finesse that pro football developed, and he was still the epitome of the unstoppable back against massed defenses. That kind would function in any era.

6. Hugh McElhenny—He generated the same kind of electricity that surrounds a magnetic actor. His only handicap was lack of national exposure when he was at his peak as the king of the open road to touchdowns. Mac had a faculty for keeping people off balance.

7. Jim Taylor—With possibly the least amount of natural gifts of any man on this list, the tough tiger of the Packers gritted his way to football greatness. A man his size, with his moderate speed, had no business breaking tackles the way he did—or producing titles.

8. Cookie Gilchrist—The character sometimes overshadows the basic talent. Cookie was the biggest of all fullbacks, and several of his best years were spent where

no one could appreciate him. But he was awesome from every angle in performing every function of a fullback.

9. Marion Motley—Again, one has to appreciate the man more than the setting. And appreciate the subordination of self to the spirit of winning. He was the instrument of pioneering techniques which modernized the running game; his execution made them work.

10. Lenny Moore—He could have been what people expect Gale Sayers to be because the instinctive ability to run past and around people was his natural gift. And if he didn't achieve perfection, he came close enough to merit rating with the all-time elite of football.

Appendix

NFL RUSHING LEADERS, BY YEARS
(since 1932)

Year		Yards	Att.	TD.
1932	Bob Campiglio, Stapleton	504	104	2
1933	Cliff Battles, Boston	737	146	4
1934	Beattie Feathers, Chicago Bears	1004	101	9
1935	Doug Russell, Chicago Cards	499	140	0
1936	Tuffy Leeman, New York Giants	830	206	2
1937	Cliff Battles, Washington	874	216	6
1938	Whizzer White, Pittsburgh	567	152	4
1939	Bill Osmanski, Chicago Bears	699	121	7
1940	Whizzer White, Detroit	514	146	5
1941	Clarence Manders, Brooklyn	486	111	7
1942	Bill Dudley, Pittsburgh	696	162	6
1943	Bill Paschal, New York Giants	572	147	10
1944	Bill Paschal, New York Giants	737	196	9
1945	Steve Van Buren, Philadelphia	832	143	15
1946	Bill Dudley, Pittsburgh	604	146	3
1947	Steve Van Buren, Philadelphia	1008	217	13
1948	Steve Van Buren, Philadelphia	945	201	10
1949	Steve Van Buren, Philadelphia	1146	263	11
1950	Marion Motley, Cleveland	810	140	3
1951	Eddie Price, New York Giants	971	271	7
1952	Dan Towler, Los Angeles	894	156	10
1953	Joe Perry, San Francsico	1018	192	10
1954	Joe Perry, San Francisco	1041	173	8
1955	Alan Ameche, Baltimore	961	213	9
1956	Rick Casares, Chicago Bears	1126	234	12
1957	Jim Brown, Cleveland	942	202	9
1958	Jim Brown, Cleveland	1527	257	17
1959	Jim Brown, Cleveland	1329	290	14
1960	Jim Brown, Cleveland	1257	215	9
1961	Jim Brown, Cleveland	1408	305	8
1962	Jim Taylor, Green Bay	1474	272	19
1963	Jim Brown, Cleveland	1863	291	12
1964	Jim Brown, Cleveland	1446	280	7
1965	Jim Brown, Cleveland	1544	289	17
1966	Gale Sayers, Chicago Bears	1231	229	8
1967	Leroy Kelly, Cleveland	1205	235	11
1968	Leroy Kelly, Cleveland	1239	248	16

LEADING LIFETIME RUSHERS
(At conclusion of 1968 season)

No.	Player	League	Yrs.	Att.	Yds.	Avg.	TD.
1	Jim Brown	NFL	9	2359	12,312	5.2	106
2	Joe Perry	AAFC-NFL	16	1929	9723	5.0	71
3	Jim Taylor	NFL	10	1941	8597	4.4	87
4	John Henry Johnson	NFL-AFL	13	1579	6806	4.3	48
5	Don Perkins *	NFL	8	1500	6217	4.1	40
6	Steve Van Buren	NFL	8	1320	5860	4.3	71
7	Rick Casares	NFL-AFL	12	1431	5797	4.1	49
8	Dick Bass *	NFL	9	1217	5416	4.4	34
9	Hugh McElhenny	NFL	13	1124	5281	4.6	39
10	Lenny Moore	NFL	12	1069	5174	4.8	63
11	Ollie Matson	NFL	14	1170	5173	4.4	40
12	Clem Daniels	AFL-NFL	9	1146	5138	4.5	30
13	John David Crow	NFL	11	1157	4963	4.3	39
14	Paul Lowe	AFL	8	1016	4962	4.9	39
15	Marion Motley	AAFC-NFL	9	828	4720	5.7	34
16	J. D. Smith	NFL	11	1100	4672	4.2	40
17	Alex Webster	NFL	10	1196	4638	3.9	39
18	Abner Haynes	AFL	8	1036	4630	4.5	46
19	Bob Hoernschemeyer	AAFC-NFL	10	1059	4548	4.3	27
20	Bill Brown *	NFL	8	1228	4438	3.6	40

* Still active.

	RUSHING			RECEPTIONS			PUNT RETURNS			KICKOFF RETURNS		
	Att.	Yds.	TD.	Rec.	Yds.	TD.	No.	Yds.	TD.	No.	Yds.	TD.
Alan Ameche	964	4045	40	101	733	4	..	..	..	6	98	0
Donnie Anderson	292	1267	13	49	697	4	15	222	1	34	759	0
Elmer Angsman	683	2908	27	41	654	5	..	..	..	81	147	0
Jon Arnett	964	3833	26	222	2290	10	120	981	1	126	3110	2
Dick Bass	1217	5416	34	204	1841	7	54	1415	0	24	263	1
Cliff Battles	846	3542	27	37	546	4	..	..	..	..	..	..
Bill Brown	1228	4438	40	208	2396	16	..	..	..	12	227	1
Jim Brown	2359	12,312	106	262	2499	20	..	..	..	29	648	0
Tim Brown	889	3862	31	235	3399	26	71	639	1	184	4781	5
Tony Canadeo	1025	4197	17	69	579	5	45	509	0	71	1626	0
Billy Cannon	601	2449	17	208	3269	43	14	178	0	67	1704	1
Rick Casares	1338	5662	49	183	1543	10	..	..	..	6	113	0
Dutch Clark	460	2757	23	29	341	8	..	..	..	..	..	..
Junior Coffey	382	1456	8	45	378	2	..	..	..	2	27	0
John David Crow	1157	4963	38	258	3699	35	2	6	0	11	330	0
Clemon Daniels	1146	5138	30	203	3314	24	8	103	0	57	1206	0
Glenn Davis	152	616	4	50	682	5	18	109	0	17	346	0
Hewritt Dixon	468	1831	14	199	2337	11	..	..	..	16	292	0
Bill Dudley	765	3057	19	123	1383	18	124	1515	3	78	1743	1
Mel Farr	334	1457	6	63	692	7	..	..	..	..	..	..
Beattie Feathers	376	1980	8	14	243	1	..	..	..	..	..	..
Tucker Frederickson	434	1456	8	53	394	3	..	..	..	3	32	0
Willie Galimore	670	2985	26	87	1201	10	..	..	..	82	1100	1
Mike Garrett	547	2452	18	94	795	5	23	165	1	14	323	0
Larry Garron	759	2981	14	185	2592	6	1	23	0	89	2299	2
Frank Gifford	840	3609	34	367	5434	43	25	121	0	23	594	0
Cookie Gilchrist	1010	4293	37	110	1135	6	..	..	..	7	104	1
Jim Grabowski	284	1111	6	34	394	2	..	..	..	..	..	..
Red Grange	170	545	5	16	288	5	..	..	..	..	..	..
Hoyle Granger	494	2430	14	69	765	4	..	..	..	..	..	..
Ace Gutowsky	917	3278	18	3	64	0	..	..	..	..	..	..
Pat Harder	740	3016	33	92	864	5	1	10	0	12	228	0
Tom Harmon	107	542	3	15	288	3	32	449	1	15	342	0
Abner Haynes	1036	4630	46	287	3535	20	85	875	1	95	2456	1
Clarke Hinkle	1171	3860	33	48	552	9	2	61	0	3	38	0
Paul Hornung	893	3711	50	130	1480	12	..	..	..	10	248	0

587

	RUSHING			RECEPTIONS			PUNT RETURNS			KICKOFF RETURNS		
	Att.	Yds.	TD.	Rec.	Yds.	TD.	No.	Yds.	TD.	No.	Yds.	TD.
John Henry Johnson	1501	6577	45	178	1328	7	1	6	0	4	59	0
Leroy Kelly	735	3736	42	83	1067	7	49	608	3	73	1747	0
Tuffy Leemans	919	3142	17	28	422	3	19	262	0	..	..	..
Keith Lincoln	758	3383	19	165	2250	19	25	342	1	39	1118	1
Paul Lowe	1016	4961	39	111	1045	7	2	0	0	58	1298	0
Tommy Mason	932	3860	31	179	1903	11	46	483	0	45	1067	0
Tom Matte	747	2950	26	162	1933	9	..	..	..	61	1367	0
Ollie Matson	1170	5173	40	222	3285	23	65	595	3	143	3746	6
George McAfee	341	1685	22	85	1357	12	112	1431	2	18	488	1
Hugh McElhenny	1124	5281	38	264	3247	20	126	920	2	83	1921	0
Johnny McNally (Blood)	107	383	4	65	1109	13	..	..	..	..	..	..
Bobby Mitchell	513	2735	18	521	7954	65	69	699	3	102	2690	5
Lenny Moore	1069	5174	63	363	6039	48	14	56	0	49	1180	1
Marion Motley	337	1688	5	40	463	3	..	..		6	148	0
Bronko Nagurski	623	2741	11	11	134	0	..	..	..	..	..	..
Jim Nance	856	3588	27	56	433	1	1	16	0	3	40	0
Don Perkins	1500	6217	42	146	1310	3	1	8	0	22	443	0
Joe Perry	1737	8378	53	241	1796	8	..	..	..	15	276	0
Nick Pietrosante	955	4026	28	141	1391	2	..	..	..	9	165	0
Eddie Price	846	3292	20	75	672	4	..	..	..	1	21	0
Dan Reeves	421	1640	19	96	1341	16	..	..	..	5	101	0
Gene Roberts	499	1904	14	64	1135	12	1	10	0	17	330	0
John Roland	547	2026	17	49	579	1	26	249	1	20	443	0
Kyle Rote	333	871	4	300	4795	48	..	..	..	6	185	0
Gale Sayers	719	3834	31	94	1197	9	27	391	2	77	2442	6
J. D. Smith	1100	4672	40	127	1122	6	..	..	..	36	882	0
Matt Snell	802	3309	19	169	1162	6	..	..	..	10	186	0
Ken Strong	385	1243	7	19	254	2	..	..	..	..	..	..
Jim Taylor	1941	8597	83	225	1756	10	..	..	..	7	185	0
Dick Todd	368	1573	13	111	1826	20	54	581	1	20	436	0
Charley Tolar	907	3277	21	175	1266	2	..	..	..	18	313	0
Dan Towler	672	3493	43	62	665	1	..	..	..	7	66	0
Charley Trippi	687	3506	22	130	1321	11	63	864	2	66	1457	0
Steve Van Buren	1320	5860	69	45	503	3	34	473	2	76	2030	3
Doak Walker	309	1520	12	152	2539	21	18	284	1	38	968	0
Alex Webster	1196	4638	39	240	2679	17	..	..	..	..	..	..
Whizzer White	387	1319	12	16	301	1	19	262	0	11	285	0
Ken Willard	776	3018	22	133	1078	7	..	..	..	..	..	..
Buddy Young	335	1275	8	119	1978	13	48	389	1	90	2514	2
Tank Younger	770	3640	34	100	1167	1	..	..	..	1	24	0

Index